CHURCHI...   ...VAR
AND COL...

CHURCHILL AND THE BOMB IN WAR AND COLD WAR

Kevin Ruane

BLOOMSBURY ACADEMIC
LONDON • NEW YORK • OXFORD • NEW DELHI • SYDNEY

BLOOMSBURY ACADEMIC
Bloomsbury Publishing Plc
50 Bedford Square, London, WC1B 3DP, UK

BLOOMSBURY, BLOOMSBURY ACADEMIC and the Diana logo are trademarks
of Bloomsbury Publishing Plc

First published in hardback 2016
This edition published 2018

Cover design: Paul Burgess
Cover images: Time & Life Pictures / David Savill / Topical Press Agency / Getty Images

A catalogue record for this book is available from the British Library.

ISBN: HB: 978-1-4725-2338-9
        PB: 978-1-4725-3080-6
        ePDF: 978-1-4725-2347-1
        eBook: 978-1-4725-3216-9

Typeset by RefineCatch Limited, Bungay, Suffolk
Printed and bound in Great Britain

To find out more about our authors and books visit www.bloomsbury.com
and sign up for our newsletters.

For Vanessa

CONTENTS

ILLUSTRATIONS

ACKNOWLEDGEMENTS

'Whilst writing, a book is an adventure', Winston Churchill reflected in 1949. 'To begin with, it is a toy and an amusement; then it becomes a mistress, and then it becomes a master, and then a tyrant. The last phase is that just as you are about to be reconciled to your servitude, you kill the monster, and fling him to the public.'[1]

Churchill, a prolific author, knew whereof he spoke. However, as my family will testify, the process of writing this particular book went very quickly to the tyrant phase. The fact that it was finished at all – never mind completed miraculously close to the contractual deadline – owes a tremendous amount to the support and understanding of my children, Niamh, Fiontan and Eimear, of my step-son, Sam, and above all of my wife, Vanessa, who made (and makes) everything possible and to whom the book is lovingly dedicated.

Although the arguments and interpretations in *Churchill and the Bomb* are all my own, the final outcome – the monster, as it were – has benefitted from the encouragement, advice and wisdom of friends, colleagues and scholars, many of whom gave generously of their time in reading all or parts of the manuscript. My thanks, therefore, to Paul Addison, Kathy Burk, Jackie Eales, Matthew Jones, Shaun Sturips, Richard Toye, Geoffrey Warner, Martin Watts and John Young. To James Ellison, I owe especial thanks: a fine historian, he is also the frankest and most penetrating of critics. All writers need an Ellison and I count myself singularly fortunate to have the original in my life – and not just as a critic and sounding-board but as the very best of friends.

I must also thank, in no particular order: Sean Greenwood who, many years ago, first inspired me to believe I could be an historian; my friends and colleagues in the History Department (as was) at Canterbury Christ Church, and indeed the University itself for its support for my research over several decades; the QR committee of the CCCU School of Humanities for financial backing for my various travels; the many archivists and librarians who have helped me track down the nuclear Churchill – in particular Allen Packwood and his team at the Churchill Archives Centre at Churchill College, Cambridge, and Finn Aaserud and Felicity Pons at the Bohr Archive in Copenhagen; Wolfson College Cambridge for granting me visiting academic status complete with a room in Sir Vivian Fuchs House; Celia Morris for her hospitality in Washington DC; at Bloomsbury Publishing, Emily Drewe, Frances Arnold and Emma Goode for the most positive and stress-free publishing experience of my career; John and Nickola Ford for a wooden retreat of great calm and contemplative value; Dr Philippe Laissue for his scientific acumen and wondrous punning; Alex Kent for his geographical pointers; Jonathan Hogg for kindly allowing me to view the pre-publication proofs of his brilliant study of *British Nuclear Culture*; Richard Smyth and Mark O'Donnell, the alternative

Acknowledgements

WSC and FDR; Jim Latham of yore for the RDM; and my CCCU 'Bomb' class of 2014–15 for demonstrating that research-informed teaching really does exist. Lastly, a second mention for Eimear who, because she lent me her digital camera, feels – rightly – that she should be formally acknowledged as my research assistant.

Kevin Ruane
Canterbury, December 2015

ABBREVIATIONS USED IN TEXT

AEA	Atomic Energy Authority, UK.
AEC	Atomic Energy Commission, USA.
AERE	Atomic Energy Research Establishment, UK.
AWRE	Atomic Weapons Research Establishment, UK.
CCS	Combined Chiefs of Staff, US-UK.
CDA	Combined Development Agency, US-UK.
CID	Committee of Imperial Defence, UK.
COS	Chiefs of Staff, UK.
CPC	Combined Policy Committee, US-UK-Canadian.
DSIR	Department of Scientific and Industrial Research, UK.
EDC	European Defence Community.
HMG	His/Her Majesty's Government.
JCAE	Joint Congressional Committee on Atomic Energy, USA.
JCS	Joint Chiefs of Staff, USA.
JPS	Joint Planning Staff, UK.
MAD	Mutual Assured Destruction.
MOD	Ministry of Defence, UK.
NATO	North Atlantic Treaty Organization.
NDRC	National Defense Research Committee, USA.
NSC	National Security Council, USA.
OSRD	Office of Scientific Research and Development, USA.
PIPPA	pressurized pile for producing power and plutonium, UK.
S-1	US codename for wartime A-bomb research and development.
SAC	Strategic Air Command, USA.
SACEUR	Supreme Allied Commander, Europe (NATO).
TA	Tube Alloys, UK.
TA-1	Bomb project.
TA-2	Power project.
UN	United Nations.
UNAEC	United Nations Atomic Energy Commission.

INTRODUCTION: SO MANY WINSTON CHURCHILLS

In April 2013, a short piece of cine-footage, a family home-movie from six decades earlier, was given a public viewing to invited guests in the state apartments of Windsor Castle. The scene depicted in the 48-second snippet was nothing out of the ordinary – a vacation, some gentle larks and picnicking – but the family was. Shot in October 1952, the washed-out colour frames show the young Queen Elizabeth II, eight months into her reign, along with her eldest child, Prince Charles, Queen Elizabeth the Queen Mother, and sundry courtiers and gillies enjoying a fishing expedition at Loch Muick on the Royal Family's Balmoral estate in Aberdeenshire. Also prominent in the film is the bulky and unmistakable figure of Winston Churchill, returned as Britain's Prime Minister a year earlier, and now, together with his wife Clementine, a guest of the Queen. A month shy of his seventy-eighth birthday, Churchill is seen sitting by the water's edge, wrapped-up warm in a grey great-coat and grey felt hat, smiling for the camera or chatting amiably to the young Prince whilst wielding a piece of club-shaped driftwood with a caveman swagger (he said he was 'waiting on the Loch Ness monster', Charles recalled many years later).[1] Churchill appears relaxed and care-free. He is on holiday. But he is not off-duty. His thoughts, we now know, regularly wandered from an autumnal Scotland to the far side of the world, to a barren, windswept, uninhabited outpost of the Commonwealth called the Montebello islands. It was there, eighty miles off the coast of north-west Australia, that Britain's first atomic bomb, its first weapon of mass destruction, a plutonium device, was about to be tested.

For Churchill, a great deal rested on a successful outcome to operation Hurricane, as the test was codenamed, not least Britain's graduation as an atomic power and its admission to an exclusive club which presently had just two members, the United States and the Soviet Union. In the months preceding Hurricane Churchill had grown fretful. 'Pop or flop?', he asked of Frederick Lindemann (Lord Cherwell), his old friend and scientific mentor. 'Pop', came the reply.[2] Even then, Churchill took nothing for granted, pestering his atomic advisors for additional reassurance, but Lindemann's confidence was merited. On 3 October 1952, at just after 9.00 am local time at Montebello, the A-bomb exploded with a violence greater than either of the weapons used by the United States against Japan in 1945.[3] Ironically, Western Australia being several hours ahead of the United Kingdom, Churchill, fast asleep in bed at Balmoral, missed registering the exact moment he became the first Prime Minister in British history to have at his disposal a nuclear weapon.[4] The overnight duty-secretary at Number 10 Downing Street, Anthony Montague Browne, a 29-year-old former fighter pilot who had only just joined the Private Office staff, received the news via the Admiralty. 'I had never met Winston Churchill', he recalled, 'but I surmised that he might not like 4 a.m. phone-calls. Anyway the explosion would presumably still have been a success at nine, so I waited until I had eaten breakfast.'[5]

There is no record of Churchill's immediate reaction when eventually informed of the test result. Nor do we know what he said to the Queen when he briefed her later in the day. What, one wonders, did this septuagenarian, a veteran of the last great cavalry charge in British military history at Omdurman in 1898, say to his young monarch? Beyond, that is, the obvious, that Hurricane had been a pop not a flop? How did a cavalry officer of the late-Victorian era make sense of the fact that now, at the dawn of the second Elizabethan Age, he had in his hands not a sword or a lance but a weapon containing the kind of pulsing, primordial energy that fuels the stars of the night sky? Did he think in military terms – of offence and defence in the Cold War struggle against an atomic-clad Soviet Union? Or in power-political terms? That the bomb granted Britain a status matched only by the other members of the old wartime Big Three? Maybe his thoughts lingered on the wonder and the horror that science had brought forth, on Hiroshima and Nagasaki in 1945, two cities, two bombs, two flashes, and 100,000 dead in an instant. For here indeed, in the words of another famous Old Harrovian, was 'the patent age of new inventions, for killing bodies, and for saving souls, all propagated with the best intentions.'[6]

If, in addition, he thought to himself, 'at last', that too would be understandable. The moment had been a long time coming – more than eleven years, in fact, since August 1941, when Churchill himself, with his country in the coils of a desperate struggle for national survival, gave the go-ahead to a top secret programme of atomic research and development. And yet, in modern popular consciousness and historical memory, this Churchill, the nuclear Churchill, remains largely unknown, certainly when compared with the many rival Churchills that are out there. 'The quandary of Winston Churchill may be simply expressed', historian Robert Rhodes James once remarked: 'there were so many Winston Churchills. Politician, sportsman, artist, orator, historian, Parliamentarian, journalist, essayist, gambler, soldier, war correspondent, adventurer, patriot, internationalist, dreamer, pragmatist, strategist, monarchist, democrat, egocentric, hedonist, romantic.'[7] This book adds three more incarnations to the list: atomic bomb-maker, atomic diplomatist, nuclear peace-maker. In truth, this triptych represents a single protean Churchill who, in the span of just fourteen years, from 1941 to 1955, altered his outlook on weapons of mass destruction to a remarkable degree. The shift, as we will see, was most obvious in the postwar era when he moved from viewing nuclear arms as a means of coercing the Soviet Union into relinquishing its authoritarian hold on Eastern Europe, to embracing, and arguably even conceiving, the concept of Mutual Assured Destruction (MAD), a global balance of terror, as the best hope of peace in a world of nuclear-primed superpowers. In the process, Churchill's hatred of communism, so deep for so long, was tempered to the extent that détente, his overriding objective by 1953–1954, required not only adherence to the principle of peaceful co-existence between the Cold War power-blocs, but an acceptance that the countries beyond what he himself had christened the Iron Curtain must be deemed lost, possibly in perpetuity. Only the genocidal fury of the hydrogen bomb, fully revealed in the spring of 1954, could have brought Churchill the great anti-communist to this painful ideological pass.

In any other statesman the gap between Churchill's nuclear starting point and ending point, between the warmonger (so his critics called him) of the early Cold War and the peacemonger of the mid-1950s, might be considered too great for credible spanning. But not so with Churchill who had always been a political shape-shifter, a man of convictions firmly held only for as long as he held them firmly: a Conservative when he first entered Parliament in 1900, a Liberal in 1904, then a Tory again in 1924; an admirer, early-on, of Benito Mussolini and even – despite the legend of his consistent opposition to Nazism – of Adolf Hitler before becoming the indomitable foe of both; a splenetic denouncer of the 1917 Bolshevik revolution and all it stood for before allying with Joseph Stalin and the USSR in the Second World War; the original Cold Warrior, the man of Fulton and the Iron Curtain, who became one of the founding fathers of European détente. We should not wonder, then, that Churchill's views on nuclear weapons existed within parameters of extremity, or that his outlook on the atomic bomb, 'the perfected means of human destruction' as he put it, or 'its monstrous child, the hydrogen bomb', altered so radically in so short a space of time.[8]

The word 'bomb', Gerard DeGroot reminds us, is ancient.

> It means, simply, a canister in which an explosive or noxious substance is placed. That canister was thrown, shot, dropped, or simply deposited for the purpose of causing mayhem. Prior to the advent of gunpowder, bombs were not explosive, they were merely annoying. A container filled with some vile substance was thrown at the enemy, who would promptly hurl one back. In fact, the concept predates the word. It is easy to imagine that prehistoric man probably took the bladder from an animal, filled it with shit and threw it at an adversary. Bombs are as old as hatred itself. But only since 1945 have we spoken of *the* Bomb.[9]

The Bomb, then, capital B. As in *Churchill and the Bomb in War and Cold War.* And not just the atomic bomb as was used against Japan but the altogether more powerful and destructive hydrogen bomb. Churchill himself offered additional nomenclatural advice in March 1955. For the 'sake of simplicity', he told MPs, he liked to distinguish between 'atomic bombs' and 'hydrogen bombs', the one a fission weapon, the other a fusion weapon, 'and . . . keep "nuclear" for the whole lot'.[10] So will this book.

Is there room, though, for yet another work on Churchill, whether on the Bomb or any other aspect of his life and times? Shelves groan under the weight of Churchillian-themed tomes – for such was his longevity, both in age and career in public office, to say nothing of the scale of the epochal events in which he participated, that studies of Churchill are seldom exercises in brevity. A big life has made for big books, although having said that, Paul Addison's *Churchill: the Unexpected Hero*, published in 2005, is a gem of a miniature.[11] The justification for adding to this historical-biographical corpus resides, first, in the tremendous importance of the development of nuclear weapons not just in terms of postwar British or international history, but for the world. As physicist and Nobel laureate I. I. Rabi observed, with the genesis of the Bomb in 1945, '[s]uddenly the day of judgment was the next day and has been ever since'.[12] Secondly, Churchill's attitude towards nuclear weapons needs to be explored and explained if we are fully to understand his views on Anglo-American and Anglo-Soviet relations, on the Cold War, arms control, détente and many other wider issues of international moment and historical significance. Thirdly, and notwithstanding the growing scholarly literature on Churchill's post-1945 career, there is still need to correct a pervasive popular perception of his 1951–1955 ministry as lame, undistinguished or lacking in substantive achievements.[13]

In public history, and even in academic studies, it is the Churchill of the Second World War who still dominates the publishing lists, followed by the Churchill of the inter-war years and the Churchill of the Great War.[14] Yet between 1941 and 1945, the nuclear Churchill, the Churchill of this book, not only launched an intensive British effort to build a super-bomb but fought long and hard to protect his country's interest when that effort was subsumed by the scientific-industrial leviathan that was the American Manhattan Project. Furthermore, in 1945, in joining with US President Harry S. Truman in giving formal approval to the unleashing of the Bomb on Japan, he ensured that the eradication of Hiroshima and Nagasaki would forever bear a British as well as an American imprimatur. In the early post-war period, at a time when many people in Britain and elsewhere looked to the newly-founded United Nations to deliver either world disarmament or at the least a system of international control of atomic energy, Churchill, now leader of the opposition, emerged as an enthusiastic proponent of the Bomb's legitimacy as an instrument of military deterrence. When the Cold War really began to bite in the late-1940s, he was to be found privately encouraging the United States to use its atomic monopoly as a lever to bring about the Red Army's withdrawal from Eastern Europe. More menacingly still, he urged the US authorities to threaten – and if necessary follow through on the threat – to deliver atomic destruction to the Soviet homelands if the Kremlin ever abandoned cold war in favour of hot war. As we know, within a year of his return to office in 1951, Churchill presided over Britain's coming of age as an atomic power, and then, in June 1954, he personally authorized the manufacture of a UK thermonuclear weapon, the first of which was tested in 1957.

By then, Churchill was two years into retirement, but the H-bomb, more so than the A-bomb, was *his* bomb. Back in 1954, he had championed its cause as the supreme deterrent of the nuclearized Cold War, as a must-have symbol of great power status, and as a means of enhancing UK influence in and over the USA, its closest, most powerful but also most worrisome ally. At the same time, the hydrogen bomb terrified him. Possessing a destructive yield hundreds and potentially thousands of times greater than the weapons which decimated Hiroshima and Nagasaki, the H-bomb, Churchill feared, could spell doom for Britain with its smallness of land-mass and density of population. This prospect not only oppressed him but goes a long way towards explaining the desperation with which he sought to arrange a Cold War summit during the last year of his peacetime ministry. Eighty in 1954, he became, as his father,

Lord Randolph, once said of Gladstone, an old man in a hurry. A summit, he maintained, was the essential first step towards chaining-up the 'nuclear monster', to establishing a basis for peaceful co-existence, and ultimately to bringing about détente with the Soviet Union.[15]

Not everyone – not the Americans, and not that many of his colleagues in the Cabinet, either – shared his sense of urgency. Stalin had died in 1953, and his successors in the Kremlin spoke increasingly of peace, but those around Churchill wanted deeds, not just words from Moscow, some tangible proofs of the Soviet Union's commitment to reducing international tension. This, though, would take time, a commodity Churchill no longer possessed. He therefore gambled: the Soviet "peace offensive" was taken at face-value. What, he argued, was the harm in talking? In the end, so driven was he by his dual obsession, by his nuclear bomb-making and Cold War peace-making, by his quest for national security and his search for global peace, by the self-belief that he was uniquely equipped to bridge the Cold War divide and by his sense of the clock running down, that in July 1954 he triggered a Cabinet crisis of such gravity that his government was brought to the very brink of collapse. This extraordinary episode in modern British political history has still to receive the detailed attention it deserves, especially in its thermonuclear dimensions. In this book, however, the crisis is recognized for what it was, the climacteric to the summer of the H-bomb.[16]

It is one of the great clichés of academic writing to refer to "gaps in the literature" in need of filling, but in the case of Churchill and the Bomb it happens to be true. The existence of the gap was brought home to me in 2012 when I was commissioned to write two articles, one on Churchill and the Cold War, the other on Churchill and weapons of mass destruction, for the Churchill Archive, a wonderful web-based resource, an 'Aladdin's cave of historical riches', as Sir Martin Gilbert described it.[17] The product of a collaboration between the Churchill Archives Centre at Churchill College, Cambridge, and Bloomsbury Publishing in London, the online facility has made available digitized images of Churchill's private and political papers, nearly a million individual pages.[18] Although Churchill's thinking on nuclear weapons is a thematic thread in the two most important book-length treatments of Churchill and the Cold War (John Young's *Churchill's Last Campaign* and Klaus Larres' *Churchill's Cold War*), it came as a surprise to discover how little focused scholarly attention had been devoted to the issue.[19]

There was, it turned out, a little-known work by Ernie Trory entitled *Churchill and the Bomb*, published in 1984 by the Hove-based Crabtree Press. A veteran British communist who died in 2000, Trory set up the press in 1946 as a dissemination vehicle for his puckishly polemical but historically suspect output.[20] Apart from this, the field seemed clear, enticingly and excitingly so. But then, in 2013, a few months after Bloomsbury issued me with a contract for the present study, the gap suddenly narrowed with the appearance to great (and it must be said justified) acclaim of Graham Farmelo's *Churchill's Bomb: A Hidden History of Science, War and Politics*.[21] That is the way of gaps. They exist to be filled. But the closing-up can take many forms. In the case of Professor Farmelo and myself, our approaches differ insofar as the former is a scientist – his doctorate is in theoretical physics – whereas I am a specialist in twentieth-century international history. Equally, where Farmelo gives extended consideration to the scientists who worked with and for Churchill during and after the Second World War, the present work takes a sustainedly Churchillian and geo-political-diplomatic approach. Hence, while covering a similar chronological span, the two works complement and in no sense rival one another.

As already noted, this book is constructed around three additions to the Rhodes James list. Churchill the bomb-maker resides in 1941–1945 when first Britain, and then the UK and USA together, sought to harness the power of nature in a weapon before Germany did so. The Allies won that race: by the time an A-bomb was combat-ready in the summer of 1945, Hitler was dead, the Third Reich in ruins and the Nazi nuclear programme shown to have been nowhere near as advanced as the Anglo-Americans had at one time feared.[22] In Asia and the Pacific, however, the war ground on. The decision to use the Bomb against Japan has generated intense historical debate, particularly amongst American scholars who have not only scrutinized with forensic acuity the motives of the Truman administration but argued passionately over the rectitude of the basic decision itself.[23] In contrast, the British, and more specifically Churchill's part in the atomic end-game is rarely given more than perfunctory consideration in the historiography.[24] This book seeks to rectify that omission. Moreover, in its focus on the wartime period, it will further show that the much-vaunted Anglo-American "special relationship" – a construct which Churchill may lay to claim to have invented or else willed into being – was not conspicuously special in the atomic field. While Churchill and US President Franklin D. Roosevelt (FDR) developed at the highest level a substantial degree of congruity on the Bomb, at the lower official level cooperation was badly blighted by tensions, arguments and suspicions on both sides. Nor, to Churchill's abiding dismay, did his various wartime agreements with FDR end up providing much protection for British atomic interests in the postwar era.

The second of our Churchills, the atomic diplomatist, first emerged at Potsdam in Germany, the setting for the last Big Three conference of the Second World War. It was there that Churchill received word of the successful first atomic test conducted in the wilds of New Mexico on 16 July 1945. Before then, he had been aware that the Bomb, if it worked, would be something unprecedented in the annals of warfare, but the graphic eye-witness accounts reaching Potsdam of the 'day the sun rose twice' nonetheless represented an atomic epiphany.[25] Churchill was instantly seized by the weapon's great value – and not just as a way to bring the war with Japan to a speedy conclusion but as a means of strengthening the diplomatic hand of the British and American governments as they sought to ameliorate, and if possible reverse the unhappy consequence of the end of the war in Europe, the USSR's politico-military domination of the eastern half of the continent. To put it crudely but not inaccurately, from mid-July 1945, Churchill favoured pressing Stalin on pain of atomic punishment to abide by the principle of national self-determination in Poland and those other countries ostensibly "liberated" by the Red Army. Potsdam is therefore the pivot-point of the book, the moment when Part I, 'War', gives way to Part II, 'Cold War'.

In the event, Churchill was denied the opportunity to indulge his newly-acquired passion for atomic diplomacy when, mid-way through Potsdam, the result of the July 1945 British General Election was declared. Taking advantage of the freedom which Churchill wished for the peoples of the Soviet sphere in Europe, British voters gave him, as he put it, 'the order of the boot'.[26] Such was the scale of the Labour landslide that the Conservatives, and Churchill with them, were banished to more than six years in opposition – years in which Moscow consolidated its control of Eastern Europe, and the Cold War, 'a peace that is no peace', disfigured the international landscape while holding within itself the potential for a hot third world war.[27] For Churchill, the years 1945 to 1949 represent the atomic showdown phase of his career, a period when he impressed upon all who would listen to him the need for the United States to take full diplomatic advantage of its monopoly and present the Soviet authorities with an ultimatum: either accept an all-European political settlement consonant with Western democratic values or face the shattering consequences. To his dismay, the US government, Truman's Democrats, refused to make atomic diplomacy an explicit feature of its Cold War strategy.

Churchill's hard-line views were mostly expressed in private for he knew how out of kilter they were with the popular hope that disarmament or international control would arrive in time to save the world from nuclear holocaust. The negative public reaction to philosopher Bertrand Russell's declared interest in an atomic-infused ultimatum to the USSR was a salutary reminder to Churchill, a man who would be Prime Minister again, of the risks attaching to nuclear stridency.[28] If, however, as Martin Sherwin argued in his seminal 1973 work, *A World Destroyed,* an atomic diplomatist is one who favours or engages in 'either the overt diplomatic or military brandishing of atomic weapons for the purpose of securing foreign-policy objectives', Churchill in his showdown phase not only came close to fitting the bill but at times resembled the war-monger that many in the Labour Party – with only his public anti-Sovietism to go on – saw him as.[29]

Today, the idea that Churchill was in any sense an atomic diplomatist is considered so revelatory, outrageous or disconcerting that it can make national newspaper headlines.[30] In fact the evidence of Churchill's minatory predilections has been around for a long time, but until now – until this book – it has never been assembled in a critical mass. However, in so doing, it becomes clear that between 1945 and 1949, Churchill regarded the threat and even the use of the Bomb as a legitimate method of dealing with the Soviet Union. Of course politicians out of power are much freer to express themselves than those in office, something Churchill knew as well as anyone.[31] Nevertheless, the persistence, vehemence and urgency with which he discoursed on the Bomb as an instrument of Cold War coercion leaves little room for the more comfortable conclusion that this was merely the posturing of a born showman.

But then, in February 1950, everything appeared to change: the atomic diplomatist exited the stage leaving the nuclear peacemaker in the spotlight. In a speech at Edinburgh during that month's General Election campaign, Churchill called for an East–West 'summit' – the first time, incidentally, that the word had been used to describe a meeting of the leaders of the great powers – to explore the potential for easing international tension.[32] The consensus amongst those historians who have considered the matter is that the Soviet Union's successful test of an atomic weapon the previous summer, together with President Truman's January 1950 announcement that the USA planned to forge ahead with building a H-bomb, wrought a profound change in his thinking. Churchill, it is argued, conscious of Britain's vulnerability to Soviet air attack and now alive to the danger that bombardment might soon be of the atomic variety, accommodated his outlook to fit the new Cold War realities.[33] However, as we will see, while there was a noticeable lessening in the anti-Soviet astringency of his speech-making after February 1950, Labour's dismissal of the Edinburgh initiative as electioneering was largely justified. Over the following eighteen months, Churchill expressed the hope, not just privately but publicly too, that the Americans would use their great atomic superiority (if no longer monopoly) to secure within a summitry framework the bulk of the Western alliance's *desiderata* in relation to the European Cold War. To that extent, the negotiations Churchill trailed in 1950 were not negotiations at all in the true sense of the word: there was to be no give-and-take, no real compromise, only dictation. Those close to Churchill in the senior ranks of the Conservative Party knew this and worried about the damaging electoral consequences if the extent of his continued attachment to atomic diplomacy became known at a time – 1950–1951 – when Labour's accusations of Churchillian warmongering were gaining popular traction.[34]

Our third Churchill, the nuclear peacemaker, only truly arrives on the scene in 1953–1954. The period from Edinburgh in February 1950, through his return to office in October 1951, to the advent of a new US government, the Republican administration of Dwight D. Eisenhower in January 1953, is a transitional one. Churchill continued to worry about the USSR's developing atomic capability and the deficiencies of Britain's national defence, but not excessively so. The Kremlin, he reasoned, was unlikely to initiate a new world war in view of the USA's greater atomic firepower and its concomitant capacity for delivering a devastating riposte. But then, in 1953–1954, a series of developments combined to transform his thinking – and not just on the Bomb but on the Cold War itself. First, the Eisenhower administration determined to rely much more heavily on nuclear weapons as the mainstay of US national security. This, in itself, might not have perturbed Churchill unduly were it not for the fact that prominent Republicans in Congress, along with several key figures in the administration, were simultaneously espousing a fire-and-brimstone brand of anti-communist fundamentalism. Previously, when Churchill contemplated the circumstances in which general war might arise, he had mainly thought in terms of a misguided act of Soviet aggression. Now he increasingly worried that an American act of provocation, even a US-initiated preventive war, was a more likely catalyst. At the same time, he was only too well aware that the United States, sitting geographically beyond the range of Soviet bombers, would not necessarily pay a high price for its actions, whereas Britain, home to US atomic bomber bases since 1948 and thus an obvious target for Soviet attack, could well be immolated.

Then came the revelation of the H-bomb's fantastic destructiveness and horrific killing-power. In August 1953, when the Soviet Union declared to the world that it had become a thermonuclear power, a distraught Churchill feared that 'we were now as far from the age of the atomic bomb as the atomic bomb itself from the bow and arrow'.[35] Yet for all the fertility of his imagination, he did not fully grasp the apocalyptic potentialities of the H-bomb until the spring of 1954 when Eisenhower confirmed that the USA, too, was a thermonuclear power and had in fact been so for at least eighteen months. The administration followed this up with a series of detailed press briefings, the release of disturbing film-footage of US weapons tests in the Pacific, and an apparent confirmation that a single H-bomb of sufficient megatonnage could destroy a modern city the size of New York. All of which, Churchill admitted, 'transformed what had been … a vague scientific nightmare into something which dominates the whole world'.[36]

Nor was this the extent of the nightmare. In March 1954, the world's press began reporting on apparently uncontrollable releases of radioactive fall-out from recent US weapons tests in the Pacific. Given that international opinion was already overwrought at the news of the annihilatory potential of the H-bomb in and of itself, the realization that toxic clouds borne on the wind could extend the killing range hundreds of miles beyond the initial point of detonation provoked widespread panic and alarm. In Britain, a country in the 'bull's eye' of Soviet targeting plans, as Churchill once described it, there was a particularly virulent outbreak of H-bomb fever, a sharp public and political reaction against the American testing of what the press dubbed 'horror bombs'.[37]

Over time the H-bomb would prove to be the great leveller – in every sense of the term. 'One consequence of the evolution from the atomic to the hydrogen bomb', adjudged Anthony Eden, Foreign Secretary in Churchill's peacetime administration, 'was to diminish the advantage of physically larger countries. All became equally vulnerable.' Writing this in 1960, Eden remembered being acutely conscious in the early-1950s 'of our unenviable position in a small and crowded island', but in the thermonuclear age 'continents, and not merely small islands, were doomed to destruction' and so 'all was equal in the grim reckoning'.[38] This might be so, but in 1954 one of Churchill's great fears was a surprise Soviet attack, for in thermonuclear war, the side which could deliver the first blow would be at a tremendous advantage. According to one top secret Whitehall estimate that passed across Churchill's desk, if Soviet bombers managed to drop just ten hydrogen bombs on UK targets – on London, Birmingham, Glasgow and other major cities – a third of the population would die instantly with millions more likely to perish in the days and weeks that followed from the baleful consequences of fall-out.[39]

It is against this terrifying backdrop that our third Churchill, the nuclear peace-maker, steps forth. In 1954 his Cold War summitry not only acquired new urgency but new sincerity: no longer was an East–West meeting to be the occasion for dictating terms to the USSR, rather he saw it as an essential first step towards regulating the Cold War in ways that would neutralize the danger of the very thing that he had favoured for more than five years after 1945, a showdown. Truly, his hope in opposition had become his fear in power. With a mind 'continually oppressed by the thermo-nuclear problem', Churchill realized that the best, possibly the only assurance of peace lay in détente. More than this, he accepted that the West must henceforward give up confronting and challenging the USSR over its totalitarian excesses beyond the Iron Curtain.[40] Peaceful co-existence, hitherto the preserve of Soviet propagandists, now entered his personal Cold War lexicon. Anti-communist extremism, such as had been his ideological stock-in-trade for much of the previous four decades, and which some in the Eisenhower administration continued to practise, could have no place in a world of H-bombs.

Henceforward, in the little time left to him, Churchill's policy became dual-containment, the pacifying of both the USA and the USSR as nuclear entities, the elimination of the risk of a direct American–Soviet clash by the removal of the conditions that could breed it, the Cold War itself. If anything, the challenge in shackling the Americans was greater: the relative invulnerability of North America to direct Soviet attack would not last and Churchill greatly feared what he called a 'forestalling' war launched by the United States before the USSR developed long-range heavy bombers or inter-continental rockets capable of carrying nuclear devastation to New York and Washington as well as to London and Paris.[41] As we will see, Churchill's decision to build a British H-bomb in June 1954 was, at its most basic level, an expression of dual-containment. The H-bomb would add to the West's overall deterrent vis-à-vis the USSR, and thus boost UK security, but just as importantly it would, he believed, provide Britain with a greater right to counsel restraint in Washington. And as long as nuclear arms stayed sheathed, and as long as the Cold War remained the Cold War, the chance for détente lived on.

This book, then, reveals a Churchill largely obscured from public view, the multi-faceted nuclear Churchill, and charts his extraordinary evolutionary journey from wartime atomic bomb-maker through Cold War atomic diplomatist to nuclear-driven disciple of détente. Along the way, his judgement sometimes proved erratic, his outlook sported contradictions, and his thinking betrayed marked inconsistencies. But the general line of advance, from 1941 to 1955, is clear and unmistakable. Historians often seek to make order out of the chaos that was the past only to end up doing the past – a messy place – a serious disservice. In the case of Churchill, the chaos, or at any rate the contradictions and inconsistences with which he was imbued, cannot be ignored, rather they must be factored into any analysis of his career, nuclear or otherwise. Does it diminish Churchill the nuclear peacemaker, for example, that he had once been Churchill the atomic diplomatist? Even Churchill the would-be atomic warrior? Hardly. It confirms instead his capacity to adapt and learn and shows that even in old age he was capable on this most vital of subjects of new and visionary thinking.

'In peace or war action is determined by events rather than by fixed ideas', he averred in 1954, the year of the H-bomb. 'One is fortunate when one has the power to decide in accordance with the factual circumstances of the day or even of the hour. I always reserve to myself as much of this advantage as I can get.' Consistency, in other words, was an overrated virtue – and even a dangerous one if it ossified into dogmatic allegiance to set positions.[42] Accordingly, as this book concludes, instead of seeking to meet the heightened Soviet nuclear threat by backing the Americans come what may in building more and bigger weapons of mass destruction, Churchill, the original Cold Warrior and atomic diplomatist, opted to call time on the Cold War.

PART I
WAR

CHAPTER 1
ONLY CONNECT . . .

In the frontispiece of his 1910 novel *Howards End*, E. M. Forster prepared his readers for what was to come with a two-word epigraph: 'only connect . . .'[1] The story of Churchill and the Bomb requires a similar connectivity insofar as many of the themes amplified in this opening chapter – among them war, science and anti-communism – provide much of the context needed to interpret in a full and rounded way Churchill's handling of the nuclear issues that came before him during the Second World War and in the Cold War that followed. But just as *Howards End* has, at its core, human relationships, there is also a vital human factor at the heart of this story, one which operates as a theme in and of itself. For to understand Churchill and the Bomb, we need also to understand his interaction with key individuals and, above all, to reflect in some detail on his remarkable friendship with Professor F. A. Lindemann, the Lees Professor of Experimental Philosophy at Oxford University.

Winston Leonard Spencer Churchill was born in Blenheim Palace, Oxfordshire, on 30 November 1874.[2] His father, Lord Randolph Churchill, was the third son of the seventh Duke of Marlborough, but the ancestry of his mother, Jennie (née Jerome), the daughter of a wealthy New York financier, ensured that Winston ended up 'half-American but all British'.[3] Throughout his long life, war was as central to Churchill – 'the very breath of life to him', according to one close associate – as it had been for his illustrious forebear, Queen Anne's lauded general, John Churchill, the first Duke of Marlborough.[4] The martial fascination began early. Rare is the biography which fails to mention that Churchill's toy soldiers were amongst his most precious childhood possessions, but while most boys of his class and generation played with soldiers, he 'organized wars', his cousin, Clare Frewen, recalled, 'and played with an interest that was no ordinary child game'.[5] At Harrow, where he was educated from the age of 13, he joined the school cadet force and developed a romantic Whiggish view of the past in which Great Men did Great Deeds, soldiers were brave and fearless in battle, and the British Empire stood as the great civilizing force in the world, *idées fixes* which never left him.[6]

His schooling over, Churchill entered the Royal Military College at Sandhurst and was commissioned in February 1895 as a second lieutenant in the Queen's 4th Hussars. This, it might be supposed, represented the fulfilment of his boyhood dream, but the mundanity of parading and exercising quickly bored him. That autumn, granted extended leave from his regiment, he journeyed to Cuba in search of excitement and adventure. The recent death of his father at the age of 45 seemed to confirm the family lore that Churchills died young and he grew anxious to make his mark on the world as quickly as possible. More prosaically, though 'well-born in terms of status', Churchill was 'not at all well-born in terms of wealth' and needed to earn some money.[7] To that end, he managed to get himself on the payroll of the *Daily Graphic* as a war correspondent and earned his keep by filing reports from Cuba on local resistance to Spanish rule. On his twenty-first birthday he came under fire for the first time in his life and the thrill of the experience would stay with him forever along with two habits acquired in Cuba, cigars and siestas.[8]

Soon after returning to his regiment in September 1896, Churchill was shipped-off to India. Based in Bangalore, the tedium of early morning cavalry exercises was partially offset by the pleasure he took from playing polo and by an exacting regime of self-improvement – he 'became his own university' – via voracious reading of works as varied as Plato, Darwin and Macauley.[9] Restless for field action, in 1897 he volunteered to take part in the North-West Frontier campaign, and then, the following year, attached himself to Kitchener's Army of the Nile and blooded himself in battle at Omdurman. By then, writing, whether journalism (building on his Cuban war-reporting) or book-length treatments of his military experiences, had begun to flow copiously, and his literary prowess would henceforward be a steady and eventually substantial earner for him. Which was just as well given his fondness for the sybaritic. 'My tastes are simple', he once confessed. 'I like only the best.'[10]

As the century drew to a close, politics increasingly exerted a more powerful pull on Churchill than the military life, as did a related desire to follow in an idolized father's footsteps, Lord Randolph having risen to become (briefly and controversially) Tory Chancellor of the Exchequer before his death. In 1899, Churchill resigned his commission and stood for Parliament as a Conservative Unionist in a by-election at Oldham. No longer a soldier, he still looked on war as a natural, even a healthy phenomenon – to die in battle for your country, he believed, was the highest and most heroic form of death – and many of his early political speeches possessed a martial patina.[11] Narrowly defeated at Oldham, he looked to journalism to tide him over until another electoral opportunity presented itself. With a lucrative contract from the *Morning Post* in his pocket, he headed for South Africa to report on the Boer War. What happened next is the stuff of Churchill legend: captured and imprisoned by the Boer authorities, he effected his escape in daring circumstances, had a price slapped on his head, but lived to tell the tale – literally in his journalism and in book-form. Between 1897 and 1900, Churchill 'reinvented the war correspondent as both fighter and writer', participating as a soldier in three of Queen Victoria's wars while jobbing as a journalist before turning his experiences into books.[12] All of which, when combined with his widely-reported South African escapade, gave him the kind of celebrity that was readily convertible into political capital.[13]

A high degree of self-regard and a gift for self-promotion were two facets of an extraordinarily multi-dimensional personality now reaching maturity. Anyone seeking a succinct summation of Churchill's qualities, both positive and negative, need only glance at the index headings of the first volume of his official biography, written by his son, Randolph. Under *characteristics* the following entries appear: 'pugnacity and rebelliousness; colossal ambition; pertinacity; love of mischief; capacious and retentive memory; extravagance; originality of mind; power of concentration; resourcefulness;

4

organising ability; talent for command; unpunctuality; self-confidence; late-maturing massive brain; thirst for adventure; egocentricity; desire for learning; cultivation of useful contacts; thirst for fame, glory and reputation; assiduity in writing books; sense of destiny; primordial thrust'.[14] Such was the composite character of the man whose six-decade parliamentary career was finally launched when, aged twenty-five, he stood again for Oldham, this time successfully, in the autumn of 1900.

However, having entered the House of Commons as a Conservative, within four years he had broken with the Tories on the issue of Free Trade and crossed the floor to join the Liberals, a defection long-remembered and hard-forgiven in Conservative circles. Establishing a close personal and political connection with David Lloyd George, the brightest star in the Liberal firmament, Churchill's career soon prospered. In 1905 he was appointed Under-Secretary of State for the Colonies; three years later he became President of the Board of Trade; in 1910 he was made Home Secretary, the youngest since Sir Robert Peel; and in 1911 he became First Lord of the Admiralty, a position he held until 1915. Churchill's personal life likewise prospered. Around the start of his political charge, he began courting Clementine Hozier and the two were wed, after a short engagement, in September 1908. The marriage, at times testy and testing, proved to be a genuinely loving partnership which provided Churchill the politician with welcome domestic stability throughout his long career.

Although home affairs were his principal professional focus until his appointment to the Admiralty, Churchill's imagination continued to be fired by notions of warfare: hero-worshipping Napoleon Bonaparte, deep-down he longed to be a great general himself. Nor did he make a secret of his passion. 'Keep your eye on Churchill', the journalist A. G. Gardiner advised. 'Remember, he is a soldier first, last, and always. He will write his name big on our future. Let us take care he does not write it in blood.'[15] In July 1911, the Agadir crisis, in which the Kaiser's growing naval muscle was flexed, led Churchill to confront the possibility of war with Imperial Germany. Before Agadir, he sometimes admitted to a conflicted military outlook. 'Much as war attracts me & fascinates my mind . . . I feel more deeply every year . . . what vile & wicked folly & barbarism it all is'.[16] After Agadir, in contrast to many of his colleagues in government, he regarded a war on the continent as a near certainty and maintained that, if it came, Britain could not hide behind neutrality but must fight with France, and if possible Russia, to thwart Germany.[17] By July 1914, his prediction poised to come true, he was almost embarrassed by the excitement he felt at the prospect. 'Everything now tends towards catastrophe and collapse', he wrote to Clementine. 'I am interested, geared up and happy. Is it not horrible to be built like that? The preparations have a hideous fascination for me. I pray to God to forgive me for such fearful moods of levity. Yet I w[oul]d do my best for peace.'[18]

For all the richness of his imagination, Churchill can scarcely have anticipated the scale of the slaughter that followed, yet he still managed to derive a thrill from being at the centre of governmental decision-making during the titanic military contest of the age. 'I think a curse should rest on me – because I *love* this war', he told his friend, Violet Asquith, daughter of Prime Minister Herbert Asquith, in February 1915. 'I know it's smashing & shattering the lives of thousands every moment – & yet – I *can't* help it – I enjoy every second of it.'[19] However, it would be wrong to infer from this that Churchill was indifferent to the suffering and agony; rather, as Roy Jenkins observed, he was 'always on a delicate edge between excitement at the prospect of great military clashes and apprehension at their consequences'.[20]

Churchill was also, by extension, a light casualty man, ever on the alert for ways to advance Britain's military objectives while simultaneously limiting losses. This brings us to our second introductory theme: Churchill's commitment to science and technological innovation in general, and to the utilization of science to improve methods of warfare in particular. Looking back on Churchill's career in the mid-1950s, the physicist and inventor Archibald Low recalled a 'soldier-scientist' whose 'appreciation of technical progress, coupled with his powerful but controlled imagination ... led him to demand weapons for the war after next'.[21] Similarly, R. V. Jones, chief scientific advisor to MI6 early in the Second World War, maintained that Churchill, '[a]lone among politicians, valued science and technology at something approaching their true worth, at least in military application'.[22]

He always had. In 1909, while at the Board of Trade, Churchill was to be found urging the Committee of Imperial Defence to get in touch with the American Wright brothers to see whether their new-fangled invention, the flying machine, could be converted for military purposes.[23] At the Admiralty from 1911, spurred by the growing threat of German sea-power, he embarked on a mission to modernize: he backed, *inter alia*, the development of a submarine fleet along with a fast division of battleships, the Queen Elizabeth class; oversaw the conversion of the Fleet from coal-fired to oil-fired engines; and identified the potential for launching aircraft from the decks of battleships. 'You have become a water creature', Lloyd George quipped, but he was also a creature of the air, 'Neptune's ally' as *Punch* magazine descried.[24] An early convert to air-power, Churchill was instrumental in establishing the Royal Naval Air Service (RNAS). Originally intended to provide protection to harbours and other naval facilities, the RNAS operated as a medium-range bombing force early in the First World War, attacking German troop concentrations and lines of communication across the Channel, and later undertook bombing missions against Zeppelin sheds at Düsseldorf, Cuxhaven, Friedrichshaven and Cologne.[25]

When it comes to his commitment to war-science, Churchill is still best remembered for the élan with which he promoted tank development. As early as September 1914 he was calling for serious investigation of the potentialities of a trench-crossing machine and engineers were soon busy working on "water carriers for Russia", the codename for the project (subsequently abbreviated to "WCs for Russia", and finally to tanks).[26] With his resignation from the government in 1915, a scapegoat in many ways for the costly failure of the Gallipoli campaign, he was deprived of any further influence over the development of the tank and was angered when 'land battleships', as he called them, were introduced 'prematurely and on a petty scale' in unsuitable crater-pocked terrain at the Somme in 1916. Only at Cambrai the following year were tanks given their 'own chance in a battle made for them ... and in which they could render the inestimable service for which they had been specially designed'.[27] In the end, the tank had 'many parents', but Churchill was 'without any question its prime *accoucheur*'.[28]

In misery following the Dardanelles disaster – 'I thought he would die of grief', Clementine recalled – Churchill decided to revert to his original calling as a soldier and made for the Western Front.[29] Following a period of training with the Grenadier Guards, in January 1916 he took command of the 6th battalion of the Royal Scots Fusiliers. Over the next few months he saw light action on the line near the Belgian village of Ploegsteert and was subjected to sporadic shelling. But much as he enjoyed the camaraderie of the army, he grew apprehensive lest his absence from Westminster hamper his chances of a political come-back, and thus, after a century of days at the front, he returned to England. A year on, when the Dardanelles Commission absolved him of sole or even principal blame for the ill-starred adventure, he was brought back into government as Minister of Munitions.[30] Although outside the War Cabinet, Churchill impressed upon all his colleagues, including Lloyd George, who had succeeded Asquith as Prime Minister, the value of '[m]echanical science . . . on the ground, in the air, on every coast, from the forge or from the laboratory' as an alternative to the bloody war of exhaustion on the Western Front.[31] In particular, he sought a great increase in the regularity and scale of aerial bombing, not just of military and economic targets in Germany but of urban centres. The war would be won, he argued, by the side which 'possessed the power to drop not five tons but five hundred tons of bombs each night on the cities and manufacturing establishments of its opponents'.[32]

Churchill also invested gas with high military value. In April 1918 he protested strongly when the French government expressed a willingness to abandon gas as a weapon if the Germans did so too. 'I am on the contrary in favour of the greatest possible development of gas-warfare', he countered.[33] He got his way. Over the next few months the production of gas shells more than doubled, from 350 tons to 795 tons a week, and by mid-year over a third of the shells fired by the British Army were gas shells.[34] 'This Hellish poison', as Churchill described mustard gas, 'will I trust be discharged on the Huns to the extent of nearly 100 tons by the end of this month', he wrote to his wife in October 1918, and 'in one dose'.[35] By now he was a 1919 man, a proponent of a massive build-up in Allied tank strength and air-power preparatory to a tremendous onslaught the following year. The government, tending towards a like view, approved what would later be termed strategic bombing, but the war ended in November 1918 before the newly-formed Royal Air Force (RAF) could make a decisive contribution in this area. However, as Secretary of State for War (and simultaneously Minister of Air) from 1919 to 1921, Churchill promoted the RAF as an instrument of air-policing in British imperial territories, and by the time he was moved to the Colonial Office in 1921 he was 'a great believer in air power' and pledged to 'forward it in every way'.[36]

Science in general, not just the marriage of science, technology and warfare, stimulated Churchill's intellect. It even shaped his choice of recreational reading with the science fiction of H. G. Wells an especial favourite. 'No more fascinating writer of philosophical romance has existed in our day', he declared in 1927. 'His imagination and foresight, almost amounting in some instances to second sight, have darted their rays through the curtains of the future.'[37] Churchill judged *The Time Machine* (1895) not only the equal of *Gulliver's Travels* but 'one of the books I would like to take with me to Purgatory.'[38] *The War in the Air* (1908), in which Wells predicted the development of aerial warfare and the extension of the traditional battlefield to towns and cities, was read with 'astonishment and delight' and clearly impacted on Churchill's thinking about air-power in the years before the Great War.[39] In *The World Crisis,* his own monumental account of that conflict, he acknowledged his debt to Wells in connection with the tank. 'There was no novelty about the idea of an armoured vehicle to travel across country and pass over trenches ... while carrying guns and fighting men', he wrote. 'Mr. H. G. Wells ... had practically exhausted the possibilities of imagination in this sphere.'[40] He was less enamoured of Wells' politics – his socialism, the welcome he gave to the Bolshevik revolution in Russia, and his critical stance on the British Empire.[41] Wells reciprocated in kind: in 1944 he would denounce Churchill publicly as a 'would-be British Fuhrer'.[42]

Churchill the wordsmith, as distinct from Churchill the politician, happily borrowed alluring phrases from Wells, incorporating them in his own speeches and writings. Whether he did this consciously or through a form of literary osmosis is unclear, although in 1931 he claimed to have read all of Wells' works with such avidity that 'I could pass an examination in them'.[43] The title of the first volume of Churchill's history of the Second World War, *The Gathering Storm*, published in 1948 (by which time Wells was dead) is an obvious example of this sampling. Employed by Churchill as a metaphor for the growing menace of Nazism, the phrase is taken from *The War of the Worlds* (1898), another of his favourite works, wherein it refers to the imminent Martian invasion of Earth. Other instances of borrowing – some might say plagiarism – have been found by historian Richard Toye who likens Churchill's penchant for Wellsian terminology to a modern-day Prime Minister 'borrowing phrases from *Star Trek* or *Doctor Who*'.[44]

As a forward-looking statesman, Churchill conceived of science as the engine of change, the driver of a modern-day Enlightenment. One of his best-known essays, 'Fifty Years Hence', published in *Strand* magazine in 1931, is an extended paean to scientific progress which, he argued, was likely to be 'constant', and happily so, 'for if it stopped or were reversed' there would be a 'catastrophe of unimaginable horror'.[45] Churchill also admired scientists, the deliverers of progress, but there was one among their number to whom he was devoted: Frederick Lindemann, Professor of Experimental Philosophy at Oxford. They first met in 1921 and their relationship would develop into one of the most meaningful of Churchill's life. As Martin Gilbert has shown, Lindemann, or the "Prof", as he was almost universally known, became 'as close to Churchill in thought, proximity and ideas as any other individual' and together they forged a partnership which lasted for more than three decades.[46] In much that follows, the Churchill–Lindemann relationship is of great importance and we need therefore to spend some time exploring the origins, nature and politico-scientific significance of this remarkable double-act.

Frederick Alexander Lindemann was the son of Adolphus Lindemann, an engineer and wealthy businessman of French-Alsatian ancestry who came to England in 1870 and was later naturalized, and an American mother, Olga née Noble. Frederick himself was born in Germany, in Baden-Baden, where his pregnant mother had gone for a rest cure only for the baby to appear prematurely on 5 April 1886. This accident of natal geography rankled with Lindemann throughout his adult life, for he suspected (with some justification) that despite his own naturalization he was never fully accepted as British by the social and ruling elite in whose midst he moved and worked.[47] Lindemann spent his early childhood in Devon, went to a Scottish public school, attended university in Germany, and in 1910 obtained his doctorate from the *Physikalisch-Chemische Institut* in Berlin for his thesis on the atomic heat of metals at low temperatures. He researched quantum physics before the Great War and soon after its close he was appointed to his chair at Oxford, was elected a Fellow of the Royal Society, and set about turning the moribund Clarendon laboratory into a research centre to rival the world-famous Cavendish laboratory in Cambridge. An accomplished tennis player, he competed at the Wimbledon championships in 1920, almost certainly the only Oxford Professor to do so, but crashed out of the men's doubles in the first round.[48]

By then – in his mid-thirties – Lindemann's political outlook had settled at the far-right of the spectrum, considerably beyond where Churchill resided. An unashamed inegalitarian, he believed in hierarchy, a fixed social order with an elite ruling class, inherited wealth (of which he possessed his goodly share), hereditary titles, and white supremacy.[49] However, despite holding pronounced right-wing views, Lindemann wholly rejected Oswald Mosley and his movement's attempts in the 1930s to ape the politics of Fascist Italy and Nazi Germany. For the Nazis in particular, he early acquired and never lost a visceral hatred. In that respect, he and Churchill shared common ground, though the two later differed insofar as Lindemann's detestation seemed to extend to all Germans while Churchill reserved his hatred for the Nazis rather than the German people as a whole.[50] This was not the only difference between them. As R. V. Jones, one of Lindemann's former students, later observed, Churchill and the Prof were the classic odd couple. 'Churchill, the older by a dozen years, ate, drank, and smoked generously, and enjoyed a happy family life', whereas Lindemann 'was a non-smoker, an abstainer from alcohol, a vegetarian, and a life-long bachelor'. Churchill had been in the midst of violent action in India, the Sudan, South Africa and Flanders but Lindemann had 'led a life so socially sheltered that it was said that he had never been on a London omnibus or the London Underground'.[51]

As a personality, Lindemann could be abrasive. To his friends he was loyal and giving but these were few compared with his enemies: arrogant in asserting his opinions, wont to lace his conversation with cutting or sarcastic asides, a striker of attitudes based on prejudice as much as knowledge, he possessed a finely honed talent for rubbing people up the wrong way.[52] His wealth, his chauffeur-driven Rolls Royce and his addiction to the society of the rich and powerful further set him apart from the majority of his scientific colleagues, whether in Oxford or later in Whitehall. Lindemann's 'main principles in life were simple and hard as a pikestaff', Lord Birkenhead, one of his biographers, later wrote, 'absolute loyalty and love for his friends, and sustained rancour towards his enemies'.[53] The Prof's physical appearance – tall, sallow, stern – and mode of dress (black coat, black hat, black furled umbrella) gave the impression that there was something of the night

Figure 1.1 Lindemann (left) and Churchill in 1940. Imperial War Museum.

about him; one Oxford student recalled a 'Dracula figure ... [w]hen he came into the room, you could feel the temperature fall'.[54] The Cabinet Office official George Mallaby, once mistaken for Lindemann by an American reporter, took pleasure in describing the real thing: 'large, erect, imperturbable, unsmiling, proceeding without haste or visible animation ... incongruous, inappropriate, strange'.[55]

The 'mystery', Ben Pimlott has written of Lindemann, 'is not why people did not like him but why his master did'.[56] To unravel the mystery we need first to acknowledge Churchill's admiration for Lindemann's 'beautiful brain', as he described it.[57] Nor was it just any brain; to Churchill's delight it was a scientific and mathematical one. Although his own scientific education ended when he left school, Churchill remained 'a scientist in the more vital sense of observing, experimenting and deducing' and his friendship with

Lindemann helped fan his amateur enthusiasms.[58] In addition, the Prof possessed the kind of personal courage that Churchill prized. During the First World War, Lindemann worked at the home of experimental aviation in England, the Royal Aircraft Factory at Farnborough, where he bent his intellect to solving the problem of tailspin – the inability of most pilots, once their aircraft entered a vertical dive, to correct the downward spiral and pull away to safety. After devising a precise mathematically-informed sequence of manoeuvres to counteract the problem, Lindemann refused to risk the life of any airmen in putting his theory to the test and instead learned to fly himself. In 1917 he took to the skies: deliberately sending his aircraft into a spin, he successfully rectified a clockwise downward-spiral before repeating the process anti-clockwise to prove that the first effort had not been a fluke. From then on, the Lindemann formula was employed as a standard drill and spin lost much of its terror for pilots.[59] This feat of daring astounded Churchill. 'It seemed certain death', he recalled many years later. 'But his theory worked . . . I did admire him so much.'[60]

Accepting Churchill's veneration of Lindemann's courage, it was science that provided the most powerful bonding agent in the first years of their relationship. Churchill's letters to Lindemann in the 1920s convey his excitement at having his own personal don to answer his questions, although he sometimes worried that Lindemann, who was 'no doubt used to the asperities of scientific discussion', would be bored by the constant inquiries of a dabbler.[61] Given the theme of this book, one early Churchill letter, dating from April 1924, is worthy of particular note. 'I have undertaken to write on the future possibilities of war and how frightful it will be for the human race', he explained. 'On this subject I have a good many ideas, but I should very much like to have another talk with you.' Lindemann agreed to help – they spent a week closeted at Churchill's recently-acquired family home at Chartwell in Kent – and this marked the beginning of a long and fruitful collaborative approach to publication.[62]

The emergent article, 'Shall We All Commit Suicide?', appeared in *Nash's Pall Mall* magazine that September. 'The story of the Human race is War', Churchill began.

> Except for brief and precarious interludes, there has never been peace in the world; and before history began, murderous strife was universal and unending. But up to the present time the means of destruction at the disposal of man have not kept pace with his ferocity. Reciprocal extermination was impossible in the Stone Age. One cannot do much with a clumsy club . . . So on the balance the life-forces kept a steady lead over the forces of death . . . It was not until the dawn of the twentieth century of the Christian era that War really began to enter into its kingdom as the potential destroyer of the human race . . . The Air opened paths along which death and terror could be carried far behind the lines of the actual armies, to women, children, the aged, the sick, who in earlier struggles would perforce had been left untouched.[63]

Yet however awful the present generation of weapons was, those of the future would likely be worse. The poison gas of the Great War was but 'the first chapter . . . of a terrible book' of destructive science, he argued in another passing nod to Wells. 'Then there are Explosives ... Has Science turned its last page on them? May there not be methods of using explosive energy incomparably more intense than anything heretofore discovered? Might not a bomb no bigger than an orange be found to possess a secret power to destroy a whole block of buildings, nay to concentrate the force of a thousand tons of cordite and blast a township at a stroke?'[64] Some twenty years later, Hiroshima and Nagasaki would provide an answer.

In 'Shall We All Commit Suicide?', the words were Churchill's but the science was the Prof's. It was a similar story in 1931 with 'Fifty Years Hence'. All the scientific statements in the article 'are supported by very high technical authority', Churchill reassured the editor of *Strand* magazine, 'and though very startling cannot be effectively disputed'.[65] That authority was Lindemann. But on this occasion much of the literary rendering was his as well. When Churchill asked for help with the piece, the Prof came up with an eleven-page document the bulk of which found its way unaltered into the final article.[66] 'We know enough to be sure that the scientific achievements of the next fifty years will be far greater, more rapid and more surprising, than those we have already experienced', Churchill/Lindemann argued, and that 'new sources of power, vastly more important than any we yet know, will surely be discovered'. The article went on to prophesy the nuclear age:

> Nuclear energy is incomparably greater than the molecular energy which we use today. The coal a man can get in a day can easily do five hundred times as much work as the man himself. Nuclear energy is at least one million times more powerful still ... There is no question among scientists that this gigantic source of energy exists. What is lacking is the match to set the bonfire alight ... The Scientists are looking for this.

But what if they found it? Or, having found it, the power fell into the wrong hands? In considering these questions, Churchill made some of his most obviously personal contributions to the article by warning at several points of the dangers of nuclear energy pressed into service by the Soviet Union, the loathed product of the 1917 Bolshevik revolution.[67]

This brings us to our third introductory theme, Churchill's anti-communism. In the era before the emergence of Hitler and the Nazis it was international communism which occupied pride of place in his personal ideological demonology. On 10 November 1918, a year after the Bolsheviks seized power in Russia, and on the very eve of the Armistice ending the First World War, Churchill warned the War Cabinet that '[w]e might have to build up the German Army' in the years to come 'as it was important to get Germany on her legs again for fear of the spread of Bolshevism'.[68] Later that same month, he spoke publicly of the 'animal form of Barbarism' practised by the Bolsheviks who maintained themselves in power 'by bloody and wholesale butcheries and murders', including those of the Tsar and his family. 'Civilisation is being completely extinguished over gigantic areas, while Bolsheviks hop and caper like troops of ferocious baboons amid the ruins of cities and the corpses of their victims.'[69]

Variations on this bestial theme punctuated many of Churchill's speeches as did the notion of a plague-riddled Russia: the Bolsheviks were likened to a 'cancer' and to 'swarms of typhus-bearing vermin' destroying 'the health and even the souls of nations'.[70] In 1919, when Russia became Churchill's professional politico-military concern as Minister for War, he went so far as to advocate a form of pest control, the use of poison gas to counteract the Red Army vermin as one element in a dynamic programme of backing for the anti-Leninist White forces battling the Bolsheviks in the Russian civil war.[71] However, when he went on to press for direct British armed intervention on the side of the Whites, albeit as part of an international coalition, he ran foul of Prime Minister Lloyd George who, in resisting Churchill's crusading zeal, better understood the parlous state of the UK economy not to mention the mood of the British public for whom overseas military adventures, after the loss of more than 700,000 war-dead in four years, had minimal allure.[72]

Aside from his ideological repugnance, Churchill had been morally outraged when the Bolsheviks concluded a separate peace with Germany in March 1918 which freed large numbers of German troops to return from the east to fight in the west. 'Every British and French soldier killed last year', he told an audience in London in April 1919, 'was really done to death by Lenin and Trotsky, not in fair war, but by the treacherous desertion of an ally without parallel in the history of the world'.[73] The Red Army's invasion of Poland and the Russo-Polish war which followed, together with worries about a possible Bolshevik surge westwards towards Germany, kept Churchill's anti-communist fervour aflame. 'The policy I will always advance', he told the Oxford Union in November 1920, 'is the overthrow and destruction of that criminal regime' in Moscow. He added, by way of a dig at his own government, that he had 'not always been able to give that clear view as full an effect as I would have desired'.[74] This was too much for Lloyd George. Concerned that Churchill had 'Bolshevism on the brain' and was incapable of fulfilling the responsibilities of his War-Air portfolio in the round, in January 1921 he moved him to the Colonial Office. Two months later, to Churchill's mortification, Anglo-Soviet trade relations were established, a move which amounted to *de facto* British recognition of the Bolshevist regime (full recognition followed in 1924).[75]

It is sometimes suggested that Churchill's anti-communism was deliberately exaggerated in order to re-establish his right-wing credentials prior to leaving the Liberals, with whom he had become disenchanted, for the Conservative benches – and indeed he duly re-crossed the floor in 1924 and was quickly rewarded when Tory Prime Minister Stanley Baldwin appointed him Chancellor of the Exchequer.[76] While there may be something in this domestic-political argument, Churchill's detestation of communism was so real and so raw that for a time it led him to see good things in fascism. In 1927, 'charmed' by Benito Mussolini after meeting him in Rome, he declared himself 'whole-heartedly' behind the Italian people in their 'triumphant struggle against the bestial appetites and passions of Leninism', and as late as the mid-1930s he was still publicly praising *il Duce,* the 'Roman genius', as 'the greatest lawgiver among living men'.[77]

This ideological mindset also led him to take a comparatively benign view when Japan invaded Manchuria in 1931 and established the puppet state of Manchukuo. 'I hope we shall try in England to understand a little the position of Japan, an ancient state with the highest sense of national honour and patriotism and with a teeming population and a remarkable energy', he told the Anti-Socialist and Anti-Communist Union in February 1933. 'On the one side they see the dark menace of Soviet Russia. On the other the chaos of China, four or five provinces of which are actually now being tortured, under Communist rule.'[78] For similarly ideologically-determined reasons, the Spanish civil war, 'the acid test of anti-fascist credentials' for many of his contemporaries, prompted no condemnation of General Franco and his anti-Republican forces.[79]

When Churchill allowed his scientific imagination to meld with his anti-communism the outcome was often disturbing. 'Fifty Years Hence' in 1931 is a prime example. Foreshadowing Aldous Huxley, whose dystopian *Brave New World* was published a year later, and revealing once more his admiration for *The Time Machine,* he warned that the 'breeding of human beings' of 'admirable physical development' but with 'mental endowment stunted' might soon prove possible. Science, in other words, could yet deliver to Soviet leader Joseph Stalin a race of genetically-engineered Morlocks ready to do his bidding:

A being might be produced capable of tending a machine but without other ambitions. Our minds recoil from such fearful eventualities, and the laws of a Christian civilization will prevent them. But might not lop-sided creatures of this type fit in well with the Communist doctrines of Russia? Might not the Union of Soviet Socialist Republics armed with all the power of science find it in harmony with all their aims to produce a race adapted to mechanical tasks and with no other ideas but to obey the Communist State? ... Robots could be made to fit the grisly theories of Communism.

Moreover, in a future 'which our children may live to see', he envisioned

[e]xplosive forces, energy, materials, machinery ... available upon a scale which can annihilate whole nations. Despotisms and tyrannies will be able to prescribe the lives and even the wishes of their subjects in a manner never known since time began. If to these tremendous and awful powers is added the pitiless sub-human wickedness which we now see embodied in one of the most powerful reigning governments, who shall say that the world itself will not be wrecked, or indeed that it ought not to be wrecked?[80]

The Cold War and the nuclear arms race were still many years off but with a predictive acuity sharpened by Lindemann's input, and a scientific imagination heightened by Wellsian immersion, Churchill anticipated both. He worried, though, that mankind might not be mature enough to handle the terrible gifts that science was poised to bestow.

There are secrets too mysterious for man in his present state to know, secrets which, once penetrated, may be fatal to human happiness and glory. But the busy hands of the scientists are already fumbling with the keys of all the chambers hitherto forbidden to mankind. Without an equal growth of Mercy, Pity, Peace and Love, Science herself may destroy all that makes human life majestic and tolerable.[81]

Throughout the remainder of the decade the hands of one particular kind of scientist, the nuclear physicist, would be busier than most, and by 1939, when Europe was pitched into war, the atomic future sketched in 'Fifty Years Hence' was well on its way to becoming the destructive present.

Until the end of the nineteenth century it was generally accepted that all matter was composed of indestructible particles, or atoms. It was further held that the atoms of one element could not be converted into those of another. From the mid-1890s, however, the inviolability of this principle was increasingly challenged. French physicist Henri Becquerel was arguably the first to note that one particular heavy element, uranium, emitted radiation which could penetrate matter. Then, in 1898, Pierre and Marie Curie isolated a new element, radium, from uranium ores, which possessed the same property – radioactivity – to a much greater degree. In 1902, the New Zealander Ernest Rutherford, widely regarded as the father of modern nuclear physics, and the English radio-chemist Frederick Soddy, contended that this phenomenon could be explained only if the atomic structure of certain elements was in fact unstable. Further research by Rutherford either side of the First World War, at Manchester and at the Cavendish, led to the proposition that the atom of one element could in theory be transmuted into that of another. As part of this process, enormous amounts of hitherto pent-up nuclear energy would be released. The chemist Francis Aston, in an extrapolation later seized upon by Churchill, surmised that if the hydrogen in a glass of water could be changed into helium, the energy released could power the 80,000-ton RMS *Queen Mary* from England across the Atlantic to America and back again at full speed. This kind of energy release could also make for an incredibly powerful explosion.[82]

In 1932, a year after Churchill's 'Fifty Years Hence' was published, two former pupils of Rutherford, the Englishman John Cockcroft and the Irishman Ernest Walton, took nuclear research to another level. After building a machine at the Cavendish that could fire a beam of high-energy protons into metal targets, they found that some of the nuclei in the target atoms of lithium disintegrated to form nuclei of helium thereby achieving artificial transmutation, the dream of alchemists down the ages. More than this, they demonstrated experimentally what Albert Einstein had so famously articulated theoretically ($E=mc^2$), namely that this whole process was accompanied by the release of energy proportionate to the weight of the material involved.[83] That same year, there occurred one of the great turning-points in atomic science when the English physicist James Chadwick, also a Rutherford protégé, discovered the neutron. Previously, there had been no known means of efficiently penetrating – as opposed to bombarding – the nucleus of an atom, where most of its mass and therefore its energy was concentrated, since charged protons, if used for this purpose, tended to be repulsed by the charged nucleus. The uncharged neutron existed only in theory until Chadwick confirmed its existence to tremendous acclaim in the scientific community (it won him a Nobel Prize) but also to some foreboding. Was this the key that would unlock the power chambers of nature? In 1933, when Hitler became Chancellor of Germany, the French physicist Paul Langevin warned that if it 'gets into the wrong hands', the neutron 'can do the world a good deal more damage than that fool who will sooner or later go to the dogs'.[84]

But what if the hands belonged to the fool himself? This dread thought, a Nazi weapon of mass destruction, would later drive Anglo-American wartime efforts to develop an atomic bomb. Initially, however, there was much scepticism in scientific circles as to the practical potentialities of atomic energy; in 1934, Einstein likened the constructive or destructive utilization of energy from nuclei to 'shooting birds in the dark, in a country where there are few birds', while Rutherford would die in 1937 convinced that '[a]nyone who expects a source of power from the transformation of … atoms is talking moonshine'.[85] Yet within a year of Rutherford's passing, two scientists working at the Kaiser Wilhelm Institute in Berlin, Otto Hahn and Fritz Strassmann, 'kicked the pebble that was to start the nuclear avalanche'.[86] Conducting their research against a glowering political and military backdrop – in March 1938 Hitler annexed Austria and by the late summer German pressure on Czechoslovakia to surrender the Sudetenland brought Europe to the brink of war – they established that uranium nuclei, when assailed by neutrons, yielded up small amounts of another and lighter element, barium. They then went beyond Cockcroft and Walton in postulating that in sundering the nucleus of a uranium atom, other secondary neutrons were liberated to invade and divide neighbouring nuclei. The energy released from this chain reaction – which their some-time collaborator Otto Frisch christened fission – was potentially awesome.[87]

In December 1938, Hahn and Strassmann published a tentatively-framed article in *Die Naturwissenschaften*, and then, after further refining their research, presented a more assertive article in the same journal in February 1939. Soon the international scientific community was abuzz with excitement as physicists at the great research centres, from Cambridge, Paris and Copenhagen to Princeton, Göttingen and Berkeley, conducted their own laboratory experiments, corroborated (and in some cases amplified) the Hahn-Strassmann findings and then disseminated their conclusions throughout the international 'republic of science'.[88] In Britain, America and elsewhere, the press latched on to the science fiction aspects of uranium fission, with H. G. Wells' 1914 story *The World Set Free*, with its theme of atomic weapons and atomic warfare in a world 'flaring … into a monstrous phase of destruction', a popular point of reference.[89] Scientists, in contrast, were loath to admit that fission must inevitably lead to apocalyptic weapons, while those who did acknowledge the theoretical potentialities were comforted by the daunting technical obstacles in the path of turning atomic energy to any practical military use. 'Of course the spectre of a bomb … was there as well', Frisch later wrote, 'but for a while anyhow, it looked as though it need not frighten us.'[90]

By the end of 1939, more than one hundred articles had appeared in scientific journals worldwide discussing, directly or indirectly, uranium fission.[91] One of the most influential of these appeared on 1 September, the day that Germany invaded Poland and brought war to Europe. Niels Bohr, the brilliant and revered Danish physicist and Director of the Institute for Theoretical Physics in Copenhagen, along with a young collaborator, the American physicist John Wheeler, published a paper in *The Physical Review* which argued, reassuringly, that it was only uranium's lighter isotope, U-235, that was fissionable. Given that U-235 was only present in natural uranium (U-238) in miniscule quantities (0.7 percent of the whole), the only chance of bringing off a chain reaction was to find a way to slow down the neutrons so that they collided more effectively with the rare U-235 instead of being absorbed to no great effect by the mass of non-fissile U-238. Slow neutron reaction, however, spoke to uranium's potential as a source of power, not as an explosive. In theory, a bomb might be realizable if some method could be found of enriching natural uranium with a much higher concentration of U-235 so that fast neutrons would hit their targets with regularity, but few scientists, including Bohr, thought this remotely practicable in view of the daunting technical-industrial obstacles.[92] Amongst the leading sceptics was F. A. Lindemann.

By the early 1930s the Churchill–Lindemann friendship had fully ripened. They saw a great deal of one another (the Prof was the most regular non-family visitor to Chartwell), took holidays together (some paid for by Lindemann after Churchill's finances took a hit in the Wall Street crash), and went on a driving tour of Germany in 1932 during which they were forcibly struck by the 'Hitler atmosphere'.[93] That Lindemann was such a fixture at Chartwell is a reminder that the decade marked for Churchill his wilderness years. After refusing to follow the modestly progressive Conservative party-line on constitutional reform for India in 1931, he spent the next eight years out of office, out of favour and out of sorts. He never forgot the Prof's devotion and constancy during this difficult time, not just as a friend but as an ally in the campaign he began to wage from mid-decade to alert government and country to the military danger posed by Nazi Germany and to the related need to commence wide-scale rearmament, especially in the air.[94] As an 'alarm clock', however, Churchill was 'a rasping one, which made most listeners more anxious to turn it off than to respond to its summons'.[95] Scarred by the searing experience of the Great War, many people in Britain looked to the League of Nations, and to disarmament rather than rearmament, as the best guarantee of peace and security. But where they saw hope, Churchill saw folly and illusion.[96]

Churchill's identification of Germany as a clear and present danger to Britain was accompanied by a remarkable change in his attitude towards the Soviet Union. The shift was not so much ideological ('I will not pretend that, if I had to choose between Communism and Nazi-ism, I would choose Communism', he averred in 1937) as geo-strategic.[97] Churchill held a nineteenth-century European statesman's view of international relations as essentially a struggle for mastery, but this outlook included due respect for the balance of power. Accordingly, from a wholly pragmatic standpoint, he was prepared from the mid-1930s to consider a tactical alliance between Britain, France and the USSR, a form of regional collective security under the aegis of the League of Nations, to deter or, should war come, contain Hitlerite aggression.[98] '[W]e all need a strong Russia', he told the Soviet ambassador to London in November 1937. 'I'm wholly for Stalin.'[99]

For many people in Britain terrified at the prospect of a new war, the appeasement of Hitler's Germany was initially preferable to Churchill's more robust approach. Churchill, too, was an appeaser in the sense that he had long maintained that the draconian economic clauses of the Versailles treaty, which had crippled the Weimar Republic, were vindictive, futile and in need of revision.[100] When, however, the Nazis 'sprang forward armed to the teeth' in the second half of the 1930s he became much more sharply critical – and not just of Germany but of Neville Chamberlain who, having succeeded Baldwin as Prime Minister in 1937, took appeasement to new heights.[101] When the Czech crisis flared in the summer of 1938, Churchill was not necessarily opposed to a negotiated solution by which the German-speaking *Sudetendeutsch* were permitted to join the Third Reich, but he did want Chamberlain to make clear to Hitler that Britain would fight if Germany pursued its aims, in Czechoslovakia or elsewhere, by force of arms.[102] He was to be disappointed. The Munich settlement that September, which gave Hitler the Sudetenland, struck him as a spineless surrender and he predicted that in the absence of any obvious will to resist in Britain (or France), Germany would grab the whole of Czechoslovakia sooner rather than later. There could never be 'friendship between British democracy and the Nazi power', he warned the Commons in the Munich debate, 'that power which spurns Christian ethics, which cheers its onward course by barbarous paganism, which vaunts the spirit of aggression and conquest, which derives strength and perverted pleasure from persecution, and uses . . . with pitiless brutality the threat of murderous force'.[103]

This was not at all what Chamberlain and his supporters wanted to hear, and the speech, along with others in like key, did little to improve Churchill's standing either with the Tory leadership or the wider parliamentary party. Six months on, however, when Hitler tore up the Munich agreement and annexed the remainder of the Czech state, Churchill's jeremiads were vindicated and the government, and the country at large, came to accept the need for a firmer line vis-à-vis Germany. Churchill himself chose the moment to renew publicly his call for an alliance with the Soviet Union, but an Anglo-French diplomatic probe, launched in Moscow's direction in the summer of 1939, was so half-hearted and desultory that Stalin chose to look elsewhere for an assurance of security.[104] In August came the news of the Nazi–Soviet non-aggression pact, a stunning development which not only rendered any further Anglo-French approaches to Moscow pointless, but made war in Europe certain.

Throughout his wilderness years Churchill remained alert to the transformative impact that modern science was likely to bring to the business of killing. 'If the Great War were resumed', he told Clementine in March 1935, 'it will be the end of the world . . . How I hope and pray we may be spared such senseless horrors'.[105] Four years later, when the Hahn-Strassmann fission experiments made world headlines, Churchill looked to Lindemann for reassurance that German science was not about to present Hitler with that fearsome bomb no bigger than an orange. Happily, the Prof was able to put his mind at ease. An atomic weapon was a theoretical possibility, he conceded, but as Bohr had pointed out, the technical difficulties in turning theory into reality were so formidable that a bomb would remain the stuff of Wellsian science fiction for the foreseeable future. When the German Foreign Minister Joachim von Ribbentrop went on to speak publicly of Germany's possession of unspecified weapons of mass destruction, Churchill was therefore relatively unfazed. On 13 August 1939, two weeks before the Nazi–Soviet pact was revealed, he sent Kingsley Wood, the Secretary of State for Air, a Lindemann memorandum which downplayed the danger of a German A-bomb. Referring to the Hahn-Strassmann experiments, the Prof felt it was 'essential' that both the government and public 'realise that there is no danger that this discovery, however great its scientific interest, and perhaps ultimately its practical importance, will lead to results capable of being put into operation on a large scale for several years'. The Lindemann memorandum went on:

> There are indications that tales will be deliberately circulated when international tension becomes acute about the adaptation of this process to produce some terrible new secret explosive, capable of wiping out London . . . For this reason it is imperative to state the true position. First, the best authorities hold that only a minor constituent of uranium is effective in these processes, and that it will be necessary to extract this before large-scale results are possible. This will be a matter of many years. Secondly, the chain process can take place only if the uranium is concentrated in a large mass. As soon as the energy develops it will explode with a mild detonation before any really violent effects can be produced . . . Thirdly, these experiments cannot be carried out on a small scale. If they had been successfully done on a big scale . . . it would be impossible to keep them secret. Fourthly, only a comparatively small amount of uranium in the territories of what used to be Czechoslovakia is under the control of Berlin.

For these reasons, the Prof concluded, 'the fear that this new discovery has provided the Nazis with some sinister, new, secret explosive with which to destroy their enemies is clearly without foundation'.[106] Churchill seconded his friend. 'I expect Lindemann's view is right in that there is no immediate danger', he told Wood, 'although undoubtedly the human race is crawling nearer to the point when it will be able to destroy itself completely'.[107]

In hindsight, what this paper shows is how far Churchill's views on atomic energy were essentially the Prof's views. Lindemann had real doubts about the practicability of a bomb and so did Churchill. Two years later, when Lindemann changed his mind and asserted that a uranium bomb was a realistic proposition after all, Churchill echoed him. But something else changed in those two years. In August 1939, Churchill was where he had been for the best part of a decade, in the political wilderness. In August 1941, he was fifteen months into his wartime premiership.

CHAPTER 2
TUBE ALLOYS

Looking back on Churchill's career, A. J. P. Taylor conjectured that if his subject had died, say, on the eve of the outbreak of the Second World War, he would probably now be remembered as 'an eccentric character, sometimes a radical, sometimes a Tory, and running over with brilliant ideas that were more often wrong than right'.[1] This is very likely true. But he did not die. Instead, when Britain declared war on Germany on 3 September, Neville Chamberlain, bowing to popular pressure to bring Churchill back into government, appointed him First Lord of the Admiralty with a seat in the War Cabinet. The story of Churchill's remarkable political comeback at the near-pensionable age of 64 has been told many times but what is not always appreciated is that the Prof was with him all the way. Lindemann became Churchill's personal advisor at the Admiralty where he established a statistical unit to compile accurate facts and figures across the naval spectrum for the First Lord's consideration. He even took rooms at the nearby Carlton Hotel so that he could join Churchill most nights after dinner and stay with him talking into the small hours as though Chartwell had come to Whitehall.[2]

Nine months later, when Hitler's *Blitzkrieg* in Western Europe was added to concurrent British reverses in Norway, the ruin of Chamberlain's premiership was complete. It was widely supposed that Lord Halifax, the Foreign Secretary, would form a new government, but in the event it was Churchill who emerged from an audience with the King on 10 May 1940 bearing that heavy commission (he had been 'full of fire & determination', the King wrote in his diary).[3] Four decades earlier, as a subaltern in search of glory on the North-West Frontier, Churchill wrote to his mother avowing 'faith in my star' and insisting that he was 'intended to do something in this world'.[4] Now, as Prime Minister and simultaneously Minister of Defence, he felt as though 'I were walking with destiny, and that all my past life had been but a preparation for this hour and for this trial'.[5] But he did not walk alone. Lindemann, slightly stoopingly, walked with him.

The Churchill version of 1940 is romantic and compelling, but as Paul Addison reminds us, it 'scarcely diminishes Churchill to point out that in some ways luck was on his side'.

Having been out of office for most of the 1930s he could not be held responsible for Britain's plight: this time the scapegoats were the 'men of Munich'. With German bombers droning overhead and blood-curdling propaganda issuing from Berlin, the threat of invasion and occupation could not have been more stark. Such were the circumstances of the time that what had previously been perceived as weaknesses or flaws in Churchill's character now became strengths. Few now complained that he was a warmonger or a would-be Napoleon: the zeal with which he waged war was now a precious asset. Nor was it any longer a black mark against him that he thought of himself above party. What better recommendation could there be for the leader of a government of national unity? . . . As for the allegation that he was an impossibilist, an impossibilist was exactly what was called for.[6]

Many years later, John Colville, assistant Private Secretary to Chamberlain, remembered the trepidation he felt at the prospect of Churchill, with his reputation for unpredictability and ghastly decision-making, taking over as Prime Minister. He also shuddered at the thought of Churchill's 'myrmidons', the likes of press baron Lord Beaverbrook, the gossipy Brendan Bracken and a certain F. A. Lindemann, being given the run of Number 10. 'The country had fallen into the hands of an adventurer, brilliant no doubt and an inspiring orator, but a man whose friends and supporters were unfit to be trusted with the conduct of affairs in a state of supreme emergency', he recalled. 'Seldom can a Prime Minister have taken office with "the Establishment" . . . so dubious of the choice and so prepared to find its doubts justified.' Yet, after just a month of Churchill's premiership, 'all was changed' and Colville was left to wonder 'if there has ever been such a rapid transformation of opinion in Whitehall and of the tempo at which business was conducted'.[7]

At Westminster, acceptance was slower in coming. Within the Conservative Party, a phalanx of resentful Chamberlainites held Churchill personally responsible for their leader's demise; those with long memories had still not forgiven his desertion in 1904; and many, perhaps a majority, seem to have regarded him as a vainglorious risk-taker.[8] In the country generally, however, Churchill's stock was high. 'Poor people', he mused. 'They trust me, and I can give them nothing but disaster for quite a long time.'[9] The Labour leader Clement Attlee, along with fellow socialist Arthur Greenwood, recognizing the need to bury partisan differences at a moment of acute national peril, agreed to serve in the War Cabinet while other Labour (and some Liberal) figures took seats alongside Conservatives at the wider Cabinet table in a new National Government. Nevertheless it would be some while before Churchill's authority as Prime Minister was established and in the interim his camarilla – 'gangsters', Halifax preferred – remained the object of deep suspicion.[10]

One myrmidon in particular, the tall, unsmiling and be-bowlered Prof, was more widely disliked than most. Those outside observers who viewed him as an unelected and unaccountable *éminence grise* would have been startled to discover just how far his writ actually ran. Lindemann not only brought his statistical team with him from the Admiralty and provided guidance to the Prime Minister on scientific matters but read and commented on many of the confidential documents that passed across Churchill's desk and was even privy to the Ultra decrypts which flowed from Bletchley Park following the cracking of the German Enigma code.[11] He also took charge of MD-1 (known as "Churchill's toyshop"), a top-secret Ministry of Defence engineering group based at Whitchurch in Buckinghamshire and responsible for developing special battlefield weapons.[12] Protected by the Prime Minister, Lindemann became a licensed gadfly, flitting across all areas of Whitehall activity, the nosy and resented Man Friday of the war leader.[13] Had he been of a sweeter disposition, the animosity towards him, which was personal as much as professional, might have been lessened. As it was, his acid tongue and tactlessness heightened the antipathy of ministers and officials and led many of them to conclude that his influence on Churchill was at least malign and possibly harmful. Looking back, Colville could remember 'no more unpopular figure in Whitehall than Professor F. A. Lindemann'.[14]

At the time, however, nothing seemed able to arrest the Prof's ascent. In June 1941, he was awarded a peerage, becoming Lord Cherwell (an elevation which prompted a fresh rash of snipes about prime ministerial patronage run amok).[15] The following year, Churchill made him Paymaster-General and secured his appointment as a Privy Counsellor, but if he thought that formalising his friend's position in government would silence the critics he was wrong.[16] Still, disliked though he was, the fact remains that Lindemann, through his friendship with arguably the greatest statesman in modern British history, exercised more influence on government and public life than any scientist before or possibly since. If, as Addison maintains, it is 'no exaggeration to say that … Churchill carried the world on his shoulders', especially in 1940, then at times Lindemann carried Churchill.[17] Indeed, as we will see, in August 1941 he would carry him right across the atomic Rubicon.

During the 1930s, a steady flow of refugee scientists from Europe, many of them German or Austrian Jews, took sanctuary in Britain. Most sought but few obtained permanent academic positions and many ended up re-emigrating, mainly to the USA. Two Jewish refugees who stayed were Austrian physicist Otto Frisch, on secondment to Birmingham University from Bohr's institute in Copenhagen when war broke out, and his friend and colleague at Birmingham, Rudolf Peierls, a German who had lived and worked in England for several years. Although uranium fission had been achieved under laboratory conditions it was an altogether different matter to repeat the process on a large scale. As for a bomb, estimates of the tonnage of uranium required to bring off an explosive chain reaction were so enormous as to rule-out construction of a remotely deliverable weapon.[18] At the start of 1940, however, Frisch and Peierls made the theoretical breakthrough which, in retrospect, began the countdown to Hiroshima and Nagasaki.

Debarred by their foreign origins from participating in research on the most secret of UK wartime scientific projects – radar, for example – the two passed a freezing Midlands winter trading ideas. After much reflection, they concluded that instead of trying to increase the amount of uranium in order to bring off a chain reaction, the highly fissionable U-235 could, in theory, be extracted. To their amazement and perturbation they estimated that just a few pounds of pure U-235 might be all that was required to produce a bomb of unparalleled violence. In alighting on isotope separation, Frisch and Peierls had reduced the scale of the challenge involved in making a weapon from the near impossible to the merely extraordinarily difficult, from 'filling the Empire State Building or the Royal Albert Hall with individual grains of sand, one by one', as Ronald Clark put it, to 'filling a barrel'.[19] In later years, Frisch was often asked why he and Peierls, knowing where their findings could lead, did not keep quiet. His answer was always the same. 'We were at war, and the idea was reasonably obvious; very probably some German scientists had had the same idea and were working on it.' Peierls agreed: 'We were desperately afraid.'[20]

In March 1940, Frisch and Peierls prepared a memorandum for their departmental head at Birmingham, the Australian Mark Oliphant, asserting the practicability of a 'super bomb' which would draw on the energy stored in a modest amount of U-235 to disburse the explosive equivalent of more than a thousand tons of dynamite. 'This energy is liberated in a small volume, in which it will, for an instant, produce a temperature comparable to that in the interior of the sun', they wrote. The blast from the explosion would destroy life in a wide area, possibly the size of the centre of a large city, while a proportion of the liberated energy would go on to emit dangerous radiations meaning that anyone entering the affected area – rescue teams, for instance – would certainly die. The memorandum also identified what we now know as fall-out. 'Some of this radioactivity will be carried along with the wind and will spread the contamination; several miles downwind this may kill people.' Their conclusions were chilling. First, as a weapon, 'the super-bomb would be practically irresistible', with no material or structure capable of resisting its force. Second, due to the 'spread of radioactive substances with the wind, the bomb could probably not be used without killing large numbers of civilians', and this, Frisch and Peierls opined (with touching naiveté), might make it 'unsuitable as a weapon for use by this country'. Third, while they had no evidence to suggest that their theories and extrapolations had occurred to other scientists, the core knowledge had been in the public domain internationally for some time and it was 'quite conceivable' that Germany had been actively pursuing weapons development for two years. Since the 'only effective reply would be a counter-threat with a similar bomb' – a view which spoke to their interest in nuclear deterrence rather than combat use – it was essential that the government start its own programme as soon as possible.[21]

Scepticism about the military potential of uranium remained widespread in scientific circles at this time.[22] Oliphant, though, was impressed and passed the memorandum on to Sir Henry Tizard, chairman of the Committee for the Scientific Survey of Air Warfare, the Whitehall body most concerned with the application of science to war.[23] A chemist by training, Tizard was dubious about the chances of anything of military value emerging from further research, at any rate within a time-frame likely to make an impact on the course of the war, but he set aside his personal misgivings and arranged for further investigation by a bespoke committee under Sir George Paget Thomson, Professor of Physics at Imperial College and amongst the minority of genuinely uranium-aware, bomb-conscious scientists in the country.[24] Falling under the sway of the Air Ministry (and from June 1940 the Ministry of Aircraft Production), the committee was small but eminent: besides Thomson himself it included James Chadwick, the discoverer of the neutron; John Cockcroft, famous for his work on "splitting the atom"; and from Birmingham, Oliphant and his deputy Philip Moon. P. M. S. Blackett of Manchester University joined the group a little later. Formally and ponderously named the Sub-Committee on the U-bomb of the Committee for the Scientific Survey of Air Warfare, the group soon acquired a shorter acronymically meaningless codename, MAUD.[25]

The first meeting took place on 10 April 1940 at the Royal Society's headquarters at Burlington House in London. Ironically, Frisch and Peierls were initially kept at arm's length for security reasons – the former was still classified as an enemy alien and the latter had only lately been naturalized – but when Peierls pointed out the absurdity of 'trying to keep our own ideas from us' the restrictions were eased and they were permitted to join the committee's technical advisory team.[26] At the outset, Thomson and his colleagues tended to share Tizard's doubts but they gradually changed their collective mind as the calculations advanced by Frisch and Peierls were shown to be sound, as MAUD's own lab-based work on isotope separation (in particular the gaseous diffusion method) yielded promising results, and as leading American physicists, consulted during the process, added their own confirmatory judgement.[27]

Events beyond the Palladian facade of Burlington House provided the MAUD scientists with an ongoing reminder of the importance of their work. The day before the committee's inaugural meeting, the "phoney war" came to an abrupt end when Germany invaded Norway and Denmark. A month later, France and the Low Countries felt the full force of Hitler's *Blitzkrieg*. Within a fortnight of Churchill becoming Prime Minister, German armies had over-run much of France and were bearing down on the Channel coast and threatening to annihilate the British Expeditionary Force (BEF). For a small but crucial period of time, the Dunkirk escape-hatch remained open and 330,000 troops, the bulk of the BEF, were able to get back to England as part of operation Dynamo (a marine 'magic carpet' Churchill later called it).[28] When, soon after, France surrendered, a Nazi invasion of England seemed sure to follow. In a speech to Parliament at the start of June, Churchill insisted that Britain would fight on 'until, in God's good time, the New World, with all its power and might, steps forth to the rescue and the liberation of the old'.[29] Even as he spoke he must have known that his country's future hinged on the most tremendous gamble – that it could survive long enough in a Nazi-dominated Europe for the American political pendulum to swing from isolation and non-intervention to internationalism and belligerency. As it turned out, it would be another eighteen months before the United States entered the war, a desperate interval when the apparent miracle of deliverance that was victory in the Battle of Britain gave way to the aerial devastation of the Blitz and to national life-threatening shipping losses in the Battle of the Atlantic.

These tumultuous developments gave the MAUD committee plenty of reason to press ahead rapidly with its programme of investigation. So did a story in the *Times* three days before Churchill entered Number 10 which suggested that a Nazi uranium project was already in train. The authorities in Berlin, it was reported, had 'ordered all German scientists in this field – physicists, chemists, and engineers – to drop all other experiments and devote themselves to [uranium] work alone'.[30] Against this, the fall of France, a strategic disaster for Britain in so many ways, produced a scientific boon with the arrival in England of a number of talented refugee physicists. For several years researchers at the

Laboratoire de Chimie Nucléaire had been investigating the fissile potential of heavy atoms and, in particular, the prospects for achieving a controlled chain reaction using uranium moderated by heavy water in a boiler (what today we would call a reactor). In June 1940, two of the leading lights in the French team, Hans von Halban and Lew Kowarski, managed to get themselves, their great knowledge and, through roundabout means, the largest stock of heavy water in the world, across the Channel. Germany's loss became Britain's gain. Initially employed at the Cavendish, the Frenchmen were later put on the payroll of the Department of Scientific and Industrial Research and their work on uranium as a source of power complemented the MAUD committee's investigation of uranium as an explosive.[31]

In July 1941, fifteen months after it began its labours, the MAUD committee delivered its verdict. An atomic bomb of incredible destructive force was not only theoretically possible, the final report contended, but if manufactured and employed as a weapon was likely to lead to decisive results in the war. Thomson admitted that he and his colleagues had 'entered the project with more scepticism than belief' but they were now prepared to state categorically that 'it will be possible to make an effective uranium bomb'. Relying on around 25 pounds of U-235 – obtained via gaseous diffusion, a process whereby uranium hexafluoride gas is repeatedly forced through ultra-fine permeable membranes to separate U-235 isotopes from their heavier U-238 counterparts – this bomb would deliver a destructive yield equivalent to 1,800 tons of TNT. In addition, it would release large quantities of radioactive substances and make the area 'near to where the bomb exploded dangerous to human life for a long period'. The report noted that uranium as a source of power (the Halban-Kowarski side of MAUD's research) was of great but long-term importance, but in the midst of a war the top priority had to be the initiation of a full-scale programme of weapons research and development. Close cooperation with the Americans, even the siting of a gaseous diffusion plant in the USA, was recommended. If a major effort was put in, a bomb might be combat-ready within two years. Meanwhile Germany was likely working on its own weapon, but even if this were not so, and even if the British project failed to achieve any results in wartime, the MAUD scientists believed that 'the effort would not be wasted ... since no nation would care to risk being caught without a weapon of such decisive possibilities' in the postwar era.[32]

For all the brilliance of Thomson and his team, the MAUD committee was only a sub-committee of a sub-committee and it was by no means certain that its recommendations would be taken seriously higher up the Whitehall chain of command. Some early reactions were in fact lukewarm. The Director of Scientific Research in the Ministry of Aircraft Production, David Pye, to whom the report was formally addressed, expressed serious misgivings: the work could take more than a decade to produce anything of military consequence, not the two years stated in the report, a view shared by Blackett, the one dissenting voice on the MAUD committee itself. Nor was Tizard bowled over. No longer directly concerned with the Committee for the Scientific Survey of Air Warfare, his opinion was still widely respected in Whitehall. Setting aside 'the physics of the problem', which were still to be 'settled', Tizard remained worried about embarking 'on this big and highly speculative industrial undertaking' at a time of desperate national danger. Would the country not be better off investing in military technologies with a greater prospect of making a difference in the current rather than a future war?[33] The MAUD recommendations thus risked being still-born. What the committee needed was a champion of standing and influence in Whitehall, someone capable of selling its prescription to the highest political authority. Someone like the Prof.

As it happened, Lindemann, like Thomson and his colleagues, had undergone a conversion. Thanks to the proselytizing zeal of Franz Simon, a brilliant German-Jewish physical chemist brought out of Germany to the Clarendon in the 1930s, Lindemann had moved from being a bomb-sceptic (witness his August 1939 memorandum) to a bomb-believer. Simon was convinced that sufficient fissionable material to fuel a bomb could be obtained by gaseous diffusion. He also thought it highly probable that the Nazis had worked this out for themselves.[34] Simon brought Peierls to Oxford to support his efforts to alert the Prof to the dangers and the possibilities. 'I do not know him sufficiently well', Peierls later wrote of Lindemann, 'to translate his grunts correctly' but he seemed 'convinced . . . that the whole thing ought to be taken seriously'.[35] This was indeed so. In July 1941, Lindemann endorsed the MAUD report. More than this, he had a close personal friend, a politician, whose long-standing fascination with the appliance of science to warfare suggested that he, too, would be most interested in the idea of an atomic bomb.

One of the qualities that Churchill especially valued in the Prof was his knack of conveying complicated subjects in simple form. 'Lindemann could decipher the signals from the experts on the far horizons and explain to me in lucid, homely terms what the issues were', he recalled.

> There are only twenty-four hours in a day, of which at least seven must be spent in sleep and three in eating and relaxation. Anyone in my position would have been ruined if he had attempted to dive into depths which not even a lifetime of study could plumb. What I had to grasp were the practical results, and just as Lindemann gave me his view for all it was worth . . . so I made sure by turning on my power-relay that some at least of these terrible and incomprehensible truths emerged in executive decisions.[36]

In August 1941, the Prof performed arguably his most important act of compression when, in just over two close-typed pages, he summarized for Churchill's benefit the MAUD report.

> I have frequently spoken to you about a super-explosive making use of energy in the nucleus of the atom which is something like a million times greater, weight for weight, than the chemical energy used in ordinary explosives. A great deal more work has been done here and in America and probably in Germany on this and it looks as if bombs might be produced and brought into use within, say, 2 years.

Owing to various complications it will probably not be quite as effective as might at first sight seem, but if all goes well it should be possible for one aeroplane to carry a somewhat elaborate bomb weighing about one ton which would explode with a violence equal to about 2,000 tons of TNT.

This estimate would turn out to be conservative: the weapons exploded over Hiroshima and Nagasaki yielded in the region of 18,000 and 21,000 tons of TNT-equivalence respectively. But no matter. In 1941, 2,000 tons – 2 kilotons – was impressive enough. *If* such a bomb could be made. The theory and extrapolations all said yes, Lindemann explained, but major obstacles remained, particularly the 'extremely elaborate and costly process' of isotope separation.

Lindemann went on to pose two determining questions. First, should Britain divert scarce money, resources and manpower away from the military needs of the moment to try to develop so futuristic a weapon? On this, he 'had no doubt whatever': the terrifying prospect of a Nazi A-bomb reduced the options here to nil. The initial financial outlay would be small, between £20,000 and £30,000, and after a further six months of experimentation it would be clear whether the Simon separation method was viable. At that point the government would need to decide whether to press ahead with building a full-scale diffusion plant. If it did, the expense inevitably would spiral. A plant capable of capturing enough U-235 to service a bomb a week might cost up to £5 million, but by the same token a plant to make 2,000 tons of TNT a week would cost even more. Second, assuming all went well in this first phase, where should the plant be built? Although the MAUD committee had worked 'in close collaboration with American scientists', he noted, 'I am strongly of the opinion that we should erect the plant in England or at worst in Canada.' He continued:

> The reasons against this course are obvious, i.e. shortage of man-power, danger of being bombed, etc. The reasons in favour are the better chance of maintaining secrecy (a vital point) but above all the fact that whoever possesses such a plant would be able to dictate terms to the world. However much I may trust my neighbour and depend on him, I am very much averse to putting myself completely at his mercy. I would, therefore, not press the Americans to undertake this work. I would just continue exchanging information and get into production over here without raising the question of whether they should do it or not.

Ministerial oversight of the project, Lindemann further recommended, should be given to Sir John Anderson, the Lord President of the Council, who 'by a strange coincidence researched uranium early in life'. Those presently theorising about a super-bomb, he ended, 'consider the odds are 10 to 1 on success within two years', but personally he 'would not bet more than 2 to 1 against or even money'. Nevertheless, it was 'quite clear that we must go forward. It would be unforgiveable if we let the Germans develop a process ahead of us by means of which they could defeat us in war or reverse the verdict after they had been defeated.'[37]

This was no simple précis. Rather, it stands as an exemplar of how Lindemann not only made complex science comprehensible for Churchill but did not hesitate to insert his personal opinion on connected political issues. Supportive of the recommendations of the MAUD report, he set out the case for UK independence from rather than partnership with the Americans. With Churchill already minded to view the war as 'a war of science, a war which could be won with new weapons', Lindemann's appeal was perfectly crafted to produce the outcome that he and the MAUD scientists wanted. 'Although personally I am quite content with the existing explosives', Churchill informed the Chiefs of Staff (COS) on 30 August, 'I feel that we must not stand in the path of improvement, and I therefore think that action should be taken in the sense proposed *by Lord Cherwell* [emphasis added]'.[38] The military men agreed. 'On the evidence put forward *by Lord Cherwell* [emphasis again added]', the Chiefs considered that 'no time, labour, material or money should be spared in pushing forward the development of this weapon, as a matter of the greatest urgency'.[39] Four years later, following the atomic bombing of Japan, Churchill acknowledged the debt that was owed to Lindemann. 'Unless he had kept me well informed upon this matter, I should not have written my minute of August 30, 1941 which turned on the full power of the State to what was then a remote and speculative project'.[40] The Prof, in short, kick-started the British atomic enterprise by kick-starting the Prime Minister. Nor was this the extent of the impact of his minute, for Churchill and the COS also agreed with him that 'the development should proceed in this country and not abroad' and that Anderson was the man to oversee the project.[41]

In going direct to Number 10, Lindemann blind-sided the normal governmental decision-making process and there was now a hiatus while the formalities were attended to. Despite the initial anxieties of the MAUD committee, the key figures in Whitehall officialdom eventually reached the same conclusion as Churchill and the Service Chiefs. On 27 August, the MAUD report began its bureaucratic progress when the Minister of Aircraft Production, Colonel J. P. C. Moore-Brabazon, submitted it to the Cabinet's Scientific Advisory Committee (SAC). In turn, Lord Hankey, the SAC chairman, handed it over to a group of independent advisors, the Defence Services Panel. Boasting Sir Henry Dale, the President of the Royal Society, and three Nobel laureates in its ranks, this august assembly spent a month weighing the MAUD findings before pronouncing them sound.[42]

So did the Hankey committee in its own report to Anderson who, as Lord President, was already responsible for overseeing much of the government's scientific and industrial research. '[W]e are strongly of the opinion that the development of a uranium bomb should be regarded as a project of first class importance and all possible steps should be taken to push on with the work', the SAC report stated, not least because of 'the probability that the Germans are at work in this field and may at any time achieve important results'. That said, Hankey and his colleagues thought that five years was a more realistic time-scale for weapons production. They further proposed that a full-scale gaseous diffusion plant might be better built in Canada than in a Britain still prey to German bombing. Lastly, the committee was unanimous that work on atomic energy as a source of power, though second in priority to building a bomb, was so critical to the future national interest that research and development should not be farmed out to the private sector.[43] This barb, Anderson knew, was aimed at Imperial Chemical Industries (ICI) whose deputy chairman, Lord Melchett, was not only aware of what was in the offing (having been a regular MAUD committee attendee) but had been privately lobbying the government to secure a monopoly for his company on the power side of any emergent scheme. As a secret ICI report observed in July 1941, atomic energy could well bring about 'the re-orientation of world industry' and it was 'essential that these ideas should be developed for the British Empire by a UK firm'. Melchett wanted ICI to be that firm.[44]

At the end of September, with the SAC verdict and the Prime Minister's outlook harmonized, the British A-bomb project was duly launched. Anderson was offered, and accepted, his atomic commission. For the next four years he would occupy a privileged position alongside Churchill and Lindemann in an atomic triumvirate, the only three people in the government with knowledge of how the various aspects of the project, scientific, technical, political, diplomatic and military, slotted together. Churchill was perhaps the least aware of the three simply because of the enormity of his other preoccupations: he could go weeks, sometimes months, without giving the issue much thought beyond taking note of the reports sent to him by the other two. Of these, the Prof enjoyed a level of personal access to the Prime Minister which the Lord President could never match, but it was Anderson who was the most important figure on an operational basis, the glue that held everything together. Yet, if he is remembered at all these days, it is for a sheet-metal garden-based construction, the eponymous Anderson shelter, 1.5 million of which were issued in 1939–1940 in the hope of affording the British public some protection during German air raids.[45]

Figure 2.1 Sir John Anderson. Popperfoto/Getty Images.

As a young man, Anderson had given serious thought to becoming a scientist. Born in Edinburgh in 1882, he graduated from his home-town university in 1903 and then spent a postgraduate year in Leipzig where, as Lindemann later noted, he wrote a treatise on the chemical properties of uranium.[46] However, in 1905, minded to marry, he opted for career stability and entered the Civil Service after winning first place in that year's entrance examinations. A string of appointments followed – at the Colonial Office, the National Insurance Commission and the Board of Inland Revenue, to name but a few – with Anderson's work-ethic and organizational prowess winning golden opinions wherever he went. In 1920, he took on a new and dangerous role as Chief Secretary for Ireland (based in Dublin Castle, he soon found himself on the IRA's hit-list) but returned to England two years later to become Permanent Under-Secretary at the Home Office. Over the next decade he forged a reputation as 'the greatest administrator of his age, perhaps of any age', and gained, in the process, the nickname 'Ja Jehovah . . . the all wise'.[47] Then, in 1932, in a dramatic shift of locale, he headed east to serve as Governor of Bengal, another perilous assignment; as Churchill later attested, he 'risked his life continually with the utmost composure' in carrying out his duties, twice narrowly escaping assassination.[48]

In 1937, Anderson returned home from India to start a new career in politics. After entering parliament as an Independent MP – albeit one supporting the National Government – his Westminster star rose rapidly. Recognizing his great organizational experience, in 1938 Prime Minister Neville Chamberlain tasked him with reviewing evacuation policy (this being the period of the *Anschluss*, the Sudeten crisis and the attendant war scare), and later appointed him Lord Privy Seal, a Cabinet-level position with special responsibility for air-raid precautions, hence the Anderson shelter. At the outbreak of war, Anderson became Home Secretary and Minister of Home Security, a daunting dual portfolio he retained in Churchill's ministry when formed in May 1940. Although not a member of the small War Cabinet, he was among those whom Churchill ordered to 'be present on all occasions'.[49] The start of the Blitz that September, with London the main target for the *Luftwaffe*, led to sharp press criticism of Anderson's refusal over the previous two years to invest in deep shelters for the protection of the capital's populace. Lacking oratorical gifts to match his administrative talents, Anderson floundered badly in defending himself and the government inside and outside of Parliament. Sensing the popular mood, Churchill moved quickly to promote him out of the firing-line.[50] Although disappointed to leave the Home Office, Anderson's new position as Lord President gave him a seat in the War Cabinet as of right and he was soon handling a wide range of unspectacular but vital domestic issues – prices, wages, rationing, food policy, social services – to such impressive effect that Churchill likened the Lord President's Committee to 'a parallel Cabinet concerned with home affairs' and even dubbed Anderson the 'automatic pilot' of the Home Front.[51]

Historians have sometimes found Churchill's 'regard for this dour and unattractive Victorian' something of a 'mystery'.[52] It is true that in dress, deportment and visage, Anderson resembled nothing so much as Mr Sowerberry, the undertaker in Charles Dickens' *Oliver Twist*, 'a tall, gaunt, large-jointed man' whose 'features were not naturally intended to wear a smiling aspect'.[53] It was also said that an Anderson speech could resemble 'a funeral oration which sounded as though he had not known the dear departed very well in his lifetime'.[54] Churchill, however, looking behind the Sowerberry frontage, discerned a man of 'far wider outlook' than his Civil Service background might suggest, the possessor of great personal courage (exemplified by his time in Ireland and India) and 'an acute and powerful mind, a firm spirit, and long experience of widely varied responsibilities'.[55] A dull dog socially, Anderson never gained admittance to Churchill's inner circle of boon companions. His 'solid gifts', Churchill's physician, Lord Moran, observed, 'were not those to set the PM's mind on fire', and though 'Winston trusted him' and 'respected his judgment … he did not always find him congenial'. Then again, for administrative and political reasons, Churchill 'has great need of such a man'.[56] In 1941, this need extended into the realm of atomic energy.

Anderson's first act as *de facto* Minister for the Bomb was to deal with ICI. Throughout the summer, Melchett had retained high hopes of a contract for the atomic power programme but these were decisively crushed in October when Anderson decreed that all work on uranium, whether for military or civilian end-use, would be conducted under direct government control.[57] 'So ended ICI's bid to become the United Kingdom Atomic Energy Authority', writes the company's official historian.[58] Anderson next gave the project a codename, Tube Alloys (TA), that was so dull that it stifled the curiosity of all but aficionados of tubes and alloys.[59] But that was the point. On the Prime Minister's orders, Tube Alloys became one of the most strenuously guarded secrets of the war with those in the know limited to a very small number. Not even the War Cabinet, the service ministers or the Chiefs of Staff (until very near the end) knew about the project, although Anthony Eden, the Foreign Secretary, Lord Halifax, now Ambassador in Washington, and a handful of other senior politico-diplomatic-military figures were periodically accorded some degree of insight. This meant that aside from the King, whom Churchill kept well briefed, the triumvirate alone was able to descry Tube Alloys in the round.[60] As John Ehrman later remarked in his Cabinet Office history, there was a 'striking contrast between the impersonal magnitude' of Tube Alloys and the 'highly personal control' exercised by Churchill, Lindemann and Anderson. 'The normal pressure of opinion and argument, from Cabinets, Departments and informed interests' was only 'indirectly' brought to bear on the A-bomb.[61]

In need of an operational base, in November 1941 a Directorate of Tube Alloys was set up within the Department of Scientific and Industrial Research (DSIR). From offices in Old Queen Street, Westminster, the Directorate was responsible for day-to-day coordination of research under the watchful eye of the Lord President. A small TA Consultative Council, chaired by Anderson and comprising scientists and administrators (Dale, Sir Edward Appleton, Head of the DSIR, and the ubiquitous Lindemann), concerned itself with matters of broad policy. A TA Technical Committee, an atomic brains trust, was also set up and included in its ranks Chadwick, Peierls, Halban and Simon, the latter also sitting on a smaller advisory Chemical panel.[62] Released from his position as research director at ICI, Wallace Akers, a chemist by training, was made

Director of Tube Alloys, chaired the Technical Committee and reported directly to Anderson. As his deputy, Akers brought with him from ICI Michael Perrin, a fellow chemist. A number of MAUD scientists were upset by these appointments. ICI, they complained, had triumphed after all given that Akers, who had helped prepare the company's failed bid to secure a monopoly on the power side, was now in charge of the country's atomic development.[63]

Anderson was having none of this. With his 'wide knowledge, un-bounded energy, even temper and absolute integrity', Akers, he maintained, was 'fitted ... admirably for a task which called for ingenuity, tact and organizing ability of a high order'.[64] Anderson also knew that there was no prospect of either the bomb project (now referred to as TA-1) or the power project (TA-2) prospering unless the government took full advantage of ICI's experience in transforming scientific theory into industrial fact. However, he repeatedly made clear that ICI was working for the government (with Akers made a civil servant for the duration) and not the other way round. This insistence, together with the innate charm and candour of Akers himself, soon dispelled the prejudices of most Whitehall-employed scientists.[65] The Americans were a different matter. As we will see, Washington policymakers would never rid themselves of the suspicion that the Churchill government and ICI were working hand-in-glove to ensure the United Kingdom's postwar pre-eminence in the field of atomic energy.

What, then, was happening in the United States? Here, the first thing to note is the disjunction between the US and UK approaches to weapons research. For while Britain, already at war, saw no reason to delay A-bomb development, the Americans, still at peace, were slower to act. In August 1939, two Hungarian émigré physicists, Leo Szilard and Eugene Wigner, sought out Albert Einstein, in exile in America from his native Germany, in the hope of persuading him to use his great eminence – he was then the most famous scientist in the world – to alert the US government to the frightening military implications of uranium fission. They succeeded to the extent that Einstein put his signature to a letter (drafted by Szilard) to President Roosevelt. Recent scientific developments in Germany required 'watchfulness and, if necessary, speedy action', the letter pointed out, for this 'new phenomenon' could also 'lead to the construction of bombs'. Following the German annexation of Czechoslovakia in the spring, Nazi occupation authorities had halted the export of uranium from the country's Joachimsthal mines. Czechoslovakia was one of the few sources of uranium in the world – the largest was the Belgian Congo – and the export ban, Einstein warned, hinted at a live German atomic programme.[66]

Szilard entrusted delivery of the letter to Alexander Sachs, a Lehman Corporation economist with a keen interest in science and, more importantly, access to the President with whom he was on close personal terms. The German invasion of Poland and the onset of war in Europe prevented Sachs from fulfilling his mission until the start of October by which time Hitler had publicly warned his enemies that he had in his possession 'a weapon which is not yet known and with which we could not ourselves be attacked'.[67] Cryptic as this statement was, it helped focus FDR's mind on what Sachs had to report. 'Alex', he said, 'what you are after is to see that the Nazis don't blow us up'.

'Precisely', Sachs replied.[68] Roosevelt acted on the instant and before the month was out an Advisory Committee on Uranium had been established to 'thoroughly investigate' atomic potentialities. Lyman V. Briggs, Director of the National Bureau of Standards and a soil physicist by training, was appointed chairman and the group soon assumed his name, the Briggs committee.[69]

It was, however, a false nuclear dawn in America. 'The job required a beaver', DeGroot has written, but the 65-year-old Briggs 'was a sloth'. Innately conservative and mistrustful of nuclear physics, Briggs proved reluctant to sanction a serious programme of experimental research and before long his committee had become a model of bureaucratic inertia.[70] The President, with myriad other urgent calls on his attention, let matters ride. Things only began to change in the summer of 1940 when Vannevar Bush, a fifty-year-old engineer, mathematician and President of the Carnegie Institution, set out to make himself the indispensable link-man between the American scientific-engineering community, the US armed forces, Congress and the White House. Self-confident and ambitious, Bush nursed genuine worries that the United States would eventually be sucked into the European war and needed to prepare accordingly. This convergence of national and self-interest led him to lobby the administration to set up a National Defense Research Committee (NDRC). After successfully selling his idea to Harry Hopkins, the President's most trusted counsellor, on 15 June 1940, with France on the brink of surrender and Hitler in control of much of the rest of Western Europe and Scandinavia, Roosevelt gave the NDRC proposal his seal of approval. By executive order, Bush became chairman. Access to the White House was – and would remain – crucial for Bush. 'I knew that you couldn't get anything done in that damned town', he later reflected, 'unless you organized under the wing of the President'.[71]

Like much of the American scientific community, Bush initially took the view that the 'great impracticability' of uranium research meant that it would be many years before it rendered anything of military value, hence the NDRC, whose primary concern was to speed the development of new military technology for use in the war that impended, did not importune the Uranium committee to exert itself.[72] Briggs himself continued to be an obstacle to action. As early fruits of a September 1940 Anglo-American agreement on scientific interchange, Briggs received several MAUD progress papers, and then, in mid-summer 1941, he was given a copy of the final report when Sir George Thomson visited Washington. For reasons attributable to a nature by turns 'slow, conservative, methodical and accustomed to operate at a peace-time government bureau tempo', and to an acute paranoia about security, Briggs declined to disseminate the MAUD findings to his colleagues and locked the report in his office safe.[73] It was still there when Oliphant arrived in the United States in August. Thunderstruck to discover that MAUD had been smothered, the irate Australian complained noisily to Bush and other influential figures in the American scientific establishment. His message was simple but alarming: an atomic bomb *was* a realistic proposition.[74]

Truth be told, there were signs of greater American urgency even before Oliphant, 'a nuclear Paul Revere', began campaigning on behalf of MAUD.[75] In June 1941, Bush was appointed to head a new and powerful executive agency, the Office of Scientific

Research and Development (OSRD), which possessed a presidential mandate to mobilize the 'scientific personnel and resources' of the United States in 'developing and applying the results of scientific research to defense purposes'. James B. Conant, President of Harvard and a chemist by training, took over the NDRC and became in effect Bush's number two. In personally specifying that the OSRD chief should report directly to him rather than through military channels, Roosevelt appeared to have found a Prof of his own, but in reality Bush never became close to the President in the manner of Lindemann to Churchill.[76] But he did have an entrée to the Oval Office and was soon using it to sell to Roosevelt the importance of a dedicated uranium research effort. The Damascene moment for Bush was the MAUD report, a draft of which he obtained in early July. Here, in cogent and persuasive form, was what the Briggs committee had failed to provide, not just the promise of something militarily significant but a programme for realizing an A-bomb within a time-frame likely to be relevant to the war.[77] Reporting to the President on 16 July, Bush revealed his new-found confidence that 'if such an explosive were made it would be thousands of times more powerful than existing explosives, and its use might be determining'. He added that if the British had worked out the potentialities of U-235, there was no reason why the Germans had not done so too. The President appeared to take the point. But Oliphant's subsequent rallying of wider scientific support for the MAUD report was unquestionably helpful to Bush and Conant in their campaign to persuade the White House to prioritize uranium research.[78]

The Bush-Conant combination, the engineer-mathematician and the organic chemist, 'two quick-witted, ambitious, no-nonsense, middle-class Massachusetts Yankees who had taken to tinkering with gadgets as teenagers and had, as adults, become well versed in academic and scientific politics', would go on to dominate the US government's military-scientific administration for the duration of the war. On atomic matters, Bush came to rely on the Harvard man's 'frank, coldly calculated appraisals' of people, prospects and progress, which he fed into his own reports, written and oral, to the President.[79] In October 1941, using both the final MAUD report and a supportive study by the US National Academy of Sciences as leverage, the duo achieved their greatest success to date when Roosevelt was persuaded to back a crash programme of research. The President's decision did not commit the United States to build an atomic bomb, only to explore whether or not a bomb was practicable. Nevertheless, looking back, without consulting Congress and probably without realizing it himself, FDR had launched the most expensive weapons programme in American history.[80]

It had taken two years for the United States to get to this point, but Roosevelt was determined not only to make up for lost time but to arrogate to himself all decision-making on high nuclear strategy. By December, a new body, the Top Policy Group, had been established to advise him 'on questions of policy relating to the study of nuclear fission', but all members served at the request of and were responsible to the President. The line-up was Vice-President Henry Wallace, Secretary of War Henry L. Stimson, the Chief of Staff of the Army, General George C. Marshall, and the two increasingly influential scientist-administrators, Bush and Conant. The Top Policy Group was, in its turn, assisted by the S-1 (A-bomb) Section of the Office of Scientific

Research and Development. Chaired by Conant, the section was reconstituted in 1942 in more compact form as the S-1 Executive Committee. By then the whole enterprise had acquired a codename, the Manhattan Engineer District, soon shortened to the Manhattan Project.[81]

Heeding Bush's advice that the United States had much to learn from the British, Roosevelt wrote to Churchill on 11 October 1941 suggesting that 'we should soon correspond or converse concerning the subject which is under study by your MAUD committee, and by Dr Bush's organization in this country, in order that any extended efforts may be coordinated or even jointly conducted'.[82] Suddenly, a bright Anglo-American atomic future beckoned. Or so it seemed. Later, writing in his history of the war, Churchill had no doubt 'that it was the progress we had made in Britain and the confidence of our [MAUD] scientists in ultimate success imparted to the President that led him to his grave and fateful decision' to launch the Manhattan Project.[83] This was largely true. At the time, however, the Prime Minister had been in no hurry to explore FDR's proposal for a coordinated Anglo-American effort. Indeed it was nearly two months before he replied, a remarkable tardiness in one who normally responded promptly and enthusiastically to all Presidential contact.[84]

On 21 November, in the interval between Roosevelt's message and Churchill's response, Frederick Hovde, the US scientific liaison officer in London, met Lindemann and Anderson. Speaking at the behest of the President, Hovde made the case for 'fuller collaboration … and for complete interchange of information'. Roosevelt wished to expedite this process 'with all possible speed'. Anderson and Lindemann agreed that collaboration 'to the fullest possible extent' was the ideal, but they confessed to worries about the level of security in an America still at peace. Nevertheless, Anderson undertook to advise the Prime Minister to reply to the President giving a 'general assurance' of cooperation.[85] This Churchill did in early December, but in the blandest manner. 'I need not assure you of our readiness to collaborate' was the extent of it. No elaboration. No enthusiasm.[86]

Historians, particularly those with an interest in missed buses, regard October to December 1941 as the key moment in US–UK wartime atomic relations. Roosevelt, it is argued, had proposed an Anglo-American partnership at a point when the more advanced state of Britain's theoretical and experimental work meant that the Churchill government ought to have been able to negotiate a merger on equal or at least highly favourable terms.[87] Whether FDR's vague words were intended to open the way to such an extensive alliance cannot be gauged with certainty. We would be a lot wiser on that score had the British bothered to probe their meaning at the time. This, though, did not happen. In view of Lindemann's position as Churchill's principal – really his *only* – scientific advisor, how far did the Prof's marked personal preference for an independent British bomb project contribute to Churchill's stand-offish response to Roosevelt? Like most of those in on the Tube Alloys secret, Lindemann believed that the work of the MAUD committee had put the British in the lead in the race for a bomb and this, in turn, encouraged his interest in a loose cooperative arrangement with the United States.[88]

Furthermore, as historian Barton Bernstein has noted, Churchill relied heavily on Lindemann and Anderson for advice, and both men entertained 'considerable doubts about tying Britain's atomic project too closely to American efforts' in case it led to the 'eclipse' of UK independence, a field in which it was presently dominant.[89] Lindemann, in fact, was more decided in this view than Anderson but the broad point holds good. Churchill did not snub Roosevelt on a whim. He can only have done so on advisement. And we know that his chief scientific advisor was firmly of the opinion that a Britain in possession of an A-bomb 'could dictate terms to the world' and should not therefore place itself at the 'mercy' of the United States.[90]

The consequences of Churchill's rebuff of Roosevelt would be costly and far-reaching: never again would Britain be given the opportunity to join with the United States as a full, as opposed to junior or associate, atomic partner.[91] But what level of personal responsibility should the Prime Minister bear for this unhappy outcome? In the most recent statement of the missed bus thesis, Graham Farmelo criticizes Churchill for passing over 'an exceptional diplomatic opportunity' and for 'allowing himself to be guided by the solid but unimaginative Anderson and by the clever but supercilious Lindemann, who both underestimated American ability and resolve'.[92] In other words, Churchill missed the bus because his advisors chained him to the bus-stop. There is something in this. Anderson, however, though he certainly misjudged how hard and fast the Americans would push uranium research going into 1942, can be removed from the equation: it is Lindemann who is the pivotal figure. Is it right, though, to blame Churchill, with all his many cares, for accepting unquestioningly what his scientific advisor told him about Britain's ability to bring off Tube Alloys on its own? As Max Hastings has pointed out, 'no human being, even Winston Churchill', could address every aspect of the war 'with the commitment which some modern historians believe should have been expected of him'.[93]

In the case of Lindemann and the Bomb, however, some fault must attach to Churchill. Had the Prof possessed an unblemished track-record of being right on all scientific questions, then censuring Churchill would be inappropriate. But Lindemann had no such record. Sometimes he was right and sometimes he was wrong.[94] Nor was his standing amongst his fellow scientists especially high. His devotion to restoring the reputation of the Clarendon had come at the cost of his own work as an experimentalist – Rutherford, an early admirer, later dismissed him as a 'scientist manqué' – and by the start of the war his professional knowledge was generally regarded as broader than it was deep.[95] Even admirers acknowledged that his mind (unusually for a scientist) could be closed to new thinking. According to R. V. Jones, Lindemann was prone to 'form a theory from a minimum of fact; and having once committed himself to the theory, he would be reluctant to accept any subsequent fact that disagreed with it'. This made it all the more important, in his privileged advisory role, to get the theory right in the first place, but 'by no means all of his advice' to Churchill 'would have been endorsed by other men of science'.[96] Nevertheless, blinded by friendship, the Prime Minister chose to rely exclusively on Lindemann's judgement rather than solicit additional or alternative viewpoints. 'If he had been killed at any point in the war', Moran later wrote of Lindemann, 'it is impossible to imagine any other scientist to whom Winston would have listened'.[97] There is the rub. The 'trouble', concluded Tizard (admittedly no Lindemann fan), 'is that the man with the wrong ideas has, to support him, all the drive and enthusiasm of Mr Winston Churchill'.[98] In late-1941, the Prof was wrong on the Bomb. And Churchill was wrong with him.

Having transmitted his lukewarm message to Roosevelt, Churchill repaired for the weekend to Chequers where he entertained a number of guests, among them the US Ambassador to London, John G. Winant. On the Sunday evening, as was his habit, Churchill, along with his party, gathered round the wireless to listen to the BBC news. The date was 7 December 1941. 'For a moment there was a jangle of music', Winant recalled, 'and then, suddenly, from the little black box, a voice announced that Japan had attacked our fleet at Pearl Harbor'.[99] On what Roosevelt called 'a date which will live in infamy', Japanese bombers and torpedo aircraft left six battleships destroyed, many other vessels crippled or sunk, 2,400 Americans dead and 1,200 wounded.[100] Pearl Harbor turned a largely European/North African war into a global conflict. The following day, the United States declared war on Japan. Three days later Germany and Italy declared war on America.

For Churchill, these tremendous developments marked the success by default of his eighteen-month campaign to bring the USA into the war. Back in the dark days of 1940 he had gambled on Britain's ability to survive until the United States joined the anti-fascist struggle. It had been a close run thing – 'touch and go', he admitted – but survive it did, aided by success in the Battle of Britain, by the inauguration of the American lend-lease scheme, by Roosevelt's stretching of the limits of American neutrality to permit the US navy to escort British Atlantic convoys as far as Iceland, and above all by the massive diversionary demands which Hitler's war from June 1941 against the Soviet Union placed on Germany's armed forces. Operation Barbarossa, the shredding of the Nazi-Soviet pact, involved in its initial surge a staggering 152 German divisions (supported by 14 Finnish divisions and the same number of Romanian divisions) and 3.5 million troops along a thousand-mile front.[101] The USSR's ordeal by fire was, for Britain, a salvation in the sense that the threat of German invasion was lifted. '[W]e have now won the war for existence', Eden remarked in August 1941, but 'we had not yet started the war for victory'.[102] That only began four months later when Japan propelled America into the Second World War and, in so doing, brought into being that great aggregation of military-industrial power – the Grand Alliance of the UK, USA and USSR – which eventually triumphed over the Axis. 'No American will think it wrong of me if I proclaim that to have the United States at our side was to me the greatest joy', Churchill later wrote. On the night of Pearl Harbor he went to bed 'and slept the sleep of the saved and thankful'.[103]

The newly globalized conflagration also acted as the sharpest of spurs in relation to the American quest for an atomic bomb. 'We'll win the war', Conant told an associate that Christmas, 'unless the Germans get S-1 first'.[104] But Pearl Harbor equally impacted on that other A-bomb race, the one between Britain and the United States. Over the next nine months, so great was the Roosevelt administration's level of commitment to the atomic project, so vast its investment of resources, so intensive its scientific endeavour, that work on S-1 not only caught up with Tube Alloys but surpassed it. In London, the triumvirate was as slow to appreciate what was happening as the Americans were swift in making up lost time and lost ground. But by the high summer of 1942, seeing was believing for British scientists visiting the United States. The bus had not just left the depot, it was over the hills and far away.

CHAPTER 3
ALLIES AT WAR

There were, to begin with, few signs that US entry into the war would completely transform the nature of Anglo-American atomic relations. Neither the A-bomb nor a Tube Alloys/S-1 merger was raised during the Prime Minister's extended post-Pearl Harbor visit to the United States, from 22 December 1941 to 14 January 1942, for talks with the President and his military chiefs. That conference, codenamed Arcadia, was critical in cementing the Anglo-American wartime alliance in a wider sense, with agreement reached on the need for a Combined Chiefs of Staff organisation, a joint Munitions Assignment Board, and (to Churchill's satisfaction and relief) to prioritise the war against Germany over the war with Japan.[1] At the lower official level, the US atomic authorities made no move to renew their offer of partnership, nor was there pressure on them to do so from Tube Alloys headquarters in London. Instead, the two projects operated in parallel rather than in any seriously connected manner, and while there was liaison between the scientific groups in the two countries, no senior scientist-administrator – Bush, Conant, Lindemann or Anderson – seemed inclined to prod their political masters in the direction of amalgamation.[2]

In laboratories all across England, Tube Alloys research pressed ahead steadily. The lodestar of the TA-1 (bomb) effort remained the Frisch-Peierls memorandum and its contention that a critical mass of U-235 would make for a weapon of superlative power. Leaving aside complex questions of bomb design and detonation, the first essential was to obtain sufficient U-235 for the fissile core. Of the various approaches explored, gaseous diffusion remained the front-runner and in early 1942 the Tube Alloys Directorate agreed contracts with ICI and the electrical engineers of Metropolitan-Vickers to build and operate a series of pilot diffusion machines at a site at Mold in North Wales.[3] The second aspect of Tube Alloys was slow neutron research. Drawing on the work of Halban and Kowarski, the MAUD report had highlighted the potential of uranium fission, if controlled and sustained in a boiler, to generate power for industrial use. This became the focus of TA-2 investigation. Initially, it was thought that a boiler, employing heavy-water as a moderator, was a long-term postwar proposition with no wartime military relevance. However, MAUD scientists acknowledged that element 94, a newly discovered and potentially highly fissile element, the by-product of uranium chain reactions, might have seriously explosive possibilities. Moreover, being chemically different from uranium, 94, or plutonium as it was soon christened, was in theory easier (though still extraordinarily difficult) to harvest compared with U-235. The TA leadership was thus cognisant of the possibility that research into the use of uranium for a bomb and for power generation might eventually converge if plutonium was confirmed as a viable explosive and if reactor development was perfected. Until that time, however, the main UK effort would continue to centre on U-235.[4]

In January 1942, leading figures in the British project, including Akers, Simon, Peierls and Halban, crossed the Atlantic to assess the state of American research. On arrival in Washington, Akers was ready to wager that in the Anglo-American race to build a bomb, the UK remained the likeliest winner.[5] Had he put money on this prediction, he would have been out of pocket. With serious encouragement from the top – Roosevelt insisted that 'the whole thing should be pushed not only in regard to development, but also with due regard to time' – an American research juggernaut was beginning to gather momentum.[6] Exploiting the USA's immense scientific and industrial resources, the administration undertook intensive study not of one (as in the UK) but four possible means of acquiring U-235: electro-magnetic separation, the centrifuge method, thermal diffusion, and its own variant on gaseous diffusion.[7] By mid-year, so great was progress on all fronts, bar centrifuge, that Roosevelt agreed that each process deserved its own pilot plant. 'Do you have the money?', he asked Bush. Bush did, plenty.[8]

The level of financing and resourcing was one obvious difference between the American and British programmes. Another was plutonium. The breeding of plutonium in piles, the American counterpart of Halban's boilers but using pure graphite as a moderator rather than the rare and difficult to produce (though more effective) heavy water, had rapidly assumed great importance. A team of researchers constellated around Arthur Compton at the Chicago Metallurgical Laboratory (Metlab) were working flat-out to prove that plutonium was every bit the equal of U-235 as a bomb core, with Berkeley physicist Glenn Seaborg, one of 94's co-discoverers, predicting that within six months of demonstrating experimentally that a controlled pile-based chain reaction was possible, a pilot plant for extracting plutonium could be up, running and delivering. While the British remained loyal to U-235, therefore, the Americans attached equal if not more importance to plutonium.[9]

By mid-summer, the consequences for Tube Alloys of all this American hyper-activity were becoming obvious to Akers. For one thing, the odds on the UK winning the Anglo-American bomb race had lengthened hugely. For another, reflecting on the scale of the Roosevelt administration's investment since the end of 1941, and considering the even greater investment that would be required to take the project forward in all its gigantic complexity, Akers and his Technical Committee concluded that an economically-straitened and war-dislocated Britain did not have the resources to compete. To Akers, it was obvious that if the UK was to remain a player in the atomic game, and if the goal was still – as surely it was – to build a bomb as quickly as possible, then partnership with the Americans was the only option.[10] Akers, though, did not make policy. The triumvirate did. Hence his challenge was to persuade Churchill, Anderson and Lindemann that a TA-1/S-1 merger, dismissed so cavalierly just a few months before, now had much to recommend it.

By coincidence, the king-pin of the triumvirate, Churchill, chose this moment to indulge in some personal top-level diplomacy the object of which – so far as we can tell – cohered with Akers' views on the need for an atomic alliance with the United States. Feeling that Roosevelt had been 'getting a bit off the rails', Churchill travelled to America in June 1942 to try and get him back on track.[11] The most vexatious Anglo-American issue was the planning date for a cross-Channel invasion to begin the process of prising Western Europe from the grip of the Nazis. US military leaders were eager for an early operation, their British counterparts much less so; instead, the Chiefs of Staff, backed by Churchill, wanted to focus on North Africa, putting off European operations until Hitler's forces had been further denuded by the Red Army and until the German war-machine itself was fatally weakened by Allied bombing. In the event, to the dismay of the American top brass, Roosevelt, keen to blood US troops against Germany as soon as possible, agreed with Churchill on an invasion of French North Africa, operation Torch, that autumn.

The atomic bomb was also considered during Churchill's visit. In *The Hinge of Fate*, the fourth volume of his history of the war published in 1951, Churchill wrote that '[o]ur research and experiments had now reached a point where definite agreements must be made with the United States'. This decision required 'personal discussions between me and the President' and these duly took place on 20 June at Roosevelt's Hyde Park home in upstate New York. Both leaders were anxious about German activity: the Nazis were known to be seeking to procure supplies of heavy water and it remained as vital as ever that the Anglo-Americans succeed in getting an A-bomb before Hitler did. To this end, Roosevelt and Churchill agreed that 'we should at once pool all our information, work together on equal terms, and share the results, if any, equally between us'.[12]

If this meeting and its outcome were as Churchill described them, then Hyde Park was one of the critical moments in UK–US wartime atomic relations. The President had renewed his offer of equal partnership and this time the Prime Minister had accepted. There are, however, problems with Churchill's account, the only record we have. For one thing, his sequencing is awry. It was only at the end of July 1942, that is to say after, not before or during his meeting with Roosevelt, that the triumvirate finally decided that the time had come to pursue atomic merger. For another, no agreement in any formal sense was concluded at Hyde Park: it was a gentlemen's understanding witnessed by just one other person, Harry Hopkins, FDR's right-hand man. By the time that *The Hinge of Fate* was published, Churchill was the only one of the three left alive, hence there was nobody to challenge the authenticity of an account that historian David Reynolds has since described as 'inaccurate' and pocked with 'serious factual errors'.[13] Indeed, were it not for the fact that the President confirmed to Bush afterwards that he had talked with the Prime Minister on the subject of the Bomb, it would be tempting to suggest that Churchill had made the whole thing up.

Accepting that an agreement *was* reached, what did it constitute? In speaking to Bush, Roosevelt confined himself to saying that he and Churchill were 'in complete accord'.[14] He offered no details but from what is in *The Hinge of Fate*, it is evident that Churchill believed that the President had committed himself to the principle of equal partnership. This, however, is the famously elusive FDR we are dealing with. 'If Machiavelli had never written', John Charmley reminds us, 'Roosevelt could have supplied the want – always

Figure 3.1 Churchill and Roosevelt, June 1942. Keystone-FranceCollection, Gamma-Keystone/ Getty Images.

supposing that anyone could have tied him down long enough to write so much and that he would have been willing to commit himself to firm opinions'.[15] The fact that the Hyde Park understanding was verbal and loose undoubtedly reflected the artful FDR's preferred method of doing business more so than Churchill's. But what, then, did he actually offer? A fully integrated enterprise? Or a recipe for the two national projects to continue to run in parallel but not in competition? Churchill's account is open to both readings.

As he conversed with the Prime Minister, Roosevelt had no idea just how far ahead of Tube Alloys the S-1 effort had got, and how unlikely it was that Britain, with its limited resources and overheating economy, would ever catch up. Nor do Bush and Conant seem to have apprehended the extent of the gulf that had opened up: the OSRD chief still considered it 'highly desirable that future action should be considered jointly' and that the British 'will undoubtedly supplement excellently' American efforts.[16] For the time being, Roosevelt probably sought to have it both ways: on the one hand, he mollified Churchill by dangling before him the prospect of intimate collaboration; on the other, the vagueness of the understanding left him ample room if he later decided to modify or even retreat from what he had said. Did the pooling and sharing of information extend to those technical processes – electro-magnetic separation, for example, or plutonium-breeding – presently an exclusive American preserve? Or was it limited to purely scientific-theoretical research? These were important questions. But they went unasked by an unbriefed Prime Minister. Within a year, as the American project began to shift from lab-based work to the construction and operation of vast industrial plants to deliver the necessary U-235 and plutonium, the consequences of Churchill's failure to pin Roosevelt down would be laid bare. He ought to have heeded the advice offered by the First Lady at the time of Arcadia. 'You know, Winston, when Franklin says yes, yes, yes it doesn't mean he agrees', Eleanor Roosevelt explained. 'It means he's listening'.[17]

Also in America in June 1942 was Michael Perrin, Akers's deputy. Convinced that a joint Anglo-American programme was the only way to go, he urged immediate action. Each day that passed, he wrote to his boss, widened the gap between the two projects; at current rates of progress it would not be long before the Americans 'completely outstrip us in ideas, research and application of nuclear energy', and then, 'quite rightly, they will see no reason for our butting in'.[18] In London, Anderson took little persuading that a merger had become necessary; he had known this moment would come, and though unhappy at the thought of giving up, for a time at least, Britain's atomic autonomy, he was realistic, if not fatalistic, about the need for an Anglo-American combine. So was the TA Consultative Committee, although Lindemann, as might be expected, put up resistance, not on grounds of logic (the case for merger was too strong for that) but for 'sentimental' reasons connected with Britain's present and future nuclear independence. By the end of July, however, even the Prof had accepted the inevitable.[19] That left only the Prime Minister to express a view.

On 30 July, Anderson wrote to Churchill making the case for merger. With the Americans 'applying themselves with enthusiasm and a lavish expenditure, which we cannot rival, to experimental work over the whole field of Tube Alloys', the Lord President and his advisors had concluded for reasons relating to expense, resourcing and general dislocation of the war effort, that a pilot plant, and in due course a full-scale complex reflecting the Simon diffusion method, should be built in the USA. 'The immediate effect of this would be that, whilst certain of the more academic research work would continue to be carried on in this country, we would move our design work and the personnel concerned to the United States'. The project would thereafter be conducted as 'a combined Anglo-American effort'. Anderson made this recommendation with some 'reluctance' but the fact was that the 'pioneer work done in this country is a dwindling asset and that, unless we capitalise on it quickly, we shall be rapidly outstripped. We now have a real contribution to make to a "merger". Soon we shall have little or none'. The prospect of a Nazi atomic weapon was an additional reason for speed, for the work currently being done in parallel in Britain and America 'is likely to come more quickly to fruition if it is pursued as a combined effort than if it is continued separately'. Looking further ahead, Anderson saw the UK's independent research and development resuming after the war, 'not where we left off, but where the combined effort had by then brought it'.[20]

This positing by Anderson of postwar considerations was no add-on to seal the Prime Minister's compliance. He was quite serious. The Bomb was not just a wartime contrivance. Britain, he recommended, should pocket the knowledge acquired from close association with the United States to advance rapidly its own atomic ambitions when the war was over. Would this stratagem, essentially nuclear main-chancery, recommend itself to the Prime Minister? The answer came in two words scribbled at the foot of Anderson's letter. 'As proposed'.[21] It is curious and possibly telling that Churchill omitted to mention that just a few weeks earlier, he and Roosevelt had mapped out, in broad terms, an atomic alliance. Perhaps he was distracted. For later that same day he left London for Cairo and thence to Moscow to explain in person to Stalin, 'the Ogre in his Den', why the Second Front that the Soviets were desperately seeking to relieve pressure on the Red Army would now take place later in the year, not in Western Europe, as the USSR wanted, but North Africa.[22]

On 5 August, as Churchill headed east, Anderson wrote to Bush outlining the triumvirate's decision and proposing that a UK-method gaseous diffusion pilot plant 'be added to your programme' and thereafter 'handled in exactly the same way as the other projects therein'. If the US authorities were agreeable, the government would 'transfer to your side' all key scientific personnel. In view of the extent of the merger, it would be necessary, Anderson added, for UK representatives to join the Manhattan Project's various oversight bodies.[23] It was an arrogant letter, unusually so for Anderson, which presumed unquestioning American acquiescence. Bush replied coyly on 1 September asking for more time to consider the matter. He was careful, however, to use the term 'interlinked' when referring to the two projects. Anderson had preferred 'incorporated'. What is in a word? A great deal, it would turn out. Bush found it 'somewhat disturbing' that a UK pilot plant was still not operational and it may be that this was the first dawning realisation that the British, despite their head-start, had not only fallen behind the United States, but in the one area where they could make an original contribution, gaseous diffusion, their technical as opposed to scientific work had yet to leave the starting-blocks.[24]

It was several weeks before Anderson heard anything more. Bush, to be fair, was busy with a major restructuring of the Manhattan Project's management. While Conant's S-1 Executive Committee remained responsible for scientific research, the US Army Corps of Engineers had been brought in to take charge of plant construction. Then, towards the end of September, a Military Policy Committee (MPC) was established. With Bush and Conant as alternate chairmen, the committee also comprised Rear Admiral W. R. Purnell of the Pentagon's Joint Committee on New Weapons, and Major General W. D. Styer, Chief of the US Army Engineers. The Top Policy Group remained unaltered but with its key politico-military figures – Wallace, Stimson and Marshall – desperately overburdened, the MPC, with its concentrated focus on the Bomb, became the Manhattan Project's operational junction box, a *de facto* board of directors.[25]

Bush eventually wrote to Anderson on 1 October but the letter was held up in transit and only reached London on the 20th, ten weeks after the British had first posed the merger question. The United States planned to prioritise three objectives, Bush revealed the rapid completion of all fundamental experimental work, the construction of three pilot plants and a heavy water plant (at an initial outlay of $7 million), and the erection of a full-scale electromagnetic separation plant (a further $25 million).[26] What, though, did this mean for a US–UK merger? Based on the advice of his 'technical people', Bush said that a decision between the comparative merits of the American and British gaseous diffusion processes should wait until the spring. This, in turn, meant that any consideration of 'further integration' must be deferred although between times there should be 'close liaison'.[27] When Conant read this letter, he was full of admiration for Bush. It was a 'masterly evasive reply', he told him, on a par with much of his other recent correspondence with London. 'You should have been a lawyer or a diplomat!'[28]

Bush was not that good. Anderson and his TA colleagues knew they were being cold-shouldered and amongst themselves they fell to pondering possible reasons for American coolness. Two stood out. The first was an anxiety bordering on paranoia on the part of S-1 administrators about the postwar Congressional inquiry into their handling of the project.[29] Roosevelt had finessed matters so that legislators on Capitol Hill had no idea where the public money underpinning research and development was going (and by the end of the war $2 billion – $28 billion in today's terms – would have been poured into the Manhattan Project from the public purse). With the US armed forces the identified recipient, few in Congress, beyond a certain Democratic senator from Missouri, Harry S. Truman, were minded to ask searching questions.[30] The postwar scrutiny, however, when it came, would be intense and it was understandable that neither Bush nor Conant wished to expose themselves to the accusation that they had conspired to give away to another power, regardless of its status as a wartime ally, information vital to the nation's security. This tendency was all the more pronounced with regard to the envoy Anderson proposed to send to Washington to negotiate the terms of an atomic partnership. As Director of Tube Alloys, Akers was the obvious choice. But having been an ICI man before the war, and likely to be so again when it was over, he was guaranteed to feed American neuroses that a Churchill government in league with a company known the world over for 'industrial omnicompetence' was bent on stealing a commercial march on the United States.[31]

The British also suspected – correctly – that the aloofness of the S-1 scientist-administrators was connected to the increased prominence of the US Army in the work of the Manhattan Project.[32] As noted, in the summer of 1942 the American atomic authorities asked the Army Chief of Engineers to take responsibility for building both pilot plants and later full-scale industrial facilities.[33] Colonel (soon to be General) Leslie R. Groves, an engineer who had supervised the building of the Pentagon, was placed in overall operational control. Groves possessed energy, drive and organisational prowess in abundance, but many people, especially the scientists into whose world he now intruded, found his brusque manner and hard-driving personality difficult to deal with. The same went for his determination to envelop the Manhattan Project in a thick blanket of secrecy and to limit the freedom of scientists to talk to one another about anything other than their very specific contribution to the overall project: everyone, Groves insisted, should 'stick to their knitting'.[34] Given that the open exchange of ideas is the first article of the scientist's creed, Bush at first feared that 'we are in the soup' with Groves on the loose, but he quickly came to accept that the bumptious General's ability to get things done more than compensated for the crudity of his methods.[35]

But what was it that Groves was keeping the Manhattan Project secure from? At the most obvious level it was the Nazis. But he perceived other dangers. There was 'never from about 2 weeks from the time I took charge of this project any illusion on my part but that Russia was our enemy and that the project was conducted on that basis', he affirmed some years later. 'I didn't go along with the attitude of the country as a whole that Russia was a gallant ally'. In light of what we know now of the extent of Soviet penetration of the Manhattan Project, Groves was right to be concerned. If anything he was less assiduous than he should have been given the damaging activities of Klaus Fuchs, David Greenglass and a number of other "atom spies" outed after the war. But Groves had a third threat in mind, not in the same category as Hitler's Germany or Stalin's Russia but the object nevertheless of deep suspicion: Churchill's Great Britain. Asked in 1954 how he had sought to advance US–UK atomic collaboration during the war, his answer was candid. 'I did everything to hold back on it . . . I did not carry out the wishes of our Government with respect to cooperation with the British'.[36]

In November 1942, Akers left an England resounding to the peal of church bells for the first time in two years – a moment of thanksgiving for victory, Churchill's first major triumph as Prime Minister, over German and Italian forces at El Alamein – and headed for the United States to try to further the cause of atomic merger. An early meeting with Conant confirmed the Tube Alloys Director in his view that the US Army was in the ascendant and that 'Bush and Conant have really been run right out of everything except pure laboratory work, so that I am really wasting my time talking with them'.[37] To be sure, the Groves factor was present and pervasive.[38] But the fact was that Akers had 'fallen victim to a typical Conant snow job'.[39] The head of the S-1 Executive Committee bowed to no-one in his determination to curb and if possible curtail a joint enterprise, something the British, fixated on Groves, were slow to divine.[40]

Back in 1940, Conant had been hugely sympathetic to the plight of Britain – 'a stouthearted population under bombardment' whose resistance to Hitler 'made me proud to be a member of the human race'.[41] Yet even then, if it came to negotiating a US–UK alliance against Germany, he wanted Washington to be 'hard-boiled and cruel', the 'majority stock-holder', and scrupulous in avoiding 'undue sacrifices to protect the British Empire'. Two years on, this outlook, a curious admixture of Anglophilia and Anglophobia, was applied more narrowly to atomic energy relations. Although committed to creating a weapon for use in the present conflict, Conant was much exercised by the long-range political, diplomatic and commercial implications of atomic energy. As the Manhattan Project moved from research to full development, he saw danger in too close an association with the United Kingdom. In the first place, an Anglo-American atomic partnership in wartime could threaten US commercial interests in the postwar era insofar as the UK would be able to use the knowledge obtained from working closely with the Americans to boost its future industrial competitiveness vis-à-vis the United States. On this count, Conant was half-right: Anderson and Lindemann *did* covet the American knowledge-bank, but for national security not commercial reasons. Secondly, at a politico-diplomatic level, Conant questioned the rectitude of the

United States limiting its freedom of manoeuvre by entering into any binding commitment to work with the British. The United States needed to guard its atomic prerogatives in the future by limiting its obligations to the United Kingdom in the present.[42]

The various strands in Conant's outlook were woven together in December 1942 in a memorandum in which he proposed – and the Military Policy Committee agreed – that the principle of "wartime use" should henceforward be the benchmark for atomic relations with the UK. In other words, the amount and nature of the information the Americans imparted would be determined by the extent to which the British could utilise it in helping develop a weapon for use against the Axis. Since the Churchill government was in no position to make an atomic bomb of its own, nor was it contributing to electromagnetic separation or the graphite pile, the Conant rules threatened to reduce drastically the level of Anglo-American interchange. From Conant's standpoint, one of the great attractions of wartime use was precisely its capacity for stymieing any British attempts to exploit American ideas and technical know-how for postwar gain.[43] The earlier Roosevelt–Churchill agreement on equal pooling and sharing might have vitiated the Conant plan were it not for the President's refusal to divulge its existence to anyone beyond Hopkins (who had witnessed it anyway). FDR's silence is a hint that he may not have considered the agreement particularly important; that he and Churchill had an atomic-themed conversation of some kind at Hyde Park in June 1942 is not in question, but for all we know it was a two-line exchange on, say, the need to push the work as fast as possible, which Churchill later expanded into a discourse on the vital necessity of a US–UK atomic alliance. Whatever the truth of the matter, it is hard to disagree with Martin Sherwin that FDR's 'secretive, idiosyncratic approach' led to 'considerable confusion' on the US side, or with Warren Kimball who concludes that the secrecy with which Roosevelt approached the agreement 'allowed the Americans in charge of the project to be, or pretend to be, ignorant of the sharing policy'.[44]

The Conant rules were signed-off by the Manhattan Project's administrative hierarchy in December 1942 and transmitted to the British at the beginning of January 1943. Unsurprisingly, the Tube Alloys establishment was shocked and distressed. Anderson and his colleagues had been seeking to use the existing level of US–UK cooperation as a springboard from which to launch a fully-fledged atomic alliance. Now an alliance had been reduced to a pipe-dream as the Americans set about marginalising the British in an enterprise to which, at the very least, UK science (or in the case of Frisch, Peierls, Simon and others, scientists working in the UK) had been the 'midwife'.[45] It is a measure of Anderson's upset that he now did something he normally tried to avoid: he sought the Prime Minister's help.

A pattern had developed with regard to Churchill's involvement with Tube Alloys, a project still too uncertain of outcome to command his regular attention. To date, he had made several decisive atomic interventions but none of these had been at his own initiative: in August 1941 he gave the green light to research and development on the back of Lindemann's seminal minute; in December 1941 he lined up with Lindemann and Anderson to snub Roosevelt's offer of a joint project; and in July 1942 he agreed that a merger with the United States was necessary after all. His June 1942 agreement with Roosevelt may or may not have been his own initiative. In between times, at the risk of stating the obvious, he had a war to run and Tube Alloys sometimes dropped off his radar for extended periods. Now, though, in a letter on 11 January 1943, Anderson placed it firmly at the centre of his concerns. And there it would stay for the next eight months, Churchill's most sustained period of atomic engagement.

'I have today been informed', Anderson wrote, 'that the United States Authorities concerned have received an order which restricts interchange of information ... by the application of the principle that they are to have complete interchange on design and construction of new weapons and equipment only if the recipient of the information is in a position to take advantage of it in this war. It appears that this principle is being interpreted to mean that information must be withheld from us over the greater part of the field of tube alloys'. This news had come as 'a bombshell', Anderson admitted, but he supposed that it was a military *diktat* which civilian S-1 leaders had no choice but to obey. Still, irrespective of its well-spring, the situation was 'quite intolerable'. Having talked the matter over with an equally appalled Lindemann, Anderson urged an immediate approach to the President to insist that 'collaboration should go ahead on a fully reciprocal basis'. The Prime Minister agreed. At the top of Anderson's note he wrote the word 'Symbol', codename for the Casablanca conference where, just a few days hence, he would be meeting Roosevelt.[46]

As Churchill prepared to journey to North Africa, the *Sunday Dispatch*, a British newspaper, ran a story speculating on the possibility of '[o]ne little bomb that would destroy the whole of Berlin ... a bomb that would blast a hole twenty-five miles in diameter and wreck every structure within a hundred miles ... The explosive in this bomb would be the energy contained in the uranium atom'.[47] This kind of Wellsian speculation had been common in the British press since news of the Hahn-Strassmann experiments first broke. However, as Churchill and Roosevelt headed for Morocco, they and their atomic advisors knew something that journalists, or indeed anybody else outside the closed TA-1/S-1 circle, did not. An A-bomb was no longer a possibility. It was a probability.

On 2 December 1942, in a converted squash court beneath the west stand of Stagg Field, the University of Chicago sports ground, Italian-born Nobel laureate Enrico Fermi employed a pile comprising graphite and uranium to bring off the world's first controlled, self-sustaining nuclear chain reaction. The pile was huge – almost 400 tons of pure graphite, 50 tons of uranium oxide, and 6 tons of uranium metal arranged in a wood-frame matrix – and took a month to build at a cost of almost $1 million. But to Manhattan Project leaders the results more than justified the expense.[48] 'There can no longer be any question that atomic energy may be released under controlled conditions and used as power', Bush informed Roosevelt.[49] At the same time, the plutonium-producing potential of Fermi's graphite pile, along with the great promise of the work going on at Berkeley on electromagnetic separation of U-235, had obvious military relevance. Although uncertainty remained about exactly how much fissile material would be required, there was still 'a very high probability', Bush concluded, of creating 'a super-explosive of overwhelming military might'.[50] Roosevelt was impressed. On 28 December, with breezy brevity ('VB-OK-FDR'), he approved the next phase of the Manhattan Project, the construction of a full-scale gaseous diffusion plant, graphite pile, heavy water pile and heavy water production facility, in addition to the electro-magnetic plant already authorised, at a cost of some $400 million. The pilot-plant stage was effectively abandoned: it was better to proceed on minimum data than delay and allow Hitler to gain a potential nuclear advantage.[51]

A fortnight later Roosevelt was in Casablanca with Churchill. The conference, an exclusively Anglo-American affair, lasted ten days, from 14 to 24 January 1943, and is best remembered for three decisions: to make the 'unconditional surrender' of the Axis the policy of the Allied powers; to again postpone a cross-Channel invasion, this time to 1944; and more immediately, to build on the recent success of Torch – when over 100,000 Anglo-American troops landed at Algiers, Oran and Casablanca – by clearing the Axis from North Africa and then set about the liberation of Italy via the springboard of Sicily. But what of atomic matters? Thanks to Anderson's prompt, the Prime Minister knew that the Americans were preparing to slam the door not only on a US–UK partnership but on any further meaningful interchange of information. When he got to Casablanca, however, Churchill passed up the chance to tackle FDR directly and opted instead to work through the President's *fidus Achates*, Harry Hopkins.

This decision was not as capricious as it might appear. Churchill first met Hopkins in 1940 and was instantly drawn to his sharp intelligence, tart humour and unerring ability to penetrate to the heart of any problem ('Lord Root of the Matter' he called him). A sincere Anglophile despite his distaste for empire and the British class system, Hopkins became Churchill's ally in the White House, regularly feeding him insights into the President's variable mindset.[52] Shortly before Casablanca, Churchill told Eden that 'my whole system is based on friendship with Roosevelt', but truth be told, it was also based on friendship with Hopkins.[53] Accordingly, drawing on tried-and-tested practice, Churchill turned to Hopkins, the 'most faithful and perfect channel of communication between the President and me', to represent to FDR the British atomic viewpoint and move him by degrees towards the end the triumvirate desired.[54]

At first, Churchill's instinct seemed sound, Hopkins declaring that the President 'knew exactly how it [the atomic question] should be handled' and that the matter would be resolved 'entirely in accordance' with British wishes.[55] In London, however, Anderson found it hard to reconcile this confident assurance with the menacing Conant rules. The restrictions, he cabled Churchill on 20 January, covered 'many of the most important processes' and he could only assume that the US military authorities 'wish to gain an advance upon us, and feel that, having now benefited from the fruits of our early endeavours, they will not suffer unduly by casting us aside'. Be that as it may, the situation was 'most serious' and he begged the Prime Minister to 'prevail upon the President to put matters right'.[56] Churchill could not see the problem. Had he not been given a personal pledge by his great friend Hopkins that all would be well? He would not trouble the President.[57] Which is a pity because if he had he might have avoided many of the arguments and recriminations which blighted Anglo-American atomic relations over the next eight months. 'It cannot be his intention that we should be treated in this way', a hopeful Anderson said of Roosevelt.[58] He was wrong.

The previous October, four months on from his Hyde Park agreement with Churchill, the President, after reviewing the field with Stimson, seconded his Secretary of War when he said that because the United States was now doing 'ninety percent of the work' there were no longer any grounds for full interchange of information with Britain.[59] Then, in mid-December, when Bush presented him with a Military Policy Committee report incorporating the new Conant-coined policy, the President 'approved' the contents in their entirety.[60] In doing so, he signalled a recalibration of the priorities which hitherto had informed American policy. The need to exercise postwar control of atomic energy, especially in weapons form but also on the power side, was now as important to the US government as the wartime imperative of building a bomb, perhaps more so. Bush and Conant thought it likely that the British would react to the new rules by withholding their own information from the Americans and thus retard the development of a weapon at a time when, for all anyone knew, the Germans might be on the cusp of acquiring an A-bomb.[61] It was impossible to estimate the length of the delay that a drying-up of UK data would cause, but whatever it amounted to the scientist-administrators considered it to be within the bounds of acceptability. In any event, the most damaging impact of any tit-for-tat would be felt in the area of gaseous diffusion and the heavy water pile, the British specialisms, but Bush and Conant were already confident that electro-magnetic separation, closely followed by plutonium-breeding, would deliver the fissile goods. Confronted, then, with a choice between a policy based on intimate wartime and, by extension, postwar partnership with Britain, or a policy predicated on ensuring a postwar US atomic monopoly at the cost of some slowing down of weapons development during the present conflict, the Manhattan Project leadership opted for the latter. So, it seemed, had the President.[62]

Leaving Casablanca, Churchill was convinced that Anglo-American relations were in good shape. There had been 'complete agreement' over 'the whole vast war scene' and the foundations laid for cooperation 'in every respect as I wished & proposed'. With Hopkins expected to work his magic on the President, Churchill's satisfaction also extended to Tube Alloys.[63] His good mood did not last long. First, he contracted pneumonia, a serious illness for anyone approaching seventy years of age, and then a whole month went by without any movement on the atomic front. On 16 February, an ailing Prime Minister cabled Hopkins reminding him of his promise that everything 'would be put right'.[64] Hopkins replied a week later. A 'casual inquiry here' with 'our people', he wrote in reference to Bush and Conant, indicated that 'there has been no breach of agreement'. He did not let on, but those same inquiries had revealed to him the President's support for the Conant rules: fulfilling his pledge to the Prime Minister would not be as easy as he first thought.[65]

Churchill continued to press. There was 'no question of breach of agreement', he agreed in a further message to Hopkins. At the same time, the basis upon which all interchange had so far occurred was 'one of complete mutual confidence and of conviction that the most certain and most rapid realisation of the project can be attained only through complete co-operation'. Referring to Hyde Park, Churchill said that 'my whole understanding' from that point onwards 'was that everything was on the basis of fully sharing the results as equal partners'. He had no written record – no agreement to breach – but he would be 'very much surprised if the President's recollection does not square with this'. 'And yours too, Harry', he might have been tempted to add. Instead he confined himself to remarking that 'if I had to justify my case on grounds of fair play, I should have little difficulty doing so'.[66]

To Churchill's disappointment, there was again silence from Washington, this time for three weeks. On 19 March, in a fit of irritation, he fired-off a telegram to Hopkins of such umbrage that it elicited a response the very next day: 'I am working on Tube Alloys and will let you know as soon as I know something definite'.[67] Then silence. For ten more days. Once more it was Churchill who folded first. 'I am much concerned about not hearing from you', he wrote to Hopkins on 1 April. His Tube Alloys experts were anxious to forge ahead. If Britain and America should ever have to 'work separately' towards the same atomic end that would be 'a sombre decision'.[68] Sombre, but maybe necessary. That same day, Churchill instructed Lindemann and Anderson to revisit the viability of an exclusively British bomb project.[69]

In his effort to restore Anglo-American cooperation, the Prime Minister had tried pleading, cajolery, appeals to US honour and an implied threat that the UK might go its own way. Yet nothing stimulated a response commensurate with the urgency he believed the issue merited. What, then, was happening in Washington? Eden was given a clue when he visited the United States in March. Much of the present difficulty, Hopkins told him, was due to the fact that Britain's 'scientific research was necessarily in the hands of persons who had been and would be again in the employ of big business, and who therefore had their eye on post-war interests'.[70] What the British did not realise – and what even Hopkins may not have known – was that for Conant, the pivotal figure in the interchange crisis, the issue went far beyond Akers, Perrin and ICI to encompass the future of America's entire foreign relations. 'The question', he reminded Bush on 25 March, 'is whether or not British representatives shall have full access to plans for the design and construction of the manufacturing plants which we are now building and full knowledge of their operation'. Conant thought not. To provide this information 'might be the equivalent to joint occupation of a fortress or strategic harbour in perpetuity'. In other words, since the fusing of US and UK defence policy was the only practicable way to share the atomic weapon, the two countries would need to conclude a full-blown postwar military alliance. This may have been Churchill's hope but it was Conant's fear insofar as such a pact was bound to compromise America's freedom, atomically and more generally, to act in defence of its national interests. Viewed in these terms, any delay to bomb production resulting from dispensing with British help during the war was a risk worth taking if the result was US atomic independence in the postwar era.[71]

In London, neither the triumvirate nor Akers and his Tube Alloys staff were aware of just how actively Conant was working against them nor the extent to which he sought to indoctrinate Bush and even Stimson with his viewpoint.[72] Continuing to hold the US Army primarily responsible for the rift in relations, the British eventually reacted in the manner predicted by Bush and Conant: scientific data was withheld, visits by UK scientists to the United States were postponed, and cooperative S-1/TA-1 ventures involving personnel already in North America were suspended.[73] In consequence, by the late spring of 1943, the Conant rules on restricted interchange had led to a situation of zero interchange. A 'shipwreck', Anderson called it.[74]

Against this troubled backdrop the triumvirate weighed the feasibility of an independent A-bomb project supposing it was given the very highest priority in terms of finance and resourcing. The prospects, the Prof concluded on 7 April, were not unpromising. Even working alone, the British could yet beat the Americans – and the Germans – to the prize. A gaseous diffusion plant remained the key: no plant, no U-235. If the government issued immediate instructions to proceed with building a full-scale facility, a final decision on whether to manufacture a bomb need not be taken until around the start of 1944, by which time Anglo-American relations might have righted themselves. In any event, Lindemann maintained, the effort, even if it came to naught in the war, would still contribute towards buttressing Britain's postwar security and ensure that the country remained at the forefront of scientific and industrial progress.[75]

Where the Prof was almost enthusiastic, Anderson was cautious. There was 'no doubt that earlier results would be obtained by the Americans and ourselves working together than by either of us working separately', he informed Churchill on 15 April. But the Prime Minister needed to understand that the Anglo-Americans were not just racing Hitler. They were racing Stalin, too. It was important to 'always remember that the Russians, who are peculiarly well equipped scientifically for this kind of development, may well be working on the Tube Alloys project somewhere in the Urals and making great progress'. An A-bomb was for future as well as present security and this was an added reason 'to make every possible effort to bring about an effective co-operation between the United States and ourselves'.[76]

Here for the first time in the Tube Alloys story, Churchill was confronted by the spectre of a Bolshevik bomb, the fell prospect of science and international communism in destructive union which had haunted him for a quarter of a century. A month later it appeared again, this time in a memorandum by Lindemann. The principles and possibilities of nuclear fission were known to scientists throughout the world, he pointed out. 'In five years undoubtedly the leading powers will possess these weapons unless forcibly prevented. Can England afford to neglect so potent an arm while Russia develops it?'[77] This must have jolted Churchill. In 1931 he had warned of a future in which dark science grafted on to 'the pitiless sub-human wickedness' of the USSR's communist leaders would pose a grave threat to 'Christian civilization'.[78] Now, just a dozen years later, his top atomic advisors told him that this forbidding future might soon be at hand. Yet regardless of the stimulus, be it Hitler or Stalin, it is hard to conceive of Churchill agreeing to embark on probably the largest single industrial construction effort ever undertaken in Britain, and at a cost in excess of £50 million, in the middle of a global war.[79]

As it happened, the matter was soon rendered academic. Access to sources of uranium and heavy water was essential to any independent work on TA-1 or TA-2, and here the triumvirate had assumed that the Canadians, in possession of both vital ingredients, would be ready to help on grounds of Commonwealth solidarity. In May 1943, however, Anderson received 'disturbing information'. Apparently without the knowledge of the Ottawa government, the American atomic authorities had sealed a deal with *Eldorado*, the company which held a monopoly on the mining and refining of uranium in Canada, giving the United States its entire output for the next two years. A similar arrangement had been negotiated on heavy water which the Chicago Metlab needed as it looked to develop its own version of Halban's boiler. The Canadian government was embarrassed but powerless to reverse the deal. Without a sufficiency of raw materials, an exclusively British bomb was a fantasy.[80]

Churchill learned of the *Eldorado* coup while he was in the United States for the third Washington conference of the war, codenamed Trident. He was livid. The Canadians, he railed (unfairly), had 'sold the British Empire down the river'.[81] Knowing that the Prime Minister intended to challenge Roosevelt on the Conant rules, Anderson cabled from London telling him to play his hand carefully, for 'if we break with the United States' in present circumstances, 'we shall be deprived of our only source of uranium and any early possibility of delivery of heavy water'. And then both the British bomb and boiler projects would be in even greater trouble.[82] Lindemann agreed. A way must be found to revive atomic relations, he told Churchill. Together, the British and Americans could speed the Bomb. Divided, the Nazis might get there first. And even if Germany was defeated before its uranium research bore fruit, what guarantee was there that the peace would last if the Soviet Union acquired an atomic capability ahead of the Western democracies? Could the United States not understand all this? 'What reason has emerged for excluding us now?'[83] Actually, at least one American, mindful of these dangers, was beginning to change his mind and move from support for British atomic exclusion to acceptance of US–UK amalgamation. It also happened to be a rather significant American.

On 24 May, towards the end of the Trident talks, Churchill broached with Roosevelt the unhappy state of atomic relations. Roosevelt suggested that Bush and Lindemann get together with Hopkins to consider the matter. This they did the following day. According to the notes compiled by Bush afterwards, the Prof, angry and accusatory, tore into the Americans for jettisoning interchange. On the defensive, Bush stuck doggedly to the ruling on wartime use, but this was not good enough for Lindemann. 'The matter finally came down to the point', Bush recorded, 'where [Lindemann] admitted rather freely that the real reason they [the British] wished this information at this time was so that after the war they could then at that time go into manufacture and produce the weapon for themselves, so that they would depend on us during this war for the weapon but would be prepared after this war to put themselves in a position to do the job promptly themselves'. Lindemann rejected the suggestion that postwar commercial as distinct from security considerations explained the UK's insistence on full access and warned that unless the restrictions were lifted, Britain might have no choice but to divert a proportion of its anti-Axis effort into building for its future security. It was a bludgeoning performance which Bush was sure Hopkins would report to the President. Here, finally, was proof of what he and Conant had been saying for months: Britain's interest in an atomic link-up was related almost entirely to postwar aims and objectives.[84]

What Hopkins said to FDR is not known. But the following day, when Churchill met Roosevelt, he discovered to his delight that interchange was back on. 'Conversation with the President entirely satisfactory', he cabled Anderson. Roosevelt 'agreed that the exchange of information on Tube Alloys should be resumed, and that the enterprise should be considered a joint one, to which both countries would contribute their best endeavours'.[85] Anderson, equally astounded, immediately arranged for Akers to fly to Ottawa to be in position to travel down to Washington as soon as the agreement was made official.[86] The extent to which a Hopkins cause-and-effect was responsible for this turn-around is hard to determine but both Churchill and Lindemann were convinced that he had made the difference.[87] Without consulting any of his atomic advisors, Roosevelt overturned the restricted interchange policy and simultaneously revived British hopes of an entangling alliance. Not that Bush or Conant or Groves knew any of this yet. Until formal guidance was issued by the White House, those in charge of S-1 continued to operate on the basis of the Conant rules.

How are we make to make sense of the President's atomic contortions? The answer is: not very easily. We need always to bear in mind that in Roosevelt we are dealing with an ends-justify-means extremist. 'I never let my right hand know what my left hand does', he once remarked. 'I may be entirely inconsistent, and furthermore I am perfectly willing to mislead and tell untruths if it will win the war'.[88] Whatever else may be said about this modus operandi, it makes pinning down the real Roosevelt a challenge. It also raises a paradox. For while the FDR presidency is 'superbly documented . . . the modern historian often needs the skills of a medievalist to infer his motives and intentions'.[89] Still, the inferring must be attempted. Setting to one side the President's failure to apprise his S-1 advisers, what lay behind his decision to renew atomic vows with Churchill? Amongst those historians who have considered this question there is broad agreement that by the spring of 1943, atomic energy had begun to impact in significant ways on FDR's thinking about the future, on his views about how postwar peace and security could be assured, and on his assessment of the kind of help that Britain might be able to give to the United States in trying to prevent another global catastrophe.[90]

These issues require elaboration. Roosevelt had started thinking about how the international system might be organised after the war before America was even in it. When he met Churchill at the Atlantic conference in August 1941, he predicted that one day both their countries might have to combine in 'an international police force' to patrol the global beat.[91] Roosevelt later extended this constabulary concept to include the Soviet Union and China, hence the Four Policemen, a Great Power consortium which would divide the postwar world into spheres of influence, with each policeman (or 'sheriff' as he sometimes called them) assuming primary responsibility for maintaining security in their respective sectors.[92] In 1942–1943, when it became clear that American public opinion would not tolerate such a crude display of power politics, Roosevelt, always on guard against any recrudescence of isolationism, dressed his hegemonic vision in Wilsonian garb, repositioning his Great Power consortium within the framework of the new world organisation he wished to see take the place of the discredited and defunct League of Nations.[93] In due course, Roosevelt became an ardent champion of the United Nations (UN), less for the idealism attaching to it than because the organisation, and a leading American role therein, would function as an anchor for his country's postwar internationalist future. However, he was never willing to make the United Nations the sole guarantor of American security, rather he continued to regard the Four Policemen (later installed, along with France, as permanent members of the UN Security Council) as the principal keepers of the peace, the only armed nations in an otherwise disarmed world.[94] But before there were four – the expansion dates from November 1943 – there were two, the USA and the UK. If, though, Britain was to play the role Roosevelt intended for it after the war, it would need to be militarily strong and financially solvent, a combination of attributes which, at the time of Trident, after nearly four years of enervating struggle, was extremely uncertain of realisation. Moreover, another of Roosevelt's guiding convictions seemed likely to add to Britain's postwar difficulties: his anti-colonialism.

FDR never hid his desire to see a dismantling of the European imperial system after the war even though this objective, if applied to the British Empire, would weaken the ally on whose strength as a postwar power the original two policemen concept partly depended. 'I can't believe that we can fight a war against fascist slavery, and at the same time not work to free people all over the world from a backward colonial policy', Elliot Roosevelt recorded his father telling Churchill at the Atlantic conference.[95] The well-known outcome of that meeting, the Atlantic Charter, in mapping out a postwar order based on universal freedoms and democratic values, was implicitly an anti-imperial manifesto, one that Churchill only supported because he was anxious to help FDR in his efforts to convince American opinion that if or when the USA became involved in the war, it would be fighting for the purest of motives and not to buttress colonialism.[96] Churchill, of course, 'had not become the King's First Minister in order to preside over the liquidation of the British Empire', and he later insisted that the Charter's reference to the right of self-determination, one of its most prominent features, only applied to countries under Axis occupation and not therefore to the British Empire. Roosevelt, with whom Churchill argued regularly and heatedly over colonial questions, was outraged. The Charter, he insisted, 'applies to all humanity' and he came to regard Churchill as a significant obstacle to the kind of new world order he hoped to fashion from the wreck of the old.[97] Like many British policymakers, Churchill suspected that behind America's ostensibly moral crusade lay grubby economic ambition, for with the break-up of the European empires, tremendous opportunities would present themselves for US trade and investment.[98] But whatever its determinant, FDR's anti-imperial vision seemed to run counter to his interest in promoting a strong postwar Britain capable of helping the United States keep the peace.[99]

Trident is where the various aspects of Roosevelt's outlook began to converge, with atomic energy the unifier. A US postwar monopoly of the Bomb must have had a certain raw nationalistic appeal for the President, but even more attractive was the weapon's value in connection with his thinking on the structure of peace. After the war, if the United Kingdom, in partnership with the United States, possessed atomic arms, this would not only go a long way towards offsetting the loss of strength and prestige accruing from its retreat from Empire but would enable it to fulfil its policing duties.[100] According to Sherwin, it was in the spring of 1943 that Roosevelt 'began to deal with atomic energy as an *integral* [original emphasis] part of his general diplomacy, linking and encompassing both the current wartime situation and the shape of postwar affairs'.[101] Cognisant of this interplay for some time, Conant opposed a US–UK atomic partnership because it might breed a broader postwar alliance containing unacceptable curbs on the freedom of American foreign and defence policy. Roosevelt now also comprehended the linkage, but where Conant was repelled by atomic intimacy, the President was drawn to it for reasons bound up with his postwar grand design. Instead of an American atomic monopoly, FDR envisioned an Anglo-American duopoly. And even when the two policemen eventually became four, Roosevelt evidently intended that only the American and British coppers would be armed with atomic truncheons.[102] The 'only reason' for Roosevelt 'acceding to the British position' in 1943 'would have been to aid them in their postwar use of atomic energy', a rueful Bush later recorded. 'This was not a war matter.'[103]

And yet, paradoxically, for the British Tube Alloys leadership the two months following the Trident conference proved to be the most perplexing and panicky of the war. Why should this be? Surely the talks had ended on the highest of highs with the President agreeing to restore interchange? The reason is simply stated but harder explained: *déjà vu*. Consider the following. A private Churchill–Roosevelt understanding is reached on equal pooling and sharing. The agreement is informal and unwritten. There is no follow-up by the President. If all this sounds like the sequencing in and after June 1942, that is no surprise: it *was* the sequencing. But it also perfectly describes May 1943 and its immediate aftermath. Looking back, we know that Roosevelt did eventually pronounce unequivocally in favour of an Anglo-American atomic alliance. That is a major difference between the 1942 and 1943 episodes. But until that pronouncement came, a full two months after Trident, the Manhattan Project leadership continued to base its approach to relations with the British according to the Conant rules. This, in turn, left those in charge of Tube Alloys confused and nervous. Why, they wondered, had the President failed to tell his atomic lieutenants that restricted interchange had been rescinded?

Again we need advanced historical-forensic skills to infer Roosevelt's thinking. Did he come to regret the extent to which he propitiated Churchill or did he perhaps conclude, on reflection, that the Conant rules had something to recommend them after all? Or was he just embarrassed to admit to his advisors that he preferred the counsel of a foreign leader to their home-spun wisdom? Whatever the reason, between May and July 1943 Roosevelt inhabited a shadowland between the old and the new policy. We may sympathise with a President burdened by so many other grave concerns for preferring drift to decisiveness – but only up to a point. For while Roosevelt dithered, the interchange crisis continued to rage with such intensity that Anglo-American atomic relations came close to complete meltdown.

CHAPTER 4
THE QUEBEC AGREEMENT

From Churchill's standpoint, Trident had been a military, political and personal success. 'My friendship with the President was vastly stimulated', he wrote to Clementine. 'We could not have been on easier terms.' His one worry was that Roosevelt might not run for the White House again in 1944. 'To me this would be a disaster of the first magnitude. There is no one to replace him, and all my hopes for the Anglo-American future would be withered for the lifetime of the present generation – probably for the present century.'[1] These hopes now unquestionably included the atomic future. When he got back to England, Churchill wrote to Hopkins recapitulating the understanding on Tube Alloys; wise by now to the President's slipperiness, he wanted written confirmation, post-facto if necessary, of what had been agreed. He was 'sure', he told Hopkins, 'that the President's decision will be to the best advantage of both our countries', and urged that '[w]e must now lose no time in implementing it'.[2] Hopkins appeared to agree – 'tube alloys is in hand', he replied – but to the consternation of the triumvirate another prolonged Washington silence then followed.[3] On 7 July, a worried Anderson begged Churchill to press the matter with Roosevelt directly. It was 'most urgent that we should either resume effective collaboration or part company *on friendly terms* [original emphasis] which will ensure for us our adequate share of vital materials on which the Americans have secured a stranglehold'. Anything was better than stasis, Anderson suggested. Even schism.[4]

Roosevelt, though, was in the shadowland. On 24 June, Bush visited the White House. It was the first time the OSRD chief had seen the President since Trident, but Roosevelt, instead of using the occasion to inform Bush of what had been settled with Churchill, gave him the impression that the Conant rules remained a going concern. As their conversation developed, Bush was surprised to discover that Hopkins had not told the President about the previous month's sparky encounter with Lindemann and he now apprised FDR of how the Prof had unashamedly made the case for access to US information 'on an after-the-war military basis'. Roosevelt listened attentively and then declared himself 'astounded' and 'amazed' that the British could hold such a point of view. Lindemann, he added, was 'a rather queer-minded chap'. Emboldened, Bush proposed that 'we ... sit tight on British relations, since our program is not suffering for lack of interchange and since the British had practically quit their efforts on the matter'. At this, Roosevelt 'nodded rather vigorously' and Bush left the meeting convinced that the President 'had no intention of proceeding farther on the matter of the [sic] relations with the British'.[5] In London, the British themselves, including the Prime Minister, were close to cracking. Distressed by the poor results from the normally reliable Hopkins channel, Churchill wrote to Roosevelt himself on 9 July expressing his upset at the failure to implement the Trident agreement.[6] FDR noted the message and passed it to Hopkins anyway. 'What should I do about this and the reply to Churchill's wire?'[7] The answer, if his agreement with Churchill meant anything, was to send an apology to Downing Street and immediately instruct his S-1 advisors to resume interchange. Instead, Roosevelt asked his chief counsellor to tell him what to do.

While Hopkins considered the options, the triumvirate looked to gain an insight into US atomic thinking when Stimson and Bush arrived in London for talks on general war matters. On 17 July, Stimson paid a courtesy call on Churchill. The US Secretary of War was 'disturbed to know that I thought we had been unfairly treated', Churchill told Lindemann and Anderson afterwards, and had vouchsafed that 'someone high up on our [the UK's] side ... had been explaining forcibly that our interest in the [atomic] matter was commercial and after the war'. The Prime Minister was appalled. 'I could not conceive how this could be', he told Stimson. 'We based our demand entirely upon the engagement entered into and the fact that this was a war secret which might yet play a great part.' On this, he insisted, 'I had the President's word.'[8]

Anderson added to Churchill's agitation by flagging the prospect of an atomic-armed Soviet Union in the postwar period. This danger, he suggested in a minute on 21 July, made it all the more important to obtain from the Americans the know-how to develop an independent UK atomic defence capability in the fastest possible time. 'Let us ourselves have no illusions', Anderson warned.

> We cannot afford after the war to face the future without this weapon and rely entirely on America, should Russia or some other Power develop it. However much, therefore, it may be tactically necessary to make use of the pretext of war-time collaboration, the Americans must realise that, failing collaboration, we shall be bound to divert manpower and materials from our work on radio, etc. in order to try to keep abreast.[9]

This, as Anderson knew, was a counsel of despair and he preferred to continue to work for the restoration of cooperation since this was the surest way for Britain to learn the art of bomb-building. As for the vexed commercial-industrial aspect, this could not be allowed to block renewed interchange and he therefore recommended that the Prime Minister accede to 'any arrangement which the President may consider fair' in this area. Anderson had no idea who the 'high up' figure reportedly stoking US suspicions might be but if there was any misunderstanding in the commercial sphere 'let us clear it up by stressing our disinterestedness'.[10]

On 20 July, Hopkins delivered his response to Roosevelt's request for direction. It was unambiguous. 'I think you made a firm commitment to Churchill in regard to this when he was here and there is nothing to do but go through with it.'[11] The President, finally emerging from the shadows, agreed. Later that same day he wrote to Bush confirming that 'our understanding with the British encompasses the complete exchange of all information', and he wished, therefore, 'that you would renew, in an inclusive manner, the full exchange of information with the British Government regarding Tube Alloys'.[12] Two days later, Stimson and Bush paid a farewell call at Number 10. Ironically, due to a garbled telegraphic transmission from Washington, Bush had yet to receive his Presidential orders and the meeting in consequence was a fraught affair.[13] Pacing the room, repeatedly trying and angrily failing to light his cigar, the Prime Minister gave full vent to his dudgeon. It was plain wrong, he told Bush, for the United States to 'claim the right to sole knowledge' in a matter of such great importance to US–UK relations. As for American suspicions of British motives, these were wholly misplaced: his government had no commercial interest in atomic energy though it was 'vitally interested' in military applications in connection with 'Britain's independence in the future as well as for success during the war'. It was imperative that neither Germany nor, Churchill added pointedly, the USSR, should win the race for the Bomb, but both 'might be in a position to accomplish this result unless we worked together'. Heeding Anderson's advice, he declared himself ready to conclude an arrangement with Roosevelt limiting UK exploitation of the commercial-industrial side of atomic energy to whatever the President deemed 'fair and equitable'. In return, he wanted a formal agreement reinstating 'free interchange' and making the project 'a completely joint enterprise'. Stimson, a mute observer of these verbal fireworks, agreed to relay the Prime Minister's views to the President.[14]

At last, on 27 July, Churchill got the news he had been waiting for when FDR cabled to say that 'I have arranged satisfactorily for Tube Alloys' and further proposing that the British send their 'top man' to Washington immediately 'to get full understanding from our people'.[15] When Bush learned that the Conant rules had been dropped he was understandably dismayed. So was their author who described Roosevelt's decision as a 'mistake'; the rules, Conant maintained, had been 'in the best interests of the war effort, the United States and the eventual peace of the world' and he feared that the President had abandoned them 'without proper understanding'.[16] Neither scientist-administrator had time to lick their wounds, however, with a British atomic envoy expected in Washington within days pursuant to the President's instructions. But who would the envoy be? In London, Lindemann knew who it could not be: Akers. The American animus was too strong. Instead he proposed – and Churchill agreed – that Anderson take on the mission. At the same time, the Prime Minister arranged for the ideas on collaboration aired in his meeting with Stimson and Bush to be converted into draft heads of agreement and these accompanied Anderson when he left for the United States on 1 August.[17]

On arrival in Washington, the Lord President was plunged into a whirl of meetings with senior figures in the Manhattan Project. He was relieved to discover that both Stimson and Marshall of the Top Policy Group were approving of restored atomic ties as this would counteract any residual hard-feelings on the part of the scientist-administrators. Of these, Bush struck Anderson as sympathetic but he gained the impression that while operational control of the Manhattan Project was still tightly in the grasp of General Groves, policy control was increasingly in the hands of the spiky Head of the S-1 Executive Committee, with Bush, he noted, 'lacking the strength to control Dr. Conant'.[18] The penny, it seemed, was beginning to drop. By the time Anderson left for Canada on 7 August, a document was ready for signature by the President and Prime Minister when they met at Quebec a few days later for the next Allied war council, codenamed Quadrant.[19]

In Ottawa, Anderson called on the Canadian Prime Minister, one of the Tube Alloys cognoscenti, and gave him an account of his time in Washington. Later, Mackenzie King wrote a detailed account of their conversation in his diary. 'Atomic weapons', Anderson avowed, 'will give control of the world to whatever country obtains them first.' He went on:

> Germany and Russia were working on the same thing ... He thought Russia with its enormous scientific development along mechanical lines might perfect discovery first of all which would be a terrific thing for that country, should such be the case. He, himself, said that, while the war might be over before the development came, it would be a terrific factor in the post-war world as giving an absolute control to whatever country possessed the secret. At the same time, if anyone of the competing nations came first, they would be sure of immediate victory, so powerful was the destruction this discovery was capable of effecting.[20]

There it was again, a Bolshevik bomb. Anderson had been the first to alert Churchill to this portentous possibility. But whereas the Prime Minister used the prospect as an additional reason to press Roosevelt to restore US–UK atomic links, and thus speed the realisation of a weapon, Anderson, as we will see, was beginning to move in a different direction; namely, to avoid a catastrophic arms race after the war, the Soviets, he felt, should not only be informed about the Manhattan Project while the conflict was ongoing, but be invited to become partners with Britain and the United States in devising a system of international control of atomic energy.

On 5 August 1943, Churchill, along with a party that included his wife, his youngest daughter Mary, the Chiefs of Staff and sundry military and diplomatic advisors, set sail for Canada aboard the *Queen Mary*. On arrival in Quebec, Churchill established himself in the Citadel, the summer home of the Governor-General on the heights overlooking the St Lawrence River. There, he received a cable from Stalin proposing that a tripartite Heads of Government meeting had become 'absolutely desirable'. Both Churchill and FDR agreed and planning commenced for first Big Three conference of the war at Tehran at the end of the year.[21] Also waiting for Churchill at Quebec was Anderson who talked him through the agreement he had worked out with the Americans before returning to London to resume watch over the Home Front.[22]

On 19 August, in a brief ceremony at the Citadel, Churchill and Roosevelt signed the 'Articles of Agreement Governing Collaboration Between the Authorities of the USA and the UK in the Matter of Tube Alloys'. The two leaders rededicated themselves to the pooling of 'all available British and American brains and resources' so as to bring the atomic project to the earliest possible conclusion. There were, in addition, four political articles in the agreement, which committed the two countries as follows:

First, that we will never use this agency against each other.

Secondly, that we will not use it against third parties without each other's consent.

Thirdly, that we will not either of us communicate any information about Tube Alloys to third parties except by mutual consent.

Fourthly, that in view of the heavy burden of production falling upon the United States as the result of a wise division of war effort, the British Government recognize that any post-war advantages of an industrial or commercial character shall be dealt with as between the United States and Great Britain on terms to be specified by the President of the United States to the Prime Minister of Great Britain. The Prime Minister expressly disclaims any interest in these industrial and commercial aspects beyond what may be considered by the President of the United States to be fair and just and in harmony with the economic welfare of the world.[23]

As we know, this last article was intended to assuage American suspicions of British commercial rapacity. However, scientist R. V. Jones later argued that the article constituted a foolish and costly surrender: Churchill, he maintained, 'would never have signed away Britain's birthright in the post-war exploitation of atomic energy had he fully appreciated the potential'.[24] More recently, and more tolerantly, historian Paul Addison has suggested that it was his 'usual concentration on the military issues at the expense of post-war questions' that led Churchill to disclaim any British interest in the industrial and commercial applications of atomic energy.[25] There is much truth in the latter observation, less in the former. The commercial-industrial concession was regarded by the triumvirate as a minimum requirement if interchange was to be resumed. And without interchange, neither TA-1 nor TA-2 was going anywhere very fast, either in the present or the future. Furthermore, singling out Churchill for yielding the national interest seems inappropriate. He did not act unilaterally in a spasm of pro-American emotionalism but on the advice of the other two members of the triumvirate.

The article so distressing to Jones was an Anderson proposition which Churchill picked up and ran with during the Stimson-Bush visit to London. 'The commercial aspect is at present secondary', Anderson argued. 'If it ever becomes important it will not be for at least 5 years, probably 10.'[26] Lindemann held the power project to be an even longer-term proposition; eight years later, in July 1951, he could still be found publicly asserting that it would be 'several decades' more before the 'peaceful uses of atomic energy' were properly realized.[27] The Prof was wrong but this matters less than the fact that in the summer of 1943, Anderson and Lindeman, as well as Akers, were of the view that 'the future industrial possibilities of TA . . . are either very small or else so remote that we need not consider them'.[28] The Prime Minister had also been told repeatedly in the months leading up to Quadrant that only through close collaboration *during the war* could Britain hope to gain access to the treasure trove of American knowledge needed to fast-track his country's own atomic weapons development *after the war*. The concession on the commercial-industrial side was the means to this security-oriented end, although we should note that Lindemann later questioned whether it had been necessary to go quite so far as to place the future of the country's power programme, remote though it was, in the hands of a multitude of as yet unknown US presidents.[29]

Beyond the counsel he was given, Churchill seems to have done some profit-and-loss calculations of his own. The bonhomie of Quadrant left him hugely optimistic about the future of Anglo-American relations generally and it would be surprising, given the high level of personal interest he had shown in Tube Alloys since the start of the year, if atomics did not impact on his thinking on this overarching subject.[30] What was surrendered in August 1943 could be recovered later if a postwar military alliance, with a Combined Chiefs of Staff at its heart, was solemnized. In such intimate embrace, what need would there be for atomic separatism? 'Our associations with the United States must be permanent', he told Lindemann a few months later when reflecting on the Quebec agreement, 'and I have no fear that they will maltreat or cheat us'. Neither Lindemann nor Anderson romanticized the US–UK relationship in quite the same way but they were agreed on the need to do whatever it took to gain re-entry to the Aladdin's cave of US atomic knowledge.[31]

To give substance to the revived relationship, the Quebec agreement established a Combined Policy Committee (CPC) responsible directly to the US, UK and Canadian governments. Based in Washington, the CPC was to be the forum within which tripartite cooperation was effected and work on the Bomb reviewed in all its varied dimensions. Stimson, designated chairman, was joined on the American side by Bush and Conant. The UK representatives were to be Field Marshal Sir John Dill, Head of the Joint Staff Mission, and Colonel J. J. Llewellin, Minister Resident in Washington for Supply. The Canadian representative was Clarence Howe, Minister of Munitions and Supply.[32] The final technical clauses of the agreement affirmed that there should be 'complete interchange of information and ideas on all sections of the project between members of the Policy Committee and their immediate technical advisers'. In addition:

> In the field of scientific research and development there shall be full and effective interchange of information and ideas between those in the two countries engaged in the same sections of the field.
>
> In the field of design, construction and operation of large-scale plants, interchange of information and ideas shall be regulated by such ad hoc arrangements as may, in each section of the field, appear to be necessary or desirable if the project is to be brought to fruition at the earliest moment. Such ad hoc arrangements shall be subject to the approval of the Policy Committee.[33]

We should note the phrase 'ad hoc arrangements' for, as will be seen, this could mean a lot or it could mean nothing.

Quadrant had 'gone off well', Churchill cabled the War Cabinet on 25 August, with the 'settlement of a number of hitherto intractable questions'. Security did not permit mention of Tube Alloys but we may be sure that this was one of the questions he had in mind.[34] On the broader Anglo-American front, the Prime Minister's conviction that relations had never been closer was given spectacular public play when he spoke at Harvard University on 6 September after being presented with an honorary doctorate by the university's President – none other than James B. Conant, architect of restricted interchange and a man whose 'long-term aim of postwar American dominance presumed leadership not only over defeated enemies but also over Washington's principal prospective ally'.[35] Churchill's aim was quite different. The USA and Britain, he declared, shared the same basic outlook on what was 'right and decent'. Both held 'a marked regard for fair play'. Both possessed 'a stern sentiment of impartial justice, and above all the love of personal freedom'. When the 'gift of a common tongue' was added to the mix, he saw no reason why, at some point in the future, there should not be common citizenship. 'If we are together nothing is impossible. If we are divided all will fail. I therefore preach continually the doctrine of the fraternal association of our two peoples.'[36]

Much has been written about Churchill's quest for an all-embracing alliance between Britain and its Empire and Commonwealth on the one side and the United States on the other, the English-Speaking Peoples as he termed them collectively (if erroneously). 'Mr Churchill by his father is an Englishman, by his mother he is an American, no doubt a blend that makes a perfect man', Mark Twain observed at the start of the century.[37] Churchill probably agreed but at Harvard he extended the blending to encompass the two nation-states. Had he been content to view this alliance as just a normal coming together of two powers, a mutually beneficial military, diplomatic and economic arrangement, albeit with the USA as the senior partner, we might have no particular cause to comment. Others in Churchill's government – not least Foreign Secretary Anthony Eden – tended to view Anglo-American relations in these kinds of terms and were realistic enough to know that when it came to a clash of national interests, the Americans would not allow sentimentality to get in the way of asserting their prerogatives even at the expense of their ally. (At Suez in 1956 Eden would learn just how right he was.) Churchill also recognized the rivalry inherent in US–UK relations. And he knew from bitter personal experience – the destroyers-for-bases deal in 1940, for example – how very hard-nosed the Americans could be in protecting their interests.[38] Nevertheless he hoped to eliminate potential flashpoints in the future by promoting a magnificently-melded US–UK combination. Sentimental or delusional as this may now seem, Churchill held to the idea as though it were a magic charm.[39] Moreover, as Elisabeth Barker has shown, his 'dream of a special relationship' explains his readiness to make short-term sacrifices to the Americans for what he hoped would be long-term gain.[40]

The Quebec Agreement may well be a case in point. Viewed in the optimistic Anglo-American context of the moment, the surrender of Britain's right to control its atomic energy destiny becomes a calculated gamble connected to Churchill's dream, for it was hardly possible for the nexus of commitments contained in the atomic agreement to be effectuated after the war (and Churchill *did* see the agreement possessing long-term relevance) unless existing military arrangements were converted into a formal alliance.

And if that came about, it would be a large down-payment on the fully-fledged fraternal association that was his ultimate aim. A few months later, pondering Quebec, Churchill told Lindemann that he was:

> absolutely sure we cannot get any better terms by ourselves than are set forth in my secret Agreement with the President. It may be that in after years this may be judged to have been too confiding on our part. Only those who know the circumstances and moods prevailing beneath the Presidential level will be able to understand why I have made this Agreement. There is nothing more to do now but to carry on with it, and give the utmost possible aid.[41]

Churchill was right to draw attention to policymakers below the President. Manhattan Project leaders had been largely resistant to a formalized US–UK atomic alliance. As of August 1943, however, their viewpoint was no longer shared by the President. The Quebec agreement, Barton Bernstein writes, 'marked the defeat of the Conant-Bush strategy', and though Roosevelt was still content to look to his scientist-administrators for technical advice, their influence on the international relations aspect of his atomic energy policy was non-existent.[42] Yet, true to the perversity of his handling of advisors generally, the President doled out the news of what had been agreed in a limited drip-feed manner. Neither Bush nor Groves had been invited to Quebec while the first that Stimson heard of the agreement was when he was told that he was chairman of something called the Combined Policy Committee. Moreover, even when ordered to renew interchange in line with the Quebec agreement, officials were never formally apprised of its political articles.[43] Nor did Roosevelt ever enlighten his atomic advisors about his reasoning. Perhaps, Bush later reflected, 'he just did not care to bring up the fact that he had been persuaded by Churchill to take a stand that would have been very unfortunate ... [and] would have made all sorts of trouble for him after the war, had he lived'.[44]

This reference to Roosevelt's mortality is germane in another sense. From August 1943, the future of Anglo-American atomic relations depended almost entirely on the personal relationship between the two men at the top. The Quebec Agreement was *their* agreement. It was not a treaty ratified by parliaments. It might even be of questionable legal and (in US terms) constitutional validity. Did Roosevelt really have the power to concede to a foreign state a right of veto over America's freedom to use the ultimate weapon? Nor was succession-planning written into this most personal of compacts. What price the future of the atomic alliance if one or other of the signatories should die or be removed from office as a result of a general election? Time, the President's health, and the voting intentions of the British people would provide an answer.

Thanks to the Quadrant feel-good factor and to the generally positive reception his Harvard speech received in the American press, the Prime Minister returned to England in high spirits.[45] It was not long, however, before they evaporated. For reasons Churchill was unable to fathom, Roosevelt appeared to cool on him – there was, for example, a certain reluctance on FDR's part to meet, or even agree to a session of the Combined

Chiefs of Staff, ahead of the Big Three conference at Tehran.[46] In retrospect, we can see that FDR was beginning his play to build a different special relationship, one with Stalin, the necessary means towards a greater Rooseveltian end, the cementing of close US–Soviet relations not just in wartime but as the bedrock of postwar peace and security. 'I can't take communism and nor can you', he once told his friend, the former US ambassador to Moscow Joseph E. Davies, 'but to cross this bridge I would hold hands with the Devil'.[47] As Tehran neared, therefore, FDR appeared anxious to avoid giving the Soviet leader the impression that there was an automatic two-thirds Anglo-American majority embedded in the Big Three structure, an objective which required some distancing between himself and the Prime Minister.[48]

In the event, Churchill and Roosevelt managed a few days together in Cairo prior to travelling to Persia, an encounter that persuaded the Prime Minister that 'amicable relations' had been restored.[49] When the Tehran conference got under way on 28 November, however, Churchill soon found 'triangular problems difficult' and after four days of often 'grim and baffling' discussions he was complaining of feeling unwell.[50] Stricken subsequently by a series of fevers which required convalescence in Carthage, he may also have been sick at heart at the way Roosevelt treated him at Tehran. In furtherance of his belief that the future peace hinged on the USA and the USSR working together, the President hit on a modus operandi which involved cosying-up to Stalin while cold-shouldering Churchill. Averell Harriman, the US ambassador to Moscow, watching from the wings, thought that the President 'unquestionably had a sadistic streak' and derived pleasure from baiting Churchill in this way.[51] No wonder the Prime Minister found Tehran a distressing experience.

The Americans and Soviets had also combined in a spoiling action to prevent Churchill advancing plans for an intensified military effort in Italy – the fascist government had surrendered that September but German forces in-country continued to put up formidable resistance – at the risk of yet another delay to operation Overlord, the cross-Channel invasion now slated for mid-1944. To General Sir Alan Brooke, Chief of the Imperial General Staff, it was obvious that Stalin not only wanted the Normandy invasion, along with a complementary invasion of the South of France, as a second front to draw German armies away from the East, but to divert Anglo-American forces from the Balkans upon which he 'cast covetous eyes'.[52] Part of Churchill's rationale for investing more manpower and resources in the Italian campaign was geo-political insofar as he hoped that Anglo-American forces would be able to advance north from Italy to arrive in central and south-eastern Europe before the Red Army claimed the area as war-booty. Roosevelt, however, offered him no support. Nor did Churchill's friendship with Hopkins avail him much. Hopkins was as sold as Roosevelt on the idea of close postwar US–Soviet relations – more so according to some British observers who viewed him as 'the champion appeaser of the Russians' always 'hotting up Roosevelt in that direction'.[53] And yet, no matter how much Roosevelt wished to make Stalin a partner in shaping and maintaining the peace, he was not prepared to tell him about the Manhattan Project. Rather, despite US intelligence concluding that the Soviets were already aware of its explosive purpose, he held to the view that the programme's importance to 'national

Figure 4.1 Stalin, Roosevelt and Churchill, Tehran, 1943. Universal Images Group/Getty Images.

safety' was so great that it must be 'more drastically guarded than other highly secret war developments'.[54]

'A bloody lot has gone wrong', Churchill complained to Moran near the end of the conference. Moran sympathized. 'Until he came here, the PM could not bring himself to believe that, face to face with Stalin, the democracies would take different courses. Now he sees he cannot rely on the President's support. What matters more, he realizes that the Russians see this too. It would be useless to try to take a firm line with Stalin. He will be able to do as he pleases. Will he become a menace to the free world, another Hitler? The PM is appalled by his own impotence.'[55] From this time onwards, Churchill was indeed prey to doubts that Roosevelt could be relied upon to stand up for the Atlantic Charter's principles of freedom and self-determination in a clash with Stalin over the political shape of postwar Europe if, in so doing, US relations with the USSR risked rupture. But what could Britain do on its own to block the projection of Soviet power and influence into the heart of Europe as the Red Army, after breaking the *Wehrmacht* at Stalingrad, began to drive Hitler's forces back towards Germany? At Tehran, he later confessed, 'I realized for the first time what a very *small* country this is. On one hand the big Russian bear with its paws outstretched – on the other the great American Elephant – & in between them the poor little English donkey – who is the only one that knows the right way home.'[56]

Historians, too, recognize Tehran as a turning-point, 'the moment when the balance of military power within the Anglo-American alliance shifted decisively in favour of the United States', when the USA 'turned its main attention … from Britain to the Soviet Union', and when American pressure for a Western European strategic focus finally trumped the UK's hopes for a continued Mediterranean and Balkan emphasis.[57] As for the personal relationship between Churchill and Roosevelt, this was probably never quite as warm as the mythology of the broader "special relationship" would have us believe, and certainly, after Tehran, their friendship seemed to operate on a more superficial level. In contrast, and as a portent of things to come, Churchill's relations with Stalin during the conference enjoyed moments of almost personal warmth.[58]

Tensions at the summit of Anglo-American relations were replicated on the lower atomic slopes. In the wake of Quebec, the Americans asked that 'a Top British Scientist, accepted and of sound judgment' be sent to Washington to act as technical advisor to the UK representatives on the Combined Policy Committee. In so doing they made clear that Akers did not fit the bill.[59] Anderson was 'distressed' by this slight on a man who had rendered 'most excellent service and about whose integrity and ability I have not the slightest doubt', but no matter how unjust, he knew that Akers must be sacrificed if collaboration was to have any future. And so it was that James Chadwick, 'liked and trusted' by the Americans and already in the United States, took on the job.[60]

From early CPC briefings, the British obtained a welcome overview of the state of the American programme: $785 million had so far been allocated to plant construction with the final outlay certain to exceed $1 billion (or $14 billion today); electromagnetic separation was confidently expected to deliver the necessary U-235, indeed a bomb might be ready as early as the start of 1945; the graphite pile as a generator of plutonium was a fail-safe, as was gaseous diffusion; and construction of a full-scale electromagnetic separation plant and an adjoining diffusion plant were well advanced. A heavy water pile was still under consideration but four heavy water production plants had been erected and were poised to begin delivering. With collaboration re-established, however, the US authorities seemed content to let the Canadian-British power team, now operating in Montreal and elsewhere in Canada under Halban (and later Cockcroft), make the running on heavy water reactor development.[61]

Starved of information on American activity for the best part of a year, these early generalised briefings represented a feast for the British. A little later, though, when they probed for hard detail, they drew several blanks. This was ominous. On the eve of the signing of the Quebec agreement, Akers had predicted that the extent to which its various scientific-technical provisions were implemented would depend on 'the good will of the Americans'. He further expected that 'nervousness' in S-1 circles about postwar Congressional scrutiny would leave the US authorities 'extremely cautious' about the release of sensitive information.[62] This proved to be a discerning assessment. General Groves settled on the view – which was shared by Bush and Conant – that if the CPC could not be magicked out of existence, it could be turned into a bureaucratic mechanism for preserving the spirit of the Conant rules. In October, after the first flush of satisfaction at being invited to sit at the atomic top-table had faded, the British awoke to the reality of life on the Groves-mediated CPC, namely that it was 'most definitely not where policy was either made or discussed'. Nor was it the place for them to learn in detail about the design, operation and technical underpinning of the vast industrial plants, veritable atomic cities, now rising up at Hanford in Washington state (plutonium production) and at Oak Ridge in Tennessee (electro-magnetic separation and gaseous diffusion).[63] Groves did his job well. He did most jobs well. 'The decisions of the Combined Policy Committee', he later reflected, 'did not at any time interfere with the United States program.'[64]

What, then, did the British get out of Quebec? It is important to recognise the agreement's dual nature, its politico-military and scientific-technical provisions. With regard to the former, the UK obtained a good deal. The use of atomic weapons, as well as the sharing of atomic intelligence with third parties (including perforce the other member of the Big Three, the USSR), rested on the principle of mutual consent. True, the British paid a price insofar as national control over civil-industrial atomic development was compromised, but the greater gain was the enmeshing of Britain and the United States at the highest levels in ways which served to advance Churchill's goal of a full Anglo-American alliance. None of these politico-military aspects, however, would be tested until an atomic bomb was close to combat-readiness. On the scientific-technical side, Anderson, while in Washington, had been obliged to compromise in order to secure his political objectives, hence full interchange, beyond gaseous diffusion, would be on an ad hoc basis as deemed 'necessary or desirable'.[65]

The arbiter of necessity and desirability turned out to be Groves, working closely with Bush and Conant, and this ensured that the CPC was neutered as a forum for meaningful exchange of information. But at least the British were *on* the CPC. The only thing worse than being the junior partner in an atomic alliance with America was not being a partner at all, and so the committee, if not its meetings (of which there were only eight in two years) remained a symbol of importance for Tube Alloys leaders.[66] There was, however, an alternative window into the Manhattan Project for the British, a way of circumventing the limitations of the CPC to obtain some at least of the information needed to realise the UK's ambitions after the war. As an outgrowth of the Quebec agreement, a British scientific mission was assigned to the Manhattan Project, including the bomb laboratory which had been set up at Los Alamos, 'the nuclear holy of holies', in New Mexico.[67] The Hill, as Los Alamos was known to its scientific residents, could yet provide the vantage point the British needed.

In September 1943, when the Chancellor of the Exchequer, Kingsley Wood, dropped dead, Anderson was appointed in his stead. Despite his new and heavy responsibilities, it was Churchill's hope that Anderson would continue as atomic overlord. Excited by the prospect of getting 'our experts in each branch of the project admitted to the United States teams', Anderson was glad to do so. Although the exodus of scientific talent across the Atlantic would denude atomic research and development in the UK, the fact was, he told Churchill, that the 'knowledge our men would acquire in this way would be greater than that which they would get working here on a necessarily smaller scale ... Only thus can we be sure of being in a position to start manufacturing here if and when that proves necessary after the war'. Lindemann concurred. 'The Americans of course fear that Congress may complain that they spent all the money and we got all the information', he remarked. Did this amount to cooperation? Or was it closer to parasitism? Either way, 'it seems likely to be the best we can get for the time being'. Churchill thought so too.[68]

An advance guard of British and UK-naturalized scientists left for North America towards the end of 1943, among them Otto Frisch, William Penney and James Tuck who made their way to Los Alamos. Eighteen months earlier, the brilliant and charismatic theoretical physicist J. Robert Oppenheimer, an early recruit to the Manhattan Project, had expressed concern to Groves that weapons design and engineering was being given less attention than the production of fissile material. The solution, he suggested, lay in the creation of a super-laboratory in which scientists could 'talk freely to each other, where theoretical ideas and experimental findings could affect each other, where the waste and frustration and error of the many compartmentalized experimental studies could be eliminated, and where we could begin to come to grips with chemical, metallurgical, engineering and ordnance problems that had so far received no consideration'.[69] Groves was initially uneasy about the security implications of such freedom of scientific interchange but his anxieties were alleviated by the geographical remoteness of the proposed location. 'My two great loves are physics and New Mexico', Oppenheimer once declared. 'It's a pity they can't be combined.' At Los Alamos, 7,000 feet up on a mesa in the Sangre de Cristo mountains, they were. In February 1943, Oppenheimer was appointed Scientific Director of the bomb lab. The following month construction work began and by the summer the first scientists had begun arriving. By the spring of 1944, the Hill and its support network boasted 3,500 employees, a figure which rose to over 6,000 by 1945, all of them contained within a security perimeter maintained by Groves and a US Army security team.[70]

The British presence at Los Alamos was comparatively small, with around a dozen front-line scientists resident and others visiting for short stays, but the UK contribution was highly valued – Tuck on the design of the plutonium implosion device used against Nagasaki, for example, and Penney in calculating blast and shock waves, measuring bomb damage and planning the first weapon test.[71] Also based at Los Alamos was Klaus Fuchs, a German-born physicist who had come to England in the 1930s, was interned as an alien in 1940, was released a year later to work on Tube Alloys, and became a British citizen in 1942. He was also a communist and arguably the most damaging of the atom spies recruited by the USSR.[72] As for the remainder of the British contingent, Chadwick became *de facto* chief of mission; Simon and Peierls worked on gaseous diffusion at Columbia and Kellex, the corporation set up to build a full-scale plant, before Peierls moved to Los Alamos; Oliphant and a team of assistants supported the work being done at Berkeley on electro-magnetic separation and later monitored the operation of the huge facility at Oak Ridge; and Alan Nunn May (another Soviet spy exposed in 1946) and more than sixty other scientists and technicians worked in Canada on atomic energy as a power source. In practice, only the great plutonium enterprise at Hanford was wholly out of bounds to the British.[73]

As Anderson predicted, by 1944 the brain-drain to America meant that work on Tube Alloys as an independent programme had to be mothballed. However, the triumvirate never doubted that research and development would be resumed following the defeat of the Axis, nor that the insights obtained from working with the Americans would provide the springboard for the re-launch.[74] 'All in all', the Tube Alloys official history concludes, 'the British were able to acquire a wide and detailed knowledge of the physics and construction of nuclear explosives' through close-up participatory experience and this went some way towards making up for the aridity of information-exchange in the Combined Policy Committee. Although impossible to quantify in any precise sense, in the two years that followed on from the Quebec agreement British scientists gained far greater knowledge and understanding than they would have been able to acquire in a UK-exclusive project undertaken in even the most favourable circumstances.[75]

Thanks to the interchange crisis, 1943 had been an unpleasant and destabilizing year for Anglo-American atomic relations, and yet, despite the tension and acrimony, the Manhattan Project's overall progress was not hampered unduly – a fact which, for some on the American side, proved their point about British expendability. One who thought that way, Conant, provided Roosevelt with an upbeat end-of-year assessment: 'everything', he reported, 'is going as well as humanly possible'.[76] The momentum carried forward into the spring of 1944 when Anderson, in a stock-take for Churchill, averred that a bomb might materialize 'at some date between the end of 1944 and the middle of 1945'.[77] In a report to Marshall, Groves was more precise: a weapon would be ready for use between March and June 1945.[78]

Meanwhile, despite the Nazi propaganda machine's occasional threats of mass destruction from unspecified super-weapons, Anglo-American anxieties about a German A-bomb began to subside as all available intelligence suggested that Hitler's uranium programme, if it existed at all in structured form, was nowhere near as advanced as the Manhattan Project.[79] This combination of developments – good progress on the Anglo-American side and an apparent lack of progress on the German side – convinced Anderson that the presently small Tube Alloys circle of knowledge needed to be widened. After all, if a weapon would be combat-ready by the summer of 1945, its operational use needed to be factored into military planning.

On 21 March 1944, Anderson wrote at length to Churchill urging that the Chiefs of Staff, and ideally the service ministers and the War Cabinet, be given 'full information'. As matters stood, only the triumvirate was *en courant* with the political, diplomatic, scientific, industrial, economic and military considerations attaching to atomic energy. Beyond Akers and his TA team in London and Chadwick and his mission in America, only a handful of individuals (Eden, Halifax and the British representatives on the Combined Policy Committee among them) possessed any real sense of the general position. However, when totted-up, Anderson argued that those in the know amounted to an insufficient quorum in view of the number and complexity of atomic-themed issues which were certain to arise as the Bomb neared delivery-point. One of the most important of these was the question of postwar international control. Other countries, Anderson told Churchill, including the Soviet Union, if possessed of the requisite scientific knowledge and access to raw materials, might well seek to fabricate their own atomic arms when the war was over. But was it sensible or even sane to allow weapons of mass destruction to proliferate? Anderson went on to sketch two possible scenarios:

> (a) Either there will be a particularly vicious form of armaments race, in which at best the United States, or the United States and the United Kingdom working as a team, will for a time enjoy a precarious advantage; or
> (b) A form of international control must be devised which will ensure that sub-atomic energy, if used at all, is used for the common benefit of mankind and is not irresponsibly employed as a weapon of military or economic warfare.

It was Anderson, it will be recalled, who first alerted Churchill to the USSR's atomic weapons potential and to the connected importance of Britain acquiring its own atomic arsenal as insurance against a future Soviet threat should the Grand Alliance collapse. That was in the spring of 1943. Since then he had done a lot of thinking, and now, a year on, he was 'convinced that we must work for effective international control'. Hitherto, the Americans had shown no especial interest in this issue but lately it had become apparent that 'one or two', notably Bush and Conant, were 'concerned about the future and are thinking of urging the President to give the problem of international control his serious and urgent attention'. It was important, therefore, that the triumvirate reach an agreed position in anticipation of an approach from the Americans. If a US–UK meeting of minds ensued and international control was taken forward to the planning level, the key question would be whether, and if so when, to inform the Soviet government about the Bomb. Anderson favoured early disclosure:

> If we jointly decide to work for international control, there is much to be said for communicating to the Russians in the near future the bare facts that we expect, by a given date, to have this devastating weapon; and for inviting them to collaborate with us in preparing a scheme for international control. If we tell them nothing, they will learn sooner or later what is afoot and may then be less disposed to co-operate. At the same time, there would seem to be little risk of the Russians, if they chose to be unco-operative, being assisted in the development of their own plans by a communication of the kind suggested.

The Chancellor's proposals had been drawn up following consultation with Lindemann and were both thoughtful and reasoned. But Churchill hated them. On bringing in the COS and the Cabinet, he retorted: 'I do not agree ... What can they do about it?' As for approaching the USSR, he was even firmer: 'On no account.'[80] The only additions to the circle of knowledge he was prepared to countenance were the Australian and New

Zealand Prime Ministers, for reasons connected with seeking alternative sources of raw materials, and his close friend Field Marshal Smuts, the South African leader, whose counsel he valued highly.[81]

Anderson must have known that winning the Prime Minister round would be an attritional process, not a one-hit wonder. Nevertheless, he found the severity of the rebuttal personally hurtful: a principled, conviction-driven politician, he genuinely believed that international control offered the best insurance against a ruinous arms race. And preparations needed to begin during the war – *before* a bomb had been built, still less tested or used against Germany or Japan – if there was to be any realistic chance of persuading the ultra-suspicious Soviet leadership to participate in a control regime when it was over. As early as August 1942, in a letter to Bush, Anderson had raised concerns about the 'misuse' of atomic power and opined that 'the utilization of nuclear energy, whether as a military weapon or for industrial purposes, will require a special and powerful system of international control' to safeguard 'the well-being of humanity'.[82] A little over a year later, Anderson met the renowned Danish scientist Niels Bohr whose work on quantum theory and complementarity, together with Einstein's theory of relativity, had transformed modern physics. Bohr was also a respected scientist-statesman and is regarded by historians as the foremost war-time advocate of international control.[83] Anderson, it has been suggested, fell under the physicist's spell.[84] He certainly had the greatest admiration for Bohr – 'worthy', he declared, 'to rank in every respect with a Newton or a Rutherford' – but the spell worked only to the extent that Bohr's idealistic vision of nuclear arms control in an open world confirmed for Anderson the rectitude of his own independently-acquired outlook.[85]

Anderson and Bohr were not just kindred spirits. In the autumn of 1943 they became co-conspirators in seeking, subtly and surreptitiously, to sell the merits of international control to the only two men in the Grand Alliance who could give life to the concept, the British Prime Minister and the American President. Bohr's part in this story is well known, that of Anderson is overlooked. Which, considering they were in many ways a team, is not right.[86]

Following the German invasion of Denmark in April 1940, Bohr received a number of offers of sanctuary from friends in Britain and the United States, but conscious of his responsibility for Jewish and other refugee scientists given asylum at his Institute for Theoretical Physics in recent years, he chose to remain in Copenhagen.[87] At first, the Nazi occupation proved less oppressive than in many other territories under German control and Bohr was mostly left alone. In the summer of 1943, however, his situation suddenly worsened when the Germans tightened their occupation policies. As part of this process, orders were issued for the round-up and deportation of Denmark's Jews. With Jewish ancestry on his mother's side, Bohr immediately recognized the danger to himself and his family. That September, with the help of the Danish underground, he and his wife (followed soon after by their four sons) were spirited across the Kattegat to neutral Sweden. Bohr was not long in Stockholm before he received a message from Lindemann inviting him to England. He gladly accepted and on 6 October 1943 he left for London in an unarmed RAF Mosquito.[88] On arrival, he was given a British passport and appointed Scientific Advisor to the Tube Alloys Directorate with an office at its Old Queen Street headquarters. His 21-year-old son, Aage, soon joined him as his assistant.[89]

In London, Bohr saw a good deal of Anderson. 'The association with Anderson', Aage later wrote, 'became of the greatest importance for my father's activities during the war and developed into a warm friendship based on mutual trust and respect.'[90] The contrast in personality-type was marked: on the one side, the dour, dry, practical Scot; on the other the warm, idealistic and loquacious Dane. Yet they established such bonds of intimacy that Bohr confessed to feeling 'almost as close to [Anderson] as a brother'.[91] Their relationship transcended a shared commitment to science, Anderson's biographer, John Wheeler-Bennett, later wrote, to encompass 'the great sense of humanity with which both men were endowed, [and] from which emerged their mutual concept of what an atomic age should be and their common fear of what it might become'.[92]

Bohr had been cut off from scientific developments in the outside world for more than three years and was excited, but also troubled, to learn of the progress made by the Anglo-Americans in uranium research. In his talks with Anderson he confided his concern that the world might soon be faced with 'an arms race that would threaten the continued existence of civilization itself'. But he also saw that, paradoxically, this terrible prospect 'offered new possibilities of giving political developments a more favourable turn ... [E]veryone would have to realize that the world was changed for better or worse, that now a comprehensive and genuine co-operation [between governments] was necessary to avoid living under the most ominous threats.'[93] While sharing Bohr's vision of an open postwar world in which atomic energy was under the jurisdiction of an international regulatory authority, Anderson knew better than anyone that his boss, the Prime Minister, was a fervent atomic monopolist and, as such, the enemy of international control.[94] Of necessity, therefore, Anderson concealed from Churchill the extent of his Bohrism, although it was plain to others, among them Chadwick who recalled that Bohr 'acted throughout [the war] not only with the best motives but with the advice and agreement of Sir John Anderson'.[95]

At the end of 1943, Bohr and his son were made *de facto* members of the UK mission and left for the United States on a tour of Manhattan Project sites. Travelling under an assumed identity – "Dr Baker" – Bohr was warmly received wherever he went, especially at Los Alamos where by 'word and deed' he boosted the morale of everyone he came in contact with.[96] Bohr also became aware of unease amongst atomic scientists, particularly at the Chicago Metlab but also on the Hill, at the thought of using the Bomb in combat when intelligence strongly suggested that the Nazi uranium project, the spoiling of which was the Manhattan Project's original *raison d'être*, was a chimera.[97] This moral queasiness would become more widespread over the next two years but the blunt reality was that scientists were employed to produce a bomb, not to determine what to do with it. That task belonged to an élite of American political and military decision-makers a majority of whom were agreed that a weapon, if or when available, would be used.

The bombing of Hiroshima and Nagasaki thus represented the implementation of an assumption dominant in S-1 circles for some time.[98] It was also, as we will see, an assumption shared by the one man on the British side likely to have a say in the Bomb's military deployment. For Churchill, war and new weapons technology were an obvious natural fit, hence 'the decision whether or not to use the atomic bomb . . . was never even an issue'.[99]

Bohr sympathized with those scientists troubled by the prospect of unleashing a bomb which he and they knew was not simply another weapon, the latest stage in an evolutionary process that began when cavemen first hurled rocks at one another, but something of a profoundly different order. Equally, and realistically, he acknowledged the existence of military imperatives and accepted that the Bomb could well have a decisive role to play in defeating the Axis.[100] But then what? The answer, he was convinced, was international control, but this required the USSR, the one member of the Grand Alliance with no atomic weapons, to have real trust in the two that did, the United States and the United Kingdom. The effort to win that trust needed to begin immediately via an approach to the Soviet government. Bohr did not propose passing on scientific or technical secrets, only the information that the Anglo-Americans were developing a super-bomb for use against the enemy and that come the end of the war they wished to work cooperatively with the USSR in establishing a system of control. If this were to happen, Bohr reflected, then the Manhattan Project 'will surely have brought about a turning point in history and this wonderful adventure will stand as a symbol of the benefit to mankind which science can offer, when handled in a truly human spirit'.[101]

"Dr Baker" kept Anderson regularly updated during his time in America; Anderson in turn asked the British Ambassador in Washington, Lord Halifax, to keep a watchful eye on Bohr. He did more than that. Soon, both Halifax and his deputy, Sir Ronald Campbell, had imbibed Bohr's thesis. 'I myself think there may be some hope in what he has in mind', the Ambassador confided to Anderson. 'I do believe that Bohr's ideas call for very urgent and deep consideration.'[102] Bohr also won an important American convert in the person of Supreme Court Justice Felix Frankfurter, a friend since the 1930s when they worked together to establish a hardship fund for 'scholar-exiles of Hitler'.[103] Aware of the Manhattan Project through contacts in the American scientific community, Frankfurter shared the Dane's fears for the future. So, it seemed, did the President of the United States. In April 1944, Frankfurter told Bohr that Roosevelt, with whom he was on intimate terms, was 'worried to death' about the Bomb and would be interested to learn more about the Dane's ideas on arms control. There was, however, the Churchill factor to consider. Roosevelt 'realizes he shares the responsibility for the handling of the matter . . . solely with the Prime Minister', Frankfurter explained to Bohr, but 'would not only welcome, but is eager for the Prime Minister to receive any suggestions for dealing with this problem'.[104]

Even by Roosevelt's unorthodox standards this was a bizarre way to operate; in essence, he asked Frankfurter to ask Bohr to ask Churchill to ask him – the President – to investigate the potentialities of international control. Perhaps it was FDR's preciousness about retaining an exclusive personal grip on the diplomatic side of atomic energy that led him to bypass the S-1 Executive Committee and the Military Policy Committee.[105] As things turned out, Bohr would have been better off going through the Bush–Conant channel as both scientist-administrators were by now giving careful thought to the postwar implications of atomic energy. Many years later, when Conant learned of Bohr's decision to deal with, and through, the White House, he offered a one-word verdict: 'mistake'.[106]

CHAPTER 5
MORTAL CRIMES

When Anderson heard of the Frankfurter gambit he urged Bohr to return to England to deliver Roosevelt's message direct to Number 10. 'We came to London full of hopes and expectations', Aage recalled, 'that Churchill, who possessed such imagination, and who had often shown such great vision, would be inspired by the new prospects.' Anderson, he added, 'shared my father's view of the problems and regarded the message from the President as a very favourable initiative'.[1] The last time Anderson tried to interest Churchill in international control he had received a sharp rebuke for his pains. Yet, as he later acknowledged, there was 'something selfless about Winston; if an idea got hold of him he would follow it up with endless enthusiasm and energy, quite regardless of whether it was going to help him personally'.[2] The trick was to get the idea to stick.

On 27 April 1944, the Chancellor had another go at the Prime Minister. He used as an opening the recent proliferation of inter-allied discussions about the shape of the post-war international order. Being divorced from any knowledge of the momentous developments taking place in the field of atomic energy, Anderson wrote to Churchill, these efforts were 'quite unreal'. When a bomb finally materialised, 'the future of the world will . . . depend on whether it is used for the benefit or the destruction of mankind. We shall be entering an entirely new era'. Obviously, while the project remained top secret it could not feature in open discourse on postwar planning, but Anderson saw no reason why a select group of those in the know in London and Washington should not consider arrangements for the *eventual* control of atomic energy. The first thing, he suggested, was for Churchill to 'break the ice' with a telegram to FDR. It was another well-reasoned presentation – Anderson was good at those – but it got him nowhere. 'I do not think any such telegram is necessary', the Prime Minister replied, 'nor do I wish to widen the circle who are informed'.[3]

Disappointed but undaunted, Anderson now opted for the indirect approach and engaged others to prepare the way for a Churchill–Bohr meeting. One ally was the President of the Royal Society and TA Consultative Committee member Sir Henry Dale who wrote to Churchill on 11 May emphasising the epochal nature of what impended. 'I cannot avoid the conviction that science is . . . approaching the realization of a project which may bring either disaster or benefit, on a scale hitherto unimaginable, to the future of mankind.' Churchill must listen to Bohr's 'own expert appraisement'. Moreover, the Dane carried 'a message which he has been charged to deliver to you in person, by a most intimate personal advisor of President Roosevelt'. It was Dale's 'serious belief that it may be in your power, even in the next six months, to take decisions which will determine the future of human history', and he beseeched Churchill to give Bohr 'the opportunity of brief access to you'. With Lindemann endorsing Dale's appeal, and with Churchill's confidant General Smuts, an unabashed fan of Bohr ('greater than Newton, greater than Faraday'), also lined-up by Anderson in support of a meeting, the Prime Minister consented to give the scientist half-an-hour of his time.[4]

Despite some last minute coaching from Anderson's private secretary 'about what he would say', Bohr's meeting with Churchill in Downing Street on 16 May went badly awry.[5] Under strain as D-Day loomed, the Prime Minister was in a foul temper from the outset. 'After all, this new bomb is just going to be bigger than our present bombs', he snapped when Bohr tried to explain his concerns. 'It involves no difference in the principles of war; and as for any post-war problems, there are none that cannot be amicably settled between me and my friend President Roosevelt.' The rest of the meeting was taken up by a squabble between Churchill and Lindemann, the only other person present, about the terms of the Quebec agreement, and Bohr, nervous and soft-voiced, was left struggling to get a word in edgeways. In the end, his only impact was a negative one with Churchill concluding – incorrectly – that he was all for giving to Stalin the secret of the Bomb *in toto*. As he was shown to the door, Bohr asked if he might put his thoughts down on paper for the Prime Minister's further consideration. By all means, Churchill said, as long as he stuck to physics.[6] When Bohr's letter arrived the following week, Churchill's instructions to his officials spoke volumes: 'This can be sealed up without being read by anyone.'[7] With the Quebec agreement in place, the Prime Minister not only valued the US–UK atomic partnership on its own terms but increasingly saw it as a means of realising a much greater objective, 'a special relationship' no less, to include a permanent Combined Chiefs of Staff organization and 'a measure of reciprocity in the use of bases … within the ambit of a world organisation'. Bohr and his ideas, insofar as they threatened the exclusivity of the Anglo-American atomic relationship, also threatened this greater Churchillian design.[8]

A deflated Bohr – 'We did not even speak the same language' – returned to the United States but he soon received a fillip when Frankfurter arranged for him to meet the President.[9] It was welcome news to Anderson, too, and in the lead-up to the Dane's date at the White House, Halifax in Washington, responding to the Chancellor's promptings from London, helped Bohr prepare to such a degree that some historians have described the scientist's encounter with FDR as 'choreographed' or even 'stage-managed' by his covert British allies.[10] The meeting took place on 26 August and was a huge improvement ('in every respect most satisfactory', Bohr told Anderson) on what occurred in Downing Street. Roosevelt was friendly and relaxed throughout the 90-minute encounter and not only allowed Bohr to set out his stall without interruption, but agreed with him that 'nothing could be lost, but very much gained by an early approach to the S[oviet] U[nion]'. FDR even undertook to raise the matter with Churchill whose rejection of international control ought not to be taken too tragically, he advised, as the Prime Minister often reacted negatively to new ideas before coming to accept them.[11] Aage later recalled the 'encouragement and gratitude my father felt at his talk with Roosevelt' and he was filled with 'optimism and expectation'.[12] So was Anderson who looked forward to Roosevelt broaching international control with Churchill

Figure 5.1 Niels Bohr. Photograph by Eric Schaal. The LIFE Images Collection/Getty Images.

when the two leaders met at the second Quebec conference, codenamed Octagon, in mid-September.[13]

While Bohr's campaign for international control played out in the summer of 1944, the triumvirate was giving thought to another important aspect of the atomic future. On 15 June, Anderson wrote to the Prime Minister to say that 'the post-war problem', specifically, whether US–UK collaboration would endure, 'must now be faced'. Overlord had begun the week before, and though there was much fighting still to be done, the launch of the cross-Channel invasion encouraged Anderson to look ahead. The idealist in him entertained visions of international control but the realist knew that Britain's security after the war, and perhaps the national interest generally, was likely to be bound up with atomic energy, hence with US–UK atomic relations.[14] Lindemann thought so too. 'I personally would like to continue and expand in peacetime our collaboration with the Americans', the Prof told Churchill, but whether the Quebec agreement provided a sufficient springboard was doubtful. At the very least, the matter needed to be thrashed out between the Prime Minister and the President.[15] This was also Churchill's view. Indeed, recalling the interchange crisis, he espied 'great dangers in opening these matters at lower and less friendly levels'.[16]

In normal circumstances, the Prime Minister might have looked to Hopkins to prepare the ground but illness had removed him from the centre of Washington decision-making while those to whom Roosevelt had recently turned for advice – Admiral William D. Leahy, his Chief of Staff, for one, Secretary of the Treasury Henry Morgenthau Jr. for another – lacked Hopkins' emotional attachment to Britain and to Churchill personally.[17] Meanwhile, influence over the direction of the war effort was more than ever linked to the military contribution of each power, and here, in Anglo-American terms, the USA had grown toweringly superior. Getting London's views heard, never mind heeded, in Washington was the challenge. 'This visit of mine to the President is the most necessary one that I have ever made since the very beginning', Churchill confided to his wife in August 1944 shortly before departing for Octagon. There were 'delicate and serious matters' which needed 'to be handled between friends in careful and patient personal discussion'.[18]

One of these was Tube Alloys. A weapon with a projected TNT-equivalence now estimated at 20,000 tons remained on track for delivery the following summer.[19] This was encouraging for British and Americans alike, but with the entire industrial development of atomic energy located in the United States, and not discounting the work of Chadwick and his mission team, there was no disguising the UK's junior-partner status. But how long would Britain continue to enjoy even that qualified position? If the Americans took a legalistic view of the wording of the preamble to the Quebec agreement, Anderson informed Churchill on 1 September, they could argue that cooperation must cease upon the defeat of Germany and Japan. A recent (June 1944) Anglo-American agreement establishing a Combined Development Trust to jointly identify, harvest and share world sources of uranium might likewise be deemed a war-time contingency. In Anderson's view, if Britain was forced to go it alone, there was no question that 'we ... now have enough knowledge to do so' and potentially sufficient raw materials. The real problem was money. Working alone, the UK would have to undertake many of the costly processes presently being conducted in the USA, 'and for this our resources would not be adequate, at any rate for some time to come'. Therefore, leaving aside all other considerations, on purely financial grounds 'it is in our material interest to seek to secure continued Anglo-American co-operation after the war'.[20]

Lindemann echoed Anderson. At Octagon the Prime Minister must 'try to discover from the President in broad outline what the Americans have in mind about work on TA after the war ends'. While cooperation on the use of atomic energy for civil purposes might well continue, would the Americans be as ready to work with the British on the military side? Could the two countries 'continue to cooperate in developing such a vital weapon unless they were united by a close military alliance?' Churchill, we know, thought (or hoped) not. The Americans must surely be aware that the UK intended to resume research and development after the war, the Prof observed, but the scope, scale and form of that programme 'depends upon whether we continue to co-operate with the USA or not'.[21]

A closet Bohrite, Anderson was also hoping that the President, rehearsed by Frankfurter and by Bohr himself, would use the Quebec conference to impress upon the Prime Minister the importance of laying the groundwork for international control. The two sides of Anderson's outlook were not yet in conflict insofar as while working in the national interest to ensure that Anglo-American atomic cooperation continued in peacetime, there was no reason why his personal hopes should not be invested in the success of Bohr's enterprise. In a paper for Lindemann's eyes only (Anderson looked on the Prof as a kindred spirit if not a paid-up Bohrite) he reprised his thinking. 'The most urgent problem in this field is ... the problem of Russia.' He went on:

Russia is well equipped in every way to work on the TA project. She may be working on it already and, if she is not, is almost certain to start doing so on the termination of hostilities in Europe. She is also likely to gain access to any information available on the subject in Germany. She will therefore be in a position to proceed independently, but if we give her an opportunity now of joining with the USA and ourselves in dealing with the problem of international security, we may place her under a sense of obligation and there will be a chance – and it may be the only chance – of avoiding a disastrous competition between us.

Like Bohr, Anderson did not propose giving very much away: 'all that would be necessary would be to indicate [to Moscow] that we have made some progress and to invite Russian collaboration in considering the resultant problem of international security'. Anderson had thought to send Churchill a paper reprising the Bohr thesis but was dissuaded by Lindemann who advised letting Roosevelt 'make the running'. The Prof did him a favour. If he had sent the paper, Anderson might have been stripped of his atomic commission.[22]

On 18 September 1944, Churchill and Roosevelt concluded their third atomic agreement of the war. They did so while relaxing in the comfortable surroundings of the President's Hyde Park home after the main business of Octagon had been completed. Hopkins, somewhat recovered, was present, as was Admiral Leahy.[23] Unlike the Quebec agreement, which had been prepared in advance by officials, the Hyde Park agreement bears the hallmarks of a hastily contrived aide-memoire – the result, Groves later quipped, of 'many glasses of brandy'.[24] Moreover, in reflecting closely the views the Prime Minister brought with him from London it was almost certainly of his own personal crafting. That said, unless he forged the President's signature, we must suppose that FDR concurred with its content.

Comprised of just three short articles, the most striking feature of the agreement is the extent to which it was an anti-Bohr declaration:

1. The suggestion that the world should be informed regarding tube alloys, with a view to an international agreement regarding its control and use, is not accepted. The matter should continue to be regarded as of the utmost secrecy; but when a 'bomb' is finally available, it might perhaps, after mature consideration, be used against the Japanese, who should be warned that this bombardment will be repeated until they surrender.

2. Full collaboration between the United States and the British Government in developing tube alloys for military and commercial purposes should continue after the defeat of Japan unless and until terminated by joint agreement.

3. Enquiries should be made regarding the activities of Professor Bohr and steps taken to ensure that he is responsible for no leakage of information particularly to the Russians.[25]

We will come to the anti-Bohrite aspects shortly but first some general observations are in order. Alongside its resounding rejection of international control, the first article spoke to anticipated difficulties in ending the war in the Pacific through an invasion of Japan's home-islands, not least the fear that the Japanese would mount so formidable a defence that Allied casualty lists would be distressingly high. The absence of any mention of Germany as a target for the Bomb is readily explicable. At the time of Octagon there was optimism in Allied circles that the end of the war was coming into view: in the east, the Red Army had made tremendous progress since its stunning victory at Stalingrad in February 1943; in the west Overlord had triumphed, Paris had been liberated and operation Market Garden, an audacious bid to secure the bridges in Holland astride the Rhine as a route into Germany, was due to begin the day after the conference. 'There is a feeling of elation, expectancy and almost bewilderment', Colville recorded. 'People are expecting the armistice any day now'.[26] Such predictions proved premature: Market Garden failed, and then, at the end of the year, the massive German counter-offensive in the Ardennes gave the Allies a severe jolt. However, back in mid-September, with an A-bomb expected within nine months, Churchill and Roosevelt, assuming the collapse of the Third Reich before then, saw no reason to include Germany in the targeting calculus.[27]

In the second article, on post-war cooperation, Churchill appeared to claw back some of the non-military concessions he had made the previous year – it spoke of equal US–UK collaboration – but the critical caveat about presidential primacy remained in place. In general, however, by affirming the principle of atomic partnership, full and enduring beyond the defeat of the Axis, Roosevelt had given Churchill the greatest part of what he wanted. As for the final article, it is tempting to suggest that in their determination to gag Bohr (who, to reiterate, had never proposed that "the world" be informed of the Manhattan Project, only the Soviets, and even then in very general terms), both Churchill and Roosevelt were already seeing the Bomb as a possible means of strengthening their diplomatic or military hand in any future confrontation with the USSR. Tempting, but premature in Churchill's case, as we will see.

For now, the Prime Minister was content. '[T]he President and I exchanged satisfactory initialled notes about the future of TA on the basis of indefinite collaboration in the post-war period subject to termination by joint agreement', he cabled Anderson on 21 September.[28] Churchill's satisfaction was Bohr's disappointment – although, having said that, the Prime Minister had at least been consistent, unlike Roosevelt who truly betrayed Bohr having assured him less than a month previously of sympathy with his viewpoint. In the absence of any written record of what passed between the two leaders, attempts to explain the President's volte-face are necessarily speculative. Nevertheless, it is clear that at the time of Octagon, FDR remained strongly desirous of maintaining the US–UK atomic monopoly and of locating it within an atomic alliance for reasons connected to his thinking on the policing of the postwar peace.[29] Roosevelt had been shocked to learn from Churchill that 'England was broke', or very close to it. If that was the case, what good would the UK be as a partner in maintaining international security in the future?[30] The 'real nub of the situation is to keep Britain from going into complete bankruptcy at the end of the war', Roosevelt told his Secretary of State, Cordell Hull, a few days after Churchill left for home. 'I just cannot go along with the idea of seeing the British empire collapse financially', a development that would render the UK a weakened European policeman and leave Germany in a position to recover its power and 'make another war possible in twenty years'. Roosevelt made no mention of any future Soviet threat: as had been the case since Tehran, he was optimistic that postwar relations with the USSR could be arranged satisfactorily.[31]

The President spoke to Lindemann in similar vein when they met in Washington a few days after the conference. Bush, who was also present, wrote of being 'very much embarrassed' when Roosevelt launched into a frank oration on atomic matters in terms not yet discussed, never mind coordinated, with his advisers. FDR declared himself 'very much in favor of complete interchange with the British on this subject after the war in all phases and in fact apparently on a basis where it would be used jointly, or not at all'. In a hint that he was even moderating his anti-colonialism in connection with his concerns for postwar security, this aim was juxtaposed with an avowal of 'the necessity for maintaining the British Empire strong'.[32] Atomic power could yet compensate for Britain's loss of power in other forms, political and economic. Nor did it matter that the UK might not have a super-bomb of its own for some years. Britain and the United States were atomic 'partners', Roosevelt affirmed, 'not only during, but after the war'.[33]

FDR's atomic agenda had never been Bohr's agenda and the hapless Dane must therefore be added to that long list of people fooled by this Janus-faced 'master of misdirection'.[34] The suggestion advanced by some historians that Roosevelt was persuaded by Churchill against his better judgement to jettison Bohr is not convincing.[35] Had the President possessed any genuine interest in the physicist's ideas it would certainly have done well to withstand the gale-force strength of the Prime Minister's opposition, but the point is moot: the interest never really existed. Meanwhile the scale of Churchill's anti-Bohrism may be measured by the telegram he sent to Lindemann from the *Queen Mary* as he sailed for England on 20 September. 'The President and I are much worried about Professor Bohr', he began.

> How did he come into this business? He is a great advocate of publicity. He made an unauthorized disclosure to Chief Justice Frankfurter who startled the President by telling him he knew all the details. He says he is in close correspondence with a Russian professor, an old friend of his in Russia to whom he has written about the matter and may be writing still. The Russian professor has urged him to go to Russia in order to discuss matters. What is this all about? It seems to me Bohr ought to be confined or at any rate made to see that he is very near the edge of mortal crimes. I had not visualized any of this before, though I did not like the man when you showed him to me, with his hair all over his head, at Downing Street. Let me have by return your views about this man. I do not like it at all.[36]

Lindemann sprang instantly to Bohr's defence. There had, he conceded, been a letter to Bohr from his old acquaintance Piotr Kaptiza, the foremost physicist in the USSR, inviting him to come and research in the Soviet Union and to bring his family with him. However, suspecting that the offer was not entirely disinterested on the part of the communist authorities (even if Kapitza's personal motives were sincere), Bohr had 'concerted a reply with our people' – the Secret Intelligence Service – 'politely declining the offer'. Beyond this, 'Bohr like many other people has some rather woolly ideas about using the existence of a super weapon to induce the nations to live in confidence and at peace', but Lindemann personally had always found him 'most discreet and conscious of his obligations to England to which he owes a great deal, and only the very strongest evidence would induce me to believe that he had done anything improper in this matter'. In Washington, he had 'thoroughly discussed' the matter with the President, Leahy and Bush, all of whom shared his view of Bohr's innocence, although Bush undertook, at FDR's behest, to 'check up' on him.[37]

It is hard to determine where Lindemann really stood on Bohr. At one level, his remark about the Dane's woolliness suggests that he had little truck with idealistic notions of international control. At another, Anderson trusted him as a confidant throughout his own back-channel Bohrite manoeuvring and it may be that the Prof's denigration of the physicist's outlook was a smokescreen to hide from Churchill the extent of his own sympathy. More likely, Lindemann had not made up his mind and neither sought to sell Bohr's ideas to Churchill nor to thwart the efforts of others to do so. As for Anderson, he was dismayed by the content of the Hyde Park agreement as it pertained to Bohr and distressed by the spitefulness of Churchill's personal attack on his friend. The tragedy of Bohr's situation, he told Lindemann, was that there was 'no doubt of the reality of the danger that preoccupies him'. Bohr had been 'brought out of Denmark and introduced into TA with my approval and in agreement with the Americans' and he (Anderson) was personally ready 'to accept full responsibility vis-à-vis the Prime Minister'.[38]

There is no record of Anderson ever speaking to Churchill on the matter, but several weeks later he was still having difficulty coming to terms with the shameful way that Bohr had been treated – more so than Bohr himself whose 'sense of humour was always stronger than his pride'.[39] Bohr would continue to promote international control during the remainder of the war but without the level of covert support from allies within the Tube Alloys establishment which he had previously enjoyed. For even the loyal Anderson had to be cautious lest his position of trust with Churchill be compromised by too obvious an association with – as the Prime Minister saw it – a near-criminous scientist.[40]

A. J. P. Taylor later wrote that Hyde Park in September 1944 was when 'one of the greatest opportunities in the history of mankind was lost'.[41] Anderson, for one, would have agreed. Shortly before his death in 1958, he fell to reminiscing with Oppenheimer about the war years. By then the Cold War and the nuclear arms race, both of which Bohr foresaw and tried to prevent, had long since despoiled the international landscape and left the world teetering precariously on a nuclear knife-edge. A forlorn Anderson, Oppenheimer recalled, confessed that he had 'never been reconciled to the fact that Bohr's counsel had not been followed'. Nor, Anderson might have added, his own.[42]

For Churchill, Quebec had been 'a blaze of friendship and unity'.[43] There did indeed seem much to cheer with the Anglo-American atomic partnership and the wider US–UK wartime alliance in good shape. However, having attended to Anglo-American relations, Churchill's next job was to see to Anglo-Soviet relations. Accordingly, on 7 October he set out on the long journey to Moscow, his second such trek of the war. So far in our atomic story the US–UK dimension has bulked large for obvious reasons, but British relations with the USSR also occupied a prominent place in Churchill's strategic outlook. How could they not? The onset of Barbarossa in June 1941 not only provided a previously isolated Britain with an ally but drew so much of German armed might eastwards that the threat of invasion was lifted, at least for as long as the Soviets kept fighting. To ensure they did, Churchill made immediate moral cause with Stalin, solemnising that commitment in treaty-form in May 1942, and then authorised the supply of vast quantities of military aid to the USSR even though Britain could barely spare the tanks, planes and guns shipped via Arctic convoys to Russia.[44] But stay fighting the Red Army did, defensively to begin with and then increasingly offensively once the tide of war in the east turned in early 1943. In battle after battle across an immense killing front, the Red Army 'tore the guts out of the German military machine', as an admiring Churchill put it a telegram to Stalin in September 1944.[45]

To fully comprehend Churchill's attitude to the USSR – and thus to understand the place of the Bomb in his Soviet policy, both in the later stages of the war and in the Cold War – we need to look beyond the imperative of keeping the Red Army in the field and give attention to two other features of his outlook: his anti-communism and his geo-political realism. Churchill's ideological abhorrence of communism dates in its most visceral form from around the time of the Bolshevik revolution. As David Carlton has shown, it was the contest with Soviet communism which 'gave his political life the greatest continuity and meaning'. In comparison, his anti-Nazi years, before and during the war, though etched deeply in the popular memory as his defining contribution to history, were 'something of a digression, however necessary, in his extraordinarily long career'.[46]

As for his geo-political realism, this existed in and of itself, independent of the Soviet Union, the product of a late-Victorian mindset which extolled the virtues of the balance of power in international relations. Interestingly, on those occasions when his geo-political realism interacted with his anti-communism it had the effect of tempering his ideological fundamentalism. In 1940, having rejected all idea of a compromise peace with Germany in favour of fighting on, and in the absence of American belligerency, Churchill essayed two strategic alternatives: either Germany would win the war and dominate all of Europe, or else the Nazi–Soviet pact would unravel, Germany and the Soviet Union would come to blows, and the USSR would emerge the victor and very likely dominant in the east.[47] For Churchill, a Western Europe free from Nazism was plainly the preferred alternative. A year on, when Germany attacked the USSR, and still with no sign of American entry into the conflict, he rushed to join forces with Stalin against their now common foe. Previously the most dedicated of anti-communists, Churchill explained his decision with his best-known statement of geo-political pragmatism. 'If Hitler invaded Hell', he told Colville in June 1941, 'he would make at least a favourable reference to the Devil!'[48]

Over the next three years, the Red Army slowly but surely expelled the Germans from Soviet territory – albeit at fearful cost – and then began the pursuit of its enemy all the way to Berlin. In due course the chase took Stalin's forces into Eastern and South-Eastern Europe, first Poland in January 1944, then Romania and Bulgaria. Was the Red Army a liberating force? Or was it to be an army of conquest? What would be the ultimate consequence of Churchill's – and Roosevelt's – reliance on the totalitarianism of the left to vanquish the totalitarianism of the right? As early as the spring of 1944 Churchill feared he knew the answer. 'The Russians are drunk with victory and there are no lengths they may not go to', he told Eden; 'very great evil will come upon the world'. But what could be done to forestall this Faustian outcome? Was there a way to reconcile Soviet security needs – Stalin's iron resolve to have Eastern Europe and the Balkans as a buffer-zone between the USSR and the capitalist West – with the Anglo-American commitment to freedom and democracy as laid down in the Atlantic Charter? Looking back, this seems scarcely possible. At the time, Churchill believed the effort had to be made. The first step, he told Eden, was to have a 'showdown' with Moscow.[49]

Showdown. We should linger on the word. Used here in May 1944, it would become Churchill's mantra: again and again in the months ahead it would crop up whenever he contemplated the fate of Eastern Europe. In this first airing, he meant a diplomatic showdown, a frank exchange of views with the Soviet authorities during which the Western democracies would make clear their expectation that the principle of self-determination would be respected in all countries liberated from Nazi control or purged of Axis affiliations. Before long, as war gave way to Cold War, this idea of a showdown would acquire a more threatening and coercive quality. As of late 1944, however, Churchill had only words to play with in dealing with Stalin. He wished that it was otherwise, that his negotiating hand was strengthened by possession of territory.

When Rome was liberated at the start of June, Churchill, and for a time the British Chiefs of Staff, sensed a 'golden opportunity' to maintain the advance into the Po valley and thence through the Ljubljana Gap and on into the plains of Hungary to threaten the upper Danube and force the Germans to divert large forces away from the Normandy front.[50] Churchill might no longer dispute the American view of Overlord as the supreme operation of the war in Europe, but he did fiercely resent the US military's insistence on a second operation in France that summer, Dragoon, a US-led and Free French-assisted invasion of southern France intended to take place at the same time as Overlord, but which, in the end, was delayed until mid-August.[51] Churchill regarded Dragoon, which took four French and three US divisions out of Italy and robbed General Alexander's campaign there of critical strength, as 'a pure waste'.[52] The Americans, he felt, never grasped the importance of success in northern Italy, either militarily as a means of drawing more Germans away from the Normandy theatre than Dragoon ever would, or geo-politically as a springboard from which to project Anglo-American forces into Austria and the Balkans and thus 'of . . . having a stake in central and southern Europe and not allowing everything to pass into Soviet hands with the incalculable consequences that may result therefrom'.[53]

As it happened, Dragoon went well – no setbacks and a rapid advance up the Rhone valley – but for Churchill this was beside the point. Alexander's army had become 'a mere lemon to be squeezed as required'.[54] Stalin 'will get what he wants', he concluded. 'The Americans have seen to that. They haven't given Alex a dog's chance'.[55] The spearhead into the Balkans (with Vienna 600 miles from Rome) was probably never remotely a realistic proposition: the logistical and diplomatic obstacles were vast and Allied casualty losses likely to be unacceptably high.[56] In its absence, however, Churchill concluded that the only hope of limiting Soviet absorption of territory and populations resided in a diplomatic showdown. 'Winston never talks of Hitler these days', Moran noticed. Instead, he was back to his vintage anti-communism, circa 1918–1921, warning of the danger of the Red Army 'spreading like a cancer from one country to another'.[57]

The Prime Minister's desire for a meeting with Stalin in autumn 1944 set him at odds with a US President in the final throes of a re-election campaign and uninterested in a Big Three conference until after the November poll. Churchill, though, was unsympathetic: the Soviet armies, he griped, 'would not stand still awaiting the result of the election'.[58] Besides, he had a further urgent and particular reason for wanting an early showdown: Greece, a country occupying a key geo-strategic position in the Mediterranean astride Britain's imperial line of communication to India and beyond to Australia and New Zealand. During the summer, with German forces beginning to withdraw from the south and a similar evacuation from the north anticipated in due course, Churchill became frantic lest the communist-led *Ethniko Apeleftherotiko Metopo* (EAM) and its military wing, *Ellinikós Laïkós Apeleftherotikós Stratós* (ELAS), effect the 'communisation of Greece in the confusion of war'.[59] With the Red Army advancing through neighbouring Bulgaria, there was the additional danger of direct Soviet intervention. The anti-communist elements of the Greek army, around 40,000 troops, reinforced by British forces (which Churchill was ready to send into Athens as soon the German withdrawal was confirmed), could probably handle the local communist guerrillas but not if the Soviets were 'boosting EAM and ramming it forward with all their force'.[60] So it was that Churchill wended his way to Moscow, without Roosevelt, in search of an understanding on the Balkans generally and on Greece in particular.

He travelled in good spirits. A long-time believer in the efficacy of personal diplomacy, Churchill held an historical-romantic view that the great men of the great powers could do great things if they could but get together in earnest council. Insofar as it touched on Stalin, this faith in personal diplomacy represents another noteworthy feature of Churchill's Soviet outlook. As a result of his two previous encounters with the Soviet dictator – Moscow in 1942 and Tehran in 1943 – he was convinced that they had connected on a human level.[61] If he could exploit this bond to persuade Stalin of the sincerity of the British and American desire for friendship, and of the Western wish to continue in peacetime the Big Three wartime cooperation, the Soviet leader might settle for a sphere of influence rather than a sphere of domination in Eastern Europe and the

Balkans. Between those two poles there was a big difference, for Churchill could live with the former, 'an amicable settlement', but not the latter.[62] 'Whatever we may think today', David Reynolds reminds us, 'Churchill saw Stalin not as the problem but the answer.'[63] The meeting – the showdown – was the thing.

Today, the 1944 Moscow conference, codenamed Tolstoy, is best remembered for the percentages deal, another piece of instant Churchillian diplomacy following on from the Hyde Park agreement, a throwback 'to an era when princes swapped chunks of territory like pieces on a chessboard'.[64] At a late-night session in the Kremlin on 9 October, Churchill proposed to Stalin a division of the Balkans based on a rough percentage estimate of ideal levels of postwar Soviet and British (or else non-communist) influence. Stalin, agreeable, approved the following formula, scribbled down by Churchill on a single sheet of paper: Romania (90 percent Soviet), Greece (90 percent British), Bulgaria (75 percent Soviet, 'others' 25 percent), Yugoslavia and Hungary (50–50). In practice, Stalin was always going to exact his percentage – the Red Army would see to that – but in Greece, the British could hardly have retained a foothold in the face of a Soviet-backed communist surge. But no such surge occurred. To the contrary, Stalin held to his promise and steered clear of any political or military interference, not just in the months following the final German withdrawal but in the years ahead.[65]

Poland did not feature in this 'naughty document', as Churchill described it, being possessed of its own separate and special importance for both the Prime Minister and the Soviet dictator.[66] In July 1944, the Soviets had established a provisional Polish administration, a Committee of National Liberation, in Lublin in the east of the country. In an unmistakable signal of how the USSR intended to handle countries "liberated" by its armies, the Lublin committee, as it became known, was populated by hand-picked communists subservient to Moscow. Stalin never disguised his determination to secure 'the most physical tangible guarantees for Russia's future security' and, to that end, in 1944 he began the construction of a *cordon sanitaire*. Poland was the first building block. Romania and Bulgaria would soon follow.[67]

If the future of Poland was, for Stalin, an issue of national security, for Churchill, along with much of public and political opinion in the UK, it was a question of national honour. This was the country whose freedom Britain had gone to war in 1939 to preserve. London was also home to the Polish government-in-exile (a bitterly anti-Soviet coalition) while large numbers of Polish airmen and soldiers went on to fight courageously alongside British and Commonwealth forces. But none of this mattered to Stalin. Opinion in Britain had been shocked by the Soviet Union's refusal to come to the aid of the people of Warsaw at the time of their rising against German control in August 1944 even though the Red Army was massed just beyond the city limits. The rebellion was cruelly suppressed and tens of thousands of Poles deported to a grim fate in Nazi concentration camps. Stalin insisted that the 'Warsaw adventure' was the work of 'criminals': what he meant was that the rising was not just against the Nazis but in support of the British-backed Polish government-in-exile and therefore, by extension, against the Lublin committee.[68] In the end, as the recent research demonstrates, the oft-levelled charge that the Soviet dictator allowed the Germans to do his work for him by liquidating a significant proportion of likely postwar opposition to his creatures is largely justified.[69]

Churchill had been 'painfully affected' by events in Warsaw but he did not make them the occasion for a break with the Soviet Union. As had been the case in April 1943 at the time of the discovery of the Katyn massacre, when Churchill strongly suspected that Stalin had the blood of 20,000 Polish officers on his hands, *realpolitik,* that most insensate of guides, counselled against falling out with a big ally for the sake of a small one.[70] At Tolstoy, Churchill reaped his reward insofar as his rapport with Stalin, unbroken despite Warsaw and Katyn, made possible an understanding on Poland which, in the Prime Minister's view, was the best that could be obtained given the Red Army's overwhelming presence in the country. Pending US sanction, the USSR would have the territory it coveted in the east, that portion of Poland accruing to it from the Nazi–Soviet pact but lost in 1941 at the time of Barbarossa, while Poland would be compensated with a comparable portion of territory hewn from Germany's eastern *länder.* As to the political complexion of the Polish government, Stalin agreed that a coalition should be formed from, *inter alia,* representatives of the London and Lublin administrations. Churchill knew that the London Poles, 'a decent but feeble lot of fools', would protest that their freedom was compromised by so forced a merger, but they too would have to learn some geo-political realism. As for the Lublin Poles, they were 'the greatest villains imaginable' but it was only by working with them that the London Poles could have any say in shaping their country's future.[71] 'The affairs go well', Churchill wrote to Clementine. 'We have settled a lot of things about the Balkans & prevented hosts of squabbles that were maturing . . . I have had v[er]y nice talks with the Old Bear . . . I like him the more I see him. Now they respect us here & I am sure they wish to w[ork] with us – I have to keep the President in constant touch & this is the delicate side.'[72]

As Churchill knew, Roosevelt felt strongly that all major decisions relating to the future territorial and political shape of Europe should be left to a grand peace conference at the end of the war. FDR was worried that revelations of unseemly secret compacts, territorial carve-ups or other evidences of old-fashioned power-politics would strengthen isolationist opposition to his internationalist agenda.[73] In reporting to the President (and to his own War Cabinet), therefore, Churchill downplayed the significance to be attached to the Balkan agreement. The percentages were no more than 'a guide', he contended.[74] In truth, as we will see, he took them very seriously. For the moment, Churchill was optimistic about the future. Anglo-American relations were in solid shape thanks to Octagon and Hyde Park. And so, thanks to Tolstoy, were Anglo-Soviet relations. More than this, he was sure that his personal relationship with Stalin had been strengthened. The Soviet leader, he began to believe, was a political moderate, maybe not even a true communist, more a benign and beneficent Bolshevik holding the line against shadowy extremists in Moscow.[75] It was a fond and foolish delusion. For one who believed so ardently in personal diplomacy, Churchill was not always very good at it.

What role, if any, did the nascence of the Bomb play in Churchill's approach to the USSR at this time? Nothing overt, it would seem, either before or during Tolstoy. But how, for instance, should we interpret his adamantine opposition throughout the war to sharing even the fact of the Manhattan Project's existence with Stalin? Roosevelt, too, held back: eager for postwar cooperation with the USSR but troubled by Soviet peremptoriness in Poland, FDR, historians have argued, saw the Bomb variously as a bargaining lever, a quid pro quo or a military counterweight should negotiations with Stalin on the European settlement, or the future of the United Nations, run into difficulty.[76] But what of Churchill? His impressive anti-communist track-record has led some scholars to infer that he was likewise minded to hold the Bomb in reserve as a means of checking Soviet ambitions. Barton Bernstein, for example, maintains that Churchill was alive from as early as 1942 to the 'likely importance' of the Bomb in the post-war world 'as a deterrent and possibly as a threat, primarily against the Soviet Union', while Martin Sherwin has written of Churchill's obsession with preserving a US–UK monopoly in terms of his search for 'a diplomatic counter against the postwar ambitions of other nations – particularly those of the Soviet Union'. Robert Dallek, Warren Kimball and Graham Farmelo had made similar claims.[77]

Was this really the case, though? After the war, Churchill would become without question an atomic diplomatist, but was he thinking in these terms during the war? He was undoubtedly a dedicated atomic monopolist. But beyond this certainty there is surprisingly little in the documentary record to prove that he gave any serious thought to how the weapon might operate as an adjunct of diplomacy – until, that is, the last Big Three conference of the war at Potsdam. There, in July 1945, privy to detailed reports of the stunningly successful first atomic test in New Mexico, he would be converted, immediately and profoundly, into an atomic diplomatist. Before then, while he appreciated that an atomic bomb would be something out of the ordinary, he may not have fully comprehended the revolutionary nature of the power that science was poised to deliver. Few, beyond Bohr and his fellow nuclear scientists, did. We also need to be careful to avoid interpreting Churchill's wartime attitude in light of his later career as a Cold Warrior and thus conclude that his extreme atomic covetousness was a conscious insurance policy, a form of containment aforethought. The danger that the Soviet Union would develop into 'a new Nazi Germany ideologically inverted' was much in his mind between 1944 and 1945.[78] But until Potsdam he does not seem to have regarded the Bomb as so staggeringly powerful as to be of decisive diplomatic benefit in helping ensure that the political future of the Balkans and Eastern Europe was settled along something approximating democratic lines. On the contrary, as Tolstoy shows, it was personal diplomacy, not atomic diplomacy, that was his preferred approach.

There is an alternative explanation for Churchill's monopolistic mania which is rarely considered: his dream of Anglo-America. As we know, Churchill invested his two principal atomic agreements with Roosevelt – Quebec and Hyde Park – with binding properties. Lindemann similarly acknowledged that these agreements could only be carried over into peacetime if US and UK defence policy was fused in a fully-fledged military alliance.[79] Even General Groves, no natural-born Anglophile, conceded that Britain and America were 'so tied up in defence matters', atomic and otherwise, 'that we should continue to act together after the war'.[80] Therefore, if atomic cooperation made possible a military alliance, this would bring nearer the realisation of the all-encompassing fraternal relationship that Churchill sought. Viewed in these terms, and notwithstanding his undeniable anti-communism, it is hardly surprising that the Prime Minister objected so strongly to opening membership of the exclusive TA-1/S-1 club to the Soviets.

Unfortunately for the Prime Minister and his hopes, the barometer reading for the Anglo-American atomic partnership at the end of 1944 pointed more towards unsettled than fair. The reason was the increasing disconnect between what Churchill and Roosevelt had agreed at the highest level and the day-to-day lower-level functioning of relations. Anderson valued the insight into Presidential thinking which Churchill's intimacy with Roosevelt afforded, but he and his TA colleagues conducted their business with the likes of Bush and Conant and here interaction was bedevilled by FDR's failure to provide his atomic lieutenants with any real policy guidance. Bush could only guess what FDR had cooked-up with Churchill – he suspected, rightly, that the President was sold on a US–UK monopoly – whereas Anderson, knowing what had transpired, was prevented from revealing his knowledge due to the secrecy which Roosevelt insisted on attaching to the agreement.[81] This situation was clearly unsatisfactory, the more so as Bush and Conant remained ill-disposed to overly-close US–UK atomic ties, a point Anderson made in a letter to Churchill at the start of 1945. With the war in Europe approaching its climax, the Chancellor supposed that American officials were more than ever chary about imparting information to Britain given that Hitler's downfall would bring nearer the worrisome Congressional inquisition.[82]

Anderson was right: Bush and Conant *were* conscious of the Senate spotlight. But they were also by now convinced that some form of international control was essential and, in this connection, that intimate American association with Britain, especially given Churchill's unyieldingly monopolistic outlook, would militate against their preferred course and even spur the Soviets into extreme efforts to obtain a bomb of their own. Ironically, the two scientist-administrators had gone from opposing an Anglo-American atomic alliance in 1942–1943 on nationalistic grounds to opposing it in 1944–1945 for internationalist reasons.[83] Lindemann was as troubled as Anderson by the Washington indicators. As long as the President and his atomic advisors ran on different rails there was a risk that Roosevelt might suddenly shift the points, veering away from atomic cooperation and towards the Bush-Conant position. With FDR, it was never wise to bank on constancy.

With these thoughts in mind, the Prof wrote to Churchill towards the end of January 1945 reminding him that with the war in Europe entering its final phase, and with recent intelligence findings all but confirming that the Nazi project had not got beyond basic research, the Bomb's future, not its potential in the military present, needed serious attention. From a national standpoint, Britain would soon be looking to resume independent research and development. The form and timing of the relaunch – the recall, for instance, of those members of the UK mission whose work was no longer contributing to the immediate job of weapons-production – needed careful handling. Opponents of a US–UK atomic alliance in Washington might argue that with Britain's principal enemy, Nazi Germany, on the verge of defeat, the London government was putting self-interest ahead of backing for America in the still intense war against Japan. If the US Congress and public should derive a similar impression, it could be very damaging for Anglo-American relations. The United States might even seek to prevent the development of atomic energy in Britain in any form. As a minimum first move, therefore, Roosevelt needed to be alerted to UK intentions. 'I think the best way of putting it would be to say that, after the war, we shall want to do work here on a scale commensurate with our resources', Lindemann advised. At Hyde Park, the President had committed himself to Anglo-American cooperation beyond the defeat of Germany and Japan. The Prof was 'pleased about this, for it seems to presuppose what must be, in effect, a military alliance'. If formalised, this alliance might see Britain host an arsenal of American-made A-bombs in the future as an accretion of strength to its security. But it would be 'dangerous', he averred, to make any proposal of this kind at the present time 'as we might be accused of shirking the effort of manufacture'.[84]

Although Churchill took note and agreed to raise the matter with Roosevelt, he may not have been unduly concerned. After all, he had the Quebec agreement, he had the Hyde Park agreement, and above all he had FDR, re-elected on 7 November 1944 for a fourth term. 'It is an indescribable relief to me that our comradeship will continue and will help to bring the world out of misery', he cabled the President on the morrow of his victory.[85] In actual fact the comradeship – and the atomic relationship that Churchill and Roosevelt personified – had precisely 155 days left to run.

CHAPTER 6
BOLSHEVIKS, BOMBS AND BAD OMENS

As 1945 opened, Churchill was in high spirits. After much chopping and changing, plans had been finalized for a second Big Three meeting, to be held at Yalta, and for pre-conference Anglo-American talks at Malta. 'No more let us falter!', he gleefully cabled FDR on New Year's Day. 'From Malta to Yalta! Let nobody alter!'[1] He was much more melancholy the following week. In the three months since Tolstoy, his confidence in Stalin's commitment to their understanding on Poland had begun to ebb and he warned Roosevelt that Yalta might be 'a fateful conference, coming at a moment when the Great Allies are so divided...I think the end of this war may well prove to be more disappointing than the last'.[2]

On 29 January, the Prime Minister and a large retinue left England on the first stage of their journey to the Crimea, the flight to Malta. When, soon after, the President arrived in Valetta harbour aboard the USS *Quincy*, many on the British side were shocked by his haggard appearance: FDR, we now know, was a dying man, and General Ismay's prediction that he 'might not last many months' was prescient.[3] After completing their pre-conference discussions, on 3 February the British and Americans flew 1,400 miles east to Saki on the Crimean peninsula. There they transferred to a convoy of motor vehicles for a five-hour road trip through a blasted landscape 'as bleak as the soul in despair' before arriving at the Black Sea resort of Yalta.[4] Stalin turned up the following day and the conference, codenamed Argonaut, got down to business in the Grand Ballroom of the Livadiya Palace, the summer retreat of the last Tsar of Russia.

For the next week, the three leaders and their advisors sought to coordinate strategy for the final assault on Germany, confirm the structures of the new world organization, and map out the geo-political contours of postwar Europe. Discussion of these issues – and others besides – took place against a military background which encouraged the belief that victory over Germany might not be long in coming. During January, the Red Army had made spectacular progress along the Vistula and into East Prussia and by the time of Argonaut, Marshal Georgi Zhukov's forces, having advanced 250 miles in three weeks, sat on the banks of the Oder river just fifty miles from Berlin. In the west, the massive German offensive in the Ardennes in December 1944 dented the prospect of an early crossing of the Rhine *en masse* – in the end the main thrust would begin towards the end of March – but US General George S. Patton's Third Army had already smashed into Germany at several points along the Belgium and Luxembourg borders.[5]

Despite the Prof's hopes, the atomic bomb did not feature in Churchill's meetings with the President. Alive to the high level of Soviet surveillance (according to one study, Roosevelt 'was bugged like no other American president in history'), the two Western leaders may have been more reluctant to talk openly about Tube Alloys than most subjects.[6] A few weeks earlier, Groves and Stimson had confirmed to Roosevelt that an A-bomb was still on course for delivery by the summer and thus likely to play a part in the war against Japan.[7] This was encouraging news from FDR's standpoint but there is no evidence that he allowed this prospect to affect his approach to the work of the conference. The same went for Churchill who was active at Yalta in promoting two decidedly non-atomic ways of bringing the war with Japan to a swift conclusion. Both would go on to feature in the US-dominated decision-making process which culminated in the bombing of Hiroshima and Nagasaki six months later and for this reason they are worthy of consideration. First, though, we need to establish the broad outline of Churchill's thinking on the war in Asia and the Pacific. Indeed such an outline is doubly necessary in view of the centrality of Japan in the final chapter of the wartime story of the Bomb.

At Casablanca in January 1943, Churchill promised Roosevelt that 'if and when Hitler breaks down, all of the British resources and effort will be turned towards the defeat of Japan.'[8] At one level, Churchill's pledge reflected a desire to avenge the humiliations the Japanese had meted out to Britain in 1941 and 1942, but at a deeper psychological level he may have been looking to exorcise some personal guilt. A few weeks before Pearl Harbor, Churchill, against the advice of Admiral of the Fleet Sir Dudley Pound, had been instrumental in dispatching the newly-built battleship HMS *Prince of Wales* and the battlecruiser HMS *Repulse* to the South China Sea in the dual belief that a show of strength by the Royal Navy would deter the Japanese from threatening British imperial interests in South-East Asia and that Japanese air-power did not pose a serious danger to capital ships. On 10 December 1941, Japanese land-based aircraft operating from Indo-China sank both ships with the loss of more than 800 lives.[9] 'In all the war I never received a more direct shock', Churchill later wrote, but the sinkings proved to be but the prelude to what Ismay called a 'cataract of disaster'.[10] On Christmas Day came news that Hong Kong had fallen; a month later Malaya had been largely over-run and Burma invaded; and then, on 15 February 1942, came what Churchill described as the 'largest capitulation in British history' when Singapore, along with 130,000 British and Commonwealth troops, surrendered.[11]

The unhappy fact of the matter is that Churchill had been consistently wrong over many years in his assessment of Japanese intentions and capabilities.[12] In the 1920s he poured scorn on strategists who warned of possible war with Japan (not 'the slightest chance of it in our lifetime'), and in the 1930s he refused to accept that the security of British interests in South-East Asia merited reinforcement at the expense of defence in Europe.[13] Right up until Pearl Harbor itself he continued to regard a Japanese-initiated conflict as a 'remote contingency' and even after this prediction was turned on its head, Christopher Thorne has shown that the Victorian imperialist in him maintained 'that such a lesser breed' as the Japanese 'could be suitably deterred by the presence in the South-western Pacific area of the *Prince of Wales* and the *Repulse*'. In quick time both vessels and their crews paid the price for disastrous civilian and strategic misjudgement, and Churchill, though by no means alone in exaggerating the deterrent power of capital ships, felt keenly the subsequent pain and humiliation.[14]

When Singapore fell, the German propaganda machine crowed that Churchill had become 'the undertaker of the British Empire'.[15] Over the next three years, though the war in the Far East never engaged his attention to the same extent as the peril closer to home in Europe ('the storm centre ... the place where the weather came from'), he determined to disprove the Nazi claim by restoring Britain's imperial position in general and by recovering Singapore, 'the supreme British objective', in particular.[16] He was also conscious of the need to support, if only rhetorically, the Americans in their campaign against Japan in the distant reaches of the Pacific. In April 1943, he told "Hap" Arnold, Commanding General of the US Army Air Forces, how the RAF 'earnestly look forward to the day when they will be able to fly side by side with their American comrades to attack Tokio [sic] and other cities of Japan'.[17] Churchill said the same thing publicly a little later in an address to a joint session of the US Congress. The day was not far off, he hoped, when British and American bombers would combine to leave 'the cities and other military centres of Japan in ashes', a statement greeted with noisy approbation from his audience. There was a deal of playing to the gallery – successfully so – in this speech: in return for US help in defeating Germany, the least he could do was show solidarity with the Americans in their desire to exact vengeance for Pearl Harbor. For the most part, however, his real interest remained South-East Asia, not the Pacific, and it would be another year before he became reconciled to the need for a British role in the final assault on Japan itself.[18]

The change in Churchill's outlook can be pinpointed to the second Quebec conference in September 1944 when he was finally won round – or worn down – by the Foreign Office-COS argument that if Britain was ever to restore its tattered prestige in the Far East, it must play a visible part in the destruction of Japanese militarism at source. This, according to Eden, was both an imperial imperative (to reassert primacy in the eyes of the peoples of Burma, Malaya, Singapore and Hong Kong) and a Commonwealth imperative (to negate the impression in Australia and New Zealand that their security was of small concern to London).[19] At Octagon, Churchill was at his most optimistic about the future of the "special relationship", but he was also correspondingly concerned to avoid any harm to its prospects. In particular, he was troubled by the potential negative impact on US opinion 'if it could be said that America had made a great contribution to the defeat of Germany, whereas the British effort against Japan had been limited to the pursuit of her own selfish interests in Burma, Malaya and Hong Kong'.[20] Consequently, Churchill abandoned thoughts of an exclusively South-East Asian focus and 'expressed strongly' to Roosevelt his desire that with the German navy no longer a threat, a well-balanced British fleet should be sent to the Pacific to join with the US navy in operations against Japan. He further hoped that when the war in Europe ended, British and Commonwealth air forces would be able to play their part in the 'severe, intense, prolonged and ever-increasing air bombardment' of Japan's cities.[21]

At this point in the war the United States hardly needed British help to defeat Japan, but a UK role in the Pacific had become, for Roosevelt, a political as much as a military issue, and for reasons not dissimilar to those exercising Churchill. 'If we allow the British to limit their active participation to recapture areas that are to their selfish interests alone and not participate in smashing the war machine of Japan', the US ambassador in London, Gil Winant, cautioned Hopkins, 'we will create in the United States a hatred for Great Britain that will make for schisms in the postwar years that will defeat everything that men have died for in this war'.[22] Hopkins took the point. So did FDR. In another signal of the importance he attached to intimate relations with Britain going into the postwar era, the President accepted the Prime Minister's offer of naval help and, by so doing, sent Admiral Ernest King, the Anglophobe US Chief of Naval Operations, 'into a swoon' at the thought of the United Kingdom intruding into 'his own pet war'.[23]

By the time he arrived at Yalta, Churchill was well aware that the end of the war in Europe would bring nearer the invasion of Japan and, with it, very great loss of life on the Allied side. For this reason, both of his war-terminating initiatives spoke to his light-casualty outlook. The atomic bomb, we should note, played no part in his calculations. Churchill's first proposal aimed, through dextrous diplomacy, to exploit Tokyo's increasingly bleak prospects. By early 1945, Japan's forces in Manchuria, South-East Asia and across the Pacific were either on the defensive or in retreat; its Imperial Navy was no longer a going concern thanks to its defeat at the Battle of Leyte Gulf in October 1944; and its home-islands were subject to a suffocating US naval blockade which made the import of oil, food and other vital supplies almost impossible. Moreover, the recent capture by the Americans of the islands of Saipan, Tinian and Guam had brought Japan's cities within range of the B-29 Superfortress, the most technologically-advanced bomber of the day, and even as the Big Three gathered in the Crimea, the US Army Air Force was commencing an air offensive predicated on fire-bombing the country's predominantly wooden-structured and over-populated cities.[24] In short, Japan was close to defeat but it was not close to surrender, a critical distinction. Final victory required another eighteen months of fighting, and dying, beyond the conclusion of the war in Europe – or so Anglo-American strategists estimated.

Within the British government, a growing body of opinion – and Churchill was of that body – held that a major obstacle to an early cessation of hostilities on terms that gave the Allies all the essentials of victory was the inability of the Japanese government and military establishment to accept the humiliation of *unconditional* surrender. Roosevelt came up with the term during a joint news conference with Churchill at Casablanca. Later he claimed that the words just popped into his head but the Americans and British had in fact been giving surrender strategy consideration for some while. 'The elimination of German, Japanese, and Italian war power means the unconditional surrender by Germany, Italy, and Japan', Roosevelt avowed.[25] At the time, Churchill enthusiastically seconded the President and remained publicly loyal to the policy over the following two years.[26] In private, however, he questioned its rectitude and these doubts accompanied him to the Crimea.[27]

On 9 February, at a meeting at the Livadiya with Roosevelt and the Combined Chiefs of Staff, Churchill proposed that an ultimatum be issued by the UK, USA, China and, if possible, the USSR (which was presently neutral in the Far East), calling on Japan to accept unconditional surrender on pain of being subjected to 'the overwhelming weight of all the forces of the four powers'. Tokyo, he surmised, might respond by seeking clarification of what, beyond the obvious, unconditional surrender meant. It would be for the US government to frame a reply. Naturally, he would follow the President's lead in a theatre where command belonged to the Americans, but 'there was no doubt that some mitigation would be worth while', some assurance to the Japanese that the Allies were not bent on destroying their society, culture and religion, 'if it led to the saving of a year or a year and a half of a war in which so much blood and treasure would be poured out'. Roosevelt did not give a flat 'no' (that was not his style) but observed that the Japanese might look upon any softening of unconditional surrender as a sign of Allied weakness and, far from hastening a capitulation, Churchill's proposal might cause them to fight on in the hope of securing further concessions. FDR also suspected that militarists in Tokyo would never face up to the reality of defeat 'until all of their islands had felt the full weight of air attack'.[28] There the matter rested. It had been a brush-off. Politely done, but still a brush-off. Churchill, though, was not easily deterred and would continue to favour a retreat from absolute unconditional surrender even as an alternative means of effecting an end to the war, the atomic bomb, moved from theory to reality.

Churchill's second Yalta initiative – this one fully endorsed by Roosevelt – was to hold Stalin to a promise he made at Tehran to abandon Soviet neutrality and declare war on Japan within two-to-three months of the end of the fighting in Europe.[29] For Churchill, this was a 'supreme object' in the Far East. 'The opening of a Russian military front against Japan would force them to burn and bleed in a manner which would vastly accelerate their defeat.' Psychologically, the shock of Soviet entry might, on its own, lever the Japanese into surrender, while at the very least, in military terms, the Red Army would help pin down the formidable Kwantung Army in Manchuria, preventing its redeployment for home-islands defence.[30] But Stalin sought, and Roosevelt and Churchill agreed to pay, a price for his help, namely the restoration of the rights and territories lost to Japan as a result of the Russo-Japanese war of 1904–1905 (the southern part of Sakhalin and its adjacent islands, the Port Arthur naval base and the commercial port of Dairen), along with the cession of the Kurile islands, a Soviet share in the running of the Chinese Eastern and South Manchurian railway systems, and acknowledgement of Moscow's pre-eminent political and economic position in Outer Mongolia. In strict secrecy, the American and British leaders accepted that all of these claims should be 'unquestionably satisfied after Japan has been defeated'.[31]

Roosevelt led from the front in propitiating Stalin but Churchill raised no objections and his signature can be found alongside FDR's and Stalin's on the single-sided piece of paper, dated 11 February 1945, confirming the Far Eastern arrangements. But he knew very well how incendiary they were. Unlike Eastern Europe, where the Anglo-Americans found themselves effectively powerless to prevent the Red Army imposing communist control, in East Asia both he and Roosevelt agreed to an extension of Moscow's influence, partly at the expense of China, an ally, without Soviet forces even leaving barracks. No wonder Churchill told Eden – who strenuously objected to bribing Stalin to enter the war when self-interest would have brought him in anyway – to keep the offending document 'in a locked box' (and not just to preserve the secret of the Kremlin's pending perfidy vis-à-vis Tokyo).[32] Then again, coming as it did on the last day of the conference, Churchill's readiness to countenance some appeasement of the USSR at the expense of China was perhaps a token of appreciation for the way that Stalin had earlier accepted that the European settlement, including Poland, would conform in broad terms to Western democratic standards. For Churchill, this was something worth paying for.

'Make no mistake', Churchill told Colville a fortnight before Yalta, 'all the Balkans, except Greece, are going to be Bolshevised; and there is nothing I can do to prevent it. There is nothing I can do for poor Poland either.'[33] And yet, when Argonaut arrived, there was Stalin, compromising. Or seeming to. On Poland, he agreed to free elections as soon as practicable. More immediately, and in keeping with what had been discussed at Tolstoy, he undertook to reconstruct the Lublin committee – despite having only just formally recognized it as the government of all of Poland – along more democratic lines by bringing in non-communists from within Poland and from London. In return, Churchill and Roosevelt agreed that the USSR should shift its borders westwards to cohere to the Curzon line, a proposed demarcation dating from 1919, and incorporate eastern Poland. They further accepted, in principle, that Poland would be accorded a comparable portion of Germany's eastern territories. Going into Argonaut, the best that Churchill and Roosevelt can have hoped for was an amelioration of Soviet control in Poland. This they seemed to have secured.[34] As a bonus, Stalin joined with his Western allies in the issuance of a Declaration on Liberated Europe in which the principles of the Atlantic Charter, including the right of national self-determination, were reaffirmed. Why would Stalin go to such lengths to accommodate the Anglo-Americans, Churchill pondered afterwards, if he were not 'anxious to work with the two English speaking democracies' in peace as well as war?[35]

Later, of course, Yalta became for many people, especially in the United States, a synonym for betrayal. Roosevelt, more so than Churchill, was castigated not only for selling out to Stalin in Asia but for failing to challenge the Soviet dictator over his totalitarian intentions in the Balkans and Eastern Europe and thus for sentencing hundreds of millions of people to a life under brutally repressive communist rule.[36] The flaw in this argument is that the Yalta agreements on Europe were not appeasement-pocked compacts. They were certainly imprecise: in order to broaden the democratic base of the Lublin committee, all Stalin had to do, technically, was add just one or two non-communists (for 'decorative purposes', as he knowingly put it to his secret police chief Lavrenti Beria). But imprecision aside, by what the President adjudged 'the right interpretation of the Crimean decision', the Soviets failed to honour their side of the bargain.[37]

A large part of the subsequent controversy surrounding Yalta was due to the way in which Roosevelt and Churchill publicly over-sold the agreements. 'I didn't say the result was good', FDR confided to Adolf Berle when he got back to Washington. 'I said it was the best I could do.'[38] That seems about right. Yet on 1 March, the President reported to

Congress on 'a successful effort by the three leading Nations to find a common ground for peace' which 'ought to spell the end of the system of unilateral action, the exclusive alliances, the spheres of influence, the balances of power, and all the other expedients that have been tried for centuries – and have always failed'.[39] *Ought*, not *will* spell. Here at least was a qualification. In contrast, Churchill's private and publicly expressed optimism was near total. On his return to London he told the War Cabinet that he was 'quite sure' that Stalin 'meant well to the world and to Poland', that the promised elections there would be 'free and fair', and that 'much rested on Premier Stalin's life'. Neville Chamberlain 'believed he could trust Hitler. He was wrong. But I don't think I'm wrong about Stalin'.[40] In the two-day Yalta debate in the Commons at the end of February, faced with a rebellion by twenty-five Conservative MPs who condemned the Polish settlement as a sham, Churchill – almost aping Chamberlain post-Munich – offered multiple hostages to fortune.

> The impression I brought back from the Crimea . . . is that Marshal Stalin and the Soviet leaders wish to live in honourable friendship and equality with the Western democracies. I feel also that their word is their bond. I know of no Government which stands to its obligations, even in its own despite, more solidly than the Russian Soviet Government.[41]

Why did Churchill commit himself in this way? The answer seems to reside in his inability, or refusal, to see Stalin for the tyrant he was. It was as if he separated the man from the totalitarian ideology he espoused, a case of loving the sinner while abhorring the sin. He was not alone in doing this – FDR, too, drew a similar distinction – but Churchill took the delineation to an extreme. 'If only I could dine with Stalin once a week, there would be no trouble at all', he remarked after Tolstoy. 'We get on like a house on fire.'[42] If Stalin was truculent or intransigent or rude, that was due, Churchill maintained, to the baleful influence of other 'Soviet leaders, whoever they may be'. Stalin himself was 'the most human of them all'.[43] He even ventilated the view that the USSR, as a result of the ordeal of total war and the experience of working alongside the Western democracies, might be in process of purging itself of its revolutionary outlook and that these 'deep-seated changes . . . in the character of the Russian State and Government', when added to 'the new confidence which has grown in our heart toward Stalin', gave grounds for believing that the Soviet Union would settle down and become a peace-loving member of the international community.[44]

Churchill's faith in Stalin was all the greater as a result of the Soviet leader's scrupulousness in abiding by the percentages agreement as it applied to Greece.[45] Doubts occasionally intruded (at the time of the Yalta debate Colville thought that 'in his heart' Churchill 'worried about Poland') but in public he held his line and refused to admit that the results of the conference could in any way be deemed appeasement.[46] With the war in Europe moving towards its conclusion, the break-up of the coalition National Government and a general election might not be far off. Ever the politician, Churchill knew that securing an honourable settlement for Poland would do himself and his party no harm electorally. Yet such domestic political pragmatism still fails to explain fully his over-selling of the Yalta agreements and the fulsomeness of his protestations of trust in Stalin. Did he not see the danger? That the smallest measure of Soviet non-compliance, never mind large-scale infractions, was bound to leave him exposed politically? Why, to repeat, did such a seasoned parliamentarian go out on so extreme a limb? And for a communist despot?

The answer, it would seem, is that he truly believed what he said about Stalin and Soviet reliability. Churchill imbued Stalin with the traits of a traditional Russian ruler, a Tsar, albeit a red one, but fatally underestimated the reach of his ambition. 'Stalin acted on a larger scale than any czar had', Vladislav Zubok and Constantine Pleshakov have shown. The Russian imperial tradition, reinforced by Marxist globalism, 'predestined Soviet expansionism'. Stalin further prioritised 'security, not cohabitation' with the West, a goal that required 'ultimate and undiluted control over territories and, ipso facto, control over the population, their households and their minds'.[47] Roosevelt was out on the same limb as Churchill, though not quite so far. But when Stalin let them both down, fate decreed that Churchill, not FDR, would be left to deal with the consequences, both geo-political and domestic-political. 'What a pity', Churchill later remarked of Stalin, 'that he turned out to be such a swine'.[48]

Figure 6.1 Churchill, Roosevelt and Stalin in the grounds of the Livadiya Palace, Yalta, during the Three Power Conference. Keystone/Getty Images.

As previously noted, Churchill and Roosevelt did not discuss Tube Alloys during their week together at Yalta – or if they did, their conversation went unrecorded except perhaps by Soviet eavesdroppers. However, the subject did crop up a few days after the conference when they were reunited in Alexandria having taken separate departure routes from the 'Riviera of Hades', as the Prime Minister dubbed Yalta.[49] At a meeting aboard the *Quincy* on 15 February, Churchill read aloud to the President the letter Lindemann sent him before he left England, the one reiterating the UK's intention of resuming its own atomic project after the war. To this, Churchill recorded, FDR 'made no objection' but merely observed that the prospects for commercial applications of atomic energy had 'receded' and that the 'first important trials' remained on schedule.[50] This was satisfactory from Churchill's standpoint. Much less so was the President's evident interest in telling Stalin about the Manhattan Project.

At Hyde Park five months earlier, FDR had been at one with Churchill in wishing to maintain Anglo-American exclusivity. Now he appeared to be wavering for reasons which, in the absence of explicatory documentary evidence, may only be guessed at. Did he perhaps feel that continuing to keep Stalin in the dark risked a serious rift when the Bomb eventually became public knowledge? That ongoing secrecy threatened his wider objective of Big Three cooperation in general and US–Soviet cooperation in particular? Against this, were he to confide in Stalin, telling him about the Bomb even in vague terms (Bohr's line), this might go some way towards buttressing mutual trust and ensure that the USSR worked with rather than against the United States after the war in devising a system of international control. Alternatively, he could attach riders, adopt a quid pro quo approach in which atomic knowledge was traded for a satisfactory resolution in Poland and elsewhere. In the end, the most obvious reason to tell Stalin – with or without strings – was that the secret was hardly a secret any more. Stimson was certain that the Soviets 'were spying on our work', although 'they had not yet gotten any real knowledge of it'; Moscow diplomats were reported to be asking loaded questions about American weapons research; and Bohr had already warned the White House (via Frankfurter) that Kapitza and other Russian scientists were assuredly engaged in atomic research. In view of all this, Roosevelt can be forgiven for feeling that secrecy had run its course.[51] However, when he attempted to broach disclosure with the Prime Minister he received a resounding knock-back: Churchill was 'shocked' by FDR's laxity and refused to give him the slightest encouragement. The President did not press the matter.[52]

According to Martin Sherwin, 'Roosevelt's ready acceptance of Churchill's view ended any possibility that the question of postwar control of atomic energy might be raised with the Russians *during* the war'.[53] From Churchill's perspective, international control, insofar as it undermined the Anglo-American monopoly, was anathema. There is, however, some evidence that FDR, troubled by the incompatibility of withholding all knowledge from the Soviets while hinging so many of his hopes for the future on US–Soviet cooperation, kept the option in play. A month after Yalta, Canadian premier William Mackenzie King visited the White House. Argonaut had gone well, Roosevelt told him, and 'he did not think there was anything to fear particularly from Stalin in the future'. As to atomic matters, the President 'thought the Russians had been experimenting and knew something about what was being done'. If this was so, continued secrecy could harm US–Soviet relations. '[T]he time had come to tell them how far the developments had gone', but Churchill 'was opposed to doing this'. Roosevelt gave no reason for the Prime Minister's obstructionism other than to suggest that he was 'considering the possible commercial use later'.[54]

In fact commercial advantage was irrelevant to Churchill. FDR also seemed to forget that the Quebec agreement prevented Britain from exploiting atomic energy for industrial purposes without his – Roosevelt's – express agreement. Beyond this, Churchill has left us with no explicit rationale for his opposition to bringing Stalin into the picture. Was his outlook connected to an appreciation of the Bomb's potential for keeping the Soviet Union in check in the future? Or was his main concern to play the monopoly in ways which might help cement a full-blown US–UK alliance in the postwar period? Did he endow the Bomb with a dual utility as the key both to containing the USSR and to ensuring long-term cooperation with the USA? As the war entered its final months – in Asia as well as Europe – the answer to these questions would become somewhat clearer.

In the month following Yalta, the Soviet Union moved with crude efficiency to strengthen its control in the Balkans. Romania was the first target, the nominally plural government set up in Bucharest the previous year succumbing to a communist coup d'état on 5 March; the Soviets, Churchill wrote to Roosevelt three days later, had succeeded in establishing 'the rule of a Communist minority by force and misrepresentation'.[55] Disturbing as Soviet behaviour was, when it came to admonishing Stalin, Churchill knew that he was badly compromised by the percentages agreement in which he had bartered virtually uncontested Soviet influence in Romania for similarly untrammelled British influence in Greece. But "influence" is the operative word. He had not sanctioned communist domination such as appeared now to be Moscow's goal. And where might it end? Was total control of the eastern half of Europe the limit of Soviet ambition? After watching film of the destruction visited on Dresden by the RAF and the US Army Air Forces in February, Churchill seemed to sense the danger of trying to defeat Germany too fully. 'What', he wondered, 'will lie between the white snows of Russia and the white cliffs of Dover?'[56]

Oppressed by such worries, Churchill moved to limit the damage – and not just in the Balkans but at Westminster where his declarations of confidence in Stalin threatened to redound against him. The day after the Bucharest coup, he warned the War Cabinet that if the Soviets continued to play false with the Yalta agreements 'it would be necessary to give the full story to Parliament'. But could Anglo-Soviet relations withstand so public a shaming of Moscow without incurring real damage and additionally jeopardizing the Big Three unity which both Churchill and Roosevelt regarded as vital to postwar peace? Could Churchill himself escape personal and political ridicule for his previous lauding of Stalin? Probably not. Better, then, from every point of view, to try quiet but firm private diplomacy. Here, however, Roosevelt's support was vital. Aside from the greater moral throw-weight of joint condemnation of Soviet actions, the Prime Minister remained wary of taking the lead himself lest Stalin accuse him of reneging on their Tolstoy pact and the Greek communists suddenly acquire a powerful benefactor.[57]

Poland had not featured in the percentages agreement and Churchill felt on firmer ground in challenging the Soviets over their failure to abide by their Yalta undertakings with regard to that country.[58] On 8 March, he wrote to Roosevelt avowing that Poland was a 'test case between us and the Russians in the meaning which is to be attached to such terms as democracy, sovereignty, independence, representative government and free and unfettered elections'. To acquiesce in what was happening – no reconfiguration of the Lublin committee, no elections, the imprisonment or deportation of anti-communist elements – would convey the impression to the world 'that you and I by putting our signatures to the Crimea settlement have under-written a fraudulent prospectus'.[59] Churchill wanted FDR to join with him in a strong protest to Stalin but to his dismay the President held back: 'I cannot agree that we are confronted with a breakdown of the Yalta agreement on Poland', Roosevelt cabled on 15 March in terms which implied that the Prime Minister had lost his sense of proportion.[60] FDR made the same point more explicitly the next day when he told his cabinet (albeit in 'a semi-jocular manner of speaking') that Churchill seemed 'perfectly willing for the United States to have a war with Russia at any time and that, in his opinion, to follow the British program would be to proceed to that end'.[61]

Roosevelt knew as well as Stalin did that a Poland at liberty to choose its political destiny would opt for a government largely hostile to the USSR. Conversely, if the Soviet Union obtained the security it craved in the form of a friendly government in Warsaw, it could only be at the expense of genuine Polish democracy. A Poland that was independent and sovereign and yet friendly to the USSR – Churchill's publicly-declared objective – was to Roosevelt (and Stalin) a geo-political oxymoron.[62] For FDR, a master of *realpolitik*, there was little value in breaking with Stalin over Poland, or Eastern Europe and the Balkans generally, when the Western allies were powerless to shape political conditions on the ground and when the mere attempt to dictate to Moscow could imperil the wider Big Three cooperation that lasting peace required. Already, in response to Anglo-American discontent over Poland, Soviet Foreign Minister Vyacheslav Molotov had announced his intention of staying away from the founding conference of the United Nations (which was due to open in San Francisco on 25 April) and to hand leadership of the Soviet delegation to his deputy. Clearly it would not take much to trigger a full-scale Soviet boycott which, in turn, might render the world organization still-born. If that happened, FDR's hopes for the USA's internationalist future could fall victim to an isolationist under-tow.[63]

No novice himself when it came to *realpolitik*, the British Prime Minister recognized the importance of holding the Big Three together in peacetime ('I see no other salvation for mankind'), but where Roosevelt seemed to feel that this end justified the means – US–UK acquiescence in the *de facto* Soviet annexation of Poland and the Balkans – Churchill had in mind a stop-line, a limit to how far the Western powers could or should go in mollifying the USSR.[64] Hence, while prepared to concede the Soviets their influence, he would not condone dominion. 'I don't mind kissing Stalin's bum', he later quipped, 'but I'm damned if I'll lick his arse'.[65] In contrast, Roosevelt at times seemed quite ready to countenance the surrender of all of Eastern Europe.[66] Stalin sensed this. 'I think Roosevelt will not break the Yalta agreements', he told Zhukov in a remark which indicated confidence that the President would be satisfied with a little democratic window-dressing in Poland, 'but Churchill, that one might do anything'.[67]

In the end, after nearly a month of prodding and pleading, Churchill managed to extract FDR's consent to a protest to Stalin – but in the form of parallel missives not a combined message.[68] Perhaps a now sick and ailing Roosevelt worried that in a co-authored cable, Churchill would lure him into using tougher language than he wanted. As it was, the President's message, sent on 1 April, was firm in places but punch-pulling in others.[69] Eden, who saw both, thought Churchill's 'a good deal rougher in tone', and so it was.[70] Stalin needed to 'come to a good understanding about Poland', the Prime Minister wrote. He should observe 'the principle of reciprocity'. And he should not 'smite down the hands of comradeship in the future guidance of the world which we now extend'.[71] But neither Roosevelt's bewilderment nor Churchill's sternness made any difference. The Soviet dictator parried both and insisted that, by his lights, he had not broken the Yalta agreement.[72]

These European tensions did nothing to lessen Churchill's opposition to sharing the secret of Tube Alloys with Moscow. Then again, as Anderson discovered at the start of 1945, the Prime Minister was against extending knowledge to *any* country. After several months weighing the matter, Anderson concluded that General de Gaulle's post-liberation provisional French government had a strong case for admittance to the Tube Alloys project, albeit as a junior partner, in view of the great contribution made by Halban, Kowarski and other French scientists to TA-2.[73] Nor was this the only reason for bringing in the French. According to Professor Frédéric Joliot – mentor to Halban and many of his colleagues, a fellow-traveller if not a communist, and presently Director of Scientific Research in the provisional government – the French had already probed the Soviet authorities about the possibility of bilateral atomic collaboration. Committed to a full-scale programme of research and development in France after the war, Joliot told Anderson that if the USA and UK were unwilling to help in this regard, his government 'would have to turn to Russia'.[74] This, for the Chancellor, was the clincher. To meet a debt of honour and simultaneously thwart Franco-Soviet atomic proliferation, the French should be invited to associate themselves formally with Tube Alloys.[75] The challenge was to secure Churchill's agreement. Scarred by previous atomic jousts with the Prime Minister, Anderson looked for an ally of kindred outlook with direct access to Number 10. Lindemann, fast acquiring a reputation as 'the most rabidly anti-French influence in London', was not the man for this particular job.[76] Eventually, the Chancellor found what he sought in the person of Anthony Eden, a Francophile by nature, who was quickly persuaded of the need to do right by the French.[77]

On 20 March, the Foreign Secretary wrote to Churchill explaining why the time had come for the authorities in Paris to be apprised of atomic developments. 'We have made use of their men, their knowledge and their material and are surely, therefore, in honour bound to admit them to participation in at any rate that side of TA work which can be represented as a continuation of their earlier endeavours.' Against this, any failure to play fair could have 'very serious' implications for Anglo–French relations. The French – or Joliot at least – were hinting that if the British and Americans shunned them, 'they will have to turn to Russia'. This, Eden observed, could lead to the existence of 'two competitive blocs on TA within the great powers, a very serious matter in itself; and, although the Anglo-American bloc would probably have a substantial lead, a Franco-Russian combination would be well equipped scientifically and industrially'. In view of the clause in the Quebec agreement preventing disclosure of atomic information to third parties without joint US–UK consent, Eden hoped that Churchill would see his way to raising the issue with Roosevelt in the near future.[78]

It was a balanced and reasoned appeal but it got Eden nowhere. In part, his timing was unfortunate as the Prime Minister was in an acutely anti-de Gaulle frame of mind. Indeed the first draft of Churchill's response contains several angry rejoinders which he later deleted. The excisions, however, are instructive and are reproduced below in italics in the body of the message as sent to the Foreign Secretary on 8 April.

I certainly do not agree that this secret should be imparted to the French. My agreement with President Roosevelt in writing forbids either party to reveal to anyone else the secret. I believe you under-rate the lead which has been obtained by the United States, in which we participate, through their vast expenditure of money – I believe above four hundred million pounds.

I was shocked at Yalta too when the President in a casual manner spoke of revealing the secret to Stalin on the grounds that de Gaulle, if he heard of it, would certainly double-cross us with Russia.

In all the circumstances our policy should be to keep the matter, so far as we can control it, in American and British hands and leave the French and Russians to do what they can ... You may be quite sure that any power that gets hold of the secret will try to make the article and that this touches the existence of human society.

I am getting rather tired of all the different kinds of things that we must do or not do lest Anglo-French relations suffer. *One thing I am sure* [of is] *that there is nothing that de Gaulle would like better than to have plenty of TA to punish Britain, and nothing he would like less than to arm Communist Russia with the secret.* This matter is out of all relation to anything else that exists in the whole world, and I could not think of participating in any disclosure to third or fourth parties at the present time ... I shall certainly continue to urge the President not to make or permit the slightest disclosure to France or Russia. *Even six months will make a difference should it come to a show-down with Russia, or indeed with de Gaulle.*[79]

A showdown. For seekers after evidence that Churchill recognized, in advance of the first successful atomic test, the Bomb's value as a means of strengthening the Western negotiating hand vis-à-vis the USSR, his minute to Eden offers something to go on. By early April, Churchill was casting about desperately for some means of retrieving the situation in

Eastern Europe. He was getting no change from Roosevelt when it came to confronting Stalin, but working on the age-old premise that territory equalled influence, he was keen for General Eisenhower, Supreme Allied Commander in Europe, to push his forces now in Germany as far to the east as possible before the Nazis surrendered. In this way, the withdrawal of US troops to previously agreed zones of occupation in the west could be deployed as a quid pro quo in negotiations with the Soviet government on, for example, Poland.[80] But did he also see the Bomb as leverage? The problem in answering this question affirmatively is that Churchill's riposte to Eden was a one-off. Over the next few months, although he regularly discoursed on the need for a showdown with the USSR, he never again juxtaposed it with a reference, direct or indirect, to the Bomb. Until Potsdam.

On 12 April, Churchill was working late in the Number 10 Annexe. As midnight neared he was forced to add an extra line to the telegram he had been composing for Clementine, then in the USSR on behalf of her Aid to Russia Fund. 'I have just heard the grievous news', he wrote.[81] Roosevelt was dead. The President had left Washington for a vacation in Warm Springs, Georgia, on 29 March. Over the following fortnight his health seemed to improve and his aides found him in excellent spirits. This may be why, when it came, the news that he had been carried off by a massive cerebral haemorrhage was such a shock to those close to him: they had let their guard down.[82]

Churchill was distraught, naturally. 'Our friendship is the rock on which I build for the future of the world', he had written to FDR the previous month.[83] Now the rock was gone. 'Ties have been shorn asunder which years have woven', he wrote to the King. 'We have to begin again in many ways.'[84] And yet, grieved though he was, Churchill declined to attend FDR's funeral citing pressure of business in London, an extraordinary decision from a man who had clocked up more than one hundred thousand air miles over the previous five years and was normally the keenest of transatlantic travellers.[85] Had Churchill 'cooled on Roosevelt to an extent which had drained away the emotional impact of his death'?[86] Certainly their post-Yalta correspondence had been tense at times and Churchill felt keenly the lack of support from FDR in confronting Stalin over Eastern Europe. Three days before the President died, Churchill had written to Eden to say that the time was ripe for a 'show-down' (that phrase again) over Poland.[87] But Roosevelt, in his last communication with Churchill (on 11 April) did not agree. 'I would minimize the general Soviet problem as much as possible', he advised, 'because these problems, in one form or another, seem to arise every day and most of them straighten out.'[88] Was it childish pique, then, of which Churchill was undoubtedly capable, that kept him away? A sense of bitterness at being let down by his friend when he – and Poland – most needed US support? Whatever the cause, Churchill later rued his decision, not because he felt he had served Roosevelt's memory poorly but because he squandered the opportunity for an early meeting with his successor. 'During the next three months tremendous decisions were made', he reflected in 1951, 'and I had a feeling that they were being made by a man I did not know.'[89]

That man was Harry S. Truman, Vice-President since January 1945 and arguably not massively better known to the American public than to the British Prime Minister.

Figure 6.2 Harry S. Truman. American Stock Archive, Archive Photos/Getty Images.

Sixty years old, dapper, bespectacled, energetic, straight-forward and straight-talking, Truman by his own admission 'felt like the moon, the stars, and all the planets had fallen on me' and he would spend his first weeks in office masking his insecurities with an outward show of confidence and by displaying a decisiveness that was often as instinctual as it was considered.[90] A Missouri Democrat with much domestic but little foreign policy experience, Truman moved quickly to make good the latter deficit. Where FDR had been a micro-manager on matters of high international diplomacy, Truman, a more natural delegator, was willing to seek and act upon advice from experts, particularly on the great issue of the moment, relations with the USSR (the complexities of which Roosevelt had avoided discussing with him).[91]

Many of the foreign policy specialists Truman turned to were less inclined than FDR had been to take a benign view of Stalin's foreign policy, and the President, initially impressed by their counsel, presided over a discernible hardening of US policy. 'My appreciation is that the new man is not to be bullied by the Soviets', Churchill wrote approvingly to Eden on 20 April. 'Seeking as I do a lasting friendship with the Russian people, I am sure this can only be founded upon their recognition of Anglo-American strength.'[92] Strength, to be sure, would be needed not only to secure what Churchill called 'a fair deal' for Poland but to prevent wholesale Soviet domination of all of Eastern Europe and the Balkans.[93] For the moment, the Prime Minister set aside thoughts of any explicit public condemnation of Soviet actions – Washington policymakers feared the damaging consequences of such a move so close to the start of the San Francisco conference – and instead gave Truman time to bed in.[94]

Before April was out, not just Roosevelt but Mussolini and Hitler were dead and the war in Europe was hurtling towards its climax. On 2 May, Berlin capitulated to the Red Army. Stalin had won the great prize – 'the lair of the fascist beast' – but only after committing

2.5 million troops to take the city ahead of his Western allies and at the cost of 350,000 casualties, a third of them killed.[95] Over the next four days German resistance ceased almost everywhere until, at Reims in the early hours of 7 May, the Chief of Staff of the German High Command, General Alfred Jodl, signed the principal instrument of surrender. Churchill received the news on waking. And yet, as Moran recorded, 'the PM does not seem at all excited about the end of the war'.[96] One reason – probably *the* reason – is to be found in a telegram Churchill sent to Clementine who was still in Moscow. 'It is astonishing one is not in a more buoyant frame of mind', he wrote, but 'I need scarcely tell you that beneath these triumphs lie poisonous politics and deadly international rivalries'.[97]

Tuesday 8 May, Victory in Europe (VE) Day, dawned in London with 'rain – intense Wagnerian rain', but this hardly dampened the euphoria and sense of collective relief felt by people in and beyond the capital.[98] At 3pm the Prime Minister delivered his much anticipated victory broadcast. The German war was at an end, he confirmed. The 'evil-doers' were 'now prostrate before us'. But Victory over Japan (VJ) Day would not necessarily follow quickly. 'We may allow ourselves a brief period of rejoicing', he said, 'but let us not forget for a moment the toil and efforts that lie ahead.'[99] That night, in an impromptu speech to a throng of revellers in Whitehall, he was again at pains to stress that there was 'another foe' out there, one 'stained with cruelty and greed – the Japanese'.[100] He returned to this theme for a third time the following week. Japan might be a 'harassed and failing' power, he told a nationwide radio audience, but it was also 'a people of a hundred millions, for whose warriors death has few terrors'. He ended with a passionate exhortation redolent of 1940. 'Forward, unflinching, unswerving, indomitable, till the whole task is done and the whole world is safe and clean.'[101] It was rousing stuff. But then it needed to be. After five years of struggle and sacrifice, the country at large found it difficult to summon the martial ardour for the task in the Far East. 'The Japanese war arouses no interest at all', Harold Nicolson noted, 'only a nauseated distaste.'[102]

Rangoon had been liberated on the eve of VE Day and with the effective end of the campaign in Burma, Admiral Louis Mountbatten's South-East Asia Command (SEAC) began planning to clear the Japanese from Malaya and open the Straits of Malacca later in the summer.[103] Meanwhile, in keeping with Churchill's promise to Roosevelt at Quebec in September 1944, a British Pacific Fleet had come into being under Admiral Sir Bruce Fraser and was operating in support of the US Navy.[104] Additionally, a British Empire and Commonwealth contribution to Downfall, the codename for the planned invasion of Japan, was earmarked to the tune of 3–5 divisions, and in June the RAF pledged ten bomber squadrons to join in the air offensive against Japan from bases in recently-captured Okinawa.[105] In sum, by mid-1945, the United Kingdom and Commonwealth were already making a valuable naval contribution to the war in the Pacific, were preparing to join in the bombing of Japan, and were intending to commit ground forces to Downfall.[106]

There was, though, one further way to hurt Japan. The Bomb. With a weapon expected to be ready by mid-summer, the British were increasingly mindful that under the terms of the Quebec and Hyde Park agreements, the weapon's combat role in the Pacific was an issue for joint Anglo-American consultation if not decision. But what standing did those Churchill–Roosevelt agreements have now that a new President was in the Oval Office? There was much more at stake for the British than simply a say in the operational deployment of the Bomb. For Churchill, Lindemann and Anderson, the Quebec and Hyde Park agreements were the twin pillars upon which a postwar Anglo-American atomic partnership, and in the Prime Minister's view a wider military alliance, would rest. If Washington no longer recognized or respected London's right to partake in decision-making on the weapon's combat role, what prospect was there that the United States would wish to work with the United Kingdom after the war in a relationship of all-encompassing atomic intimacy? The Bomb's present and future were, for the Churchill government, inextricably enmeshed.

CHAPTER 7
TRINITY AND POTSDAM

By the early summer of 1945, fissile material was beginning to come out of Hanford (plutonium) and Oak Ridge (U-235) in meaningful quantities and the bomb lab at Los Alamos was consequently working overtime to resolve the remaining technical problems connected with the production of a weapon of mass destruction. Oppenheimer and his team were confident that a gun-type detonation mechanism – the perfectly-timed coming together of two pieces of sub-critical material, the one fired bullet-like into the heart of the other – would be effective in setting off a chain reaction in a uranium bomb but they had known for some time that this method would be ill-suited to a plutonium device the core of which was so fissionable that it could easily pre-detonate. The solution arrived at was to implode a plutonium sphere by exploding chemical lenses around its surface, but this required extraordinary precision and needed to be tested. In contrast, the uranium bomb had no need of a trial.[1]

The news that a weapon was '99% certain' to materialize was welcomed in London by the triumvirate, but Lindemann was apprehensive about what the recent change at the top in Washington portended for Anglo-American atomic relations.[2] On 25 April, the day coincidentally that Truman received his first detailed briefing on the Manhattan Project, the Prof warned Churchill that the new President was likely to be 'more sensitive than his predecessor' to the probings of a Congressional inquiry, and that 'Conant & Co.' might try to take advantage of this to 'move' Truman 'towards a cancellation, covert or otherwise, of the Quebec Agreement'. Until the Prime Minister was able to ascertain Truman's views for himself it would be unwise to resume serious work on Tube Alloys in the UK lest Washington opponents of atomic partnership charge the British with acting with indecent haste to profit from US investment. On the other hand, if it became clear that Truman did not feel bound by Roosevelt's pledges, 'we should immediately go ahead in this country on the largest scale which our resources permit'.[3]

Other senior Tube Alloys figures were not quite as anxious about American reactions, especially to the early establishment of a UK experimental research centre, but they entirely shared Lindemann's estimate of the importance of ensuring a smooth transition from war to peace. The cost of pressing ahead with a full-scale national programme would be high, Chadwick warned, possibly more than a war-ravaged economy could bear, and it was thus imperative that bilateral cooperation, hence continued British access to US knowledge and technical expertise, be maintained.[4] The problem with Chadwick's prescription was that most Manhattan Project leaders continued to display markedly unilateralist tendencies. Anderson and Lindemann quickly picked up the danger-signs: if cooperation with the USA was at a premium in wartime, when the UK was a recognized partner, whither the chances of close atomic relations in peacetime?

Churchill, believing that the Quebec and Hyde Park agreements retained their binding properties, was slower to face up to this issue.

The most obvious pointer to how relations were likely to develop was the readiness of the Truman administration to abide by the Churchill–Roosevelt agreements in connection with the combat use of a bomb. On 20 April, the British Ambassador Lord Halifax met with Secretary of War Stimson and asked if the US government intended issuing an ultimatum to Japan to accept unconditional surrender or face the atomic consequences. Stimson would not be drawn. According to the Hyde Park agreement, a bomb 'might perhaps, after mature consideration, be used against the Japanese, who should be warned that this bombardment will be repeated until they surrender'. This wording did not commit the Americans, or the British, to the issuance of a prior warning to Japan, although it did foreshadow a warning pursuant to the first bombing and promising further destruction. More generally, the reference to 'mature consideration' presupposed top-level consultations. So what did Stimson's evasiveness imply? Were the Americans intending to determine the role of the Bomb in the war with Japan entirely on their own? Based on comparative levels of investment, the Americans were far and away the majority shareholder in the atomic enterprise, but did this give them the right to decide unilaterally all matters relating to military end-use?[5]

On 30 April, General Marshall confirmed to Field-Marshal Sir Henry Wilson, Head of the British Joint Staff Mission and a member of the Combined Policy Committee, that an atomic bomb would be used against Japan 'some time in August'. He made no mention of a warning, or of discussing operational details with the British, or indeed of seeking UK consent under the terms of the Quebec agreement. With the administration poised to establish a bespoke committee to consider 'the whole range of political questions' attending to the Bomb, it might be, Wilson opined, that such issues would be jointly considered in due course.[6]

The so-called Interim committee came into being at the start of May. Chaired by Stimson and comprising high-level political, military and scientific figures, its remit was to study and report to the President on 'the whole problem of temporary war controls and later publicity, and to survey and make recommendations on post-war research, development and controls, as well as legislation necessary to effectuate them'. The Bomb's combat role did not feature in the terms of reference since, strictly speaking, that was a military matter, but nobody on the Interim committee seriously questioned whether it should be used or not, rather its employment against Japan was taken for granted. Furthermore, though Stimson was in the chair, it was James F. Byrnes, President Truman's personal representative, who dominated the committee. Holding no official position in the government until the start of July, when he was appointed Secretary of State, Byrnes nonetheless enjoyed great access to and arguably influence over Truman. A highly-cultivated political animal, Byrnes was 'a master manipulator of people and the levers of government, easing his way with geniality, informality, and a certain amount of Harper and Old Taylor bourbon whiskey'.[7] Crucially, it was Byrnes who, early on, settled the debate in the committee between those like Stimson, Bush and Conant who were attracted to the idea of working with the Soviets on international control, and those who favoured retaining an atomic monopoly for as long as possible. Byrnes was very much of the latter stripe – the Bomb, he told Truman, 'might well put us in a position to dictate our own terms at the end of the war' – and his strong and pervasive influence militated against the advancement of even diluted Bohrism in Washington, inside or outside of the Interim committee, in the summer of 1945.[8]

From London, Anderson used "Jumbo" Wilson, a soldier with a hearty appetite and a flair for diplomacy, to alert the US authorities to the UK's desire for some say in decision-making on the Bomb's combat role as well as its expectation of ongoing cooperation after the war.[9] To Anderson's dismay, Wilson discovered that while the Quebec agreement was familiar to Manhattan Project leaders, nobody in Washington knew anything about the content of the Hyde Park agreement: no copy could be found anywhere and Stimson asked Wilson to supply one 'so as to avoid any possibility of misunderstanding or of the partners proceeding on different assumptions'.[10] Eventually, some *years* later, Roosevelt's copy popped up in the files of his naval aide: the FDR White House was famously chaotic (Eden called it a 'mad house') and it seems that a hapless filing clerk, believing Tube Alloys to refer to some secret naval experiment, misfiled the document.[11] Wilson eventually furnished Stimson with a copy on 20 June.[12] By then, senior S-1 figures had worked out the gist of what it contained – Stimson wrote that it 'did not bring any bombshell' – but the agreement, like Roosevelt, was now history.[13] With a new president in place, Manhattan Project leaders were presented with an opportunity to recalibrate US policy in ways that negated much of what Churchill had worked out with Roosevelt. To those policymakers worried about imminent Congressional scrutiny or minded from a nationalist standpoint to regard the A-bomb as almost entirely American (as well as those whose outlook encompassed both viewpoints), delimiting cooperation with the British during the war as the prelude to possibly cutting loose entirely when it ended had much to recommend it. In addition, Bush and Conant continued to believe that an overly close US–UK association would diminish the chances of winning Soviet backing for a postwar international control mechanism.[14]

Sensing that something was not right, in mid-May Anderson wrote to Eden, who was attending the San Francisco conference, identifying three atomic-themed issues requiring urgent and high-level attention in Washington. The first was joint US–UK agreement on what to say publicly after the weapon was used in combat (or possibly sooner if the result of the test made it impossible to conceal its existence); more specifically, how was the Soviet Union to be handled as part of this disclosure strategy? Second, once the secret was out, the USA and UK would have to decide once and for all between 'sole control' and 'international control'. Lastly, thought needed to be given to the eventual industrial uses of atomic energy. The government, he suggested, needed a worked-out position on all these issues, especially the first two, in advance of consultations with the Americans.[15]

As to the military deployment of the Bomb, Anderson had already (2 May) written to Churchill recommending that he remind the US authorities of the mutual consent principle.[16] The reply from Number 10 – which took three weeks to materialize –

disappointed him. Churchill did not wish to press Truman. Instead he hoped that some kind of 'machinery for consultation' would emerge naturally from discussions in and beyond the Combined Policy Committee. He was 'anxious', he added, 'to avoid having to insist . . . on any legalistic interpretation of the second [mutual consent] provision of the Quebec Agreement'.[17] Evidently, as far as Churchill was concerned, it made no difference whether Roosevelt or Truman was President; his 1943–1944 atomic understandings were transferable.

In the absence of any pressure from London for a part in decision-making, the Americans went their own way. On 1 June, the Interim committee unanimously agreed with a suggestion by Conant that 'the bomb should be used against Japan as soon as possible; that it be used on a war plant surrounded by workers' homes; and that it be used without prior warning'.[18] Truman endorsed the decision a few days later. Nobody on the US side felt any overwhelming need to discuss options with the British. On the contrary, on 21 June the Interim committee took what Sherwin calls 'the incredible step' of proposing that the President revoke entirely the mutual consent clause of the Quebec agreement. The intention was to inform, not debate with London.[19] Setting aside previous hesitancy about telling the Soviet authorities, the committee also recommended that Truman use a suitable opportunity at the next Big Three meeting – plans for the Potsdam conference were now evolving – to 'advise the Russians that we were working on this weapon with every prospect of success and that we expected to use it against Japan'. Truman might, in addition, assure Stalin that there would be discussions in the near future on 'insuring that the weapon would become an aid to peace'. In suggesting that Truman talk tactics with Churchill ahead of meeting with Stalin, Stimson and his colleagues nodded towards the Quebec agreement's clause on non-disclosure of information to third parties unless by mutual consent. But it was a negligible gesture. All the important decisions had been taken. The Interim committee's disregard for the Quebec agreement – never mind the Hyde Park agreement – was reflective of the fact that Roosevelt's undertakings to Churchill were not regarded by Washington decision-makers as binding on his successor.[20] As of 21 June, the Truman administration had decided, of its own volition, the target for the Bomb, that no advance warning would be issued to Tokyo, that Stalin should be told about the Manhattan Project, and that the prospect of international control might be dangled before the Soviets at Potsdam.

The silence from Washington made Anderson uneasy. Did the Truman administration's lack of interest in discussing the Bomb's use betoken a more general retreat from cooperation? At the end of June, as the Big Three meeting drew nearer (mid-July was now in the diary), Anderson encouraged Churchill to tackle Truman directly on atomic questions when they met.[21] Based on what we know of Churchill's views, had he been consulted by the Americans he would have agreed with the targeting decision but advised that an advance warning to the Japanese be given serious consideration. Against this, he would have objected to telling Stalin anything in advance of the Bomb's first combat use and positively bridled at the idea of international control. The Prime Minister, though, was not invited to offer a view. Instead, on 22 June, Groves informed Wilson that either Stimson or Marshall 'would soon be consulting us . . . as to the best method of recording concurrence by HMG to the operational employment of TA'. In other words, UK agreement was regarded as a given. The only consultation related to bureaucratic convenience: should London's concurrence be recorded in a Combined Chiefs of Staff minute or in a Combined Policy Committee minute?[22] On 28 June, Halifax and Wilson, having met with Stimson, cabled Anderson asking for permission to agree to 'the implementation of Provision II of the Quebec Agreement' at the next CPC meeting. Both men recognized a *fait accompli* when they saw one.[23]

So, reluctantly, did Anderson. The next day, he sent a minute to Churchill recommending endorsement of the decision to hit Japan. By this time, the Chancellor was in receipt of the drafts of two statements which the US government intended to issue in the wake of the bombing, a short one by the President and a longer one by Stimson rehearsing the history of the project. Neither statement, Anderson noticed, made any reference to Quebec or Hyde Park. The Chancellor then cabled Halifax to warn him that in view of these ominous indicators, the Prime Minister might yet decide that the matter 'was so important that he ought to deal with it himself direct with the President' and that his combat-use approval would therefore be reserved until Potsdam. Was this Anderson's unspoken wish? He certainly questioned whether the CPC's remit extended to deciding formally on the use of the Bomb which, he averred, was a matter for the President and Prime Minister to determine between them.[24]

If Anderson did harbour the hope that Churchill would delay a green light, it came to nothing. On 2 July, his enabling minute came back to him inscribed with the Prime Minister's initials and the date. There was no comment. And so, in this passive and quiescent manner, and without consulting either the War Cabinet or the Chiefs of Staff, Churchill became the first (and so far the only) British Prime Minister to approve the use of nuclear weapons against human beings.[25] Twenty years earlier, in an article in *Strand* magazine, Churchill had predicted that military leaders in 'a future world-agony' might 'extinguish [. . .] some London or Paris, some Tokio [*sic*] or San Francisco, by pressing a button, or putting his initials neatly at the bottom of a piece of foolscap'. If so, they would 'have to wait a long time for fame and glory'.[26] Now, in July 1945, with uncanny exactitude, he performed his own premonition. Anderson dutifully relayed the decision – along with the Prime Minister's expectation that the Bomb would still be a live topic of discussion between himself and Truman at Potsdam – to the British embassy in Washington.[27] Churchill can only have had in mind future policy. The present was decided. At the next meeting of the Combined Policy Committee at the Pentagon on 4 July, Wilson confirmed his government's (or more precisely the Prime Minister's) assent to US plans.[28]

Questions remain. Churchill might have initialled Anderson's piece of foolscap, but what did this actually signify? Had the Prime Minister *agreed* to the use of the Bomb? Or had he simply rubber-stamped an American decision? According to a Whitehall assessment prepared in November 1945, while '[w]e were consulted before the bombs were dropped on Japan . . . there can be little doubt that this consultation was a formality' and that 'it would have been beyond our power to have restrained the American Government from using the weapon had we so wished'.[29] Here, though, is the rub. The UK did not so wish. Twenty years later, A. J. P. Taylor denied the existence even of quiescence when writing that the decision to use the Bomb, 'being purely American, [was] not of direct concern in British history', a view echoed by Martin Gilbert.[30] This represents one end of an historiographical spectrum. At the other extreme is Jacques Hymans who maintains that it is 'an underappreciated fact that the formal authorization for the atomic bombings ... was given not just by the United States, but also by the United Kingdom ... the British leadership of the day chose explicitly to agree to the bombings', an interpretation which suggests some pro-activism on Churchill's part.[31] Somewhere in the middle is Kathleen Burk: the decision was taken by the United States with Britain 'simply asked to agree to what was arguably the single most significant act of the war'.[32]

Where does the truth of the matter reside? In seeking to answer this question, reliance on Churchill is not helpful. Ten days after Hiroshima, he insisted in the House of Commons that he had played an active role in the decision-making process. 'Great Britain had a right to be consulted in accordance with Anglo-American agreements', he explained. 'The decision to use the atomic bomb was taken by President Truman *and myself* at Potsdam, and *we* approved the military plans to unchain the dread, pent-up forces [emphasis added].'[33] Leaving aside the fact that Churchill decided nothing at Potsdam, with or without Truman, and disregarding the by no means minor detail that the military plans were drawn up entirely by the Americans, what did his assent, signalled so limply on 2 July, amount to?

If the decision appeared to be a purely American one – to revert to the Taylor-Gilbert thesis – that was because of Churchill's consciously *laissez-faire* approach. The Truman administration did not solicit British views. But equally the Prime Minister did not offer any. In his 1954 Cabinet Office study, John Ehrman concluded that the British 'gave their formal consent to the use of the bomb apparently without hearing the arguments for its use'. Churchill simply wrote the Americans 'a blank cheque' insofar it was accepted in London that the deployment of the Bomb, being a weapon for use in a theatre of war where the Americans reigned supreme, was a matter, like the decision to invade Japan, for the US Joint Chiefs of Staff (JCS), not the Combined Chiefs of Staff. 'The balance of power, both in Tube Alloys and in the Pacific, lay too heavily with the United States for the British to be able to oppose this particular decision.'[34] This is quite true, but it misses the point. Churchill was never going to veto the use of the Bomb. But he could – and maybe should – have insisted on a more prominent British role in the decision-making process, especially on the question of a warning to Japan which the Hyde Park agreement had posited as a question for mature Anglo-American consideration.[35] By standing on the terms of the FDR–Churchill agreements, the British might have irritated the Truman administration, but given the transcendent importance of atomic energy, annoying Washington was arguably a small price to pay if it prised from US policymakers an acceptance that the UK deserved fair treatment. But Anderson could do nothing. Only Churchill could give a lead. And so no lead was given.

The Prime Minister's lack of engagement obliges us to consider again the possibility that he failed to grasp the significance of atomic energy – beyond, that is, his appreciation, rooted in his scientific imagination, that an A-bomb promised to make an unprecedented bang. At times, he seemed fully clued-up: in April, in rejecting Eden's plea for French involvement in Tube Alloys, he described the A-bomb as a 'matter . . . out of all relation to anything else that exists in the whole world'.[36] Against this, Anderson sometimes thought that Churchill's 'mind was so far from being of a scientific nature that he had difficulties in viewing the project in its proper perspective'.[37] For some historians, the possibility that Churchill never truly comprehended that the atomic bomb contained not just more ordnance than any previous bomb but the very power of nature itself explains his semi-detached approach to the issue of consent.[38] The Prof ought to have made good any deficit in his master's understanding but there is evidence that a few shards of his old scepticism remained. 'No one can be sure that it will go off – there's many a slip "twixt cup and lip"', he remarked to R. V. Jones in March 1945. 'Think what fools the Americans will look if the bomb does not work.'[39] On a visit to Los Alamos the previous October, Lindemann's atomic acumen left Oppenheimer underwhelmed: 'That guy will never understand a thing', he reflected.[40] If the Prof did not understand, how could Churchill?

Despite all this, it remains a wonder that the Prime Minister, in light of his almost obsessive referencing of the Quebec agreement over the previous two years, did not seek a greater say in the decision-making process. As we know, Churchill's failure to take advantage of Roosevelt's offer of atomic partnership in October 1941 is seen by many historians as the great "missed bus" moment in the Tube Alloys story.[41] But what of his refusal to invoke Britain's right to proper consultation in the summer of 1945? Should this not also fall into the category of missed opportunities? Churchill did not need to exercise that right in any determining way, only to remind the Americans of its existence and, by so doing, to test the new administration's allegiance to Quebec and Hyde Park. Did he perhaps put his faith in the "special relationship" which, despite the change in President, he continued to venerate? Was Churchill relying on Truman to do the honourable thing and uphold his 1943–1944 agreements with Roosevelt? If so, he misread the Americans, and not for the first time. Or was there some method behind his seemingly meek acquiescence?

Looking back, Lindemann remembered Churchill being 'anxious' in the period before Potsdam 'that nothing should be done by us to retard the use of the TA weapon'.[42] Did that include, for Churchill, intruding himself into US deliberations? It may be argued that from a British standpoint what happened to Japan was of less consequence than securing acceptance by the new men in Washington that the Quebec and Hyde Park agreements should be the foundation stones of a US–UK atomic alliance. Allowing the Americans their head in the death-throes of the war in the Pacific was as nothing compared to the securing Britain's atomic future in partnership with the United States. Moreover, on the wider geo-strategic plane, unquestioning backing for the USA in the Pacific might bank goodwill in Washington and generate greater American support for Churchill's efforts to contain the Soviet threat in Europe. In the end, however one evaluates the evidence, Churchill's claim before Parliament in the aftermath of Hiroshima and Nagasaki that 'the decision to use the atomic bomb was taken by President Truman and myself' is a distortion.[43] To Anderson's disappointment, the Prime Minister chose neither to discuss the matter telegraphically with the President nor elbow his way into the general American decision-making process. Rather, he left the Americans to their own devices.

If Churchillian ignorance of the nature of atomic energy is accepted – if, as Graham Farmelo contends, he was 'poorly prepared for the imminent arrival of the nuclear age' – where does this leave the argument that Churchill was a proto-atomic diplomatist, determined to keep the secret from Stalin in order to use the Bomb to strengthen the Anglo-American negotiating position vis-à-vis the USSR over the future of Central, Southern and Eastern Europe?[44] Hanging by a thread, it would seem. The proof of Churchill's lack of A-bomb awareness is to be found in the ten weeks between the end of the war in Europe (8 May) and the opening of the Potsdam conference (17 July). In this period, his anxiety about Soviet expansionism peaked as did his desire for a showdown, a frank face-to-face encounter with Stalin in which he would make clear his opposition to Soviet behaviour in Poland and elsewhere. At the same time, thanks to briefings by Anderson and Lindemann, he knew that an atomic test was imminent and that one or two weapons were likely to be ready for use against Japan by mid-summer. It follows that if ever there was a moment for Churchill to invest the Bomb with diplomacy-enhancing properties, this was it. But there is nothing in the documentary record: not in his correspondence with Truman, in his dealings with Anderson or Lindemann, in his copious minutes and telegrams to Eden, or in his discussions with Ismay or the Chiefs of Staff. Nothing. Until Potsdam.

As we have seen, the toughening of US policy towards the Soviet Union in the first weeks of the Truman presidency gave Churchill hope that a united Anglo-American front might be reconstituted and that Stalin, faced with Western firmness, would draw in his horns in Poland. The new and the old American administrations resembled one another in desiring continued cooperation with the USSR, but the Truman administration, to begin with at least, was more inclined than its predecessor to insist on Soviet respect for the Declaration on Liberated Europe and the other Yalta agreements. This unsettled the Kremlin but pleased Churchill who looked forward to his showdown with Stalin.[45] Convinced that personal diplomacy could end the Polish deadlock and settle amicably other differences, he importuned Truman to agree to a Big Three meeting – what became the Potsdam conference – at the earliest possible date.[46]

At the same time, in considering ways to strengthen the Anglo-American bargaining position, Churchill stuck to his conviction that territory equalled influence. A week after Truman became President, he wrote to him urging that US forces finding themselves inside the agreed Soviet control zone in Germany when the war ended should stand their ground pending a Big Three conclave.[47] He held tenaciously to this viewpoint over the next month as American armies did indeed penetrate deep into Soviet-mandated territory. Simply to fall back, he told Eden at the start of May, 'would mean the tide of Russian domination sweeping forward 120 miles on a front of 300 or 400 miles' and leave Stalin in control of half of Germany, the Baltic States, Czechoslovakia, a good swathe of Austria and the whole of Poland, Yugoslavia, Hungary, Romania and Bulgaria. In seeking to prevent this outcome, the Anglo-Americans had 'several powerful bargaining counters', including territory in the Soviet zone. It was thus to an 'early and speedy showdown and settlement with Russia that we must now turn our hopes'.[48] There was, we should note, no mention of the atomic bomb in connection with showdowns and bargaining counters.

Truman was unmoved by Churchill's entreaties. Taking the view that an agreement was an agreement', whether big or small, and that the Soviets would have no reason to abide by previous undertakings unless the Western powers set a good example, the President affirmed on 12 June that US forces in eastern Germany would begin withdrawing before the end of the month. When the news reached him, Churchill recalled, it 'struck a knell in my breast'. Here, perhaps, was the first intimation that Truman was not going to be a consistent hawk.[49] Churchill was also distressed by the President's seeming lack of urgency in settling a date for the Big Three conference – for, that is, the showdown – and his messages to the White House became shrill in their insistence that delay was permitting the Red Army to embed itself deeper and deeper in Eastern Europe.[50] It says much for Churchill's lack of Bomb-consciousness that it did not occur to him that Truman might be putting off his first encounter with Stalin until it was confirmed that the A-bomb was a real weapon in America's military (hence its diplomatic) arsenal.[51]

In Washington, Manhattan Project leaders attached increasing importance to the forthcoming test – scheduled for mid-July – of a plutonium device. As Stimson reflected vis-à-vis the European situation, over 'any such tangled weave of problems the S-1 secret would be dominant' and yet 'it seems a terrible thing to gamble with such big stakes in diplomacy without having your master card in your hand'.[52] The impact of this diplomatic requirement made itself felt at Los Alamos where Oppenheimer recalled coming under 'incredible pressure to get it done before the Potsdam meeting'.[53] And all the time at the back (and more often than not the front) of Churchill's mind was the late-President's insistence that US military forces – those not earmarked for transfer to the Pacific – would remain in Western Europe only for a year or so after the defeat of Germany.[54] Nothing in Truman's demeanour suggested that he had an alternative time-table in mind. Eventually, on 4 June, the President committed to a Big Three meeting in 'the vicinity of Berlin' in mid-July. Although placated, Churchill confided to Ismay that he would have to tell Truman when they met 'that if his armies go too soon' from Europe, 'they will probably have to come back pretty quick'.[55]

The most striking proof of Churchill's anxiety about Soviet intentions, hence, by extension, the most striking example of the absence of any hint of atomic diplomacy in his mind-set, is the instructions he issued to the Chiefs of Staff within a week of the end of the war in Europe to plan for a surprise Anglo-American military assault on the USSR. The Chiefs were astonished. 'Winston ... gives me the feeling of already longing for another war!', Field Marshal Brooke, the Chief of the Imperial General Staff, wrote in his diary, '[e]ven if it entailed fighting the Russians!'[56] Field Marshal Montgomery and the British Ambassador to Moscow, Archibald Clark-Kerr, likewise remarked on Churchill's 'sudden and temperamental change of attitude since Yalta – from a convinced philo-Russianism ... to regarding her as Public Enemy No. 1', and how he 'talks quite seriously of the possibility of having to fight her'.[57] This was also the message that the Soviet Ambassador in London, Fedor Gusev, received loud and clear when he called on the Prime Minister on 13 May. 'Churchill was extraordinarily angry', he reported to Moscow. 'His remarks were full of threats ... We should recognise that we are dealing with an adventurer who is in his element in war, who feels much more at ease in the circumstances of war than those of peace.'[58]

Pressed by the Prime Minister, the Joint Planning Staff (JPS) set to work on what became known as operation Unthinkable. By late May an outline concept was in place. The objective, so far as the JPS could divine Churchill's wishes, was to 'impose upon Russia the will of the United States and the British Empire' and, more specifically, to secure 'a square deal for Poland'. Unthinkable envisioned ten German divisions press-ganged into supporting a projected forty-seven American and British divisions (fourteen of them armoured) in an immense operation with a provisional launch-date of 1 July 1945. Success, though, was hardly to be expected. Indeed unless the Red Army was quickly ousted from Poland, the planners warned that 'we must be prepared to be committed to a total war' against numerically superior Soviet land forces in the vast inner spaces of Russia 'which will be both long and costly'.[59] Brooke was appalled – the plan was 'fantastic and the chances of success quite impossible' – and at the beginning of June he and his fellow service chiefs told the Prime Minister in no uncertain terms that it was a non-starter.[60]

Churchill bowed to the force of military objections but could not quite let go of Unthinkable. Rather, he asked the Chiefs to reconfigure the plan as a defensive concept. 'If the Americans withdraw to their zone [in Germany] and move the bulk of their forces back to the United States and to the Pacific, the Russians have the power to advance to the North Sea and the Atlantic', hence it was critical, he reasoned, to 'have a study made of how then we could defend our Island'. By retaining the codeword Unthinkable, the Prime Minister wished it to be understood that 'this remains a precautionary study of what, I hope, is still a purely hypothetical contingency'. At the same time, he had 'never in his life' been 'more worried by the European situation than he was at present'.[61] This concern spawned other desperate military injunctions. Montgomery, for instance, was ordered to gather up surrendered German weapons for stockpiling against a future crisis.[62] Moreover, despite the end of the war with Germany, and notwithstanding the demands of the struggle in Asia and the Pacific, Churchill was loathe to countenance any major demobilization of British forces in Europe. 'I do not wish to be left alone with no troops at all and great Russian masses free to do whatever they choose', he told Ismay. Some 'solution in the main field of international relations', perhaps at Potsdam, was required before UK forces, especially the RAF, were scaled back. As the date of the conference drew near, Churchill relaxed a little when he learned of the retirement eastwards of large numbers of Red Army troops in preparation for war with Japan, but even so, he did not want to go to Potsdam 'with too little in hand'.[63]

In the reworked Unthinkable, military planners downplayed the likelihood of a Soviet airborne assault and anticipated, if it came to conflict, a massive rocket bombardment, a more destructive version of Hitler's V-2 assault. To provide an effective defence, an estimated 230 squadrons of fighters, 100 of tactical bombers, and 200 of heavy bombers would be required.[64] However, when the Truman administration made clear that there was not the slightest possibility of the United States reversing its decision on troop withdrawals, the file on Unthinkable was closed.[65] Without strong support from the United States there was no prospect of Britain, on its own, prising Poland from Stalin's grasp: Truman 'botched things', Churchill later complained, and together with Eisenhower 'gave away, to please Russia, vast tracts of Europe'.[66] Whether this is right or not, Truman certainly sent Harry Hopkins to Moscow at the end of May with instructions to find a compromise that would neutralize the Polish issue before it completely poisoned Big Three relations. Given American worries that European tensions might cause Stalin to reconsider his pledge to enter the war in East Asia, any compromise was likely to be to the USSR's advantage. And so it proved.

In June, Stalin reaffirmed his intention of declaring war on Japan (he was also looking forward to gaining an occupation zone), while in Poland a reshuffle of the government, which had now relocated to Warsaw, gave four cabinet seats to non-communists in a finessing rather than diminution of Moscow's control. This, though, was good enough for the United States which recognized the Polish government on 5 July.[67] So did the British, reluctantly, in order to maintain a façade of Anglo-American unity, and resentfully so on Churchill's part ('Truman wouldn't wait', he sniped).[68] For Count Edward Raczynski, the Polish ambassador in London, the matter was settled 'in a manner unworthy of great powers and inconsistent with the Yalta decisions'.[69] But what could Churchill do other than recommend that the London Poles make the best of the situation?[70] He had run out of levers.

On 15 July, the Prime Minister and his party arrived in Berlin for the final Big Three conference of the war, appropriately codenamed Terminal. The venue was the 176-room Celienhoff palace at Potsdam, home to the last Crown Prince of Prussia, situated some fifteen miles south-west of Berlin, a city of ruination and death, 'Hitler's folly' Truman called it when he saw it.[71] In this mock-Tudor palace the three leaders, together with their military staffs and sundry political advisors, attempted to settle the geo-political future of Europe and agree on how best to bring the war against Japan to a swift conclusion. Also in attendance on the British side was Clement Attlee, the Labour leader. The outcome of the General Election held on 5 July remained in doubt while the votes of service personnel overseas were gathered and counted. Quietly confident of victory, Churchill nevertheless deemed it appropriate for Attlee to attend as an observer; the election would be declared on 26 July, mid-way through Terminal, and if, despite his hopes, there should be a change of government, he wished the transition to be seamless as far as the business of the conference was concerned.[72] The following day, Churchill visited the shattered Reichstag and what was left of Hitler's Chancellery and bunker before watching a parade of British troops on Charlotten Strasse. It was only at the end of the march-past that George Mallaby, a member of the UK delegation, realized that Attlee had also been present on the viewing stand. Diffident and unassuming, the Labour leader, Mallaby remembered, 'was more warmly cheered [by the troops] than Mr. Churchill, and for the first time I saw the writing on the wall'.[73]

Churchill himself noticed neither wall nor writing. Instead he focused his thoughts on Truman, Stalin and a week of critical negotiations on which the 'future of Europe, and indeed the peace of the whole world, may turn'.[74] On the morning of the parade he travelled the short distance from his residence at No. 23 Ringstrasse to Truman's villa at Babelsberg. It was the first meeting between the two men. 'He is a most charming and a very clever person – meaning clever in the English not the Kentucky sense', the President wrote afterwards. 'He gave me a lot of hooey about how great my country is and how he loved Roosevelt and how he intended to love me ... Well, I gave him as cordial a reception as I could – being naturally (I hope) a polite and agreeable person. I am sure we can get along if he doesn't try and give me too much soft soap'.[75] Despite what, for Churchill, was a distressingly early 11.00 am start (his daughter Mary, acting as his ADC, remarked that he had not been up so early in years), he emerged from the encounter in high spirits. '[H]e likes the President immensely', Mary observed, 'they talk the same language.'[76]

As for Churchill's relations with Stalin at Potsdam, whenever he allowed his mind to dwell on communism, or on the power of the Red Army to advance Soviet aims by force of arms, he was his old rampant anti-Bolshevik self, yet when he spoke of Stalin the man it was with warmth, respect and an almost romantic sentimentality.[77] Others in the British delegation, being more convinced of Stalin's 'wicked side' and unnerved by his 'cold, basilisk glare', grew anxious that the Prime Minister – tired, inconsistent, not on top of his briefing papers – would be outmanoeuvred by "Uncle Joe", a master of detail and an accomplished negotiator.[78] Churchill was 'again under Stalin's spell'. Eden wrote in his diary. 'He kept repeating "I like that man" & I am full of admiration of Stalin's handling of him.'[79]

On the morning of 17 July, Churchill visited Frederick II's Summer Palace at Sans Souci and then returned to his residence where he was joined at lunch by Stimson. Towards the end of the meal, the US War Secretary passed him a piece of paper on which was written a brief message: 'Babies satisfactorily born'. Churchill was bemused. 'It means', Stimson said, 'that the experiment in the Mexican desert has come off. The atomic bomb is a reality.'[80] The previous day, at 5.29 am local time in New Mexico, some sixty miles from Alamogordo, the world entered the atomic age when a plutonium device was successfully detonated. Codenamed Trinity, the test exceeded expectations in producing an explosive yield equivalent to 18,600 tons of TNT. William L. Laurence, the only reporter present, shocked by the blast and horrified by the sight of the broiling mushroom cloud that followed, wrote of 'an elemental force freed from its bonds after being chained for billions of years ... It was as though the earth had opened and the skies had split.'[81] Physicist Hans Bethe, a member of the Los Alamos bomb team, beheld a sight that 'briefly resembled the state of the universe moments after its first primordial explosion'. Otto Frisch, whose work with Rudolf Peierls in Birmingham in 1940 had set the whole project in motion, thought that 'somebody had turned the sun on with a switch' to illuminate the early morning desert, while the UK mission's James Chadwick was 'filled with awe' at 'a vision from the Book of Revelation . . . a great blinding light lit up the sky and earth as if God himself had appeared among us'.[82] Oppenheimer, struggling to come to terms with what he had witnessed, remembered alighting on a verse from Hindu scripture, the Bhagavad Vita: 'Now I am become Death, destroyer of worlds'.[83] Physical chemist Henry Linschitz eschewed esoterics. 'My God', he exclaimed, 'we're going to drop that on a city?'[84]

Far away in Potsdam, Churchill was denied the visual spectacle of Trinity but he was still 'intensely interested and greatly cheered up' when told of the outcome.[85] Later, in *Triumph and Tragedy*, the final volume of his history of the war, Churchill wrote of how the news created in his mind's eye a 'vision – fair and bright indeed it seemed – of the end of the whole war in one or two violent shocks'.[86] From this, most readers would infer that, immediately on being told of the test result, he invested the new weapon with war-winning qualities. In fact the extant contemporary record shows that Churchill's understanding of the Bomb's military, never mind its diplomatic import, developed only gradually over several days as more detailed information reached Potsdam from Los Alamos. The Americans had been similarly thrilled by the initial reports but Truman and his advisors preferred to wait to read the full account of the test being prepared by General Groves before getting too carried away. That only reached Berlin on 21 July, five days after Trinity. Until then it was business as usual for the Anglo-Americans. Sticking to his original brief, Truman sought confirmation from Stalin that the USSR still intended to declare war on Japan. In this, he was successful. 'I've gotten what I came for – Stalin goes to war August 15 with no strings on it', he wrote to his wife on 18 July. 'I'll say that we'll end the war a year sooner now, and think of the kids who won't be killed! That is the important thing.'[87] In his diary the President added, vis-à-vis Soviet entry, 'Fini Japs when that comes about'.[88]

Nor did Churchill alter his basic position in the days immediately following the birth of the Bomb. Rather, as at Yalta, he continued to look for a diplomatic rather than a military means of bringing the war with Japan to a speedy conclusion. Planning for Downfall had been gathering pace since June when Truman gave the operation his formal approval. The invasion would be an American-directed show in two acts, an amphibious assault on Kyushu (codenamed Olympic), provisionally scheduled for 1 November 1945, the prelude to the massed attack on Honshu and the Tokyo Plain (Coronet) which was tentatively set for March 1946.[89] The problem for Churchill as he searched for a diplomatic solution remained unconditional surrender which Truman, desirous of demonstrating policy continuity with his predecessor, had publicly reaffirmed on several occasions since taking the oath of office.[90] On 18 July, the Prime Minister channelled his misgivings into a direct appeal to the President to reframe Allied policy. Invoking 'the tremendous cost in American life and, to a smaller extent, in British life which would be involved in enforcing "unconditional surrender" upon the Japanese', he begged Truman to consider whether Anglo-American aims might be expressed 'in some other way' in communicating with Tokyo 'so that we got all the essentials for peace and security, and yet left the Japanese some show of saving their military honour and some assurance of their national existence, after they had complied with all safeguards necessary for the conqueror'. Truman, crackling with indignation, 'did not think the Japanese had any military honour left after Pearl Harbor', but Churchill pressed gamely on. The Japanese 'had something for which they were ready to face certain death in very large numbers', namely their emperor. Some reassurance about the Mikado's future – which 'might not be so important to us as it was to them' – could reap spectacular dividends.[91]

Churchill also carried over from Yalta his belief that a Soviet declaration of war might, on its own, hasten Japan's surrender. That same evening he met privately with Stalin. From what the Soviet leader said, it was evident, Churchill wrote afterwards, 'that Russia intends to attack Japan soon after August 8', a conclusion which tallied with the American understanding and one which he welcomed.[92] Truman, however, in receipt of additional information from Los Alamos, was growing more certain about the value of the Bomb. 'Believe Japs will fold up before Russia comes in', he wrote in his diary. 'I am sure they will when Manhattan appears over their homeland.'[93] The President's confidence was given its greatest boost yet when the Groves report finally arrived at Potsdam late on the morning of 21 July. Stimson was the first to see its contents. It was 'an immensely powerful document', he wrote, 'and revealed far greater destructive power than we expected'. At 3.30 that afternoon, Stimson met with Truman and Byrnes and read the report out loud to them. 'They were immensely pleased', he noted. The President in particular 'was tremendously pepped up by it and spoke to me of it again and again when I saw him. He said it gave him an entirely new feeling of confidence.'[94] Later, in his diary, Truman wrote of possessing 'the most terrible bomb in the history of the world' and wondered if it might turn out to be 'the fire destruction prophesied in the Euphrates Valley Era, after Noah and his fabulous Ark'.[95]

The Groves report was an eye-opener for Churchill, too. Stimson passed it on when he called at the Prime Minister's residence on the morning of 22 July. 'He [Churchill] told me that he had noticed at the meeting of the Three yesterday that Truman was evidently much fortified by something that had happened and that he stood up to the Russians in a most emphatic and decisive manner', Stimson recorded. 'He said "Now I know what happened to Truman yesterday. I couldn't understand it. When he got to the meeting after having read this report he was a changed man. He told the Russians just where they got on and off and generally bossed the whole meeting." Churchill said he now understood how this pepping up had taken place and that he felt the same way.' Harvey Bundy, Stimson's aide, who was also present, confirmed Churchill's amazement. 'Stimson', the Prime Minister intoned, 'what was gunpowder? Trivial. What was electricity? Meaningless. This atomic bomb is the Second Coming in Wrath.'[96]

The next day, 23 July, Churchill told Eden that it was now obvious that the Americans 'do not at the present time desire Russian participation in the war against Japan'.[97] Then again, nor did Churchill. 'The end of the Japanese war no longer depended upon the pouring in of their armies', he later wrote. 'We had no need to ask favours of them.'[98] It would be no easy diplomatic task, however, to wriggle out of a deal with Stalin that had been solemnized only a few days previously to American (and British) satisfaction. Perhaps the Bomb would solve the dilemma – if it was used quickly enough. For Byrnes, newly installed as Truman's 'able and conniving' Secretary of State, atomic arms were fast becoming the ultimate panacea, the means by which the United States could defeat Japan before the deadline for the Red Army's entry into the war, without the need for the mass blood-letting of an invasion, and without having to honour the Yalta Far Eastern agreement or concede an occupation zone to the USSR.[99] Truman apparently felt the same way. Within 72 hours of the Groves report reaching Potsdam he had approved a written military order permitting the use of atomic weapons against Japanese cities. Hiroshima, Kokura, Niigata and Nagasaki were specified. The order made no mention of purely military objectives or of sparing civilian lives.[100]

Contrary to his later public testimony, Churchill was not involved at Potsdam in any decision-making process relating to the Bomb. To the distress of Brooke and the other service chiefs, the British were excluded by the Americans from almost every important strategic decision connected with the final phase of the war in the Pacific.[101] Churchill having given his consent to the Bomb's operational deployment a fortnight earlier, this exclusion policy extended to the atomic sphere.[102] Yet Truman, far from controlling events, was himself being borne along by the gathering momentum. The 'initial decision and the primary responsibility' for using the Bomb 'were Mr. Truman's', Groves later maintained. 'As far as I was concerned, his decision was one of non-interference – basically, a decision not to upset the existing plans.'[103] Churchill did not interfere with Truman's policy of non-interference. And so the countdown began. Leaving aside the two devices, one uranium (nicknamed Little Boy), the other plutonium (Fat Man), that were now being primed, Truman's 25 July directive also settled the question of subsequent deployments. A separate order would not be required. 'Additional bombs' could be used 'as soon as made ready by the project staff'.[104]

In his diary, the President wrote that 'military objectives and soldiers and sailors are the target and not women and children'.[105] He was deluding himself. Or else he was poorly briefed by his military advisors. Stimson, in contrast, knew the targets to be cities and civilians more than military bases. In the weeks preceding Potsdam this concern led the Secretary of War to recommend to Truman that unconditional surrender be ameliorated to permit a continuation of the Royal House and the retention of the Emperor as a constitutional monarch. In this way, Stimson suggested, the war might be ended speedily without an invasion (his main concern) and without the use of new weapons. A number of other senior US policymakers shared this view, among them Admiral Leahy, Acting Secretary of State Joseph C. Grew, Assistant Secretary of War John J. McCloy, Secretary of the Navy James V. Forrestal and his Under-Secretary Ralph A. Bard, and even (at times) General Marshall. Japan, Stimson was sure, 'is not a nation composed wholly of mad fanatics of an entirely different mentality than ours' and might yet be 'susceptible to reason'. The effort, he felt, was worth making.[106]

When Churchill arrived at Potsdam he had been of a similar mind – to bring the war to a swift end, the folly of unconditional surrender needed to be addressed – but he would leave the conference content to see the Bomb employed. At no point in this transition process did Churchill experience the moral torture which wracked Stimson.[107] The pivotal moment for the Prime Minister was his reading of the Groves report. Only then, on 22 July, does he seem to have truly awoken to the Bomb's politico-diplomatic as well as its military potentialities. The report, he told Parliament a few weeks later, left 'no doubt in the minds of the very few who were informed, that we were in the presence of a new factor in human affairs, and possessed of powers which were irresistible ... From that moment our outlook on the future was transformed.'[108] A qualification is needed. More than Groves' statistic-driven observations and utilitarian prose, it was the eye-witness account of Brigadier Thomas F. Farrell, Groves' deputy, that made the deepest impression on Churchill. Farrell had been in the observation bunker closest to the detonation and his vividly-drawn description of Trinity was embedded in the main report.

> The effects could well be called unprecedented, magnificent, beautiful, stupendous and terrifying. No man-made phenomenon of such tremendous power had ever occurred before. The lighting effects beggared description. The whole country was lighted by a searing light with the intensity many times that of the midday sun ... It was that beauty the great poets dream about but describe most poorly and inadequately. Thirty seconds after the explosion came first, the air blast pressing hard against the people and things, to be followed almost immediately by the strong, sustained, awesome roar which warned of doomsday and made us feel that we puny things were blasphemous to dare tamper with the forces heretofore reserved to The Almighty.[109]

Having digested all this, Churchill began his transformation into an atomic diplomatist. Before 22 July, he had been buoyed by the reports from New Mexico, sketchy as they were, but there is no evidence that they left him so thunderstruck that he instantly seized on the Bomb as a high-value advantage in the fraught negotiations with Stalin over the future of Europe. When he read the Groves report, however, something clicked. And once started, the metamorphosis was rapid. The very next day – 23 July – he told Moran everything. This, in itself, was ironic. For four years Churchill had been the most implacable opponent of widening the circle of Tube Alloys knowledge, but now he could barely contain himself. The 'PM turned to me with great solemnity', Moran recorded:

> I am going to tell you something you must not tell to any human being. We have split the atom. The report of the great experiment has just come in. A bomb was let off in some wild spot in New Mexico. It was only a thirteen-pound bomb, but it made a crater half a mile across. People ten miles away lay with their feet towards the bomb; when it went off they tried to look at the sky. But even with the darkest

glasses it was impossible. It was the middle of the night, but it was as if seven suns had lit the earth; two hundred miles away the light could be seen. The bomb sent up smoke into the stratosphere . . .

It is the Second Coming. The secret has been wrested from nature. The Americans spent £400 million on it.[110] They built two cities. Not a soul knew what they were working at. All scientists have been busy with it. I have been very worried. We put the Americans on the bomb. We fired them by suggesting that it could be used in this war. We have an agreement with them. It gives the Americans the power to mould the world . . . If the Russians had got it, it would have been the end of civilization. Dropped on London, it would remove the City. It is to be used in Japan, on cities, not on armies.

The extent to which Farrell's observations permeated the Prime Minister's thinking is obvious. To Moran, however, it was 'H. G. Wells stuff' and he asked 'what would happen if the Russians got the idea and caught up[?]'. That was possible, Churchill conceded, 'but they wouldn't be able to do it for three years, and we must fix things up in that time'. Quite what he meant by 'fix things up' was unclear, although he added, cryptically, that the 'Americans and ourselves . . . were the only nations with principles'.[111]

Later that same day, Brooke encountered the Prime Minister in a state of fevered excitement:

I was completely shattered by the PM's outlook! He had seen the reports of the American results of the new TA secret explosive experiments which had just been carried out in the States. He had absorbed all the minor American exaggerations, and as a result was completely carried away! It was now no longer necessary for the Russians to come into the Japanese war, the new explosive alone was sufficient to settle the matter. Furthermore we now had something in our hands which would redress the balance with the Russians! The secret of this explosive, and the power to use it, would completely alter the diplomatic equilibrium which was adrift since the defeat of Germany! Now we had a new value which redressed our position (pushing his chin out and scowling), now we could say if you insist on doing this or that, well we can just blot out Moscow, then Stalingrad, then Kiev, then Kuibyshev, Karhov . . . Sebastopol etc, etc. And now where are the Russians!!! . . . I *shudder* to feel that he is allowing the half baked results of one experiment to warp the whole of his diplomatic perspective!

Reviewing his diary in later years, Brooke accepted that

Winston's appreciation of [the Bomb's] value in the future international balance of power was certainly more accurate than mine. But what was worrying me was that with his usual enthusiasm for anything new, he was letting himself be carried away . . . He was already seeing himself capable of eliminating all the Russian centres of industry and population without taking into account any of the connected problems, such as the delivery of the bomb, production of the bombs, possibility of Russians also possessing such bombs etc. He had at once painted a wonderful picture of himself as the sole possessor of these bombs and capable of dumping them where he wished, thus all-powerful and capable of dictating to Stalin![112]

In truth, the dictating – the attempt to fix thing up – began at Potsdam. The Second World War was almost done. The Cold War beckoned.

PART II
COLD WAR

CHAPTER 8
HEAVY METAL, IRON CURTAIN

On 18 July, the second day of the Potsdam conference, Churchill lunched alone with Truman. The President spoke of his desire to tell Stalin about the Bomb. The Interim committee had recommended an approach and now that Trinity confirmed the Bomb as a real as opposed to theoretical weapon, Truman wondered what Churchill thought. Twenty-four hours earlier, when Stimson told him of the birth of the "babies", Churchill remained, as he had been throughout the war, 'strongly inclined against any disclosure'. Now, in the presence of a President from whom he was hoping to secure financial help to overcome Britain's crippling war debt, and mindful of Lindemann's pre-conference advice that it might be politic to concede the point if the Americans pressed it strongly, he shifted his ground. If Stalin was to be told, 'it might well be better to hang it on the experiment, which was a new fact on which he and we had only just had knowledge'. In this way, the Anglo-Americans 'would have good answer to any question, "why did you not tell us this before?"'. Truman, he felt, 'seemed impressed . . . and will consider it'.[1] Churchill's support for disclosure had been negatively-framed; he went along with the idea, not because he felt it had any great merit but because he did not wish to argue with Truman. Then, on 22 July, he read the Groves report. The following day, Admiral Sir Andrew Cunningham, the First Sea Lord, found the Prime Minister 'most optimistic and placing great faith in the new bomb' and beginning to think 'it a good thing that the Russians should know about it' insofar as it 'may make them a little more humble'.[2]

The Terminal plenary session on 24 July was a bruising encounter in which Churchill rounded on Stalin over Soviet behaviour towards the countries of the Balkans and Eastern Europe. 'An iron fence has come down around them', he said. 'Fairy tales!', Stalin retorted.[3] As the meeting broke up, Truman sidled up to Stalin. Churchill, observing from a few yards away, recalled the encounter in his war memoirs.

> I knew what the President was going to do. What was vital to measure was its effect on Stalin. I can see it all as if it were yesterday. He seemed to be delighted. A new bomb! Of extraordinary power! Probably decisive on the whole Japanese war! What a bit of luck! This was my impression at the moment, and I was sure that he had no idea of the significance of what he was being told. Evidently in his immense toils and stresses the atomic bomb had played no part. If he had the slightest idea of the revolution in world affairs which was in progress his reactions would have been obvious . . . But his face remained gay and genial . . . As we were waiting for our cars I found myself near Truman. 'How did it go?' I asked. 'He never asked a

question,' he replied. I was certain therefore that at that date Stalin had no special knowledge of the vast process of research upon which the United States and Britain had been engaged for so long . . . .[4]

Truman's odd manoeuvre was hardly the serious and open-handed approach that advocates of international control – the likes of Bohr, Anderson, Conant and Bush – had envisaged. Although the President was convinced that Stalin 'knew no more about it than the man in the moon' we now know that the Soviet leader's poker-faced performance was due to substantial atomic foreknowledge courtesy of informants within the Manhattan Project, including Klaus Fuchs of the British mission.[5] Apprised by intelligence sources of the existence and import of the Anglo-American effort, in 1943 the USSR's State Defence Committee had approved an atomic development programme under the direction of physicist Igor Kurchatov, but the debilitating demands of the war with Germany meant that the focus and resources available for research and development were limited. By the start of 1945, however, Moscow was receiving intelligence direct from Los Alamos, a scientific-technical coup which eliminated the need for the Soviets to pursue expensive experimentation already proven irrelevant or unsatisfactory by the Anglo-Americans, and by the time of Potsdam, Stalin, knowing a weapon was imminent, was anticipating some form of approach from his allies – he even rehearsed with Beria, whom he had put in overall charge of the bomb project, how he should react when the moment came ('pretend not to understand').[6]

It follows that the failure of Truman, and Churchill, to brief him fully about the Bomb, let alone invite him to join in a Big Three partnership devoted to the international control of atomic energy, probably convinced Stalin of their malign intentions. And that being so, Robert Dallek may be right in pinpointing 24 July 1945 as a strong contender for 'the beginning of the Cold War'. On the Soviet side, fears of American intentions and military power heightened. On the US and UK side, inflexible Soviet diplomacy on many of the issues before the conference, from Germany and reparations to self-determination in Eastern Europe, helped crystallize negative perceptions and, in consequence, diminished interest in international control.[7]

As for Churchill, from 22 July onwards he had in mind a dual use (or dual hope) for the Bomb. In addition to bringing the war with Japan to a swift conclusion, he saw it serving as a demonstration of American military might which – as a corollary – would strengthen the US and UK diplomatic hand in the confrontation with the USSR over the settlement of Europe. He had, as we have seen, been thinking in terms of a showdown with Stalin for some time. At Potsdam, post-Trinity and armed with the Groves report, he was once again in a showdown frame of mind, only now he believed that he and Truman possessed a potentially winning diplomatic hand. The tenor of his comments to Moran, Brooke and others show that finally he understood the awesomeness of atomic power and confirm too how eager he was to integrate the Bomb into his Soviet policy. And yet, ironically, he was to be denied the opportunity to play that hand as a consequence of British voters exercising the democratic right which he so wanted the Poles and other peoples in the Soviet-occupied territories to enjoy.

*

On 25 July, the day that Truman issued the atomic bombing order, the Potsdam conference went into recess and Churchill flew home for the announcement of the result of the British General Election. Before departing, he approved the final wording of the Potsdam proclamation in which, for the first time, the Japanese were given an indication as to what unconditional surrender actually involved. The impetus for a statement came from Stimson, 'a deeply moral man faced with terrible and difficult choices', and like-minded supporters in Washington, but to the extent that the Prime Minister's interest in a diplomatic solution during the early phase of the conference encouraged the US War Secretary, Churchill, despite his subsequent conversion to atomic diplomacy, may be considered one of the proclamation's originators.[8] An initial draft, prepared by Stimson and deemed 'sound' by the President, stated that after the war Japan would be permitted 'a constitutional monarchy under the present dynasty' as long as militarism and aggression were renounced. This early effort also proposed that the USSR, still officially neutral in the war in the Far East, should join the US, UK and China in issuing the proclamation. At this point, Byrnes got hold of the draft and began editing out almost every hint of compromise. The US Secretary was by no means the only member of the American delegation to take a hawkish view but he was the most committed believer in the Bomb's value not just as a means of ending the war quickly but as an instrument of diplomacy vis-à-vis the USSR: as he remarked to physicist Leo Szilard prior to Potsdam, 'our possessing and demonstrating the bomb would make the Russians more manageable in Europe'.[9]

Thanks to the success of Trinity, by mid-July America was in possession. But without a combat target, there could be no demonstration, hence timing was everything for Byrnes. The Japanese could surrender whenever they wanted, as long as it was *after* the atomic bombs had been used. Beyond this, Byrnes was concerned that diehard militarists in Tokyo would connect any softening of surrender terms to the recent Okinawa blood-bath – in taking the island-redoubt the US Navy lost 4,907 men killed, the army 4,675, the Marines 2,928, with some 36,000 troops wounded ashore – and thus conclude that US resolve was weakening, that Washington could be pressed to make more concessions, and that far from ending the war, a retreat from unconditional surrender might prolong it. Once the Bomb was dropped, however, Byrnes expected Japan to capitulate and this in turn would mean that 'Russia will not get in so much on the kill'. The final version of the proclamation, therefore, made no explicit reference to the position of the Emperor. Nor, thanks to Byrnes, was the USSR any longer an issuing power. That Churchill did not register any dissent to the wording confirms both his abandonment of his earlier commitment to a diplomatic solution and his embracing of the Bomb as a winning weapon.[10]

'The time has come for Japan to decide whether she will continue to be controlled by those self-willed militaristic advisers whose unintelligent calculations have brought the Empire of Japan to the threshold of annihilation, or whether she will follow the path of reason', ran the proclamation as issued on 26 July. 'We call upon the government of

Japan to proclaim now the unconditional surrender of all Japanese armed forces ... The alternative for Japan is prompt and utter destruction.'[11] The document 'was not unreasonable', Paul Ham notes. Unconditional surrender, as defined, was aimed at the armed forces rather than the country at large: the Japanese would not be enslaved as a race or destroyed as a nation. But what did this portend for Hirohito as titular head of the armed forces? Was he to be safe or would he go down with his commanders? Moreover, with the shattering US strategic bombing campaign in the process of razing 60 Japanese cities to the ground, it is to be wondered why the drafters of the proclamation thought the prospect of 'prompt and utter destruction' would so alarm the Japanese as to tip them into accepting unconditional surrender.[12] Truman, in the privacy of his diary, seemed to recognize this: he was 'sure' they would not capitulate, 'but we will have given them the chance'.[13]

Today, seventy years on, historians continue to debate (and many to doubt) whether an explicit assurance about the Emperor would have made any difference in view of the determination of a majority of the Supreme Council for the Direction of the War to fight to the bitter end.[14] On 28 July, the Japanese Prime Minister, Kantaro Suzuki, told a news conference that his government 'does not find any important value in it [the proclamation], and there is no other recourse but to ignore it entirely and resolutely fight for the successful conclusion of this war'.[15] The Soviets, meanwhile, having assumed that they would be co-signatories to any warning, were aggrieved at being outmanoeuvred by the Americans (and by extension the British) who, it seemed, had appropriated the right to preside over the Japanese end-game without Soviet assistance. According to Nikita Khrushchev's later testimony, Stalin began to worry that the Far Eastern concessions promised at Yalta might not materialize. The Soviet leader had 'doubts as to whether the Americans would keep their word ... What if the Japanese had surrendered before we entered the war against them? ... [They might say] since you didn't participate, we are not obliged to give you anything.' Accordingly, the Soviet High Command's preparations for war accelerated.[16]

The recess at Potsdam was due to last forty-eight hours. Truman and Stalin were both sure that Churchill would be back. So was Churchill. But by 1.00 pm on 26 July it was obvious that the Conservatives had been routed and that Attlee, not Churchill, would be returning to Germany. 'We lunched in Stygian gloom', Mary Churchill remembered. 'Papa struggled to accept this terrible blow – this unforeseen landslide.'[17] That evening, Churchill drove to Buckingham Palace to tender his resignation. 'It is a strange feeling, all power gone', he confided to Moran. 'I had made all my plans ... It is no use, Charles, pretending I'm not hard hit.'[18] At Potsdam, the Soviets were flabbergasted. Stalin had predicted a Tory majority of eighty seats, while years later Molotov was still shaking his head in disbelief. '[T]o this day I cannot understand how he lost the election in 1945! ... I need to know English life better.'[19] Molotov was unfamiliar with the way that free elections functioned having never experienced one. Churchill, in contrast, knew the rules. 'They are perfectly entitled to vote as they please', he said of the electorate. 'This is democracy. This is what we've been fighting for.'[20] Truman, meanwhile, wrote to Churchill wishing him 'the happiest possible existence from now to the last call'. He added, with obvious sincerity, 'we shall always remember that you held the barbarians until we could prepare.'[21]

The final few days of the resumed conference were devoid of any atomic-themed drama, the key decisions, along with the issuance of the proclamation, having occurred in the first phase. Now that he was Prime Minister, Attlee was given a detailed briefing on Tube Alloys and then conferred with Truman who told him that 'Uncle Joe had not cross-examined him at all' about the A-bomb.[22] On the evening of 27 July, the BBC carried a statement by Churchill in which he thanked the British people for their 'unflinching, unswerving support' over the previous five years. His only 'regret' was that 'I have not been permitted to finish the work against Japan', but even here, 'all plans and preparations have been made, and the results may come much quicker than we have hitherto been entitled to expect'.[23] He knew whereof he spoke.

On 2 August, with the Potsdam conference ended, President Truman travelled from Berlin to Plymouth where the USS *Augusta* was waiting at anchor ready to take the American delegation home. First, though, he and Byrnes had a luncheon appointment with 'the limey King', George VI, aboard HMS *Renown*.[24] According to Sir Alan Lascelles, the King's Private Secretary, Byrnes was 'clever as a wagon-load of monkeys' and a tremendous 'chatterbox' who 'began discussing in front of the waiters the impending release of the atomic bomb'. The King, whom Churchill had kept fully informed about Tube Alloys, was mortified. 'I think, Mr Byrnes', he interjected, 'that we should discuss this interesting subject over our coffee.'[25] Four days later, on 6 August, a Bank Holiday Monday, people in Britain – including monarchs and waiters – who tuned-in to the BBC Home Service at 6.00 pm heard the following: 'Here is the news: President Truman has announced a tremendous achievement by allied scientists. They have produced the atomic bomb. One has already been dropped on a Japanese army base. It alone contained as much explosive power as two-thousand of our great ten-tonners. The President has also foreshadowed the enormous peace-time value of this harnessing of atomic energy.' At which point the newsreader moved on to describe a Bank Holiday of inclement weather, with sunshine interspersed with thunderstorms.[26]

The weather in Hiroshima that day had been better, Andrew Rotter tell us. To begin with.

> From a clear blue sky on a radiantly hot summer morning came a single American B-29 bomber (warily flanked by two observation planes), carrying a single bomb. The plane was called the *Enola Gay*, after its pilot's mother; the bomb bore the innocent nickname 'Little Boy'. There were no Japanese fighter planes to challenge the *Enola Gay*, no airbursts of flak in its way . . . The target of the bomb was the Aioi Bridge, which spanned the Ota River at the heart of the city. At 8.15 Hiroshima time the crew of the *Enola Gay* released the bomb. Forty-three seconds later, at an altitude of about 1,900 feet, Little Boy exploded. One plane, one city, one morning in August, one atomic bomb: simple.[27]

A city of 350,000 people in western Honshu, Hiroshima had so far been spared in the American bombing campaign. Now, as the uranium weapon disbursed the equivalent of between 16,000 and 18,000 tons of TNT, the reason became clear: the United States had wanted an unsullied target so as the better to assess the destructive power of the Bomb. Two days later, on 8 August, the USSR declared war on Japan and sent its armies pouring into Manchuria, a shattering military and psychological blow to the Japanese which wrecked the hope of a number of Emperor Hirohito's senior civilian advisers that the Soviets might be prevailed upon to play the role of peace intermediary with the Americans.

Truman was still aboard the *Augusta* on his way back from Europe when Hiroshima was hit but a pre-prepared press release was issued by the White House at 10.45 am Washington-time, 6 August, in which the President made public the news of the Bomb. 'The Japanese began the war from the air at Pearl Harbor', he observed, factually.

> They have been repaid many fold. And the end is not yet. With this bomb we have now added a new and revolutionary increase in destruction to supplement the growing power of our armed forces. In their present form these bombs are now in production and even more powerful forms are in development. It is an atomic bomb. It is a harnessing of the basic power of the universe. The force from which the sun draws its power has been loosed against those who brought war to the Far East.

He went on to warn that America was prepared 'to obliterate more rapidly and completely every productive enterprise the Japanese have above ground in any city'. If Tokyo did not accept the terms of the Potsdam proclamation there would follow 'a rain of ruin from the air, the like of which has never been seen on this earth'. Truman paid due tribute to Anglo-American cooperation from which 'many priceless helps to our victories have come ... With American and British scientists working together we entered the race of discovery against the Germans.' The United States eventually spent $2 billion (around $28 billion in today's terms) on 'the greatest scientific gamble in history', but it paid off with victory in the 'battle of the laboratories'.[28]

On 9 August, before the Japanese government could properly comprehend what had happened at Hiroshima, a plutonium bomb, Fat Man, was detonated over Nagasaki, a city of 260,000 inhabitants on the island of Kyushu, with a blast equivalent to 20,000 tons of TNT. Like Hiroshima, Nagasaki had hitherto been off-limits to American bombers. Bad weather and poor visibility saved Kokura, a sprawling military-industrial complex that was top of the target list for that day, but Nagasaki was a more than acceptable substitute. Home to the Mitsubishi Corporation, which operated shipyards, steel mills and an arms factory in the city, in the age of total war this was more than enough to make it a target of military importance.[29] Truman, now back in Washington, issued a second atomic-themed statement that same day, but referring not to Nagasaki but to Hiroshima.

> The world will note that the first atomic bomb was dropped on Hiroshima, a military base. That was because we wished in this first attack to avoid, insofar as

possible, the killing of civilians. But that attack is only a warning of things to come. If Japan does not surrender, bombs will have to be dropped on her war industries and, unfortunately, thousands of civilian lives will be lost.[30]

The time difference between Washington and Nagasaki is 14 hours, so that even as Truman spoke, expressing concern for the fate of Japanese civilians, Fat Man had already done its worst. For this reason, perhaps, and in advance of the formal announcement of the second attack, the President felt the need to add several layers of justification. Alongside the routine denunciation of Japan's attack on Pearl Harbor, he insisted that the Bomb was used 'against those who have starved and beaten and executed American prisoners of war, against those who have abandoned all pretense of obeying international laws of warfare'. The overall aim 'was to shorten the agony of war, in order to save the lives of thousands and thousands of young Americans'. This being so, atomic weapons would continue to be deployed 'until we completely destroy Japan's power to make war'. Only the unconditional surrender of Japan would halt the death and destruction. Truman also referred to the possibility of international control of atomic energy.

> The atomic bomb is too dangerous to be loose in a lawless world. That is why Great Britain, Canada, and the United States, who have the secret of its production, do not intend to reveal that secret until means have been found to control the bomb so as to protect ourselves and the rest of the world from the danger of total destruction ... It is an awful responsibility which has come to us. We thank God that it has come to us, instead of to our enemies.[31]

The tallying makes for grim consideration. At Hiroshima, the immediate death-toll has been put in the region of 60,000–70,000, but many more would die in the months ahead from burns and radiation sickness, the hidden killer that destroys the body from the inside out. According to one survey, by November 1945 the dead had nearly doubled to 130,000. Nagasaki experienced a comparable incremental increase in casualties. The postwar US Strategic Bombing Survey estimated that 35,000 people were killed by the initial blast and heat, and subsequent estimates, factoring in post-bombing deaths, put the figure at 60,000–70,000 by the end of 1945. Around 90 percent of all fatalities were non-combatants, a statistic which underscores the fact that both cities were not in any sense exclusively military targets.[32] A third atomic weapon had been primed for use – the target list, in descending order of priority, was Sapporo, Hakodate, Oyabu, Yokosuka, Osaka and Nagoya – before Truman imposed a moratorium on further bombing. Henry Wallace, the Secretary of Commerce, met the President on 10 August and made a note in his diary afterwards. 'He [Truman] said the thought of wiping out another 100,000 people was too horrible. He didn't like the idea of killing, as he said, "all those kids".'[33] On the other hand, Truman chose to continue the conventional bombing – 'to go ahead with everything we've got' in raids which caused an estimated 15,000 further fatalities in the final days of the war – which suggests that he drew a moral distinction, if only sub-consciously, between the A-bomb and ordinary explosives.[34]

Figure 8.1 Hiroshima, 6 August 1945. Universal History Archive, Universal Images Group/Getty Images.

Churchill had begun working on his own Bomb statement during his last month as Prime Minister and added the finishing touches over his first post-premiership weekend.[35] His initial inclination had been to make direct reference to his wartime agreements with Roosevelt, but Lindemann thought this 'very undesirable' since it was bound to lead to demands for publication which, if met, would be 'very embarrassing to the Americans and perhaps even to us'. The Truman administration was preparing for the moment when the Manhattan Project would come under the Congressional microscope and had already signalled its anxiety that 'this particular aspect should be handled with considerable care as very difficult political issues may be involved'. Churchill heeded Lindemann's advice, though he would later regret doing so.[36]

The statement was released on the evening of 6 August and was printed in full in the British press the following day. Churchill began by rehearsing the history of the project before rejoicing that by 'God's mercy' the USA and the UK had 'outpaced all German efforts' in the atomic field. As might be expected, he paid fulsome tribute to the Americans on to whose shoulders 'the main practical effort' involved, 'and virtually the whole of its prodigious cost', had fallen. The burden of execution, the setting up of the giant industrial plants and the perfecting of the technical processes had likewise been taken by the United States and represented 'one of the greatest triumphs of American – or indeed human – genius of which there is record'. While generously acknowledging the Canadian role as a supplier of uranium and heavy water, Churchill was at pains to stress that British science had been the progenitor of the bomb, and that even though the UK contribution to research and development was eventually dwarfed by that of the USA, the successful outcome still owed much to the United Kingdom. The 'smoothness' of Anglo-American war-time atomic cooperation was 'a happy augury', he added, an observation which must have occasioned a wry smile from Akers and other TA veterans. Turning to the war in the Pacific, Churchill said it was 'now for Japan to realize in the glare of the first atomic bomb which has smitten her what the consequence will be of an indefinite continuance of this terrible means of maintaining a rule of law in the world'. Finally, he looked to the future.

> This revelation of the secrets of nature long mercifully withheld from man should arouse the most solemn reflections in the mind and conscience of every human being capable of comprehension. We must indeed pray that these awful agencies will be made to conduce to peace among the nations and that, instead of wreaking measureless havoc upon the entire globe, they may become a perennial foundation of world prosperity.[37]

Press reaction in Britain to Churchill's statement was overwhelmingly positive: there was gratitude to him personally, to British science and to the USA for helping beat the Nazis in the race for the Bomb, but there were also expressions of apprehension – a 'range of nuclear anxieties' – as to what the unloosing of atomic energy would mean for the future of the world.[38] At a wider level, a lot of people felt morally confused or ethically challenged by the Bomb. As the Archbishop of Canterbury, Geoffrey Fisher, observed, for nearly six years Britain had 'fought for the light against spiritual darkness, that we and those who came after us might walk in the light', but in so doing, 'we had to enter the darkness ourselves, to use the weapons of darkness, to turn every endeavour of mind and body to deadly and destructive ends'. The Bomb was 'a terrible and shocking reminder that war must be an unclean business, and that none could touch it even in a righteous cause, even to defend, as we had had to defend, the sanctities of life, without defilement'.[39] For most people, however, the unconditional surrender of Japan just five days after Nagasaki vindicated the deployment of the weapons of darkness. Laurens van der Post, who was captured in Java in 1943 and held prisoner (and tortured) by the Japanese over the next two years, later maintained with 'an absolute conviction' that had the atomic bombs not been used 'the war would have dragged on, the Japanese would have fought as they had fought everywhere else to the bitter end', and under such circumstances, 'apart from many more Japanese dead, hundreds of thousands of Americans and their allies would have died as well'. This conviction was widely held and not just by POWs freed from their terrible ordeal or by soldiers who, throughout the summer of 1945, had daily contemplated what they feared would be their certain doom when the anticipated invasion of Japan was launched, but by countless numbers of ordinary people.[40]

What, though, of historical reality as distinct from popular perception? Was bomb-surrender cause-and-effect so clear cut? In the immediate aftermath of the second bombing and the Soviet declaration of war, Emperor Hirohito convened a conference of his highest-ranking military and political advisors. After listening to the case for and against surrender he intervened decisively. The time had come, he said, 'to bear the unbearable'.[41] On 10 August, the Japanese government relayed a message to Washington via the Swiss embassy in Tokyo expressing readiness to accept the Potsdam proclamation subject to one critical rider: that this action did not prejudice the prerogatives of the Emperor as a sovereign ruler.[42] The offer was repeated – apparently without official sanction – via Japanese radio and was soon common knowledge around the world. In England, there was great excitement. Strolling down Whitehall, Churchill found himself mobbed 'by a frenzied crowd' who cheered 'Churchill for ever' and 'We want Churchill'. All of which, Clementine reflected, was nice but a little late.[43]

Nor was the war quite over. In replying to Tokyo, the US government, strait-jacketed by unconditional surrender, was obliged to concoct a form of words which gave the Japanese what they asked for while appearing to remain loyal to established policy. This, it will be recalled, is precisely what Churchill had proposed to Truman early on at Potsdam. After deciphering the American démarche, the Japanese government signalled (on 14 August) its acceptance of the Potsdam proclamation.[44] Although many historians today regard the Bomb and Soviet entry as combined shocks in bringing about Japan's surrender, when Hirohito spoke to his people over the radio on 15 August he drew especial attention to the atomic dimension. The 'enemy has begun to employ a new most cruel bomb, the power of which to do damage is indeed incalculable, taking the toll of many innocent lives', he explained. 'Should we continue to fight, it would not only result in ultimate collapse and obliteration of the Japanese nation, but also it would lead to the total extinction of human civilisation.'[45]

Just over a fortnight later, on 2 September, Japanese representatives signed the Instrument of Surrender aboard the USS *Missouri* anchored in Tokyo Bay. The war in Asia and the Pacific was over but for historians the debate about the precise role of the atomic bombs in bringing about Japan's surrender was about to begin. Today, the arguments continue. In a judicious judgement representative of the middle ground in an often polarized historiographical debate, Richard Frank suggests that '[w]ithout atomic bombs, it is by no means clear that the Emperor would have intervened to provide the essential first step in the process of an organized capitulation of Japan's government and armed forces. Without an organized capitulation, it is not clear whether the final end of the war would have come in months or years.'[46] This, as it happens, is close to what Churchill thought at the time. Speaking in the House of Commons on 16 August, he said it was 'to this atomic bomb more than to any other factor that we may ascribe the sudden and speedy ending of the war against Japan'. But that was already the past. What of the future?

> The bomb brought peace, but men alone can keep that peace, and henceforward they will keep it under penalties which threaten the survival, not only of civilisation but of humanity itself. I may say that I am in entire agreement with the President that the secrets of the atomic bomb should so far as possible not be imparted at the present time to any other country in the world. This is in no design or wish for

arbitrary power, but for the common safety of the world ... So far as we know, there are at least three and perhaps four years before the concrete progress made in the United States can be overtaken. In these three years we must remould the relationships of all men, wherever they dwell, in all the nations. We must remould them in such a way that these men do not wish or dare to fall upon each other for the sake of vulgar and out-dated ambitions or for passionate differences in ideology, and that international bodies of supreme authority may give peace on earth and decree justice among men. Our pilgrimage has brought us to a sublime moment in the history of the world. From the least to the greatest, all must strive to be worthy of these supreme opportunities.[47]

All of which sounded noble and high-minded but in private at Potsdam just three weeks before he had struck a very different chord: the Bomb, he argued, should be used to strengthen the Anglo-American negotiating position in a diplomatic showdown with the Soviet Union. Here, then, in August 1945, a pattern was established that would endure for several years. In public, Churchill played the atomic statesman, speaking the words that an anxious and confused domestic (and international) audience needed to hear. Privately, he was the atomic diplomatist, convinced that the Bomb was a prize asset, the key to breaking the Soviet hold on Eastern Europe. In this, he resembled the American Secretary of State. Approaching the first meeting of the Council of Foreign Ministers, the construct established at Potsdam to handle unfinished business connected with the making of the new international order, Byrnes was described by Stimson as keen to have 'the presence of the bomb in his hip pocket ... as a great weapon to get through the thing'.[48] However, while the US Secretary is recognized as an atomic diplomatist, Churchill is rarely labelled in the same way even though, in some respects, he was an even more extreme proponent of A-bomb bargaining.[49]

Had he been re-elected and returned to Potsdam, Churchill later wrote, he would have had his 'show-down' with Stalin and accepted a 'public break' rather than be party to the Sovietization of Poland.[50] He did not vouchsafe the role he intended the Bomb to play but there is little doubt that it would have featured prominently in his diplomacy. The day after Hiroshima, he called on his old and trusted friend Lord Camrose, proprietor of *The Daily Telegraph*. 'Churchill is of the opinion that, with the manufacture of this bomb in their hands, America can dominate the world for the next five years', Camrose wrote afterwards.

If he had continued in office he is of the opinion that he could have persuaded the American Government to use this power to restrain the Russians. He would have had a show-down with Stalin and told him he had got to behave reasonably and decently in Europe, and would have gone so far as to be brusque and angry with him if needs be. If the President and his advisers had shown weakness in this policy he would have declared his position openly and feels certain that the American people would have backed the policy on the grounds that it would have been carrying out the Atlantic Charter.[51]

Which, then, was the real Churchill? The atomic statesman or the atomic diplomatist? As we will see, the persistence of his advocacy (albeit in private) of an atomic-themed showdown with the USSR over the next five years points strongly to the latter appellation. That he would go on in the mid-1950s to become a disciple of détente, a true believer in peaceful co-existence between the two nuclear-armed Cold War blocs, is not in question. But his transformation is rendered all the more striking – and worthy of serious study and explanation – when viewed against his earlier career as a proto-atomic warrior.

If the Bomb's military and diplomatic potentialities were recognized by Churchill, they were increasingly obvious to Stalin as well. The Soviet leader did a good job at Potsdam in feigning indifference when Truman told him about the Trinity shot, but as soon as he returned to his villa that evening (24 July) he consulted with Kurchatov and then held a meeting with Foreign Minister Molotov and Andrei Gromyko, the Ambassador to Washington. Hitherto slow – like Churchill – to appreciate the role that the Bomb might play in international relations, Stalin had been jolted by Truman's revelation.[52] 'Our Allies have told us that the USA has a new weapon', he observed. Both the Americans and British 'are hoping we won't be able to develop the Bomb ourselves for some time ... [and] want to force us to accept their plans. Well that's not going to happen'. He then cursed the Anglo-Americans in what Gromkyo called 'ripe language'.[53]

Two weeks later, Stalin learned of the destruction of Hiroshima. 'War is barbaric', he reflected, 'but using the A-bomb is a super-barbarity. And there was no need to use it. Japan was already doomed!'[54] Why, then, *was* it used? To Molotov, the answer was obvious. The bombs 'were not aimed at Japan but rather at the Soviet Union. They [the Americans] said, bear in mind you don't have an atomic bomb and we do, and this is what the consequences will be like if you make the wrong move!'[55] Stalin agreed. Meeting with Beria and top scientists soon after, he told them that 'Hiroshima has shaken the whole world. The balance has been destroyed. That cannot be.' Beria was ordered to press on at top speed to accomplish 'Task Number One', to deliver a bomb as soon as possible. 'A-bomb blackmail', Stalin concluded, 'is American policy.'[56] It was certainly Churchill's policy.

Before we follow Churchill into the postwar era, it is only right that the other two members of the triumvirate be acknowledged. Both are little known today (though Anderson at least has a bomb shelter to his name). Even in 1945 their roles in the drama barely registered with the public even though they both issued statements addressing the bombing of Japan and the future of atomic energy. Rarely remarked upon, their views deserve consideration for the simple reason that, between them, Anderson and the Prof probably knew as much about the atomic bomb as anyone in Britain, Churchill included.

Anderson was first to air his opinions. The day after Hiroshima – the day that Churchill outlined to Camrose his thinking on atomic diplomacy – he spoke on the BBC Home Service. 'What must be realised is that this is no mere extension of an existing field of enquiry', he told his listeners.

A new door has for the first time been prised open. What lies on the other side remains to be seen. The possibilities for good or ill are infinite. There may on the one hand be a veritable treasure-house awaiting fruitful development in the interests of mankind. There might, on the other hand, be only the realisation of a maniac dream of death, destruction and desolation. God grant that it may not prove to be so.

These are problems calling for statesmanship of the highest order. The establishment of any organ for the maintenance of world peace and security would obviously be sheer mockery if means could not be found of guaranteeing the effective international control of war of such potency. There could be no higher task for the statesmen of the United Nations gathered round the Conference table.[57]

His great friend Niels Bohr, who made the same points in an article in the *Times* a few days later, no doubt approved.[58] Moreover, Anderson's views were echoed in a statement signed – but not made public – by most of the British scientists working at Los Alamos. Banning the Bomb was useless, they maintained. International control was the 'only hope'.[59]

On 21 August, Attlee announced that Anderson was to chair a committee of experts to help the Labour government frame an atomic energy policy.[60] The appointment, a tribute to Anderson's high ability and political independence, left a confirmed Bohrite at – or close to – the centre of atomic decision-making in Whitehall. Not that Attlee (unlike Churchill) needed much persuading that international control was the way forward: unless something was done about the Bomb, and done quickly, Attlee feared he would have to 'direct all our people to live like troglodytes underground as being the only hope of survival, and that by no means certain'.[61] To Churchill's dismay, the Prof was not on the committee. It was 'important', Anderson explained to him, 'that someone who knows the subject thoroughly should be available, free and untrammelled, to advise you and other opposition leaders on any proposals that may be made'. Since Anderson and Lindemann were 'the only two people who could play that part', it would be unfortunate if both of them were 'to some extent sterilised' by membership of a confidential government committee.[62]

Neglected and probably peeved, the Prof returned to Oxford. Never greatly given to expressing himself in public, his first statement of note on atomic issues came two months after the bombing of Japan. His message, however, was stark. '[W]e are only at the beginning of the story and there is very little doubt that enormous improvements in the power and efficiency of the bombs to be used will be made', he told the House of Lords. 'If we enter upon an arms race with the nuclear weapons culminating in a world war, the end of civilization as we know it is almost inevitable. I do not think that anyone will disagree with the thesis that the most important thing in the world to-day is to find some way of preventing such a race'. The obvious answer was international control, but Lindemann took issue with those who – like Anderson, Bohr, and many others – believed that the United Nations, or any other world authority, could simply take over and administer the atom. There was too much wishful thinking involved. Until such time as an appropriate international agency had been established, he felt that those in possession of the secret of the Bomb should continue to hold it close. That some system must eventually be developed, though, he was quite certain.

> Perhaps the threat of this new weapon may in the end bring home to the various nations the overriding need of finding means, at no matter what cost and sacrifice, of reaching agreement without resort to force. We must pray that this will be achieved in time, for if it is not then the end of civilized life on this planet is at hand.[63]

Going into the peacetime period, then, two out of the three members of the triumvirate favoured international control of atomic energy, but whereas Anderson, steeped in Bohrism, veered towards the idealistic, Lindemann was more pragmatic, even cynical. As for the third member of the group, he remained very much the atomic monopolist. And the atomic diplomatist.

At the start of September, Churchill flew from London to Italy for a vacation at Lake Como. He was joined by his daughter, Sarah, and by Lord Moran, Clementine having decided to stay in England to de-mothball Chartwell. After the trauma of his election defeat, the beauty and tranquillity of the surroundings had a restorative effect. 'It has done me no end of good to come here', he wrote to his wife. But though he claimed he was 'not worrying about anything', this was not true.[64] Towards the end of September he moved on to the French Riviera where he caught up on international events by wading through back issues of English newspapers. What he read disturbed him. 'The Bolshevization of the Balkans proceeds apace and all the cabinets of Central, Eastern and Southern Europe are in Soviet control, excepting only Athens', he wrote again to Clementine. 'I regard the future as full of darkness and menace . . . Very little is known as to what is happening behind the Russian iron curtain.'[65] The one bright spot on the horizon was the Bomb and he 'thank[ed] God that the secret of the atom was in the right hands' and took comfort from the knowledge that it would take the USSR 'three years to discover and act upon the discovery'.[66] In the interim the Americans needed to make the most of their monopoly. 'Russia has altered her tune since the atomic bomb', he told Moran. 'She sees she can't just do what she likes with the world.'[67]

While Churchill looked on the Bomb as a good thing in light of the deteriorating international situation, his successor as Prime Minister continued to take a contrary view. Attlee had established a top-secret ministerial committee to handle atomic energy questions; known formally by its Cabinet Office reference GEN.75, it was referred to by its select membership as the Atom Bomb Committee. Attlee had agreed with the decision to use the Bomb against Japan but he instantly recognized its revolutionary nature. In a paper for the Atom Bomb Committee three weeks after Hiroshima, he argued that the entire concept of war must be 'banished from people's minds and from the calculations of government'. In the future, if the great powers all possessed atomic weapons, they were bound to use them in the event of a new world war and, in so doing, doom themselves and possibly the entire planet to oblivion. It had taken Attlee four weeks to pick up what Churchill had failed to see in four years: international control, not short-term monopolistic fixations, offered the best hope of lasting peace. 'The new World Order', Attlee insisted, 'must start now.'[68]

In September, the Prime Minister marshalled his thoughts in a draft letter to President Truman which, as a courtesy, he forwarded to Churchill at Como along with a request for comment. The essence of Attlee's message was that the United States should make an 'Act of Faith' and surrender its atomic knowledge to the United Nations in order to benefit all mankind and pre-empt a calamitous arms race. Maintaining Big Three cooperation was the Labour government's declared policy and the Prime Minister's views on the Bomb dovetailed with this wider objective.[69] 'I am in general agreement with the sentiments you express from feeling with you the appalling gravity of the matter', Churchill replied, but on specifics he took issue with almost everything in Attlee's letter. What, he wondered, did an 'Act of Faith' actually mean? That the Americans should give over to the United Nations not just their scientific knowledge but their technical know-how and their uranium stocks? 'I do not believe they will agree and I personally should deem them right not to and will certainly have to say so.' He went on:

The responsibility for propounding a world policy clearly rests with the USA. I imagine they have two or three years lead, and will have got still further on at that time. I am sure they will not use their advantage for wrong purposes of national aggrandisement and domination. In this short interval they and we must try to reach some kind of security based upon a solemn covenant backed by force viz the Atomic bomb. I therefore am in favour, after we and the USA have reached agreement, of a new United Nations Conference on the subject. I do not however consider we should at this stage at any rate talk about "acts of faith". This will in existing circumstances raise immediate suspicion in American breasts.

Churchill's reply also showed that he still looked on the Bomb as an important Anglo-American unifier:

Moreover we have a special relationship with them [the Americans] in this matter as defined in my agreement with President Roosevelt. This almost amounts to a military understanding between us and the mightiest power in the world. I should greatly regret if we seemed not to value this and pressed them to melt our dual agreement down into a general international arrangement consisting, I fear, of pious empty phrases and undertakings which will not be carried out ... Nothing will give foundation except the supreme resolve of all nations who possess or may possess the weapon to use it at once unitedly against any nation that uses it in war. For this purpose the greater the power of the US and GB in the next few years the better are the hopes. The US therefore should not share their knowledge and advantage except in return for a system of inspection of this and all other weapon-preparations in every country, which they are satisfied after trial is genuine.[70]

Attlee acknowledged the force of Churchill's arguments but still sent his letter to Washington substantially unaltered.[71]

The Truman administration was also struggling to set an atomic course, but eventually, on 3 October, the President announced its destination. 'The hope of civilization lies in international arrangements looking, if possible, to the renunciation of the use and development of the atomic bomb, and directing and encouraging the use of atomic energy ... toward peaceful and humanitarian ends', he told the Congress. Pending discussions with the UK and Canadian governments, the United States proposed to explore the exchange of scientific information as a first move towards such international regulation. There would, though, be no 'disclosures relating to the manufacturing processes leading to the production of the atomic bomb itself'.[72] At a news conference a few days later, Truman expanded on his thinking. While the basic science was already familiar to physicists in many countries, the knowledge and understanding of the complex technical processes involved in fabricating a weapon of mass destruction were currently the sole preserve of the United States. That was the way it would stay. If other countries wanted to 'catch up with us on that, they will have to do it on their own hook, just as we did'. Where this left Britain and Canada was unclear, though Truman still referred to both countries as 'our partners'.[73] For the moment, international control was the US government's goal, which pleased Attlee. But until such time as a fool-proof system of regulation and inspection was established, the American monopoly would remain, which pleased Churchill.[74]

In October, after several weeks of 'painting and picnics', Churchill returned to England.[75] Over the next few months he made up his mind to continue as leader of the Conservative Party and to fight the next General Election. By 1950 – the likely date of the poll – he would be seventy-five years old but he was sustained in his ambition by a keen desire to avenge his defeat at the hands of Labour. In the meantime, he delegated the daily grind of opposition to his deputy, a none-too-happy Anthony Eden, thus freeing himself to travel, set about writing his war memoirs, and pick his moments to intervene in the business of the House of Commons.[76]

As the most famous statesman in the world, Churchill was also much in demand on the international lecture circuit. Waiting for him on his arrival home was one invitation, from Westminster College in Fulton, Missouri, in the American Mid-West, which stood out from the pack insofar as it was endorsed by the President of the United States. 'This is a wonderful school in my home State', Truman wrote. 'Hope you can do it. I'll introduce you.'[77] Churchill eagerly accepted and three months later, on 9 January 1946, accompanied by Clementine, he set sail across the Atlantic. 'I have a Message to deliver to your country', he told Truman, and to 'the bewildered, baffled and breathless world'.[78] That message was not unconnected with the worrying international scene. 'Russia was grabbing one country after another', he complained to Mackenzie King. The Soviets 'should have been stood up to more than they were'.[79]

Churchill spent the better part of three months in the United States, initially in the sunshine of Miami where one local journalist, impressed by his vigour, wrote him up as an 'atomic bomb of an Englishman'.[80] He left Florida on 2 March and headed for Washington to stay at the British embassy. Two days later, he and Truman boarded a special train for the twenty-four hour journey to Jefferson City, Missouri, and thence by car the twenty miles to Fulton. There, on the afternoon of 5 March, atop a temporary podium in the gymnasium of Westminster College, he was introduced to his audience by the President as 'one of the great men of the age'. He then began to speak. The population of this small college town had been swollen by the presence of a huge press corps which, together with a live radio transmission, ensured that his words resonated (as he intended) not just throughout America but globally. His speech has since been dissected and debated by historians from every conceivable angle, although most often in terms of its role in the origins of the Cold War.[81] And yet, to the wider public today, the title that Churchill gave his address, 'The Sinews of Peace', arouses little recognition compared with its informal moniker, the "iron curtain" speech. The original title is instructive. Churchill believed he was serving up a blueprint for peace not war, be it hot or cold. In this connection, he called for a 'fraternal association of the English-speaking peoples' which would have at its core 'a special relationship between the British Commonwealth and Empire and the United States'. It was his 1943 Harvard vision recast for the postwar era. Like most people, Churchill hoped that the United Nations would help to ensure peace, in which case this special relationship would complement the UN's work. But if the UN went the way of the League of Nations, the US–UK–Commonwealth partnership would come into its own. As for the USSR, while avowing his admiration for the Soviet peoples and sympathy for their security needs, he warned that the Kremlin's expansionist policies constituted a real and present danger. This provided the backdrop to the best remembered and most quoted passage of the speech:

> From Stettin in the Baltic to Trieste in the Adriatic, an iron curtain has descended across the Continent. Behind that line lie all the capitals of the ancient states of Central and Eastern Europe. Warsaw, Berlin, Prague, Vienna, Budapest, Belgrade, Bucharest and Sofia, all these famous cities and the populations around them lie in what I must call the Soviet sphere, and all are subject in one form or another, not only to Soviet influence but to a very high and, in many cases, increasing measure of control from Moscow.

To contain further Soviet expansion, the free world needed to unite behind US leadership. But Churchill was careful to stress that armed conflict was not inevitable; he believed that the USSR wanted 'the fruits of war and the indefinite expansion of their power and doctrines', not war itself. This meant that negotiations had a role to play. Indeed he anticipated a general international settlement which would safeguard Western interests, provide the USSR with adequate security, and restore independence to the countries currently imprisoned behind the iron curtain. The military strength of the US–UK combine he envisioned – resting on the atomic bomb, the coordination of strategy and the sharing of air and naval bases around the globe – would either induce such a settlement or else bestow 'an overwhelming assurance of security' if relations with the

Soviet Union continued their downward spiral. He did not call it a formal military alliance, preferring to talk of fraternalism, but we know from the war, and from his more recent Como cable to Attlee, that his hopes lay in this direction.[82]

While Fulton is best remembered for the Iron Curtain, Churchill had important things to say about the Bomb. During the previous few months the idea of international control had gained traction both in and beyond the United States. In Washington in November 1945, Truman, Attlee and Mackenzie King issued a declaration expressing their readiness to exchange 'fundamental scientific information and the interchange of scientists and scientific literature for peaceful ends with any nation that will fully reciprocate'. However, they were not prepared to release any of the 'specialized information' currently in their keeping unless or until 'effective, reciprocal, and enforceable safeguards' had been established that would 'contribute to a constructive solution of the problem of the atomic bomb'.[83] Taking its cue from the declaration, the Council of Foreign Ministers meeting in Moscow called for the establishment of a United Nations agency to explore the viability of international control and in January 1946 the UN General Assembly duly convened an Atomic Energy Commission (UNAEC) comprising six permanent members (the USA, UK, USSR, France, China and Canada) and six other rotating members.[84] This was the backdrop against which Churchill spoke at Fulton. Based on past precedent, his first instinct may have been to condemn international control outright, but aware of the hopes of people around the world that UN regulation was the way to prevent a doom-laden arms race, he confined himself to warning against premature action:

It would . . . be wrong and imprudent to entrust the secret knowledge or experience of the atomic bomb, which the United States, Great Britain, and Canada now share, to the world organization, while it is still in its infancy. It would be criminal madness to cast it adrift in this still agitated and un-united world. No one in any country has slept less well in their beds because this knowledge and the method and the raw materials to apply it, are at present largely retained in American hands. I do not believe we should all have slept so soundly had the positions been reversed and if some Communist or neo-Fascist State monopolized for the time being these dread agencies . . . God has willed that this shall not be and we have at least a breathing space to set our house in order before this peril has to be encountered: and even then, if no effort is spared, we should still possess so formidable a superiority as to impose effective deterrents upon its employment, or threat of employment, by others. Ultimately, when the essential brotherhood of man is truly embodied and expressed in a world organization with all the necessary practical safeguards to make it effective, these powers would naturally be confided to that world organization.[85]

Looking back, Fulton contained several themes that would infuse Churchill's approach to the Cold War in the next few years: the seriousness of the Soviet threat to peace and security, and the need to counter it; the vital necessity from this standpoint of the closest

Figure 8.2 Churchill, Fulton, 5 March 1946. Popperfoto/Getty Images.

cooperation between Britain, the Commonwealth and the United States; the need for general Western political cohesion and military strength, the latter to include atomic weapons over which the USA (ideally in harness with the UK) should exercise a monopoly for as long as possible; and yet, at the same time, the hope for some kind of negotiated settlement with the USSR and the establishment of a basis for lasting peace.

As we know, Churchill's anti-communism ran deep. But he was pragmatic enough to recognize the value of compromise with Moscow when it stood to benefit Britain's strategic interests (1941 immediately springs to mind). Nevertheless, it is hard to look on the negotiations he alluded to at Fulton as anything other than a forum within which the Anglo-Americans, with the Bomb to bolster their diplomacy, could dictate terms to the USSR.[86] By the same token, it is hard to see why Moscow would respond constructively. Nor did it. *Pravda* was soon condemning Churchill's 'slanders' and reminding its readers that this was the same Churchill who, three decades earlier, had been 'the sharpshooter and standard bearer of the anti-Soviet campaign'. Now he was at it again, promoting 'an Anglo-American military alliance'.[87] In an interview with the same publication, Stalin denounced Churchill as a 'firebrand of war' and took exception to the notion of a US–UK–Commonwealth special relationship. Churchill, he sniped, was aping 'Hitler and his friends' by promoting the 'racial theory' that 'only nations speaking the English language are fully valuable nations'.[88]

In conceiving 'The Sinews of Peace', Churchill had hoped to snap the United States out of what he saw as its postwar complacency about international affairs and alert the American people to the way in which the Soviet menace had replaced the fascist threat. More than this, he wanted the US government to assume the leadership of the free world in responding to the danger. However, based on initial American reactions, it was by no means clear that his speech had achieved the desired result. More praised than commonly allowed, there was still substantial and sharp criticism. Typical of the harsher strain was *The Nation*, which editorialized that a bellicose Churchill had added 'a sizeable measure of poison to the already deteriorating relations between Russia and the Western powers', and Eleanor Roosevelt who accused him of wanting to wreck the United Nations and replace it with a transatlantic military alliance. Influential columnist Walter Lippmann, writing in the *Washington Post*, bridled at the idea of the United States in effect buttressing Britain's rickety imperial position in the world under the guise of an anti-Soviet alliance or a crusade for freedom. The 'line of British imperial interest and the line of American vital interest are not to be regarded as identical'. Similar views were aired in the US Congress.[89] Shown a copy of the speech in advance, Truman had pronounced it 'admirable' but predicted it would 'make a stir'. Yet he was still taken aback by the scale of the negativity and in an act of political self-preservation he publicly denied having had any foreknowledge of what Churchill proposed to say.[90]

There had in fact been a decided hardening of US administration attitudes towards the Soviet Union over the previous few months, a growing desire to challenge Moscow over its expansionist designs not just in Europe but the Near East. A fortnight before Churchill spoke, diplomat George Kennan, based in the US embassy in Moscow, sent the State Department his famous Long Telegram which set in motion the process that would lead in quick time to the United States embracing "containment" as its Cold War strategy. 'Impervious to the logic of reason', Kennan argued, the USSR 'is highly sensitive to the logic of force' and 'can easily withdraw – and usually does – when strong resistance is encountered at any point'.[91] Truman himself privately condemned Soviet actions in Poland as a 'high-handed outrage', confessed to being 'tired babying the Soviets', and maintained that unless the USSR was 'faced with an iron fist and strong language another war is in the making'.[92] But in harbouring these views, the President and his top advisors were several laps ahead of wider American opinion. There was, in sum, a lag in threat-perception; the US public was uninterested or apathetic, the administration anxious and attentive. Churchill's speech was, for Truman, a trial balloon to test the popular reaction to a toughening of official US policy, albeit one that was popped before it gained any great height.[93]

In Britain, too, the speech received mixed reviews. The *Times* was critical of Churchill's implication that the East–West ideological contest might have to be settled by force of arms, but the *Manchester Guardian* preferred to focus on his hopes for an eventual rapprochement with Moscow.[94] At Westminster, ninety-three Labour MPs tabled a motion of censure against the leader of the opposition for promoting a 'sectional alliance' injurious to good relations between America, Britain and the USSR. Significantly, though, when the Prime Minister was asked to repudiate the speech, he declined to do so. Attlee still hoped that East–West differences could be mediated peaceably, but both he and his government, if not yet the rank-and-file of the Parliamentary Labour Party, were becoming pessimistic about the prospects for long-term cooperation with Stalin, especially over Germany.[95] The Conservative Party had also been disquieted by Fulton. As shadow Foreign Secretary, Eden was incensed by the lack of consultation about a speech which, in its 'polemics' against the Soviet Union, stood in marked contrast to his own ameliorative approach to East–West differences. He even expressed the wish that Churchill would relinquish the Tory leadership if he was intending to embark on 'an anti-Russian crusade, independent of us'.[96]

But Churchill was going nowhere. As he put it to his old crony Brendan Bracken, he was 'determined to lead the Tory Party until he becomes Prime Minister on earth or Minister of Defence in Heaven!'[97]

CHAPTER 9
WARMONGERING AND PEACEMONGERING

Following Fulton, Churchill's public statements on East–West relations initially struck a balance between denunciations of the 'Sovietising' of half of Europe and expressions of hope that 'friendly cooperation with the Soviet Government and the Russian people' was still possible.[1] By the summer, however, the balance had given way to a more persistent and strident anti-Sovietism. 'He has what I consider very wrong ideas', Duff Cooper, the British Ambassador to France, wrote after talking to him in July. 'He is absorbed by the Russian menace and is all for helping the Germans to recover, with a view to making use of them against the Russians.'[2]

When Parliament returned in the autumn, senior figures in the Conservative Party worried that their chief's uncompromising approach was so at odds with the popular mood in Britain as to be politically damaging. Most people continued to hope that statesmen on all sides, their minds focused by the horrors of two world wars in little more than a generation, would never allow their differences to degenerate to the point where another global holocaust threatened. Nor was there any prospect of Churchill and his anti-Sovietism voluntarily disappearing from the political scene, however much Eden, his eyes fixed on the party leadership, might 'wish the old man would go'.[3] All of which left Rab Butler – who, together with Eden, was doing his best to hold a demoralized Tory opposition together at Westminster – 'dreading' what Churchill, 'bursting with vigour and vengeance', would say in the Foreign Affairs Debate that October. Butler was particularly worried lest he 'trot out the Bolshevik bogey . . . and do much harm' by giving the impression that the Conservatives were hopeless ideologues, merchants of doom and even war-mongers at a time when Labour Foreign Secretary Ernest Bevin was striving manfully to compose differences with the USSR.[4]

These qualms were not misplaced. In the debate, Churchill harked back to Fulton and his view that the Soviet Union did not want war, only the fruits of war. Six months on, he was no longer so sure. Without vouchsafing his source (one historian suggests he was possibly being fed information from the Chiefs of Staff or officials in the Ministry of Defence[5]), he claimed that some 200 battle-ready Soviet divisions were positioned on or behind the iron curtain yet the Labour government seemed more interested in promoting voter-pleasing social initiatives at home than in maintaining the country's defences against the threat from the East.[6] Predictably, the speech did little to harmonise the international mood music with Stalin denouncing Churchill as a rampant militarist. On the other hand, by admitting publicly to having sixty divisions in place, Stalin went some way towards vindicating Churchill's warning; even sixty divisions, the Tory leader calculated, would 'greatly exceed' the combined British and American forces in Europe.[7]

Atomic weapons also featured prominently in Churchill's thinking about the Soviet danger. 'It is clear to me that only two reasons prevent the westward movement of the Russian armies', he wrote to Attlee prior to the debate. 'The first is their virtue and self-restraint. The second, the possession by the United States of the Atomic Bomb.'[8] Never mind that the United States did not yet have the numbers of weapons or the delivery capacity to do serious damage to the USSR, for Churchill it was the *idea* of the Bomb that would keep the peace.[9] The Soviets, he insisted, 'were realists to the extreme'. They would soon work out the new constellation of power. The USA had the Bomb. The USSR did not, for now. That was enough. Deterrence through symbols. The Red Army 'could march to the Atlantic in a few weeks, practically unopposed', he told Moran. 'Only the atomic bomb keeps the Russians back.'[10]

The Bomb's offensive potential excited Churchill as much as its defensive properties. Indeed the four years following on from Fulton constitute the nuclear showdown phase of his Cold War career, the period when he held to the view that the United States should use its atomic muscle to compel the Soviet Union to accept a European settlement based on democratic values. He knew that the US monopoly could not last and that the time-frame for dictating to Stalin – for exercising atomic diplomacy – was limited. 'You think there will be another war?' Moran probed him in August 1946 at a point when the USSR was menacing Turkey. 'Yes', he replied. 'You mean in ten years' time?' Moran asked. 'Sooner. Seven or eight years.' Churchill then spoke of pre-emption. 'We ought not to wait until Russia is ready. I believe it will be eight years before she has these bombs . . . America knows that fifty-two per cent of Russia's motor industry is in Moscow and could be wiped out by a single bomb. It might mean wiping out three million people, but they [the Soviet leadership] would think nothing of that.'[11]

For some historians, the callousness of these views is reprehensible, 'an astonishing confession of acquiescence in the possibility of a nuclear war that would indiscriminately kill millions of civilians'.[12] In Churchill's defence, it could be argued that he was taking advantage of Moran's allegiance to the Hippocratic Oath to air in confidence frustrations born of recent events and that in reality, as Roy Jenkins has argued, he was 'far from bomb-happy'.[13] The problem is that the views he expressed to his physician were not a one-off. Over the next few years he would regularly express himself in a similarly threatening manner, albeit in private for he knew how poorly his views would be received in the public domain. But he thought the thought, and often.

In the summer of 1947, Churchill met the US Republican senator Styles Bridges, who was on a visit to England. 'Churchill was very much concerned about the Russian picture', Bridges informed the FBI later, 'and stated that the only salvation for the civilization of the world would be if the President of the United States would declare Russia to be imperilling world peace and attack Russia'. Churchill believed that 'if an atomic bomb could be dropped on the Kremlin wiping it out, it would be a very easy problem to handle the balance of Russia, which would be without direction'. Against this, if nothing was done, 'Russia will attack the United States in the next two or three years when she gets the atomic bomb and civilization will be wiped out or set back many years'.[14]

That autumn, when Mackenzie King met Churchill in London, he was given a vivid insight into what a showdown entailed. When the talk got round to the USSR, King wrote in his diary, the 'gleam' in Churchill's 'eyes was like fire'. If the Soviets were unwilling to co-operate in a settlement in Europe based on democratic principles, Stalin should be told that 'the nations that have fought the last war for freedom, have had enough of this war of nerves and intimidation'. Churchill went on:

We do not intend to have this sort of thing continue indefinitely. No progress could be made and life is not worth living. We fought for liberty and are determined to maintain it. We will give you what you want and is reasonable in the matter of boundaries. We will give you ports in the North. We will meet you in regard to conditions generally. What we will not allow you to do is to destroy Western Europe; to extend your regime further there. If you do not agree to that here and now, within so many days, we will attack Moscow and your other cities and destroy them with atomic bombs from the air. We will not allow tyranny to continue.

Churchill was convinced that if the Soviets 'were told that this is what would happen, they would yield and put an end to their bluff' for he believed that they were 'hoping to increase their territories as Hitler had sought to increase his by bluff'. King's account continues:

He [Churchill] sat back and said that war can be saved if we stand up to them now. 'I can see as clearly as can be, that, if that stand is not taken within the next few weeks, within five years or a much shorter time, there would be another world war in which we shall all be finished'. His whole face and eyes were like those of a man whose whole being was filled with the belief which he had. He turned to me and said: '. . . I am telling you now what I see in the future'.[15]

It has been suggested that this was 'the zenith of Churchill's nuclear bellicosity' and that from this point onwards he 'softened his line' on the bomb.[16] In fact, as we will see, he remained an unreformed atomic diplomatist for quite some time to come.

Given Churchill's view of the Bomb's value to the West, the last thing he wanted to see happen was for the US monopoly to be subsumed in an international control mechanism. Yet, to his consternation, throughout 1946 the Truman administration, with the backing of the British and Canadian governments, continued to search for ways to internationalize and pacify the atom. On 17 March, less than a fortnight after Churchill had urged the United States at Fulton to think carefully before giving up its secrets to any international agency, the US Secretary of State, James Byrnes, received a report prepared by Dean Acheson, his deputy, and David E. Lilienthal, Chairman of the Tennessee Valley Authority, who themselves had taken advice from a number of top scientists including Oppenheimer. The report argued that while atomic developments could not be reversed, they could be channelled towards constructive ends. As their centre-piece proposal, Acheson and

Lilienthal wished to see established an Atomic Development Authority (ADA) to conduct a global survey of fissile materials and thereafter supervise both their mining and the purposes (peaceful not violent) towards which they were put. In eschewing intrusive inspections of national territory and plant, and in rejecting sanctions for rule-breaking, the report presupposed considerable Soviet–American trust and cooperation, an approach that won Bohr's warm approval. No timetable was advanced for the dismantling of the extant US atomic arsenal but this was nevertheless the crowning objective of the Acheson–Lilienthal plan.[17] A few days later, Byrnes authorized the report's publication but in doing so he stressed that it represented a 'starting point for . . . informed public discussion' and not an administration wish-list.[18]

The Acheson–Lilienthal proposals contrasted sharply with Churchill's outlook insofar as they would surrender America's great atomic advantage while affording the Soviets ample scope to evade ADA rules and secretly build an A-bomb arsenal of their own. The extent of Churchill's dissatisfaction may be gauged by the countervailing delight he exhibited on learning (also in March 1946) that Truman had appointed a half-deaf, six-foot-five-inch, septuagenarian Wall Street tycoon, Bernard M. Baruch, to be the USA's representative on the newly-established UN Atomic Energy Commission. Baruch was one of Churchill's oldest friends and there was 'no man in whose hands I would rather see these awful problems placed', he declared. 'All God's children may sleep comfortably in their beds for the next few years' knowing that Bernie Baruch was in charge of the atom's destiny.[19] Others were much less enamoured of the President's choice, among them the Acheson–Lilienthal group to whom it was immediately apparent that their proposals, which hinged on frank, open and constructive dialogue with the Soviets, were unlikely to find favour with an anti-communist ideologue like Baruch. 'We're lost', said Oppenheimer. The impeccably liberal Lilienthal just felt 'sick'.[20]

By June, Baruch had a plan in place. While broadly endorsing the Acheson-Lilienthal proposal for a supranational development authority, it being easier to control raw materials than information, Baruch refused to invest in such a doubtful commodity as Soviet honesty and pressed for full and unfettered UN inspection of all national nuclear facilities.[21] The Baruch plan also made the production or possession of atomic weapons an international crime calling for 'swift and sure punishment', a tenet which implied UN police action against violators. Nor would the five permanent members of the Security Council be allowed to retain their power of veto when it came to deciding on sanctions against nations engaging in prohibited activities. Finally, when the ADA and the inspection and policing regime were fully operational – and only then – would the United States consider dismantling its atomic arsenal.[22] In sum, there was absolutely nothing in the Baruch plan to recommend it to a Soviet government hyper-sensitive about foreign interference in its internal affairs and secretly determined to acquire its own atomic arms as soon possible.[23] The trick from Baruch's standpoint was to promote his proposals to the American public and world opinion generally as a sincere attempt to prevent an atomic arms race while ensuring that the odium for the failure of the ADA attached to the Soviets when, as was to be expected, they torpedoed the initiative. At that point the United States could legitimately proceed with building more and more weapons. Asked by a rather idealistic associate what would happen if his plan failed to get off the ground, Baruch seemed unconcerned. 'Anyway', he said, 'we've got the bomb!'[24]

When the Baruch plan was unveiled at the UNAEC's first meeting in the Empire State Building in New York on 14 June 1946 it triggered the anticipated Soviet reaction with *Pravda* condemning America's 'atom diplomacy', especially the threat of what Baruch called 'condign punishment' of ADA infractions by a self-appointed UN/US police force. The plan, Moscow further argued, would perpetuate the American monopoly while denying other nations the chance to enhance their security with atomic weapons.[25] By the end of the month, the Soviet AEC delegate, Andrei Gromyko, had tabled a counter-plan which called for a UN convention to ban the production, stockpiling and use of atomic weapons, ensure early destruction of all existing (that is to say American) A-bombs, allow for the full sharing of nuclear secrets with a view to peaceful development, and defer consideration of issues of inspection and verification to a later date.[26]

In its way, this Gromyko plan was also posturing. The Soviet A-bomb programme was more advanced than the United States appreciated: the extraction and refining of uranium had begun in January 1946 and by the end of the year the first Soviet experimental reactor would go critical; eighteen months later and a full-scale reactor would be up and running; and in February 1949 the first batch of weapons-grade plutonium would be on the stocks. The Soviet government also attached priority to assembling a long-range heavy bomber force and to developing a system of interlocking strategic air defences. For Stalin, the A-bomb was a must-have status symbol. In public he downplayed its importance as a weapon of war, and this may have been his privately-held view, too, at least in the first years of the Cold War, but what he found intolerable, and an affront to the USSR's great power status, was the American monopoly.[27] As Gerard DeGroot concludes, the Baruch plan, insofar as it maintained that monopoly, was guaranteed a reception in Moscow 'as cold as a Siberian wind'.[28]

Over the next six months there was much sterile debate at the United Nations while, at Bikini Atoll in the Pacific, the United States conducted a series of highly-publicized atomic weapons tests, codenamed Crossroads. Finally, on 30 December, the Baruch plan was put to the vote in the UNAEC. Unanimity was required if it was to have a future. Ten of the twelve members voted affirmatively. The Soviet Union and Poland, citing the inconsistency of American advocacy of atomic restraint at the UN while testing weapons of mass destruction in the Pacific, abstained.[29] And that was that. Five days later Baruch resigned amidst 'the fanfare reserved for victors, heroes, and those statesmen who protect the national interest'.[30] He did so 'thoroughly convinced' of the need for 'some system of punishment' in dealing with 'malevolence'.[31] For the Truman administration, and for most of the US press and public opinion, it was a watershed moment. Discussion of international control would continue at the United Nations but the United States was increasingly of the view that its national security hinged on the size of its atomic arsenal and not, by extension, in surrendering its monopoly to any world body.[32]

It is easy with hindsight to criticize the appointment of Baruch but even if Truman had chosen the sainted Niels Bohr instead of a 'stuffed shirt' with enough ego 'to run the world, the moon and maybe Jupiter', the result would have been no different.[33] Stalin, as Vladislav Zubok has shown, 'was ready to thwart the Baruch Plan long before it was announced'.[34] Churchill, though, was content enough with this outcome: as he later acknowledged, the Americans needed to jump through the hoop of proposing an outwardly attractive international control package in order that, when the Soviet veto came, they would have the support of public opinion for getting on with the business of bomb building.[35] Baruch, however, was not a one-man-show, he was an instrument of the Truman administration's will. 'I am of the opinion that we should not under any circumstances throw away our gun until we are sure the rest of the world can't arm against us', the President had told him. 'I think we understand each other on this subject'.[36] Baruch himself regarded the bomb as 'our "winning weapon" – a weapon which we give up only when we are sure the world will remain safe ... If we cannot be sure, we must arm to the teeth with the winning weapon.'[37] This, as we know, was Churchill's view too.

The Fulton speech was never intended to be a declaration of Cold War, only a 'signpost', as Churchill later put it, a prediction of what might – and did – come to pass.[38] During 1946 and into 1947, the USSR tightened its grip on Eastern Europe while probing for geo-political advantage in the Mediterranean, the Near East and East Asia. As it did so, the United States gradually emerged as the leader and coordinator of the free world's response. In March 1947, a year on from Fulton, came the Truman Doctrine ('it must be the policy of the United States to support free peoples who are resisting attempted subjugation by armed minorities or by outside pressures'), followed three months later by Secretary of State George C. Marshall's announcement of a far-reaching initiative for the economic recovery of Europe in order to eradicate the socio-economic conditions in which communism, as a political contagion, was believed to breed.[39] These two developments betokened in a much more definitive way than Fulton the onset of the Cold War.

The Soviet Union responded with the so-called "left-turn", a decisive shift away from even the semblance of cooperation with its former wartime allies, the adoption of a more vitriolic anti-Western propaganda line, and the promulgation of the theory of a world divided into "two camps", the capitalist and the socialist. The establishment by the USSR of the Communist Information Bureau – Cominform – in September 1947 as a coordinating vehicle for the left-turn, and the final and complete consolidation of communist dictatorships in the countries beyond the Iron Curtain, was presented by Moscow as a defensive reaction to threatening Western moves, but recent research confirms that Stalin used the Truman Doctrine and the Marshall Plan as the excuse, or justification, to implement policies long-since decided upon. The Western powers, in their turn, raised the stakes by announcing plans to create a separate West German state at the heart of a consolidated Western Union, and by early 1948 the division of the continent between capitalism and communism, democracy and totalitarianism, had hardened. From a Western standpoint this was bad enough, but was worse to come? With the Red Army apparently gaining in strength at the same time as the Western powers were running-down their military forces from their wartime highs, concern mounted that Stalin might be preparing to extend his power and influence, and with it the line of the iron curtain, further westwards.[40]

Churchill had rejoiced when the United States rejected a return to the isolationism of the inter-war years and donned the mantle of free world leadership.[41] Following the announcement of the Marshall Plan, he wrote to Truman to thank him 'from the bottom of my heart for all you are doing to save the world from famine and war'.[42] The spirit of internationalism radiating out of Washington from the time of the Truman Doctrine onwards, he later reflected, offered 'the best hope for the salvation of Christian civilisation and democracy from Communist and Russian conquest and control'.[43] He was much less happy about parallel developments in the atomic sphere. In August 1946, Truman signed the Atomic Energy Bill into law. Shepherded through Congress by the "Atomic Senator", Democrat Brien McMahon, apparently in ignorance of the Churchill–Roosevelt wartime agreements but with the tacit approval of the administration, the McMahon Act (as it was more popularly known) outlawed the sharing of American atomic secrets and technical know-how with other countries. The Act also provided for the transfer of control and management of atomic energy, including the US weapons project, from the military to a five-member civilian Atomic Energy Commission (AEC) which itself would be advised by a nine-member scientific body, the General Advisory Committee. Monitoring everything from Capitol Hill was an eighteen-member statutorily bipartisan Joint Committee on Atomic Energy (JCAE), 'one of the most powerful joint committees in congressional history'.[44]

The McMahon Act, which came into force on 1 January 1947, was a tremendous blow to the Labour government which had been banking on American help in furthering Britain's atomic ambitions.[45] From the autumn of 1945, Attlee and his atomic advisors had pursued a twin-track approach, publicly supporting international control while privately preparing for its failure. The government authorized the setting up of an Atomic Energy Research Establishment (AERE) and the building of an experimental reactor at Harwell in Berkshire alongside the creation of a production organization at Risley in Lancashire to oversee the construction of a gaseous diffusion plant and a plutonium-producing pile. Thanks to the McMahon Act, further progress on these several fronts would occur without the benefit of US advice and support. The same went for the UK atomic weapons programme when it was finally given the go-ahead in January 1947. National security and national prestige were obvious drivers but the Labour government also saw a British bomb as an expression of independence from excessive military reliance on the USA – the country, Bevin boomed, needed an A-bomb with 'the bloody Union Jack flying on top of it'.[46] The Ministry of Supply was made responsible for development via its Research Division at Woolwich and the Armament Research Establishment at Fort Halstead in Kent before – in 1949–1950 – all work on the bomb came to be concentrated in an Atomic Weapons Research Establishment (AWRE) at Aldermaston.[47] International control was never abandoned as a noble ideal, but as Bevin later lamented, in the context of the developing Cold War, all efforts in this direction tended to be 'defeated by the intransigence of Soviet Russia'.[48]

As for Churchill, while most of his long life and political career are richly chronicled (by himself or others), there is a lacuna when it comes to his immediate reaction to the McMahon Act. Of one thing, though, we may be certain: when Truman, in seeking to justify the Act, told his atomic advisors that he 'remembered distinctly Churchill's saying that the Quebec Agreement did not extend beyond the war', he remembered distinctly incorrectly.[49] Based on Churchill's later comments, it is plain that he was distressed by the Truman administration's abandonment of the principle of US–UK partnership, as well as angered by the Attlee government's failure to fight more effectively to defend Britain's atomic inheritance. In a letter to Dwight D. Eisenhower after he became President in 1953, Churchill expressed 'regret' that "Ike" had not been in power in 1946 to veto the McMahon Bill. 'If the agreement signed between me and FDR had not been shelved we should probably have been able to add a substantial reinforcement to your vast and formidable deterrent power', but as things turned out, the delay to Britain's atomic energy programme 'must ... be regarded as a severe misfortune to our common cause.'[50]

As we have seen, at the end of the war, as he prepared to speak in Parliament on the atomic bombing of Japan, Churchill had been minded to make public the details of the Quebec agreement. In the event, both Truman and Lindemann, working separately but in consonance, persuaded him to stay silent. His solicitude to Truman's anticipated difficulties with Congress was commendable but the unintended consequence was that the secrecy attaching to Hyde Park and Quebec made it easier for the US Senate, and indeed the Truman administration, to substitute an American closed-shop for the US–UK combine that Churchill had wanted.[51] Much as he later griped about Attlee caving in to the Americans, his own mute compliance in August 1945, and even more so his earlier failure to invoke the Quebec agreement to permit full consultation on the operational use of the bomb against Japan, contributed significantly to Britain's later atomic exclusion.

Leaving aside his disappointment and displeasure over the McMahon Act, Churchill continued to derive comfort from the American atomic monopoly. Moreover, as the Cold War worsened between 1947 and 1948 – Truman opined that the Fulton speech appeared 'more nearly a prophecy every day' – the gap between Churchill's private and public outlook on the Bomb narrowed.[52] Against a backdrop of communist-inspired violence in Greece, Churchill told the Commons in January 1948 that the 'best chance of preventing a war is to bring matters to a head and come to a settlement with the Soviet Government before it is too late'. With Moscow presumed to be bending might and main to get its own A-bomb, he could not conceive 'that any serious discussion which it may be necessary to have with the Soviet Government would be more likely to reach a favourable conclusion if we wait till they have got it.'[53]

The following month, Cold War tensions increased when the politically plural (if communist-biased) government of Czechoslovakia was subverted in a communist-engineered coup and the whole country slipped behind the iron curtain. Initially, Jan Masaryk, the son of the Czech state's first president and a friend of Churchill's, retained his position as Foreign Minister, the only non-communist in the new cabinet, but on 10 March his body was found on the pavement beneath an upper window of the Foreign Ministry in Prague. His death – accident, suicide or murder? – came to symbolize the extirpation of Czech liberty and shocked opinion in Western Europe. The reverberations extended across the Atlantic and helped speed up Congressional approval of start-up funding for the Marshall Plan. 'Since the close of hostilities', Truman told Congress the week after Masaryk's death, 'the Soviet Union and its agents have destroyed the independence and democratic character of a whole series of nations in Eastern and Central Europe. It is this ruthless course of action, and the clear design to extend it to the remaining free nations of Europe, that have brought about the critical situation in Europe today'. Congress agreed and within a few weeks the necessary legislation and appropriations were in place for the launch of the European Recovery Programme, the Marshall Plan in action.

Churchill had been distraught over the passing of Masaryk (a 'resolute, unflinching soul') and, with him, Czech freedom. Fearful that a similar fate awaited other countries in Western Europe unless they drew together in unity, in March he applauded Bevin's successful negotiation of the Brussels Pact, a treaty of mutual assistance between the UK, France, Belgium, Luxembourg and the Netherlands. But more of the same was needed if Churchill's wider goal of a United States of Europe (or of Western Europe at any rate) was to be realized.[54] At the same time, though approving of Truman's tough rhetoric, he was dismayed by Washington's apparent acceptance that Eastern Europe was now lost. The Truman Doctrine and Marshall Plan were manifestations of containment. They were not vehicles for the liberation of Eastern Europe and the making of a Europe-wide political settlement based on democratic values. In Churchill's view, the United States possessed the ability to go beyond containment, to achieve liberation, if only policymakers in Washington would act with boldness.

In April 1948, Churchill told the US ambassador to London, Lew Douglas, that a third world war was almost certain when, rather than if, the USSR acquired atomic weapons. He had developed a close friendship with Douglas (so much so that Bevin came to question the ambassador's political impartiality) and often spoke frankly in his company. 'He [Churchill] believes that now is the time, promptly, to tell the Soviets that if they do not retire from Berlin and abandon East Germany, withdrawing to the Polish frontier, we will raze their cities', Douglas reported to the State Department. 'It is further his view that we cannot appease, conciliate, or provoke the Soviets; that the only vocabulary they understand is the vocabulary of force; and that if, therefore, we took this position they would yield.'[55] Churchill was not to know it, but the USA had only a dozen or so viable atomic bombs (though a production drive would push the figure to fifty by the end of 1948), too few to give effect to this kind of blistering high-stakes diplomacy.[56] Then again, if what Styles Bridges told the FBI the year before is to be believed – and it certainly tallies with what Churchill was saying to others – all that was needed was a single bomb so long as it could be dropped directly on to Stalin's desk in the Kremlin.

In June 1948, the Cold War took its most hazardous turn to date with the onset of the Berlin crisis. Reacting to proposals by the USA, UK and France to further merge their occupation zones into a separate West German state, the Kremlin imposed a road, rail and canal blockade that cut off the city, rooted inside communist-controlled eastern

Germany, from the outside world.[57] Until this point, writes Sean Greenwood, the two sides in the Cold War 'had engaged largely in shadow-boxing using bluff, subversion or economic weaponry'. Now the super-heavyweights seemed poised to trade real punches. Neither wanted war, but 'each was prepared to contemplate action which skirted the risk of open conflict'.[58] Churchill took a keen interest in the crisis (nothing less than the 'soul of Germany' was at stake), was publicly supportive of the American and British governments in their refusal to be bullied or browbeaten, and applauded the eventual US–UK-led riposte, a mammoth airlift to keep the 2.4 million inhabitants of the western half of the city supplied with food, fuel and other essentials. In private, however, he feared that political leaders in Washington and London, frightened by the hot war danger of the situation, might lose their nerve if the crisis dragged on and settle for a 'Munich', a craven compromise that would cede the whole city to the Soviets. By far the better course of action, he maintained, was for the United States to take advantage of the fact that it was Stalin who had brought on the crisis in the first place and prepare the ground for a showdown.[59]

High summer found Churchill in the south of France seeking 'paintacious' places and a little peace and quiet to work on his war memoirs.[60] Berlin, however, was never far from his thoughts. 'I would have it out with them [the Soviets] now', he told Tory MP Robert Boothby who visited him in Aix-en-Provence in August. 'If we do not, war might come. I would say to them, quite politely: "The day we quit Berlin, you will have to quit Moscow." I would not think it necessary to explain why.' He thought the Americans too hesitant, bashful even, about flaunting their atomic power with the result that the Kremlin leadership could be 'absolutely certain that we shall behave decently' and forego the atomic option. 'With me around they would not be quite so sure.'[61] In a letter to Eden on 12 September, Churchill again urged 'a real showdown with the Kremlin' before the Soviet Union's A-bomb programme came to fruition, for '[o]nce that happens nothing can stop the greatest of all world catastrophes'. But he now seemed to feel that the West could afford to wait a year or so. It was doubtful that the USSR would have the Bomb before 1950 and by then the Americans 'will have a third more atomic bombs and better, and far more effective means of delivery both by airplanes and the bases they are developing'.[62]

Churchill was referring to the air bases in East Anglia which the Labour government had given over to the US Air Force shortly after the Berlin crisis flared. The bases brought the Soviet homelands within range of B-29 bombers, three groups of which (around 70 aircraft) were sent to the UK. This was no knee-jerk move on either the American or British side. Since 1946 the United States had predicated its hot war strategy on a massive air offensive against the USSR from forward bases, and those in East Anglia had already been extensively developed for use in an emergency. The Attlee government welcomed the B-29s as a high-profile expression of America's commitment to the security of Western Europe, and the following year – coinciding with the publication of George Orwell's *1984* with its vivid depiction of a Britain of the future reduced to the status of Airstrip One – the US Air Force was granted four more bases in Oxfordshire, Gloucestershire and Berkshire. What began as a temporary expedient soon assumed an air of permanence. The arrangement was still in place in February 1951 when Attlee told Parliament that it would continue for as long as the two countries considered it to be 'in the interest of their common defence'.[63] At the time of the initial deployment it was popularly assumed that the B-29s, whose flights from their home bases in Kansas and Florida were brashly publicized, were atomic-capable. There was, though, an element of bluff at work since we now know that Silverplate B-29s (those converted to carry atomic payloads) did not arrive in Britain until mid-1949 and that actual A-bomb components, including the all-important fissile core, were not stored at US bases in combat-readiness until 1952. Nevertheless, the presence of the aircraft, Silverplate or otherwise, though intended as a deterrent to Soviet adventurism, made the United Kingdom an obvious and early target for Soviet air assault if the Cold War ever heated up.[64]

Churchill ended his letter to Eden by affirming that 'while we should not surrender to Soviet aggression or quit Berlin, it may well be that we and the Americans will be much stronger this time next year' and he was 'not therefore inclined to demand an immediate showdown, although it will certainly have to be made next year'. He added, as a postscript: 'None of this is fit for public use'.[65] This was stating the obvious: first, his views would not sit well with a large section of British opinion; and second, they would be a political gift to Labour. As it was, the Attlee government's accusations of Churchillian war-mongering were on the increase. 'Mr. Churchill is a great war leader, of course he is, that's why he wants another war', Emmanuel Shinwell, the Secretary of State for War, told a Labour Party meeting in Oxford in October. 'He is a danger to peace'.[66]

The Shinwell jibe was prompted by Churchill's address to his party's annual conference at Llandudno. Best remembered for the unveiling of his three interlocking circles (America, Empire, Europe) concept of Britain's place in the world, the speech also contained his most hard-hitting attack on the Soviet Union since the end of the war and was the closest he had yet come to a public call for an atomic showdown. After warming-up his audience with critical remarks about Soviet 'aggressiveness and malignity', Churchill focused attention on the mighty atom.

> It is my belief, and I say it with deep sorrow, that at the present time the only sure foundation of peace and of the prevention of actual war rests upon strength. If it were not for the stocks of atomic bombs now in the trusteeship of the United States there would be no means of stopping the subjugation of Western Europe by Communist machinations backed by Russian armies and enforced by political police ... Of one thing I am quite sure, if the United States were to consent in reliance upon any paper agreement to destroy the stocks of atomic bombs which they have accumulated, they would be guilty of murdering human freedom and committing suicide themselves.

If, as they professed, the Soviets wished to see established a system of international control and the outlawing of all military applications of atomic energy, Churchill demanded that they first reassure the free world of their peaceful intentions. Deeds, not words, were required, specifically the granting of liberty to all the countries under Moscow's sway in Eastern Europe, an end to the oppression and exploitation of East Germany and Austria, the release of 'the million or more' German and Japanese prisoners held as 'slaves', the lifting of the Berlin blockade, a cessation of support for communist insurgents in Malaya and Indonesia, an end to meddling in the Chinese civil war to the advantage of Mao Zedong and the Chinese Communist Party, and the surrender of the Kremlin's controlling influence in the northern half of Korea. Only if Stalin fulfilled all of these conditions would it be safe for the USA to contemplate giving up to an international body its atomic monopoly, the free world's 'one vast ... , sure and overwhelming, means of security'. Changing tack, Churchill wondered aloud what would happen when rather than if the USSR got a bomb of its own. 'You can judge for yourselves what will happen then by what is happening now', he decided. 'If these things are done in the green-wood, what will be done in the dry?' With the life of the US monopoly already ebbing away, '[w]e ought to bring matters to a head and make a final settlement'. The Western powers 'will be far more likely to reach a lasting settlement, without bloodshed, if they formulate their just demands while they have the atomic power and before the Russians have got it too'.[67]

Rapturously received by the Tory faithful – and commended by Eden, whose views on the USSR were now beginning to catch up with Churchill's in terms of toughness – the speech troubled the *Times*. The idea of using the US monopoly to intimidate the USSR was 'dangerously simple', the paper editorialized, for even if it 'were true ... that it is the atomic bomb which alone prevents the victory of Communism, it is extremely unlikely that just the threat of the bomb would make Russia consent to a settlement on western terms. No great and proud nation will negotiate under duress; Britain and the United States have rightly refused to do so in the case of Berlin. It is unreasonable to suppose that Russia will willingly negotiate on the division of the world under the threat of atomic bombardment. And if she does not, is the United States to drop the bombs? Mr Churchill, it should be emphasized, did not say.' A Soviet withdrawal from Eastern Europe and an end to Moscow's campaign of subversion and pressure elsewhere in the world was infinitely desirable, 'but Mr Churchill cannot seriously imagine them happening by arrangement'.[68]

'Only the Communists and the *Times* seem to dislike your speech!', Sarah Churchill wrote to her father.[69] She was right on both counts. Alongside the criticism from Printing House Square, the *Daily Worker* proclaimed him the 'atom gangster', *Pravda* likened him to a 'bison of British reaction', and Moscow Radio called him a 'warmonger' who 'rattles the US atom bomb'.[70] The Labour government, too, found the speech unhelpfully provocative at a time of inflamed tensions over Berlin.[71] Churchill, though, was unapologetic. In Parliament on 28 October he reiterated many of the points he had made at Llandudno and cautioned that whatever military preparations Britain and its allies undertook during the next few years to improve their security must be 'quite subsidiary to the deterrent power of the atomic bomb', for it was this alone that 'prevents the rebarbarisation and enslavement of Europe by the Communist forces directed from the Kremlin'.[72]

*

Tame by comparison with what Churchill had been saying privately since July 1945, the Llandudno speech and its Commons follow-up were still at root atomic diplomacy. He remained convinced of the Bomb's power to achieve great things, not least the liberation of Eastern Europe and the roll-back of the communist tide a full four years before John Foster Dulles, Secretary of State in the Eisenhower administration, ventilated such ideas. Churchill wanted a settlement with the USSR in keeping with Western democratic precepts, an outcome he thought achievable if the United States invoked the threat of the Bomb. But what would happen – as the *Times* asked – if Stalin refused to accept the humiliation that yielding to an atomic démarche would involve? Would the United States then be committed to attack the USSR?

Clearly, much depended on Moscow's reaction to Western pressure, but given Stalin's publicly-stated views, together with what we now know of his private thinking, meek compliance was unlikely. 'Not atomic bombs, but armies decide the war', he told the Polish Communist leader, Wladyslaw Gomulka, in November 1945, and further contended that a major conflict between the capitalist and communist blocs, though inevitable according to his ideological lights, would not happen for twenty years at least.[73] He held to this position for some time. 'I do not believe the atomic bomb to be as serious a force as certain politicians are inclined to regard it', he told Alexander Werth of the *Sunday Times* in September 1946. 'Atomic bombs are intended for intimidating the weak-nerved, but they cannot decide the outcome of war.'[74] According to later testimony from Gromyko, Stalin had been undeterred by the US atomic monopoly when it came to launching the Berlin blockade.[75] As late as 1952, he was to be found telling the Italian Socialist leader Pietro Nenni that 'America has the technical potential for war, but not the human. She has the planes, the atomic weapon, but where would she find the millions of soldiers necessary to face up to war? It wouldn't be enough for America to destroy Moscow any more than it would be for us to destroy New York. Armies are needed to occupy Moscow and New York.'[76] Allowing for an element of bravado and propagandistic purpose in these statements – after all, Moscow was never going to admit to feeling intimidated – Stalin may well have questioned whether the A-bomb was a wholly revolutionary development in modern warfare. The Soviet leader would die before the H-bomb, a genuinely transformative weapon, wrought a fundamental shift in the way that the Cold War's principals thought about hot war, and we are thus left to conclude that in the face of overt US atomic threats in the late 1940s, the USSR would not have buckled.[77]

At the time, however, Churchill deplored what he held to be US atomic timidity. As Marc Trachtenberg has shown, support for a 'preventive' war against the USSR, launched while the USA retained sole possession of the Bomb, was 'surprisingly widespread' in the Congress, the military (especially the air force) and the press, but the Truman administration preferred the 'long-term, patient but firm and vigilant containment' of Soviet communism.[78] According to Truman biographer Alonzo Hamby, the deployment of B-29 bombers to Britain in 1948 was 'as close as Truman ever came to playing the nuclear card during his presidency'.[79] And even then it was a bluff. 'This was no time to be juggling an atomic bomb around', the President insisted. After Nazism and Fascism, 'World Communism . . . is our next great problem' and he hoped to 'solve it without the "blood and tears" the other two cost'. To Truman, the Bomb was a way to counterbalance the USSR's superiority in conventional arms: it was a weapon of containment.[80] Churchill, in contrast, while accepting the Bomb's great deterrent value, also saw it as an engine of liberation which, if grafted on to Western diplomacy, could be the key to freeing Eastern Europe from Stalinist tyranny. Yet, to his disappointment, the US government, far from rattling its atomic sabre, seemed content to downplay its very existence. When US Defense Secretary James Forrestal met Churchill in November 1948 he found him fearful that the US monopoly was becoming a wasting asset. He 'deprecates what he feels to be a dangerous tendency to "write down" the atomic bomb', Forrestal wrote, and worried that if the Soviet Union gained the impression that atomic power was 'simply a substantial extension in damage potential to an ordinary bomb', the A-bomb deterrent would be robbed of its credibility. Given the denuded state of Western Europe's defences, it was the Bomb alone which, to Churchill's mind, shackled the Red Army. To that end, Stalin needed to believe that, in a moment of crisis, the United States would not hesitate to unloose its atomic arsenal.[81]

In March 1949, Churchill, accompanied by his wife and youngest daughter, visited America for the first time in three years. The highlight of his trip was to be a meeting in Boston with Truman who, to Churchill's relief, had been elected to the presidency in his own right the previous November.[82] He had an additional cause for satisfaction in the rapid progress in the negotiations, inspired by the Prague coup and the Berlin crisis, on an Atlantic pact to bring the USA and Canada into a military alliance with Britain and the other West European states; by the time he arrived in America, a treaty was almost ready for signature.

During a three-week stay, the theme of many of his pronouncements was the Soviet threat which, in contrast to his last visit at the time of Fulton, played well with most of his audiences. In a speech at New York's Ritz-Carlton Hotel on 25 March, he declared that the only way to 'deal' with the communists was to have 'superior force on your side on the matter in question'. Nobody could have doubted what he meant. 'You have not only to convince the Soviet Government that you have superior force – that they are confronted by superior force – but that you are not restrained by any moral consideration if the case arose from using that force with complete material ruthlessness. And that is the greatest chance of peace . . . Then, the Communists will make a bargain.'[83] On 28 March, Churchill dined at the office of *The New York Times*. Journalist James Reston kept 'careful notes' of the conversation. If it was ever discovered 'that the Russians were really manufacturing the atom bomb with any rapidity', Churchill said, 'he would put serious pressure on them and force a showdown'. As a preliminary, he would 'send aircraft over the major cities of the Soviet Union, dropping leaflets in order to put pressure on the Soviet government to reach a general settlement'. When Reston observed that this 'seemed vaguely alarming', Churchill had a ready retort. 'You must take the occasion to let them know that if they exceed certain limits it is your intention to use the bomb without hesitation – if indeed that is your intention.[84]

From New York, Churchill travelled to Massachusetts to deliver the centre-piece speech of his trip. Briefed by the Prof before he left England, on 31 March he spoke to 14,000 people at Boston Gardens on the twinned themes of scientific and technological progress.[85] If he noticed the knot of 75 protestors outside the venue carrying placards daubed with 'We Want Peace, Churchill Wants War', they did not deter him from taking time out from his main text to once again attack the USSR. The Soviet leaders 'have their anti-God religion, and their Communist doctrine of the entire subjugation of the individual to the State, and behind this stands the largest army in the world, in the hands of a Government pursuing Imperialist expansion as no Czar or Kaiser has ever done'. The fact was that 'Europe would have been Communised like Czechoslovakia, and London under bombardment some time ago, but for the deterrent of the Atomic bomb in the hands of the United States'. The aim now should be to build on the Marshall Plan and the imminent Atlantic pact to forge even tighter Western political cohesion and military strength in order to prevail in what, for the first time in public, he termed 'the cold war'. Alongside the belligerence he offered some pacific words. 'War is not inevitable', nor was he suggesting that 'violent or precipitate action should be taken now, rather his wish was for a settlement with the Soviets from whom '[w]e seek nothing but goodwill and fair play'.[86]

Few noticed these placatory caveats. 'CHURCHILL DECLARES ATOM BOMB ALONE DETERS RUSSIA FROM WAR' ran the banner headline in *The New York Herald Tribune* the next day. British newspapers reported in similar vein.[87] Truman did not attend the Boston event: he 'ran out of coming' at the last moment, Clementine tartly observed.[88] It may be that Truman had grown nervous about sharing a public platform lest his physical proximity to Churchill be taken as support (as it was by some in March 1946) for his views. 'I am sure he must have thought about the implications of such a conjunction as is now arranged', Churchill himself mused. 'This will inevitably recall Fulton, about which I have nothing to retract. Three years have seen a melancholy confirmation of what I then said, with his approval.'[89]

The Western unity that Churchill put such store by was greatly strengthened with the formal signature in Washington on 4 April of the North Atlantic Treaty – and even more so by its evolution over the next year from a paper pact into the North Atlantic Treaty Organization (NATO).[90] Buoyed by this development, he urged Truman to seize the moment to make plain to the USSR, and publicly so, that the United States would not recoil from using the Bomb to safeguard democracy.[91] In the end, the nearest Truman came to issuing the kind of ultimatum sought by Churchill (and it really was not that near) was two days after the Atlantic pact signing ceremony. Addressing newly-elected Democratic members of Congress, he said it was his hope, and prayer, that he would never again have to take the kind of decision he took in 1945 to use the atomic bomb, but 'if it has to be made for the welfare of the United States, and the democracies of the world are at stake, [I] wouldn't hesitate to make it again'.[92] 'I was deeply impressed by your statement', Churchill wrote to him a little later. 'I am sure this will do more than anything else to ward off the catastrophe of a third world war ... Complete unity, superior force and undoubted readiness to use it, give us the only hopes of escape.' In fact Churchill read too much into the President's remarks. 'I am not quite so pessimistic as you are about the prospects for a third world war', Truman replied. 'I rather think that eventually we are going to forget that idea, and get a real world peace. I don't believe even the Russians can stand it to face complete destruction, which certainly would happen to them in the event of another war.'[93] By now, the United States possessed around 150 atomic bombs, most of a power-equivalence similar to the Hiroshima device, nowhere near enough to wreak 'complete destruction', as Truman put it, but if the stockpile kept growing in quantity and explosive power, and if delivery systems were perfected, that moment might arrive.[94] Provided, of course, that the atomic arms race continued to have just one runner.

On 12 May 1949, the Soviet authorities lifted the Berlin blockade. It was unquestionably a humiliation for Stalin who had underestimated both the possibilities of supplying west Berlin by air (an average of 13,000 tons had been flown in every day for the best part of a year) and the determination of the Western powers to proceed with their plans for a West German state. With an ever-present risk of war but little likelihood of achieving a worthwhile outcome, the Soviet leader cut his losses.[95] When, a few days later, the Federal Republic of Germany was formally established, the Western alliance, with the freshly-minted Atlantic pact at its heart, seemed to be shaping up well – as was, from Stalin's perspective, an American-led anti-Soviet Western bloc. The end of the crisis lessened the immediate danger of war in Europe but the continent remained as geo-politically riven as before and in this sundering the potential for a new flashpoint was ever-present.

On the day the blockade was raised Churchill spoke in Parliament. The outcome was a victory for Western firmness and unity, he declared, and he hoped that Europe would now enjoy a period of stability. Elsewhere, however, especially in Asia, tensions were rising: in China, the communists were nearing victory in the country's bitter civil war, while in South-East Asia a spate of communist-led insurgencies from Malaya to Indonesia had melded with the on-going French war in Indo-China to 'bring home to us the magnitude of the great struggle for freedom which is going on under the conditions of what is called the cold war'. Over this broiling scene 'reigns the power of the atomic bomb, ever growing in the hands of the United States'. It was 'this alone that has given us time to take the measures of self-protection.'[96] What, though, had the Labour government done with the breathing-space bestowed by the Bomb? Not enough, he maintained. For two years he had condemned the Attlee administration's neglect of defence and its corresponding and, in his opinion, excessive investment in domestic social initiatives. This concern had grown acute during the Berlin crisis when, for twelve months, war seemed only a miscalculation away.

In July 1949, Churchill and a delegation of senior Conservatives called at Number 10 to tell the Prime Minister to his face that his government had been dangerously negligent in continuing to estimate the country's defence requirements on the quixotic assumption that a modus vivendi with the USSR was still to be had. In this way, Churchill supposed,

Labour justified robbing defence to pay for the Welfare State. The reality was that an East–West settlement was nowhere in sight. Lindemann was part of the Tory team. Although much absorbed by life at the Clarendon, the Prof was a member of the Conservative consultative committee, the *de facto* shadow Cabinet, and had prepared the data that Churchill now deployed to prove Labour's neglect of national security in general and of anti-aircraft defence in particular. The situation was as puzzling as it was distressing, Churchill told Attlee, since the government claimed to be spending around ten times as much on air forces as before the war. 'Our only hope as usual seems to be the atomic bomb.'[97] That hope, however, was about to be severely dented.

CHAPTER 10
TO THE SUMMIT

On 3 September 1949, a specially equipped US Air Force B-29 on a mission over the North Pacific picked up atmospheric indications that an atomic explosion had recently occurred somewhere in Soviet Asia. The samplings did not lie. Five days earlier, the USSR had detonated its first nuclear weapon, a plutonium device similar to the Nagasaki bomb, at the Semipalatinsk-21 test-site on the Kazakhstan steppes with a blast-yield of 22 kilotons.[1]

The world was informed of the test, not by the Kremlin but in a press release from the White House on 23 September in which President Truman added a new appeal for international control (the Baruch plan and the Gromyko counter-plan remained on the table at the UN, if inertly so).[2] 'We are all feeling depressed', wrote Harold Nicolson. 'We were told that they would not have one for five years, and they have got it in four.'[3] Nudged by Truman's announcement, the Kremlin issued its own confirmation and further claimed (fallaciously) that it had in fact acquired an A-bomb two years earlier. Anxious to deter any thoughts in Washington of a surprise attack before the Soviet stockpile grew to serious proportions, the message put out by Moscow was that Western Europe would no longer be able to escape the atomic consequences of war, nor, in time, would the United States.[4] For his part, Stalin seemed more impressed by the power of the A-bomb now that he had one of his own and may even have anticipated a future balance of terror. 'Atomic weapons', he suggested, 'can hardly be used without spelling the end of the world', and nobody, he implied, wanted that.[5] Being less sure, the editors of the *Bulletin of the Atomic Scientists* moved the time on the Doomsday Clock, the bulletin's logo, from seven to three minutes to midnight, the Armageddon hour.[6]

In Washington, the twin jolts of the Soviet bomb (referred to in the West as Joe-1) and the birth of the communist People's Republic of China on 1 October (which added 500 million people to the human reservoir of world communism) led the Truman administration to undertake a root-and-branch review of its national security strategy. As early earnest of the seriousness with which the United States viewed the altered international situation, at the end of January 1950 the President announced plans to press ahead with 'work on all forms of atomic weapons, including the hydrogen or so-called super-bomb'.[7] According to a Gallup poll, Americans believed by a factor of four-to-one that the contest with a now atomic-armed USSR justified the H-bomb, the destructive power of which dwarfed that of the A-bomb hundreds and potentially thousands of times over.[8] '[I]f we let the Russians get the Super first', Senator McMahon, chairman of the Joint Congressional Committee on Atomic Energy, warned the President, 'catastrophe becomes all but certain – whereas if we get it first, there exists a chance of saving ourselves.'[9] Theoretical physicist Edward Teller, the most ardent champion of the "super", was prepared to bet that he 'would be a Russian prisoner of war in the United States within five years' unless the H-bomb was built.[10] Truman took little persuading. 'There actually was no decision to make on the H-bomb', he reflected. '[W]e had to do it ... though no one wants to use it.'[11]

There were dissenting voices, including church leaders, political commentators and ethically-troubled scientists.[12] In the end, though, as AEC chief David Lilienthal remarked, the institutional momentum, both military and political, in favour of the H-bomb was so great that opposition was as pointless as trying to 'say "No" to a steamroller'.[13] Morality, to the extent that it was present in the thinking of decision-makers (George Kennan warned that a H-bomb, '[n]o matter how we might wish to use it ... could not fail to be a weapon of mass destruction' rather than an instrument of 'purely military employment') was trumped by the security imperative: 'it is folly to argue whether one weapon is more immoral than another', the Joint Chiefs of Staff pointed out, for 'in the larger sense it is war itself which is immoral'.[14]

In Britain, too, there was unease. 'In spite of the original estimates of "total destruction" by atomic bombs, it has come to be accepted by most authorities that the atomic bomb would not necessarily be a decisive weapon in war', a leader in the *Times* commented.

> It has grave limitations in practice and, even if it came to the worst, a great nation like Russia or the United States might survive an atomic war without irreparable damage. Whether this would also be true of the hydrogen bomb is more doubtful. It seems possible that war waged with hydrogen bombs would be so obviously, so demonstrably ruinous that not even the greatest nation with the widest spaces could embark on it.[15]

The H-bomb headline in the *Illustrated London News* made the same point more succinctly: 'A Possible Destroyer of the World'.[16] Geoffrey Fisher, the Archbishop of Canterbury, spoke for the conflicted emotions of many people when he suggested that no responsible government could forgo development of this 'hideous engine of destruction', not when its enemies were almost certainly working to the same end, but the appearance of the H-bomb nonetheless 'reveals how evil and insane things are, and how essential it is that they should be changed'.[17] Churchill made no recorded comment on Truman's H-bomb announcement, though later he would have a great deal to say on matters thermonuclear. Indeed, by 1954, he would have made the Fisher thesis his own.

In January 1950, Attlee called a General Election. Despite the mood of public nervousness occasioned by the H-bomb there was little reference to foreign policy during the first weeks of campaigning as the parties focused on domestic issues. However, on 14 February, a dour election sparked into life when Churchill spoke to a packed Usher Hall in Edinburgh. His twin theme was the Cold War and the nuclear danger. The 'two worlds', the capitalist and the communist, were ranged against one another 'more profoundly and on a larger scale than history has ever seen before', he observed. The Soviet bloc possessed 'by far the greatest military force, but the United States have the atom bomb; and now, we are told that they have a thousandfold more terrible manifestation of this awful power. When all is said and done it is my belief that the superiority in the atom bomb, if not indeed almost the monopoly of this frightful weapon, in American hands is the surest guarantee of world peace tonight'. So far, it could be said, so familiar. The departure from the norm came near the end. 'The idea appeals to me', Churchill declared, 'of a supreme effort to bridge the gulf between the two worlds, so that each can live their life, if not in friendship at least without the hatreds of the cold war. You must be careful to mark my words in these matters because I have not always been proved wrong. It is not easy to see how things could be worsened by a parley at the summit.'[18]

Reaction to the speech varied considerably. Hitherto, the *Times* observed, Churchill had urged the Western powers

> to take advantage of their temporary lead in atomic weapons to 'bring things to a head' and seek 'a final settlement' with Russia. It was not always clear exactly what he meant by this and there were some who feared that he wished to use the atomic bomb to force Russia to withdraw from Europe and to accept the western terms on pain of war. If he ever meant this – and it seems unlikely that he did – it is clear that he does not mean it now.[19]

In Conservative circles there was 'thankfulness' that Churchill had 'given a lead on Russia', but in Labour ranks he was accused of political sharp practice: Herbert Morrison, deputy Prime Minister, sniped at his 'soap-box diplomacy', while Bevin derided 'stunt proposals' and an obvious 'electoral manoeuvre'.[20] Harold Nicolson concurred. To suggest a summit 'inevitably makes people think, "Winston could talk to Stalin on more or less the same level. But if Attlee goes, it would be like a mouse addressing a tiger. Therefore vote for Winston". No – I agree with Bevin, it was a stunt, and unworthy of him'.[21]

With Churchill repeating his call for a summit on at least two further occasions prior to polling day, it is legitimate to ask whether the atomic diplomatist had undergone a genuine conversion. Had the Soviet A-bomb test, as Paul Addison suggests, really 'put an end to Churchill's vision of an ultimatum that would make or break the world' and brought him to embrace 'a new approach to the Soviet Union'? Had he 'assuredly changed his views' on the role of the Bomb in relation to the USSR, never again to speak of showdowns or attacks on Moscow, as Graham Farmelo and a number of other historians have argued?[22] Between Potsdam in July 1945 and Edinburgh in February 1950, Churchill argued repeatedly in private (unless Llandudno counts as a public expression) that Western diplomacy vis-à-vis the Soviet Union should be strengthened by atomic menaces and that if the USSR refused to settle the political future of Eastern Europe according to Western democratic norms, or agree to nuclear disarmament, the US Air Force should be unleashed to do its worst. This much is clear. And yet, around the end of

1949, Churchill's broad outlook on the Cold War does seem to have begun – note, *begun* – to change.

The gap is most discernible in a toning-down of his anti-Soviet rhetoric. There is, for example, a huge gulf between the ideologically-raw invective of the speeches he delivered on his March 1949 trip to the United States and the ameliorative strains of his Usher Hall address eleven months later. In the absence of any recorded explanation by Churchill himself it is tempting to invest the Soviet A-bomb test with determining properties. If war came, the United Kingdom was a certain target for Soviet air attack and, thanks to Joe-1, that assault could soon be of the atomic variety. On its own, this would have given Churchill pause for thought. But then, in the pausing, came Truman's H-bomb announcement. Whatever level of destruction Churchill believed an atomic attack would visit on Britain he seems to have persuaded himself (as others did) that an atomic war, though hideous in its manifold consequences, was at a certain level survivable: as Marc Trachtenberg has shown, this was 'still not a period when it was taken for granted that all-out war meant the destruction of whole societies'.[23]

This brings us back to Edinburgh on Valentine's Day, 1950. It would be easy but erroneous to conclude from this one speech that Churchill the atomic diplomatist was no more. In the first place, electoral opportunism – the Bevin–Morrison–Nicolson argument – cannot be removed from the equation, not when Jan Smuts, Churchill's confidant, was convinced that the Edinburgh initiative 'was taken for political reasons' in the context of a close election campaign in which Labour had labelled the Tory leader a 'war-monger'.[24] Nor when Lord Beaverbrook claimed that it was only at his psephological prompting that Churchill decided to go vote-hunting by floating the prospect of 'direct negotiations with Stalin'.[25] Beyond this, the idea of a showdown, far from being jettisoned in February 1950, remained in Churchill's thoughts for much of the next two years. As we will see, he certainly became less strident in its advocacy, even in private, and more realistic about what could be achieved now that the USSR was an atomic power. But a showdown retained its allure. Prior to Edinburgh, he believed that the US atomic monopoly, if applied as an adjunct of American diplomacy, could secure a satisfactory settlement in Europe. After Edinburgh, he altered his outlook to the extent that he hoped that the USA's massive atomic superiority would strengthen its diplomacy sufficiently to secure most (if no longer all) of the West's desiderata. It follows that those historians who regard Edinburgh as a Damascene moment, the point at which Churchill abandoned all thoughts of a showdown and dedicated himself to East–West reconciliation, are chronologically premature.[26] That he would go on to become, by 1954, a conviction-driven apostle of peaceful co-existence and détente is not in question. But his journey was only beginning in February 1950. He had a long way to go and more than once he would double-back on himself.

The election, which took place on 23 February 1950, saw Labour returned with a wafer-thin overall majority of six seats. Churchill was disappointed but not devastated as he had been in 1945, for he knew that another election beckoned, possibly within a few months, and in the meantime he determined to maintain maximum pressure on a fragile government.[27] In a speech to the new Parliament on 16 March he focused on what he still viewed as Labour's Achilles' heel, defence. The public, he warned, should not 'nurse foolish delusions that we have any other effective overall shield at the present time from mortal danger than the atomic bomb in the possession, thank God, of the United States'. He then reprised his recent electoral theme. 'Let us … labour for peace, not only by

Figure 10.1 WSC and Attlee, February 1950. IPC Magazines/Picture Post/Getty Images.

gathering our defensive strength, but also by making sure that no door is closed upon any hope of reaching a settlement which will end this tragic period when two worlds face one another in increasing strain and anxiety.'[28]

A fortnight later in a Foreign Affairs Debate, Churchill proposed that some of the gap in Western European defence be plugged by raising West German troops. Coming just five years after the end of the war, this suggestion excited controversy not just in Britain but in France, the Benelux states and even in the German Federal Republic, but Churchill, a champion of the fullest rehabilitation of the Germans ('[m]y hate had died with their surrender'), was prescient; the same idea was already being discussed in secret by the British Chiefs of Staff, and within a few months it would be openly embraced by NATO.[29] In the spring of 1950, however, his support for German rearmament was hardly best timed to convince the Soviets, with their memories of more than 25 million war-dead, of his summitry sincerity. Nor was his approach to the Bomb helpful in this regard. 'There is no doubt now that the passage of time will place these fearful agencies of destruction in Soviet hands, that is to say, where there is no customary, traditional, moral or religious restraint'. Thankfully, there was bound to be an 'interlude between the discovery of the secret and the effective large-scale production of the article'. In other words, the US stockpile would remain much greater than the USSR's for some time to come and it was thus important to seek a summit while the West held the atomic advantage. 'Therefore, while I believe there is time for a further effort for a lasting and peaceful settlement, I cannot feel that it is necessarily a long time or that its passage will progressively improve our own security. Above all things, we must not fritter it away'.[30]

On the basis of these two Parliamentary performances, was there, we may ask, a great difference between pre- and post-Edinburgh Churchill? The way in which he framed his appeal for a summit suggests that his main interest was in establishing a forum within which Western objectives could be secured. From Moscow's standpoint, there was nothing in Churchill's public stance to encourage the belief that negotiations in the true sense of the term – a search for compromise and common ground involving give-and-take on both sides – was what he had in mind.[31] To the contrary, his summitry still seemed predicated on atomic diplomacy. There was no mention, for example, of peaceful co-existence (nor would there be for at least another three years) and he continued to believe that the USA's atomic supremacy, if factored into its Soviet policy, could fashion a settlement of Cold War differences favourable to the West. The 'only way to deal with Communist Russia', he maintained, 'is by having superior strength in one form or another, and then acting with reason and fairness'.[32] The USSR had itself been calling for 'peace' for some time, largely as a reaction to the ideological broadsides of those in the West whom Moscow classified as warmongers, and the Kremlin evidently had difficulty believing that Churchill, the warmonger-in-chief according to its propaganda, was remotely serious about East–West bridge-building.[33]

Nor was Washington enthusiastic about Churchill's summitry, albeit for different reasons. The Truman administration never actually came out against negotiations with the Soviet Union at this time but did make clear that diplomatic engagement was contingent upon the full launch of its new national security strategy forged in the aftermath of the Soviet bomb and the communization of China. The blueprint for much of America's approach to the Cold War over the next four decades, National Security Council document number 68 (NSC-68), on Truman's desk in April 1950 and formally signed-off a few months later, called for a massive increase in military spending on the part of the United States and its allies in order to develop a position of conventional and nuclear superiority that would thwart 'the Kremlin design for world domination'.[34]

Beyond this, the State Department maintained that discussions with the Soviets, if they took place, should be at Foreign Minister level and not, as Churchill envisaged, between heads of government. This was partly an elitist response by a Foreign Service determined to keep high international diplomacy in the hands of professional diplomats, and partly a reflection of popular disillusionment in the USA with "top table" meetings on the wartime Big Three model. As a principal at Tehran, Yalta and Potsdam, Churchill naturally held a different opinion. The sterility of the Council of Foreign Ministers process – the last full-scale encounter had been in London at the end of 1947 – did not strike him as any kind of recommendation for second-tier dialogue. Furthermore, while agreeing with the Truman administration that negotiation from strength must be the West's goal, as of early 1950 he believed that America's great atomic advantage over the USSR meant that there was sufficient strength already to permit safe summitry. Against this, to allow the Cold War to continue year-on-year would only increase the danger of a shift to hot war, a contingency which neither Britain nor the Western alliance generally was remotely prepared for.[35]

In this connection, Churchill wrote to Attlee in May 1950 urging immediate action to narrow the alarming disparity between Western and Soviet bloc conventional forces in Europe. With the USSR thought to possess between 70 and 100 divisions, the Western powers, by Churchill's reckoning, could muster barely ten. 'The only thing that keeps the peace is the American possession of the atomic bomb.' Now, though, no less a figure than the chairman of the US Joint Chiefs of Staff, General Omar Bradley, was warning publicly that within four years the Soviet Union could possess enough atomic weapons 'to cause a major catastrophe at any time they so decided'. By 1954, the United Kingdom would be 'a prime target for attack' from a USSR with 'overwhelming military superiority in Europe and a formidable supply of atomic bombs'. And yet, under Labour, defensive preparations had been allowed to slide. 'In my long experience I have never seen a situation so perilous and strange.'[36]

Churchill's European concerns were set aside, at least temporarily, when the Korean War – the first major shooting-war of the Cold War – broke out on 25 June 1950. In London, the Labour government made common cause with both the United States and the United Nations in condemning communist North Korea's invasion of its southern neighbour. The commitment went beyond words. Inspired by President Truman's offer of American military assistance to South Korea, within 48 hours of the start of hostilities the government had placed the British Pacific Fleet at the disposal of the US Navy. The lessons of the 1930s, in particular the need to stand-up to aggression, were the initial analogue for the Attlee administration. However, when the UN Security Council went on to approve direct military intervention to save South Korea, the British Chiefs of Staff, along with several Cabinet ministers, proved less than enthusiastic about committing land forces to an American-led UN Command (UNC). This hesitancy derived not from any reluctance to uphold the rule of international law but from recognition of the already onerous burden the United Kingdom was bearing in trying to maintain security commitments in Western Europe, the Middle East and South-East Asia with limited military resources in a time of economic difficulty. In the end, in late July, Attlee and Bevin joined forces to overcome Cabinet and COS qualms and a decision was taken to commit two infantry battalions; taking the negative view, both Prime Minister and Foreign Secretary feared that a failure to act would damage Anglo-American relations; more positively, as a military stakeholder Britain might be able to exert some influence over US decision-making on the war.[37]

As the conflict developed, this last consideration bulked increasingly large for London policymakers. A wider war involving the People's Republic of China was not the policy of the Truman administration, still less that of the United Nations, and it was certainly not the policy of the Labour government. At times, however, it seemed to be the preference of the commander of UN forces in Korea, General Douglas MacArthur. The hero of the Philippines campaign in the Second World War and more recently the *shogun* of the US occupation regime in Japan, the seventy-year-old MacArthur was a brilliant but maverick soldier of such towering ego that he was said to have attended 'the same prep School as God – but, of course, in a higher form'.[38] For the Attlee government, the worry was that if the situation in Korea escalated into a general Far Eastern conflagration, Hong Kong and other important British regional interests would be at the mercy of China. Worse still, if the Soviet Union, having recently signed a mutual security treaty with the Central People's Government, became drawn in to the struggle, then a local East Asian crisis could explode into global war. Thanks to established ties of friendship, shared experiences in war and Cold War, and intersecting strategic needs, the British possessed a fair claim on the USA's attention when it came to expressing their views, but Attlee and Bevin concluded that putting troops on the ground in Korea was the best guarantee that those views – especially on reining-in MacArthur and limiting the fighting geographically to the Korean peninsula – were not just heard but heeded.[39]

Over the next three years, the British and Commonwealth contribution to the UNC would be second only to that of the United States, but whether this brought – or bought – the hoped-for influence in Washington is debateable. Meanwhile, the Conservative opposition fully supported the government's decision to back the United Nations. But it was a strange bipartisanship, Churchill acknowledged. 'The old man is very good to me', told his shadow Cabinet. 'I could not have managed this situation had I been in Attlee's place. I should have been called a war-monger.' Asked what 'old man' he meant, he replied: 'God'.[40] The Soviet Union was widely assumed to have approved the North Korean attack – an assumption since proven to be sound – but Churchill was initially relaxed about the risk of escalation into a clash between the major Cold War powers.[41] The Soviet 'bear', he maintained, would launch a third world war for its own reasons and in its own time and not merely to protect a Chinese or North Korean 'cub'. Against this, he was aware that even the coolest of Kremlin calculations could fall victim to 'accident, passion, folly or madness' and that local crises like Korea contained the potential to throw up a Sarajevo moment.[42]

With this in mind, and still troubled by General Bradley's estimate of the USSR's medium-term nuclear weapons prospects, Churchill told the Commons on 5 July that '[w]e should endeavour to come to a settlement' with the Soviets 'before they become possessed of this devastating power'. The successful repulse of the North Korean aggression, and the restoration of the status quo ante bellum, might provide the occasion for negotiations. Conversely, '[t]here could be no more certain way of bringing about the destruction of civilisation than that we should drift on helplessly until the Soviets are fully equipped with the atomic bomb.' Vague on details, Churchill's talk of peace and summits was an easy political points-scorer at a time of public anxiety over Korea. But stripped back to its essentials, the settlement he favoured required the USSR, faced with the prospect of American atomic punishment, to agree to freeze or reverse its A-bomb programme and relinquish its grip on Eastern Europe. In sum, there was nothing in Churchill's atomic-infused prescription to attract the Soviet authorities.[43]

On 27 July, Churchill again spoke in Parliament. The emergency was now in its fifth week and UN forces – around 140,000 troops – were struggling to retain a foothold in South Korea around the port of Pusan. Was there not a danger, he asked, of the Soviet Union making an aggressive move on Western Europe while world attention was centred on East Asia? If so, there was presently 'no effective defence ... beyond the Channel'. A Red Army thrust through Germany into France and Belgium 'would bring us under air bombardment, apart from the atomic bomb, far worse than we have ever endured'. That this danger was not an immediate prospect was due entirely to the United States whose superiority in atomic weapons was 'so vast that a major act of Russian aggression is still subject to an effective and even perhaps decisive deterrent'. It was for this reason that he had 'ventured on several occasions to express the opinion that a third world war is not imminent'. Still, the fact remained that five years after the end of the Second World War, the Labour government had yet to produce a single atomic weapon and the country was left 'dependent upon the United States both for the supply of the bomb and largely for the means of using it. Without it, we are more defenceless than we have ever been. I find this a terrible thought.'[44] It was a 'searching, probing, fearless speech' listened to in an 'atmosphere [which] grew increasingly grim', the *Times* parliamentary correspondent wrote.[45] Many MPs were left in a state of 'paralysed shock' and all too sensible of the parallels with the 1930s.[46] 'Sometimes', wrote Harold Macmillan, a future Prime Minister, 'when one shuts one's eyes, one believes oneself back in 1937–1939'.[47]

The following week, Churchill met with Attlee to discuss defence. According to Macmillan, he came away from the interview 'much depressed' having learned that 'to scrape together 3,000 men and their equipment for Korea will take two months!'[48]

Churchill left two notes with the Prime Minister, one setting out his thinking on security, the other, authored by Lindemann, focusing on atomic research. In his own paper, Churchill agreed to support the government in all action necessary to improve national defence, but equally, as leader of the opposition, he would not shirk from pointing out gaps and failings. The priority was the raising of a European/NATO combined force of thirty-five divisions: the French would contribute fifteen divisions, the British and Americans between them six, the West Germans five and the balance made up by the Benelux states. However, while this force was being formed the United Kingdom remained in danger, and he wanted Attlee to request that the United States supply up to one thousand fighter aircraft as a quid pro quo for allowing the US Air Force to operate from British soil.[49]

Lindemann's memorandum, the contents of which Churchill endorsed, argued that the UK atomic project, which had not only failed to produce any weapons but been lapped by its Soviet counterpart, should be liberated from the Ministry of Supply, into whose charge it had been placed in 1946, and put in the hands of a new dynamic organization on the lines of the American Atomic Energy Commission. Without the Bomb, Lindemann lamented, Britain was 'a second-class nation armed with inferior weapons', while any chance of overturning the McMahon Act and restoring meaningful atomic collaboration with the United States 'will vanish unless we have something of our own to show'.[50]

The Cold War Lindemann was as passionate an advocate of an independent British nuclear capability as the wartime Lindemann had been. But while his criticisms of the Ministry of Supply were not without some merit, the UK bomb programme was more advanced than he, or Churchill, appreciated. As we have seen, the Attlee government took the decision to manufacture an A-bomb in January 1947. While most political observers, including Churchill, assumed that Tube Alloys had been taken up again at the end of the war, the government was initially coy about admitting publicly to the existence of a dedicated bomb project. The nearest it came to a public acknowledgement was in May 1948 when the Minister of Defence, A. V. Alexander, told the House of Commons, almost as an aside, that 'research and development continue to receive the highest priority in the defence field' and that 'all types of modern weapons, including atomic weapons, are being developed'.[51] It says much for the state of the Cold War by then that the revelation made scarcely a ripple in the press: what would have made a splash was the news that the government was *not* building a bomb.[52]

Two years on, in August 1950, Churchill, insensitive to the hugely damaging impact of the McMahon Act, tore into the government for its failure to produce 'a single specimen' and accused it of squandering 'all the knowledge we had amassed in the course of our joint work with the Americans during the War'.[53] This proved to be the opening salvo in a regular atomic-themed barrage against the government. At a partisan political level, Churchill was out to erode public confidence in Labour's credibility as the guardian of British national security, but he was also genuinely perturbed by the country's nuclear nakedness. The Labour riposte was to add atomic rabidity to the standing accusation against Churchill of war-mongering, while Attlee, though bewildered by Tory tactics, derived electoral comfort from 'the strongly held fear' in the country 'that, if Winston got in, he would lead us into war'.[54]

In a speech to Parliament on 12 September, Churchill introduced some significant variations into what had become his familiar tune. Once NATO was strong in conventional arms, and accepting the continued existence of the American atomic shield, he argued that two factors would then determine whether war or peace ensued. The first was the 'calculations and designs of the Soviet autocracy'. The second was 'the anger of the people in the United States' at the strains, stresses and costs of the Cold War and its bloody offshoots like Korea. What would happen, Churchill wondered, if American anger led to an upsurge of support for a preventive war against the USSR while the USA remained superior in atomic weapons and – crucially – out of range of Soviet bombers? It was one thing to rely on the Bomb to buttress diplomacy, which was what his own showdown philosophy was presently about, but quite another to eschew diplomacy in favour of a premeditated nuclear attack on the USSR, especially when the United Kingdom and Western Europe, not the United States, would bear the brunt of any Soviet retaliation. For the time being, as long as there was a NATO conventional rearmament drive, Churchill trusted that the Americans would exercise caution and the Soviets likewise restrain themselves from embarking on courses of action that would bring about 'the most frightful of world wars yet waged'.[55] Still, he had sent out a signal that his previous hope that the United States would assert, and if needs be employ its atomic power in dealing with the Soviet Union, was undergoing some revision. But that is all it was, a signal. A transitional staging-post. An atomic diplomatist since Potsdam, Churchill had by no means conquered his showdown addiction and in moments of high international tension his first instinct, as we will see, was to reach for his old comforter.

For all Churchill's focus on the Korean War's European impact, he was fully alert to its importance in its own Asian setting. On 15 September, the tide of war, hitherto flowing strongly in North Korea's favour, began to turn as a result of the Inchon landings, MacArthur's audacious outflanking manoeuvre involving 75,000 troops and over 250 naval vessels. Within a fortnight, Seoul had been recaptured and the North Koreans all but evicted from the south. Containment, Washington's Cold War policy for the previous three years, required only the restoration of the status quo ante bellum, but the prospect of building on the success in the south by liberating the north was an intoxicating one for a Truman administration smarting from recent foreign policy set-backs, not least the Soviet A-bomb and the "loss" of China. Armed with a UN resolution (sponsored by an equally intoxicated Britain) in support of a unified, independent and democratic Korea, and with instructions from the US Joint Chiefs of Staff to destroy North Korea's military establishment, at the start of October MacArthur led his forces across the 38th parallel.[56] The advance made impressive progress: Pyongyang was taken on 19 October and a month later UN forces were bearing down on the Yalu river, the frontier between southern China and North Korea. Warnings from Beijing that the offensive constituted a direct threat to PRC national security were either ignored or downplayed by MacArthur, that 'supreme egoist' as Truman once described him.[57] Then, on 26 November, the war was utterly transformed when China intervened in force, committing over 250,000 troops in the first wave and sending UN forces into headlong retreat. The US Eighth Army, the core of the UN Command, was threatened with annihilation, while in the United States there were calls to abandon Korea and muster all military strength for war with China instead.[58]

With this darkening Asian prospect as his backcloth, Churchill spoke in the House of Commons on 30 November 1950, his seventy-sixth birthday. Back in 1948, he recalled:

> I hoped that we might come to terms with them [the Soviets] before they gained the secret of the atomic bomb. Now I hope that we may come to terms with them before they have so large a stockpile of these fearful agencies, in addition to vast superiority in other weapons, as to be able to terrorise the free world, if not, indeed, to destroy it.

He was still 'in favour', he said, 'of efforts to reach a settlement with Soviet Russia . . . and of making those efforts while the immense and measureless superiority of the United States atomic bomb organisation offsets the Soviet predominance in every other military respect'. Churchill wanted a summit at which 'decisive conversations' could take place 'in confidence, in privacy and even in secrecy'. At a moment of popular anxiety following China's entry into the war, this restatement of his Edinburgh initiative was well-timed to garner favour with public opinion, but equally his transparent desire to negotiate while the USA held the upper-hand in nuclear throw-weight was unlikely to convince the Soviets that détente rather than dictation was on the summit agenda.[59]

According to Hansard, Churchill started to speak at 3.41 pm. At that very moment, on the other side of the Atlantic, President Truman was in the midst of one of the most controversial news conferences of his career. His text was also nuclear-themed. With US forces in Korea involved in the longest retreat in American military history, Truman said that he was giving 'active consideration' to the use of the atomic bomb. MacArthur, the commander in the field, 'will have charge of the use of the weapons, as he always has'. The President quickly checked himself by adding that 'I don't want to see it [the Bomb] used', which was no doubt true, but the damage was done. At home and abroad his comments caused such tumult that the White House rushed out a clarification to the effect that only the President, by law, and not therefore MacArthur, could authorize the use of the Bomb, but this made little difference at Westminster where flash reports of the news conference produced such upset that Macmillan wrote of 'a day unlike anything since Munich'.[60] Handed a petition signed by seventy-six Labour MPs demanding immediate withdrawal of British troops from Korea if the use of the Bomb was even a remote possibility, an anxious Attlee invited himself to Washington to take part with Truman in 'a wide survey of the problems which face us today'. The news of his transatlantic journey – it would be the Prime Minister's first meeting with the President in five years – was greeted with loud cheers in the Chamber of the Commons.[61]

Churchill had assumed that, amongst other things, Attlee would remind Truman of the article in the Quebec agreement making the use of the atomic bomb a matter for mutual consent. To his great distress, however, he received a letter from Attlee on 3 December, the day the Prime Minister left for Washington, revealing that the agreement no longer held. Truman and his atomic advisors had been anxious to liquidate all the wartime arrangements, Attlee explained, because their existence 'put them in a very embarrassing position with Congress'. The Quebec agreement in particular went much further than the normal scope of an Executive agreement such as the President was permitted to conclude under the Constitution. Since an Anglo-American treaty embodying similar terms stood no chance of securing Senate ratification, the Quebec agreement had been allowed to wither. A new agreement had been initialled in January 1948 known simply as the *modus vivendi*. With the McMahon Act casting its baleful shadow, the *modus vivendi* omitted (on US insistence) all reference to the political features of the FDR–Churchill compacts, including mutual consent, and instead specified just nine permissible areas of technical cooperation.[62]

As it happened, the Labour government had been keen to eliminate the fourth article of the Quebec agreement, the one preventing Britain from making use of atomic energy for industrial purposes except on terms sanctioned by the US President, and to the extent that these commercial manacles had been unlocked, the loss of the mutual consent provision – which was unenforceable anyway – struck Attlee as a fair trade. And besides, the congruity of Anglo-American thinking on so critical an issue as the combat use of the Bomb depended on 'the degree of friendship and understanding prevailing between our two countries and not on any written agreement, one of the original authors of which was no longer alive'. The Quebec agreement, Attlee averred, had served its purpose but in the 'quite different circumstances of peace the secret war-time agreement no longer had the same character as a binding understanding between the two countries'.[63]

Attlee did not draw attention to it but the case of the atom spy Klaus Fuchs added greatly to his government's difficulty in reaching an agreement both to replace the Churchill–Roosevelt understandings and expand the cooperation embodied in the *modus vivendi*. By the end of 1949, after many months of negotiations, and with Joe-1 and the intensification of the Cold War having made the Americans more receptive to a resumption of cooperation, a new deal appeared in prospect, one which would permit a stock of American atomic weapons to be held in the UK under British government control.[64] However, the nationalistic outlook of the JCAE first operated as a brake on the Truman administration and then came the outing of Fuchs.[65] The scandal, complete with a high-profile Old Bailey trial, occurred at the worst possible moment for the Labour government: the February 1950 Sino-Soviet treaty, which gave rise in the West to panicked visions of a monolithic communist bloc, and the simultaneous 'attack of the primitives', as US Secretary of State Dean Acheson described the onset of the McCarthyite hunt for communists or communist sympathizers in the US government, combined to make it politically impossible for the Truman administration to enter into any serious collaborative atomic relationship with a security-compromised United Kingdom.[66] In

Parliament, Attlee, with typical understatement, described the Fuchs affair as an 'unfortunate incident', but privately he suspected that the Truman administration welcomed the scandal as an excuse to terminate atomic dialogue.[67] Either way, as the door of Fuchs' cell in Wormwood Scrubs clanged shut – he was sent down in March 1950 for 14 years, but was released after nine – so the Americans triple-locked their own door to further interchange with Britain.[68]

Nine months on, in December 1950, Churchill was in no mood to empathize, let alone sympathize with the Prime Minister's difficulties. Quite the opposite. He would never forgive Attlee for his 'feeble and incompetent' capitulation and from this point onwards, the publication of the Quebec agreement, for which the permission of the White House was required, became his burning obsession.[69] At one level, he was motivated by national interest; to make the agreement known might tap into the American sense of fair play and lead to the restoration of the US–UK partnership. At another and more base level, he was out for personal and political revenge, and believed that publication would show him to have been the defender and Attlee the betrayer of Britain's nuclear heritage. But he needed patience; the chance for retribution would not come until April 1954.

In the meantime, the news that Britain no longer possessed a veto on the exercise of US atomic power led Churchill to dust-off his showdown thesis. Why this should be is unclear. Perhaps he felt that with an unrestrained America on the loose it was only a matter of time before it took an atomic pot-shot at the Soviet Union, and in that case, it might be better to have it out with Stalin sooner rather than wait until the USSR's atomic capability had burgeoned. Whatever the causal factor, atomic diplomacy, for a time at least, was again his favoured policy. At a shadow Cabinet meeting on 6 December, Churchill delivered a soliloquy on the Bomb the gist of which was recorded by Macmillan.

> If we wait for the show-down with Russia, we may well be weaker (relatively) in 3 years than we are now. For the degree (if any) that we have caught up in conventional weapons may be more than balanced by Russia's increased power in unconventional weapons. Should we then hurry on the conference and the show-down now. Peace by ultimatum! Either you agree to our terms, covering the whole field, including Central and Eastern Europe – or we destroy you![70]

Later that month, an article appeared in the US press by the influential columnists Joseph and Stewart Alsop claiming (approvingly so) that Churchill was keen for the United States to engineer a showdown in this, its time of nuclear plenty. Macmillan, who had become very close to his leader, thought the piece 'certainly reflects a good deal that I have heard Churchill say in private conversation'. But, equally, those private opinions 'sh[oul]d certainly not be published'.[71] This was the view of others privy to Churchill's thinking as well. The Chief of the Air Staff, Air Marshal Sir John Slessor, concluded that 'Winston' had 'far too high an appreciation of the effect of the atom bomb' if he thought that 'a fortnight's unpleasantness' would be 'followed by 100 years of peace'. Churchill's ideas on 'preventive war' were 'balls'.[72]

*

Attlee, meanwhile, undertook his mission to Washington. Over four days – 4–7 December – he pressed Truman and his advisors for an assurance that atomic weapons would not be employed without consultation with London. He also stated his government's opposition to any widening of the war from Korea to China and stressed the UK's strong interest both in a peaceful resolution in Korea and, thereafter, an all-encompassing Far Eastern settlement with China. For his part, Truman accepted the principle of consultation insofar as it was practicable in an emergency but in most respects the discussions were a disappointment for Attlee – 'one of the least effective encounters between the Americans and a British premier', according to one veteran observer of the phenomenon.[73] Few of Whitehall's cognoscenti would have disagreed. 'We appear not to have convinced the Americans of the need to make a serious effort to reach a political settlement with the Chinese and not to have shaken them in their intention to undertake some form of "limited war" against China', the Foreign Office's Pierson Dixon wrote to Bevin.

> If matters are left like this, it seems inevitable that the United States at least will be drawn into war-like operations against China. Two results seem certain to flow from this: (a) the Far Eastern theatre will inevitably take priority over the European theatre, however much the Americans say that they put Europe first; (b) the temptation to Russia to act in Europe will be greatly increased.[74]

According to the Chiefs of Staff, their American counterparts, being convinced that general war with the USSR was inevitable, felt that 'the sooner we got it over the better'.[75]

Near the end of the conference, Truman repeated his assurance that, as far as circumstances allowed, he would always seek to consult with London before authorizing the use of the Bomb, but the President's advisors immediately intervened to ensure that this understanding remained personal and private rather than official and open. Also on US insistence, the communiqué issued at the close of the talks was limited to recording Truman's anodyne 'hope that world conditions would never call for use of the atomic bomb' and his concomitant 'desire to keep the Prime Minister at all times informed of developments which might bring about a change in the situation'.[76] Back in London, Attlee tried to put an optimistic construction on the outcome. He was 'completely satisfied' the Americans would give the 'fullest weight' to British views when it came to the general conduct of the Korean campaign, he told Parliament on 14 December, while on the specific issue of the use of the Bomb he considered the assurances in the communiqué 'perfectly satisfactory'. For Churchill, still seething about the loss of the Quebec agreement, this was never going to be good enough. There was 'no guarantee' in the communiqué 'even of consultation', he cavilled, whereas during the war 'we were on equal terms with the United States in the whole business of atomic research ... In 1943 I made an agreement with the President. Since then I understand other arrangements have been made.' What were they? Parliament should be told. 'After all, this matter has become one of very real and vital consequence to us since the decision of the Government to afford the United States the bomber base in East Anglia.'[77]

He also took exception to the government's position on non-first use of the Bomb. With public opinion alarmed by the hot war dangers of the Korean crisis, and with MacArthur adding to anxiety levels with bellicose statements about war with China, the Attlee ministry's attitude was in keeping with the popular mood. Churchill, however, took a different view. 'The argument is now put forward that we must never use the atomic bomb until, or unless, it has been used against us first. In other words, you must never fire until you have been shot dead. That seems to me undoubtedly a silly thing to say and a still more imprudent position to adopt.' Moreover, 'such a resolve would certainly bring war nearer. The deterrent effect of the atomic bomb is at the present time almost our sole defence. Its potential use is the only lever by which we can hope to obtain reasonable consideration in an attempt to make a peaceful settlement with Soviet Russia.' Once again Churchill anticipated John Foster Dulles who, four years later, would advance – and become the public face of – the concept of brinkmanship, the idea that the credibility of the US nuclear deterrent hinged on the Soviet Union's belief that America would actually fire-off its arsenal, a belief to be inculcated by a clear readiness to go to the very brink of war. For now, Churchill ended with his routine complaint about the government's failure to produce an atomic bomb, something which 'astonished me very much when I remember how far we were advanced . . . in 1942 and 1943'. Overall, his message was that the nation's security, never mind its atomic future, was no longer safe in Labour's hands.[78]

Churchill spent Christmas and the New Year in Marrakesh working on his war memoirs, but much as he tried 'to put the world out of my thoughts . . . somehow it intrudes its ugly face from time to time'.[79] Korea was the ugliest invader. By mid-December the initial Chinese onslaught had been stemmed and there was a lull in the fighting. In a letter to Clementine on Christmas Day, Churchill said he was looking forward to a MacArthur counter-offensive and to teaching 'the Chinese the sort of lessons we learned upon the Somme and at Passchendaele'.[80] On 27 December he cabled the UN commander himself in similar terms: 'Remembering the Somme and Passchendaele I have many hopes'.[81] But they proved misplaced. On 1 January 1951, the PRC renewed the attack, sweeping south across the 38th parallel in strength and capturing Seoul before the offensive petered out mid-month. By March, UN forces had recaptured the South Korean capital and in April the failure of a further Chinese offensive marked, in retrospect, the end of attempts by either side to obtain an outright military victory. The front-line settled on or around the 38th parallel and by July 1951 the two sides had set out on what would be a protracted two-year period of fighting and negotiating. Kaesong was the initial venue for peace talks before they transferred to Panmunjom, which became their permanent home. There, on 27 July 1953, an armistice was finally signed.

Back at the start of 1951, Churchill could no more anticipate the course of events than anyone else. The loss of life on the UN side, including British troops, grieved him, but he was also 'terribly alarmed' at the prospect of the United States becoming 'bogged down' on the Asian mainland for years to come and thereby denuding Western Europe – which was where 'the world cause will be decided' – of military resources and manpower vital for its security.[82] In addition, whenever his mind pondered the possibility of the Korean situation escalating into a general war with the USSR, he was reminded of what had been lost with the demise of the Quebec agreement. On his return to London from Marrakesh he wrote to Attlee to say that publication of the agreement would be in the 'national interest' insofar as it would put moral pressure on the United States to give Britain due consideration in atomic matters.[83] But it would also manifestly serve his personal-political interest. As Roy Jenkins reminds us, Churchill was a politician to his bootstraps, always alive to how foreign and defence issues played domestically, and in early 1951, with Labour defending a paltry majority, 'few holds were barred' in his harrying of the government. If publishing the agreement showed him to have been the wise atomic statesman and Attlee the craven compromiser, so much the better. This, of course, was a gross distortion of the truth but it would still be political capital in the bank to draw on come election-time.[84]

Attlee had no personal objection to publication but proposed, as a matter of courtesy, to seek Truman's view.[85] Churchill, though, was impatient. As co-signatory of the original accord he felt he had the right to approach the President directly and in fact did so on 12 February. The agreement, 'although made in wartime, was . . . intended to cover more than the wartime period'. If it was now placed in the public domain, he was sure that Congress would concede the legitimacy of the British case in favour of mutual consent, certainly as far as atomic-primed B-29s in East Anglia were concerned. Churchill sent Attlee a copy of the letter. The Prime Minister was not pleased. 'I do not understand the basis of your communication to the President', he wrote. 'While the Quebec Agreement was made between Roosevelt and yourself, it was, of course, in your capacities as President and Prime Minister. I do not see that a personal communication of this kind which you have made will advance a matter which is at present under discussion between Governments'.[86]

The extent to which Churchill was questing for domestic political advantage is further demonstrated by the vote of no confidence he now moved against the government's defence policy.[87] In many ways he was delighted at the manner in which the Korean crisis had catalysed European security. That September, the Truman administration, pursuant to NSC-68, pressed its European allies to embark on a large-scale rearmament drive with the aim of narrowing the Soviet bloc's conventional superiority on the continent. The fear was that with attention centred on Korea, the Red Army might make a move on Western Europe where, as things stood (and as Churchill repeatedly warned), there was not much in the way of a defensive barrier. As the UK's contribution, the Labour government agreed in October to a £3,600 million defence programme, a figure upped in January 1951 to £4,700 million spread over three years. In return, the United States began working to convert the North Atlantic Treaty into a fully-fledged defence organization, to confirm General Eisenhower as NATO's first supreme commander (SACEUR), and to commit to the defence of Western Europe *in* Western Europe by stationing several US divisions in the German Federal Republic. As a further accretion to NATO's overall strength, plans were finalized for the raising of 12 West German divisions within a supranational European Defence Community (EDC).[88] Despite all this, in February 1951 Churchill refused to commend Labour for its huge effort in the common cause. Instead he proposed a vote of no confidence on the dubious grounds that Attlee and his colleagues, based on past experience, were bound to mismanage their own enhanced defence programme.

Going into the debate, Churchill would have dearly liked Truman's sanction to quote from the Quebec agreement, but as the President had yet to respond to his appeal he could only hint at its history. Mutual consent on the use of the Bomb, he told MPs, had become a matter both of national sovereignty and national security since 'we have made ourselves the target, and perhaps the bull's eye of a Soviet attack' by hosting the US Air Force.[89] In the event, Churchill suffered a double set-back. On 15 February, the government survived the vote, and then, twenty-four hours later, Truman vetoed publication of the Quebec agreement. 'I am making a sincere effort to carry out the Atlantic Treaty with opposition in the Congress which might be termed vicious and unfair under present emergency conditions', he wrote to Churchill in a reference to the Great Debate then raging on Capitol Hill. In its effort to put the O into NATO, the Democratic administration was seeking to commit substantial US forces to Western Europe in time of general peace, a controversial undertaking which raised important constitutional questions as to whether the President or the Congress had the greater right to determine the fundamental shape of US foreign policy. If the Senate rejected the "troops to Europe" plan, NATO could yet be still-born and Truman was consequently anxious that any public raking-over of secret Executive agreements entered into by a previous Democratic President, especially on a matter so vital to US national security as atomic energy, could be damaging. 'I hope you won't press me in this matter', he ended. Publication could 'ruin my whole defense program both here at home and abroad'.[90] The message was terse and brooked no appeal. And it pleased Attlee no end.[91]

The Truman administration eventually prevailed and in March 1951 the Senate approved the dispatch to Europe of four American divisions (to add to the two already in Germany). It was a relieved Truman who wrote again to Churchill at the end of the month to explain in more depth the reasoning behind his decision on non-publication of the Quebec agreement which, he said, would have led to calls for disclosure of each and every atomic understanding between the USA and Britain.[92] Churchill replied on 11 April confirming that he would not be 'pressing the question any more at present'.[93] That same day, Truman stripped MacArthur of all his commands, the punishment for multiple acts of insubordination connected with the prosecution of the war in Korea. It was a courageous decision in view of the General's tremendous popularity in America. 'I didn't fire him because he was a dumb son of a bitch, although he was', Truman later told Merle Miller. 'I fired him because he wouldn't respect the authority of the president'.[94] Churchill appreciated and applauded the political risk the President had taken in 'asserting the authority of the civil power over military commanders, however able or distinguished'. The dismissal of MacArthur, he told him, 'will receive universal approval in England'.[95]

So disturbed had British opinion become over the MacArthur "problem" – the danger that one man's megalomania and military recklessness could trigger a general Far Eastern war which, in turn, could bring on a global confrontation with the USSR – that the news of his removal was met with cheering in the House of Commons.[96] Before long, though, Churchill was worrying that hostility towards MacArthur could backfire if American opinion mistook it for an attack on the USA in general by an ungrateful ally. In the Commons in May, he warned against 'girding at the United States' which, in the name of the United Nations, was bearing the brunt of the fighting and doing the bulk of the dying in Korea. He also condemned the unwarranted sympathy shown by the anti-American left wing of the Labour Party for 'Red China' and counselled against giving the American people 'the impression that they are left to do all the work, while we pull at their coat tails and read them moral lessons in statecraft and about the love we all ought to have for China'. Criticism of America might even generate a groundswell of opinion in the United States in favour of isolationism or possibly an Asia-first foreign and defence policy. Yet where would Western Europe be, he wondered, if the United States had second thoughts about NATO?

> What would be our position . . . if Europe were overrun, as it would be but for the immense American ascendancy in the atomic bomb, and the deterrent effect, not necessarily upon the Russians but upon the Communist Kremlin regime, of this tremendous weapon? . . . It is said that we are getting stronger, but to get stronger does not necessarily mean that we are getting safer. It is only when we are strong enough that safety is achieved.[97]

The prospect of a Churchill return to Number 10 was brought closer when the Prime Minister – whom Churchill had been lampooning for months as a 'lion-hearted limpet' – called an autumn election.[98] Approaching 77 years of age, this was clearly Churchill's last chance to wield political power and exert direct influence on the course of international affairs. Polling day was set for 25 October. It would be the fourteenth national campaign of his career and his seventeenth parliamentary joust in all. If 1900 was the "Khaki" election, and 1918 the "coupon" election, 1951 is remembered today as the "warmonger" election. Soviet propaganda had been routinely condemning Churchill as 'an aggressor, clanking with atomic weapons' for some time, but this theme was now taken up and amplified by the Labour-supporting *Daily Mirror*, which portrayed the Tory leader as a reckless opportunist determined to launch an atomic war against the USSR.[99] 'Whose finger do you want on the trigger . . .?', the newspaper asked its four million readers early in the campaign, 'Attlee's or Churchill's?'[100]

The *Mirror*'s attacks on Churchill, while politically motivated, chimed with what many people felt, or feared, and not just Labour supporters. Even in Conservative circles there was doubt. 'Winston has wound up [the campaign] with an impassioned defence of himself as a lover of peace', wrote Leo Amery. 'I am sure he does in principle, but he has always thoroughly enjoyed a war.'[101] Macmillan, while despising the *Daily Mirror* for its 'bunk and bawdiness', later calculated that the war-mongering accusations 'must have swayed hundreds of thousands, perhaps even millions, of votes'.[102] Needless to say, Churchill denied the charge, referring back several times in the campaign to his Edinburgh initiative by way of exculpation.[103] In a speech in Plymouth two days before polling, he dismissed the 'false and ungrateful charge' of war-mongering and maintained that, on the contrary, the quest for a summit was one of the main reasons he remained in public life. Rearmament, which he supported, was necessary not to fight but to 'parley'. From negotiations with the Soviet Union he hoped that some kind of settlement, 'the last prize I seek to win', would emerge. The maintenance of Empire and Commonwealth, the need to rebuild close Anglo-American relations after several years of alleged neglect under Labour, and the ongoing need to improve Western European defence and develop NATO, were themes which regularly featured in his statements on the stump, but his principal foreign policy goal was 'a friendly talk' with Stalin from which might emerge 'a fruitful and durable peace'.[104]

The *Daily Mirror* was unimpressed. On polling day, the paper devoted its front page to a picture of a hand holding a gun set above photographs of Attlee and Churchill. 'WHOSE FINGER?', the headline asked. 'Today YOUR finger is on the trigger. SEE YOU DEFEND peace with security ... VOTE FOR THE PARTY YOU CAN REALLY TRUST'.[105] Churchill immediately called in his lawyers and secured a full and grovelling apology, the *Mirror*'s owners claiming that the criticisms were made 'in the heat of the Election' and were, on reflection, 'unfair' and 'deeply wounding'. But that was seven months later. The damage, Macmillan reflected, had been done in the voting booths on 25 October where a projected comfortable Tory victory by fifty-plus seats was whittled down by the effectiveness of Labour sloganizing to an overall majority of just 17.[106] Still, Churchill was back. 'It's likely to be my last innings', he conceded. 'So it had better be a good one.'[107]

CHAPTER 11
ATOMIC ANGLES

In constructing his peacetime administration, Churchill set such store by familiarity and experience – Eden was back at the Foreign Office, General (now Lord) Ismay was given Commonwealth Relations, General (Viscount) Alexander would soon to be brought in as Minister of Defence – that Colville, himself a returnee to the Number 10 Private Office, could almost hear the strains of 'Auld Lang Syne' ringing round Whitehall.[1] But how long could this 'vast commemorative pageant' for the great days of the war last?[2] In truth, few people thought that Churchill would see out a full five-year term and most of his political associates expected – and his wife hoped – that he would hand over to Eden sooner rather than later. According to Colville, to begin with this was also Churchill's intention.[3] Yet despite mounting health problems, increasing deafness and bouts of depression, Churchill, who 'always believed in staying in the pub until closing time', developed other ideas.[4] Over the next three-and-a-half years he would drive his ministerial colleagues to distraction by his stubborn determination to soldier on even after a near-fatal stroke in June 1953 left him, according to Roy Jenkins, 'gloriously unfit for office'.[5] The principal reason (or excuse, according to some historians) for his clinging so tenaciously to power was a sense of personal mission, a conviction that with his unique experience and immense renown as a world statesman it fell to him to try to bring about 'an abatement of what is called "the cold war" by negotiation at the highest level'.[6] More bruised by the *Daily Mirror*'s campaign than he let on publicly, and possessed of what Paul Addison calls a 'sublime and persistent egotism', Churchill regarded the convening of a Yalta-esque conference as the ultimate affirmation of his credentials as a man of peace.[7]

There was one former colleague from the war years whose services Churchill was keener than most to re-engage. 'I must have Prof', he insisted. 'He is my adder. No. I can add – he is my taker away.'[8] Lindemann, however, sixty-five years old and in poor health, had no burning desire to substitute 'the hurly burly of political life' for the 'peace of Oxford'.[9] But Churchill wheedled and cajoled until, finally, his old friend agreed to become Paymaster-General, not always a Cabinet-level position but designated so on this occasion. Bonds of loyalty and friendship contributed to the Prof's capitulation, but so did the prospect of helping shape the country's atomic future.[10] Writing to the Vice-Chancellor of Oxford University to obtain Lindemann's release, Churchill explained that alongside the Paymaster-General's normal duties he was to 'supervise on my behalf the organization of our atomic energy work'.[11] Here was the opportunity. Over the previous two years, Lindemann had tried but failed to persuade the Labour government to set up a body similar to the American Atomic Energy Commission to manage all research and development. It was scandalous, he felt, that the United Kingdom had still not produced a single A-bomb, and he placed most of the blame on the Ministry of Supply, wherein a combination of suffocating red-tape and the ultra-cautious outlook of career civil servants had robbed the enterprise of vital dynamism.[12] In opposition, Churchill had supported the idea of a semi-independent corporation based on the BBC model, and Lindemann, in answering the call to serve, had cause to believe that prime ministerial backing for his plan was assured.[13]

Churchill had also been keen to re-engage the services of Sir John Anderson – he offered him the position of Chancellor of the Duchy of Lancaster with overlordship of the Treasury, Board of Trade and Ministry of Supply – but to his regret, the prospect of reviving the Tube Alloys triumvirate, even informally, came to naught.[14] Anderson had continued as an Independent MP after the war and even attended meetings of the shadow Cabinet, but in 1950, when his University seat was abolished, he decided to leave the Commons. In itself, this was not an impediment to ministerial office in a Churchill administration but when the call came, Anderson still declined to serve. 'He [Churchill] needs you in the Cabinet', Lord Moran admonished, to which Anderson, looking like 'a prim elder of the kirk', replied 'quietly' that he 'could not afford to join the Cabinet'. What he meant was that it was impossible to provide his wife, the trilling social climber Ava, 'Becky Sharpe personified', with the lifestyle she expected on a ministerial salary. Instead, he accepted a peerage, becoming, in 1952, Lord Waverley.[15]

To begin with, the new government's most urgent priority was not atomic energy but the desperate plight of the economy (although, having said this, the two issues would soon converge). The gravity of the economic position had been obscured by Labour during the election, but once the Conservatives came into their inheritance the financial facts of life were immediately laid bare. On his first day as Chancellor, Rab Butler was treated to lunch at the Athenaeum by senior Treasury officials. The tale they unfolded – 'of blood draining from the system and a collapse greater than had been foretold in 1931' – robbed him of his appetite.[16] Britain had experienced balance-of-payments crises in the recent past but it was the impact of the Korean War which had brought the economy to its knees. As a consequence of the Labour government's rearmament programme, defence spending leapt in the space of a year from 8 per cent to more than 14 per cent of GNP while the concomitant diversion of resources from the productive economy swiftly transformed a balance of payments surplus of £300 million into a deficit of £370 million. By the time that Churchill formed his ministry it was clear that huge reductions in public spending would be needed to keep the economy from going under. Despite having been Chancellor for more than four years in the 1920s, Churchill's grasp of the finer points of economic theory was not always the surest but he could recognize a crisis when he saw one. 'Never in my life have I faced an ordeal of this kind', he told Moran. 'It was worse than 1940.' All areas of government activity, at home and abroad, needed to be scrutinized from the standpoint of affordability and value for money. And that included the atomic programme.[17]

On returning to office, the Conservatives discovered that their predecessors had accomplished far more in the atomic sphere than they had credited. A uranium metal plant and two plutonium-producing piles at Windscale in Cumbria were working well; a further Windscale plant for chemical separation of plutonium would soon be in operation; and a gaseous diffusion plant to enrich uranium to feed the reactors and speed up plutonium breeding was under construction at Capenhurst in Cheshire. With the design and mechanics of an A-bomb – a plutonium-implosion device – also perfected, and with the first billet of weapons-grade plutonium on schedule for delivery in the spring of 1952, the United Kingdom was close to becoming the world's third nuclear power.[18]

Lindemann passed on the good news to Churchill in a briefing paper on 13 November. He further revealed that a weapon would be tested within the next twelve months in Australia. All that was needed was for the Prime Minister to give the final go-ahead and preparations for the test, codenamed Hurricane, could be completed. It would be good, he suggested, if the matter was sewn-up before Churchill left for the United States at the end of December for talks with President Truman since Britain was 'much more likely to get American cooperation in the future if we show we are not entirely dependent on them now'.[19] When it came two days later, Churchill's response gave Lindemann a jolt. 'I have never wished since our decision during the war that England should start the manufacture of atomic bombs', he wrote, although research 'must be energetically pursued'. The country 'should have the art rather than the article' and he intended to use his visit to Washington to obtain from the Americans 'a reasonable share of what they have made so largely on our initiative and substantial scientific contribution'. When Truman was shown the Quebec agreement, a copy of which he would bring with him with a view to early publication, he was sure 'we shall get very decent treatment'.[20]

The Prof found all this very disturbing. In the first place, he had supposed that Churchill was as desirous as he was for Britain to have its own deterrent. As far back as November 1945, Churchill told the Commons that 'we should make atomic bombs, and have them here, even if manufactured elsewhere, in suitable safe storage with the least possible delay'.[21] There was, though, a clue to his underlying thinking in the words 'if manufactured elsewhere'. For if the US–UK atomic relationship endured, he seemed to be suggesting, Britain should receive, as of right, a quota of American-made bombs. The subsequent passage of the McMahon Act was a set-back to these hopes but Churchill persuaded himself that it was American suspicion of the Attlee government's socialism that had prompted the legislation in the first place and that if, or when, he and the Conservatives were returned to power, Anglo-American trust, and with it atomic intimacy, would be restored. This belief contributed to his ambivalence about a separate UK atomic arsenal. Why go to the enormous expense of building an independent deterrent when a share of the American deterrent was Britain's atomic birthright?

In October 1946, Churchill had reminded Attlee that the UK, as a result of his wartime agreements with FDR, was entitled to 'a share of [American] bombs as they are produced, and this might well be an economical alternative to our making them ourselves'.[22] More recently, in February 1951, following a series of sharp exchanges with Attlee in Parliament, Churchill drew up a press release clarifying his position. The first draft (written in the third person) included the following sentence: 'Mr Churchill wishes to make it clear that he has never urged, nor does he now advise the large scale manufacture of the atomic bomb in this country, which our danger from air attack renders specially unsuitable'. After consulting Lindemann, whose opinion was the diametric opposite, this sentence was removed.[23] The fact that it was inserted in the first place ought to have put the Prof

Figure 11.1 The Prof, November 1951. Fred Ramage, Hulton Archive/Getty Images.

on alert but he was still shocked when, eight months later, Churchill appeared to come out in opposition to an independent deterrent. It was as though the Prime Minister was rooted in 1943, hankering after a "special relationship" in which notions of independence were irrelevant: the British and Americans would be as one, atomically-speaking.

To Lindemann, this was the greatest nonsense and in a long letter on 21 November he accused Churchill of living in atomic Wonderland. The Quebec and Hyde Park agreements were dead, he wrote. Under the terms of the 1948 *modus vivendi*, the Labour government had traded the mutual consent principle for the freedom (severely restricted under the wartime arrangements) to develop atomic energy in the UK for industrial purposes. This struck Lindemann as a good deal since in a crisis the Americans were unlikely to desist from using the Bomb simply because the British waved a piece of wartime-vintage paper under their noses holding no legal or constitutional standing in the postwar context. Attlee had hoped that a comprehensive agreement would follow but when the Fuchs scandal broke the Americans went into atomic lock-down and Britain had been 'limping along on the remnants of the modus vivendi' ever since. Turning to Churchill's desire to publish his wartime compacts with Roosevelt, the Prof pointed out that the Truman administration had already shown them (albeit in camera) to the Joint Congressional Committee on Atomic Energy, and the 'threat of publication' now would achieve little other than to irritate the White House. As to the Prime Minister's view that American A-bombs were to be had simply for the asking, 'the ferocious penalties' of the McMahon Act, including at the extreme end of the scale the death penalty, made this a non-starter. (Against this portion of the letter an irked Churchill scribbled 'no'.)[24]

Looking to the future, Lindemann explained that the Labour government had undertaken to manufacture weapons 'on a medium scale' with a view to accumulating by 1957 a stockpile 'not without military significance'. This decision he supported. In contrast, Churchill's idea of looking to and depending on the USA was potentially ruinous. 'If we are unable to make the bombs ourselves and have to rely on the American army for this vital weapon we shall sink to the rank of a second class nation, only permitted to supply auxiliary troops like the native levies who were allowed small arms but not artillery.' He ended with an urgent plea for confirmation that Australia would be the locale for Hurricane: until there was prime ministerial approval preparations would remain on hold.[25] Churchill duly signalled his assent – Hurricane could proceed – but it took him a month to do so.[26] On all the other issues raised in Lindemann's letter, he offered no comment.

Leaving aside Churchill's profound, even quasi-mystical faith in the "special relationship" to make everything right, was there also a pragmatic economic calculation undergirding his thinking? In view of the magnitude of the balance-of-payments crisis, the government could not have the defence policy it wanted, only the policy it could afford. This much he knew. To test an atomic bomb – to prove possession of the art – was one thing. To go on from there to invest countless further millions in developing and maintaining a fully-fledged atomic article was another matter altogether. In the long run, nuclear weapons might prove to be superbly cost-efficient, but at the time, in the midst of a severe economic downturn, they struck Churchill as a questionable diversion of scarce national resources – and an unnecessary one if the United States donated a stock of A-bombs to be carried by suitably-adapted RAF bombers.

Churchill had not been back in Number 10 very long before he discovered that the Labour government had spent in excess of £100 million on the atomic bomb project, a revelation that prompted an interestingly variegated reaction: he marvelled at (and probably admired) Attlee's sorcery in hiding this expenditure from Parliament; he griped about Labour's hypocrisy in accusing him of being a warmonger while secretly developing weapons of mass destruction; and he bridled at the scale of the follow-on investment that would be required to produce enough weapons to make a UK deterrent credible. And where were the votes in Bomb-building? Always the politician, he knew that trying to explain publicly a massive financial outlay on atomic development when staples like meat, butter, cheese and tea were still rationed would hardly be voter-pleasing. The only possible justification was national security, but on this count, if the United States could be brought to honour its wartime undertakings, Britain could have security not only in depth but on the cheap.[27]

On 6 December, Churchill spoke in Parliament on atomic matters and also looked ahead to his Atlantic crossing. In the past, he admitted, 'I commented unfavourably on the fact that the Socialist Government had not been able to make a specimen atomic bomb although they had been trying to do so for four years'. Now he learned that 'a great deal of work had been done' and his government was prepared to take on from Labour this 'very costly production'. Churchill refused to divulge the extent to which atomic weapons might be integrated into the country's defence in the future but he did remark that there were 'certain aspects of this delicate subject which I hope we may clarify by discussions with the United States authorities'. He was much more explicit when raising his concern – first flagged in public a fortnight earlier – about 'the great and ever-growing American air base in East Anglia'. The Attlee government had done right by offering the US Air Force a home, but three years on the reality was that the United Kingdom had become an American 'aircraft carrier', and though the atomic-capable B-29s contributed significantly to the overall efficacy of the NATO deterrent, they also placed Britain 'in the front line should there be a third World War'. The extent to which the government had a right to prior consultation, and even a veto, if the United States contemplated launching bombers at the USSR from British soil, was another issue ripe for discussion in Washington.[28]

Absent from Churchill's Commons statement was any hint of a showdown with the USSR. More than two years on from Joe-1, the UK's vulnerability to Soviet atomic bombardment meant that showdown had exceeded its natural life. In November 1951, Churchill told the Australian Foreign Minister, Richard Casey, that while he did not believe that 'total war' was likely in present circumstances, he worried that the Americans might one day tire of having to 'pay for the maintenance of Europe [and] … would say to the Russians you must by certain dates withdraw from certain points and meet us on certain requirements: otherwise we shall attack you'. This, as we know, was what Churchill had wanted the Truman administration to do for at least five years after 1945. But the atomic diplomatist had now retired from the field. If war resulted from US pressure on the Soviet Union, Churchill fretted, Moscow's 'first target would be the British Isles', a compelling reason, he judged, to bury any further thought of a nuclear showdown.[29]

But what could be done to hold back the Americans? In the specific instance of the East Anglian B-29s, the UK possessed some right to advise caution, but on the wider strategic plane the Truman administration continued to arrogate to itself sole responsibility for determining when and where the Bomb should be employed even though its European allies would be (literally) in the firing-line of any Soviet retaliation. Two further Soviet A-bomb tests had been detected during the 1951 General Election campaign and pointed to ominous momentum in Moscow's weapons programme, hence the Tory government, no less than its Labour predecessor, sought to lock the United States into a commitment to consultation whenever and wherever the atomic option was contemplated.[30] To Churchill, the obvious means to this end was to reconstitute the Anglo-American partnership as set out in the Quebec and Hyde Park agreements. Nor was this the only throwback to attitudes he had borne in the war. The counterpoise of his interest in a US–UK atomic alliance was a strong aversion to international control. In December, when the UN General Assembly's Disarmament Commission considered issuing a declaration to the effect that it was 'the duty of every state to accept, and act in aid of, an effective system of international control', and to work for the eventual elimination of all atomic weapons, Churchill was horrified. Convinced that there could never be a truly fool-proof system of inspection and detection, he wanted the proposal vetoed. 'This resolution, if it became effective, would be our death', he told Eden. 'Without the US supremacy in the Atomic weapon we and Europe would be defenceless, and war perhaps very near.'[31]

On New Year's Eve 1951, Churchill boarded the *Queen Mary* for his voyage to America. His party was 30-strong and included three Cabinet ministers (Eden, Ismay and Lindemann), the First Sea Lord, Admiral Sir Rhoderick McGrigor, and the Chief of the Imperial General Staff, Field-Marshal Sir William Slim. Also aboard was Moran who recalled how he and Churchill had made the same voyage ten years earlier in the aftermath of Pearl Harbor. 'The indomitable spirit of the PM of those years, battling against a deadly threat to the world's freedom, is now struggling only with the humiliations of old age and with economic problems that are quite beyond his ken', Moran wrote.[32] During the crossing, the eleventh of his life, Churchill showed little interest in the briefing papers his advisors had prepared, especially the economic ones. He was going to America, he insisted, 'to re-establish relations, not to transact business'.[33]

The *Queen Mary* docked in New York on 4 January 1952 and from there Churchill flew to Washington where the President was waiting to greet him. This was the first meeting between the two men as heads of their respective governments since Potsdam. At that time, Churchill told Truman, 'I held you in very low regard. I misjudged you badly ... you more than any other man have saved Western civilization.'[34] Since then, Truman had grown into an assured leader whereas Churchill struck administration observers who remembered him from the war as visibly aged and far from his pomp.[35]

A substantial section of the US Congress and press, however, refusing to believe that age had dulled Churchill's diplomatic edge, suspected that with the British economy in trouble he was 'coming over here to trade the shirt off the United States'. Similarly, the White House mail-bag bulged with warnings to Truman to be on guard lest Churchill 'play you for a schoolboy' or 'take you for a ride like he did Roosevelt'.[36]

The administration hardly needed the advice. Although Truman later wrote of 'a welcome reunion with an old friend', for more than a month his advisers had been preparing for the Prime Minister as though a typhoon was heading their way, with brief after brief encouraging the President to batten-down US policy and weather the storm.[37] Churchill wanted to 'buttress Britain's waning prestige and influence by demonstrating a special relationship between the UK and the US', Truman was told, but from America's standpoint, though a strengthening of bilateral ties and cooperation to achieve joint objectives was desirable, it was important to accomplish these ends 'without impairment of relations with other friendly governments'. The French, so critical to the success of top US priorities in Europe (the EDC) and South-East Asia (a non-communist Indo-China), were an obvious case in point. Hence 'informal consultation' rather than any explicit affirmation of Anglo-American specialness was the most that Churchill should be offered.[38]

As to the Prime Minister's interest in a summit, this was held to be premature while the Western defence build-up remained incomplete, although American policymakers conceded that the USA, being geographically removed from the immediacy of Soviet attack, held a different outlook from the Western Europeans. Because the consequences of war for the United Kingdom 'could be so much more catastrophic' than for the United States, Charles Bohlen of the National Security Council's Senior Staff observed, the British evinced a 'tendency to play down the extent of the Soviet menace' and an accompanying propensity, its natural corollary, 'to play up the possibilities of settlements through diplomatic means'. Churchill epitomized this outlook. A statesman with a track-record of favouring 'spheres of influence' as a method of settling differences between the great powers, his hankering for a summit struck many in America as redolent of an 'appeasement' mindset but evidently played well in Britain where both the public and the political elites had become conditioned over many generations 'to expediency and power realism in their foreign relations'. The administration, Bohlen concluded, should 'lose no opportunity to endeavour to bring the British to an acceptance of a more realistic estimate of the nature of Soviet power'.[39]

Ironically, as the Americans braced themselves to resist Churchill's siren songs, some on the British side were anxious that the Prime Minister's avidity for harmonious US–UK relations might lead him to sell the pass in important areas. Eden was especially worried lest his chief offer unduly fulsome support for US policy in Asia, an area of the world that counted for little in Churchill's sense of global priorities, if in return the Americans were ready to back UK policy in the Middle East, a region which, in comparison, he rated highly. To Eden, the American approach in Asia was disturbingly adventuristic. Just a few weeks earlier, Dean Acheson, his US counterpart, told him that if an armistice was reached in Korea only to be broken by the Chinese, that would be 'the trigger . . . we should have to go after them . . . if they jump on us, they will be for it . . . no holds will be barred'. Eden was left in 'no doubt that the United States would rise in its wrath if there was a major attack' and for that reason he was determined, as were the UK Chiefs of Staff, to retain the right to judge an Asian crisis on its merits and to question, and if necessary challenge, American policy. Moreover, with the current generation of Soviet bombers known to be able to reach London but not Washington, it would be the United Kingdom not the United States that felt the heat of Soviet nuclear retaliation if a crisis in the Far East spiralled out of control.[40] However, despite his best efforts, Eden could not prevent Churchill pledging to Truman that 'the UK will do its utmost to meet US views and requests' in the Asian Cold War.[41]

Others besides the Foreign Secretary were 'a good deal concerned by the PM's readiness to give away our case', and not just on the Far East.[42] Apprised of Churchill's doubts about the need for an independent British atomic capability, Air Chief Marshal Slessor, the Chief of the Air Staff, had written to him before he left for Washington to warn that if hot war erupted there was presently no guarantee that the US Strategic Air Command (SAC), which had sole responsibility for the Allied atomic air offensive, would hit those targets in the USSR most critical from the standpoint of British as opposed to American national security. The Ministry of Defence knew little of SAC targeting plans, and Slessor, recalling disputes between the RAF and the United States Army Air Forces during the Second World War over priority bombing targets, feared that the Americans might overlook bomber bases or submarine pens from which Soviet air and naval forces could operate against the UK. Even if the United States executed a volte-face and opened-up to the British the contents of SAC's guidance book, he still urged Churchill not to 'surrender our capacity for strategic initiative, even to so loyal and powerful an Ally as the United States'.[43] This was also Lindemann's view and he begged the Prime Minister to focus not on Quebec and the past but on the present. In particular, the American Strategic Air Plan could not be accepted 'blind-fold'.[44]

The first meaningful atomic discussions took place at the White House on 7 January 1952. Although charged under US law with ultimate responsibility for using the Bomb, Truman told Churchill that he hoped 'the time would never come when he might have to give the decision to wipe out a whole population not in the fighting line'. He added that it had 'always been his personal feeling that allies should be consulted on this matter'. The US Secretary of Defense, Robert Lovett, also present, then surprised the British by offering to provide an 'extensive' briefing on SAC war plans. A visit to the Pentagon by Churchill and one or two advisors would be arranged. The Prime Minister, when he spoke, appeared to have heeded Lindemann's advice to avoid bringing up the Quebec agreement insofar as he insisted that he sought only the fullest level of cooperation permitted by US law. A recent – October 1951 – amendment to the McMahon Act allowed for a somewhat greater interchange of technical data (though nothing whatsoever connected with weapons design or fabrication), and with this in mind, and prompted by Lindemann, he proposed, and Truman agreed, that Anglo-American experts should get together outside the formal meetings to explore the potentialities in this regard. The Prof would lead for the UK.[45]

As Lindemann quickly discovered, Pentagon officials, notwithstanding Lovett's offer of a SAC briefing, maintained that there was no real distinction to be drawn between military and non-military information and were consequently loathe to share any data with the British even under the loosened-up McMahon Act, especially in view of London's poor (Fuchs-personified) security record.[46] In contrast, the attitude of civilian authorities was more forthcoming. On 8 January, Churchill and Lindemann lunched with Senator McMahon. Face-to-face with Britain's atomic nemesis, Churchill could not resist bringing up the past. 'We have been grossly deceived', he growled as he handed McMahon copies of his agreements with Roosevelt. 'There has been a breach of faith.' McMahon appeared genuinely taken aback. 'If we had known this the Act would not have been passed', he told Churchill. 'Attlee never said a word.' However, with 1952 a US presidential election year, McMahon downplayed the chances of any 'large forward step in Anglo-American cooperation' until after the November poll. Churchill took note and then spent the remainder of the lunch talking about the UK atomic programme and offering an upbeat assessment of the prospects for Hurricane later in the year.[47]

As expected, the question of American bases in Britain came up for discussion while Churchill was in Washington. Less expectedly, the matter was disposed of relatively easily. The Pentagon, the Joint Chiefs, the State Department and the JCAE had all grown nervous lest the Prime Minister, having made such a public issue of the bases, rescind the existing arrangements unless he was given satisfaction. Accordingly, the Americans accepted with minimal demur a compromise sketched out some months earlier by the British ambassador to Washington, Oliver Franks, affirming that the launch of US atomic bombers from East Anglia 'in an emergency' would be a matter for 'joint decision ... in the light of the circumstances prevailing at the time'. Recalling Attlee's difficulties in December 1950, the Prime Minister insisted that the understanding be made public, which it duly was.[48] Beyond this, Churchill fared no better than the Labour leader in pinning the Americans down to a firm commitment to consultation if or when they were minded to employ atomic weapons generally. Even in the case of the East Anglian B-29s, the conditional 'in the light of the circumstances prevailing at the time' was so nebulous that there was nothing to stop Truman launching US bombers without British consent if he judged those circumstances sufficiently ominous or urgent.[49] Deep down, Churchill probably knew this. The matter was still preying on his mind when he left Washington for New York on 9 January to stay with Bernard Baruch. 'Britain ought to be consulted ... before an atomic bomb was sent off from airfields in East Anglia', he insisted. 'If the American Government take the line that they need not consult us, then they had better begin removing them now.'[50]

From New York, Churchill went on to Ottawa before returning to Washington for the climax of his North American visit, an address to a joint session of the US Congress on 17 January. As on the two previous occasions he had been accorded this honour, his principal theme was the importance of the closest possible Anglo-American relations. On more specific matters, he described the Bomb as 'the supreme deterrent against a third world war and the most effective guarantee of victory in it'. He also implored the

United States (as he had at Fulton six years before) 'not to let go of the atomic weapon until you are sure, and more than sure, that other means of preserving peace are in your hands'. There was no reference to his newer ambition, the convening of a great power summit, but when he spoke of the Cold War in Asia there was just a hint of the old atomic diplomatist. Praising the Americans for their massive military effort in Korea and their patient diplomacy at Panmunjom, he said that Britain stood four-square behind the United States in seeking to contain Communist China and, to that end, 'if the [Korean] truce we seek is reached only to be broken' by the PRC or North Korea, 'our response will be prompt, resolute and effective'.[51]

On 18 January, his last full day in Washington, Churchill attended the promised briefing on the Strategic Air Plan. As Lindemann had discovered, the President's enthusiasm for greater interchange did not extend to the Defense Department, even on the non-military aspects of atomic energy, hence the briefing afforded the British a last chance to gain some real insight into one aspect at least of US nuclear strategy.[52] For more than a year the Truman administration had been urging its NATO partners to concentrate on producing forces for the conventional defence of Western Europe while it got on with planning – entirely in secret – the atomic air offensive. To date, all British requests for information had been rebuffed. Privately, the Joint Chiefs of Staff were dismissive of the contribution the UK could make to NATO's atomic firepower. They also questioned why a financially-straitened Britain was wasting scarce money in a poor man's effort to ape what SAC was already doing, resented British competition for vital fissionable materials, and derided London's security procedures in light not just of the Fuchs scandal but the defection the previous year of the Foreign Office's Guy Burgess and Donald Maclean.[53] For their part, the British Chiefs of Staff were bitter at being so excluded when the presence of US bases in England put the United Kingdom in the atomic front-line. The Americans, they insisted, 'cannot keep their hands free in this matter, which is one of life or death to this country'.[54]

The Pentagon briefing was restricted, on the British side, to Churchill, Lindemann, McGrigor and Air Chief Marshall Sir William Elliot, Head of the Joint Staff Mission. No official record has come to light but according to Elliot's report to the Ministry of Defence, Churchill had been greatly impressed by the scale of destruction that SAC promised to visit upon the Soviet Union. At the same time, the Prime Minister worried that Britain would pay a terrible price in any future war and pleaded with the Americans to think most carefully before resorting to atomic arms. 'He foresaw that a crisis might arise when we might wish to have a talk with the Russians', Elliot wrote.

If this talk were refused or failed, the danger of war would be closer, and the fear of atomic attack greater. In that event he proposed an operation which would be in the nature of an intervention between the talk and the blow – an intensification of the cold war in a final attempt to avert the hot war. The purpose of the operation would be, in the words of the Prime Minister, 'to carry truth instead of death' by leaflets in fast aeroplanes to 50 or 60 cities in Russia warning the people of the danger in which they stood.

Churchill the politician might have been impressed by SAC's plans but Elliot the professional soldier was 'disappointed' by the generalized nature of the briefing and concluded that it was mostly a sop to a Prime Minister who had raised publicly a question mark over the presence of US bombers in the UK.[55] Over the next few months, the Chiefs of Staff would continue to pump their American opposites for information, but ironically, such insights as they obtained, mostly from General Hoyt Vandenberg, the sympathetic US Air Force Chief, could not easily be factored into military planning due to the ongoing restrictions of the McMahon Act.[56] Nevertheless, it was clear that the United States intended to trump the Red Army's conventional advantage with its own unconventional superiority. 'We don't have to match them man for man', Lovett insisted. 'We aren't going to square-dance with them.'[57]

As he prepared to leave for home, Churchill reflected on 'the most strenuous fortnight I can remember'. The visit had been a 'gamble' that had paid off.[58] True, the Americans offered little support for a summit, but that was hardly unexpected in an election year. And besides, Churchill had not pushed his agenda with any great vigour having accepted the American view that NATO's conventional build-up must first obtain critical mass.[59] Overall, though, he was confident that the visit would 'do a lot of good' in reconstituting the "special relationship" and he confessed to liking Truman 'fearfully'.[60] Others aboard the returning *Queen Mary* read the runes differently. 'It was impossible not to be conscious that we are playing second fiddle', wrote Evelyn Shuckburgh, Eden's private secretary. Even Churchill's 'powerful and emotional declarations of faith in Anglo-American co-operation' were regularly cut-off by Truman with a 'Thank you, Mr Prime Minister. We might pass that to be worked out by our advisers.' All of which was 'a little wounding', Shuckburgh thought.[61] The President and his team had stuck to their pre-planned strategy of courteous inflexibility, but while Churchill had been moved by the courtesy, Eden was 'horrified' by the inflexibility. 'They are polite [and] listen to what we have to say', he noted, 'but make (on most issues) their own decisions.'[62]

So far as the Bomb was concerned, Churchill left Washington content with the agreement on US bases – as long as it was respected in a crisis. The SAC briefing had been an eye-opener, for which he was appreciative, but he was as disappointed as Lindemann at the failure to expand technical interchange. He also continued to pine for the Quebec agreement and with it the UK's right to determine, as a partner of the USA, when or whether atomic weapons should be deployed.[63] Ultimately, Churchill was reliant on the good sense and judgement of Truman who had personally assured him that he had no interest whatsoever in a confrontation with the USSR.[64] This being so, one wonders what Churchill would have made of the President's diary entry for 27 January 1952, a mere nine days after their last meeting. Truman often used his diary as a pressure-release but this particular entry, occasioned by reports that the Chinese were planning a new offensive in Korea while supposedly talking peace at Panmunjom, is unusually angry. The time had come, Truman wrote, to target the source of communist aggression rather than continue to commit blood and treasure in combating its symptoms, as in Korea.

It seems to me that the proper approach now would be an ultimatum with a ten day expiration limit, informing Moscow that we intend to blockade the China coast from the Korean border to Indo-China, and that we intend to destroy every military base in Manchuria, including submarine bases, by means now in our control and if there is further interference we shall eliminate any ports or cities necessary to accomplish our peaceful purposes ... We did not start this Korean affair but we intend to end it for the benefit of the Korean people, the authority of the United Nations and the peace of the world ... This means all out war. It means that Moscow, St. Petersburg, Mukden, Vladivostok, Pekin[g], Shanghai, Port Arthur, Dairen, Odessa, Stalingrad and every manufacturing plant in China and the Soviet Union will be eliminated. This is the final chance for the Soviet Government to decide whether it wants to survive or not.[65]

Two years earlier, Churchill would have applauded this approach. Now, had he known that Truman entertained such minatory thoughts, even in private, he would have shuddered. But they were just thoughts. 'The Truman administration ... never worked out a clear strategy for deriving political benefits from its possession of nuclear weapons', John Gaddis concludes. 'Certainly the administration was at no point willing deliberately and publicly to threaten their use.'[66]

The Prime Minister arrived back in England on 28 January 1952 to find himself facing a Parliamentary vote of censure called by the opposition in reaction to the 'prompt, resolute and effective' retaliatory rhetoric of his address to Congress. Well-received in America, the speech garnered mixed reviews at home; the *Times* called it 'frank, robust, and admirably phrased' but the *Manchester Guardian* accused him of giving way 'to the MacArthur policy of carrying the war to China', while the *Daily Herald* warned that his tacit approval of an American attack on China could yet spell 'ruin for us all'.[67] Labour left-winger Richard Crossman, writing in the *New Statesman*, claimed that the US government not only planned to bomb China if a Korean armistice was signed and then violated, but even if the present negotiations at Panmunjom collapsed without result. And where US conventional bombing went, atomic bombing seemed sure to follow. Crossman, who claimed to have insider-information (though presumably not Truman's diary), asserted that 'Mr. Churchill and Mr. Eden did very little to moderate this policy. Indeed, it looks as though they acquiesced in it.'[68]

Churchill relished the prospect of a parliamentary duel. One of the constants during a long and mercurial political career was the pleasure he derived from 'smashing his opponents up in debate' and from this standpoint the atomic bomb was just another means to 'hit the Labour front bench for six'.[69] In preparing for the debate – delayed until the end of February following the death of King George VI – he was initially inclined to play his master-card and reveal Attlee's abandonment of the Quebec agreement. Lindemann, however, pinioned him: the revelation, he advised, would put Truman 'in a very difficult position' and would probably 'embarrass our friends in America who are anxious for greater collaboration'.[70] Nevertheless, it was a belligerent Prime Minister who entered the Commons chamber on 26 February. After re-stating the satisfactory terms of the agreement on East Anglian air-bases he proceeded to lob a political hand-grenade into the opposition trenches. Referring to the charge that he had signalled to the Americans his agreement to expand the Korean fighting to China, he announced to an astonished House that the principle of limiting the war geographically to the Korean peninsula had already been compromised by the previous government. In May 1951, the Labour Cabinet had secretly approved the bombing of China, albeit in certain prescribed contingencies (if, for instance, UN forces came under heavy aerial attack from Chinese aircraft launched from bases inside the People's Republic). It followed, Churchill observed, that his words to Congress hardly signified 'any new designs or decisions' but were instead a public reaffirmation of Attlee's hitherto secret undertaking.[71] The Labour rank-and-file, for whom the geographical containment of the war was a sine qua non of support for the US-led UN campaign, were stunned to discover how far their leadership had departed from this principle. 'There was pandemonium', wrote Tory MP Nigel Nicolson. 'I was sitting directly opposite Attlee. He was sitting hunched up like an elf just out of its chrysalis and stared at Winston, turning slowly white. The Labour benches howled – anything to make a noise to cover up the moment of shock'.[72]

For Churchill the Westminster scrapper, it was a sweet moment. 'We put them on their backs', he exulted. 'Why, it was one of the meanest things in public life to withhold from their followers their commitment over Korea, and then bring in a vote of censure on me'.[73] He had won. Handsomely so. But as he would discover in the not too distant future, playing party politics with the Bomb was a risky business.

Looking to take advantage of Churchill's good mood, Lindemann chose this moment to advance formally his plan for an atomic energy corporation but he quickly found himself embroiled in a bitter bureaucratic turf-war with a Ministry of Supply determined to retain its prestigious commission. Adding piquancy to the contest was the fact that the Minister of Supply, Duncan Sandys, a politician of vaulting ambition and married to Churchill's eldest daughter, Diana, was one of the Prof's great enemies: possessing a 'Sicilian memory for a slight', Lindemann had never forgiven Sandys for challenging his scientific authority during the war over the scale of the potential threat posed by German V-2 rockets.[74] On 9 March, while weekending at Chequers, Lindemann pressed the merits of his corporation plan with such vigour that, there and then, Churchill dictated a minute approving the immediate transfer of responsibility for atomic energy from the Ministry of Supply to the Ministry of Defence, an interim move pending legislation to establish a new organization. Satisfied, Lindemann headed back to Oxford in his Rolls Royce. Within the space of a few hours, however, Churchill changed his mind and rescinded the minute. Instead, he issued new instructions that the atomic programme should stay where it was, albeit with the Paymaster-General given a greater say in strategic decision-making.[75] Lindemann was livid and made his feelings plain. On 16 March, Colville's diary tells us that Churchill was 'irritated with the Prof who is being tiresome about atomic matters'. A week of argumentation later and Colville was writing that the Prime Minister had become 'angry, almost to breaking point, with the Prof'.[76] Rarely if ever in thirty years had their friendship been so sorely tested.

How do we explain Churchill's about-turn? His stated reason – that even a temporary shift to the MOD implied only a 'warlike use' of atomic energy – must have infuriated Lindemann in view of his previous and largely unavailing efforts to engage the Prime Minister's interest in anything but military usage.[77] We are thus left to speculate. It may be that Churchill, hectored by his friend but sensible of their long comradeship, took the course of least resistance in dictating the original minute, but later, with the Prof no longer hovering at his shoulder, he judged that in parliamentary terms the change was likely to be more trouble than it was worth. Political expediency transcended friendship. With full-scale legislation required to effectuate the Prof's plan, and with the government defending a slim majority, Churchill knew there was no guarantee that such a potentially contentious amendment to Labour's 1946 Atomic Energy Act would secure safe passage through Parliament. Furthermore, the Chancellor of the Exchequer was concerned about the rectitude of entrusting annually a huge amount of tax-payers' money (perhaps as much as £40 million) to what could be deemed to be a private-sector enterprise.[78]

The Prime Minister may also have come under family pressure from a son-in-law whom he 'esteemed and liked' and who was determined to hold on to his full ministerial portfolio.[79] But whatever Churchill's motives, the Prof was choleric when Sandys won this first round of their struggle. Churchill sought to sweeten the pill by assuring his old friend that henceforward 'you will have the fullest power to guide and direct with my authority and constant access to me on all the practical steps which must be taken in the next critical six months'. The Ministry of Supply was there to relieve him of the burden of mundanity in areas like the issuing of contracts, overseeing staffing and general accounting, freeing him to think strategically. Sandys, Churchill added, apparently without irony, 'is quite ready to serve you'.[80]

Had Lindemann not been so intimately involved with the preparations for Hurricane at this time he might well have resigned.[81] Instead he carried on and in April the Cabinet approved a revised atomic role for the Paymaster-General based on Churchill's offer. Lindemann would be responsible for advising the Cabinet on 'policy matters relating to atomic energy' and would preside over an Atomic Energy Board made up of the key figures in the British project. Subject to any directives issued by the Cabinet, he was to take 'all Ministerial decisions' with regard to research, development and production of atomic weapons and power, while the Ministry of Supply was tasked with implementing the administrative action necessary to give effect to policy decisions.[82] Whether Lindemann wished for this level of authority is doubtful. Always happier in the background as an adviser, prompter or critic, it was his firm intent to return to Oxford in the autumn of 1953. And such satisfaction as his new role may have afforded him was largely negated by his 'intense depression' that the atomic programme was still subject to the dead hand of the Civil Service.[83]

Superficially, relations between Churchill and Lindemann recovered, but the Prof was now a scientist on a mission. After a period of reflection, he concluded that the only way to overcome the Prime Minister's obstructionism was to take him on and defeat him in

Cabinet. The decision was not arrived at lightly. If he failed to win a majority, his plan – which he was convinced was in the national interest – would founder. If he won, whither his friendship with Churchill? During the war the two had been the closest of allies in Cabinet, a formidable double-act as Herbert Morrison later testified. 'There would be a voluminous report from a minister, and beside it the single sheet of paper with the Prof's comments on the official memorandum'. Churchill would 'keep his eye more on the Prof's report than on the official one' and sometimes 'unintentionally reveal, by the nature of his queries, that he had studied the Prof's comments but not the minister's paper … The result could be annoying or amusing, according to the temperament of the minister involved.'[84] Now it would be Churchill's temperament put to the test when the Cabinet was asked not just to take a view on the Lindemann plan but to take sides.

The Prof intended to time his Cabinet démarche for the autumn, to coincide with Hurricane, the preparations for which now intensified. The test was planned as a joint military operation under the direction of the Admiralty. The Royal Navy was to transport the Hurricane expedition and its vital cargo to Australia while the Army undertook the bulk of the civil engineering and construction, the RAF provided air transport from the United Kingdom, and the Australian government locally contributed ships, aircraft, men, logistics and communications. Rear-Admiral David Torlesse, whose naval career began as a sixteen-year-old in the Grand Fleet at Scapa Flow, was in overall command but he worked intimately with William Penney, head of High Explosive Research at Aldermaston and regarded by Lindemann as 'absolutely the key-man'.[85] An expert in mathematical physics and a veteran of the British mission to the Manhattan Project, the genial Penney had acquired the nickname 'the smiling killer' while working at Los Alamos, but in truth, as Graham Farmelo shows, he was 'so peaceable that he would think twice about crushing an ant'.[86] In the context of the Cold War, however, Penney was convinced that Britain's national security and status as a front-rank power hinged on possession of the most advanced weapons that science and technology could deliver.[87]

Churchill began taking an increased interest in the preparations for Hurricane from the time of his return from America. If all went to schedule, Britain would graduate as an atomic power at about the same time as US voters were electing Truman's successor. Fully cognizant of the opportunity presented by this conjunction, Churchill planned to approach the new American administration as soon as it took office with a view to restoring the Anglo-American atomic partnership.[88] On 17 February, the government, responding to press speculation, confirmed that a test would take place towards the end of the year in an unspecified location in Australia. One of the first to react to the news was Senator McMahon:

The achievement of an atomic explosion by Great Britain, when an accomplished fact, will contribute to the keeping of the peace because it will add to the free world's total deterring power. This event is likely to raise in still sharper focus the problem of atomic cooperation between ourselves and Great Britain. The British contributed heavily to our own war-time atomic project. But due to a series of unfortunate circumstances the nature of the agreements which made this contribution possible was not disclosed to me and my colleagues on the Senate special atomic energy committee at the time we framed the law in 1946. Now we may consider rethinking the entire situation with all the facts in front of us.

This was 'no more than he said to you' in Washington, Lindemann wrote to Churchill. 'But I think it very satisfactory that he has stated it publicly'.[89]

The prospect of a British bomb rekindled Churchill's enthusiasm for the marriage of science and weaponry. As soon as Hurricane was publicly confirmed, General Sir Frederick Morgan, Controller of Atomic Energy, remembered, the Prime Minister decided that 'nothing would do but that a committee to control the affair must be formed under his personal chairmanship'.[90] So was born the APEX committee, which held its first meeting in March. Membership was small. In addition to Churchill in the chair, it comprised Lindemann, Sandys and Lord Alexander, the Minister of Defence, although Morgan, Penney, Torlesse and Salisbury, the Lord President, were regular *ex officio* attendees.[91]

'You may wonder why I have called this the APEX Committee', the Prime Minister opened the first meeting. 'The other day I saw a cartoon – two ape-like creatures in a blasted landscape, the male approaching the female with an ingratiating look on his face, and she saying, "No! We are not going to start all that over again!"'. That explained the APE. 'The X, of course, stands for the unknown quantity'.[92] On a more serious note, Churchill said that the

success of the test was of the utmost importance, since it would put the United Kingdom in a far better position to secure the full co-operation with the United States which was essential to the success of a strategic air plan in war. Once our equality was established, we should be able, not only to exchange technical and scientific information more freely, but also to initiate joint consultations on targets and methods of attack.[93]

Hurricane, in other words, was the skeleton key that would unlock all those American doors slammed shut when Fuchs was exposed. Provided, of course, that the bomb went off.

CHAPTER 12
HURRICANE WARNING

The APEX committee met just four times. Preparations for Hurricane were already being managed perfectly well by the Hurricane Executive Committee (HUREX), established in May 1951, and from the start APEX was resented as an unwelcome distraction by those forced to attend to satisfy the curiosity of a Prime Minister uninterested in reading briefing papers. On one occasion Salisbury fell asleep and had to apologize afterwards for being 'gaga'. On another, Lindemann and Sandys locked horns: the two of them 'sat either side of the PM', Torlesse recalled, 'and conducted their war across him until told to desist'.[1] Nobody was sorry, save perhaps Churchill, when APEX fell into abeyance, but Hurricane itself continued to gather strength.

In May, the government confirmed that the test would take place in the remote Montebello islands off the north-west coast of Australia, and the following month, Torlesse and his task force – the aircraft carrier HMS *Campania* and support vessels, a vast tonnage of stores and scientific equipment, and an assemblage of physicists, mathematicians, chemists, botanists, doctors and engineers, set sail from Portsmouth on their 10,000-mile voyage.[2] In the hold of one of the vessels, the frigate HMS *Plym*, was the bomb save for its plutonium core which followed by air. Bill Moyce of the Atomic Weapons Research Establishment chaperoned the core as it made its way in an RAF Hastings from England to Singapore and thence, in a Sunderland flying boat, to Montebello. Moyce was under orders that if his aircraft was ever at risk of crashing he should clutch the plutonium container to his body and bail out – presumably to sink to the ocean's depths along with Britain's nuclear treasure. Fortunately for Moyce, both he his fissionable hand-luggage reached their destination safely.[3]

As the APEX committee was folding, another and altogether more consequential Whitehall committee was taking a decision of great national importance. On 9 July 1952, the Cabinet's Defence Committee, with Churchill in the chair, agreed that the Chiefs of Staff's recently completed Global Strategy Paper (GSP) should form the doctrinal basis of Britain's defence policy for the next several years.[4] Much had changed in the thirty months since the Attlee government had committed the country to a £4,700 million defence programme, the GSP pointed out. Aside from the economic downturn, the US stock of atom bombs and the American long-range bomber force (hence the effectiveness of the West's overall deterrent) had become so formidable that it was hard to believe that the USSR would risk its existence by deliberately initiating war in the near-to-medium-term future. Accordingly, Labour's defence programme, with its emphasis on rapid, large-scale and costly conventional rearmament over three years needed a new completion schedule, one that stretched some way beyond 1954. At the same time, the

Chiefs warned that the 'Free World' remained 'menaced everywhere by the implacable and unlimited aims of Soviet Russia'. Employing communism as 'a convenient and dynamic instrument', the Kremlin sought nothing less than 'world-domination'. Faced with this threat, the two cardinal objects of Allied policy were to stop international communism from 'infiltrating and disintegrating the Free World' and 'to prevent war': in other words, to manage the Cold War while avoiding hot war. This last aim was of especial relevance to the United Kingdom which would be 'the first and principal target of the Russian atomic attack'. In the absence of any fully effective defence against aerial bombardment, deterrence assumed supreme importance. 'The knowledge that atomic attack would be swift, overwhelming, and certain' would do much, the Chiefs maintained, to dissuade the USSR from starting a war, hence the Western powers 'must keep their lead in atomic weapons and in the means of their delivery, and must retain the liberty to use them'.[5]

The paper also argued for a 'complementary deterrent' – a sufficiency of land and tactical air forces at readiness in threatened areas, particularly Western Europe, which would combine with the atomic deterrent to further reduce the likelihood of general war, or else, if war materialized, to retard any Red Army surge to the Channel. Working on the happier assumption that hot war could and would be successfully deterred, the GSP anticipated a 'prolonged period of Cold War'. Importantly, in economic terms, if greater emphasis was given to developing cost-effective atomic strike-power, in due course this would permit reductions in the complementary deterrent and produce savings in overall defence expenditure. As recently as February 1952, NATO had reaffirmed its determination to build a combined conventional force of 96 divisions and 9,000 aircraft by 1954. The designated UK contribution was nine divisions and 1,550 aircraft. Now, with the Cold War expected to endure, there was much less justification for breakneck rearmament at the risk of national bankruptcy than had been the case during the Korean-induced hot war scare of 1950–1951.[6]

If the United Kingdom was to contribute meaningfully to the Allied air offensive, the GSP continued, it would be necessary to expand the current RAF programme to cater for a larger proportion of four-engined medium jet-bombers. Concurrently, Britain's atomic research and development programme needed to be prioritized with 'the small penetrating atom bomb' earmarked as a possible mainstay. At present, the Chiefs reiterated, responsibility for the Allied air offensive rested entirely with the Americans. In the absence of even a modest atomic capability of its own, and in ignorance of the details of SAC planning, Britain was obliged to trust the United States to attack those targets in the USSR of critical importance from the standpoint of UK defence. It was assumed that SAC would concentrate on military, industrial and urban centres, but the United Kingdom needed to be able to choose and destroy targets of direct relevance for its own survival. In the end, a British atomic arsenal, independent of but dovetailing with the US arsenal, was a high security imperative.[7]

On the political level, the Chiefs argued that a UK deterrent would ensure that London's views were taken more seriously in Washington, whereas 'to have no share in what is recognised as the main deterrent in the Cold War, and the only allied offensive in world war, would seriously weaken British influence on American policy and planning in the Cold War, and in war would mean the United Kingdom would have no claim to any share in the policy or planning of the offensive'. This, then, was the essence of the review. The defence programme launched by Labour was not to be abandoned but it could be slowed down and potentially scaled back. Much would depend on persuading the United States that its burgeoning stockpile of A-bombs, when considered alongside NATO's conventional arms build-up, was already an effective deterrent to Soviet aggression, certainly in Europe. At the same time, the Chiefs echoed Churchill in cautioning that America's pre-eminence in nuclear weapons could yet spell danger if it bred 'a mental outlook' in Washington 'tending to the view that war is preferable to the indefinite continuation of the Cold War and thus to a demand for a show-down'.[8]

In its discussion of the allied air offensive and the UK's part therein, the Global Strategy Paper reads today as a curious mix of reality and idealism, of aspiration and anticipation. For one thing, Britain had still to test its first atomic bomb, and though it would soon do so, it was bound to be some time before it could hope to accumulate even a small stockpile of its own. For another, even when it had the Bomb, the country would lack any means of getting it to enemy targets since the V-bomber force, the projected delivery mechanism, was not expected to enter service for another three years. On the eve of the outing of Fuchs, the GSP observed, the Labour government had been close to reaching an agreement with the Truman administration whereby in return for UK-produced plutonium, the Americans would provide a stock of atom bombs to be held 'under British control in this country'. Even now it was 'probable that if war came a stock of American atom bombs would be made available for use by the Royal Air Force'. This issue, the Chiefs of Staff advised, was one for early discussion with whatever administration took office in Washington in January 1953. What they left unsaid was that for the next few years the UK would have to rely on the USA to supply it with A-bombs. The same went for a delivery means, probably B-29 bombers, around seventy of which had been on loan to Bomber Command since 1950 (and renamed the Washington B-1 when in RAF service). However, none of these aircraft were Silverplated and in any event, by the time they were needed as an atomic strike-force, they would probably be operationally obsolescent. These qualifications left a large question mark over the independence of any British deterrent.[9]

Churchill pronounced the GSP 'a state paper of the greatest importance'.[10] Several of its headlines chimed with his own outlook: the expectation that a Britain with its own bomb would be able to exercise greater influence in and over Washington, for example, and the hope that if the US–UK atomic partnership could be forged anew, Britain might receive a quota of US weapons. However, though content to approve the GSP as a road-map for Britain's defence over the next few years, it remained to be seen whether Churchill and the service chiefs were truly of one mind. The Prime Minister was on record as stating that possessing the art of making a bomb – for which purpose the successful test of a single device was all that was required – might open the way to revived US–UK cooperation and, with it, to a share of American A-bombs. Churchill, in other words, might yet settle for the article being US-made, particularly in view of the still disconcerting economic indicators which left him on high-alert for short-term savings in defence expenditure. The Chiefs of Staff, in contrast, though fully cognizant of the economic context of their deliberations, were reluctant to invest anything like this degree of faith in the United States and wanted home-manufactured A-bombs in significant numbers both to improve national security and complement the American arsenal.

Three months after Churchill endorsed the Global Strategy Paper, the United Kingdom tested its first atomic weapon. The plutonium device was designed to detonate below the water-line of HMS *Plym* and thereby assess the impact of a bomb smuggled aboard a merchant ship and set off by time-fuse while docked in a large port like London, Liverpool or Portsmouth.[11] Almost to the last minute Churchill fretted that the bomb would be a dud. Asked by Lindemann to comment on the wording of the official statement to be released in the wake of the blast, he advised (with only part of his tongue in his cheek) to '[m]ake sure it has gone off before you issue the communiqué. Otherwise we might look silly.'[12] For the same reason he had two personal telegrams drafted for immediate dispatch following the test: 'Thank you, Dr Penney', if it was a failure, and 'Well done, Sir William', if it was a triumph.[13] The government also worried that 'would-be spies and saboteurs' might intercept Moyce and his plutonium cargo in transit to Montebello, prevent or usurp intelligence-gathering after the blast, or in some nefarious way suborn nuclear scientists into divulging vital secrets, hence elaborate deception plans were devised to suggest that the test would take place later than actually scheduled.[14]

In the end, all such anxieties were without foundation. At 9.15 am local time on 3 October 1952, Ieuan Maddock, a chemist with the Hurricane task force, began the final countdown (thus earning himself the nickname the Count of Montebello). The official film of the test, *This Little Ship*, included the moment when the initial eyewitness assessment of the blast was cabled to the Admiralty in London: 'PLYM, OBLIVION. REPEAT, OBLIVION. OBLIVION.'[15] Penney had been on the flight deck of HMS *Campania* with Admiral Torlesse when the explosion occurred. 'Suddenly there was an intense flash, visible all round the horizon … The sight before our eyes was terrifying – a great, greyish black cloud being hurled thousands of feet into the air and increasing in size with astonishing rapidity.' Despite the violence of what he beheld, Penney hoped that the test would 'bring us one step nearer the day when world war is universally seen to be unthinkable'.[16]

As we know, the Prime Minister was staying at Balmoral as the guest of the Queen when he learned of the outcome. Over the following 48 hours he sent his thanks to the Hurricane task force, approved the release of a somewhat bland public statement confirming that the test had been a success (a more excitable *Times* leader referred to the 'historic bang'), and dispatched the knightlier of his two Penney cables.[17] Apart from this, Churchill made no noteworthy public comment until 23 October when he addressed a cheering House of Commons. 'Thousands of tons of water and of mud and rock from the sea bottom were thrown many thousands of feet into the air and a high tidal wave was caused', he revealed. 'The effects of blast and radio-active contamination extended over a wide area and HMS *Plym* was vaporised except for some red hot fragments which were scattered over one of the islands and started fires in the dry vegetation.' The weapon 'behaved exactly as expected' and subsequent observations and measurements showed that the bomb did not contradict 'the natural expectation that progress in this sphere would be continual'.[18] Churchill did not disclose that the weapon was more efficient and – at 25 kilotons – more powerful than the early American bombs, not just those used against Japan but also the ones tested at Bikini in 1946.[19]

It had taken seven years and much toil, trouble and expense – probably about £150 million (some £3.6 billion today) – but Britain had finally caught up with the United States and the Soviet Union, not in size of arsenal or in delivery methods, obviously, but in basic possession of the article. 'The explosion seemed to the project, to most politicians and probably to most members of the public ... a proof of Britain's status as a great, if not super, power', the official historian of the UK bomb has written. 'It would surely win greater respect from the United States, and Britain would surely be militarily more secure through possession of the supreme deterrent of the day.'[20] Yet just six weeks later, the United Kingdom was again left standing in the nuclear arms race when the Atomic Energy Commission in Washington announced the outcome of operation Ivy, a series of tests at Eniwetok Atoll in the Pacific including, portentously, 'experiments contributing to thermo-nuclear weapons research'.[21] In Britain and America the press immediately concluded that the United States possessed, or would very soon do so, a hydrogen bomb, but the Truman administration, when pressed for confirmation, would not be drawn.[22]

We now know that the US test of 1 November 1952, codenamed Ivy-Mike, involved a monstrous device the size of a house weighing over 60 tons and with a power equivalence of 10.4 megatons – that is around five hundred times more powerful than the bomb used against Hiroshima. In comparison, the Hurricane device was Lilliputian.[23] The British government had neither been informed about the test in advance nor received confirmation from the US authorities afterwards as to the precise nature of what had taken place.[24] Lindemann, however, advised Churchill that Ivy-Mike undoubtedly involved thermonuclear science and that it was only a matter of time, and perhaps not much at that, before the USA, and then the USSR, had deliverable hydrogen bombs.[25] As a reality check, Ivy-Mike took some beating.

Lindemann had always planned to re-launch his campaign for an atomic energy corporation around the time of Hurricane and on 30 September, three days before the test, he submitted a paper for consideration by the Cabinet. Atomic energy was of such overwhelming importance, he argued, that it required 'all the imagination and drive which we, as a nation, can furnish', not to mention 'efficiency, elasticity and rapidity of decision', to realize its full potential. These qualities were more often found in the private-sector, among those 'who control large and growing industrial enterprises', than the public and he therefore urged the earliest possible creation of a national atomic corporation, run by a small executive board and financed by a government grant-in-aid. Because the emphasis of the UK programme was bound to shift sooner or later from weapons to power production, it was even more 'essential that industry should be brought in – unless the Government wishes to monopolise the production and distribution of electricity and perhaps of heat just because it happens to be generated by nuclear machines'. Lindemann wanted a bill laid before Parliament in its next session. Hesitation would be fatal. '[T]he new industrial and military revolutions will pass us by', he warned. 'Quietly and imperceptibly we shall lose our place among the nations of the world.'[26]

Several weeks went by without Lindemann's paper appearing on the Cabinet's agenda. Suspecting that Sandys was the source of the obstruction, he wrote to Churchill on 24 October urging him to be on guard against 'the tactics of those with a vested interest in the present organisation' and reminding him of his backing for the scheme whilst leader of the opposition. He added a handwritten addendum ('you will I am sure not wish to place me in the invidious position of carrying out a policy which I notoriously consider to be wrong') that was a thinly-veiled resignation threat. The Prime Minister took it badly. 'I certainly do not feel that I am pledged in this matter', he replied, 'and still less that I made a bargain with you about it when you took office.'[27] Churchill had not read Lindemann's paper – Colville had been complaining for some time that 'the PM is not doing his work' and demanding single paragraph summaries of even the lengthiest documents.[28] Nor did he read it now. Instead he asked the Cabinet Secretary to "do a Prof" and précis it for him. Brook, however, '*the* great technician of cabinet government in mid-twentieth-century Whitehall', was wholly behind Lindemann and the summary he prepared for Churchill was consequently laced with leading remarks.[29]

The Paymaster-General made a strong case, Brook felt, for even 'the most besotted admirer of the Civil Service would hardly claim that it is the best instrument for improvising and developing new industrial processes'. Having taken soundings amongst ministers, Brook advised that notwithstanding the established objections of Sandys and Butler, there was so much support for a corporation that it was no longer a case of '*whether* this should be done, but *how* it can be done'.[30] As was evident when the Cabinet finally took Lindemann's paper on 6 November, Brook had done his work well in moving a 'tired and visibly ageing' Churchill towards compliance.[31] In discussion, Sandys insisted that his object was not 'to defend a preserve of his Ministry' while advancing arguments intended to achieve that very end. Butler, for his part, remained perturbed about the financial (and political) accountability of a body in receipt of £40 million per annum from the Exchequer. But otherwise, as Brook predicted and Churchill now accepted, the 'balance of opinion' was strongly in favour of change. Due to the complexities involved, however, the Cabinet agreed to set up a small ministerial committee to consider the issue in detail.[32]

Even though 1952 was fast coming to a close, there was still time for atomic issues to add further discord to the Churchill–Lindemann relationship. In September, the Prof had urged the Prime Minister to extend the super-priority status attached to the A-bomb to cover reactor development for civil-industrial purposes, but by December, to his dismay, no green light had been forthcoming. Worse still, in the military realm, Churchill's commitment to an independent British deterrent, apparently secured following his approval of the Global Strategy Paper, was wavering.[33] The revival of the Prime Minister's interest in the art rather than the article was triggered by the election of Dwight D. Eisenhower as US President on 4 November. Here, Churchill believed, was a wonderful opportunity to work with the 'beloved Ike of wartime memory' to make the Anglo-American relationship special again.[34] Moreover, having planned since the summer to 'have another shot at making peace by means of a meeting of the Big Three' once the US vote was out of the way, he hastily arranged to visit the President-elect to put his views across before Republican policies crystallized.[35] The US election result was also welcomed by Eden and the Foreign Office as a chance to re-establish the principle of consultation, not just on atomic energy but on all issues of Anglo-American concern. Latterly, the Truman administration's negligence in this area had prompted 'endless complaints by the British at every level'.[36]

At the same time, there was considerable nervousness in Whitehall about the shape that US foreign policy might assume under Eisenhower. Churchill embodied this duality: on the one hand he was delighted that his old wartime comrade would soon be resident in the Oval Office; on the other, he thought that 'this makes war much more probable'.[37] What lay behind this observation? As Geoffrey Best has noted, 'just as he could be sentimental and ignorant about Americans and their country', preferring instinct to analysis, Churchill could also be 'realistically worried about them and the dangers they presented'.[38] Accepting this proposition in general terms, Churchill harboured more specific fears that the Republicans, out of power for twenty years, lacked the experience to handle a volatile international environment. This concern was accentuated by the Republican foreign policy platform as it revealed itself during the campaign. Senior party figures, including John Foster Dulles, the man poised to take charge of the State Department and much disliked by Churchill, spent a good deal of time promising to roll back the communist tide and liberate the enslaved states of Eastern Europe. There was also talk about relying much more heavily on atomic weapons as instruments of US foreign policy. Intended to distance the Republicans from the Democrats, whose passive containment policy was derided by Dulles for perpetuating rather than seeking to win the Cold War, and to unnerve the Kremlin and keep Stalin guessing as to the nature of Republican policy, this rough-house rhetoric would have been welcomed by Churchill a few years earlier but now it left him edgy. The fact of the Ivy-Mike test, the prospect of both the USA and the USSR soon having H-bombs, the United Kingdom's position as the primary target for Soviet attack, and the election of a politically inexperienced President who could yet end up as the plaything of extreme Republican anti-communists, all combined to create in Churchill's mind a sense of foreboding.[39] Indeed, as Martin Gilbert has shown, it was around this time that Churchill became seized by 'a new sense of mission'. Reneging on several promises to Eden that he would soon stand down as Prime Minister in his favour, he determined to stay on in order to 'bring about, by his own exertions, a reconciliation of the two Great Powers'.[40]

Whatever else a Republican administration might bring, Churchill was convinced that having Eisenhower in the White House meant that the prospects for a revival of the old wartime atomic intimacy were more favourable than they had been for some time. He was also sure that the UK's recent emergence as an atomic power in its own right would strengthen the case for restored cooperation. The Prof, in contrast, was sceptical as to whether an Anglo-American partnership would necessarily be in Britain's best interests – supposing one was even attainable. On 11 December the Defence Committee considered two Lindemann-authored papers. The first leant strong backing to the Chiefs of Staff who sought a doubling of plutonium output over the next four years to facilitate the stockpiling of A-bombs. To this end, two more reactors would be required, modern dual-purpose piles that could produce not just plutonium for weapons but power for civil purposes. Operating in tandem with the existing Windscale reactors (which were dedicated exclusively to breeding plutonium for weapons), the new piles would cost an estimated £25 million spread over the four years. The second paper sought approval for another atomic test in Australia in 1953. In both cases, Lindemann plotted a carefully-reasoned course. But while the committee agreed to the test – operation Totem would take place the following autumn – the Prime Minister flatly refused to sanction any further reactor development until he had spoken with Eisenhower. The combination of a new US government and the success of Hurricane had altered the atomic equation, he maintained, and it would be 'unwise' to 'embark upon costly expansion', either in reactors or weapons, 'until a further approach had been made to the Americans'. The committee agreed to postpone a decision on the reactors until the outcome of Churchill's transatlantic probe was known, though Lindemann – silent, according to the minutes, but assuredly upset – was asked to prepare detailed costings and blueprints.[41]

After simmering for a fortnight, the Prof boiled over in an angry stream of minutes in which he berated Churchill for his excessive military focus on atomic energy, his negativity towards the power project, and his seemingly fantastical view of how Anglo-American atomic relations were likely to develop under the Republicans. With coal reserves certain to dwindle over the next century, Britain's industrial future and national prosperity 'may depend upon learning how to exploit the energy latent in uranium'. Unless the country was to sacrifice 'all hope of holding our own in this vital field of the exploitation of nuclear energy, which I refuse to believe you contemplate, we shall have to spend almost the same amount of money whether we make bombs or not'. In other words, the investment levels for civil use would be comparable to those required for weaponry. Either way, the essential starting point was plutonium, hence more reactors, something which Churchill evidently failed to grasp. 'I was shocked by the line you took at the Defence Committee', Lindemann wrote. Looking to the Americans to dole out A-bombs was preposterous and took no account of political reality in the United States. In any event, even if the McMahon Act was suddenly conjured out of existence, and even if Eisenhower proved personally amenable to donating atomic weapons, Britain would still need dual-purpose piles if it was not to 'lag behind instead of leading in the industrial use of nuclear power'. The extra cost (an estimated £6 million per annum over four years) was 'negligible' compared with the £1,500 million the UK spent annually on defence. A decision against developing a British arsenal of A-bombs would save perhaps £7 million per annum, but there would be no further major claw-back unless the UK gave up work on atomic energy in all its forms and Lindemann could scarcely believe that Churchill would contemplate 'such a disastrous line which might well in the long run spell national suicide'.[42]

As he had done on several occasions in the war, Lindemann called for a declaration, if not of atomic independence then of substantial distancing from America. Britain 'should no more rely entirely on the Americans to supply our forces with this war-winning weapon than we should depend on them to protect our homes from bombs or our imports from U-boats'. The Prime Minister should stop chasing 'the will-o'-the-wisp of full American collaboration' and look instead to develop atomic relations with Australia and South Africa whose sources of uranium and thorium could yet underpin a 'great Commonwealth enterprise'. Far better that Britain got on with acquiring the raw materials vital to its military and industrial programmes than wait for the McMahon Act to wither away or a revivified Quebec agreement to take its place. In fact immediate action was required to cement a Commonwealth partnership lest Canberra and Pretoria 'succumb to the attraction of American dollars' and offer their ores to the United States.[43]

Whether Churchill read Lindemann's multiple missives – surely the severest he ever sent to his friend – before he left for the United States is uncertain, but if he did, he ignored much of the advice they contained. Within a few hours of his arrival in New York on 5 January 1953 he was dining with Eisenhower and preaching to him on 'the vital importance of a common Anglo-American front' on all issues, not least the Bomb. When Eisenhower claimed never to have seen the Quebec agreement, the Prime Minister whipped a copy out of his pocket and passed it over. Eisenhower seemed impressed and undertook to explore the whole question of atomic relations once he was properly in the saddle. 'There can be nothing but good in this', Churchill reported to Eden. As to obtaining atomic weapons, he had the 'feeling ... that we might easily get a supply from the United States. 'These are not his [Eisenhower's] words', Churchill admitted, 'but my impression'.[44] As we will see, his instinct was basically sound: Eisenhower *was* sympathetic, even to providing the British with arms, a prospect that Lindemann had derided as chimerical. Eden, too, thought the President-elect's reaction was 'encouraging' but echoed the Prof in advising the Prime Minister that Britain would be able to 'negotiate the more successfully' with the Americans 'the stronger we grow' as an independent atomic power.[45] Churchill had a second meeting with Eisenhower on 7 January as a result of which he was confident they had reconnected meaningfully: he went so far as to tell Colville that 'he had felt on top of him ... Ike had seemed to defer to his greater age and experience to a remarkable degree'. On the other hand, his animus towards Dulles, 'whose "great slab of a face" he disliked and distrusted', deepened.[46]

From New York, Churchill headed to Washington where he hosted a dinner at the British embassy in honour of the outgoing President. It was by all accounts an evening of real warmth and bonhomie during which Churchill spoke movingly of Truman who, he said, would 'go down in history as a great President if only for the courage of the great personal decisions' he had taken. Of these, Hiroshima and Nagasaki, together with the founding of NATO and the campaign in Korea, stood out.[47] The next day Churchill flew to Jamaica for a holiday. While there, he was visited by his old friend Lord Beaverbrook who found him 'tired and disappointed over his American journey'.[48] The reasons are not hard to descry. For one, his hopes for a resounding public reaffirmation of the "special relationship" went unrealized: privately, Eisenhower described such a relationship as 'completely fatuous' given the USA's other important international relationships with the likes of France and West Germany.[49] For another, Churchill had been depressed to find his presentiment about gung-ho Cold Warrior Republicans largely confirmed. Dulles enjoyed top-billing in this regard but he now anticipated 'rough weather ... ahead in dealing with the Republican party' in general.[50] As for his dream of a summit, Eisenhower and the Republicans evinced no more interest in a meeting with Stalin than had Truman and the Democrats.[51]

According to Harold Macmillan, it was a 'sombre' Prime Minister who returned to England at the end of January 1953. 'He talks a good deal about American foreign policy – the atomic bomb – and the hydrogen bomb. Will the Americans be prepared to wait or will they force the issue? Will they wait until, either by their own skill or by treachery, the Russians have learned the secret of the hydrogen, as they have of the atom, bomb[?]'.[52] To Churchill, it mattered less how war started than the fact that Britain would suffer terribly. Back in London, he collected his thoughts in a paper for the Cabinet which, though never completed, provides an insight into his thinking at this time. On balance, he felt that if war broke out in the near future it would be because the USSR, working to a 'settled plan', struck the first blow, which was 'never of so much importance as in the atomic age'. But there was also a chance that the new US administration might seek to convert its roll-back rhetoric into reality and launch a preventive war. Anticipating '48 hours' notice' from Washington, Churchill considered what should be done with this precious time. Since Britain had no means of contributing to the atomic air offensive it could only focus on preparing for Soviet retaliation – on making sure its armed forces at home and abroad were battle-ready, its anti-aircraft defences primed, the Queen and the rest of the Royal Family spirited to safety along with as many civilians as could be evacuated from London and other large cities. Yet no matter how assiduous the preparations, nothing could prevent 'immense destruction of life' once the bombs began to fall.[53]

Three months later, a top secret report by the Cabinet's Home Defence Committee (HDC) provided Churchill with statistical corroboration. Assuming that 132 Soviet atomic weapons 'of the Nagasaki type' managed to penetrate the country's air defences, 1,378,000 people would die immediately, 750,000 would be left badly injured, over 2 million homes would be destroyed and a further 10 million left uninhabitable. By way of comparison, 450,000 Britons (armed forces and civilians combined) died during the Second World War and 750,000 homes were levelled or badly damaged by German bombing.[54] We know now that the USSR in the early 1950s possessed nothing like this level of destructive power: the Soviet Long-Range Aviation Force comprised three armies and one independent bomber corps equipped with the piston-engined Tupolev Tu-4, an inferior but still effective variation on the US B-29, which held all of Western Europe within its operational range, but these bombers were mostly devoid of atomic payloads until 1954.[55] This, though, was known neither to Churchill nor to the Anglo-American intelligence community whose efforts at estimating Soviet capabilities were based on a combination of faulty guesswork and pessimistic prognostication.[56] Even if the real facts and figures had been laid before a US or UK intelligence officer, David Gordin suggests, 'he would not have believed it and accused you of wilfully deflating your figures'.[57] The same goes for the British Prime Minister. To Churchill, perception represented morbid reality.

During the remainder of 1953, Anglo-American cooperation continued to be the touchstone of Churchill's atomic outlook. In February, he wrote to Eisenhower restating his hope that 'now that we are making the bomb ourselves, we could interchange information to mutual advantage'. He added an appeal that was general in its sentiment but had especial relevance to the Bomb. 'What I do hope is that where joint action affecting our common destiny is desired, you will let us know beforehand so that we can give our opinion and advice in time to have them considered ... I am resolved to make our cooperation with the United States effective over the world scene.'[58]

As it happened, Eisenhower remained genuinely desirous of closer atomic ties, not from any particular sense of obligation to honour wartime undertakings (although he did feel that Britain had been badly treated in this regard) but because a pooling of knowledge and expertise would benefit US national security. However, on the atomic front, he could only go as hard and fast as the law and Congress would allow him, something the British did not always appreciate. Visiting Washington in March, Eden asked the President straight-out for a firm assurance that he would not use atomic arms without consultation with the United Kingdom. Ike demurred. With the law militating against any curb on US freedom to deploy its own weapons of mass destruction, he asked that Eden 'trust him in the general handling of his policy'. It would be little short of 'treasonous' for him to give 'a binding assurance' to consult in all circumstances. Then again, it would 'also be treasonous if he were not to consult ... if the time factor in any way permitted'.[59] What the British 'really want to know', the President confided to Dulles, 'is that we are not starting a war'.[60]

When Lindemann learned of Eisenhower's "trust me" plea he concluded that there had been no advance on the situation that had prevailed under Truman – indeed things might soon worsen. In a letter to Churchill on 19 March he warned that opinion in Washington generally, if not in the White House, was 'less favourable to Anglo-American cooperation than heretofore'. Under its new chairman, Republican Representative W. Sterling Cole, the Joint Congressional Committee was 'less flexible and more nationalist' and 'far less well disposed towards us' than it had been when the Democrats were in charge. The situation was unlikely to improve when Lewis L. Strauss took over as chairman of the Atomic Energy Commission in the summer. A one-time shoe salesman who had made good, Strauss was familiar to the Prof through his friendship with his brother, Charles Lindemann, and based on this family knowledge he described Strauss as 'friendly to England in conversation' but also well-known for 'adhering meticulously to all the provisions of the McMahon Act when Anglo-American cooperation has threatened to become a reality'. In sum, with Britain getting 'little if any benefit' from the US atomic connection in the present, and unlikely to get much more in the future, he advised Churchill that the time was approaching 'when we ought to free our hands from some of the restrictions it imposes in order to build up a great Commonwealth enterprise'.[61]

This was not at all what the Prime Minister wanted to hear (increasingly, little of the Prof's atomic advice was to his taste) and he still put his faith in an Anglo-American arrangement. By April, though, with no sign of movement in this direction, Churchill was thinking once more of publishing the Quebec agreement to demonstrate to US opinion Britain's moral claim to fair treatment. What he overlooked, or chose to ignore despite frequent reminders from Lindemann, was that the Quebec agreement had never provided for full US–UK cooperation. Moreover, fixated on the mutual consent aspect, and on the broader concept of partnership, he failed to appreciate the potential damage to his reputation at home arising from the revelation that he had surrendered to Roosevelt and his successors the United Kingdom's freedom to develop atomic energy for civil-industrial purposes. It was 'an astounding sell-out', Hugh Dalton remarked when he first learned of the offending clause, 'an Atomic Bomb on Churchill's reputation'.[62]

Meanwhile, against this backcloth, the saga of a UK atomic energy corporation played itself out. On 7 January 1953, with Churchill in New York conversing with Eisenhower, the ministerial committee tasked with examining the viability of the Lindemann plan pronounced in its favour.[63] The following week – with Churchill now in Jamaica – the Cabinet approved 'in principle' the removal of the atomic energy programme from the Ministry of Supply and established a body of experts under Tube Alloys veteran Lord Waverley (the ennobled Sir John Anderson) to consider how a corporation might function in practice.[64] A delighted Lindemann soon had additional cause for satisfaction. On 25 February, the Defence Committee, with the returned Churchill in the chair, agreed to proceed with the construction of a new dual-purpose reactor, a pressurized pile for producing power and plutonium (PIPPA). The Prime Minister had evidently gained insufficient encouragement from Eisenhower to maintain his opposition to another reactor, while PIPPA marked, for Lindemann, another small but significant move in the direction of UK atomic independence in as much as the reactor would produce not only electricity but plutonium for the weapons he hoped would form a British deterrent.[65]

In April, the Prof tabled a paper in Cabinet advocating early negotiations with the Australians both to secure the country's unallocated uranium output and also, on a wider level, to begin the process of creating a Commonwealth atomic partnership. Once a regular supply of fissile material was assured, Britain would be able to take 'a rather stiffer line' with Washington, he told fellow ministers. At stake was nothing less than the United Kingdom's 'freedom'. However, while the Cabinet agreed to exploratory talks with Canberra (as well as with Brussels on Congolese uranium), Churchill was uneasy.[66] Until this point he had allowed himself to be borne along by the tide of Lindemann's convictions, but he now expressed concern that a Commonwealth grouping could prove injurious to his hopes for Anglo-American fusion. In a minute on 1 May, he reminded Lindemann 'that our lives depend upon the atomic bomb power of the United States and that many years must pass before we can become independent of them. By that time the Russians will be far more powerful than they are now or we are likely to be.'[67]

Lindemann denied that he was seeking to break away from the Americans. On the contrary, while Britain sought to cooperate to the maximum extent permissible under the terms of the McMahon Act, the United States clearly preferred minimal interchange and continued to prize nuclear unilateralism. If proof were needed, Lindemann drew Churchill's attention to recent public comments by Sterling Cole. 'I do not feel that we can safely share our vital secrets with the British', Cole remarked. 'They were too lenient with traitors to suit me.' Although Fuchs was safely locked away, and though British security vetting had been greatly improved in recent times, Cole's attitude confirmed for Lindemann the American 'aversion to cooperating with us'.[68] Nor, as Churchill soon discovered, was this the only vital area of Anglo-American Cold War activity where congruity of outlook was wanting.

On 1 March 1953, Peter Lozgachev, Deputy Commandant at Stalin's dacha at Kuntsevo on the fringes of Moscow, brought the Soviet leader a package of documents requiring his attention. Stalin had retired to bed at around 4.00 am that morning, 'pretty drunk' by all accounts, but even when nursing a hangover he usually stirred by mid-afternoon. It was now 10.00 pm. Lozgachev made his way through the dacha until he reached the dining room where, he recalled, 'a terrible picture' presented itself. Stalin was lying on the floor in soiled pyjama-bottoms and vest, leaning up on one hand 'in a very awkward way'. After an effort to speak he gave a snort and appeared to fall asleep. He died four days later, carried off by the massive stroke that had floored him.[69]

On 5 March, as Stalin prepared to breathe his last, Churchill was telling Parliament that while a third world war could never be ruled out, it was more likely that '[w]hat is called the cold war' would continue for many years.[70] A few hours later, when it was confirmed that Stalin was no more, Churchill tore up this prediction: suddenly he sensed the possibility of a 'relaxation' in East–West tensions, perhaps even an end to the Cold War itself. The demise of Stalin presented an 'opportunity that will not recur'.[71] The last time Churchill had seen Stalin was at Potsdam. Midway through the conference, the British diplomat Pierson Dixon recorded in his diary a 'debate' in the Anglo-American camp 'on the perennial question whether Russia was peaceful and wanted to join the Western Club but is suspicious of us, or whether she is out to dominate the world and is hoodwinking us. It is always safer to go on the worse assumption.'[72] Eight years on, Churchill, who had spent most of his career adhering to the Dixon axiom, rushed to embrace the philosophy of the best assumption. There was no objective reason why a change of regime in Moscow should mean a change in basic Soviet foreign policy. Instead, Churchill went on an admixture of hunch and hope. For in the atomic age, his ideological detestation of communism, though still profound, might yet be considered a dangerous indulgence when world peace, even world preservation was at stake. Impelled by such thoughts, on 11 March he wrote to Eisenhower with a bold proposal: a joint Anglo-American invitation to the USSR to attend a Big Three summit. The President, however, a pragmatist not an intuitive emotionalist, rebuffed him. No need to rush, he advised.[73]

Over the next month a collective leadership emerged in Moscow, with Georgi Malenkov, Chairman of the Council of Ministers, and NKVD chief Lavrenti Beria, in charge of the Ministry of Internal Affairs, evidently primus inter pares. Vyacheslav Molotov was back as Foreign Minister and Nikolai Bulganin was appointed Defence Minister. Attracting comparatively little attention in the West was the rise of Nikita Khrushchev, not to the top but near to it; within two years he would have completed his ascent to become the sole undisputed leader of the post-Stalin USSR. What did make the headlines in the West was a series of remarks by top Soviet figures hinting at the need for improved East–West relations, which the press in Britain hailed as the onset of a 'peace offensive'.[74]

During this same four-week period, Churchill's initial hopeful reaction to Stalin's death hardened into a conviction that détente was now a real prospect. He did not stop to ask himself whether Soviet peace talk was genuine or whether perhaps the Kremlin needed a period of international tranquillity to allow it to focus on pressing problems at home. He put out of his mind the way that Stalin had deceived him into believing the sincerity of his commitment to the Yalta agreements. And he failed to weigh the extent to which Moscow's ameliorative strains were intended to wreck the European Defence Community (for if détente was on the cards, it could be argued that there was no longer a need for rearmed German or even a European army). Instead, Churchill went on gut-feeling. At the very least, he wrote to Eisenhower on 5 April, there should be a probe to discover 'how far the Malenkov regime are prepared to go in easing things up all round'.[75] The President agreed in principle but being of Dixonian bent, he wanted proof of Soviet sincerity before he would consider any serious diplomatic trysting. In the meantime, the NATO build-up, including West German rearmament, should continue.[76]

Eisenhower went public with these views in an address to the Society of Newspaper Editors in Washington on 16 April. The speech, entitled 'The Chance for Peace', was one of the most impassioned of his presidency. Condemning the 'perpetual fear and tension' of the Cold War, he warned that the world was set on a 'dread road' towards nuclear conflict. 'This is not a way of life at all', he intoned. 'Under the cloud of threatening war, it is humanity hanging from a cross of iron.' He then appealed to Malenkov and his colleagues to demonstrate their commitment to peace by working constructively for an early settlement of the Korean war, ending their backing for communist movements in South-East Asia, and ceasing their stalling on an Austrian peace treaty.[77] Publicly, Churchill praised a 'bold and inspiring initiative', but privately he was concerned that making explicit demands of the Soviets – the very approach he himself had advocated at Llandudno five years before – could backfire and arrest the progress of détente. Indeed, when Soviet news agencies criticized the tone of Eisenhower's address, Churchill was confirmed in his view that US policy was hopelessly 'freezing' and 'negative, if not bankrupt'.[78] The next day, in a speech of his own in Glasgow, he offered an alternative line of advance. Whether there was truly a chance for peace remained to be seen, but 'we must not cast away a single hope, however slender, so long as we believe there is good faith and goodwill'. There was no mention of Ike-style pre-conditions or demands for proofs of Soviet sincerity. It was an open, not a closed invitation.[79]

The Eisenhower administration was by no means alone in questioning the motives of the new men in the Kremlin, or in exhibiting concern at Churchill's overly-eager reaching out to Moscow. Within the British government, too, there was scepticism. Macmillan, the 'Captain' of Churchill's 'Praetorian Guard', applauded the skill of Soviet propagandists in sowing dissension in the West. The peace offensive, which Churchill took so seriously, struck Macmillan as a cynical move to weaken the resolve of the public, and by extension the governments of the European NATO powers to press on with rearmament and the EDC.[80] This was also the view of those in the Foreign Office who suspected that when the Soviets talked of peaceful co-existence 'they visualize it as the co-existence of the snake and the rabbit'.[81] Additionally, the Foreign Secretary, while supporting the Americans in establishing summitry pre-requisites, preferred that any emergent encounter with the Soviets should be at Foreign Minister level rather than, as Churchill wished, between heads of government. It may well be true that Eden, 'essentially more vain than most politicians', craved the spotlight for himself, but he was also genuinely apprehensive that Churchill, in his desperation to be the peace-maker, would give away too much, and he would surely have applied a brake on the Prime Minister's summitry had a serious life-threatening illness not sidelined him from April to October.[82] Taking over the Foreign Office himself, Churchill was soon revelling in his freedom. Despite Eden's parting plea to officials 'not to allow too much appeasement of the Russian bear in my absence', Sir William Strang, the FO Permanent Under-Secretary, struggled to keep tabs on a 'secretive' caretaker boss whom he strongly suspected was planning 'to seize whatever opportunity there may be for a lessening of tension' in international affairs.[83]

The opportunity occurred – and was taken – on 11 May when Churchill issued a new clarion call for a summit, one that elicited wide interest and sympathy throughout Europe.[84] In a speech to Parliament, he proposed a heads of government conference to be 'confined to the smallest number of Powers and persons possible', by which he meant three, meeting with 'a measure of informality and a still greater measure of privacy and seclusion. It might well be that no hard-faced agreements would be reached, but there might be a general feeling among those gathered together that they might do something better than tear the human race, including themselves, into bits'.[85] 'Thank God you said it all', Lord Swinton, the Commonwealth Relations Secretary, wrote to him afterwards. 'You have given a lead to the whole world'.[86] The US ambassador in London, Winthrop Aldrich, cabled Washington to say that in 'delivery, tone, and content' it was possibly 'Churchill's greatest performance since [the] war' as he 'touched the whole range of emotions of [the] British people'.[87] In that respect, the Prime Minister achieved one of his main aims, namely to circumvent opposition within Whitehall to his Soviet policy by recruiting public opinion as an ally. Neither the Foreign Office nor the Cabinet were apprised in advance of what Churchill intended to say mainly because, as he knew, for every Swinton there were perhaps two sceptics who worried that he was moving towards a 'super Munich'.[88]

The US government had likewise been kept in the dark about a speech in which the Prime Minister distanced himself from American policy. For the first time in a major address on foreign affairs, Aldrich commented, 'Churchill did not mention [the] Anglo-American alliance or necessity [of] solidarity with United States' and was at times 'implicitly critical' of Washington's handling of the Soviet Union.[89] A Gallup poll indicated that 78 per cent of ordinary Americans broadly supported the idea of a summit, but the Congress and many newspapers condemned the potential for appeasement inherent in Churchill's proposal, while the Eisenhower administration, though publicly neutral, privately deplored the way that the Prime Minister had unilaterally raised public expectations of peace while ignoring the President's April pre-conditions.[90] As for the convalescing Eden, he not only worried about the American reaction but was fearful of the impact on the EDC's prospects in France: it was 'long in history', he adjudged, 'since one speech did so much damage to its own side'.[91]

Churchill, though, cared nothing for the EDC.[92] Nor was he unduly bothered about criticism from the Foreign Office or elsewhere in Whitehall. What mattered was that the public was on his side and he was now ready, Macmillan believed, to play his 'big game' at the risk of 'a serious rift' with his Cabinet at home and his allies abroad, including Eisenhower.[93] The President, Churchill decided, was 'a nice man, but a fool' who had been both 'weak and stupid' in wrapping his olive branch in thorns.[94]

CHAPTER 13
A PILL TO END IT ALL

Following Churchill's Commons performance, the French government, worried about being frozen out of a British or Anglo-American sponsored détente process, proposed that the three Western powers get together to discuss the international situation. Churchill preferred to keep 'the bloody Frogs' out of it but Eisenhower was insistent on French participation and so planning went ahead on a tripartite basis for a conference at Bermuda later in the summer.[1] There was, however, one issue that the Prime Minister intended to ring-fence from the French; as he wrote to Eisenhower on 21 June, Bermuda offered an opportunity to discuss 'atomic matters' and for that reason he would be bringing two additional items of luggage, 'a document I showed you when we met last January' and a man in a bowler hat who 'explains things to me I cannot otherwise understand'. This combination of the Quebec agreement and the Prof signalled to Eisenhower in unmistakable terms that he would face further pressure to do something to improve the level of US–UK atomic cooperation.[2] In the event, the President was spared a Churchillian buffeting because the Prime Minister never made it to Bermuda.

On 23 June, Churchill hosted a dinner at Number 10 for his Italian counterpart. Towards the end of the evening, he appeared unwell – one or two observers thought him a little drunk – and by the next morning, with his left leg and arm and the left side of his face paralysed, it was obvious that he had suffered a stroke.[3] This would surely have been the end of his premiership had Eden been well. As it was, a small group of politico-medical crisis managers – Salisbury, Butler, Moran, Colville and Churchill's son-in-law Christopher Soames – took it upon themselves to defer any constitutional decision until his condition became clearer. Bermuda, though, was off. An obfuscatory medical bulletin explained the cancellation on the grounds that the Prime Minister 'has had no respite for a long time from his very arduous duties and is in need of a complete rest'.[4] The reality of his condition was further concealed from the public when the Fleet Street press barons, apprised of the situation, agreed to avoid comment or speculation in their papers, at least for the time being.[5] In the end, only Churchill's family, closest friends and political intimates knew the truth – and for that same reason, they were the only witnesses to his astonishing recovery. 'The shock of seeing a great oak tree felled is as close as I can get to describing what I felt', his daughter Sarah wrote of her father a day or two after the stroke, and yet by 1 July he was cabling Eisenhower to say that he was 'not without hope' of carrying on as Prime Minister. He even nudged the President about a summit. 'After all', he suggested, 'ten years of easement plus productive science might make a different world.'[6]

By mid-1953, the political leadership of the United Kingdom had devolved to the survival of the least unfit with both Churchill and Eden vowing to resume active service by the autumn. In the interim, Butler, the most senior Cabinet member left standing, became acting Prime Minister while the 'calm and aristocratic' Salisbury took over the Foreign Office.[7] Macmillan, a regular visitor to Chartwell and Chequers, thought that the Prime Minister's recovery was not only miraculous but connected, in a psychologically-sustaining way, to his 'sense of mission to be the "peacemaker"'.[8] In this regard, the sudden dismissal of Beria from the ruling group in Moscow at the end of June – he was later executed for treason – was taken by Churchill as a good omen. Beria represented 'the worse forms of the Communist police state', he maintained, and his downfall was 'a helpful sign' that moderates were in the ascendant and that a summit was a real prospect.[9] 'Great things seemed within my grasp' before illness struck, he confided to Moran. 'Not perhaps world peace, but world easement ... I have not given up hope of attending a Four Power Conference in, say, September ... Malenkov is, I feel, a good man.'[10]

In August, the recently retired British ambassador to Moscow, Sir Alvary Gascoigne, was summoned to Chequers. Peppered with questions about the Soviet outlook, he was unable to tell Churchill what he wanted to hear: 'there had been no "change of heart" on the part of the new Kremlin leaders', Gascoigne insisted, 'but the new team in power wished to have some time in which to settle down'. Churchill, he wrote afterwards, 'has evidently very much in mind the power of the bomb' which, insofar as it presently deterred the Kremlin from contemplating war, offered an opening for peace.[11] Clementine, anxious and worried about her husband, found the thought of a summit hateful and confided to a friend her hope that he would soon retire. 'She said, truly, that the Conference with the Russians, which he longed for w[ou]ld not be just one Conference. It w[ou]ld be the start of a long struggle which might last for years.'[12] Then again, Churchill undoubtedly knew this and welcomed the prospect of 'some final triumph, like Disraeli at the Congress of Berlin in 1878' that would 'light the way to the end of the Cold War'.[13]

In Churchill's and Eden's absence, the 'Government of all the invalids' took two important decisions on the future of the British atomic energy programme.[14] On 21 July, the Defence Committee, with Alexander in the chair, considered a paper by Lindemann which again made the case for a big increase in the annual output of plutonium to meet the Chiefs of Staff's new target of 240 A-bombs by 1957. Over the previous few months the economy had turned a corner and the Treasury, having weighed costs and benefits, had no objection to further investing in the programme. Accordingly, the committee agreed that a second dual-purpose reactor – the first having been approved in February – was required. Before the year was out, two PIPPAs had begun to rise up at Calder Hall off the Cumbrian coast. Although the original inspiration had been the need for plutonium to feed the weapons programme, the ultimate dividend was as much civil as military when, in 1957, the Calder Hall piles became the first in the world to feed electricity directly into a national grid.[15]

Lindemann was given additional cause for satisfaction when the Waverley committee came up with a viable plan for how an atomic energy corporation should function. In essence, while the government would provide the new organization with direction on matters of high policy, all technical questions would be handled by an autonomous board. A designated Cabinet minister would inform Parliament in broad terms about policy decisions and account for the corporation's budget and expenditure.[16] The Waverley report delighted Lindemann who wrote to Churchill warmly endorsing its recommendations. Atomic energy, however, remained the fault-line in their relationship. When the Prof observed that 'Waverley has clearly approached the matter in an impartial way and taken an enormous amount of trouble and I should hesitate very much to set my opinion against him in matters of this sort', the recovering Churchill scribbled a tart marginal heckle: 'esp. when he takes your view!'[17]

The Prime Minister was in fact minded to reject the Waverley report in its entirety. 'We have learned by bitter and prolonged experience in both world wars that it is a fundamental error in principle to separate research from production, or not to have one Minister directly responsible for the combined functions', he wrote in a draft minute to Butler on 9 August. He therefore preferred to keep atomic research and production with the Ministry of Supply but designate a small but powerful committee of the Cabinet to monitor the project. Before sending the minute, however, he spoke with Lindemann and as a result of that conversation he set it aside. What passed between them is unknown, but the following day, the Cabinet approved in principle the report's recommendations with one important adjustment; while the Atomic Weapons Research Establishment would henceforward fall under the jurisdiction of the corporation, the development and production of the atomic core of weapons would be subject to contracts placed with the corporation by the Ministry of Supply. In this way, Sandys and his Ministry not only retained responsibility for the conventional components of A-bombs but, on paper at least, continued to operate as the sole supplier of atomic weapons to the Armed Services. This curious compromise – a bureaucratic no-man's-land between the extremes of a Lindemann resignation and a Prime Ministerial veto of the Waverley report – possibly gives the clue to what passed between Churchill and the Prof the day before.[18]

On 16 August, Churchill returned to London 'like Tiberius returning from Capri' and chaired his first Cabinet since June.[19] He also presided the following week when ministers gave their final assent to the establishment of what would become the UK Atomic Energy Authority (AEA).[20] Despite his earlier ambivalence, the Prime Minister was now keen to lay the matter to rest. Accordingly, Lord Salisbury was given Cabinet oversight of the AEA and in September Sir Edwin Plowden, late of the Treasury, agreed to become its first chairman. Plowden would go on to become the public face of the atomic programme but to those in the know it was Lindemann who was the AEA's 'founding father'.[21] His goal achieved and his two-year sabbatical expired, in October the Prof announced his resignation and prepared to return to Oxford. Informally, he would continue to offer his wisdom to the Prime Minister (including his adamantine opinion that 'in the world of today only countries with atom bombs rank as great powers').[22] Lindemann's formal responsibilities were added to Salisbury's growing atomic portfolio, and then, in November, a government White Paper was published detailing the changes and confirming Plowden's appointment. Nine months later, the Atomic Energy Act was entered in the Statute Book and shortly thereafter (in August 1954) the AEA came into being.[23]

During the summer of 1953, as his recovery continued, Churchill sometimes succumbed to dark forebodings about the nuclear future. 'That hydrogen bomb can destroy two million people', he told Moran on 16 August. 'It is so awful that I have a feeling it will not happen.'[24] He was wrong. Four days later Moscow announced to the world that it had successfully tested a weapon 'many times greater than the power of atomic bombs'. The claim was verified by the US Atomic Energy Commission's new chief Lewis Strauss but beyond this the Eisenhower administration refused to comment.[25] We now know that the Soviet device was a hybrid bomb (a fission bomb incorporating and boosted by lithium deuteride) rather than a true H-bomb, which would only come in 1955: at 400 kilotons, it was around 20 times greater than the weapons used against Japan, but about 25 times smaller than the Mike blast.[26] Churchill, however, drew no distinctions in kind or quality. Visiting him shortly after the Soviet announcement, Macmillan found the Prime Minister '[g]reatly depressed by thoughts on the hydrogen bomb' and these anxieties inevitably fed into his thinking on a summit.[27] Hitherto, he had spoken of moving forward in unison with Eisenhower, but following the Soviet announcement he seemed more willing to consider a solo visit to Moscow and 'a talk with Malenkov myself'.[28]

In its public statements on the H-bomb, Moscow evinced pride in Soviet science but also reaffirmed its interest in 'peaceful co-existence', a juxtaposition which British Kremlinologists interpreted as a signal that the USSR believed it was 'playing from strength and not from weakness'.[29] Consequently, the Foreign Office, already nervous about a multilateral summit, was mortified at the thought of a unilateral Churchill approach to Moscow. Convinced like the Americans that any change for the better in Soviet behaviour was due not to Stalin's death but to the unity of the West and the success of its containment policy, officials worried that if Churchill – erratic, emotional, consumed with playing the peace-monger on the global scene – should ever meet with Malenkov on his own it would 'be regarded in Europe as another Munich and sow deep distrust between us, the United States and our European allies'.[30] With Churchill in the habit of citing his 1944 percentages deal as a model of personal diplomacy ('You see', he maintained, 'the people at the top can do these things, which others can't do'), Foreign Office fears of appeasement, including the trading of the EDC for improved relations with Moscow, had some provenance. Nevertheless, for the time being, Anglo-American unity remained Churchill's preferred way forward. To that end, the Korean armistice, signed on 27 July, one of Eisenhower's summitry pre-conditions, was encouraging. 'Before I lead the British people into another and more bloody war', Churchill remarked on the day of the armistice, 'I want to satisfy my conscience and my honour that the Russians are not just play-acting. I believe they mean to do something. I believe there has been a change of heart.'[31]

When Eden visited Churchill at Chequers at the end of July, he thought him 'a tragic wreck of one of the greatest men in our history'.[32] Two months later, however, confounding his doctors, dismaying his wife and once again thwarting his Foreign Secretary's hopes of the succession, he was still Prime Minister and showing no sign of giving up. Churchill's political come-back began at the Conservative Party conference in Margate on 10 October.

Pepped-up with stimulants supplied by his doctor – he took to calling them his "Morans" – his leader's speech, including a renewed call for a summit, was 'magnificent', Macmillan recorded, '50 minutes, in the best Churchillian vein'. Ten days later he got through his first Prime Minister's Questions since his stroke, albeit with more help from his GP ('You hit the bull's eye with your pill', he told Moran), but his biggest test was always going to be the Debate on the Address at the start of November.[33]

Looking back, his speech in the debate ranks as one of the earliest – and quite possibly the first – public articulations of Mutual Assured Destruction (MAD), a concept most often associated with the nuclear arms race in the 1960s and 1970s. A summer spent reflecting on his own mortality and brooding about nuclear war, along with Eisenhower's recent announcement that 'the Soviets have the capability of atomic attack on us, and such capability will increase with the passage of time', provided Churchill with his central theme: the universality of annihilation.[34] Six months had passed since his great play for détente and he did not hide from MPs his bitter disappointment that a summit had yet to materialize. At the same time, he wondered whether the 'continual growth of weapons of destruction' might, paradoxically, prove to be a source of salvation. 'I have sometimes the odd thought', he admitted, 'that the annihilating character of these agencies may bring an utterly unforeseeable security to mankind'. He went on:

> When I was a schoolboy I was not good at arithmetic, but I have since heard it said that certain mathematical quantities when they pass through infinity change their signs from plus to minus – or the other way round ... It may be that this rule may have a novel application and that when the advance of destructive weapons enables everyone to kill everybody else nobody will want to kill anyone at all. At any rate, it seems pretty safe to say that a war which begins by both sides suffering what they dread most – and that is undoubtedly the case at present – is less likely to occur than one which dangles the lurid prizes of former ages before ambitious eyes.

All nations, he ended, 'stand, at this hour in human history, before the portals of supreme catastrophe and of measureless reward. My faith is that in God's mercy we shall choose aright'.[35]

It was 'one of the speeches of his lifetime', wrote Chips Channon. Churchill left the Chamber 'flushed with pride, pleasure and triumph' and afterwards sat in the Smoking Room for two hours 'sipping brandy and acknowledging compliments. He beamed like a school-boy.'[36] An editorial in the *Times* the next day echoed Channon; in 'one of his most memorable performances' he had demonstrated his 'complete authority over the Commons'.[37] Not bad, Macmillan reflected, for a recovering stroke victim.[38] But beyond proving to himself, and to others, that he was still (literally) fit to govern, the speech was a means to one end. 'That's the last bloody hurdle', he told Moran. 'Now, Charles, we can think of Moscow ... I must see Malenkov. Then I can depart in peace.'[39]

A summit was easier contemplated than brought into being. During the summer, the boost that the Korean armistice gave to Churchill's hopes had been effectively cancelled out by the decision of the US and French governments to invite the USSR to a four-power Foreign Ministers meeting focused exclusively on European issues. Salisbury, charged with running foreign policy while both Foreign Secretary and Prime Minister were laid up, found no support in Washington or Paris for a top-level Potsdam-type conference and thus yielded to the Franco-American preference for second-tier diplomatic reconnaissance.[40] Churchill was furious at this whittling down of his grand conception – 'They've bitched things up', he snapped – but had no option but to await the Soviet response.[41] In conversation with Lord Woolton, the Tory party chairman, Salisbury complained that Churchill thought he was 'the only person who could bring peace to the world by dealing with Molotov', a self-conceit which reminded Woolton of 'him [Churchill] telling me that he could manage Stalin ... Roosevelt suffered under the same delusion'.[42]

Moscow eventually pronounced on 3 November, the day of Churchill's Commons triumph, in the form of a counter-proposal for a *five*-power Foreign Ministers meeting, with the People's Republic of China (with whom neither the Americans nor the French had diplomatic relations) added to the mix and with an agenda devoted to global as opposed to European problems.[43] When the Eisenhower administration rejected this suggestion, Churchill grabbed the chance to revive his top-table alternative. The first essential was to get Eisenhower on board and that required a face-to-face meeting. 'We are confronted with a deadlock', he wrote to the President on 5 November. 'So why not let us try Bermuda again?'[44] Having consented to the first – abortive – conference, Eisenhower could hardly say no, but he again insisted that the French be brought along. A date was set for the start of December. 'I put my paw out to Ike, and it was fixed up at once', Churchill purred. 'My stock is very high. There is a feeling that I am the only person who could do anything with Russia. I believe in Moscow they think that too.'[45]

For Churchill, Bermuda was not just an opportunity to promote his summitry agenda but an occasion for serious Anglo-American discussion of nuclear matters. Indeed the two issues were increasingly conjoined in his thinking. If war came, he knew that Britain would be 'shattered, but, I hope, not subjugated', whereas a summit might help to minimize the chances of conflict.[46] On the wider atomic plane, the President had been working steadily – if too slowly for Churchill's liking – to give substance to his earlier promise of closer US–UK cooperation. In March, he had tasked the AEC, along with the State and Defense Departments, with drawing up proposals for major revisions to the McMahon Act. In June, however, when he went public with his view that the Act was outmoded, he ran into strong opposition on Capitol Hill. There was also resistance to increased cooperation with the UK from Eisenhower's two most influential civilian atomic advisors, Dulles and Strauss. On the other hand, the Joint Chiefs of Staff backed the President on the grounds that military plans for the future defence of Western Europe, to the extent that they would eventually involve large numbers of tactical battlefield nuclear weapons then in production, required not just the UK but probably NATO generally to comprehend American intentions and capabilities. Inter-governmental agreements would also be needed with several partner-powers to permit US tactical atomic-armed units to be based in their territory. The announcement of the Soviet H-bomb that August strengthened the hand of the President and other proponents of increased nuclear exchange while previous dissenters, inside and outside of government, began to recognize the value of a united Anglo-American if not NATO-wide response to this troubling development.[47]

While the US government busied itself with devising a new Atomic Energy Bill to put to Congress, the President continued to search for ways to expand the amount of US–UK interchange within the parameters of the law as it stood. In November, with Eisenhower's encouragement, Lindemann, in his last days as Paymaster-General, undertook a mission to Washington. In talks with Strauss and other members of the US nuclear elite, the Prof secured an agreement permitting the British access to American data on the effects of atomic blasts which could be put to use in shaping UK civil defence measures.[48] When the news of the agreement was made public it was welcomed on both sides of the Atlantic as rational and sensible, while even the JCAE intimated that in the wake of the Soviet H-bomb it might be time to consider 'whether the balance which had been struck in security was to-day the one which would keep the United States ahead of Russia tomorrow'.[49] Eisenhower was keen to extend cooperation further. 'If we are forced to do battle with an enemy equipped with modern weapons', he confided to Strauss, 'it would not make much sense to expect allies covering our flanks to use bows and arrows' and he was increasingly minded to allow the British to draw on the US stock of A-bombs.[50] Accordingly, when Churchill told Eisenhower that he would bring Lindemann with him to Bermuda 'as I want to talk over with you our "collusion" on atoms', the President immediately added Strauss to the American delegation.[51]

On 1 December, Churchill left London by air for Bermuda. At a public relations level, the aim of the conference was to reaffirm Anglo-Franco-American unity at a moment of international tumult, and if the communiqué issued at the end of four days of talks is taken as a guide, it was a case of mission accomplished.[52] The truth, however, was very different. Bunkered-in at the Mid-Ocean Golf Club, the three delegations struggled to find common ground on many of the issues confronting them at what Lord Ismay, now NATO Secretary-General, called 'a sod' of a conference.[53] Matters were not helped by Churchill's bad form; occasionally sparkling, he was mostly irritable or distracted. The US Secretary of State particularly got on his nerves. 'This fellow preaches like a Methodist Minister, and his bloody text is always the same: that nothing but evil can come out of meeting with Malenkov.' Dulles, Churchill decided, was a 'bastard'. As for the French, they were treated like gate-crashers at an Anglo-American party and American observers were left embarrassed by the Prime Minister's barely disguised contempt for the 'Bloody Frogs'.[54]

Inevitably, Churchill's mood impacted on his own side. 'I am hating the whole thing', Eden wrote to his wife, Clarissa. Thanks to his boss's behaviour, the proceedings were often 'a complete circus' and sometimes 'a nightmare'. Churchill 'hears nothing . . . which doesn't help my problems'. And then there was the 'old theme song' about the change for the better in the USSR, a claim 'for which [Churchill] adduced no evidence whatsoever'.[55] Eisenhower, too, found 'Winston's deafness' difficult to deal with, especially when employed tactically 'to avoid hearing anything he does not want to hear', and the President came to resent the Prime Minister's egocentric posturing as 'the world's only statesman today'.[56]

Much of Churchill's irascibility derived from his failure to win Eisenhower's support for a summit. A few days before Bermuda, the USSR abruptly abandoned its insistence on the inclusion of China in any East–West meeting. In response, the American and French governments wanted to reissue the original invitation to Moscow to join in a four-power Foreign Ministers conference limited to Germany. This rankled with Churchill who used the opening plenary at Bermuda on 5 December to expatiate at length on his thesis that the 'new look' in the USSR could only be properly exploited by a Heads of Government summit on the wartime model.[57] This was too much for Eisenhower who was goaded into 'a short, exasperated & vulgar rejoinder'.[58] Colville was on hand to take it down word-for-word. 'Russia was a woman of the streets, and whether her dress was new, or just the old one patched, it was certainly the same whore underneath. America intended to drive her off her present "beat" into the backstreets.' It was crude. But it was also unequivocal. 'He has been chewing this over for months', Ike muttered to Eden as he stalked off in search of a whiskey and soda.[59] An invitation to the USSR to attend a four-power Foreign Ministers meeting in Berlin in January 1954 was duly sent to (and quickly accepted by) the Kremlin, and thereafter British officials found it hard to get the Prime Minister, mired in his disappointment, to focus on many of the other important issues before the conference.[60]

Beyond a summit, one of the few topics capable of engaging Churchill's attention was atomic energy. Yet even here his behaviour was so quixotic that Eden was left in despair. Immediately on arrival at Bermuda on 4 December, Eisenhower had secreted himself away with Churchill for a one-to-one talk about Korea, the Bomb and the linkage between them. More than four months on from the armistice, the Americans were anxious that the Korean Political Conference, which was to draw up a peace treaty, had yet to convene due to communist dilatoriness. Were the Chinese surreptitiously planning to resume the fighting? If so, Eisenhower said, the United States would not be sucked into another meat-grinder war – too many Americans, around 33,000 of them, had died already – but 'would expect to strike back with atomic weapons' against the Chinese People's Republic. The Prime Minister not only failed to raise any objections, but according to the American record (the only one we have) he told the President that their conversation 'put him in a position to say to Parliament that he had been consulted in advance and had agreed'.[61]

Unless deafness prevented him hearing properly, it is difficult to understand why Churchill acquiesced so meekly. Perhaps he hoped that UK support for US policy in East Asia would redound in American backing for the British position in the Middle East. If this was his calculation (and he had long hankered after such a trade), it blinded him to the dangers inherent in Eisenhower's proposals. For if, as Churchill maintained, a summit was needed to prevent the Cold War degenerating into hot war, why give advance sanction to the unleashing of the US atomic arsenal in ways that could start the very conflagration his summitry was intended to avert? His failure to raise even the slightest question about American policy on Korea is all the more puzzling given that just twenty-four hours earlier he had suffered 'one of his black days, when his imagination conjures up what might happen to mankind if he fails with Malenkov ... London, men, women and children, might be destroyed overnight'.[62]

The rest of the British party were shocked by US plans and upset that Churchill had approved them. Eden was especially distressed by the implications ('too horrible for the human mind to contemplate').[63] On a visit to London in October, Dulles had forewarned Eden that the United States, as a result of an overhaul of its national security strategy, was looking to 'use atomic weapons in military operations in repelling aggression whenever it is of military advantage to do so'. Having had this talk with the Foreign Secretary, Dulles seemed to think that US bombers in East Anglia could henceforward be unleashed in a crisis by a decision of the President alone since the joint consultation specified in the 1952 base agreement could be considered to have taken place. Eden, needless to say, strongly disagreed.[64] Now, two months on, the Americans returned to the charge in seeking advance British sanction to employ atomic weapons in and beyond Korea as they saw fit.[65]

Late on the evening of 4 December, Eden wrote to Churchill acknowledging that Britain was committed to a forceful response to a communist breach of the armistice through, *inter alia*, the August 1953 Joint Policy Declaration (in which the powers that made up the UN Command had warned that if hostilities resumed, 'in all probability the conflict could not be confined to Korea'). By the same token, 'we have never given, or been asked to give, approval to widespread bombing of China proper nor, of course, to the use of the atom bomb, or to a [naval] blockade', all of which were now mooted by Eisenhower. In case Churchill had somehow convinced himself that war with China could be contained geographically, Eden reminded him that if the USSR came to the PRC's aid, it would be in Europe, not Asia. This would place the United Kingdom in 'immediate danger' because, as the Prime Minister himself had said on numerous occasions, the presence of American bases had propelled the country to the top of Moscow's hit parade.[66]

The Foreign Secretary's hope was that a bad situation would not worsen when Churchill, accompanied by Lindemann, met Eisenhower for further atomic-themed discussions the next morning while he himself was otherwise engaged with Dulles and the French Foreign Minister Georges Bidault.[67] This time, however, Churchill did him proud. Indeed leaving aside Korea, Eisenhower's forthcoming attitude meant that the meeting was a positive one for the British on several counts. According to Strauss' record, Churchill welcomed the recent agreement by which the Americans would provide the British with data on their testing programme, but like a nuclear Oliver Twist, he asked for more. Ideally, he said, the Quebec agreement should be recognized as the foundation-stone of US–UK atomic relations, but failing that he had a more practical request. The V-bomber force was currently being developed in ignorance of the weight, dimensions and ballistics of American A-bombs, yet if Britain was to receive in the future the quota of bombs he believed to be its due, these aircraft would be unable to carry them to targets in the Soviet Union. This anomaly needed to be rectified, and quickly. Turning to the UK atomic programme, Churchill confirmed that the first *Blue Danube* A-bomb had now been delivered to the RAF, while Lindemann added (somewhat speciously) that there were presently no plans to develop a hydrogen bomb.

Responding, Eisenhower sidestepped the Quebec agreement and avoided making any promises to provide A-bombs even though, as we know, his mind was moving in this direction. Instead he reiterated his intention of amending the McMahon Act to ease the restrictions on general cooperation and expressed his hope that there would soon be greater reciprocity in sharing and analysing intelligence on Soviet nuclear activity. He also observed, *en passant*, that atomic weapons 'were now coming to be regarded as a proper part of conventional armament and that he thought this a sound concept'. To this, Strauss wrote, 'Sir Winston concurred'. If he did, it was his only rogue moment. For the most part, he had taken to heart Eden's cautionary advice. Any use of atomic weapons in

Figure 13.1 Churchill and Eden, Bermuda, December 1953. Photograph by Leonard McCombe. The LIFE Images Collection/Getty Images.

East Asia, Churchill avowed, would risk a general war in which 'all we hold dear, ourselves, our families and our treasures', risked incineration. '[A]nd even if some of us temporarily survive in some deep cellar under mounds of flaming and contaminated rubble, there will be nothing left to do but to take a pill to end it all.' Eisenhower 'sympathized' with these concerns but maintained that bombing, atomic or conventional, as long as it was limited to military targets in China, would not bring on a third world war. Sensing that he was straying into dangerous territory, Churchill pulled down the shutters. He would say no more 'until Mr. Eden was brought into the talks'.[68]

This encounter proved to be the prelude to what Colville described as 'grim conversations' that evening when Churchill, Eisenhower, Eden and Dulles dined together.[69] The US Army, Navy and Air Force were all being equipped with the Bomb, the President announced. 'If war came or if there were to be a serious breach of the armistice in Korea, the people of the United States would never understand it if the weapon were not used.' Eden countered that automatic recourse to weapons of mass destruction, as opposed to retaliation to a surprise attack by the USSR, was so 'morally repellent' that the Prime Minister's earlier blank-cheque approval of US plans for Korea no longer obtained. Rather, if a crisis erupted, there should be Anglo-American consultation regarding the most appropriate response.[70] Afterwards, in a letter to his wife, Eden revealed his 'fear' that 'we shall end up committed to new perils without any advantage to peace anywhere'.[71] At least he could console himself that his chief was back on-message. All the other problems besetting the Western alliance 'shrink into insignificance by the side of the one great issue which this conference has thrown up', the Prime Minister reflected.[72]

Eisenhower had his own rather different perspective. 'The British thinking – apparently both governmental and personal thinking – still looks upon the use of the atom bomb as the initiation of a completely new era in war', he confided to his diary. He continued:

This feeling unquestionably arises out of the fact that up until this time the British have had no atom bombs and because of their experience in World War II, they see themselves as the initial and possibly principal, target of a Soviet bomb offensive. They apparently cling to the hope (to us fatuous) that if we avoid the first use of the atom bomb in any war, that the Soviets might likewise abstain. Our thinking, on the other hand, has come a long ways past this kind of conjecture and hope. Specifically we have come to the conclusion that the atom bomb has to be treated just as another weapon in the arsenal. More important than this, we are certain in our own minds that the Soviets will do whatever they calculate their own best interests dictate. If they refrain from using the atom bomb, it will be for one reason only – because they believe that their position would be relatively worse in atom warfare than if this type of warfare were not employed. This is one point in which there seems to be no divergence whatsoever between Eden and Sir Winston. I told them that quite naturally in the event of war, we would always hold up enough to establish the fact before the world that the other was clearly the aggressor, but I also gave my conviction that anyone who held up too long in the use of his assets in atomic weapons might suddenly find himself subjected to such wide-spread and devastating attack that retaliation would be next to impossible.[73]

The next morning, the British were in 'rather a state', Colville recorded, and not just because of US plans for Korea.[74] Eisenhower had asked Churchill to comment on the draft of a major address he was to deliver at the United Nations immediately after the conference ended. Entitled 'Atoms for Peace', its central proposal was that the three nuclear powers should contribute a proportion of their fissile material to a pool to be regulated by the UN and drawn upon by other countries to facilitate civil projects. The draft perplexed Eden and his advisors who found it difficult to marry its peaceful intentions with American insistence that the A-bomb, through a process of evolution beginning with the rock, the club and the sling-shot, had achieved conventional status, and with Eisenhower's assertion of America's right to use its nuclear weapons as it saw fit.[75] Churchill, however, despite his long-standing aversion to all forms of international control, applauded 'a great pronouncement' that would 'resound through the anxious and bewildered world'.[76] Maybe he felt he owed Ike after running out on him over Korea. If so, it again fell to Eden to remind him of the atomic facts of life, namely that approval of the draft as it stood would make Britain 'accessories before the act' if the United States ever loosed its nuclear arsenal – an act, moreover, that could bring Soviet atomic retaliation raining down on the British Isles.[77]

Churchill got the message and returned the paper to Eisenhower with a note explaining certain 'reservations' he had inserted 'in the light of our exposed position'.[78] Colville was the courier. The President was 'friendly' but 'never smiled', he noticed, but agreed to substitute the phrase 'reserving the right to use the atomic bomb' for the original wording that had so bothered Eden; to wit, that the USA was 'free to use the atomic bomb'.[79] In this, Shuckburgh felt, 'we have definitely had a success in restraining the Americans, not only perhaps over the speech but on actual policy'. Events, however, would prove otherwise.[80]

After the French departed there was time for what Churchill, in reporting to the Queen afterwards, described as a 'highly important' Anglo-American meeting on Korea. Alongside the Prime Minister were Eden and Brook, while Eisenhower and Dulles were joined by Walter Robertson, Assistant Secretary of State for Far Eastern Affairs. The Americans again pressed for British support for 'a vigorous offensive – using the atomic weapon against military objectives north of the Yalu river' if the communists broke the armistice. Eisenhower and Dulles were keen on an early and explicit warning to Moscow and Beijing that atomic punishment awaited them if they stepped out of line. Churchill and Eden objected that it was the United Nations, not the United States, which should determine whether a warning was warranted. In any event, there could be no question of advance UK assent. Even in a crisis, the Cabinet, and if possible the Commonwealth countries contributing to the UN Command, should be given the chance to consider the matter. In the end, as Churchill put it to the Queen, the issue was 'so grave' that he had no option but to reserve his government's position. He was confident, however, that the Americans had been 'impressed by the dangers' which had been drawn to their attention.

(He omitted to mention that he had earlier backed the US policy he now so strongly opposed.)[81]

Eden, in contrast, doubted whether the Americans had really been deflected from their purpose, which was to 'hit back with full power' and 'go for China with all the weapons at [their] command'.[82] If, as was likely, a global war then threatened, Churchill and Eden wanted to know what say the United Kingdom would have over the use of the Bomb, both generally and in the specific instance of atomic-capable US bombers in East Anglia. 'Certainly', Eisenhower reassured them, 'there should be consultation on the circumstances in which it [the Bomb] may be used and the targets against which it should be employed.'[83] Circumstances. That could mean anything – or nothing.

For Churchill, Bermuda had been a dispiriting conference but rather than head home he opted to stay on for a few days of recuperative sunshine.[84] In Stockholm, meanwhile, Clementine accepted the Nobel Prize for Literature on her husband's behalf. The accolade brought Churchill little pleasure: the prize he truly coveted was the one for peace, but on that score, Bermuda had been the setting for what Martin Gilbert calls 'his greatest disappointment since the war'.[85] The cause of much of that regret, President Eisenhower, had gone on to New York to deliver his Atoms for Peace address to the UN General Assembly. The proposal on pooling came towards the end. Before then there was some passive-aggressive referencing of America's nuclear prowess which jarred badly with the supposedly peaceful intentions of the speech. Sounding like a modern-day Stanley Baldwin, Ike declared that the 'awful arithmetic of the atomic bomb', the yearly multiplying megatonnage of destruction, brought no comfort to a world in which there was no real defence against an atomic-laden bomber bent on delivering its deadly payload. From there he segued into a warning that pretended not to be a warning. 'Should such an atomic attack be launched against the United States, our reactions would be swift and resolute. But for me to say that the defense capabilities of the United States are such that they could inflict terrible losses upon an aggressor – for me to say that the retaliation capabilities of the United States are so great that such an aggressor's land would be laid waste – all this, while fact, is not the true expression of the purpose and the hope of the United States.' Only then did he call for the establishment of an international Atomic Energy Agency to direct atomic power towards the needs of agriculture, electricity, medicine and other constructive ends.[86]

Atoms for Peace was given a tremendous ovation in the General Assembly and was well received in and beyond America. But looking back, and without questioning the basic sincerity of Eisenhower's motives, it is hard to disagree with Shuckburgh who, when shown the draft at Bermuda, descried a two-faced policy. 'The speech is not very clever', he wrote, and 'pretends willingness to internationalise atomic weapons, coupled with the threat to use them.'[87] Historians have sometimes succumbed to hyperbole in describing Atoms for Peace – 'the most generous and the most serious offer on controlling the arms race ever made by an American President', according to one – but no more so than Churchill at the time. The speech, he told the House of Commons, was 'one of the most important events in world history since the end of the war'.[88]

Given Churchill's efforts to re-establish a "special relationship" with the United States, he was hardly going to come out against Atoms for Peace. But his public endorsement masked inner ambivalence. During the war, whenever the idea of international control was raised, he reacted like a bucking bronco. He carried this animus with him into the Cold War. Moreover, Britain was now an atomic power in its own right and from a narrow national self-interest perspective, Atoms for Peace, insofar as it required the UK to give up a proportion of its precious but scarce (not to mention incredibly expensive) fissionable material, had limited appeal.[89] The only grounds for UK involvement in an atomic bank, Churchill privately argued, was if the USSR took part and the plan therefore made some real contribution to general peace.[90] When, however, the Soviets ended several months of dithering by declaring in March 1954 that they would have nothing to do with Eisenhower's proposal unless or until there was an international agreement banning the production of atomic weapons, the British were privately relieved in that they could now stand aloof from America's flagship initiative while blaming the Soviets for undermining its viability.[91] In the end, it would be another three years before an international Atomic Energy Authority came into being, a delay which owed much to the inconsistency in the US approach that first revealed itself to the British at Bermuda. Was Eisenhower an atomic peacemaker? Or was he an atomic warrior? At times he seemed to want to be both.

Churchill was seventy-nine when the new year opened and while Eden and many of his other colleagues supposed, and maybe hoped, that he would soon retire, the prospect of a meeting with Malenkov made him more determined than ever to stay on in Number 10. Paradoxically, while Bermuda had been a severe disappointment to his summitry hopes, the disturbing insight he gained into American atomic thinking served to deepen his worries about nuclear war and to intensify his interest in brokering détente. Bermuda is now a forgotten, or at any rate neglected Cold War moment, but its importance so far as Anglo-American nuclear relations are concerned is great. For Churchill and Eden, the memory of those four days in December – the casualness with which Eisenhower and Dulles contemplated employing atomic weapons – would inform their thinking on the twin issues of war and peace for some time to come.

What the British had been given at Bermuda was a preview of the Eisenhower administration's new national security strategy. Nine months in the making, the so-called New Look was only signed-off by the President in October 1953 and had not yet been made public. Insofar as it aimed to contain and weaken the Soviet bloc over the long-term by maintaining global defensive positions of great strength, the New Look's ends cohered with those of the Cold War strategy pursued by Truman and the Democrats. In terms of means, however, the Republican approach was quite different. The Eisenhower administration set itself the goal of maximizing America's military power while balancing the budget. To achieve this, the New Look emphasized reliance not on expensive conventional forces but on more cost-efficient nuclear arms, both strategic and tactical. The deterrent value of such weapons was obvious. But if, nonetheless, the communist powers committed overt acts of aggression, the Republican administration was prepared to consider an atomic response with a seriousness that the Truman administration never got close to. '[T]he US had come to a point where it could not back away from atomic weapons', the President reflected. 'Both the US and the other side are in too deep.'[92]

Eisenhower appreciated that it would take the rest of NATO some time to adjust to the New Look but he had still been disappointed by the British reaction at Bermuda to American plans for Korea. Churchill in particular had shown himself to be 'a curious mixture of belligerence and caution, sometimes amounting almost to hysterical fear', Eisenhower wrote privately. 'When he really wants to do something, he pooh-poohs and belittles every word or hint of risks involved. On the other hand, if he is in opposition to an argument – as for example the thought that we would count on using the atomic bomb to repel massive aggression in Korea – he can rake up and expand upon every possible adverse effect on Russian intentions and reaction, and on public opinion throughout the world.'[93] According to Dulles, the problem was the ignorance of European allies as to the value of the new generation of tactical weapons being developed by the USA. Washington policymakers had arrived at an 'understanding about atomic warfare . . . earlier than any other people so far'. Bermuda showed that 'other nations were not yet ready to take the position which we were taking' – specifically, that local use of atomic arms would not add greatly to the risk of general war – 'and . . . if we were not careful about what we said about that position, we would frighten them so that they would "fly the coop"'.[94] Education would be needed. A lot of it.

The New Look was gradually unveiled to the American people – hence to the USA's allies and enemies – in the weeks following Bermuda.[95] It fell to Dulles, however, to launch the New Look in all its menacing glory in a widely reported speech to the Council on Foreign Relations in New York on 12 January 1954. Referring to the 'massive retaliatory power' now at America's disposal, he said that the administration had taken a 'basic decision' to 'depend primarily upon a great capacity to retaliate, instantly, by means and at places of our choosing'. A direct attack on the United States or its allies by the USSR would be an obvious trigger moment, but Dulles warned that local communist aggression, as had occurred in Korea, would also henceforward merit nuclear punishment both on the battlefield and against its more distant source, be it the USSR or China. 'Local defense will always be important', he conceded. 'But there is no local defense which alone will contain the mighty landpower of the Communist world. Local defenses must be reinforced by the further deterrent of massive retaliatory power.' Under the New Look, the best way to prevent communist aggression was to leave both Moscow and Beijing in no doubt that direct nuclear attack, swift, brutal and crippling, would be their certain fate if they transgressed. As a bonus, the strategy promised value for money insofar as prioritizing nuclear weaponry over comparatively expensive conventional arms would make possible cuts in overall defence spending without jeopardizing national security. In sum, Dulles said, America would have a 'maximum deterrent at a bearable cost', the proverbial "bigger bang for the buck".[96]

Intended to impress and therefore contain the USSR and China, the New Look ended up badly spooking America's allies. The British, post-Bermuda, were edgier than most. Following Dulles' speech, nervous Foreign Office officials concluded that the 'likelihood of atomic warfare (by the USA or the Soviet Union) in the event of new armed conflict involving Communist forces is increased', while 'the very nature of the retaliatory power at the Americans' disposal is such that any decision to retaliate becomes one of cataclysmic potentialities'. Perhaps, they told themselves, the Dullesian rhetoric was just a 'brand of sales talk' designed to appeal to domestic opinion, particularly the Republican right-wing, and in practice the administration would implement the strategy in a carefully measured manner.[97] However, for those like Eden, privy to the atomic discussions at Bermuda, the rhetoric appeared indistinguishable from reality. In a memorandum on Korea prepared for the Cabinet's Defence Committee on 1 February, the Foreign Secretary rated it a near certainty that the Americans would employ 'the most effective weapons at their disposal', including atomic bombs, if the communists destroyed the peace. Given the potentially ruinous implications of this policy for the United Kingdom, he intended to make it plain to Washington that 'we cannot agree to such action in advance and must insist upon being consulted at the time before it is taken'.[98]

At Bermuda, Eisenhower had re-pledged himself to extend Anglo-American atomic cooperation and Churchill duly returned to London anticipating a 'closer, more agreeable and more fertile relationship'.[99] The President did not tarry in making a down-payment on his promise: first, in his annual budget statement in January 1954 he signalled his intention to amend the McMahon Act, and then, the following month, he formally apprised Congress of his wish 'to permit our allies to have more tactical knowledge of the use of atomic weapons and their effects so that they themselves, in their planning with their general staffs, can take into account the use of atomic weapons'. In a public iteration of what he had told the British privately at Bermuda, Eisenhower added that 'atomic weapons . . . have today achieved conventional status'. Looking further ahead, he observed, almost as an aside, that the 'hydrogen bomb' in its turn 'dwarfs in destructive power all atomic weapons'.[100]

In London, the Churchill government welcomed the news of the proposed changes to the McMahon Act but the President's casual but loaded reference to the H-bomb caused disquiet. That the United States was developing the "super" had been an open secret since 1950 but there had been no categorical confirmation that it actually possessed a thermonuclear capability until 2 February 1954 when Eisenhower publicly affirmed that the 1952 Ivy-Mike shot had been 'the first full-scale thermo-nuclear explosion in history'.[101] A week later, the President sent Churchill a long and very personal letter in which the H-bomb featured as a frightening *leitmotif*. Depicting the Cold War as an epic contest between the forces of good and evil, Eisenhower littered his message with emotive references to the 'stupid and savage individuals in the Kremlin', to the 'Russian menace', and to the need to 'throw back the Russian threat and allow civilization, as we know it, to continue its progress'. Evidently, the President's objections to a summit remained strong. But whatever disappointment Churchill felt in this regard was outweighed by his unease when the letter went on to describe a future in which communism bestrode the globe in triumphant dominion.

It is only when one allows his mind to contemplate momentarily such a disaster for the world and attempts to picture an atheistic materialism in complete domination of all human life, that he fully appreciates how necessary it is to seek renewed faith and strength from his God, and sharpen up his sword for the struggle that cannot possibly be escaped. Destiny has given priceless opportunity to some of this epoch. You are one of them. Perhaps I am also one of the company on whom this great responsibility has fallen.[102]

Coming hard on the heels of the H-bomb revelations, the President's words were too redolent of Churchill the anti-Bolshevik crusader circa 1918–1921 for the comfort of Churchill the present-day summiteer. Accordingly, before replying, he sought the advice of his inner circle. 'He showed me a very queer letter from President Eisenhower, obviously not prepared by or even seen by the State Department, written in a strange mystical mood', Macmillan recorded in his diary. At any other time, Ike's message might have been dismissed as a confessional think-piece, but in the thermonuclear moment it possessed a more disturbing quality. Churchill 'broods a great deal about the atomic and hydrogen bomb', Macmillan wrote. 'The destructive power of the latter is frightful. All London in one night ... Will the Americans put off the "show down" again until the Russians have caught them up for a second time? Or will they go for pre-emptive war?'[103] Salisbury, who thought the letter 'most sinister', had been convinced for some time that it was the United States, not the USSR, which posed the most immediate threat to peace. 'Russia knew that she could be attacked with terrible power by America, with no power of retaliation (except in Europe)', he maintained. 'America knew that for an interval of several years she was safe. She might be tempted or provoked into rash action.'[104] Eden, so scarred by Bermuda, shared this anxiety and insisted that Churchill reply to Eisenhower thus: 'I take it that you are referring ... to the spiritual struggle. Otherwise your words might suggest that you believe war to be inevitable. I certainly do not think so and I am sure you do not either.'[105] As events would soon show, both Churchill and Eden were unwise to bank on certainties.

CHAPTER 14
H-BOMB FEVER

Churchill spent a month considering how best to reply to Eisenhower's sword-sharpening message. At one level, he had been flattered to be the recipient of such a frank exposition which confirmed, he felt, the closeness of their personal relations. At another, he disagreed profoundly with the proposition that nuclear weapons had transformed themselves into conventional arms to be used with abandon in the event of war.[1] However, any reticence he may have felt about challenging Eisenhower evaporated in the space of a week. On 11 February 1954, the Foreign Office was given a copy of the US record of the discussions at Bermuda on consultation on the use of US bombers in East Anglia. The British minutes – already quoted – had Eisenhower stating that '[c]ertainly there should be consultation', albeit only on the 'circumstances' in which the Bomb might be used. According to the American minutes, nothing whatsoever had been agreed. 'It was not possible', they recounted, 'to go into all the details of the problem at this time, and the experts should consult further together.'[2]

Then, on 17 February, the JCAE's Sterling Cole issued a public statement in Chicago which added disconcerting detail to the President's earlier bald statement about the 1952 Ivy-Mike shot. The explosion had completely destroyed the test island of Elugelab and left a crater in the ocean floor a mile in diameter and 175 feet deep at its lowest point, a hole big enough, Cole helpfully noted, to hold '140 structures the size of our nation's Capitol'. A similar weapon used against a modern city would wreak 'absolute destruction over an area extending three miles in all directions' and 'severe-to-moderate damage' for up to seven miles from ground-zero. He made no mention of the human cost (his listeners could do their own arithmetic using a Hiroshima-Nagasaki calculus) but added, portentously, that it was 'beyond any question' that the USSR would have the capacity to deliver such an attack on the United States in 'one or two or three years from now'.[3]

Next morning, when Colville entered Churchill's bedroom at Number 10, he found him reading Cole's statement in the *Manchester Guardian*. The Prime Minister had just got off the telephone to Eden, Brook and the Chiefs of Staff, none of whom, he complained, 'had had the slightest idea of what had happened'. Here, if it is needed, is proof of just how effectively the McMahon Act kept the British in the nuclear dark. It was 'lucky', Churchill snapped, 'that at least one person in Whitehall read the newspapers'.[4] Looking back, Churchill remembered being 'astounded' by Cole's statement. He felt as though 'the entire foundation of human affairs was revolutionised, and mankind placed in a situation both measureless and laden with doom'.[5] Suddenly, America's lead in the nuclear arms race, such a comfort to him since Joe-1, counted for little. 'A nation that had one-tenth as many hydrogen bombs as another', he worked out, 'can nevertheless win the war by being the first to attack and thereby completely destroying the 10 to 1 advantage which the other nation has got'.[6]

Nine years on from Churchill's reading of the Groves report, his moment of atomic enlightenment, the Cole statement was his thermonuclear epiphany and he spent the next three weeks pouring his perturbation into draft after draft of his response to Eisenhower. The final version was cabled to the White House on 9 March. The H-bomb – its present testing, future operational use, and deadly radioactive consequences – dominated.

> You can imagine what my thoughts are about London. I am told that several million people would certainly be obliterated by four or five of the latest H-Bombs. In a few years these could be delivered by rocket without even hazarding the life of the pilot. New York and your other great cities have immeasurable perils too, though distance is a valuable advantage at least as long as pilots are used. Another ugly idea has been put in my head, namely, the dropping of an H-Bomb in the sea to windward of the Island or any other seaborne country, in suitable weather, by rocket or airplane, or perhaps released by submarine. The explosion would generate an enormous radio-active cloud, many square miles in extent, which would drift over the land attacked and extinguish human life over very large areas. Our smallness and density of population emphasizes this danger to us.

Churchill was surprised that Cole's statement had attracted so little public or press comment. The reason, he supposed, was that 'human minds recoil from the realization of such facts' and that people, including the well-informed, 'can only gape and console themselves with the reflection that death comes to all anyhow, sometime'. Yet this 'merciful numbness' was not permitted to 'the few men upon whom the supreme responsibility falls' and in whose number he counted himself and the President. 'They have to drive their minds forward into these hideous and deadly spheres of thought. All the things that are happening now put together, added to all the material things that ever happened, are scarcely more important to the human race. I consider that you and, if my strength lasts, I, cannot flinch from the mental exertions involved'. Using the outline wording recommended by Eden, he then pressed Eisenhower to clarify his thinking on preventive war. 'I understand of course that in speaking of the faith that must inspire us in the struggle against atheistic materialism, you are referring to the spiritual struggle, and that like me, you still believe that War is not inevitable.' In closing, Churchill maintained that détente offered the only antidote to nuclear catastrophe and that, as the initial means to that end, there must be a summit. 'Men have to settle with men, no matter how vast, and in part beyond their comprehension, the business in hand may be. I can even imagine that a few simple words, spoken in the awe which may at once oppress and inspire the speakers might lift this nuclear monster from our world.'[7]

It was a 'powerful and dramatic letter, which I admit only WSC could have written', Shuckburgh recorded.[8] But would his plea for nuclear restraint and a summit move

Eisenhower? The day after Churchill sent his message, the President was asked at a news conference whether he shared the Prime Minister's desire for a meeting with Malenkov. Eisenhower swatted the question with disdain. 'Here, in this one, I will put it this way: I fail to see at this moment what good could come out of it.'[9] This was a foretaste of what he wrote on 19 March in his reply to Churchill, for while sharing the Prime Minister's 'grave concern at the steady increase in methods of mass destruction', there were no grounds for a meeting with the Soviets in the immediate future.[10] That was it. No more, no less.

For Churchill, increasingly gripped by 'Russian monomania', this was never going to be good enough. If war came, both sides might begin by employing conventional weapons but escalation to the atomic and thermonuclear levels remained an inherent possibility, if not a likelihood. Far better, then, to regulate great power relations in ways that minimized the risk of war. And that, to Churchill, meant starting with a summit. 'His only interest', he told Rab Butler, 'was in high level consultations with the Russians, & in the future of the atom bomb.'[11]

On 1 March 1954, the US Atomic Energy Commission announced that a series of nuclear tests had begun that day in the Pacific. No details were given but the press in America and elsewhere assumed – rightly – that a thermonuclear device was involved. Operation Castle, unlike operation Ivy in 1952, aimed to test actual weapons that could be carried by US bombers. The first blast in what was intended to be a sequence of seven, codenamed Castle-Bravo, produced a fireball nearly four miles in diameter, a cloud that reached a height of 114,000 feet in four minutes, and an explosive yield of 15 megatons, around 900 times as great as the Hiroshima weapon and nearly twice as powerful as American experts predicted. Theoretical physicist Marshall Rosenbluth watched the shot from a destroyer thirty miles away. It was, he recalled, a 'shattering experience'. The fireball kept 'rising and rising, and spreading . . . It looked to me like what you might imagine a diseased brain of some mad man would look like . . . And it just kept getting bigger and bigger . . . it was pretty brutal.'[12]

While ready to make public the fact of the test, the Eisenhower administration had no plans to discuss its nature or impact. Very soon, however, this policy of minimal disclosure was in trouble. On 14 March, a Japanese trawler, the 100-ton *Lucky Dragon No. 5* (*Daigo Fukuryū Maru*), reached its home port of Yaizu, thirty miles south-west of Tokyo, with its 23-man crew suffering from varying degrees of radiation sickness. The worst affected had blistered skin, bleeding gums, hair falling out, headaches, nausea and watering eyes. As a result of previous experimentation – notably the Upshot-Knothole test in Nevada in 1953 – American authorities were aware of the danger of fall-out and in the lead-up to Castle-Bravo the US Navy had been assiduous in warning vessels to avoid the area in which radioactive contamination was assessed to be a potential hazard.[13] On the eve of the test, however, the wind stiffened and shifted direction but Castle-Bravo went ahead regardless and the unlucky crew of the *Lucky Dragon*, fishing for tuna on or just beyond the fringe of the exclusion zone, were subsequently showered in whitish flakes of ash. Given Japan's heightened nuclear sensitivity, the fate of the fishermen provoked instant 'radioactivity hysteria' with anti-US protests across the country and the press full of stories warning of the dangers of skin cancer from American 'death ash' and of radio-active fish in the food chain.[14]

Beyond Japan, the *Lucky Dragon* quickly became the focus of widespread international criticism of the Eisenhower administration and its testing regime.[15] The USA's public relations image was not helped at this moment of global anxiety by Cole's announcement that America possessed a H-bomb deliverable to any target in the world, or by Strauss who confirmed that an additional $1 billion had been set aside to ensure the 'variety and versatility' of the nation's already 'very great' nuclear arsenal.[16] At a news conference on 24 March, the President added to the alarm. 'It is quite clear that this time something must have happened' in the Pacific 'that we have never experienced before, and must have surprised and astonished the scientists'.[17] This was not reassuring. If the nuclear experts did not know what was going on, then who did? When, soon after, the Indian leader Jawaharlal Nehru likened the H-bomb to 'the genie who came out of the bottle, ultimately swallowing man' and called for 'some sort of standstill agreement' on the testing of 'all dreaded weapons of war', he found a sympathetic echo in many countries, not least Britain.[18]

In London on 22 March, the Cabinet decided that the Prime Minister needed to make a 'general statement' to Parliament 'about the appearance of this new horror' even though, by so doing, he risked revealing the extent to which nuclear decision-making of direct consequence for Britain's national security was 'largely in the hands of the Americans'.[19] The following day, however, in speaking to MPs, Churchill fudged the issue: using words redolent of Attlee's in December 1950, he said he was perfectly satisfied with the existing 'smooth and friendly' arrangements for consultation on the use of the Bomb.[20] What else could he say? That no formal mechanism for consultation existed? That despite his 1952 agreement with the Americans, the US government could still take action likely to expose Britain to nuclear devastation without political authorities in London having any say in the matter? Notwithstanding the confident tones of his parliamentary statement, Castle-Bravo forced Churchill to confront these questions head-on. The next day, in a cable to Eisenhower, he observed pointedly that the H-bomb, and the 'rapid progress the Soviets are said to be making with it', was the 'peril which marches towards us and is nearer and more deadly to us than to you'.[21]

Ignoring the international furore, the United States held its course and carried out the second test in the Castle series on 26 March, the news being announced by Strauss three days later.[22] The possibility of a moratorium on testing was given consideration in Washington, and in fact remained on the National Security Council's agenda until June when it was finally and decisively rejected: US security in the thermonuclear age was more important than courting international goodwill.[23] The Eisenhower administration's one concession to world opinion was to extend the Pacific exclusion zone to 450 miles from the proving ground, but in Britain, a country, unlike the United States, within the operational ambit of Soviet bombers, this gesture only heightened public concern about the H-bomb, 'not as a nightmare of the future', as Lord Salisbury put it, 'but as a hideous reality of today'.[24] The new Pacific 'danger zone', the *News Chronicle* worked out, covered an area equivalent to the whole of the British Isles, most of France, all of Holland and Belgium, and Germany as far east as Frankfurt. The message seemed clear. In the event of war, if you managed to survive the blast and the heat of the H-bomb itself, the death-cloud would get you anyway.[25]

'Very great excitement everywhere', Evelyn Shuckburgh wrote in his diary, 'as if people began to see the end of the world'.[26] Time to pray then? Billy Graham, the young American evangelist, had launched his Greater London Crusade at the start of March and by the end of the month he was filling the 12,000-seat Haringey arena night after night while landline relays ensured that his message of salvation and God's redemptive love reached packed churches, halls and cinemas far beyond East London. In all, over 12 weeks, an estimated 1.7 million people witnessed Graham preach. The crusade culminated on 22 May with consecutive gatherings of 65,000 people at White City and 120,000 at Wembley Stadium. It was, writes David Kynaston, a 'phenomenon' explicable in part by mass fear of what Graham himself called 'this hell bomb'.[27]

On 30 March, Churchill delivered a political sermon to his own congregation at Westminster. For nearly a fortnight the opposition had been pressing the government to declare its position on the great issue of the moment and now, finally, the Prime Minister obliged. There was, he insisted, no scientific basis to the suggestion in the more sensationalist newspaper accounts that H-bomb testing was running amok. The earth's atmosphere was not about to catch fire. As everybody knew, the US government was prohibited by law from discussing its testing procedures with other countries and he was not going to harangue Eisenhower on that matter. Naturally he hoped that the pending relaxation of the McMahon Act would allow for greater access to information about American activities and that this in turn would be of value in shaping UK civil defence policy. But if Labour kept up its incessant anti-American criticism, the President and Congress, he warned, might have second thoughts. This brought Churchill to his principal theme, the need to show trust in the wisdom and discretion of the Americans in handling the H-bomb. Consistent with this view, he said there were no grounds for pressing Eisenhower to agree to a moratorium on testing. On the contrary, the 'experiments which the Americans are now conducting ... are an essential part of the defence policy of a friendly power without whose massive strength and generous help Europe would be in mortal peril'. The US nuclear arsenal, he reminded MPs, 'provides the greatest possible deterrent against the outbreak of a third world war'.[28]

'You handled yourself in your very best style yesterday ... on the Hydrogen Bomb', his old friend Bernard Baruch wrote to him. 'You are still the champ'.[29] This, though, was a far from universally-held opinion in Britain, particularly on the left. A *Daily Mirror* editorial, 'Twilight of a Giant', described the Prime Minister as disconnected from the anxieties of ordinary people. Britain needed to show international leadership 'in facing the horror-bomb problem' and should be challenging not backing the United States over testing. But what, the paper asked its 4.5 million readers, had the Prime Minister served up? 'Old and tired, he mouthed comfortless words ... His battles are past ... This is the Giant in Decay'.[30]

At the end of March, the Labour opposition called for a full-dress debate on the H-bomb.[31] Churchill was happy to take them on not merely to defend his "trust America" position but to prove that he remained literally fit to govern. For months the *Daily Mirror* had been calling for his resignation on grounds of age and decrepitude, but left-wing

Man goeth forth unto his work and to his labour until the evening.

Figure 14.1 Churchill by Illingworth, *Punch*, 3 February 1954.

needling caused him little concern. It was a different matter when, in February, *Punch* published a deeply unflattering cartoon of him sitting listless at his desk, rheumy-eyed and crumpled with age. The cartoon, by Leslie Illingworth, not only upset Churchill on a personal vanity level but left him feeling politically vulnerable. Unlike the *Mirror*, he told Moran, '*Punch* goes everywhere. I shall have to retire if this sort of thing goes on.'[32] A month later, thanks to the H-bomb, he saw his chance to hit back. 'It is obvious that the Opposition – or the less responsible part of it – feel that at last they have found something to cling on to', Macmillan wrote. 'I have no doubt that Churchill will accept the challenge.'[33] He did. On 31 March he told the Cabinet that 'in view of the public anxiety which these experiments had aroused' he would grant Labour its wish.[34] The Prime Minister was in 'rampaging' form, Brook told Moran, and looking forward to putting 'Attlee on his back'.[35]

In Washington, the Eisenhower administration had started to panic about the panic. 'Some feel the British Isles could be wiped out, and so they better make a deal on the best terms possible with the Russians', a disconcerted Dulles told Strauss on 29 March. Something needed to be done to 'moderate [the] wave of hysteria' which was 'driving our Allies away from us. They think we are getting ready for a war of this kind. We could survive but some of them would be obliterated in a few minutes. It could lead to a policy of neutrality or appeasement' and the break-up of NATO.[36] On 31 March, however, Strauss single-handedly made matters a lot worse. During a joint news conference with Eisenhower at the White House he read out a prepared statement denying in impressively measured terms that testing was 'out of control', but then, in answering a question from a reporter, ruined the effect by remarking that the hydrogen bomb could be made 'as large as you wish, as large as the military requirement demands'. Just one bomb, he added, could 'destroy a city'. When the press corps chorused '*What?*' in disbelieving unison, he repeated the claim and offered up New York City, including the metropolitan area, by way of illustration. 'Lewis, I wouldn't have answered that one that way', Eisenhower muttered as they left the podium.[37] Within a few hours, the administration had put out a clarification; apparently only the island of Manhattan would be devastated and not, as Strauss had suggested, the metropolitan area with its 3,500 square miles. But it was too late. 'H-BOMB CAN WIPE OUT ANY CITY, STRAUSS REPORTS' ran the headline in the *New York Times* the next day.[38] 'In his own backhand way', writes Robert Divine, 'Lewis Strauss had quieted the nation's concern over fallout by raising the spectre of nuclear holocaust.'[39]

According to Manhattan Project veteran Vannevar Bush, the US public had hitherto been 'prone to think of atomic bombs only in terms of offense'. This, he felt, explained the popular 'surprise' and 'shock' when confronted by the H-bomb and the linked realization that offensive action was as much a Soviet as a US prerogative.[40] In Britain, a country within range of Soviet bombers, the danger of attack had been recognized for some time but popular disquiet was ratcheted to new heights by the news of the incredible destruction which the H-bomb threatened to deliver. Indeed when Strauss' comments were carried in UK papers they added greatly to the febrile state of public opinion and created a context that was as much emotional as political for the pending H-bomb debate.[41]

Churchill sensed this. In preparing for the debate, he asked Eisenhower for permission to quote the contents of the Quebec agreement. 'Our Opposition, especially its anti-American Left Wing, are trying to put the blame for the present restriction of information on to me and this increases my difficulty in defending, as I have done and will do, your claim to keep your secrets as agreed with the late Socialist Government', he explained on 1 April. 'I am also supporting, as you will have seen, your continued experiments'. Publishing the agreement 'will prove decisively that the Opposition, not I, are responsible for our present position'.[42] Eisenhower replied promptly. 'Of course some of this history is not fully known to me but I certainly would not feel disposed to interpose any objection'. He was 'confident' that Churchill had 'weighed this matter with the wisdom which you always bring to bear on these momentous occasions'.[43]

Wisdom, alas, is not the word that springs most readily to mind when evaluating Churchill's performance in the debate on 5 April. So focused was he on political points-scoring, so determined was he to reassert his parliamentary primacy and leadership credentials, that he seemed to forget that for most people, even MPs, the threat to the future of civilization from the H-bomb was the ultimate non-partisan issue. In consequence, he caused 'one hell of a row'.[44] Attlee opened by moving a Labour motion proposing a summit 'for the purpose of considering anew the problem of the reduction and control of armaments and of devising positive policies and means for removing from all the peoples of the world the fear which now oppresses them'. He was not, he said, animated by 'party spirit'. Churchill, responding, began in a similarly high-minded manner before suddenly rounding on Attlee for 'losing' the Quebec agreement. When he left office in 1945, the agreement, including the principle of mutual consent to the use of the Bomb anywhere and at any time, had been in force. Now, thanks to Attlee, it was gone. Viewed in this light, Churchill thought it rich of the Labour Party to criticize him for not doing more to restrain the Americans when its own leader had thrown away the United Kingdom's veto power.

This was political debating of the most barbed kind and well before Churchill reached his peroration the Commons had descended into uproar. Labour members were appalled, not by the lesson in recent history, inaccurate as it was, but by the grubby political opportunism that lurked within. 'You have sacrificed the interests of humanity to make a cheap party point', shouted Labour MP Sydney Silverman, a future founding member of the Campaign for Nuclear Disarmament, while the normally mild-mannered Attlee was described as red in the face and spluttering with rage. Tory MPs sat rooted in uneasy or embarrassed silence (apart from the maverick Robert Boothby who stalked out) as their chief was buffeted by opposition boos and catcalls. 'Look at the faces behind you', Labour left-winger Bessie Braddock yelled at one point, but on Churchill went, eyes down, ploughing through his prepared text, his voice barely audible, until he got to the end. At which point he slumped back down into his seat.[45]

Watching from the gallery, Lord Woolton rued 'a party speech, tremendous in its attack, and relentless'. What should have been Churchill's 'greatest hour' ended up as an 'extraordinary flop ... the most distressing thing I have ever seen in the House'. The Prime Minister was 'out of touch with what the country, and indeed the world, wants from him'.[46] Ironically, given that the speech was designed in part as a public reminder that age had not withered him, Churchill had to be rescued by his young(ish) heir-apparent. Disregarding *sotto voce* advice from some of his own supporters to abandon his leader to his fate, Eden wound-up the debate in so masterly and soothing a manner that much of Labour's animosity dissipated.[47] After the division – a vote in favour of the Labour motion on a nuclear-themed summit, hence indirectly a victory for Churchill's policy – the Prime Minister insisted on going to the Commons smoking room and stayed there 'chatting to the "boys" till nearly midnight' as if it had been an ordinary day at the office.[48] He was kidding himself. 'It was the nightmare scene which all Parliamentarians dread and which on a small scale nearly all of them have to endure once or twice in their careers', Roy Jenkins later reflected. 'But in his case it was writ large, with a full House and the prospect of a devastating press the next morning.'[49] So it proved. According to the *Times*, the Prime Minister's sense of occasion, 'usually one of his greatest strengths', had 'deserted him sadly' and he was roundly blamed for transforming the debate into 'a sterile, angry and pitiful party wrangle'. The *Manchester Guardian* was pithier: the Prime Minister 'blundered'.[50]

Attlee, meanwhile, could not understand why Churchill chose to play party politics. 'I had given him the opportunity to make a great speech on a high level – to give a lead to the world', he wrote to his brother. Instead, he misjudged the 'atomicsphere' [*sic*] and 'plunged into the gutter to everybody's disgust'.[51] The truth is that from the moment he learned, from Attlee himself in December 1950, that the Quebec agreement had been allowed to lapse, he not only blamed the Labour leader for a dereliction of national duty but was determined to hold him publicly to account. Publication of the agreement became his obsession. Even that wisest of Whitehall owls, Norman Brook, could not believe that foreknowledge of the agreement would have prevented the US Congress passing the McMahon Act. But long before April 1954, Churchill had lost all sense of perspective.[52]

Looking back, the most extraordinary aspect of the fiasco was the Prime Minister's ability to hunker down, see out the storm and then resurface and carry on as if nothing out of the ordinary had happened. It may be that, as Moran at the time and Jenkins later observed, he was simply incapable of registering the magnitude of his humiliation.[53] More likely, he knew very well that he had got it wrong but, as Macmillan observed, 'his natural reaction will be to fight on' to redeem himself.[54] To a large extent, Churchill's fate was in Eden's hands. If ever there was a moment for the Foreign Secretary to wield the political knife, this was it. He had the motive, the opportunity and the support of many Tory ministers and MPs desperate for a change at the top. All he lacked was the killer instinct. Or else he was too loyal or too weak or too principled. The Prime Minister had chosen his successor wisely. 'Had Macmillan been the recognised heir apparent instead of Eden at this moment', Richard Thorpe concludes, 'Churchill might not have lasted the week.'[55]

Churchill had little time to lick his wounds before he and his government were swept up in a major international crisis as the eight-year war in French Indo-China reached its violent climax. Coming when it did, the crisis immediately acquired a determining thermonuclear dimension which, despite the large body of historical literature on the war, has been largely overlooked by scholars. For the British government, events in Viet-Nam, and even more so the Eisenhower administration's efforts at crisis management and resolution, brought their nuclear anxieties to the highest pitch and, as a consequence, exposed Anglo-American relations to tremendous strain.

The war had begun in 1946 as a colonial conflict, an attempt by France to reassert its imperial supremacy in the face of determined nationalist resistance, before being transformed into a Sino-American war-by-proxy in 1950 when the United States started supplying France with military assistance and the newly-founded People's Republic of China did likewise for the communist-led Viet-Minh. Had the Korean War not intruded, Indo-China might have become a catalyst for conflict between the rival Cold War blocs sooner than it did. As it was, the flashpoint arrived with the onset of the battle of Dien Bien Phu on 13 March 1954. A remote valley in north-west Viet-Nam, Dien Bien Phu was the site of a large *base aéro-terrestre* garrisoned by around 14,000 French and French Union soldiers. Within 48 hours of the start of the fighting, the airstrip, the garrison's lifeline to the outside world, had been knocked-out by shelling and the fortress found itself in a noose which the Viet-Minh commander, General Vo Nguyen Giap, along with 40,000 siege troops, steadily tightened.[56]

The Eisenhower administration, shouldering 80 per cent of the total financial cost of the French war effort, now had something else to worry about besides the worldwide outcry over H-bomb testing. So great was the level of French investment in the battle (emotionally and in terms of prestige as much as manpower) that policymakers feared that the loss of the fortress would shatter French morale and lead to a military collapse throughout Viet-Nam. Even if the French managed to hold the line beyond Dien Bien Phu, the Americans essayed the possibility of a French political capitulation when a scheduled international conference on the Asian Cold War opened in Geneva on 26 April. If French negotiators arrived at the *Palais des Nations*, the former home of the League of Nations, with the Dien Bien Phu garrison annihilated and defeatism wracking the metropole, some US officials predicted a cut-and-run deal by which the safe evacuation of French forces might be traded for Viet-Minh control of Viet-Nam. In sum, whether through French defeat on the battlefield or French surrender at the conference table, Viet-Nam, and probably neighbouring Laos and Cambodia too, would be lost. To US Cold War strategists, this was the stuff of nightmares. 'We could lose Europe, Asia and Africa all at once if we don't watch out', a fraught Dulles told Admiral Radford.[57] He did not use the term "domino theory" – Eisenhower would adumbrate that concept publicly for the first time at a news conference on 7 April – but it was plainly in his mind.[58]

As it scrambled to find a means of keeping the French fighting, the Eisenhower administration concluded that the nuclear aspect of the New Look was not the solution. Threatening wholesale retribution against China, or the USSR, when the issue was indirect communist aggression, was an obviously disproportionate response, one that risked global war while doing nothing to save the garrison at Dien Bien Phu or bolster the French position in Indo-China generally.[59] In the end, after intensive inter-agency debate, the Eisenhower administration settled on a conventional response: a military coalition comprising the United States and such allies as it could recruit to intervene directly in Viet-Nam, not at Dien Bien Phu, the fate of which seemed sealed, but elsewhere in a morale-boosting show of solidarity with the French that would hopefully prevent the loss of one battle leading to communist victory in the war itself. In a widely-reported speech to the Overseas Press Club in New York on 29 March, Dulles unveiled the plan.

> Under the conditions of today, the imposition on Southeast Asia of the political system of Communist Russia and its Chinese Communist ally, by whatever means, would be a grave threat to the whole free community. The United States feels that that possibility should not be passively accepted, but should be met by united action. This might involve serious risks. But these risks are far less than those that will face us a few years from now, if we dare not be resolute today.[60]

Dulles' speech marks the point at which the Indo-China crisis became, simultaneously, a crisis in Anglo-American relations. For, as we will see, the Churchill government not only set out to resist US plans but to thwart them for reasons intimately connected with the contemporaneous 'panic and hysteria' over the hydrogen bomb.[61]

The H-bomb fever of spring 1954 not only infected British public, press and parliament but spread to Whitehall, to the Chiefs of Staff and to the Cabinet. As the situation in Viet-Nam worsened, the Prime Minister and his chief advisors fell prey to a variety of nuclear-related anxieties. The confirmation of the staggering power of Ivy-Mike and even more so Castle-Bravo, the alarming fall-out phenomenon and the fate of the *Lucky Dragon* were unsettling enough but they were only part of it. UK political and military leaders understood only too well that if general war broke out, US bases in East Anglia would likely be a lightning rod for Soviet atomic bombers – bombers which could hit London but not Washington or New York. In addition, the demise of the Quebec agreement left the British without any real influence over Washington's nuclear decision-making. And then there was the New Look, a huge worry all on its own.

In Cabinet on 22 March, a week before Dulles issued his call for united action, Eden warned ministers that in the event of general war the Americans might well turn to nuclear arms as weapons of first resort. Such was the logic of the New Look, he said, that the 'US will soon assume that *any* action by them is atomic. They will have all their armaments attuned & fitted for atomic weapons *only*.' He was seconded by Salisbury. The Strategic Air Command was 'turning over to H. bomb as standard weapon', and with East Anglia hosting several SAC bases he reminded colleagues of the literal life-and-death difference between the UK and US situations, namely that the 'US can't be attacked with this by R[ussia] for 5 years or so' but Britain could. The Foreign Secretary still bore the marks of Bermuda: even though it was Viet-Nam, not Korea, which had emerged as the Asian tinderbox, the parallels were too close for comfort. In both cases, Eden suspected, war with the People's Republic was the real if undeclared object of US policy. Direct Chinese intervention in Viet-Nam on a scale that would justify US retaliation, nuclear or conventional, against targets inside the PRC, was unlikely given how well the Viet-Minh was doing on its own. But US-led united action, if it provoked Beijing into counter-intervention, could create the conditions that would merit, by Washington's lights, a nuclear bombardment of China. And that might be the overture to a third world war.[62]

From the outset, the Eisenhower administration identified British support as the 'key' to realizing united action. Where the UK led, Dulles believed, other states, in a diplomatic version of the domino effect, would follow. With Congress still bitter over the way that the United States had done the bulk of the fighting, dying and paying in Korea, the administration doubted whether it would be successful in securing the war powers necessary to move forces into Viet-Nam unless the Senate was persuaded that a genuinely burden-sharing coalition was in prospect.[63] Here it was hoped that Britain would take a lead. A year before, Dulles had spoken privately of the pitfalls of relying too heavily on allies. The United States, he averred, 'must strike a balance between allied unity and American freedom of action . . . To be committed to "consultation" on every step is to be exposed to veto by those consulted, with consequent handicaps on freedom of action.'[64] Now, in spring 1954, the need to win round a Korea-damaged Congress to military action in Viet-Nam led the Eisenhower administration to gift that very veto power to a British government predisposed to exercise it to the full.

On 1 April, three days after Dulles launched united action, Eden approved an Indo-China guidance paper prepared by the Foreign Office in liaison with the Chiefs of Staff, which set London and Washington on a collision course. 'Any direct intervention' in Viet-Nam 'by the armed forces of any external nation . . . would probably result in Chinese intervention, with the danger that this might ultimately lead to global war', the paper argued. 'Our influence should therefore be used against these more dangerous forms of deeper United States involvement'. Instead, the negotiating option offered by the imminent Geneva conference should be exploited to bring about a peaceful settlement based on the partition of Viet-Nam.[65]

Over the next three weeks, as the outlook for the Dien Bien Phu garrison grew darker and the Eisenhower administration intensified the pressure on London to fall in with united action, the Conservative government held to its non-interventionist position.[66] Consequently, Anglo-American relations reached one of their lowest points since the Second World War – and on the watch of Winston Churchill, the great guardian, the inventor even, of the "special relationship".[67] Normally Churchill would have been first in line behind the Americans. When Washington felt so strongly about something – in this case the preservation of a non-communist Viet-Nam – he usually took the view that British questioning or quibbling could only aggravate relations. In particular, he was never happy when the general harmony of the Anglo-American Cold War partnership was disturbed by specific disagreements over the PRC.[68] The Americans not only knew this. They banked on it.

Deliberately by-passing Eden and the Foreign Office, on 4 April Eisenhower wrote to Churchill imploring him to support united action. Based on past precedent, he must have had a high expectation of success. 'If I may refer . . . to history, we failed to halt Hirohito, Mussolini and Hitler by not acting in unity and in time. That marked the beginning of many years of stark tragedy and desperate peril. May it not be that our nations have learned something from the lesson?'[69] It was a carefully-crafted appeal which deliberately played on Churchill's vanity, his reputation as an anti-appeaser, and his romantic sense of himself as one of the great figures in history. And, to repeat, in normal circumstances it would surely have elicited the response Eisenhower sought. But these were not normal circumstances. They were thermonuclear circumstances. 'I am more worried by the hydrogen bomb than by all the rest of my worries put together', Churchill confessed to Moran.[70] And so Ike was deflected, politely but effectively.[71]

At the very moment it was seeking UK support for a military adventure in Viet-Nam with clear escalatory potential, the Eisenhower administration inadvertently added to the already high level of thermonuclear anxiety in Britain in ways which further militated against the success of united action. On 26 March, the White House approved the release of the AEC's film of the November 1952 Ivy-Mike test, a commendable act of open government which went badly awry when, on the eve of its airing on coast-to-coast American primetime, Strauss announced that a single H-bomb could wipe out New York.[72] In Britain, too, there was alarm and despondency. On 8 April, a Pathé newsreel, 'H-bomb', a six-minute distillation of the AEC film, started showing in cinemas around the country. Over the following three weeks – the high-tide of the Viet-Nam crisis – movie-goers were treated to jaw-dropping footage of thermonuclear destructiveness set to a disturbingly discordant orchestral score and accompanied by a dramatic commentary from American actor Reed Hadley. 'In less than a minute the first hydrogen bomb ever set off on earth will explode before your very eyes', Hadley intoned. And then there it was, a colossal bubble of pulsing violence filling the screen as the music became shrill and menacing. 'Mike was power, the kind of titanic energy released by stars'. In an unintentional homage to Strauss, a silhouette of the Manhattan skyline was transposed on top of the fireball. A hydrogen bomb dropped on any other comparable-sized city would achieve an identical result, Hadley asserted: 'complete, utter, absolute annihilation'.[73]

Thanks to Castle-Bravo and the *Lucky Dragon*, British audiences, like their American counterparts, knew that the blast and heat were the beginning not the end of the horror: there was also fall-out, radioactive clouds and poisonous rain to ensure that the H-bomb continued killing in staggeringly high numbers far beyond ground-zero.[74] In Coventry, a city which had suffered badly from bombing in the Second World War, the local council refused to implement the government's requirement to train a local civil defence corps because, it claimed, the hydrogen bomb made all defence pointless. The story soon made national headlines and served, along with the activities of the Hydrogen Bomb National Campaign Committee (chaired by the Reverend Donald Soper and with Labour MPs Fenner Brockway, Sydney Silverman and Anthony Wedgewood-Benn in positions of prominence) to maintain public awareness of thermonuclear war.[75]

Against this fraught background, American pressure on the British government to join in military action in Viet-Nam reached a peak. On 24 April, with the French at Dien Bien Phu seemingly doomed and French public and political support for a continuation of the war ebbing fast, Dulles approached Eden at a NATO meeting in Paris with a proposition. If the UK was prepared to stand with the USA, Eisenhower would immediately request from Congress 'war powers' to permit large-scale American armed intervention in Viet-Nam, not at Dien Bien Phu but more generally in support of the French position.[76] United action had come down to Anglo-American action. Eden was stunned. Begging leave to consult Churchill and his other colleagues, he returned to London that night. If Dulles took this as a hopeful sign he was in error. Bilateral or multilateral, it made no difference: military action in and of itself was the problem. 'Anthony says he won't agree', Clarissa Eden wrote in her diary, 'and if they [the Americans] go in it will mean fighting China & setting off a Third World War.'[77]

This was precisely the line Eden adopted when the Cabinet and Chiefs of Staff assembled in emergency session in Downing Street at 11.00 am on 25 April, a Sunday. The latest American proposal must be rejected, he argued, for the dangers of a wider war were too great. With the Geneva conference due to begin the very next day, it was 'inevitable', Eden argued, 'that large parts of Indo-China should fall under Communist control' and the 'best hope of a lasting solution lay in some form of partition'. Churchill agreed – the government would 'clearly be ill-advised to encourage the Americans to take precipitate military action' – as did the other ministers and soldiers in the Cabinet room.[78] Unanimity achieved, the meeting broke up, but the participants had barely digested their Sunday lunches before they were summoned back to Number 10 to be told that the Eisenhower administration had now abandoned its reluctance to take action at Dien Bien Phu and stood ready to launch air-strikes against the Viet-Minh besiegers within 72 hours if the British gave their public blessing for the operation. Incensed, Eden charged the Americans with wanting war with China. Air action at Dien Bien Phu could not possibly affect the outcome of the battle but it would wreck the Geneva conference before it began and invite large-scale Chinese intervention, which the United States might well use as an excuse to hit back at the PRC with nuclear weapons. There would then be 'a grave risk that the Soviet Union would feel obliged to intervene' and this could be 'the first step towards a third world war'. No-one around the table dissented. '[W]hat we were being asked to do', Churchill summed up, 'was in effect to aid in misleading Congress into approving a military operation which would itself be ineffective and might well bring the world to the verge of a major war.' Personally, he had 'no doubts that this request must be rejected'.[79]

Eden flew direct to Geneva that evening. On landing, he informed Dulles of the Cabinet's decision. It was, wrote Shuckburgh, a 'disagreeable' meeting.[80] However, before Eden could settle down to peacemaking, the Americans made one last desperate bid to secure British backing for military action. Tellingly, they concentrated on what they still saw as the weak link in the UK chain of resistance: Churchill. Waiting until the Foreign Secretary was safely out of London, Eisenhower dispatched as his emissary of persuasion the gung-ho chairman of the Joint Chiefs, Admiral Radford. When Eden learned that Radford, whom he was convinced was 'spoiling for a war with China', was to dine alone with Churchill at Chequers on 26 April, the opening day of the Geneva conference, he had a fit of the 'terrors' lest the Prime Minister's attachment to the "special relationship" result in eleventh-hour approval of US air action at Dien Bien Phu.[81] He would have been even more alarmed had he known that Radford's mission was in obedience of Presidential instructions to dissuade the British from attempting 'a second Munich'.[82]

At the dinner, the Admiral gave Churchill the full treatment. The fall of Dien Bien Phu would be 'a turning point in history', he warned. Dominos would tumble, South-East Asia would be lost, the Middle East imperilled. Yet late as the hour was, disaster could still be averted. Congress stood ready to approve armed intervention if 'England were willing to co-operate'. The Soviet Union was 'frightened of war' and would not help the PRC. This, Radford concluded, was 'the critical moment at which to make a stand against China'. It was quite a performance and there had been a time, not so long ago, when Churchill might have responded positively. But not now. The loss of Dien Bien Phu might indeed be 'a critical moment in history', he acknowledged, but the fact was that the 'British people would not be easily influenced by what happened in the distant jungles of S. E. Asia; but they did know that there was a powerful American base in East Anglia and that war with China, who would invoke the Sino-Russian Pact, might mean an assault by Hydrogen bombs on these islands. We could not commit ourselves at this moment, when all these matters were about to be discussed at Geneva, to a policy which might lead by slow stages to a catastrophe'. There was 'nothing more important' than Anglo-American unity, Churchill declared, but 'we could not allow ourselves to be committed against our judgement to a policy which might lead us to destruction'.[83] Deflated and disappointed, Radford returned to Washington ruing that Churchill's position had been 'in exact accord' with Eden's.[84] In Geneva, meanwhile, the Foreign Secretary, being far from sure that the Prime Minister would stand firm, waited anxiously for news. When, finally, he received Colville's account of the dinner, his relief was great but concisely-expressed: on the bottom of the report he wrote just one word, 'Good'.[85] The H-bomb had set limits even to Churchill's commitment to the "special relationship". Now Eden could get on with ending the Indo-China war.

There is a further aspect – a paradox, even – to the summer of the H-bomb which demands examination. Amidst the swirl of crisis in South-East Asia, and in the strictest of secrecy, Churchill, together with a small group of senior military and political figures, agreed that Britain must possess its own H-bomb. The Prime Minister was closely involved at every stage of the decision-making process. Repelled as he was by the H-bomb's genocidal properties, he was equally drawn to its deterrent power, a combination of fear and fascination which informed his thinking for the remainder of his time in office.

The H-bomb decision itself, arguably the most important in terms of UK national security since the war, was taken (in typical Whitehall fashion) by a committee – or rather by two complementary committees brought into existence for the purpose. Churchill chaired both. The first, known simply by its Cabinet Office prefix GEN.464, convened for the first time on 13 April, a week after the Prime Minister's mauling in the H-bomb debate. In addition to Churchill, the committee comprised just five other ministers: the Foreign Secretary, Eden; the Lord President of the Council, Salisbury; the Chancellor of the Exchequer, Butler; the Minister of Defence, Alexander; and the

Secretary of State for Commonwealth Relations, Swinton. The latter's involvement reflected the committee's principal concern, namely the acquisition of the raw materials vital to the production of a hydrogen bomb, in particular thorium which was believed to be present in South Africa in significant but untapped quantities. To begin with, the committee's discussion was anticipatory, with ministers expressing concern that if it was ever decided to proceed with H-bomb development, the country could find itself starved of the basic raw ingredients unless a procurement strategy was already in place. Churchill, however, had a much more immediate time-frame in mind. He intended, he said, to invite the Cabinet 'at an early date' to decide 'in principle that hydrogen bombs should be made in the United Kingdom'.[86]

The second committee – which proved to be the key body – came into being at the initiative of Cabinet Secretary Norman Brook. As disturbed as anyone by the H-bomb, Brook requested a briefing from three nuclear knights, Sir Edwin Plowden (Controller of Atomic Energy), Sir William Penney (of the AWRE and Hurricane fame), and Sir John Cockcroft (head of the Harwell atomic research establishment), the tripartite core of the government's advisory Atomic Energy Group. Meeting with Brook in mid-March, the knights thought it probable that that the Soviets 'have already developed the material for an attack on this country, the intensity of which far exceeded previous assumptions'. Startled, Brook immediately recommended to the Prime Minister that a high-powered ministerial committee be established to re-examine the fundamental bases of British national security.[87] Discreet, politically-neutral and devoted to the national interest, Brook had early on acquired and never lost Churchill's ear and it was not long before a Defence Policy Committee (DPC) had come into being.[88] Aside from the Prime Minister in the chair, the committee (not to be confused with the Cabinet's existing Defence Committee) was composed of the Foreign Secretary, the Lord President, the Chancellor, the Ministers of Defence and Supply and the Home Secretary. The Chief of the Imperial General Staff, Field Marshal Sir John Harding, and his fellow service chiefs were not only regular attendees but undertook, at Brook's request, to prepare a detailed review of defence policy.

At the DPC's first meeting on 4 May, Churchill offered a series of sombre observations about the international situation and the impact of the H-bomb on the American approach to the Cold War. In the process, he confirmed his abhorrence for what had one time been his favoured nuclear policy.

The Prime Minister said that there was little doubt that the Soviet Government would seek to avoid world war for so long as they continued to be able to achieve so much of their aims without it. They now had vast opportunities to extend world Communism in Asia, without themselves engaging openly in armed conflict ... So long as this situation continued, there seemed to be little risk of world war – unless the United States should succumb to the temptation to bring matters to a head before the Russians had built up their strength in atomic weapons and their power to deliver them against targets in North America. It was arguable that the United States would better serve their own interests by an early trial of strength with Russia than by committing their forces successively, in different theatres, in support of efforts to check Communist encroachment into the free world. The great question was whether the United States would withstand the temptation to initiate what we would prefer to call a 'forestalling' war, rather than a 'preventive' war, before the Russians had built up the power to deliver an effective atomic onslaught against North America.

Churchill said he was concerned about the activities of certain prominent individuals in America – he singled out Sterling Cole and anti-communist demagogue Joseph McCarthy – who seemed to be working to create a 'climate of opinion which would be favourable to an early trial of strength' with the USSR. If a US-engendered war broke out, Britain 'could not afford to follow a neutralist policy . . . Even if it were practicable for the United Kingdom to stand aside in a war between the United States and the Soviet Union, her fate would be determined by it. If Soviet forces overran Europe, the United Kingdom would not go unscathed.' The Prime Minister had, it seemed, come round to the Eden-Salisbury view that the United States was more likely than the USSR to bring the Cold War to the brink of hot war in the next few years. This was a remote possibility, he conceded, but it was still that, a possibility. Indo-China proved as much. And in global war, no matter how it started, the United Kingdom would be decimated while the United States went comparatively unscathed. Britain needed to do everything it could to curb the exercise of US nuclear power in all circumstances short of retaliation against a surprise Soviet assault. With its own H-bomb, Churchill maintained, the country would have the nuclear standing in Washington to demand a say 'in determining the major issue of peace of war'.[89]

At the DPC's second meeting on 19 May, the Prime Minister developed his thesis. Hitherto ambivalent about the need for an independent British *atomic* deterrent, he was entirely sold on the idea of an independent *thermonuclear* deterrent. 'Influence depended on possession of force', he argued. In the short-term, '[w]e must avoid any action which would weaken our power to influence United States policy' while in the medium-term, '[i]f . . . we were able to show that in a few years' time we should be possessed of great offensive power, and that we should be ready to take our part in a world struggle', then it 'would not be impossible to reconcile reductions in defence expenditure with the maintenance of our influence in world councils'. As his reference to expenditure indicates, Churchill saw the H-bomb as cost-efficient in ways that he had not done with the A-bomb: in drawing up the committee's terms of reference, he urged members 'to keep prominently in mind the aim of securing a total saving of £150 million on defence expenditure in 1955, as compared with the expenditure forecast for that year', a figure subsequently raised to £200 million. The H-bomb could help in this connection, not immediately but over the next several years, and he 'hoped' for this and the other reasons he had advanced, that 'the Cabinet would agree we should proceed with the development of the hydrogen bomb'.[90]

It is often argued that Churchill saw the H-bomb as a prop to shore-up Britain's flagging world status.[91] This was certainly a broad consideration ('the price we pay to sit at the top table', as he once put it) but in a more specific sense he believed that thermonuclear weapons, as the core of a British independent deterrent, would add weight to UK influence in Washington.[92] The crisis in Indo-China underlined this need. While the Prime Minister and his colleagues on the DPC pondered how a H-bomb would aid British efforts to dissuade the United States from effecting a showdown with the Soviet Union in the future, Eden was working at Geneva to prevent an American showdown with China in the present. Whether the Foreign Secretary's task would have been made easier had Britain already been a member of the H-bomb club, this being the logical extension of Churchill's argument, is open to doubt. At best, a UK thermonuclear capability, including a means of delivery, would have given the USSR, not the USA, pause for thought. But it was the Americans, not the Soviets, the British most worried about.

If H-bombs were deemed necessary to help contain the United States, they were most urgently needed between 1954 and 1958, the accepted window of vulnerability for the United Kingdom, the period when US policymakers, aware that a new generation of Soviet long-range bombers or rocket technology would soon bring North America within the USSR's nuclear reach, were most likely to be tempted to use their strategic advantage to launch a forestalling war which might in turn see atomic (if not thermonuclear) devastation rain down on the UK. With no prospect of a British hydrogen bomb before the back end of that time-frame, the immediate priority was to keep the Cold War cold. This, though, a troubled Eden confided to Salisbury, might not be so easy. 'You know that Radford's policy has for some time been intervention in Indo-China, and in China too', he wrote from Geneva. 'Some aspects of American policy are only comprehensible to me if that view is held by others in addition to Radford.'[93]

CHAPTER 15
THE JULY DAYS

After sending Radford on his way on 26 April, Churchill told Parliament the next day that his government was 'not prepared to give any undertakings about United Kingdom military action in Indo-China in advance of the results of Geneva'. Should these turn out to be satisfactory, Britain would play its 'full part in supporting them in order to promote a stable peace in the Far East'.[1] At Geneva, however, Eden found the Americans less interested in a diplomatic solution than in preparations for military action which would court 'the third world war'.[2]

The Cabinet continued to offer the Foreign Secretary strong support for his peacemaking while Churchill blamed Dulles for most of the tensions besetting Anglo-American relations. 'He is a dull, unimaginative, uncomprehending, insensitive man', he railed. 'I hope he will disappear.'[3] He did, though only from Geneva. After a week disporting himself with 'the pinched distaste of a puritan in a house of ill-repute', on 3 May Dulles handed leadership of the US delegation to his deputy, Walter Bedell Smith, and headed home.[4] 'The trouble with you, Foster', Eden told him as he bade him adieu, 'is that you want World War Three.'[5] On a personal level, Eden and Bedell Smith, who were old friends, got on well and there was a not unconnected improvement in Anglo-American atmospherics. But in terms of policy differences nothing changed. The British were ready to compromise with the communists, and ultimately settle for peace based on partition of Viet-Nam. The Americans were not. To the contrary, the Eisenhower administration encouraged the French to hang tough in the negotiations and kept alive the prospect of military intervention if or when the conference collapsed.[6]

On 7 May, news reached Geneva of the fall of Dien Bien Phu. After 55 days of resistance and with more than 2,000 dead and 5,000 wounded, the remainder of the French garrison, around 9,000 troops, surrendered. It was a stinging humiliation for France.[7] Churchill immediately sent a message of condolence to his French counterpart, Joseph Laniel, and counselled that the 'doom' of the fortress need not foreclose 'the hope of extracting an honourable settlement' at Geneva.[8] The Eisenhower administration, believing otherwise, now began secret talks with the French about the terms and conditions under which the USA would join the war as a co-belligerent. By 17 May, Dulles had ready a draft Congressional resolution authorizing the President to send US air and naval forces into Indo-China if invited to do so by the Laniel government.[9]

Unaware of the extent of American war preparations, Eden wrote to his wife on 22 May to say that the chances of an armistice were 'even money' but he would keep working to improve the odds because he was 'more than ever convinced of dangers of 3rd world war' if the conference failed.[10] So, it appeared, were the communists. At the start of June, the Chinese, hitherto inflexible in the negotiations, tabled a number of concessions which encouraged Eden to believe that a settlement was still to be had.[11] However, the biggest boost to peace came mid-month when Pierre Mendès-France, a long-standing critic of the war, replaced Laniel as French Prime Minister. Declaring his intention to take personal charge of his country's delegation at Geneva, Mendès-France set himself a stiff deadline: peace by 20 July or he would resign.[12] The British were delighted. Here at last was a French government which knew its mind. More than this, the advent of Mendès-France ruled out any prospect of US or US-led military action before Geneva had run its course.[13] On 20 June, the conference went into recess but when the negotiations resumed in early July, Eden was now hopeful that a settlement would emerge which would end the war, guarantee the security of South-East Asia and 'greatly strengthen peace throughout the world'.[14]

While Eden laboured at Geneva, in London his colleagues on the Defence Policy Committee were nearing a final decision on the H-bomb.[15] On 16 June, the Chiefs of Staff's review of defence policy was the subject of extended discussion. 'More than ever the aim of United Kingdom defence policy must be to prevent war', the Chiefs argued. 'To this end we must maintain and strengthen our position as a world Power so that Her Majesty's Government can exercise a powerful influence in the counsels of the world.' The global situation had been altered radically by recent advances in weapons technology with some of the newest American thermonuclear bombs estimated to be 1,500 times more powerful than the Nagasaki device. At present, the USA was ahead of the USSR in the nuclear arms race, but 'we must reckon that within one or two years' the Soviets 'will have weapons of devastating power, even by American standards'. What that would mean for the United Kingdom in the event of global war was chilling. Aside from the physical destruction, the predicted kill-factor from ten thermonuclear weapons used against ten major cities was put in the region of 5 million dead if the bombs were of 100 times nominal (Nagasaki) A-bomb power, rising to 12 million if the bombs were of 1,000 times nominal power. This tally took no account of the deadly properties of fall-out but according to a contemporaneous assessment by the Atomic Energy Group, the Chiefs needed to insert a macabre value-added factor into the equation.

The review further observed 'that a country which can equip itself with the means of delivery needs only a comparatively small stockpile of [thermonuclear] weapons in order to be able to deliver a devastating attack on an enemy'. To the USSR, Britain was that enemy until such time as Soviet bombers, or rockets, were built to reach North America. There were no grounds for believing that moral or ethical considerations would render the use of nuclear weapons taboo. On the contrary, 'if war came in the next few years, the United States would insist on the immediate use of the full armoury of nuclear weapons with the object of dealing the Russians a quick knock-out blow'. In consequence, the United Kingdom needed to 'plan on the assumption that, if war becomes global, nuclear bombardment will become general'.

But plan to what purpose? Not defence, for there was none that would truly protect the nation. The councillors of Coventry had been right. 'Indeed, the real problem might well be one of physical survival', the COS conceded, and their overriding conclusion was that 'short of sacrificing our vital interests or principles, our first aim must be to prevent global war'. To this end, the government and armed forces needed to work to 'strengthen our position and influence as a world power and maintain our alliance with the United States'. The country must also possess 'the means of waging war with the most up-to-date nuclear weapons', for if deterrence should fail, an 'immediate and overwhelming counter-offensive with the most powerful nuclear weapons offers the only hope of preventing an enemy from completely devastating this country'. The United Kingdom could and should contribute to the general NATO deterrent 'by producing a stockpile of nuclear, including hydrogen, weapons and the means of delivering them'. Given that the US Strategic Air Command could not deal effectively with every target of prime importance for Britain's security, it was anticipated that the RAF's contribution, though framed in the context of NATO's overall war plans, would result in the country's core defence resting in its own hands. But with the current *Blue Danube* A-bomb a mere 10-kiloton weapon – a limitation connected to the scarcity of fissile material – and insufficiently powerful to assure total destruction of priority UK targets in the USSR, a 5–10 megaton H-bomb, built for delivery by V-bombers, had obvious strategic attraction.[16]

The ensuing DPC discussion of the review elicited a high level of agreement with its conclusions, but an unidentified figure – possibly Salisbury – wanted to know what would happen if the United States, the great and powerful ally in whom the service chiefs invested so much faith, should decide on a forestalling war while it held the nuclear advantage over the USSR. It must be a 'primary aim of United Kingdom policy', Field Marshal Harding answered, 'to restrain the United States from doing this'. Churchill agreed. Dual deterrence – dual containment – had become necessary, a means of keeping the Soviet Union at bay *and* of preventing the United States taking precipitate action. From this the committee moved towards its unanimous decision to initiate a programme for production of hydrogen bombs. The government's Working Party on the Operational Use of Atomic Weapons had already assessed that the country could produce annually around ten hydrogen bombs of the 5–10 megaton class, starting in 1959, if the order was given 'at once and all goes as planned'. That order was now issued.[17]

Although Salisbury, the Cabinet's nuclear supremo, set to work immediately on preliminary planning, the DPC's decision was kept a tightly-guarded secret. How to explain such a controversial move, both to Parliament and the country at large, required careful consideration. In May, Sir George Thomson, who had chaired the MAUD committee in 1940–1941, declared publicly that the hydrogen bomb, 'being a weapon of annihilation', was 'the most serious danger' facing the world. If the aim was to destroy enemy munitions factories or military bases in time of war, the A-bomb was more than sufficient whereas the 'only target for a hydrogen bomb is a big city, and its effect is indiscriminate slaughter'.[18] Soon after, the annual Methodist conference resolved that with the coming of the H-bomb, 'the world had now passed beyond the stage of debating pacifism and non-pacifism' and people everywhere – inside and outside of the church – were looking to governments to take a 'courageous lead' and outlaw all weapons of mass destruction.[19] The Thomson statement and the Methodist resolution were reminders to

Churchill and his colleagues of the popular anxiety still attending the H-bomb. A disclosure strategy was needed to insure against a repeat of the panic of the spring, but this, in turn, required time and thought. For the moment, the H-bomb decision was to be kept from Parliament and thus from the public. But what of the full Cabinet? Although Churchill had announced at the DPC's first meeting that he intended to seek collective ministerial sanction for the H-bomb, he delayed doing so for three weeks following the committee's crossing of the thermonuclear threshold.[20] Not long, really. But as we will see, given the enormity of the issue involved, this tardiness proved to be a serious error of judgement.

Towards the end of June, Churchill paid the third and final visit of his peacetime ministry to the United States. Back in the spring, he had all but invited himself to Washington to discuss with Eisenhower ways in which the USA and the UK could 'co-operate more fruitfully in the atomic and hydrogen sphere'. In addition, he still hoped to win the President round to a summit, the pre-requisite, he maintained, to an 'easement' in East-West relations.[21] By the early summer another more general item had been added to the agenda, namely the healing of the rift that had opened up over Indo-China.[22] On 5 June – fully seven weeks after arrangements had been made – Churchill revealed to the Cabinet his travel plans. Because he was 'specially concerned' to discuss the H-bomb, Lindemann would be joining him. Ideally, he would have liked Eden at his side but with Geneva approaching a critical juncture he feared that this might not be possible. Ministers, Macmillan wrote afterwards, were 'frankly horrified' at the thought of Churchill spending time in the USA without Eden as a chaperone for there was no knowing what he might give away in an effort to repair Anglo–American relations.[23]

In the event, to general ministerial relief, the Geneva recess enabled Eden to accompany the Prime Minister after all. The Washington talks opened on 25 June and continued for four days in a cordial atmosphere. Tensions remained on Viet-Nam but they fizzled rather than flared ('Dulles outwardly quite correct & almost friendly', Eden noted, 'but I suspect otherwise within').[24] Churchill was relaxed and in good form although he appeared to American eyes to be diminished both physically and mentally (White House Press Secretary James Hagerty thought him 'almost in his dotage').[25] Erratic, emotional, inconsistent. Churchill was all of these things. But he was still capable of giving riveted attention to nuclear questions. When he read Cole's statement on the H-bomb in February, he told Eisenhower on the first day of the talks, it 'made his eyes start out of his head'. The description of Ivy-Mike 'transformed what had been to him a vague scientific nightmare into something which dominates the whole world'. Before the Cole revelations he felt that 'war could have been fought with the A-bomb'. A war now would be the end of all things. The 'H-bomb is something totally different' and he was inclined, in the manner of the good burghers of Coventry, to abandon all work on air-raid shelters in Britain since they would plainly 'prove useless in a thermonuclear attack'. When Eisenhower vouchsafed that the US hydrogen bomb arsenal 'at the present time was several times that of the Russians', Churchill was glad to hear it. The 'safety of the world depended on this deterrent – on the capacity for an overwhelming retort'.[26]

Later in the talks, Churchill informed Eisenhower of British plans to build a H-bomb. The President raised no objections. On the contrary, on nuclear issues generally, including granting the British greater access to technical information, he was extremely forthcoming. As it was, Ike reminded Churchill, the 1948 *modus vivendi* was being stretched to the limit to permit the passing on of data on the impact of nuclear tests 'on human beings and their environment', a reference to the Lindemann–Strauss understanding. Churchill was grateful but wanted more, to wit, the specifications of American nuclear weapons so that RAF V-bombers could be adapted to carry them.[27] Eisenhower was minded to give him what he wanted. 'If we ever get into trouble when we need these bombs it is our duty to provide them as quickly as possible to the British air force', he remarked to Hagerty the day before Churchill arrived. 'I don't want to see American crews and American crews alone take the punishment they will have to take to deliver those bombs.'[28] Now, responding to the Prime Minister's request and at the President's prompting, Strauss confirmed that the United Kingdom would be given 'all information necessary to use United States type bombs, i.e. dimensions, attachments, but *not* information on how to make them', and indeed before the year was out the US Air Force and the RAF had begun working together.[29]

Advised by Strauss that these undertakings to the British did not infringe the McMahon Act, the President was still guarded in public; the communiqué issued at the end of the conference referred obliquely to the importance of 'technical cooperation on atomic energy' and attested that 'both our countries would benefit from such cooperation to the fullest extent allowed by legislation'.[30] Shortly after the Prime Minister left for home,

Figure 15.1 Dulles, Churchill, Eisenhower, Eden, Washington 1954. Popperfoto/Getty Images.

Eisenhower renewed pressure on the Congress to ease the restrictions of the McMahon Act (of which he was 'personally ashamed') and on 30 August a new Atomic Energy Act was promulgated. The Act hardly constituted the restoration of Anglo-American atomic relations as existed during the war, but then again those relations were never as extensive at the technical (as distinct from the political) level as Churchill remembered them. When Eisenhower first proposed the legislation, British Ambassador Roger Makins observed that the new Act 'is not going to give us all we would like to have' but it was 'quite likely to give us all we could reasonably expect'. That turned out to be right. The US government could now release to privileged allies previously classified data on the external characteristics of nuclear weapons though nothing on design and fabrication. This information, however, would enable US allies to be trained in the use of and defence against nuclear weapons. The Act also opened the way to Anglo-American sharing of intelligence on the nuclear capabilities of the USSR and made possible the interchange of non-military nuclear information to assist not just Britain but any of America's close allies in building reactors for research purposes and for power generation.[31]

Eisenhower had been generous in many nuclear matters but he gave absolutely nothing away to Churchill on the linked issues of consultation and consent in connection with the actual use of weapons of mass destruction. In that respect, the Quebec agreement remained a dead letter. Against this disappointment, however, Churchill balanced not only the other nuclear plusses but the President's apparently encouraging attitude towards a summit. The 'vast surprise' on day one of the conference, Colville recorded, was that Ike 'at once agreed to talks with the Russians'.[32] Churchill was cock-a-hoop and more than ever convinced that if he could just get Malenkov to the conference table, the Cold War would begin to thaw.[33]

In truth, the Prime Minister had got ahead of himself – and of Eisenhower. There was undoubtedly an increased appreciation in the White House and State Department (if not the Pentagon) for Churchill's summitry ambition, as well as the wider nuclear concerns informing the British Cold War outlook. The day before the British party arrived in Washington there occurred what Matthew Jones describes as a 'pivotal' meeting of the National Security Council.[34] With the Joint Chiefs of Staff still seeking to exploit US nuclear superiority by putting pressure on the USSR, Dulles cautioned that 'our "tough policy" was becoming increasingly unpopular throughout the free world; whereas the British "soft policy" was gaining prestige and acceptance both in Europe and Asia'. If the JCS approach continued to inform national policy,

> very few of our allies would follow us ... The tide is clearly running against us in the channel of this tough policy. If we are to continue to pursue it we shall lose many of our allies, and this in itself compels a reappraisal of our basic policy ... We must recognise the fact that we can no longer run the free world.

With the President in agreement, the Eisenhower-Dulles combination proved too strong for those in favour of a forceful, pro-active and nuclear-injected Soviet policy.[35]

At the same time, there were limits to how far the US administration was prepared to go in support of an actual summit. Indeed, having excited Churchill on the first day of his visit, Eisenhower spent the next three rowing-back from his initial endorsement of an early meeting. Much careful preparation was needed, he maintained.[36] The Prime Minister, however, left Washington convinced that even if Eisenhower would not take part himself in a top-level meeting in the near future, he had no objection to a bilateral UK–Soviet leaders' meeting, a 'reconnaissance in force'. In fact Eisenhower harboured substantial reservations. Whether he failed to make these clear to Churchill, or whether his guest did not hear or would not listen, is uncertain.[37] 'Winston has a wonderful way of turning conversations at some later time into ironclad agreements', the President noted on the eve of the Churchill's arrival. 'We surely want to avoid that.'[38]

Beyond the general contribution that a summit could make to lightening the glowering Cold War atmosphere, a meeting with the Soviets remained, for Churchill, the key to preventing nuclear war. His thoughts were 'almost entirely thermo-nuclear', he confessed while in Washington. 'I spend a lot of time thinking over deterrents.' As long as the East–West contest remained at the level of Cold War, there existed the prospect, through high-level negotiations, of preventing hot war. But 'time is short', he insisted. The search for détente had to begin immediately.[39] Time must have seemed short in every sense to a man on the cusp of 80 years of age and convinced that he – and maybe he alone – could make the world a safer place.[40] So short, in fact, that en route home from America, somewhere in the middle of the Atlantic, Churchill dispatched a telegram to Molotov sounding him out on the likely Soviet attitude to a top-level conference in the early autumn supposing (and it was a crafty conditional) the British government was to propose one formally. To his delight, the Soviet Foreign Minister replied in encouraging terms.[41]

The Prime Minister's visit to North America is noteworthy for another reason rarely if ever mentioned in the literature. It was now, for the first time in the Cold War, that Churchill comprehended that détente and its corollary, the reduction of the danger of nuclear war, were unattainable unless or until the Western powers took seriously the Kremlin's calls (dating from the time of Stalin's death) for peaceful co-existence. From Washington, Churchill had travelled to Ottawa where, on 30 June, irritated by stories in the American press likening his summitry to communist appeasement, he clarified his position. 'We have to live with all sorts of people in this wicked world', he told a news conference, and 'hatred of communism' should not be allowed to get in the way of improved diplomatic (and trade) relations with the Soviet bloc, and even more so a broad settlement that would assure global peace. The two ideologies, capitalism and communism, had to learn to live 'side-by-side'.[42] For a man who had made a career out of demonizing communism, this was quite a statement. In the five years after Potsdam Churchill's atomic diplomacy had been predicated on liberating Eastern Europe from Soviet control. Even his summitry from 1950 rested on the belief that the USA's great nuclear advantage over the USSR, if deployed diplomatically, would at least attenuate if not eliminate communist control beyond the line of the Iron Curtain. At no point between 1945 and 1954 did he ever concede that Eastern Europe was lost. Now he did.

On the five-day voyage home aboard the *Queen Elizabeth* Churchill refined his thinking. Because of the holocaustic H-bomb, avoidance of war was now the overriding priority. Nuclear deterrence was one means to that end: Britain, the USA and the rest of the Western alliance must be strong enough to exorcise from the minds of Kremlin strategists even the thinnest sliver of belief that aggression could pay. But what Churchill called easement – or, in its most advanced state, détente – was another means. This was the view he took with him to Washington. And then, at some point during his North American sojourn, quite possibly as an off-the-cuff remark during his Ottawa press conference, he hit on a correlation which had previously eluded him: if détente was ever to be realized, the West must cease challenging and confronting the USSR over what it was doing in Eastern Europe. This did not require moral approval of Soviet communism. But it did mean acknowledging that the Kremlin's hegemony could neither be wished away nor forcibly extirpated without incurring wholly unacceptable risks.

Having alighted on peaceful co-existence, Churchill could talk of almost nothing else to his shipmates. In doing so he seemed keen to project his own new thinking on to Eisenhower. 'I am planning to go to meet the Russians, if they would like it', he told Moran on 2 July. He had the President's blessing. 'Ike has crossed a gulf of thought . . . He has made up his mind that Communism is not something which we must at all costs wipe out, but rather something we have got to learn to live with, and alongside – peaceful coexistence.' He returned to this theme on several other occasions.

> I am counting on the Russians wanting a better time; they want butter, not bombs, more comfort. For forty years they have had a pretty tough life. They may have given up dreams of world conquest and be ready for peaceful co-existence. Anyway, Ike has crossed the gulf which separates a mission to destroy Bolshevism from living side by side in peace. I must admit that I myself have crossed that gulf. I would like to visit Russia once more before I die.

Nearing Southampton, he had a wobble, not about his own gulf-spanning but Ike's. The Americans could easily 'become enraged – violent' in their handling of the USSR. 'I know them very well.' A forestalling war could yet ensue. On the other hand, a summit, if it bred peaceful co-existence and détente, would eliminate the reason for American rage.[43]

Churchill's choice of off-duty reading, Harold Nicolson's *Public Faces*, which he devoured during the voyage, further nourished his nuclear thought processes. Published in 1932, eight years after Churchill had written of a time when bombs no bigger than oranges might destroy entire cities, Nicholson's futuristic novel described a similarly compact device – the size of 'an ink-stand' in his case – housing an explosive mineral that 'could by the discharge of its electrons destroy New York'. The book sold tens of thousands of copies in the early 1930s, feeding the public's morbid fascination with modern science's potential for delivering destruction.[44] A devotée of science fiction since his teens, Churchill had somehow missed *Public Faces* when it first came out, but reading it now he pronounced it a 'very remarkable book'.[45] One of Nicolson's sub-themes was the capacity of nuclear research to generate political controversy and threaten the lives of governments. Over the next tumultuous month, Churchill would have plenty of cause to reflect on the sometimes blurred line between fiction and reality.

The Prime Minister arrived back in London on the evening of 6 July 1954. The following morning he chaired his first Cabinet for a fortnight. No minister beyond the chosen ones of the Defence Policy Committee knew anything about the H-bomb decision. No minister apart from Eden and those whom Churchill privately informed the night before (Butler, Macmillan and Salisbury) knew anything about the mid-Atlantic Molotov telegram. By the time the Cabinet broke for lunch, everyone was a lot wiser and a lot more disturbed. It was not immediately apparent, but Wednesday 7 July marked the beginning of a three-week Cabinet crisis which, at its severest, threatened to bring down the government. And all because of the politically toxic convergence of Churchill's bomb-making and his peace-making.

How could this be? How, from the best of intentions, could Churchill imperil the life of his own government? In seeking to reconstruct the crisis three sources are of especial value. First and most obviously there are the official minutes produced by the 'omni-competent' Norman Brook and his Cabinet Office team.[46] Here, though, we do well to heed Macmillan's good-natured rebuke of Brook. 'Historians reading this [record] fifty or a hundred years hence will get a totally false picture', he observed. 'They will be filled with admiration and surprise to find the Cabinet were so intellectually disciplined that they argued each case methodically and logically through to a set of neat and precise conclusions. It isn't like that at all.'[47] Happily, we now have access to Brook's original notebooks, the second key source. These include verbatim quotes, consistent attribution of viewpoints identifiable to named individuals, and entire conversational threads omitted from the official minutes. By blending the notebooks and the final record, we are thus able to get a little closer to the reality of events. Lastly, we have Macmillan's detailed diary account of the Cabinet meetings which, in combination, he considered 'the most extraordinary which I can remember since the Government was formed – or indeed at any time which I can recall'. Allowing for the caution historians must apply in handling any diary, and accepting that Macmillan was a political diarist in every sense of the term, his record adds important context and insight that cannot be found elsewhere.[48]

The meeting on 7 July began slowly – MPs' expenses headed the agenda – before, as Macmillan wrote, 'we came to the "bombshell"'. Churchill unfurled the circumstances behind and content of his seaborne message to Molotov. The telegram, he insisted, was entirely informal, a 'personal' sounding-out of the Soviet attitude to 'a friendly meeting' with no object other than to find 'a reasonable way of living side by side in growing confidence, easement and prosperity'. The Prime Minister was 'obviously nervous', Macmillan thought, and as he spoke the initial look of 'blank surprise' on the faces of most ministers was replaced by a sense of grievance on two connected grounds: first, that he had acted without the unequivocal approval of Eisenhower; and second, that for all the supposed informality of the cable, the positive Soviet response had left the government all but committed to an Anglo-Soviet summit which a number of ministers, had they been asked for an opinion, would have opposed because of the known American animus. However, since Churchill had written that morning to Eisenhower explaining his actions, the Cabinet deferred any further discussion until the President's response had been received.

At this point, Lindemann joined the meeting to review the atomic energy discussions in Washington before Churchill took up the running once more. Three weeks earlier, he explained, the Defence Policy Committee had approved a proposal by the Chiefs of Staff that the UK atomic weapons programme be extended to include the production of hydrogen bombs. His talks in Washington and Ottawa had therefore been conducted on the basis that Britain was a thermonuclear power in the making. The case in favour of an H-bomb was irrefutable, Churchill believed. First, there was its great deterrent value. The best hope of preserving world peace 'was to make it clear to potential aggressors that they had no hope of shielding themselves from a crushing retaliatory use of atomic power'. To this end Britain must possess 'a sufficient supply of up-to-date nuclear weapons'. Second, there was the retaliatory aspect: the UK needed to be in a position 'to ensure that no surprise attack, however large, could wholly destroy [its] power of effective retaliation'. Lastly, there was prestige. Britain, Churchill maintained, could not hope to wield serious influence in world affairs unless it was a member of the H-bomb club. Added together, these factors made it 'essential that we should manufacture hydrogen bombs in the United Kingdom'.[49]

The way in which Churchill laid out his stall suggests that, as during the war, he expected 'compliance with my wishes after reasonable discussion'.[50] But whether because of the magnitude of the moral and ethical considerations involved, or else because ministers were already upset at the way that collective Cabinet responsibility had been trampled by the Molotov telegram, he did not receive automatic approval. Harry Crookshank, the Lord Privy Seal, was especially distressed. The Cabinet 'had had no notice that this question was to be raised' and Crookshank 'hoped they would not be asked to take a final decision on it until they had had more time to consider it'. Cornered, Churchill agreed to discuss the matter at a further meeting the next day.[51]

The official minutes hint at the tensions in the Cabinet room but Macmillan's diary confirms them. 'It was dramatic . . . a most extraordinary scene' when Churchill

> dropped his second bomb . . . Harry Crookshank at once made a most vigorous protest at such a momentous decision being communicated to the Cabinet in so cavalier a way, and started to walk out of the room. We all did the same and the Cabinet broke up – if not in disorder – in a somewhat ragged fashion. Walter Monckton [Minister of Labour] and Woolton [Minister of Materials and Tory Party Chairman] seemed especially shocked! Not, I think, at the decision (which is probably right) but at the odd way in which things are being done.[52]

This was certainly Crookshank's sense. 'I feel that I should not conceal from you the shock which I – and other of your colleagues – experienced this morning', he wrote to Churchill afterwards. '[W]e had a right to be consulted in even so secret a matter.'[53]

After what we may fairly assume was a disturbed night, the Cabinet reassembled the next morning – 8 July – for round two. In a sprawling discussion, the H-bomb was subjected to questioning from a number of angles with Crookshank acting as chief scrutineer. He began by asking about the expense. Not prohibitive, said Butler and Sandys. The capital cost would not exceed £10 million while hydrogen bombs could be made 'in lieu of atomic bombs at a relatively small additional production cost'. Crookshank next raised the basic morality of building an H-bomb. Not germane, countered Lord Simonds, the Lord Chancellor, backed by Lord Alexander. Besides, all ethical objections were undercut by the fact that 'we had already embarked on the production of atomic weapons'. National prestige, that amorphous yet essential consideration for any country with great or even front-row power pretensions, provided a further rejoinder to Crookshank. 'No country could claim to be a leading military Power unless it possessed the most up-to-date weapons', the official minutes record (without ministerial attribution, thus implying consensus), 'and the fact must be faced that, unless we possessed thermo-nuclear weapons, we should lose our influence and standing in world affairs'. The record continues:

> At present some people thought that the greatest risk was that the United States might plunge the world into war, either through a misjudged intervention in Asia or in order to forestall an attack by Russia. Our best chance of preventing this was to maintain our influence with the United States Government; and they would certainly feel more respect for our views if we continued to play an effective part in building up the strength necessary to deter aggression than if we left it entirely to them to match and counter Russia's strength in thermo-nuclear weapons.

According to Brook's handwritten notes, this passage was a conflation of views expressed by Eden and David Maxwell-Fyfe, the Home Secretary. Brook also shows that while most ministers, impressed by these arguments, were becoming reconciled to the need for a hydrogen bomb, there was still considerable upset over the manner in which Churchill had broached the matter. There was also concern about the public relations aspect of the decision. Secret for now, it could not remain so for ever and ministers were conscious that an announcement that the government had decided to start work on a thermonuclear weapon at the very moment that public and parliamentary opinion was experiencing paroxysms of anxiety about "horror" bombs could be very damaging politically in the run-up to the next General Election. Time was needed to allow frayed nerves to settle prior to a campaign to educate the country about the H-bomb's deterrent value. With this, the discussion drew to a close. On the substantive issue, the official minutes record, there was 'general support' (not, therefore, unanimous backing) 'for the proposal that thermo-nuclear bombs should be manufactured in this country'. Crookshank pleaded for a further opportunity to 'reflect' before any irreversible decisions were taken and the Prime Minister duly agreed to a third round on the H-bomb towards the end of the month.[54]

'Cabinet explosions', Crookshank wrote afterwards. 'Winston very shamefaced – he knew he had been wrong.'[55] In fact Churchill knew no such thing. Permitting his colleagues a little more time for reflection was a necessary pressure-release but it was unlikely to change anything. There was 'very little doubt', he went on to inform the Queen in one of his regular political dispatches to Buckingham Palace, 'that the government would agree to the development of thermonuclear weapons' and that the first bombs would be ready within 'some two years'.[56] However, Churchill seriously underestimated the level of upset in the Cabinet. 'I thought the decision too grave to be taken by 3 or 4 ministers, without informing the others', Macmillan recorded. 'Either we were a responsible Cabinet or not.'[57] This, it so happens, was also the issue exercising ministers with regard to the Prime Minister's unilateral action in seeking an Anglo-Soviet summit. Churchill may well have been correct in what he told the Queen – a majority of the Cabinet was likely to go with the H-bomb – but he does not seem to have apprehended that he had a dual crisis on his hands.[58]

This brings us back to the Cabinet meeting on 8 July. Having disposed of the H-bomb (for now), ministers turned to the Molotov telegram. Overnight, Eisenhower had sent Churchill a cable of muted but unmistakable displeasure. 'You did not let any grass grow under your feet', he wrote. 'When you left here, I had thought, obviously erroneously, that you were in an undecided mood about this matter, and that when you had cleared your own mind I would receive some notice if you were to put your program into action. However, that is now past history, and we must hope that the steps you have started will lead to a good result.'[59] In his reply – sent to Washington before the Cabinet assembled – Churchill was contrite ('I hope you are not vexed with me') but insistent that Molotov's 'cordial and forthcoming' response excused all and 'strengthens my view' that the Soviet Union was 'anxious about the thermo-nuclear future'. The H-bomb not only justified his search for peace, it made possible its realization.[60]

The Cabinet, once apprised of these exchanges, was much less ready to accept that the end justified the means and Churchill was again forced to defend his right to approach foreign leaders on a personal basis. Naturally, he said, it had been his intention to consult the Cabinet if or when his informal Soviet sally had elicited a substantive response. Now it had. And here he was, consulting. This did not impress Lord Salisbury. The Prime Minister had taken 'a decision of policy which involved the collective responsibility of the whole Government without prior consultation'. This meant that 'any of his colleagues who dissented from the decision' – and Salisbury did – 'might thereby be forced to the remedy of resignation'. It came down to a question of 'constitutional' propriety. And why, Salisbury wondered, had Churchill sent his message to Moscow from the high seas rather than wait until he got back to London when he could have sought proper counsel? The answer, he heavily implied, was that the Prime Minister wished to outflank colleagues who might have opposed him. Now, though, the Cabinet was snared. If the Soviets went public with Churchill's offer, the government would be committed to a bilateral meeting of which the Americans, along with Salisbury and several other ministers, disapproved.[61]

The second most powerful figure in the room, Anthony Eden, now entered the fray. He had approved the cable composed by Churchill aboard the *Queen Elizabeth* – albeit in return for another (and purportedly definite) promise that the keys to Number 10 would be his following an autumn Churchill–Malenkov tête-à-tête – but had supposed, he told his colleagues, that the message would be put to the full Cabinet before dispatch. At this, Butler interjected. Left minding the shop in London, the Chancellor recalled receiving the telegram from Churchill but thought that he was being asked for a personal comment. Accordingly, rather than solicit a general ministerial reaction, he made a few textual tweaks and sent it back to the *Queen Elizabeth* from whence it wended its way to Moscow. On this point of clarification, the meeting adjourned until the next day.[62]

'Cabinet were very quiet, but rather grim', Macmillan wrote afterwards. There was 'a sense of drama' throughout, 'as of a Government about to break up'.[63] Certainly the Prime Minister, the Foreign Secretary and now the Chancellor were all at odds, while Salisbury was on the brink of a resignation which might encourage others to follow suit. If, that is, Churchill did not jump first. Absent from the official record but prominent in Brook's original notes is a prime ministerial resignation threat. It would be 'unfortunate if the Cabinet broke on such an issue', he said, particularly as 'opinion w[oul]d be divided in the country' (a remark suggestive of some confidence that the public, as well as the opposition, would be on his side). If he continued to find himself 'at variance' with his colleagues 'he w[oul]d resign'.[64] Churchill's desperation to convene a summit now threatened the very existence of the government. But that desperation, lest we forget, was entirely thermonuclear-generated.

Just after noon on 9 July the Cabinet met again, this time in the Prime Minister's room in the House of Commons. 'What a Friday!', wrote Macmillan, 'the most dramatic Cabinet which I have attended'.[65] It was also the shortest of the crisis. Churchill opened in fence-mending form. In seeking to arrange a meeting with Malenkov he would not travel to Moscow after all. The venue must be neutral. He also agreed to seek 'some definite proof' of Soviet sincerity – an Austrian treaty or agreement to cooperate in launching Eisenhower's Atoms for Peace plan – as a prerequisite to a meeting and would so inform the White House immediately after the Cabinet. To Salisbury, however, this missed the point. The Lord President remained 'unalterably opposed' to *any* high-level meeting with the Soviets without the participation of the United States. It mattered not a jot that Ike had now given his (grudging) consent. If the Cabinet endorsed the Prime Minister's policy, he would have no choice but to resign.[66] There was 'a tense, dramatic silence', Macmillan wrote. 'After a few moments, PM said – with great dignity and emotion – "I should deeply regret a severance. But I hope our private friendship would survive".'[67] It was a cool response but Churchill must have been taken aback. At any rate he now played for time: further discussion, let alone decisions, should be deferred until Eisenhower's 'final views' were known, likewise the results of Geneva conference. Nobody in the room dissented.[68]

As Churchill went off to compose his message to Eisenhower, his colleagues took stock.[69] For Macmillan, Eden, Salisbury, Crookshank and several others, the worry now was that even if the government held together, an Anglo-Soviet summit, should it ensue, would serve no positive purpose. To the contrary, it would drive a wedge between the UK and the USA, destabilize NATO, and expose to the world Churchill's failings – his refusal to read briefs, his poor concentration, his deafness, his emotionalism, and his readiness to compromise on key issues for the sake of currying favour with Malenkov. 'In thinking this all over, I am persuaded that Churchill is now quite incapable – mentally, as well as physically – of remaining Prime Minister', Macmillan wrote.

> Like many men who had had their strokes, his judgment is distorted. He thinks about one thing all the time – this Russian visit and his chance of saving the world – till it has become an obsession ... He has forgotten what barbarians the Russians are ... Of course, with his brilliance and charm and gallantry and astonishing resilience, he can still put in a performance – Parliamentary questions, an after-dinner speech ... or even a press conference ... But it's a tremendous effort and takes more and more out of him. For a great part of the day, he doesn't really function ... Now it looks as if, in the last days of his career, he may destroy his reputation, his Government, and the party of which he has accepted the leadership.[70]

Oliver Lyttelton, the Colonial Secretary, doubted it would come to that. Churchill, he observed, had painted his colleagues into a corner. To join with Salisbury to bring down the government on a détente initiative just as the H-bomb was scaring people out of their wits would leave the dissenters looking like 'a bunch of stone-heads led by a reactionary marquess who had let his gun off before September 1st and shot the dove of peace in a turnip field'.[71]

The Geneva recess having ended, Eden now returned to Switzerland to resume the search for peace in Indo-China. In consequence, the Cabinet crisis went into stasis. On 12 July, Churchill reported to Parliament on his visit to Washington where, he said, he 'never had the feeling of general good will more strongly borne in upon me'. He also spoke at some length on his new-found belief that peaceful co-existence, a 'fundamental and far-reaching conception', and détente must be regarded as as complementary halves of a single approach to Cold War peace-making:

> What a vast ideological gulf there is between the idea of peaceful co-existence vigilantly safeguarded, and the mood of forcibly extirpating the Communist fallacy and heresy. It is, indeed, a gulf. This statement is a recognition of the appalling character which war has now assumed and that its fearful consequences go even beyond the difficulties and dangers of dwelling side by side with Communist States. Indeed, I believe that the widespread acceptance of this policy may in the passage of years lead to the problems which divide the world being solved or solving themselves, as so many problems do, in a manner which will avert the mass destruction of the human race and give time, human nature and the mercy of God their chance to win salvation for us.[72]

In asserting his credentials as a peace-monger, Churchill further straitjacketed those ministers contemplating resignation over the Molotov telegram. But this was a consequence, not the reason for him speaking as he did. The driving force was conviction. A public statement of this kind had been brewing for a while. Hydrogen bombs and ideological extremism – the kind of anti-communism that he had espoused for nearly forty years – were, he now saw, a deadly mix.

That same day, Churchill received a message from Eisenhower approving his setting of preconditions for an Anglo-Soviet summit and reassuring him that, while he bore no personal grudge, he could not vouch for the reaction of US opinion when news of a Churchill–Malenkov rendezvous broke. Still, he promised to 'do my best to minimize whatever may be the immediate and unfavorable reaction'.[73] Churchill was 'much gratified' by this message, he told the Cabinet on 13 July, but though politically strengthened by its contents, he accepted that any further move – another message to Molotov being the obvious one – must await Eden's return from Geneva.[74] The 'general feeling' was 'relief', Macmillan wrote, but Salisbury 'looked glum and worried'.[75]

No wonder. From Salisbury's standpoint, the President's message altered nothing. As Colville noted, the Lord President's resignation remained 'hanging over everybody' as was 'the still more alarming possibility that Winston, if thwarted, would resign, split the country and the party and produce a situation of real gravity'. If that happened, Colville, for all his loyalty to his master, knew where the fault rested. On the voyage back from America, Churchill had spoken openly to him of making a meeting with Malenkov 'a matter of confidence with the Cabinet ... If they opposed the visit, it would give him a good occasion to go.' In composing the Molotov telegram, therefore, Churchill had been deliberately devious. Salisbury was right. 'He [Churchill] admitted to me', Colville wrote, 'that if he had waited to consult the Cabinet after the *Queen Elizabeth* returned, they would almost certainly have raised objections and caused delays. The stakes in this matter were so high and, as he sees it, the possible benefits so crucial to our survival, that he was prepared to adopt any methods to get a meeting with the Russians arranged.' Churchill, and nobody else, had brought the government – *his* government – to a point of implosion.[76]

On 20 July, after three months of intense negotiations, the Geneva conference finally succeeded in bringing the Indo-China war to a close. Under the terms of the settlement, Viet-Nam was divided at the seventeenth parallel, the Viet-Minh regrouping north of that line and the French and the Viet-Namese government forces to the south. However, this territorial delineation was only temporary. Internationally-supervised nation-wide elections were scheduled for July 1956 out of which it was intended that a single Viet-Namese government would emerge to preside over a reunified and independent state. 'The result was not completely satisfactory', Eden acknowledged in closing the conference, 'but we had stopped an eight-year war and reduced international tension at a point of instant danger to world peace. This achievement was well worth while.'[77] Those in Britain and beyond who had worried that a failure at Geneva would lead to a wider war gladly seconded the Foreign Secretary's verdict. At home especially, Eden was lionized as the peacemaker-in-chief and showered with accolades including the Order of the Garter and the title 'Politician of the Year' by the normally reliably anti-Tory *Daily Mirror*.[78] Thanks to Geneva, he was at the zenith of his career as an international statesman.

Significantly, the Geneva settlement also marked a victory for British diplomacy over the USA's early hopes for a military solution and its later unhelpful approach to the peace process. Eden was the vehicle of American diplomatic defeat but the cause was the Eisenhower administration's failure to educate its allies effectively as to the nuclear utility of the New Look. In May, following his departure from Geneva, Dulles told the National Security Council that the 'basic cause for the British weakness with regard to Southeast Asia was their obsession over the H-bomb and its potential effect on the British Isles'.[79] Dulles was right. Nor did anything change over the next two months. As the US ambassador in London noted at the close of proceedings at Geneva, it was the doctrine of 'massive retaliation' that made the British 'hesitant' about involvement in any 'local engagements' carrying a risk of general war, and it was conceivable that 'thermo-nuclear neutralism' might henceforward gain substantial traction both in the UK and Western Europe. More immediately, now that Indo-China was settled, Aldrich expected Churchill to renew his call for a summit.[80] This was prescient. But there would be no summit, bilateral or multilateral, unless Churchill could hold his government together.

There were more spectators than usual in Downing Street on 23 July as ministers entered through the famous black door for that day's scheduled Cabinet. Most had come to glimpse the Foreign Secretary, the hero of the hour. None of them realized that the fate of the government hung in the balance. Eden, though, knew well enough what was at stake. Taking leave of Geneva, he confessed to Bedell Smith how 'very worried' he was about Churchill's 'solitary pilgrimage' and 'afraid [the] Cabinet will resign' if the Prime Minister did not back down.[81] This, in its turn, might lead to a snap General Election that would let in Labour, a point Eden tried to get across to Churchill when warning him that Salisbury's departure would be 'a political loss which it is of the first importance to avert'. The loss would also be personal: Eden wanted to succeed Churchill as Prime Minister, not as leader of the opposition.[82] As well as Salisbury and Crookshank, Woolton was said to be considering his position, while Simonds and Lord Swinton were reportedly planning to turn the constitution on its head by asking the Queen to intervene to prevent the government folding.[83] At Macmillan's instigation, Clementine had begged her husband to be less uncompromising but judging from the telephone call Macmillan received from Churchill ('a long and often violent defence of his conduct') she got nowhere.[84] Moran called by Number 10 early on 23 July. Churchill told him he had been 'very tired last night'. That was only natural, Moran said, it had been a 'grim' week or two. Churchill 'repeated the word "grim" and nodded his head'. He then fell silent for a time before suddenly snapping out of his reverie. 'Today's Cabinet will be decisive', he proclaimed. 'They must support me or I shall go.'[85]

Overnight, Eisenhower had sent another letter, this one wishing Churchill well and expressing regret that he could not 'bring myself to believe wholeheartedly in the venture' due to an 'utter lack of confidence in the reliability and integrity of the men in the Kremlin'.[86] Now, when the Cabinet got down to business, the Prime Minister exploited this non-objection (it could not be classed as positive approval) in seeking backing for another message to Moscow requesting a time (September, ideally) and a place (Berne, Stockholm or Vienna) for a meeting with Malenkov. The message, he once more insisted, would be personal and private, and once more his opponents contended that such a missive inevitably engaged the collective responsibility of the Cabinet. At this, Churchill played his trump. 'If I have lost the confidence of my colleagues', he intoned, 'there can only be one end to it.' Leaving this implied threat hovering in the air like cigar fug, he then changed tack. The original cable had been sent with the Foreign Secretary's approval and thus with the Cabinet's *de facto* sanction since Eden was the minister in charge of foreign policy. An outraged Eden reacted as though cattle-prodded. 'You cannot say this', Macmillan's diary records him snapping. 'You know that I did everything possible to dissuade you for one whole day at least on the voyage. I told you that if you sent the telegram "it would be against the advice of the Foreign Secretary". I told you that it ought to be referred to the Cabinet. What else could I do? Resign on board the ship, I suppose?' Notoriously highly-strung, Eden nonetheless rarely if ever expressed himself so intemperately to Churchill in an open forum. The 'outburst was rather a shock to C', Macmillan wrote. 'But he went on gallantly enough.'[87]

Macmillan himself attempted to alter the trajectory of the discussion by voicing the view – which was shared by others – that instead of dwelling on the past the Cabinet should address the situation which now confronted it. Salisbury agreed: he had been 'the first to raise the constitutional aspect' but the most pressing concern now was the destabilizing international consequences of a Churchill–Malenkov meeting. The unity of NATO and, at its heart, the closet possible Anglo-American relationship, was the best deterrent to a war which would bring appalling devastation to the United Kingdom, he reminded Cabinet colleagues. But with the Soviet Union's post-Geneva propaganda viciously traducing American policy in South-East Asia, the Prime Minister's rush to sup with Malenkov, the man in charge of the propaganda-machine, risked imposing new strains on a barely restored US–UK relationship. With Indo-China hopefully at peace, this was a moment for transatlantic healing not wound-opening. Furthermore, the need for Britain to exercise influence over US foreign policy – for which purpose relations needed to be in good working order – had never been greater given the 'risk . . . that the United States might decide to bring the East–West issue to a head while they still had overwhelming superiority in atomic weapons and were comparatively immune from atomic attack by Russia'. Eden took Salisbury's part: he 'did not himself believe that any good would come from a bi-lateral meeting with the Russians at the present time'. The Prime Minister did not respond and the Cabinet ended in agreement to postpone a final decision on a Churchill–Malenkov encounter (and thus by extension on Salisbury's future along with that of the government) for another seven days.[88]

It had been a 'painful . . . even shattering' ordeal, Macmillan wrote.[89] Crookshank thought it simply 'terrible'.[90] Afterwards, Macmillan found Eden 'really shocked by Winston's *supressio veri, suggestio falso*' performance. The 'old man is really a crook!', Eden railed. 'He hasn't told the truth.' And with that the Foreign Secretary took to his bed. For two whole days. Nor was he disturbed by telephone calls from Number 10. 'Dead silence from Winston', Clarissa noted; 'unheard of from him'.[91] Was Churchill really giving thought to resignation? Quite possibly. From the outset, his handling of the Cabinet had involved substantial brinkmanship as he sought, through emotional and political ruses, to build support for his summitry. Now he was on the brink itself: he had to decide whether to retreat or forge ahead regardless of the consequences. Later, Colville maintained that Churchill was 'seriously considering an appeal over the heads of his Cabinet colleagues to the conscience of his countrymen'.[92] This was also the view of the US embassy in London. After talking to several Cabinet members, Aldrich informed Washington that Churchill had 'actually threatened to form a coalition government with the opposition for the purpose of insuring peace if his present colleagues should be unwilling to support him'. There was 'little doubt', the ambassador added, that 'the opposition would join such a government because of existing fears in Britain of [the] result to this country of atomic warfare'.[93]

All through his long political career Churchill had been a natural coalitionist ('non-party', according to Clementine, 'he makes up his mind on questions as they strike him').[94] However, even though Labour had voted for a summit in April at the climax of the H-bomb debate, it is unlikely that Attlee, his shadow Cabinet or Labour's National Executive would have gone along with the idea of a one-issue emergency coalition.[95] But however one looks at this extraordinary three weeks in British politics, it is hard to disagree with John Young's conclusion that Churchill had been 'ruthless and devious' throughout in seeking to get his own way.[96] If only that energy and focus could have been directed towards all of the major issues confronting his government at home and abroad. As it was, he had only enough in reserve for his conjoined obsession, a summit and the reduction of the nuclear danger.

Nor were the July days quite played-out. Salisbury, though emotionally drained himself, did not have the luxury of taking to his bed as Eden did. The 'only man for many years who had openly challenged Churchill in Cabinet and induced him to consider resignation', he was also the minister responsible for nuclear policy and in that capacity he prepared for the third and decisive Cabinet discussion of the hydrogen bomb by circulating two papers.[97] The first was the appreciation of the Chiefs of Staff which had made such an impression on the Defence Policy Committee in June. Now, for the first time, the Cabinet as a whole was given a copy (albeit with certain sensitive details, such as the numbers of H-bombs involved, excised). The second was a paper of his own outlining the DPC's thinking and seeking approval not only to proceed with the manufacture of a British weapon but for the strategic concept it was intended to support. 'Our primary aim must be to prevent a major war', he wrote. 'To that end we must strengthen our position and influence as a world Power and maintain and consolidate our alliance with the United States.' In keeping with this broad outlook, the UK's defence objectives were to possess the most modern means of waging war 'so that we may hold our place in world councils on the issue of peace or war and play our part in deterring aggression'; to continue to play its part globally 'in checking the spread of Communism'; to preserve the security and political stability of its Colonial territories; and to support its world-wide trading interests.[98]

However, when the Cabinet assembled on 26 July, the H-bomb had to be set aside temporarily while ministers dealt with an unexpected twist in the saga of the Molotov telegram. The previous day the USSR had issued a call for an early conference of all European governments, along with the United States, to consider a new system of collective security. This was, at first sight, a crude attempt to neutralize what Moscow called the 'special danger' of German rearmament within the EDC.[99] The Prime Minister, without prompting, told the Cabinet that the announcement had created 'a new situation' and he was 'satisfied that he could not proceed with his proposal for a bilateral meeting with the Russians while this suggestion of a much larger meeting of Foreign Ministers was being publicly canvassed'. A message, he suggested, should to be sent to Molotov stating that the Soviet initiative superseded his own idea of an Anglo-Soviet summit. His colleagues must have listened to this in varying degrees of slack-jawed wonder. For three weeks, Churchill's brazen and bull-headed behaviour had brought the government close to extinction. Now he pulled back from the brink as did his opponents in collective and relieved reaction. The Prime Minister's proposed course was approved but, as a safety net, ministers insisted that his message to Molotov be firmed-up to the effect that until this all-Europe conclave was convened (which few in Cabinet thought would ever happen), a Churchill–Malenkov encounter must be considered 'in abeyance'. And so the government survived, for the time being at least, saved indirectly and ironically by its great Cold War adversary.[100]

With the apparent resolution of the crisis over the Molotov telegram, ministers could be forgiven for approaching the H-bomb decision, grave though it was, with a certain lightness of being. The official minutes note only a 'short discussion' before agreement was reached that 'we should possess a stock of the most up-to-date thermo-nuclear weapons'. In Brook's notebook, Crookshank is quoted as being 'not wholly persuaded' but gave his assent 'reluctantly'. Ministers agreed that much serious consideration needed to be given to how and when to release and then justify the decision to the public. For now, it would remain secret.[101] The next day the Cabinet endorsed the strategy underpinning the H-bomb as recommended by the DPC.[102] A little under three years later, Britain detonated its first hydrogen device. It was Churchill's bomb.

CHAPTER 16
STURDY CHILD OF TERROR

It had been a gruelling month for the Prime Minister, one in which he received 'probably his roughest ever treatment at the hands of his full cabinet'.[1] Compared with his 'exhausting life as a peacetime Prime Minister', he told Walter Graebner, 'I had an easier time of it during the war ... Now everything is different. There is so much patter, patter, patter, chatter, chatter, chatter, it's a wonder anything ever gets done.'[2] Still, he had got through his ordeal by patter-chatter and on 27 July he informed Parliament that a top-level meeting with the USSR must await the outcome of Moscow's proposal for an all-European conference.[3] This prompted a swift response from Moscow – the two gatherings, the small and the big, were not mutually exclusive, Molotov insisted – but to the Cabinet's relief the Prime Minister held his position.[4] With this, Martin Gilbert suggests, 'Churchill's last great foreign policy initiative was at an end', a judgement that is sound enough in terms of hindsight (there would be no summit during the remainder of his premiership) but which understates the extent to which Churchill, at the time, retained hope that he could still get Malenkov to the conference table.[5] And because he had not given up hope, he was not ready to give up the premiership. 'It's really this business of meeting the Russians that keeps him from going', Brook reflected.[6] That and the Bomb.

On 2 August, in a memorandum for the Cabinet, Churchill explored with lucidity and cogency the linkage between the nuclear peril and the imperative of détente. Remarkably, he wrote – or dictated – the paper in just two hours.[7] Stressing that the purpose of his mooted meeting with Malenkov had always been to prepare the ground for a great power summit involving the USA (and possibly France), Churchill was convinced that the Soviet Union, being 'far weaker in the thermo-nuclear sphere, including especially power of hostile delivery', would welcome the prospect. Moscow, surely, would agree that a period of 'peaceful co-existence', lasting perhaps twenty years, had much to recommend it. And why stop at twenty? If the two sides used their Cold War sabbatical to learn to understand each other and work out a basis for a permanent modus vivendi, so much the better. More immediately, Churchill accepted that the main danger to peace lay not in a major act of Soviet aggression but in the troubling thought processes entertained by American policymakers. In a role-play diversion, he described these as follows:

> We alone have for the next two or perhaps three years sure and overwhelming superiority in attack, and a substantial measure of immunity in defence. Merely to dawdle means potential equality of ruin. Ought we not for the immediate safety of

our own American people and the incidental rescue of the Free World to bring matters to a head by a 'show-down' leading up to an ultimatum accompanied by an Alert?

A showdown. How he had come to hate the term. Reverting to himself, Churchill predicted that if another local crisis in Asia or elsewhere should escalate into a showdown, it could trigger a global nuclear war in which Britain and its Western European neighbours 'might well be victims whatever we thought, said or did'. There was, he conceded, a possibility that Moscow, undertaking a profit and loss analysis, might capitulate and accept a settlement on Western terms, but realistically 'Total War' was the more likely outcome. There was, though, another way of managing the Cold War, one which would avoid prestige-engaging showdowns: peaceful co-existence and détente. Therefore, while conscious of the dangers of being 'taken in or out-manoeuvred' by the Soviets, Churchill's aim remained the convening of a top-level summit brought about, if needs must, by a preliminary Anglo-Soviet encounter.[8]

'Impressed but not convinced' was how Montague Browne summed up the Whitehall response to the paper. 'The FO dislikes it. They say if we seem to appease Russia, other countries, like France, will say let us all hasten and make our own peace with her, and we shall see the break-up of NATO.' Salisbury and Crookshank were also reportedly 'very much against'.[9] Beyond its summitry merits, Churchill's paper was a manifesto for his continuance in office. He sent a copy to the vacationing Foreign Secretary who still laboured under the impression that the keys to Number 10 would be his in the autumn. 'I feel sure', Churchill wrote in a covering note, 'that I can be a help in the cause of peace'. Which must have sounded ominous to Eden.[10] The Prime Minister conveyed the same message to Eisenhower. 'One has to do one's duty as one sees it from day to day and, as you know, the mortal peril which overhangs the human race is never absent from my thoughts. I am not looking about for the means of making a dramatic exit or of finding a suitable Curtain.' On the contrary, he was driven by the belief that '[n]ow ... is the moment for a parley at the summit'. The interest of 'both sides' in the Cold War had become 'Survival' and, as an added attraction, the 'measureless material prosperity of the masses' if or when nuclear energy was diverted from destructive to constructive ends.[11]

During the torrid summer of 1954, Churchill had also developed the idea that a summit could perform a vital educative role. Did Malenkov and his comrades *truly* understand the realities of the nuclear age? Did they *really* know what they were up against in a thermonuclear-armed USA? It was only through a face-to-face meeting that Churchill could check and, if required, remedy any deficit in their comprehension. Full and reciprocal nuclear awareness would aid the cause of détente. Indeed, as he told Eisenhower when they met in June, 'what might be the doom of the world' could yet prove to be 'its salvation'.[12] Was Churchill once again trail-blazing on behalf of mutual assured destruction? Almost certainly. In some ways he had been gravitating in this direction since 1924 when, in 'Shall We All Commit Suicide?', he first essayed a future of '[r]eciprocal extermination'.[13] Thirty years on, when Bedell Smith stopped by

Downing Street on his way home to Washington from the Geneva conference, he was treated to a Churchillian lecture on the 'importance of a final try for peaceful co-existence' with the Soviets. The Prime Minister said 'that "these people" must be convinced that while *we* could not make a surprise attack on them, and they could, and would, make a surprise attack on us, it was inevitable that "even though they should slaughter ten million of us in Britain and the United States, they could not prevent the devastating counterstroke" . . . this meant that we must have "many bases, more and more of them – some camouflaged and concealed – all over the world", and that we must reduce the size of "these frightful things" so that they can be carried on smaller planes which can take off from any airfield or from any of our carriers'.[14] This might not have been a fully worked-out treatise on MAD, but it was getting close and Churchill would continue to hone his thinking in the months ahead.

With the collapse of his hopes for a September conference with Malenkov (for which, incidentally, he blamed the Foreign Office, Salisbury and 'that impudent Crookshank' much more than Molotov and his pan-European peace proposal), Churchill ceased speaking in riddles and made clear his absolute determination to carry on. 'You will, I am sure, be glad to hear that I am not thinking of retirement at the present time', he wrote to Baruch at the end of August. 'I feel earnestly I still have something to contribute to the cause of "Peace through Strength" . . . My mind is continually oppressed by the thermo-nuclear problem, though I still think it is more likely to bring War to an end than mankind.'[15] Baruch was delighted by the news. Not so the Foreign Secretary. 'Winston said he feels better all the time and he has no intention of retiring until a fortnight before the General Election', Clarissa Eden wrote in her diary. If the parliament ran its full course, that would be October 1956. 'Poor Anthony absolutely stunned.'[16]

On 30 November 1954, Churchill celebrated his eightieth birthday. No Prime Minister since Gladstone had been serving in office at that great age. He was the only MP in the House of Commons to have been elected in the reign of Queen Victoria. It was fifty-six years since he had charged with the Lancers at Omdurman, forty-nine since he entered Sir Henry Campbell-Bannerman's Liberal government as Under-Secretary of State for the Colonies, and forty-four years since he became a Privy Counsellor. Now, though, time was finally catching up with him. 'Towards the end of 1954', Norman Brook recalled, 'there were signs that he would not be able to carry on for much longer.' He could still rise to the big occasion but 'in the daily round of his responsibilities he no longer had the necessary energy, mental or physical, to give to papers or to people the full attention which they deserved'.[17]

There were, however, two notable exceptions to the general malaise: his quest for a summit and his search for ways to protect his country, and the world, from the danger of nuclear war. 'I have cherished the hope that there is a new outlook in Russia, a new hope of peaceful co-existence', he told his party's annual conference that autumn. 'While I have life and strength I shall persevere in this'. But he was not so fond or foolish as to let down his guard. 'Peace through Strength . . . founded on the unity, precautions and vigilance of the free nations of the world' was embedded in a policy which, he said, took full account of the USA's superiority in nuclear weapons, still 'the decisive deterrent against communist aggression'.[18]

By this time one of the great obstacles to a summit, the European Defence Community, had been removed, though not in the way that the scheme's champions had wanted. After two years of vacillation, the French National Assembly finally put the EDC treaty to the vote on 30 August 1954 – only to throw it out. Since the EDC, and with it West Germany's rearmament and sovereignty, could not be fully realized without unanimous ratification by all six proposed member states (the Federal Republic, Italy and the Benelux countries having already approved the treaty), the French vote plunged the Western alliance into crisis.[19] The British, with Eden in the van, moved decisively to hold NATO together. Instead of replacing the EDC with another complex supranational body, the Foreign Secretary proposed, and the West Europeans and Americans accepted, a looser inter-governmental alternative, a Western European Union (WEU), within which German rearmament could be safely effected. In October a new treaty was initialled allowing for the Federal Republic to join the WEU and thus to enter NATO on terms of approximate equality with the existing members. However, by December, the French Assembly, reluctant to sanction German rearmament in any form, was cavilling over WEU ratification, the pre-requisite, NATO collectively agreed, to any top-level meeting with the Soviet Union.[20]

Writing to Eisenhower, Churchill decried the 'tyrannical weakness of the French Chamber' but trusted that an affirmative vote would be forthcoming early in 1955. At that point, he said, he would relaunch his campaign for a summit. Indeed it was mainly in the 'hope' of bringing about an East–West meeting 'that I am remaining in harness longer than I wished or planned'.[21] In his reply, the President smothered that hope. The launch of the WEU was, for Eisenhower, an end in itself, not just a means to a summit. Before he would contemplate a heads of government meeting he wanted the Foreign Ministers of the USA, UK, France and the USSR to come together to survey the Cold War landscape. But since he could see no prospect of such a gathering 'for some considerable period' it followed that 'I cannot see that a top-level meeting is anything which I can inscribe on my schedule for any predictable date'.[22] This was a real body-blow to Churchill – the more so in light of public hints from Moscow that the Soviets would be receptive to a formal Western offer of a summit.[23]

While Churchill clung to what remained of his summitry dream, his government wrestled with the problem of how to present to Parliament and public the decision to build a hydrogen bomb. The tumult of the spring had died down by the autumn and policymakers, nervous about stimulating a new outbreak of H-bomb fever, were inclined to let matters drift. In November, Lindemann wrote to Churchill from Oxford to say that enough was enough: work on the H-bomb was ongoing and 'a policy of permanent silence' was hardly 'feasible, even if it were desirable'.[24] Prodded by the Prof, the Prime Minister agreed to enfold the thermonuclear revelation in a general Defence White Paper to be put to Parliament early in the New Year.[25]

The task of preparing the paper fell to Macmillan who had recently succeeded Alexander as Minister of Defence. Macmillan accepted that the statement must emphasize the obvious deterrent value of the H-bomb and refer, in broad terms, to the civil defence implications of thermonuclear warfare, but he was reluctant to comment in detail on fall-out until more was known about the phenomenon.[26] On 10 December he wrote to Churchill recommending that a small group of officials, including representatives of the Ministry of Defence, the Cabinet Office and the Home Office, begin work immediately on a report for consideration by ministers. The Prime Minister agreed and before the year was out, William Strath, a respected Cabinet Office official, had been appointed to lead the group which, for short-hand, became known as the Strath committee.[27]

The presentational aspect of the H-bomb decision was not the only nuclear-themed public relations issue exercising the Churchill government. Towards the end of the year, the United States advanced proposals in NATO which had as their ultimate object the nuclearization of a large part of the organization's armed forces. The Americans also wanted the SACEUR, General Alfred Gruenther, to have the right to use tactical nuclear weapons – atomic artillery, for the most part – at his sole discretion in the event of a Red Army ground invasion of Western Europe.[28] 'I fear that the public will be rather alarmed to discover that we really cannot fight any war *except* a nuclear war', Macmillan recorded in his diary. He continued:

It is quite impossible to arm our forces with *two* sorts of weapons – conventional and unconventional. The Air Force and in course of time, the Army will be largely equipped with nuclear weapons of one sort or another. That means that if the Russians attacked (which is *very* unlikely) with conventional weapons only, in the first instance, we should be forced into the position of *starting* the nuclear war, with all that is implied – including the counter-attack on UK. From a purely military point of view, there is no way out. We should be utterly crushed in a conventional war. But, politically, it is full of danger, at home and abroad, and may lead to a fresh burst of defeatism or neutralism.[29]

Churchill, too, was disturbed about the direction in which the Americans were pushing NATO. Nuclear weapons should be used in retaliation for a like attack, he maintained, and he deprecated the Eisenhower administration's emerging first use philosophy.[30] In tandem with intelligence estimates suggesting that the Soviet nuclear weapons programme was 'large, efficient and scientifically up-to-date', US plans for NATO underscored for Churchill the urgency of a summit before the American and Soviet nuclear juggernauts careered out of control.[31] He had, in addition, personal political reasons for hastening a meeting. With a General Election likely within eighteen months, the frustration of senior Conservatives at his refusal to stand down had burgeoned into anxiety and resentment.[32] On 21 December, a delegation of ministers, including Eden, Butler and Woolton, called at Number 10. The ostensible purpose of the meeting was to discuss the date of the election but the reality of the situation quickly dawned on Churchill. 'I know you are trying to get rid of me [but] it is up to me to go to the Queen and hand her my resignation', he snapped, 'but I won't do it.'[33] Still, when he calmed down, he must have realized that a summit needed to happen early in 1955 lest political pressure, never mind Eisenhower's opposition, finally put pay to his hopes.

Since the time of his stroke in 1953, Churchill unquestionably used the prospect of a meeting with Stalin's successors as an excuse, or justification, for putting off the dread moment of retirement, his 'first death ... a death in life', as Clementine described his feelings on the subject.[34] This has earned him criticism, some of it sharp, from historians.[35] However, while acknowledging his cunning and unworthy manipulations, Robert Rhodes James rightly reminds us that Churchill's search for détente, far from being the 'quasi-senile dreams of an old man still wanting to hold centre stage in world affairs', possessed 'a nobility and vision about them that are admirable'.[36] A summit might succeed or it might fail in establishing a basis for peaceful co-existence, but unless a meeting was had, there was, in Churchill's view, no way of finding out. In the meantime, Britain and its allies needed to attend to their security. Such was the thrust of the last major Cabinet paper on nuclear issues that he composed during his premiership.

Dated 14 December 1954, 'Notes on Tube Alloys', a sophisticated discourse on the place of nuclear weapons in international affairs, was very far from the work of a statesman in decline. The 'only sane policy is Defence through Deterrents', Churchill argued, but this would never guarantee safety in a world of nuclear imbalance. Over the next two-to-three years the real 'danger' would come from 'a forestalling nuclear attack on Russia' by a more powerful United States. On balance, he suspected that the Americans would be restrained 'by their strong moral and spiritual convictions from such an act', and might even adopt, as he hoped they would, a non-first use policy. But what of the USSR? Would the Soviets deliberately embark on war? This was by no means 'improbable', he averred. Fearing a thermonuclear assault before its own arsenal of weapons had acquired critical mass, the Kremlin might be tempted to 'bridge the gulf by a surprise attack'. The defence here – 'our only hope' – was that same US nuclear superiority, reinforced by the British stockpile of atomic and eventually hydrogen bombs, maintained at such a high level that the USSR would know that any attack would be met with 'immediate retaliation on a far larger scale'. Radioactive fall-out, such a worry to people the world over since Castle-Bravo and the *Lucky Dragon* incident, would itself serve to 'increase the deterrent upon Soviet Russia by putting her enormous spaces and scattered population on an equality or near-equality of vulnerability with our small densely-populated Island and with Western Europe'. Indeed a stage of reciprocal – mutually assured – destruction might soon be reached with 'safety ... the child of terror, and existence the twin brother of annihilation'.[37]

In weighing the future, Churchill was adamant that NATO conventional forces must also remain strong in order to hold back a Red Army invasion of Western Europe long enough for the impact of nuclear retaliation to make itself felt. 'If during and in spite of the confusion of the nuclear war, they [the Soviets] were able to occupy Paris and Brussels and spread themselves out over the conquered lands, they would have an important counter for negotiation, and bases for the discharge at Britain of missiles very injurious and additional to their atomic stockpile.' Even then it was 'probable' that the Allies 'would be shy of dropping a Hydrogen bomb on the Bois de Boulogne, and thus destroying the population of Paris'. This led him to pronounce on the sovereignty of nuclear decision-making. The current American proposal to give SACEUR the right to decide when tactical battlefield weapons should be employed was unacceptable. Governments must be the decision-making bodies – but not necessarily, in the NATO context, *all* governments. To avoid delay in an emergency, he recommended that the USA and Britain, as the only two nuclear powers in NATO, take the decision on behalf of all members. Churchill ended by uniting his twin obsessions. The art of deterrence was to ensure that those you would deter are fully aware of your military-nuclear strength and your determination to use that strength if sufficiently provoked. To this end, Britain and the United States ought to use a summit to instruct the Soviet leadership. 'Time', he implored, 'should not be wasted.'[38]

Churchill was proud of a paper in which, as John Young notes, he showed 'a remarkable grasp' of future nuclear developments.[39] Beyond the Cabinet, he sent copies to a number of interested parties, including Attlee, Montgomery (deputy SACEUR) and Ismay (NATO Secretary-General), all of whom commended its clarity and realism.[40] He even dispatched one to the Queen.[41] Then, in January 1955, having obtained 'a very large measure of agreement' from Cabinet colleagues, he sent the paper to Eisenhower.[42] The President, too, praised the way that Churchill conceptualized the nuclear issue but disagreed with his view that governments, even if only the US and British governments, must be the ultimate decision-makers in a crisis. It was all about speed of reaction. Where, Eisenhower wondered, would the time be found for inter-governmental consultation? 'I think it possible that the very life of a nation, perhaps even of Western civilization, could … come to depend on instantaneous reaction to news of an approaching air fleet; victory or defeat could hang upon minutes and seconds used decisively at top speed or tragically wasted in indecision'. Beyond this, Eisenhower agreed generally with Churchill's thesis on deterrence but felt that considerable thought needed to be given to 'the conditions under which we would find it necessary to react explosively'. In other words, what actions on the part of the communist bloc would merit a full nuclear response? 'A concomitant problem would be how we could inform the enemy of the first decision so that he would not, through miscalculation, push us to the point that global war would result'.[43]

To Churchill, the answer was obvious: educative summitry. But Ike was still not ready. On the vexed question of command and control, NATO subsequently agreed that war-planning should henceforward be predicated on the wide use of nuclear weapons, that the organization's forces should be equipped accordingly, and that SACEUR should, in a situation likely to involve nuclear weapons, seek political guidance 'when appropriate'. This, though, was a fudge insofar the supreme commander himself was to decide on the question of appropriateness and was free to (and very likely would) bypass governmental machinery in time of crisis. For the moment, though, it left politicians, including Churchill, with the comforting feeling they were in control of the Bomb, but in the event of war it was obvious that NATO's central command, and by extension the United States, would quickly assert itself.[44]

*

At the start of February 1955, the government's White Paper, and within it the rationalization for the H-bomb, was complete. It did not pull many punches. A thermonuclear assault on the British Isles 'would cause devastation, both human and material, on an unprecedented scale', while for those who managed to escape the blast, heat and fall-out there would be 'a struggle for survival of the grimmest kind'. However, in homage to the Prime Minister's convictions, the paper also posited the H-bomb as the great deterrent, a weapon, therefore, 'not of despair but of hope'.[45] With Commonwealth leaders assembled in London for one of their periodic conferences, Churchill took it upon himself to inform them of the paper's import ahead of publication.[46] The Canadian Lester Pearson has left us a richly descriptive account of how the Prime Minister went about his business.

> He really let himself go on the H-Bomb – the shattering implications of which, on our society, he has fully grasped. His sweeping imagination and range of mind has sensed that this discovery has made all the old concepts of strategy and defence as out of date as the spear or the Macedonian phalanx. He is horrified and comforted at the same time by the immensity of the bomb, and by its value as a deterrent against Russia. He finds solace in the fact that the Moscow men are cold-blooded realists who know what power means and don't wish to be destroyed. So he thinks the bomb may mean the destruction of war, not of humanity.

Drawing on his recent Cabinet memorandum, Churchill ended by underlining the 'ironic fact' that 'we had reached a stage where safety might well be the child of terror and life the twin of annihilation'.[47]

The Prime Minister also spoke to Commonwealth leaders of his dim but still flickering hopes for a summit, but just a few days later, on 8 February, came the news that Malenkov, the man he had built up in his mind as a moderate, a communist with whom he could do business, had been removed from power and his authority transferred to a Bulganin-Khrushchev diarchy. When Molotov, who retained his position as Foreign Minister, immediately launched a personal attack on the British Prime Minister as scathing as anything heard from the Kremlin since Stalin's death, it seemed as though the new Kremlin set-up was going to be more anti-Western, and therefore more opposed to diplomatic engagement, than the Malenkov regime.[48] As it turned out, this was by no means the case, but at the time appearances equalled reality for Churchill whose decision – taken a fortnight later – to set a firm date for his hand-over to Eden owed much to the upheaval in Moscow.[49] At the end of February it was confirmed that the Queen would do Churchill the signal honour of attending a farewell dinner at Downing Street on 4 April. His resignation would follow the next day. Royalist that he was, Churchill knew that the diaries of monarchs were not things to be trifled with. There could be no more backsliding.[50]

Having taken his decision, the Defence Debate, scheduled for the start of March, suddenly acquired added importance as his final major parliamentary outing as Prime Minister. 'I want it to be one of my best speeches', he told Moran, to prove that he was 'still fit to govern' and was retiring not because he could no longer carry the burden but 'to give a younger man his chance'.[51] By rights, given the subject of the debate, the opening statement ought to have been made by the Minister of Defence, but Churchill pulled rank. He was 'very apologetic', Macmillan wrote. 'He felt he must do so. It might be his last big speech; and since he had taken the burden of responsibility on himself about the Hydrogen bomb, he should open.'[52]

After revisiting his writings on nuclear issues in the 1920s and 1930s, Churchill was minded to make his concept of an atomic orange more apposite for his Westminster audience. Hence, in one early draft of his speech, he described how the dispatch box in the Chamber of the Commons could contain enough plutonium to destroy much of London. Macmillan was uneasy. The allusion, he felt, was too simplistic as well as factually incorrect. Moreover, by arguing, in effect, that nuclear disarmament was impossible because no inspection regime would ever be able to locate such easily concealable explosive material, Churchill's view was out of step with public opinion. 'What worries me is that it will be said you have taken away the last hope of the world', Macmillan wrote to him. 'You have denigrated disarmament. Please think about this. It might really have most serious effects both at home and abroad – particularly at home.' The previous autumn, an *Economist* editorial observed that 'Disarmament, in our world, means virtually the same thing as peace' and that to 'decry progress towards disarmament is ... to brand oneself a war-monger'. This was Macmillan's concern. With a General Election drawing closer, the Conservatives, he hinted heavily to Churchill, could really do without a re-run of the 1951 "whose finger on the trigger?" campaign. The Prime Minister took the point and softened his phraseology.[53]

The debate itself, a two-day affair, opened on 1 March 1955. That morning, Moran called at Number 10. He found the Prime Minister's mind 'full of foreboding, his mood dark and sombre'. The burden of what he proposed to say was the cause. 'You are unhappy about the hydrogen bomb?', Moran asked. 'Terrible, terrible', Churchill answered. 'Nothing so menacing to our civilisation since the Mongols.'[54] The Strath committee's work was almost complete – the final report would be ready by mid-month – but Churchill had asked to be 'informed of the details of every step' and he was well aware of its shocking headline findings.[55] An attack by ten H-bombs on the UK's major cities could unleash an explosive force equivalent to 100 million tons of TNT, forty-five times as great as the total tonnage of bombs dropped by Allied bombers in the whole of the European theatre during the last war. Some 12 million people would die instantly, with a further 4 million grievously injured. In total, this accounted for one-third of the population. The cities would be left smouldering toxic ruins, and the survivors, such as there were, would be prey to fall-out that would further poison air, soil and food and add countless more to the death-toll. Agriculture, industry and the economy would be obliterated; fire-fighting, medical, transport, water and food supply services would cease to function along with the machinery of government and civil society itself.[56] None of this information found its way into the White Paper, or into Churchill's speech other than in allusive or very sanitized form, but the Strath committee's findings still added to the 'nagging pain' in the Prime Minister's head, 'robbing him of all peace of mind' in the lead-up to the debate.[57]

By the time Churchill entered the Chamber it was already full to the rafters with those unable to find a seat forced to stand in the side aisles or sit on the floor. The House expected a Churchill special. At 3.45 pm he rose from his seat and began to speak. For the next forty-five minutes he held MPs rapt: there was not a single interruption. The purpose of his speech was to explain the government's decision to build the hydrogen bomb but he took advantage of the occasion to offer a series of 'observations of a general character on which I have pondered long', all of them connected to the 'obliterating weapons of the nuclear age'. He began with a warning. 'There is no absolute defence against the hydrogen bomb, nor is any method in sight by which any nation ... can be completely guaranteed against the devastating injury which even a score of them might inflict on wide regions.' What, then, should be done?

> Which way shall we turn to save our lives and the future of the world? It does not matter too much to old people; they are going soon anyway; but I find it poignant to look at youth in all its activity and ardour and, most of all, to watch little children playing their merry games, and wonder what would lie before them if God wearied of mankind.

The ideal remained world disarmament, but 'sentiment', he cautioned, 'must not cloud our vision'. Aside from the practical fact that nuclear disarmament required a system of inspection which, to judge from previous efforts to give effect to international control, would certainly be rejected by the Soviet authorities, there was peril in banishing nuclear weapons without also outlawing conventional arms in which, presently, the USSR enjoyed 'immense superiority'. Universal disarmament was 'in all our hearts', Churchill conceded, but until it came to pass there was 'only one sane policy for the free world in the next few years' and that was 'defence through deterrents'.

This in fact had been NATO's policy for some time but in order that Britain could make a decisive contribution to the Western deterrent, Churchill believed that 'we must ourselves possess the most up-to-date nuclear weapons, and the means of delivering them'. Here the hydrogen bomb stood supreme. In addition to the weapon's insensate destructiveness, the spectre of fall-out, the stuff of so many nightmares, added grim value to the deterrent and, in the process, gave rise to 'a curious paradox':

> Let me put it simply. After a certain point has been passed it may be said: 'The worse things get, the better'. The broad effect of the latest developments is to spread ... to a vast extent the area of mortal danger. This should certainly increase the deterrent upon Soviet Russia by putting her enormous spaces and scattered populations on an equality or near-equality with our small densely populated island and with Western Europe. I cannot regard this development as adding to our dangers ... On the contrary, to this form of attack continents are vulnerable as well as islands ... This is why I have hoped for a long time for a top level conference where these matters could be put plainly and bluntly ... Then it may well be that we shall by a process of sublime irony have reached a stage in this

story where safety will be the sturdy child of terror, and survival the twin brother of annihilation.

This arresting phrase, already trialled in his Tube Alloys paper in December and in his more recent briefing of Commonwealth Prime Ministers, was here perfected. But he was not finished yet. The threat of H-bomb attack on the British Isles, he reassured MPs, still lay some three-to-four years in the future. In the present, only the United States was capable of delivering a full-scale nuclear attack, an 'important fact' that was 'not entirely without comfort' insofar as the Kremlin ought to know that a surprise Soviet assault on the West would be met with immediate and devastating retaliation. But in due course the USSR would itself possess not just a sufficiency of H-bombs but the ability to deliver them to the United States as well as Western Europe. Was the advent of mutual assured destruction, the reaching of what Churchill called 'saturation' point, something to be feared? Not really. 'Major war of the future will differ ... from anything we have known in this one significant respect: that each side, at the outset, will suffer what it dreads most, the loss of everything that it has ever known of.' World-wide comprehensive disarmament remained the Holy Grail of the nuclear age but if it continued to be beyond reach, then perversely, the growth in the scale and scope of *both* the Western and Soviet nuclear deterrents offered a compensation. 'In the past an aggressor has been tempted by the hope of snatching an early advantage', Churchill pointed out. 'In future, he may be deterred by the knowledge that the other side has the certain power to inflict swift, inescapable, and crushing retaliation.'

In closing, Churchill made two final points. First, Western deterrence could not rest on nuclear weapons alone. 'We must, together with our NATO allies, maintain the defensive shield in Western Europe', for without effective forces on the ground 'there would be nothing to prevent piecemeal advance and encroachment by the Communists in this time of so-called peace'. Second, Britain must possess its own independent nuclear deterrent rather than rely on the protection of the United States. At this, the Prof, watching from the gallery, must have allowed himself a thin smile and a reflection that, at last, his old friend understood what he meant about national sovereignty and nuclear autonomy being practically synonymous. Also implicit in Churchill's argument were lessons learned at Bermuda in 1953 and during the Indo-China crisis of 1954. 'Personally', he said of the Americans, 'I cannot feel that we should have much influence over their policy or actions, wise or unwise, while we are largely dependent, as we are today, upon their protection. We, too, must possess substantial deterrent power of our own.' Then came the peroration. 'All deterrents will improve and gain authority during the next ten years. By that time, the deterrent may well reach its acme and reap its final reward. The day may dawn when fair play, love for one's fellow-men, respect for justice and freedom, will enable tormented generations to march forth serene and triumphant from the hideous epoch in which we have to dwell. Meanwhile, never flinch, never weary, never despair.'[58]

The product of years of nuclear learning, Churchill's speech is today regarded as amongst the finest of his long career.[59] At the time, too, there was an outpouring of praise.

Apart from the *Daily Mirror* and the communist *Daily Worker*, the press was everything Churchill could have wished: the headline in the *Daily Express* picked up on his 'sturdy child' metaphor while the *News Chronicle* preferred 'Never Despair' and the *Daily Sketch* chose 'Churchill names it H for Hope'.[60] There was also appreciation from his political opponents that, unlike April 1954, he had approached the issue in a non-partisan manner; indeed on this occasion he had lauded Attlee for his great 'initiative' in launching the Hurricane programme.[61] Against this, while accepting the H-bomb as a necessary deterrent evil, the Labour front bench took issue with the comparatively low priority given to civil defence in the White Paper and to Churchill's over-emphasis on nuclear deterrence at the expense of detailed discussion of how the defence programme would impact on the three services.[62] A Labour motion of censure on both grounds was voted on, and defeated, on the second day of the debate, the division's arithmetic affording Churchill much satisfaction. 'Considering we only have a majority of sixteen', he wrote to Eisenhower, 'the fact that the Opposition ... censure was rejected by 107 votes was a remarkable event and entitles me to say that our policy of "Defence through Deterrents" commands the support of the nation'.[63]

This was very largely correct, as the *Times* pointed out afterwards.[64] However, Emmanuel Shinwell, the shadow Defence Secretary, had been disappointed that there was no 'prospect of peace' written into Churchill's prescription. Where was the great play for a summit? Where, indeed, was peaceful co-existence?[65] When left-wing Labour MP Aneurin Bevan repeated these criticisms on 2 March – inserting the added barb that a summit would have occurred by now if the government had not been in thrall to a US veto – the Prime Minister was stung into delivering a sustained riposte in which he revealed for the first time in public the 'sudden illness which paralysed me completely' in 1953 and how it was this, not American dictation, which had retarded summitry progress. Since that time he had tried his 'utmost' to bring about a conference, on a bilateral or multilateral plane, and he still hoped that a summit would happen as soon as WEU ratification was complete and West Germany was locked into NATO.[66] But in any case, Shinwell was wrong: peaceful co-existence, implicit in Churchill's H-bomb speech and asserted more explicitly the following week in a debate on disarmament, remained central to the Prime Minister's Cold War outlook.[67]

On the evening of 4 April, Churchill was the host of a grand dinner party to mark his retirement the next day. Alongside the pre-booked guests of honour, the young Queen Elizabeth and the Duke of Edinburgh, were 'an inspired jumble' of family, friends, political colleagues and social grandees.[68] '10 Downing Street can seldom if ever have looked so gay', Colville recorded, 'or its floorboards ... have groaned under such a weight of jewels and decorations'. Also there was Anthony Eden who, after more than a decade as Churchill's acknowledged successor, was poised to fulfil his dearest political ambition. The evening was a 'splendid occasion', Colville wrote, although not without its incidents, one of which involved Eden and his wife Clarissa (Churchill's niece) who tried to jump the queue advancing to shake hands with the Queen. In the ensuing kerfuffle the Duchess of Westminster put her foot through Clarissa's train. 'That's torn it, in more than one

Figure 16.1 Churchill leaves for the Palace, 5 April 1955. Topical Press Agency, Hulton Archive/ Getty Images.

sense', quipped the Duke of Edinburgh. Around midnight, after the Queen and the other guests had left, Churchill went upstairs to his bedroom, and there, still wearing his Garter, Order of Merit and knee-breeches, he sat down on his bed. Colville watched him closely. 'For several minutes he did not speak and I, imagining that he was sadly contemplating that this was his last night at Downing Street, was silent. Then suddenly he stared at me and said with vehemence: "I don't believe Anthony can do it".[69] At noon the following day, Churchill presided at his final Cabinet and was then driven to Buckingham Palace where, dressed in the top hat and frock coat he always wore for audiences, he tendered his resignation to the Queen.

In light of Eden's fate – personal humiliation and political oblivion as a result of the 1956 Suez crisis – Churchill's assessment of his successor seems startlingly prophetic. Yet in his truncated premiership Eden achieved one thing that had been beyond Churchill: he attended a heads of government summit. 'How much more attractive a top-level meeting seems when one has reached the top', Churchill sniped in reference to Eden's earlier preference for engagement at the Foreign Minister level.[70] His bitterness and regret are understandable but in fairness to Eden it was only in May 1955 – some six weeks after Churchill's resignation – that the WEU had been fully established and West Germany's admission to NATO confirmed, both of which the Americans had made pre-conditions for a summit.[71] Moreover, it is evident from the release of Soviet-era documents that the Kremlin all along had been extremely suspicious of the motives of Churchill, the legendary anti-communist, in promoting détente, and that Soviet leaders were only really interested in summitry feelers from the Americans which, until early 1955, were not greatly in evidence.[72]

'I feel sure that the Western nations could not, with self-respect, have earlier consented to a Four-Power Summit meeting', Eisenhower wrote to Churchill on 15 July on the eve of the conference at Geneva. 'Yet I cannot escape a feeling of sadness that the delay brought about by the persistently hostile Soviet attitude toward NATO has operated to prevent your personal attendance at the meeting . . . But your long quest for peace daily inspires much that we do.'[73] Churchill appreciated the message. 'I have never indulged in extravagant hopes of a vast, dramatic transformation of human affairs', he replied, 'but my belief is that, so long as we do not relax our unity or our vigilance, the Soviets and the Russian people will be increasingly convinced that it is in their interests to live peaceably with us.'[74] Alas, the only evidence of nascent détente at Geneva was the preference of the Soviet leaders for 'driving around in open cars instead of in the usual dark-windowed, heavy Soviet saloons'.[75] Mostly the summit failed to resolve any of the outstanding Cold War issues, including curbing the nuclear arms race, although the fact that diplomatic interchange of any kind had taken place gave some hope for the future.[76]

In retrospect, the Soviets were never going to consider serious nuclear limitations until they had caught up with the Americans in the arms race, qualitatively if not quantitatively, and could negotiate as equals. To Churchill, this prospect, the coming of strategic parity, was not a reason for concern. On the contrary, once it was accepted as an 'undoubted fact' that a 'full scale nuclear war means not the mastery of one side or the other but the extinction of the human species', he told Eisenhower at the time of the Geneva summit, 'it may well be that a new set of deterrents will dominate the soul of man'.[77] Over the next two years, in a world in which universal disarmament remained a pipe-dream, Churchill seemed at times to be willing the onset of mutual assured destruction because with it would come a countervailing assurance, or semi-assurance of peace. In April 1956, he wrote to Eisenhower to suggest that the creation of a balance of terror 'would certainly be the end of nuclear war, except, of course, for accidents, which all nations have an equal interest in preventing'.[78] Eisenhower demurred. It was 'unsafe to predict that, if the West and the East should ever become locked up in a life and death struggle, both sides would still have sense enough not to use this horrible instrument'. To illustrate his point the President fell back on recent history. 'You will remember that in 1945 there was no possible excuse, once we had reached the Rhine in late '44, for Hitler to continue the war, yet his insane determination to rule or ruin brought additional and completely unnecessary destruction to his country, brought about its division between East and West and his own ignominious death.'[79]

Churchill was unconvinced by Eisenhower's argument and in retirement he continued to pin his hope on an eventual nuclear balance between the Cold War blocs and, by extension, to fret about the dangers inherent in an American preponderance of nuclear destructiveness. He also read a great deal. One novel, Nevil Shute's *On the Beach* (1957), with its chilling evocation of nuclear war and radioactive fall-out on such an apocalyptic scale that eventually all life on earth is extinguished, especially impressed him: he read it twice and declared it 'a remarkable work'.[80] Staying with Lord Beaverbrook in the South of France in September 1957, he spoke admiringly of Shute's work. James Lees-Milne, who was also a guest, recorded the dinner-table conversation in his diary. 'I think the earth will soon be destroyed', Churchill remarked. 'And if I were the Almighty I would not recreate it in case they destroyed him too the next time'. As for Shute's novel, it was so stunning he was minded to send a copy to Khrushchev. 'And Eisenhower?' he was asked. He thought not. Judging by what he knew of Ike's thinking, it would be 'a waste of money'.[81]

CONCLUSION: '. . . IF GOD WEARIED OF MANKIND'

Churchill the bomb-maker, Churchill the atomic diplomatist, Churchill the peacemaker. Three Churchills in one. But have we, in the nuclear realm, missed a fourth Churchill? 'The atom is amoral', Lewis Strauss once remarked. 'The only thing that makes it immoral is man.'[1] Leaving aside man, plural, what of our man, singular? Where did Churchill stand on the morality of the Bomb?

In attempting an answer to this question it is right to begin with Hiroshima and Nagasaki, the destruction of which marked the culmination of the first phase of the nuclear Churchill's career. The bombings remain immensely controversial, 'the worst atrocities ever committed in the history of warfare' in the view, not of sensationalist bloggers on the internet, but two respected historians, Campbell Craig and Sergey Radchenko.[2] Churchill's public position on Hiroshima and Nagasaki was uncomplicated, consistent and entirely at odds with the Craig-Radchenko thesis. Beginning with the statement he issued on the night of Hiroshima and continuing into his six-volume *The Second World War*, he maintained that in war, weapons get used; that the A-bomb was a weapon; that the Allies were at war with Japan; and that *ipso facto* the A-bomb was a legitimate military option.[3] Moreover, seemingly immune from moral doubts himself, he deprecated those whose consciences were less strongly fortified.

Take Cuthbert Thicknesse, Dean of St. Albans. For most people in Britain in August 1945, such moral unease as the Bomb aroused was probably cancelled out by the sense of relief that the war had ended so quickly. Thicknesse, however, chose publicly to denounce the 'indiscriminate massacre' of civilians at Hiroshima and Nagasaki and banned a service of thanksgiving in the city's Abbey because victory over Japan had been achieved by 'devilish' means.[4] Known for a 'force of character of volcanic power' and with a pulpit at his disposal, Thicknesse stood at the clangourous end of the spectrum of moral disquiet.[5] At the other end was Gladys Langford, a middle-aged school teacher from London whose diary quietly records the moral ambiguities of the moment. It was noticeable, she wrote, how many people seemed 'very proud of the Atomic bomb *we've* dropped on Japan and yet those same people cursed the Germans for *their* cruelty when they bombed us'.[6] Similarly, twenty-four-year-old Joan Wyndham, stationed with the Women's Auxiliary Air Force in Nottinghamshire, wrote of her perplexity on hearing that somewhere called Hiroshima, and then Nagasaki, 'had been wiped out'. Many of her friends felt the same way. There were no 'wild parties, hardly any drunken celebrations' such as accompanied VE Day. The end of the war had been 'too unheroic'.[7]

In Parliament on 16 August, Churchill spoke directly to the Thicknesses of the world, the voluble moral questioners, but also indirectly to the Langfords and the Wyndhams. 'There are voices which assert that the bomb should never have been used at all', he told MPs. 'I cannot associate myself with such ideas.' He went on:

Six years of total war have convinced most people that had the Germans or Japanese discovered this new weapon, they would have used it upon us to our complete destruction with the utmost alacrity. I am surprised that very worthy people, but people who in most cases had no intention of proceeding to the Japanese front themselves, should adopt the position that rather than throw this bomb, we should have sacrificed a million American and a quarter of a million British lives in the desperate battles and massacres of an invasion of Japan. Future generations will judge these dire decisions, and I believe that if they find themselves dwelling in a happier world from which war has been banished, and where freedom reigns, they will not condemn those who struggled for their benefit amid the horrors and miseries of this gruesome and ferocious epoch.[8]

This statement set the tone for much of his subsequent public comment on Hiroshima and Nagasaki. In war, Churchill suggested, moral qualms were a luxury to be enjoyed by other people, not by those tasked, as he had been, with the defence of Britain, the Empire and the Commonwealth.

Churchill touched on the morality of the A-bomb decision again in *The Gathering Storm*, the first volume of his history of the war, published in 1948. There was, he maintained, an inter-connection between the conventional bombing of Germany, in which Allied aircraft dropped 1.3 million tons of explosives over a five-year period, and the unconventional bombing of Japan. This 'hideous process of bombarding open cities from the air, once started by the Germans, was repaid twenty-fold by the ever-mounting power of the Allies, and found its culmination in the use of the atomic bombs which obliterated Hiroshima and Nagasaki'. He seemed to be suggesting, defensively, that any ethical line which existed had been crossed long before Little Boy and Fat Man came into the world, but in a more assertive sense he was espousing an age-old morality: the Germans, by crossing the line first, deservedly reaped what they had sown.[9]

Triumph and Tragedy, the sixth and final volume of Churchill's history dealing, *inter alia*, with Trinity, Potsdam and the Bomb, was published in the USA in autumn 1953 and in the UK the following spring. By then, the British public, like people in many other countries, had become nuclear-sentient: not only was the scale of the death and destruction at Hiroshima and Nagasaki more fully comprehended, but the power of the latest weapons tested by the USSR and the UK as well the USA were regularly calculated in the press and scientific journals in multiples of the TNT-equivalent of the bombs used on Japan.[10] The defiling presence in the world of nuclear arms continued to offend the moral sensibilities of many people, not least church leaders, but for the British public at large, weapons of mass destruction were not so much moral, immoral or amoral as simply there, the horror in waiting should the Cold War flare into hot war. International control, and better still universal disarmament, would obviously reduce the danger of catastrophe, but failing this utopian outcome few people, in or out of government, believed that ethical or moral constraints would limit a third world war to conventional arms alone.[11] This may be why the H-bomb, together with its grim value-added factor, radioactive fall-out, when brought fully to world attention by the misfortune of a

Japanese trawler in March 1954, prompted such upset: if it should come to war, there was no reason to suppose that the superpowers would be any more restrained in using H-bombs than A-bombs even though the former were manifestly engines of genocide.

In *Triumph and Tragedy*, Churchill offered his readers neither remorse about what happened to Japan in 1945 nor hope that a Hiroshima or a Nagasaki would never occur again. 'British consent in principle to the use of the weapon had been given on July 4 [1945]', he wrote. 'The final decision now lay with President Truman, who had the weapon; but I never doubted what it would be, nor have I ever doubted since that he was right. The historic fact remains, and must be judged in the after-time, that the decision whether or not to use the atomic bomb to compel the surrender of Japan was never even an issue.'[12] At first sight, Churchill's handling of the Bomb in this volume appears to operate against the subtextual methodology he had adopted in the previous five. As David Reynolds has demonstrated, Churchill 'made history as statesman and as historian', the words he used to shape the past being carefully chosen to make a contemporary impact or to serve present-day political needs. *The Gathering Storm*, for example, written as the Cold War began to grip and published during the Berlin blockade, spent a good deal of time on the 1930s with Churchill stressing the lessons of that dismal decade, above all the need for democratic powers to unite politically, militarily and in time whenever freedom was threatened by totalitarian states; the relevance of this lesson for 1948 was plain.[13]

As it happens, there is atomic contemporizing in *Triumph and Tragedy* but it is extremely subtle. Churchill omitted any reference to the Quebec and Hyde Park agreements, thus passing up the opportunity to arraign the United States for failing to honour his wartime agreements with Roosevelt. This, though, was a politic move insofar as criticism was certain to produce a negative reaction from the Atomic Energy Commission and the US Congress and thereby jeopardize any chance that a sympathetic Eisenhower, elected president a year before *Triumph and Tragedy* appeared, would be able to effect a restoration of close US–UK atomic ties. However, only those who knew about Quebec and Hyde Park in the first place – and they were few – would have appreciated Churchill's self-denying ordinance. Similarly, if we consider the international context in which Churchill was writing, an additional Cold War message can be deciphered. Published in 1953–1954, his main intellectual investment in the book came earlier, in 1950–1951, when the nuclear Churchill was in transition: the atomic diplomatist was on the wane, the peacemaker yet to wax. As such, he continued to argue, publicly as well as privately, that the effectiveness of the American nuclear deterrent depended on inculcating in the minds of Soviet leaders the USA's absolute determination to unloose its arsenal if provoked. His account of the bombing of Japan in 1945 would not serve this Cold War need if he admitted to the slightest moral queasiness or suggested that nuclear weapons were anything other than a legitimate means of defence or, if it came to it, attack. Needless to say, had he still been writing or refining at the time of Bermuda, the New Look, Castle-Bravo and the *Lucky Dragon* in 1953–1954, his contemporizing of the past would probably have taken a very different form. As it was, *Triumph and Tragedy* set the seal on Churchill's version of Hiroshima and Nagasaki and of himself as a warrior-statesman, an atomic decision-maker for whom the Bomb had been a military necessity to hasten Japan's defeat and limit Allied casualties; the lives of a million American and half-a-million British and Commonwealth servicemen had been saved, he told Parliament in August 1945, a figure which, though pure guesswork, was faithfully reproduced eight years later in his history of the event.[14]

This was the public Churchill, however, the image of himself he wished the world to see. The private Churchill seems to have been rather more morally-conflicted, or at least not quite as comfortable with what befell Hiroshima and Nagasaki as his outward-facing persona suggested. This is not to say that he had any doubts about the military necessity of using the Bomb while the war with Japan was ongoing – his memoirs are sound on that score – only that he experienced, quite quickly after the event, a degree of unease about his part in the bombing. The clues to his feelings on this subject are to be found, somewhat unexpectedly, in his relationship with God.

Brought up in the Anglican communion and 'saturated' in the Christian tradition, by his early twenties Churchill was evincing views which, if not atheistic were certainly in conflict with the doctrinal bases of Christianity.[15] As a young subaltern in India he had sought to compensate for his lack of university-level education by binge-reading of the great works of history, science and philosophy, among them Plato's *Republic*, Gibbon's *Rise and Fall of the Roman Empire*, Darwin's *Origins of the Species*, Winwood Reade's *Martyrdom of Man* and Lecky's *Rise and Influence of Rationalism*. As a consequence of this programme of self-improvement, the religious and the rational came to vie for primacy in his evolving intellectual outlook: in the end, the rational won. '[I]f the human race ever reaches a stage of development . . . when religion will cease to assist and comfort mankind . . . Christianity will be put aside as a crutch which is no longer needed, and man will stand erect on the firm legs of reason', he wrote to his mother in January 1897. This would be no bad thing for the 'cold bright light of science & reason will shine through the cathedral windows . . . The great laws of Nature will be understood – our destiny and our past will be clear. We shall then be able to dispense with the religious toys that have agreeably fostered the development of mankind.'[16] The following year, contemplating the possibility of death at Omdurman, he wrote again to his mother, this time advising that if he perished in battle, she should avail herself of 'the consolations of philosophy' and 'reflect on the utter insignificance of all human beings'. He added, apparently conclusively, that 'I do not accept the Christian or any other form of religious belief'.[17]

As it turned out, throughout the remainder of his long life Churchill was not without religion *per se*, but as Geoffrey Fisher, Archbishop of Canterbury from 1945 to 1961, later observed, his was 'a religion of the Englishman': he had 'a real belief in Providence, but it was God as the God with a special care for the values of the British people'.[18] If Churchill appeared more devout than he was, this was due to his visible presence at St Paul's or Westminster Abbey on state occasions, to regular attendance at church weddings, christenings and funerals, and to a prodigious memory which allowed for perfect quoting from dozens of Anglican hymns or the recitation of long passages of the King James

Bible. During the Second World War, Churchill's speeches often referenced the Almighty in the sense of beseeching God's deliverance of country, Commonwealth and Christian civilization from Axis evil, but his piety was strategic, an oratorical device rather than an expression of any deeply-held religiosity.[19]

At the very end of his career in front-line politics, in his speech on the H-bomb in the House of Commons on 1 March 1955, we have seen how Churchill, now a very old man, spoke movingly of watching 'little children playing their merry games, and wonder[ing] what would lie before them if God wearied of mankind'.[20] Accepting that Churchill was 'a non-believer, at least in any conventional theological sense', Roy Jenkins later found it puzzling that he 'should have thought of the most divinely apocalyptic phrase for depicting the terror' that the H-bomb threatened to visit upon the earth.[21] In fact it was not uncommon for Churchill to juxtapose God and the Bomb in his nuclear-themed reflections. Setting to one side his private reaction at Potsdam to the Groves report ('the Second Coming in Wrath'), the public referencing began early with his statement on the night of Hiroshima (it had been by 'God's mercy' that the Anglo-Americans had beaten the Germans to the Bomb) and proceeded to take in Fulton in 1946 (when he thanked God that the secret of the Bomb was 'at present largely retained in American hands') and the launch of his Cold War summitry in 1950 (when he again thanked God, this time for the US superiority in atomic arms).[22] The announcement of the Soviet H-bomb in 1953, coinciding with the heightening of his sense of the UK's vulnerability to nuclear assault, led him publicly to avow 'faith' in 'God's mercy' that mankind would be granted the wisdom to step back from the thermonuclear abyss, and then the following year, by which time the hydrogen bomb had established itself at the epicentre of his concerns, he once more sought the 'mercy of God' but this time 'to win salvation for us'.[23]

It may of course be argued that Churchill's oratorical religiosity during the Cold War served much the same purpose as its wartime equivalent, namely to meet the spiritual and psychological needs of a still largely Christian British public by holding out the possibility of divine intercession to save the country, and the world, from a fiery fate. 'Whether you believe or disbelieve', he once remarked, 'it is a wretched thing to take away Man's hope.'[24] However, when we delve into the private Churchill we find not just a rich vein of Bomb-induced religious contemplation but evidence that as the Cold War deepened, and with it the danger of nuclear Armageddon, his earlier agnosticism, and even at times his atheistic impulses, were challenged. Churchill claimed not to believe in an after-life. 'I expect annihilation at death', he wrote in 1898. 'I am a materialist – to the tips of my fingers.'[25] More than half a century later, recovering from a stroke, he still maintained that there was nothing to come but 'black velvet', eternal sleep.[26] And yet, for all this, he spent a surprising amount of time worrying about how his responsibility for the atomic bombing of Japan would be judged if he was wrong and there was a God waiting for him after all.

In May 1946, Mackenzie King met Churchill in London and later recorded their conversation in his diary. What began as two elderly statesmen pondering philosophically but humorously 'the present life and the life hereafter' took a more serious turn when

Churchill suddenly launched into a disquisition on the atomic bombing. King's account continues:

> The way Churchill put it ... was [that] he expected that he would have to account to God as he had to his own conscience for the decision made which involved killing women and children and in such numbers. That God would ask him why he had done this and he would reply he had seen the terrors of war. He knew something of what the Japanese method of war-fare was like. That there were these thousands of lives – fine American soldiers – all of which would likely be destroyed or tortured. War might go on for another year or so with cities destroyed and numbers so much greater than could possibly be foreseen and with a breaking down of civilisation bit by bit. He had had to decide what in the end would be best for mankind and felt that he, regardless of what the consequences might be, had done what was right. He said something to the equivalent of welcoming a chance to be judged in the light of omnipotent knowledge.[27]

What is notable about this sequence of statements, apart from Churchill's erroneously reductionist view that the choice in 1945 was a binary one, invasion or the Bomb, is his absolute certainty that he had played a full and equal part alongside Truman in determining the fate of Hiroshima and Nagasaki. The truth, as we know, is that Churchill's sanctioning of the bombing was given in the most casual and even careless manner. He might have *approved* the use of the Bomb in a moment of foolscap-initialling, but the *decision* itself was an all-American one. Nevertheless, in his own mind, he was just as responsible as Truman and, by extension, equally answerable to God.

This expectation of divine judgement persisted. In July 1946, Churchill lunched with Lord Mountbatten. According to Alan Campbell-Johnson, Mountbatten's aide who was present and recorded the table-talk, Churchill argued that Japan's military power had been akin to 'the lighting of fire on ice': it was superficial and never likely to burn for long. The Japanese 'were nothing like as strong as we thought them to be and ... had been crippled by American power long before the Atom Bomb was dropped'. This was not, as Churchill saw it, a reason against using the Bomb; on the contrary, it spoke to Little Boy and Fat Man as the critical blows that tipped the Japanese into surrender. At the same time, however, he admitted when it came to his war record, the 'decision to release the Atom Bomb was perhaps the only thing which history would have serious questions to ask about ... I may even be asked by my Maker why I used it but I shall defend myself vigorously and shall say – Why did you release this knowledge to us when mankind was raging in furious battles?' At this, Sir John Anderson, another luncheon guest, interjected with characteristic drollness to remind Churchill that '[y]ou cannot accuse your judges'.[28]

While confident that he could defend himself, the regularity with which Churchill spoke of being judged by God points to a mind, if not a conscience, not quite as comfortable with the A-bomb decision as his public statements suggested. Hiroshima and Nagasaki were still in his thoughts seven years later – in January 1953 – when he hosted a dinner at the British Embassy in Washington in honour of President Truman.

Margaret Truman, the President's daughter, has left a detailed account of a lively evening of reminiscing, with the Prime Minister in sparkling form. At one point, however, without conversational prompt or warning, Churchill suddenly turned to Truman and said: 'Mr. President, I hope you have your answer ready for that hour when you and I stand before Saint Peter and he says, "I understand you two are responsible for putting off those atomic bombs. What have you got to say for yourselves?"'. Before Truman could reply, Robert Lovett, the US Defense Secretary, stepped in. 'Are you sure, Prime Minister, that you are going to be in the same place as the President for that interrogation?' Churchill sipped his champagne and then intoned: 'my vast respect for the creator of this universe and countless others gives me assurance that He would not condemn a man without a hearing . . . in accordance with the principles of the English common law'. This was the cue for a role-play game in which the other guests – among them the Chairman of the Joint Chiefs of Staff, General Omar Bradley, and Secretary of State Dean Acheson – formed a jury composed of some of the great figures of history (Alexander the Great, Julius Caesar and Socrates to name but a few). 'Dad was appointed judge', Margaret Truman wrote. 'The case was tried and the Prime Minister acquitted.'[29]

It was a darkly humorous moment redolent of Michael Powell and Emeric Pressberger's 1946 cinematic classic, *A Matter of Life and Death*, but leaving aside the questionable taste of a skit in which Truman, a co-defendant in the real 'case' of the A-bomb, acted as Judge in acquitting Churchill and therefore himself of any wrong-doing, two things about the evening are noteworthy: first, Churchill's still adamant insistence that he and Truman were equals in the A-bomb decision; and second, his concomitant fretfulness that a reckoning of some kind awaited him. This last concern was evident again the following year, although in a different form and context. In May 1954, with international tension over Indo-China peaking and with H-bomb fever still raging, Churchill had what can only be described as a 'God moment' when he asked Billy Graham to look in on him at Number 10. Fresh from his spectacularly successful Greater London Crusade, attendances at which had been boosted by public anxiety about the 'Hell bomb', the American evangelist was only supposed to have ten minutes with the Prime Minister but got forty-five – and this despite Churchill's next visitor, the Duke of Windsor, the former King Edward VIII, impatiently kicking his heels in an ante-room. Frightened and depressed by the H-bomb, Churchill described himself to Graham as 'an old man . . . without any hope for the world . . . unless it is the hope you are talking about, young man . . . We must have a return to God'. Afterwards, a giddy Graham felt as if he had met 'Mr History', while Churchill, in a letter to Clementine, confirmed that Graham had made 'a very good impression'.[30] In some accounts, it is suggested that the two men prayed together, a rather fanciful notion in view of Churchill's previous track-record of impiety.[31] Then again, if anything could bring him to his knees, it was the H-bomb.

From all this it seems clear that Churchill expected to be judged in some form or other as a nuclear decision-maker. In which case, in closing, let us weigh him in the scales – not in any Biblical sense but objectively and, so far as possible, according to his own lights. 'Men in power must be judged not by what they feel, but by what they do', he wrote in

1933 in his life of his illustrious forebear, the first Duke of Marlborough.[32] So what did the nuclear Churchill *do*?

In August 1941, Britain became the first country in the world to possess a dedicated government-backed programme of research and development with the explicit objective of building an atomic bomb; in comparison, the Nazi project was halting, disjointed and lacking in serious or consistent government encouragement.[33] Tube Alloys was Churchill's doing. A life-long fascination with science and new military technologies came together in his approval of the MAUD committee's recommendations. Had he determined otherwise – that the investment of money, manpower and resources in so futuristic an enterprise was simply too great in view of the pressing military needs of the moment – it is hard to see how Tube Alloys could have been pursued other than on a small and mostly theoretical scale with obvious negative implications for the UK's emergence as a nuclear power after the war.

But Churchill did something else in August 1941: he took advice, specifically that of F. A. Lindemann, his friend, counsellor and nuclear mentor. Three months later, he found himself being probed in Parliament about the extent of Lindemann's influence – the Prof being an unelected and unaccountable advisor. That influence, as we have seen, was pervasive and penetrating and by no means limited to science, not that Churchill admitted this. 'Winston's almost blind loyalty to his friends is one of his most endearing qualities', wrote Chips Channon, a witness to the exchanges in the Commons.[34] Endearing but also problematic. For as Churchill was standing up for his friend at Westminster, he was also in the process of deflecting President Roosevelt's proposal for a jointly-conducted Anglo-American atomic weapons programme. The evidence strongly suggests that Lindemann's views on the politico-military necessity of an independent British project were determining. Implicitly trusting of his friend's judgement and uninterested in seeking alternative scientific opinions, Churchill effectively rejected FDR's offer of merger because the Prof did not approve.

With this, as the official historian of the Tube Alloys project, Margaret Gowing, along with many others have contended, the proverbial bus was missed: when, less than a year later, the British decided that a TA-1/S-1 merger was necessary after all, the Americans had leapt ahead in the race for the Bomb and were no longer interested in intimate collaboration. The chance for Britain to work with the United States as an equal in an atomic alliance had gone.[35] But what if the bus had been boarded? This question is seldom asked, even though Churchill – more so than Lindemann – has been reproved for his apparent lack of foresight. As with any counter-factual, there are no sure answers but we may still speculate. Due to the extreme secrecy surrounding the Bomb, there was no prospect of US–UK cooperation, if pursued with seriousness in late 1941, being formalized in a treaty requiring Congressional ratification. Rather, in line with the generalized nature of FDR's proposal, some kind of memorandum of understanding might have been drawn up providing for the pooling and sharing of knowledge on a basis of equality, a written version of the verbal Hyde Park understanding of June 1942. However, the mere existence of such a document would not have altered some very salient facts. One was the tremendous disparity between the two countries in terms of the money and resources subsequently invested in the Bomb. Another – a corollary – was the emergent view of senior Manhattan Project administrators in 1942–1943 that because the United States was responsible for 90 per cent of the supposedly joint effort, the end-product, when it materialized, would in practice be all-American not Anglo-American. Nor would the intimate and cohesive personal nature of the atomic alliance at the very highest (FDR–Churchill) level have been replicated lower down where interaction between Tube Alloys and S-1 administrators, though effective in some areas, was much more impersonal and often hindered by strong mutual mistrust. Above all, in the critical three months preceding the Bomb's realization, Roosevelt would still have died, Churchill would still have been voted out of office, and the atomic partnership they had come to personify would still have withered in the absence of institutionalized roots or a treaty legally obligating the Truman administration to extend wartime collaboration into the peace.

Our hypothetical 1941 understanding, therefore, being on the American side an Executive agreement, would not have compelled Truman to follow Roosevelt's policy any more than the 1943 and 1944 agreements had done. Nor, realistically, would an additional FDR–Churchill understanding have prevented a nationalistic and proprietorial US Congress legislating in 1946 to terminate meaningful cooperation with Britain – or any other country – in the further development of atomic energy for military purposes. In sum, Churchill may have missed the bus in 1941 (albeit on advisement), but even if he had hopped aboard there is no guarantee that it would have taken him to the destination he desired.

As we know, Churchill fought fiercely to protect the UK's atomic interests during the war. Later, in his opposition years, he came to regard the Quebec agreement, his 1943 reward for fighting so well, as the functional equivalent of a treaty. If, as he hoped, he became Prime Minister again, he wanted Quebec to be recognized by the Americans as the foundation-stone of a restored alliance. This, though, could and would never be. Leaving aside its non-treaty status – for one who was such an admirer of the United States, Churchill often displayed considerable ignorance about its governance and Constitutional processes – the Quebec agreement was not the lodestar he took it to be. Focusing only on the generalized commitment to cooperation embodied in its various articles, he failed to read the small-print insofar as the technical-industrial articles never provided for full and unfettered cooperation. Hence, at best, an additional Churchill–Roosevelt understanding, negotiated in 1941 when the British were ahead in theoretical and basic experimental research, might have given UK scientists an all-areas pass when the Manhattan Project got into its stride in 1942. If this pass allowed for access to information on the design, construction and operation of the plutonium-breeding piles and chemical separation plants at Hanford, it would have added substantially to the British body of knowledge ahead of what would still in all likelihood have been the shut-down of interchange when the McMahon Act came into force.

In his wartime bomb-maker phase, Churchill did something else: he positioned himself as the arch-enemy of international control. It is hard not to feel sympathy for

Niels Bohr – and for his secret Whitehall champion, the unjustly unsung Sir John Anderson – whose wartime efforts on behalf of postwar arms control were so blithely dismissed by Prime Minister and President alike. Still, it is important to try and see the issue from Churchill's standpoint rather than rush (as A. J. P. Taylor did) to lay upon him a measure of blame for the later Cold War nuclear arms race.[36] Did Churchill really regard the Bomb as nothing more than an extreme aggregation of existing explosives which, as he snapped at Bohr when they met in May 1944, 'involves no difference in the principles of war'?[37] This seems improbable when we remember how well-schooled he was in the basic principles of nuclear physics thanks to Lindemann's educative efforts since the late-1920s. More likely, Bohr fell victim to Churchill's pre-existing and pronounced mistrust of other-worldly scientists who tried to tell real-world politicians how to do their jobs: as he once quipped, scientists should be 'on tap and not on top'.[38] Even Lindemann, the notable exception to Churchill's animus towards politicized scientists, knew his place in the pecking-order. Furthermore, Churchill only agreed to meet Bohr under sufferance, having been ganged-up on by the Prof, Anderson, Dale and Smuts. Lastly, to the extent that he listened to Bohr at all, he concluded erroneously that the Dane wanted him to do the very thing that he absolutely did not want to do, namely, tell Stalin all about the Bomb. Already, therefore, in weighing what the nuclear Churchill did, we find ourselves equally drawn to what he did not do.

On this question of keeping Stalin in the dark, Churchill's motives may not be quite as straightforward as historians have often suggested. His atomic covetousness is usually ascribed to a combination of dyed-in-the-wool anti-communism and anxiety (peaking in 1944–1945) about Soviet intentions in the Balkans and Eastern Europe. Churchill's thinking, it is argued, was akin to containment aforethought – the holding of the Bomb as insurance lest the Grand Alliance crash and there developed a need for a powerful diplomatic instrument or military weapon to stem the spread of Soviet communism.[39] All of this is perfectly plausible in light of Churchill's anti-communist history, but when it comes to finding evidence to prove the claim, the wartime documentary record is threadbare – until, that is, we get to Potsdam. There, having read the Groves report, Churchill became, almost on the instant, an atomic diplomatist and remained so for some years thereafter. Before Potsdam, even in the weeks immediately preceding the conference when his concern for the fate of Poland and the other countries in the Red Army's zone of control had become acute, the Bomb, as a potential check on the USSR, is conspicuous by its absence from his recorded mindset. As late as June 1945, when he was thinking militarily Unthinkable thoughts, planning a diplomatic showdown with Stalin at Potsdam, and fully aware that the first A-bomb test was scheduled for the following month, he still does not seem to have thought about or even recognized the Bomb's diplomatic value.[40] Secrecy does not explain Churchill's failure to leave us with any hard evidence of an interest in atomic diplomacy prior to Potsdam: he was perfectly happy at other times in the war to discuss the Bomb with those in the know.

If Churchill did not consciously bank on the Bomb as insurance against a breakdown in relations with the USSR, why then did he maintain his objection to disclosure to the Soviets even after Roosevelt, in February 1945, concluded that secrecy had probably run its course? Recalling Churchill's often extreme efforts to maintain close personal relations with Stalin, an attempt to inform the Soviet leader about Tube Alloys in general terms might have been helpful. It would also have insulated Churchill against Soviet accusations of bad faith when the secret of the Bomb was finally revealed. One answer – the evidence does not permit its positing as *the* answer – brings us back to Churchill's dream of a postwar Anglo-American "special relationship", the fraternal association of America, Britain and the Commonwealth. If the exclusivity of the US–UK atomic partnership lasted to the end of hostilities – which, perforce, required keeping the Soviets out – the continued sharing of the Bomb in peacetime, something Churchill believed was assured by Quebec and Hyde Park, would only be practicable within the framework of a formal military alliance. If such an alliance materialized, this in turn would open the way to the fully-fledged melding of the USA, UK and Commonwealth, the veritable Anglo-America that was Churchill's overarching aim.[41] Arguably, then, his passion for atomic secrecy can be explained as much by trans-Atlanticist considerations as by a conscious desire to retain the Bomb as protection against a future Soviet threat.

In weighing what the wartime nuclear Churchill did we must also revisit his approval of the use of the Bomb against Japan. Churchill was later adamant that the decision had been a joint one and, in consequence, that he and Truman were equally answerable before History, and to God, for what took place at Hiroshima and Nagasaki. However, the evidence presented in this book suggests that Churchill either mis-remembered or deliberately exaggerated the extent of his contribution to the policy-making process in the weeks leading up to the bombings. Churchill may have approved, but he did not decide, jointly or otherwise. Instead, possibly distracted in May and June by the demands of a General Election campaign, he left the Americans to their own devices. Ignoring Anderson's counsel, he refused to invoke the Quebec agreement to demand from the Truman administration a right to full and formal consultation. Nor did he stand on the wording of the Hyde Park agreement to request an opportunity for 'mature reflection' with Truman, be it on the Bomb's combat role or the desirability of a warning to Japan.[42]

Had this consultation and reflection occurred, the minutes of the meeting of the Combined Policy Committee on 4 July 1945 would still have recorded UK approval of the bombing. There was never a question of a British veto. Rather, by summoning forth his agreements with Roosevelt, by intruding himself into the decision-making process instead of leaving the field clear for the Americans, Churchill would at the least have compelled the Truman administration to make an early declaration of its position on the future of US–UK atomic relations. If the Americans accepted the validity of the Quebec and Hyde Park agreements going into the peacetime period, all well and good; if they did not, then Churchill would have been free to reveal their details – as he was initially minded to do – when he spoke to Parliament on 16 August in the wake of Japan's surrender. No doubt some on the American side would have resented British interference in a theatre of military operations in which the United States exercised exclusive command, but given the importance of the Bomb, some Anglo-American friction was a small price to pay for obtaining clarity as to the true state of atomic relations.

Reflecting on the Quebec agreement in May 1944, Churchill admitted that it might be seen in later years as 'too confiding on our part' but he was sure that the Americans would not 'maltreat or cheat us'. Given the way that Anglo-American atomic relations developed after 1945, it is hard to escape the conclusion that he had indeed been too confiding – or else inordinately naive in believing that his agreements with FDR would hold good come what may. It is worth recalling in this connection Senator McMahon's later confession to Churchill that had he and the JCAE known about the Quebec agreement, the 1946 Atomic Energy Act would not have been passed in the form it was. Instead of later blaming Attlee for losing the Quebec agreement, therefore, Churchill might perhaps have done more to protect it himself while he was still Prime Minister.[43]

Moving into the postwar period, what did Churchill accomplish in the "showdown" phase of his nuclear career? Nothing – thankfully. The question of the degree of seriousness to be accorded to his views on the need for an atomic showdown in the five years following Potsdam has already been pondered at length and there is no need to reprise the arguments here. However, Henry Kissinger's later verdict on Churchill the atomic diplomatist invites comment. If Churchill had won the 1945 election and gone on to advocate a showdown, not impotently as leader of the opposition but determinedly as Prime Minister, Kissinger contends that 'he might well have given the emerging Cold War a different direction provided that America and the other allies had been willing to risk the confrontation which seemed to underlie Churchill's preferred strategy'.[44] We will come to the Americans in a moment but it is likely that Churchill would have been subject to home-grown constraints as well. The Chiefs of Staff, although quick after the war to identify the USSR as the successor to Nazi Germany as a real and present danger, would surely have straight-jacketed Churchill: we have seen how Brook and his colleagues vetoed Unthinkable on the ground that it was just that, unthinkable, and there is no reason to believe that they would have been any better disposed towards an atomic variation of the same theme. Churchill might also have had trouble with his Cabinet just as he did in 1954 when he sought ministerial backing for his solo mission to Moscow along with post-facto validation of his H-bomb decision.

However, as Kissinger indicates, the Americans would have been the greatest obstacle. A showdown was never in Churchill's gift. Only the United States possessed the power of atomic punishment which needed to accompany an ultimatum to Stalin over Soviet behaviour in Eastern Europe. But as we have seen, the Truman administration, to Churchill's disappointment, never made the Bomb an explicit feature of its Cold War diplomacy, nor did it particularly over-indulge in implicit atomic menaces. It thus seems most unlikely that Churchill, for all his immense renown and experience, could have persuaded US leaders to adopt a more minatory position on the Bomb against their better judgement or in variance with what they determined to be the preponderant needs of American national security.

Churchill's interest in a showdown retained at least a half-life rather longer than historians have supposed; it remained in his mind even after he publically declared himself a summiteer in February 1950, and as late as autumn 1951 there were some in the shadow Cabinet who worried that the next election could be lost if their leader's abiding attachment to atomic diplomacy became public knowledge. In the event, despite the *Daily Mirror*'s best efforts to make the charge of warmonger stick, Churchill and the Tories won the General Election that October, although not by much. Keen to reprise his dual wartime role, Churchill promptly made himself Minister of Defence, 'an extraordinarily maladroit move', a distressed Macmillan wrote in his diary. 'It almost justifies the *Daily Mirror*!'[45] Within a few months, the workload having proven too much, Churchill brought in Lord Alexander to run the MOD, but looking back now, Macmillan's concern, though understandable at the time, was unwarranted. Churchill would never again refer to an atomic showdown, at least not in positive or welcoming terms. Was this a case of high office taming the opposition maverick? Partly, perhaps, but as Churchill knew, a showdown was only really viable while the USA held its atomic monopoly, or possibly for a short time thereafter while a newly-atomic Soviet Union remained inferior in weaponry and delivery capacity.

By October 1951, the time for atomic-infused ultimata had passed. The announcement from Moscow during the election of two more successful A-bomb tests underscored the progress made by the Soviets in the two years since Joe-1 and served as a reminder to Churchill (not that he needed the prompt) that the USSR might already be in a position to deliver terrible devastation to Britain in the event of general war. As the idea of a showdown faded, Churchill, as Prime Minister, had plenty of other nuclear calls on his attention: he undertook to see the previous Labour government's weapons programme through to a conclusion; concerned by the security and sovereignty implications of US air bases in East Anglia he sought and secured from the Truman administration a commitment (with caveats) to consultation if it was ever proposed to launch atomic-laden bombers at the Soviet Union from British soil; and he accepted, though with bad grace, the Lindemann plan for transferring direction of the UK atomic programme to a bespoke Atomic Energy Authority.

Beyond this, Churchill's overriding atomic goal was the revival of the old wartime Anglo-American partnership, an objective rendered more attainable, he believed, by the success of Hurricane in October 1952. When, the following month, Eisenhower was elected President, Churchill launched his bid for renewed cooperation. To his delight, Ike not only regretted the passage of the McMahon Act but was personally convinced that US national security stood to gain from closer atomic associations with the United Kingdom. Against this, the President-elect made clear that there was not the remotest chance of a resuscitated Quebec agreement, including the restoration of the principle of mutual consent, being approved by Congress. Nor would he ever propose such an extensive curb on US nuclear independence.

For Churchill, the positive that was Eisenhower's largely encouraging atomic outlook was balanced against a more general but substantial negative. The President headed an administration populated (or so Churchill believed) by anti-communist ideologues and atomic sabre-rattling militarists desperate to roll-back the communist tide in Europe and Asia. Ironically, this was very close to the kind of approach that Churchill, in his opposition years, had wanted the Truman administration to embrace. Now, though, back in Downing Street, with the USSR presumed to be building a modern atomic bomber fleet, and with the UK in easy range of those bombers while the USA stood safely beyond the danger ambit, the provocative posturing of prominent Republicans left him nervous and insecure. And his edginess only increased. In August 1953, the Soviet Union acquired a thermonuclear capability, and though Churchill did not immediately appreciate just how far the H-bomb's megatonnage outstripped the A-bomb's kilotonnage, his concern for his country's safety deepened. Then, at the end of 1953, came the Bermuda conference and with it evidence that Republican rhetoric and Republican policy were worryingly similar. Atomic weapons, Eisenhower insisted, would henceforward be regarded by his administration as conventional arms to be used against the Sino-Soviet enemy as and when circumstances required. Which was all very well, Churchill and Eden reflected, when Britain, and Western Europe, not America, stood to pay the ultimate price for any US strategic blunder.

What did Churchill do in response to these troubling developments? Boldly and ultimately bullishly, he set out to end the Cold War. For only if détente obtained would Britain, and the rest of the world, be safe from the doom that nuclear weapons threatened to unleash. Churchill's summitry had been in the doldrums for some time: Edinburgh in 1950 had been a false (and in reality insincere) start, but even his genuine post-Stalin efforts to convene a heads of government meeting had been thwarted by his own poor health and American insistence (seconded by Eden and the Foreign Office) on Soviet compliance with a raft of summitry prerequisites. Then, in March 1954, a convergence of Sterling Cole's descriptive powers, the terrifying film of Ivy-Mike and the shocking fall-out from Castle-Bravo seared into Churchill's consciousness – along with that of millions of people around the world – the H-bomb's true annihilatory character. From this time on, a summit ceased to be an aspiration and became for Churchill a life-or-death imperative. But he was held back. To his dismay, Eisenhower continued to insist on deeds, not just words, as the clinching proof of the Kremlin's commitment to easing Cold War tensions. This was also the view of his own Cabinet wherein ministers, though equally disturbed by the H-bomb, were reluctant to agree to a meeting with the Soviets before the Western defence programme had been completed and the German Federal Republic safely ensconced in NATO.

Angry, frustrated and only too aware that time was against him, Churchill struck out on his own. In the Cabinet, key figures, appalled at the dangers inherent in his 'solitary pilgrimage' to Moscow, rebelled against his peace policy and for a time it looked as though the government would implode.[46] Does the innate nobility of Churchill's cause – world peace and the elimination the nuclear danger – excuse his reckless unilateralism? Does it mitigate his arrogant underhand subversion of the principle of collective Cabinet responsibility or his conscious parting of the ways with the Americans and Britain's other Cold War allies? To a Cabinet minister in July 1954, or a Western leader dedicated to the unity of NATO, the answer was probably no. On the other hand, in view of the extent of H-bomb fever, the British public and wider international opinion might well have backed his solo peace effort.

As we know, Churchill never made it to the summit. But what if he had? What would have happened if he had sat down opposite Malenkov at the negotiating table? Here, the prognosis, admittedly retrospectively applied, is not encouraging. For someone who truly believed that great men could achieve great things if only they could meet in intimate council, Churchill was not really very good at top-level personal diplomacy. His dealings with Roosevelt and Stalin in the war are hardly models in the art, while his citing of the percentages agreement as an exemplar of the high value of inter-leader summitry was quixotic. In addition, when we consider that in the summer of 1954 Churchill was nearly 80 years of age, in poor health, easily tired, possessed of limited concentration, allergic to reading briefs and increasingly governed by emotion, sentiment and gut-instinct, it becomes possible to see – as Eden, Macmillan, Salisbury and others did – the potential for personal humiliation and strategic mishap in any encounter with hard-bitten Soviet interlocutors. Then again, Churchill being Churchill, he might have worsted the doubters and risen splendidly to the summitry occasion. '[W]as he the man to negotiate with the Russians and moderate the Americans?', Colville asked himself in his diary in March 1955, just a week before Churchill retired. Eden and the Foreign Office, and many, perhaps most in the Cabinet, thought not, Colville conceded. The public, however, might have said yes. 'And I, who have been as intimate with him as anybody during these last years, simply do not know.'[47]

There are historians who view Churchill's obsessive focus on a summit in the 1950s as simply an excuse for his clinging to power far beyond the point he was capable of fulfilling his prime ministerial duties to the necessary standard on all fronts.[48] Unquestionably, Churchill's hubristic conceit in maintaining that as the last survivor of the wartime Big Three it was beholden upon him to try to heal the East–West rift, not to mention his egoism in viewing himself as uniquely qualified for the role of Cold War peacemaker, must have helped rationalize in his own mind his continuation in office. Yet, excuse or not, it must also be acknowledged that from 1954 to 1955, his time of supposed dotage, there was a real clarity and wisdom in his shifting nuclear outlook. Regrettably, the energy and focus he poured into his nuclear-driven peacemaking left little in his reserves for all his other responsibilities. From that standpoint, he was not living up to the prime ministerial job specification. But his accomplishments in those areas of foreign and defence policy where he did still function effectively deserve to be evaluated fairly and in their own right; his summitry was not merely selfish sophistry; his nuclear learning was not pressed into the service of personal-political or psychological needs alone.

In 1954, Churchill pushed the H-bomb through Cabinet in the face of significant opposition – a weapon, we should note, which went on in adapted form to provide a mainstay of the UK independent nuclear deterrent for much of the rest of the Cold War. Subjectively, the H-bomb scared him half-to-death. Objectively, he knew it was a necessary evil both to improve Britain's national security and buttress its flagging great-power status. It may come as a surprise to some readers of this book to learn that on returning to office in 1951, Churchill was largely opposed to a British independent atomic deterrent. He evinced no doubts whatsoever about the thermonuclear variety. What, though, was the H-bomb actually deterring? Leaving aside the Soviet Cold War enemy, in some ways Churchill was also seeking to arm the United Kingdom against the United States, not in the sense of military protection, obviously, but in politico-diplomatic terms.

Back in 1941, Churchill had launched Tube Alloys in order to build an atomic bomb before the enemy of the moment, Nazi Germany, managed to do so. Later, when the Cold War set in and the USSR became the next great foe, he saw atomic arms both as a defensive shield and, potentially, a hot war-winning weapon. Intriguingly, however, by 1954–1955, while the Soviet danger remained live and active, Churchill's principal argument in favour of the H-bomb (beyond security, status and cost-efficiency) was framed in the context of relations with the USA, an ally. The H-bomb, he believed, would enhance British influence in and over Washington and provide thermonuclear *locus standi* to restrain the Americans if they ever contemplated a forestalling war against the USSR. Eisenhower declared publicly in August 1954 that 'preventive war … is an impossibility … I wouldn't even listen to anyone seriously that came in and talked about such a thing'.[49] The problem was that Churchill did not entirely believe him. Consequently, he succumbed to the attractions of nuclear dual-containment. In different ways, a British H-bomb would deter *both* the USA and the USSR from embarking on actions which could result in the immolation of the United Kingdom.

By April 1955, Churchill was convinced that the longer hot war was deferred, the greater the chance that sanity would prevail and peaceful co-existence and détente come to be recognized by the main Cold War protagonists as infinitely preferable to the earth-shattering, civilization-threatening results of a third world war. However, in holding this view, he exited Number 10 a disappointed man; a summit had proven beyond his power to effect while peaceful co-existence, never mind détente, seemed far from realization. And yet, in the dying weeks of his ministry, he came to derive a compensatory comfort from the thought of the USSR's developing nuclear strength.

Strange as it may seem today given that Churchill was then one of the two most important leaders of the Western alliance, he regarded the USA and the USSR as co-threats to world peace, a view which developed in earnest during the 1954 Indo-China crisis and went on to inform his thinking on dual-containment. Whether the threat of conflict arose from the best of intentions (American over-zealousness in containing communism) or the worst (Soviet aggressive expansionism), Churchill contemplated the possibility of a third and this time nuclear world war with unbridled horror. By 1955, America's nuclear superiority, for so long his comfort and consolation, was especially worrying. The strategic imbalance between the superpowers was dangerous in that it kept alive the prospect of an American preventive war against the USSR, the consequences of which for the UK, in terms of Soviet retaliation, could be catastrophic. The alternative to imbalance was US–Soviet strategic parity. If, in due course, a point of mutual assured destruction was reached, that in Churchill's view would be no bad thing. Détente offered the best assurance of peace and security, but failing that, a nuclear balance, rooted in MAD, was an acceptable alternative.

This was the 'sublime irony' which he had in mind when predicting that one day 'safety will be the sturdy child of terror, and survival the twin brother of annihilation'.[50] These quotes are taken from his H-bomb speech in Parliament on 1 March 1955. That speech also marked the end of a nuclear journey which began for Churchill on 30 August 1941 when he approved what became the Tube Alloys programme. In combination, the three Churchills presented in this book make up the nuclear Churchill: subtle yet crude, sane and sensible but at times irrational and aggressive, an atomic diplomatist-cum-warrior and yet also a thermonuclear peacemaker. Of the three, it is perhaps easiest to admire and laud the peacemaker, but that particular Churchill would not have existed without the inspired risk-taking bomb-maker or the threatening atomic diplomat. 'If my devils are to leave me', the German poet Rainer Maria Rilke once wrote, 'I am afraid my angels will take flight as well'.[51] So it was with the nuclear Churchill.

ABBREVIATIONS USED IN NOTES

For full publication/archival information see Bibliography

AB   UK Atomic Energy Authority files.

ALSOP   Joseph and Stuart Alsop papers.

ATTLEE   Attlee papers.

BAE   *Britain and Atomic Energy, 1939–1945*, Margaret Gowing.

BAS   *Bulletin of the Atomic Scientists.*

BMFRS   *Biographical Memoirs of Fellows of the Royal Society.*

BOHR   Niels and Aage Bohr papers.

BUSH   Bush papers.

BUTLER   Butler papers.

CAB   Cabinet Office files.

CEC   *Churchill–Eisenhower Correspondence*, Peter Boyle, ed.

CHAR   Churchill papers, Chartwell collection.

CHUR   Churchill papers.

CROOK   Crookshank papers.

CSC   Clementine Spencer Churchill.

CSFS   *Churchill: The Struggle for Survival*, Lord Moran.

DDEL   Dwight D. Eisenhower Library.

DEFE   UK Defence Ministry files.

DNB   *Dictionary of National Biography*, Oxford, online.

DO   Dominions Office files.

DTS   *Descent to Suez*, Evelyn Shuckburgh diary.

DULLES   Dulles papers.

EG   UK Atomic Energy Policy files.

EMRYS   Emrys-Evans papers.

ES   UK Atomic Energy Research Establishment files.

FDR   Franklin D. Roosevelt.

FDRL   Franklin D. Roosevelt Library.

FOP	*Fringes of Power*, John Colville diary.
FR	*Foreign Relations of the United States*, followed by volume details.
FRANK	Frankfurter papers.
HCD	*House of Commons Debates*, Hansard.
HLD	*House of Lords Debates*, Hansard.
HO	Home Office files.
HSTL	Harry S. Truman Library.
ID	*Independence and Deterrence*, followed by volume, Margaret Gowing.
JRO	J. Robert Oppenheimer papers.
LRB	*London Review of Books*.
LEAHY	Leahy papers.
LIND	F. A. Lindemann (Lord Cherwell) papers.
LUNG	Lunghi papers.
MAC	Macmillan papers.
MART	Martin papers.
MJS	Martin J. Sherwin collection.
NYRB	*New York Review of Books*.
OSRD	US Office of Scientific Research and Development files.
OTR	*Off the Record*, Truman diary, Ferrell, ed.
PEIERLS	Peierls papers.
PPP	*Public Papers of the Presidents*.
PREM	Prime Minister's Private Office files.
SCOTT	Scott papers.
SFT	*Speaking for Themselves*, Soames, ed.
SHER	Sherfield papers.
T	Treasury files.
TMSN	Thomson papers.
TRHS	*Transaction of the Royal Historical Society*.
USAEC	US Atomic Energy Commission official history, followed by volume.
WAVE	Lady Waverley papers.
WOOL	Woolton papers.
WSC	Winston Spencer Churchill.
WSC	Official Churchill biography, followed by volume details.

NOTES

Acknowledgements

1. WSC speech, London, 2 November 1949, CHUR5/28 (images 7–11).

Introduction: So Many Winston Churchills

1. *Chartwell Bulletin*, No. 58 (2013), 'New Colour Film of Churchill with Royal Family'.
2. CC(52)15, 11 February 1952, CAB195/10.
3. In general on Hurricane, see Cathcart, *Test of Greatness*.
4. Hennessy, *Having It So Good*, pp.183–184
5. *WSC/VIII*, p.764.
6. Lord Byron, *Don Juan* (1819).
7. Rhodes James, 'Enigma', p.6.
8. 'Epilogue', in WSC, *Second World War: Abridged One-Volume Version*, p.963.
9. DeGroot, *The Bomb*, p.2, original emphasis.
10. *HCD* Vol. 537, col. 1894, 1 March 1955.
11. Addison, *Churchill*.
12. Sherwin, 'Old Issues in New Editions', p.40.
13. For a recent example, Heffer, 'Churchill myth', p.23.
14. Zoller, *Annotated Bibliography*.
15. WSC to Eisenhower, 9 March 1954, *CEC*, pp.122–123.
16. Among the few historians who do give the crisis serious coverage are Young, *Last Campaign*, pp.266–289; Larres, *Churchill's Cold War*, pp.341–355; Leaming, *Churchill Defiant*, pp.272–299; and Hennessy, *Having It So Good*, pp.335–356.
17. www.churchillarchive.com.
18. All references to Churchill's papers in these notes (those prefixed with CHUR or CHAR) conform to the Churchill Archive Centre referencing system, but I have added, for those subscribing to the online Archive, precise image numbers for ease of access.
19. Rosenberg, 'Before the Bomb and After', pp.171–193, is a short but estimable exception. For details of Young and Larres, see Bibliography.
20. Trory, *Churchill and the Bomb*.
21. Farmelo, *Churchill's Bomb*.
22. On the German project see Rose, *Heisenberg*; Powers, *Heisenberg's War*; Walker, *German National Socialism*.

23. On the debate, the following review essays are good starting points: Walker, 'Decision to Use the Bomb', pp.97–114, and his follow-up, 'Recent Literature', pp.311–334; Kort, 'Historiography of Hiroshima', pp.31–48; Yagami, 'Bombing Hiroshima and Nagasaki', pp.301–307.

24. Hymans, 'Britain and Hiroshima', is one of the few historians to evaluate the British role with real seriousness.

25. Amrine, 'Day the Sun Rose Twice'.

26. Charmley, *Churchill*, p.647.

27. Orwell, 'You and the Atomic Bomb'.

28. Russell, 'The Atomic Bomb and the Prevention of War' (1946); 'Fight Before Russia Finds Atom Bomb', *Observer*, 21 November 1948; Perkins Jr., 'Bertrand Russell and Preventive War', pp.135–153.

29. Sherwin, *World Destroyed*, p.192, note; 'Labour Criticism of Mr. Churchill', *Times*, 11 October 1948.

30. 'Winston Churchill's "bid to nuke Russia" to win Cold War – uncovered in secret FBI files', *Daily Mail*, 8 November 2014.

31. WSC, 'Epilogue', p.959.

32. WSC speech, 14 February 1950, CHUR5/32A–C (images 567–579); Young, *Last Campaign*, p.1.

33. See for example Farmelo, *Churchill's Bomb*, p.355; Young, *Last Campaign*, p.29; Jenkins, *Churchill*, p.834; Best, *Churchill*, p.289.

34. Macmillan, 20 December 1950, 20 and 27 October 1951, in *Diaries/I*, pp.34–45, 109, 111.

35. Colville, August 1953, *FOP*, pp.675–676.

36. WSC-Eisenhower meeting, 25 June 1954, *FR1952–4/VI*, pp.1085–1086.

37. *HCD* Vol. 484, cols 623–641, 15 February 1951; 'Horror Bombs: A Policy for Survival', *Sunday Pictorial*, 28 March 1954; 'Twilight of a Giant', *Daily Mirror*, 1 April 1954.

38. Eden, *Full Circle*, p.368.

39. DP(54)6, COS memorandum, 1 June 1954, CAB134/808; GEN.465/2nd meeting, 19 March 1954, CAB130/101.

40. WSC to Baruch, 29 August 1954, CHUR/2/210A-B (images 458–460).

41. GEN.465/1st and 2nd meetings, 12 and 19 March 1954, CAB130/101; WSC, 'Notes on Tube Alloys', C(54)390, 14 December 1954, CAB129/72.

42. WSC to Salisbury, 21 August 1954, PREM11/669.

Chapter 1 Only Connect . . .

1. Forster, *Howards End* (1910).

2. The 'Leonard' was soon dropped leaving the well-known set of initials WSC, which are employed throughout these notes. The biographical portrait in this chapter is a conflation of the early volumes of the official Churchill biography, his *Oxford Dictionary of National Biography* (*DNB*) entry written by Paul Addison (as well as Addison's *Churchill*), Roy Jenkins' *Churchill* and Geoffrey Best's *Churchill and War*. Specific quotes from these sources, along with additional information, are cited in the normal way.

3. Murphy and Davenport, 'Lives of Winston Churchill', p.97.

4. King, in Dilks, *Churchill and Company*, p.69.

5. Best, *Churchill and War*, p.2.

6. Young, *Last Campaign*, p.3.

7. Cannadine, *Churchill's Other Lives: Money* (2011). In general, Lough, *Churchill and his Money*.

8. Addison, *Churchill*, p.14.

9. *WSC*/I, p.334.

10. Graebner, *Churchill*, p.48.

11. Best, *Churchill and War*, p.ix; *Finest Hour*, No. 93 (1996–1997), p.20.

12. Schama, 'Rescuing Churchill'. The books were *The Story of the Malakand Field Force* (1898) and *The River War* (1899, two volumes), and *London to Ladysmith via Pretoria* (1900).

13. Toye, *Roar of the Lion*, p.18.

14. *WSC*/I, p.561.

15. Reynolds, *Command of History*, pp.xxii–xxiii; Rose, *Literary Churchill*, p.116.

16. WSC to CSC, 15 September 1909, *SFT*, p.30.

17. WSC to Grey, 30 August 1911, and WSC to Lloyd George, 31 August 1911, *WSC*/II, pp.529–532.

18. WSC to CSC, 28 July 1914, *SFT*, p.96.

19. Bonham-Carter, 22 February 1915, in Pottle, ed., *Champion Redoubtable*, p.25, original emphases.

20. Jenkins, *Churchill*, p.213.

21. Low, 'Churchill and Science', p.306.

22. Dilks, *Churchill and Company*, p.45.

23. Report of the CID Sub-Committee on Aerial Navigation, 25 February 1909, *WSC*/II, p.688.

24. *WSC*/II, p.576; *Punch*, 25 May 1914.

25. Gilbert, 'Churchill and Bombing Policy', pp.1–3.

26. *WSC*/III, pp.535–538.

27. WSC to Fisher, 16 September 1916, and WSC to Conan Doyle, 1 October 1916, *WSC*/III, p.810; WSC, *World Crisis*, Vol. II, pp.1218–1221.

28. Howard, 'Churchill and the First World War', p.136.

29. *WSC*/III, p.473.

30. Addison, *Churchill*, p.86.

31. WSC, *World Crisis*, Vol. II, p.971.

32. WSC, Cabinet paper, 5 March 1918, *WSC*/IV, p.146.

33. WSC to Loucher, 6 April 1918, *WSC*/IV, p.105.

34. *WSC*/IV, p.105.

35. WSC to CSC, 15 October 1918, *SFT*, p.215.

36. WSC minute, June 1921, *WSC*/IV, p.797.

37. WSC, 'Mr. H. G. Wells and the British Empire', November 1927, proofs, CHAR8/215 (images 10–14).

38. Moran diary, 7 December 1947, *CSFS*, p.328.

39. Farmelo, *Churchill's Bomb*, pp.24–25.

40. WSC, *World Crisis*, Vol. I, p.514.

41. *WSC*/IV, pp.441–442; WSC, 'H. G. Wells', *Sunday Dispatch*, 21 June 1942, CHAR8/706 (image 2).

42. Hastings, *Finest Years*, pp.528–529. See also Toye, 'H. G. Wells and Winston Churchill'.

43. WSC, 'H. G. Wells', *Sunday Pictorial*, 23 August 1931.

44. *Independent*, 27 November 2006. See in general Toye, *Churchill's Empire*, pp.162–164.

45. WSC, 'Fifty Years Hence', *Strand*, December 1931.

46. *WSC*/VI, p.593.

47. Colville in Wheeler-Bennett, ed., *Action This Day*, p.102.

48. Wimbledon online archives, 1920 tournament.

49. *DNB*, 'Cherwell'; Fort, *Prof*, p.108; Birkenhead, *Prof*, pp.23–24.

50. Colville diary, 6 January 1941, *FOP*, p.329; Moran diary, 13 September 1944, *CSFS*, p.177.

51. Jones, 'Churchill and Science', p.429.

52. *DNB*, 'Cherwell'; Rhodes James, *Churchill*, p.242; Birkenhead, *Prof*, p.169.

53. Birkenhead, *Prof*, p.162.

54. Best, 'Momentous Conjecture', p.37.

55. Mallaby, *From My Level*, p.40.

56. Pimlott, '"I must have Prof"', *Guardian*, 25 October 2003.

57. Moran diary, 4 July 1957, *CSFS*, p.729.

58. *DNB*, 'Cherwell'; Low, 'Churchill and Science', p.305.

59. Birkenhead, *Prof*, p.73.

60. Moran diary, 4 July 1957, *CSFS*, p.729.

61. WSC to Lindemann, 21 April 1924 and 4 April 1926, LIND/K62/2 and 4, and 22 February 1927, K63/5.

62. WSC to Lindemann, 3 April 1924, K62/1.

63. WSC, 'Shall We All Commit Suicide?', *Nash's Pall Mall*, 1924, CHAR8/200A-B (images 225–229).

64. WSC, 'Shall We All Commit Suicide?', *Nash's Pall Mall*, 1924, CHAR8/200A-B (images 225–229).

65. WSC to Shaw, 4 July 1931, CHAR8/292 (image 77).

66. Lindemann to WSC, and enclosure, 18 February 1931, CHAR8/301 (image 3).

67. WSC, 'Fifty Years Hence'.

68. War Cabinet, 10 November 1918, CAB23/14.

69. WSC speech, Dundee, 26 November 1918, CHAR9/56 (images 147–163).

70. Capet, 'Creeds of the Devil', *Finest Hour online* (2009).

71. Milton, *Russian Roulette*, pp.250–255.

72. Lloyd George to WSC, 16 February 1919, *WSC*/IV, p.251.

73. Kinvig, *Churchill's Crusade*, p.164.

74. 'Criminal Bolshevist Regime', *Times*, 19 November 1920.

75. Toye, *Churchill's Empire*, p.137; Carlton, *Churchill and the Soviet Union*, pp.18, 21.

76. Young, *Last Campaign*, p.11.

77. WSC press conference, Rome, 20 January 1927, CHAR9/82A-B (images 166–177); *Times*, 21 January 1927; *WSC/V*, p.457.

78. Carlton, *Churchill*, p.41.

79. Ramsden, *Churchill*, pp.44, 208.

80. WSC, 'Fifty Years Hence'.

81. WSC, 'Fifty Years Hence'.

82. DeGroot, *Bomb,* p.9; Ehrman, *Atomic Bomb,* pp.9–10.

83. 'Splitting the Atom', *Times,* 21 November 1932.

84. De Ropp, *New Prometheans*, p.22.

85. Keas, 'Rutherford', p.53; Farmelo, *Churchill's Bomb*, p.71.

86. Clark, *Greatest Power*, p.78.

87. Rotter, *Hiroshima*, pp.12–14.

88. Polanyi, 'Republic of Science', pp.54–74.

89. Wells, *World Set Free*, p.240.

90. Frisch, *What Little I Remember*, pp.118–119.

91. *USAEC/*I, p.13.

92. Bohr and Wheeler, 'The Mechanism of Nuclear Fission' (1939), pp.426–450; Bohr, 'War Years', p.191.

93. WSC, *Gathering Storm*, p.75.

94. WSC, *Gathering Storm*, p.72.

95. Jenkins, *Churchill*, p.474.

96. WSC, *HCD* Vol. 295, col. 865, 28 November 1934.

97. WSC, *HCD* Vol. 322, col. 1063, 14 April 1937.

98. Young, *Last Campaign*, p.7; WSC, *HCD* Vol. 322, col. 1064, 14 April 1937 and Vol. 347, cols 1840–1849, 19 May 1939; *Manchester Guardian,* 10 May 1938.

99. Maisky, 16 November 1937, in Gorodetsky, ed., *Maisky Diaries*, p. 89.

100. Best, *Churchill,* p.153.

101. WSC, 'Hitler and his Choice' (1935), reprinted in WSC, *Great Contemporaries*, p.208.

102. Lukacs, *Churchill,* p.24; Jenkins, *Churchill,* pp.464–467, 525.

103. WSC, *HCD* Vol. 339, col. 371, 5 October 1938.

104. WSC, *HCD* Vol. 345, col. 2502, 3 April 1939.

105. WSC to CSC, 8 March 1935, *SFT*, p.391.

106. Lindemann letter, 10 August 1939, in Gilbert, ed., *Volume V Companion*, p.1587.

107. WSC to Wood, 13 August 1939, in Gilbert, ed., *Volume V Companion*, p.1586.

Chapter 2 Tube Alloys

1. Taylor, 'What Was Winston Churchill?', p.296.

2. WSC, *Gathering Storm*, pp.420, 663–664; Fort, *Prof*, p.201.

Notes

3. George VI diary, 10 May 1940, in James, ed., *Spirit Undaunted*, p.193.

4. WSC to Lady Randolph, 5 September 1897, CHAR/28/23/52 (images 1–3).

5. WSC, *Gathering Storm*, pp.599–600.

6. Addison, 'Three Careers of Winston Churchill', p.195.

7. Wheeler-Bennett, ed., *Action This Day*, p.49.

8. Jenkins, *Churchill*, p.588.

9. Ismay, *Memoirs*, p.116.

10. Howard, *RAB*, p.94.

11. *WSC/VI*, p.593; Fort, *Prof*, p.205; Wheeler-Bennett, ed., *Action This Day*, p.103.

12. In general, McCrae, *Churchill's Toyshop*.

13. Richardson, *Churchill's Secret Circle*, p.52.

14. Colville, *Churchillians*, p.35.

15. Channon, 13 June 1941, in James, ed., *'Chips'*, p.307; Pownall, 25 July 1941, in Bond, ed., *Chief of Staff*, p.34. For consistency, Lindemann will continue to be used rather than Cherwell.

16. Dalton, 5 January 1943, in Pimlott, ed., *Second World War Diary of Hugh Dalton*, p.543; Reith, 7 July 1944, in Stuart, ed., *Reith Diaries*, p.323.

17. Addison, *Churchill*, p.182.

18. Newhouse, *Nuclear Age*, p.17.

19. Clark, *Greatest Power*, p.89.

20. DeGroot, *Bomb*, p.24; Frisch, *What Little I Remember*, p.126; Peierls, *Bird of Passage*, p.168.

21. Frisch-Peierls memorandum, March 1940, *atomicarchive.com*.

22. *BAE*, p.37.

23. Oliphant to Tizard, March 1940, in Clark, *Tizard*, p.218.

24. *BAE*, p.35.

25. For the curious origins of the name MAUD see Farmelo, *Churchill's Bomb*, p.161.

26. Frisch, *What Little I Remember*, pp.131–132.

27. Ehrman, *Atomic Bomb*, p.21; Rhodes, *Atomic Bomb*, p.330.

28. Moran diary, 2 September 1945, *CSFS*, pp.292–293.

29. *HCD* Vol. 361, col. 796, 4 June 1940.

30. *Times*, 7 May 1940.

31. Chadwick to Lindemann, 20 June 1940, LIND/D230/8; Edgerton, *Britain's War Machine*, p.118.

32. MAUD Committee Report, 15 July 1941, *fissilematerials.org*.

33. Farren, 'Tizard', *BMFRS*, Vol. 7 (1961), p.338; Clark, *Tizard*, pp.298–299.

34. Simon to Lindemann, 7 May 1940, LIND/D230/1; Clark, *Greatest Power*, pp.109–110.

35. *BAE*, p.47.

36. WSC, *Finest Hour*, p.338.

37. Lindemann to WSC, 27 August 1941, CAB126/330.

38. WSC to Ismay, 30 August 1941, PREM3/139/8A.

39. Ismay to Anderson, 4 September 1941, CAB126/330

40. WSC to Anderson, 22 August 1945, CHUR2/3 (images 140–141).

41. Ismay to Anderson, and Anderson annotation, 5 September 1941, CAB126/330; Hollis to WSC, 2 September 1941, PREM3/139/8A.

42. SAC(DP)(41) 13th meeting, CAB90/8, 19 September 1941.

43. SAC/DSP report, 25 September 1941, Ehrman, *Atomic Bomb,* pp.356–366.

44. 'Note by Imperial Chemical Industries Limited', 3 June 1941, AB1/175; Reader, *ICI*/II, p.290.

45. An hour-long episode of *Archive on 4* in 2015, devoted to the British wartime atomic project, ignored Anderson entirely. 'Destroyer of Worlds', *Archive on 4,* BBC Radio 4, 11 July 2015.

46. The following character sketch is a conflation of Wheeler-Bennet, *Anderson,* Anderson's (Lord Waverly) *DNB* entry and his obituary in *The Times* and the *BMFRS.* Additional sources are indicated in the notes.

47. Scott, *Obedient Servant,* pp.63–64; *DNB,* 'Waverley'.

48. WSC, *Closing the Ring,* p.145.

49. WSC, *Gathering Storm,* p.374.

50. Overy, *Bombing War,* pp.148–152; WSC, *HCD* Vol. 365 col. 295, 8 October 1940.

51. Taylor, *English History,* p.482; Attlee, *As It Happened,* p.14; WSC, *HCD* Vol. 378, col. 39, 24 February 1942; WSC, *Finest Hour,* p.326.

52. James, *Spirit Undaunted,* p.241.

53. Dickens, *Oliver Twist,* p.23.

54. Jones, 12 July 1941, in Jones, *Diary With Letters,* p.489.

55. WSC, *Closing the Ring,* p.145.

56. Moran diary, 22 September 1943, *CSFS,* p.121.

57. Pye to Thomson, 10 October 1941, TMSN/6; Clark, *Greatest Power,* pp.129–130.

58. Reader, *ICI*/II, p.291.

59. There are other claimants to authorship of the codename but Perrin to Gorell Barnes, 24 November 1943, CAB126/300, and to Lindemann, 28 July 1949, AB16/266, confirm Anderson as the originator.

60. Lindemann memorandum, n.d., July 1945, PREM3/139/9; Anderson (OZ3879) to JSM Washington, 25 November 1943, AB1/140; *BAE,* pp.106–107.

61. Ehrman, *Atomic Bomb,* p.9.

62. Brook to Hovde and enclosure, 30 January 1942, CAB126/41.

63. Chadwick to Appleton, 27 and 30 October 1941, Oliphant to Chadwick, 27 October 1941, CHAD/I/19/3 and IV/11/2.

64. Waverley and Fleck, 'Akers', *BMFRS,* Vol. 1 (1955), p.1.

65. Chadwick to Oliphant, 10 November 1941, and Oliphant to Chadwick, 14 January 1942, CHAD/I/19/13; Reader, *ICI*/II, pp.287–294.

66. Einstein to FDR, 2 August 1939, FDRL, Atomic-02/pp5-6.

67. *Times,* 20 September 1939.

68. Sachs testimony, 27 November 1945, p.558, FDRL, Atomic-Sachs1945/p57.

69. FDR to Einstein, 19 October 1939, FDRL, Atomic-02/p1.

70. DeGroot, *Bomb*, p.23; *USAEC*/I, pp.33–41.

71. FDR to Bush, 15 June 1940, FDRL, Atomic-02/pp21–23; Bundy, *Danger and Survival*, p.40; Sherwood, *Hopkins*, Vol. I, pp.156–158.

72. Zachary, *Endless Frontier*, pp.190–191

73. Compton (K) to Bush, 17 March 1941, MJS/58/3; Clark, *Greatest Power*, p.75.

74. Oliphant, 'The Beginning', p.17.

75. Bundy, *Danger and Survival*, p.49.

76. FDR Executive Order, 28 June 1941, *PPP*.

77. *USAEC*/I, pp.42–43.

78. Bush to FDR and enclosure, 16 July 1941, FDRL, Atomic-02/pp58–63.

79. Hershberg, *Conant*, pp.127, 148.

80. Bush to Conant, 9 October 1941, Bush report to FDR, 6 November 1941, NARA, Bush-Conant file, RG227/OSRD/M1392.

81. Rhodes, *Atomic Bomb*, pp.378–379; Sherwin, *World Destroyed*, p.43.

82. FDR to WSC, 11 October 1941, FDRL, Atomic-02/p64.

83. WSC, *Hinge of Fate*, pp.340–341.

84. See Colville, 2 May 1948, *FOP*, p.624, on this.

85. Anderson-Lindemann-Hovde meeting, London, 21 November 1941, PREM3/139/8A.

86. WSC to FDR, December 1941 (n.d.), PREM3/139/8A.

87. On the missed bus see Farmelo, *Churchill's Bomb*, pp.6–7, 203–204; Rotter, *Hiroshima*, p.117; Clark, *Greatest Power*, pp.134, 138; Hershberg, *Conant*, p.179; Bernstein, 'Uneasy Alliance', pp.202, 206; Gowing, 'Bohr and Nuclear Weapons', p.119.

88. *BAE*, pp.85, 92–94.

89. Bernstein, 'Uneasy Alliance', pp.202, 206.

90. Lindemann to WSC, 27 August 1941, CAB126/330.

91. Bernstein, 'Uneasy Alliance', p.206; *BAE*, p.123.

92. Farmelo, *Churchill's Bomb*, pp.195, 207.

93. Hastings, *Finest Years*, p.560.

94. *DNB*, 'Cherwell'.

95. James, *Churchill*, pp.241–242; Farmelo, *Churchill's Bomb*, p.46; Clark, *Tizard*, pp.243–245.

96. Jones, *Nature*, Vol. 180 (September 1957), pp.579–580.

97. Moran diary, 4 July 1957, *CSFS*, p.728.

98. Clark, *Tizard*, pp.243–245.

99. Winant, *Letter from Grosvenor Square*, p.198.

100. FDR to Congress, 8 December 1941, *PPP*.

101. Moran diary, 10 July 1945, *CSFS*, p.261; Jenkins, *Churchill*, pp.667, 680; Roberts, *Stalin's Wars*, p.82.

102. Colville diary, 30 August 1941, *FOP*, p.434.

103. WSC, *Grand Alliance*, pp.539–540.

104. Hershberg, *Conant*, p.155.

Chapter 3 Allies at War

1. *WSC*/VII, pp.23–41.

2. Anderson to Bush, 23 March 1942, and Bush reply, 20 April 1942, AB1/207.

3. Peierls memorandum, n.d., July 1945, CAB126/1.

4. TA(42)1st meeting, 16 January 1942, and 2nd meeting, 12 June 1942, CAB98/47; Peierls to Gowing, 30 October 1961, PEIERLS/NCUACS57.6.95/A17.

5. Akers letter to Brook, 9 January 1942, CAB126/330.

6. FDR to Bush, 11 March 1942, FDRL, PSF/Box97/Bush/p3.

7. *USAEC*/I, p.260.

8. FDR to Bush, 23 June 1942, and Bush reply, 24 June 1942, FDRL, PSF/Box97/Bush/pp5–7.

9. *BAE*, pp.84, 127, 131; Rhodes, *Atomic Bomb*, p.389.

10. Farmelo, *Churchill's Bomb*, pp.212–214.

11. Brooke diary, 13 June 1942, in Danchev and Todman, eds, *War Diaries*, p.265.

12. WSC, *Hinge of Fate*, pp.336, 341.

13. Reynolds, *Command of History*, p.334.

14. FDR to Bush, 11 July 1942, *USAEC*/I, p.261.

15. Charmley, *Churchill*, pp.459–460.

16. Bush to Anderson, 20 April 1942, CAB126/41; Bush to Conant, 19 June 1942, MJS/58/4.

17. Goodwin, *No Ordinary Time*, p.311.

18. *BAE*, pp.133, 137.

19. Akers memorandum, TA(42)10, 22 July 1942, and TA(42) 4th meeting, 29 July 1942, CAB98/47; *BAE*, p.144.

20. Anderson to WSC, 30 July 1942, PREM3/139/8A.

21. WSC marginalia, 31 July 1942, PREM3/139/8A.

22. CSC to WSC, 4 August 1942, *SFT*, p.466.

23. Anderson to Bush, 5 August 1942, and Anderson to MacDonald, 6 August 1942, CAB126/41.

24. Bush to Anderson, 1 September 1942, CAB126/41.

25. *USAEC*/I, pp.80–83; Groves, *Now It Can Be Told*, p.24.

26. Almost $100 million and $330 million respectively in 2015 terms.

27. Bush to Anderson, 1 October 1942, CAB126/41.

28. Hershberg, *Conant*, p.180, and p.809, note 27.

29. Lindemann memorandum, July 1945, PREM3/139/9; Akers to Perrin, 21 December 1942, AB1/128.

30. Rhodes, *Atomic Bomb*, p.379; Malloy, *Atomic Tragedy*, p.93.

31. Reader, *ICI*/II, p.292; *USAEC*/I, p.275; Ehrman, *Atomic Bomb*, pp.68–69.

32. *BAE*, p.140.

33. *USAEC*/I, p.75.

34. Groves, *Now It Can Be Told*, p.140.

35. Goldberg, 'Groves Takes the Reins', p.36.

36. US AEC, Groves testimony, Oppenheimer hearing, 1954, *archive.org*.

37. Akers to Perrin, 16 November 1941 and 21 December 1942, AB1/128.

38. Oppenheimer to Bethe, 19 October 1942, JRO/20/1.

39. Hershberg, *Conant*, pp.181–183.

40. Conant to Bush, 26 October 1942, MJS/52/3.

41. Conant, *Several Lives*, p.252.

42. Hershberg, *Conant,* pp.143–144, 178–180.

43. Bernstein, 'Uneasy Alliance', p.209.

44. Sherwin, *World Destroyed,* pp.67–68; Kimball, *Forged in War,* p.147.

45. *ID*/I, p.1.

46. Anderson to WSC, 11 January 1943, and WSC marginalia, PREM3/139/8A.

47. *Sunday Dispatch*, 10 January 1943.

48. *USAEC*/I, p.112.

49. Bush to FDR, 16 December 1942, NARA/RG227/OSRD/M1392/Bush-Conant file.

50. Bush to FDR, 16 December 1942, NARA/RG227/OSRD/M1392/Bush-Conant file.

51. *USAEC*/I, p.115; Hershberg, *Conant*, p.164. Centrifuge had fallen by the wayside. $400 million = approximately $5.5 billion today.

52. Moran diary, 16 November 1943, *CSFS,* p.126; WSC, *Grand Alliance*, pp.21–22.

53. Reynolds, *Command of History,* p.414; Harbutt, 'Churchill, Hopkins, and the "Other" Americans', p.237.

54. WSC, *Grand Alliance*, p.21.

55. Note by Rowan, 18 January 1943, PREM3/139/8A.

56. Anderson (Telescope 151) to WSC, 20 January 1943, and Conant memorandum, 7 January 1943, PREM3/139/8A.

57. WSC (Stratagem 196) to Anderson, 23 January 1943, PREM3/139/8A.

58. Anderson to WSC, 11 January 1943, PREM3/139/8A.

59. Bernstein, 'Uneasy Alliance', p.210.

60. Bush to Hopkins, 31 March 1943, confirming FDR's earlier 'approval', FDRL, Atomic-03/pp11–15.

61. Bush to FDR, 16 December 1942, and Conant to Groves, 9 December 1942, NARA/RG227/OSRD/M1392/Bush-Conant file.

62. Sherwin, *World Destroyed,* pp.73–76.

63. WSC to CSC, 24 January 1943, *SFT*, pp.474–475.

64. WSC (T.178/3) to Hopkins, 16 February 1943, PREM3/139/8A.

65. Hopkins (T.218/3) to WSC, 24 February 1943, PREM3/139/8A.

66. WSC (T.233/3) and enclosure (T.234/3) to Hopkins, 27 February 1943, PREM3/139/8A.

67. Rowan to WSC, 17 and 18 March 1943, WSC (T.336/3) to Hopkins, 19 March 1943, Hopkins to WSC, 19 March 1943, PREM3/139/8A.

68. WSC telegram (T.434/3), 1 April 1943, PREM3/139/8A.

69. *BAE*, p.161.

70. Eden to Hopkins, 13 April 1943, and Halifax to Eden, 14 April 1943, in Eden, *Reckoning,* p.569.

71. Conant to Bush, 25 March 1943, FDRL, Atomic-03/pp125–132.

72. Hershberg, *Conant,* p.180. In a reflection omitted from her official history of Tube Alloys, Margaret Gowing thought that 'Conant's attitude to the British was in general rather unworthy and was not wholly caused by his dislike of the ICI influence'. Gowing to Chadwick, 11 July 1963, CHAD/IV/12/5.

73. Clark, *Greatest Power,* p.147; Bernstein, 'Uneasy Alliance', p.212.

74. Anderson to WSC, 26 July 1943, PREM3/139/8A.

75. Lindemann to WSC, 7 April 1943, PREM3/139/8A.

76. Anderson to WSC, 29 April 1943, PREM3/139/8A.

77. Lindemann to WSC, n.d., May 1943, PREM3/139/8A.

78. WSC, 'Fifty Years Hence'.

79. £50 million = approximately £700 million in 2015.

80. Anderson (Alcove 197 and 236) to WSC, 13 and 15 May 1943, PREM3/139/8A; Akers-Perrin memorandum, 7 May 1943, CAB126/56; Eggleston, *Canada's Nuclear Story,* p.79.

81. Sanger, *MacDonald,* p.245.

82. Anderson (Alcove 236) to WSC, 15 May 1943, PREM3/139/8A.

83. Lindemann to WSC, n.d., May 1943, PREM3/139/8A.

84. Bush–Hopkins–Lindemann meeting, 25 May 1943, FDRL, Atomic-03/pp62–64.

85. WSC (Pencil 251 and 405) to London, 26 May 1943, PREM3/139/8A.

86. Ehrman, *Atomic Bomb,* p.75.

87. WSC to CSC, 28 May 1943, *SFT,* pp.482–483; Lindemann to Hopkins, 30 May 1943, FDRL, Atomic-03/p252.

88. Kimball, *Juggler,* p.7.

89. Reynolds, 'Had He Not Run', p.29.

90. For example, Sherwin, *World Destroyed,* pp.84–85; Kimball, *Forged in War,* p.214; Dallek, *Roosevelt,* p.417.

91. FDR-WSC meeting, 11 August 1941, *FR1941/I,* p.363.

92. Kimball, 'Sheriffs and Constables, *Finest Hour online* (2008–2009), pp.36–42.

93. Hilderbrand, *Dumbarton Oaks,* p.21.

94. Woods, *Changing of the Guard,* p.105; Costigliola, *Roosevelt's Lost Alliances,* pp.184–185.

95. Roosevelt, *As He Saw It,* p.37.

96. Atlantic Charter, 14 August 1941, *NATO online.*

97. WSC, Mansion House speech, 10 November 1942, *Churchill Society online;* Clymer, *Quest for Freedom,* p.122.

98. Burk, *Old World, New World,* p.516.

99. Kimball, *Forged in War,* pp.233–234.

100. Pierre, *Nuclear Politics,* p.60.

101. Sherwin, *World Destroyed,* pp.84–85.

102. On this see Sherwin, *World Destroyed,* pp.88–89; Bernstein, 'Uneasy Alliance'. p.204; Kimball, *Forged in War,* p.214.

103. Bush, *Pieces of the Action,* p.284.

Notes

Chapter 4 The Quebec Agreement

1. WSC to CSC, 28 May 1943, *SFT*, pp.482–483.
2. WSC telegram (T.760/3) to Hopkins, 10 June 1943, PREM3/139/8A; Gorell-Barnes to Anderson, and Anderson minute, 8 June 1943, CAB126/145.
3. Hopkins telegram (T.837/3) to WSC, 17 June 1943, CAB126/145.
4. Anderson to WSC, 7 July 1943, PREM3/139/8A.
5. Bush memorandum, 24 June 1943, *FR1943/Washington-Quebec*, pp.631–632.
6. WSC to FDR, 9 July 1943, PREM3/139/8A.
7. FDR to Hopkins, 14 July 1943, FDRL, Atomic-03/p36.
8. WSC (M.486/3) to Lindemann and Anderson, 18 July 1943, CAB120/842.
9. Anderson to WSC, 21 July 1943, PREM3/139/8A.
10. Anderson to WSC, 21 July 1943, PREM3/139/8A.
11. Hopkins to FDR, 20 July 1943, *FR1943/Washington-Quebec*, p.633.
12. FDR to Bush, 20 July 1943, *FR1943/Washington-Quebec*, p.633.
13. Bush memorandum, 4 August 1943, *FR1943/Washington-Quebec*, p.645; Bush, *Pieces of the Action*, p.282.
14. WSC (M.507/3) to Anderson and Lindemann, 23 July 1943, CAB120/842; Bundy record of meeting, 10 Downing Street, 22 July 1943, *FR1943/Washington-Quebec*, pp.634–636.
15. FDR (telegram 326) to WSC, 27 July 1943, PREM3/139/8A.
16. Conant to Bush, 30 July 1943, *FR1943/Washington-Quebec*, p.639; Bush, *Pieces of the Action*, p. 284.
17. Lindemann to WSC, 28 July 1943, Anderson to WSC, 29 July 1943, WSC (T.1149/3) to FDR, 30 July 1943, PREM3/139/8A; WSC to Stimson, 30 July 1943, CAB126/145.
18. Gorell-Barnes memorandum, 4 August 1943, CAB126/164; Akers to Perrin, 31 August 1943, AB1/376; Bush to Anderson, 6 August 1943, and Anderson reply (same date), and Anderson to WSC, 10 August 1943, PREM3/139/8A.
19. Ehrman, *Atomic Bomb*, pp.79–85.
20. King diary, 8 August 1943, in Pickersgill, ed., *Mackenzie King Record*/I, pp.531–532.
21. WSC (Concrete 81) to London, 10 August 1943, CHAR20/117 (images 23–24).
22. Gorell-Barnes minute, 13 August 1943, and enclosure, CAB126/145.
23. British copy of Quebec Agreement, signed by Churchill and Roosevelt, 19 August 1943, in PREM3/139/10.
24. Jones, 'Churchill and Science', p.438.
25. Addison, *Churchill*, p.212.
26. Anderson to WSC, 21 July 1943, PREM3/139/8A.
27. *HLD* Vol. 172, col. 670, 5 July 1951.
28. Perrin to Akers, 12 August 1943, and Akers reply, 19 August 1943, AB1/376.
29. Lindemann to WSC, 6 December 1950, CHUR/2/28 (images 260–261); Clark, *Greatest Power*, p.175.
30. On Churchill's thinking at this time see Reynolds, 'Rethinking Anglo-American Relations', p.94.

31. WSC (M.662/4) to Lindemann, 27 May 1944, PREM3/139/11A.

32. The composition altered somewhat over the next two years. In late 1943, Sir Ronald Campbell replaced Llewellin, and Campbell himself then made way for Halifax in 1945. Dill died in December 1944 and was replaced by Field Marshal Sir Henry Maitland Wilson.

33. Quebec Agreement, 19 August 1943, in PREM3/139/10.

34. WSC (Welfare 421) to London, 25 August 1943, CAB120/113.

35. Hershberg, *Conant,* p.143.

36. WSC speech, Harvard, 6 September 1943, CHAR9/196A-B (images 81–87).

37. Gilbert, *Churchill: A Life*, p.137.

38. Reynolds, '1940', p.251.

39. Best, *Churchill*, p.280. See also Gilbert, *Churchill and America*, p.363.

40. Barker, *Churchill and Eden at War*, p.199.

41. WSC (M.662/4) to Lindemann, 27 May 1944, PREM3/139/11A.

42. Bernstein, 'Quest for Security', p.1006.

43. Groves, *Now It Can Be Told,* pp.131, 135–136; Bush to Conant, 6 April 1954, BUSH/27/5; *USAE*/I, p.280.

44. Bush, *Pieces of the Action,* p.284.

45. US press comment, September 1943, CHAR9/196 (images 131–137).

46. Sainsbury, *Turning Point*, pp.124–125.

47. Gaddis, *Strategies of Containment,* p.3.

48. Kimball, 'Wheel within a Wheel', p.299; Butler, ed., *My Dear Mr Stalin,* 'Introduction', *passim*.

49. WSC to CSC, 26 November 1943, *SFT,* p.487.

50. WSC (Frozen 515 and 530) to Clementine, 29 and 30 November 1943, CAB120/120.

51. Kimball, *Forged in War*, p.18.

52. Brooke diary and commentary, *War Diaries,* 28 November 1943, pp.483–484.

53. Harbutt, 'Churchill, Hopkins'. pp.250–252; Gladwyn, cited in Charlton, 'Eagle and the Small Birds', p.23; Kaiser, 'Limits of Power', p.211.

54. FDR to Oppenheimer, 29 June 1943, JRO/62/9; Kimball, *Forged in War*, p.243.

55. Moran diary, 28 and 29 November 1943, *CSFS*, pp.136, 140–141.

56. Bonham-Carter, 1 August 1944, *Champion Redoubtable*, pp.312–314.

57. Sainsbury, *Turning Point*, p.307.

58. Kimball, 'Wheel within a Wheel', p.300; Jenkins, *Churchill*, p.729.

59. WSC (Welfare 450), 25 August 1943, PREM3/139/8A; Bush to FDR, 23 August 1943, FDRL, PSF/Box97/Bush/p47; Bush memorandum, 23 August 1943, PREM3/139/8B.

60. Anderson (Concrete 616 and 690) to WSC, 28 August 1943 and 2 September 1943, and Anderson to WSC, 15 October 1943, PREM3/1 39/8A; Anderson (OZ3454) to Llewellin, 29 October 1943, CAB126/331.

61. TA Technical Committee report, 9 October 1943, PREM3/139/8A.

62. Akers to Perrin, 14 August 1943, AB1/376.

63. Edgerton, *War Machine*, p.120; Anderson to WSC and enclosure, 15 October 1943, PREM3/139/8A.

64. Groves, *Now It Can Be Told*, p.136.

65. Quebec agreement, 19 August 1943, PREM3/139/10.

66. Ehrman, *Atomic Bomb*, p.158.

67. Clark, *Greatest Power*, p.134.

68. WSC (M.607/3) to Anderson, 27 September 1943, LIND/F247/1; Anderson to WSC, 15 October 1943, Lindemann to WSC and WSC annotation, 19 October 1943, PREM3/139/8A.

69. Rhodes, *Atomic Bomb*, pp.447–448.

70. DeGroot, *The Bomb*, pp.40–42; Szasz, *Manhattan Project*, p.26; Conant to Oppenheimer, 25 February 1945, JRO/27/7–8.

71. *BAE*, p.265.

72. See in general, Laucht, *Elemental Germans*.

73. *BAE*, p.240.

74. Ehrman, *Atomic Bomb*, pp.94–96.

75. *BAE*, p.267–268.

76. Conant to FDR, 30 December 1943, FDRL, Atomic-03/p97.

77. Anderson to WSC, 21 March 1944, PREM3/139/2.

78. *USAEC/I*, p.252

79. 'Huge reprisal blow threatened by Nazis', *New York Times*, 4 December 1943; Anderson (CANAM3) to Dill, 8 January 1944, CAB126/177.

80. Anderson to WSC and enclosure, 21 March 1944, and WSC annotations, PREM3/139/2.

81. Ehrman, *Atomic Bomb*, p.119.

82. Anderson to Bush, 5 August 1942, CAB126/41.

83. See in general, Sherwin, 'Niels Bohr', pp.41–45; Aaserud, 'Scientist and the Statesman', pp.1–47.

84. Wheeler-Bennett, *Anderson*, p.297.

85. *BAE*, p.245.

86. Szasz, *Manhattan Project*, p.77, for an example of the Bohr 'one man crusade' line of argument.

87. Bohr to Chadwick, Feb. 1943, BOHR/J1.5.

88. Moore, 'Niels Bohr ', pp.253–260.

89. Appleton to Bohr, 19 October 1943, BOHR/J3.6.

90. Anderson (OZ.3798) to Washington, 19 November 1943, CAB126/39; Bohr, 'War Years', p.197.

91. Wheeler-Bennett, *Anderson*, pp.296–297.

92. Ibid.; Bohr to Lady Waverley, 5 January 1958, BOHR/18/12.

93. Bohr, 'War Years', p.199.

94. Bohr to Anderson, 26 January 1956, BOHR/18/1.

95. Chadwick to Ehrman, and enclosure, 18 December 1952, CHAD/IV/12/5.

96. Oppenheimer to Groves, 17 January 1944, JRO/36/16.

97. Goudsmit, *ALSOS*, pp.76–77.

98. Sherwin, *World Destroyed*, p.5; Bernstein, 'Atomic Bombings Revisited', p.138; Bernstein, 'Roosevelt, Truman, and the Atomic Bomb', p.62.

99. WSC, *Triumph and Tragedy*, p.553.

100. Bohr to Anderson, 16 February 1944, BOHR/J2.2.

101. Bohr, 'Notes on the TA Project', 18 April 1944, CAB126/39.

102. Halifax to Anderson, 18 February 1944, CAB126/39.

103. Frankfurter to Oppenheimer, 23 November 1962, FRANK/b127/r77–78.

104. Bohr note on contacts with 'American friends', n.d., April 1944, and Halifax to Anderson, 20 April 1945, enclosing Frankfurter memorandum, 18 April 1945, CAB126/39.

105. Bohr suspected this was the case. Bohr to Anderson, 9 May 1944, CAB126/39.

106. Hershberg, *Conant,* pp.198, 206–207.

Chapter 5 Mortal Crimes

1. Bohr to Anderson, April 1944, n.d., BOHR/J4.; Bohr, 'War Years', p.203.

2. Moran, diary, 16 August 1956, *CSFS,* pp.703–704.

3. Anderson to WSC, and Rowan to Barnes (conveying Churchill's response), 27 April 1944, PREM3/139/2.

4. Dale to Lindemann and Dale to WSC, 11 May 1944, Lindemann minute to WSC, n.d., May 1944, PREM3/139/2; Bohr, 'War Years', p.204; Wheeler-Bennett, *Anderson,* p.297.

5. Gorell-Barnes to Anderson, 13 May 1944, CAB126/39.

6. Bohr, 'War Years', p.204; Jones, 'Meetings in Wartime and After', p.281; Brooke, 8 and 17 May 1944, *War Diaries,* pps. 545, 547.

7. Bohr to WSC, 22 May 1944, BOHR/J2.1; Lindemann to WSC, 24 May 1944, and WSC reply, 27 May 1944, PREM3/139/11A.

8. WSC (M.125/4) to Law, n.d., February 1944, CHAR20/152/2 (image 14); Gorell-Barnes to Anderson, 26 April 1944, CAB126/145.

9. Frankfurter to FDR, 26 June 1944, JRO/34/7; Bohr to Anderson, 13 July 1944, BOHR/J2.2.

10. Costigliola, *Lost Alliances,* p.222; Hymans, 'Britain and Hiroshima', p.778.

11. Frankfurter to FDR, 10 July 1944, enclosing Bohr memorandum (3 July 1944), FDRL, Atomic-03/pp117–126; JSM (ANCAM100) to AMSSO, 27 August 1944, CAB126/39; Bohr to Anderson and enclosure, 12 September 1944, BOHR/J2.2.

12. Bohr, 'War Years', pp.206–207.

13. Anderson (AMSSO 4949) to JSM, 1 September 1944, CAB126/39; Washington telegram 41 to Anderson, 10 September 1944, CAB126/39.

14. Anderson to WSC, 15 June 1944, PREM3/139/11A

15. Lindemann to WSC, 30 June 1944, PREM3/139/11A.

16. WSC (M.868/4) to Anderson, 16 July 1944, PREM3/139/11A.

17. Harbutt, 'Churchill, Hopkins', pp.252–261, *passim.*

18. WSC to CSC, 17 August 1944, *SFT,* p.501.

19. Bush-Conant to Stimson, 30 September 1944, MJS/31/1.

20. Anderson to WSC and enclosures, 1 September 1944, PREM3/139/11B; Anglo-American Declaration of Trust, 13 June 1944, *nuclearfiles.org.*

Notes

21. Lindemann to WSC, 12 September 1944, PREM3/139/8A.

22. Gorell-Barnes to Anderson, and Anderson Note, 1 September 1944, CAB126/145.

23. Martin diary, 19 September 1944, MART/2/p156.

24. Groves in Bernstein, 'Uneasy Alliance', p.224, note 104. In his diary, Leahy wrote, erroneously, of an 'oral agreement' on a 'new weapon project in which I have no confidence'. Leahy diary, 19 September 1944, LEAHY/6/p85.

25. Hyde Park agreement, as signed by Churchill and Roosevelt, 18 September 1944, FDRL, Atomic-03/p155.

26. Colville diary, 1 and 4 September 1944, *FOP*, pp.507–508.

27. Hyde Park agreement, 18 September 1944, FDRL, Atomic-03/p155.

28. WSC (Gunfire 293) to Admiralty, 21 September 1944, PREM3/139/8A.

29. Sherwin, *World Destroyed,* pp.112–114.

30. Morgenthau diary, 19 August 1944, FDRL/MPD/17.

31. Beschloss, *Conquerors: Roosevelt*, p.148.

32. Bush to Conant, 22 and 25 September 1944, NARA/RG227/OSRD/M1392/Bush-Conant file.

33. *BAE*, p.341.

34. Bush to Conant, 26 September 1944, MJS/52/5; Kimball, *Forged in War*, p.119.

35. Costigliola, *Lost Alliances,* p.223; Szasz, *Manhattan Project,* p.79; Clark, *Greatest Power*, p.178.

36. WSC to Lindemann, 20 September 1944, CAB127/201.

37. Lindemann to WSC, 23 September 1944, CAB127/201; Kaptiza to Bohr, 28 October 1943, and Bohr reply, 29 April 1944, BOHR/J9.4–5.

38. Anderson to Lindemann, 25 September 1944, CAB126/39, and 29 September 1944, CAB127/201.

39. Campbell to Gorell-Barnes, 19 October 1944, and Anderson to Halifax, 10 November 1944, CAB126/39; *BAE*, p.359.

40. On this point, Hymans, 'Britain and Hiroshima', p.783.

41. Taylor, 'War in our Time', pp.8–9.

42. Oppenheimer, 'Niels Bohr', *NYRB* (17 December 1964).

43. WSC (T.1778/4) to Australian PM, 18 September 1944, CHAR20/186/1 (image 5).

44. Edmonds, 'Churchill and Stalin', pp.312–315.

45. WSC (T.1828/A/4) to Stalin, 27 September 1944, PREM3/397/6.

46. Carlton, 'Evil Empires', p.351.

47. Lukacs, *Churchill*, p.11.

48. Colville diary, 21 and 22 June 1941, *FOP*, pp.404–406.

49. WSC (M.497/4 and M.497/5) to Eden, 4 May 1944, and (M.537/4), 8 May 1944, CHAR20/152/5 (images 4 and 10).

50. COS committee No 205, 22 June 1944, *WSC*/VII, p. 816; WSC (T.1706/4) to Smuts, 31 August 1944, CHAR20/171/8 (image 11).

51. It was planned that Allied forces would move from the Riviera up the Rhone River valley and then link up with Allied armies advancing across France from Normandy.

52. Colville diary, 1 September 1944, *FOP*, p.507. Due to the demands of Dragoon, Alexander's Fifth Army of 250,000 was reduced by nearly 100,000. *WSC*/VII, p. 887.

53. WSC (T.1676/4) to Smuts, 25 August 1944, CHAR20/170 (image 98); WSC (D(O)4/4A) to Ismay, 9 September 1944, CHAR20/153 (images 37-38); Ismay, *Memoirs*, pp.362–363.

54. WSC (D.215/4 and 218/4) to Ismay, 5 and 6 July 1944, CHAR20/153/1 (images 5–6).

55. Moran diary, 4 August 1944, *CSFS*, p.161, and commentary (September 1944), p.190.

56. Reynolds, *World War to Cold War*, pp.126–133.

57. Moran diary, 21 August 1944, *CSFS*, p.173.

58. *CSFS*, p.191, October 1944, n.d.

59. WSC (M.932/4) to CIGS, 6 August 1944, CHAR20/153 (image 26).

60. WSC (T.1342/4) to FDR, 23 June 1944, CHAR20/167 (images 50–51); WSC (T.1625/4) to FDR, 17 August 1944, CHAR20/170 (image 32); WSC (M.1001/4) to Eden, 4 October 1944, and (D.315/4) to Ismay, 31 December 1944, CHAR20/153/4 (image 4) and -/6 (image 15).

61. *WSC*/VII, p.664; Hugh Lunghi, 'Tribute to Sir Winston Churchill', 1 March 1997, CAC/LUNG/1/4.

62. Moran, diary, October 1944, n.d., *CSFS*, p.191.

63. Reynolds, *Command of History*, p.470.

64. Kimball, *Forged in War*, p.285.

65. Carlton, *Churchill*, p.116.

66. Rose, *Churchill*, p.312.

67. Eden, *Reckoning*, p.289.

68. WSC (T.1662/4) to FDR enclosing Stalin message, 23 August 1944, CHAR20/170 (image 79); *WSC*/VII, pp.923–927.

69. Khlevniuk, *Stalin*, p.244.

70. WSC (T.1634/4) to Eden, 18 August 1944, CHAR20/170 (image 43); WSC to CSC, 18 August 1944, *SFT*, p.503; Reynolds, *Command of History*, p.457; Addison, 'Three Careers', p.197.

71. WSC to the King, 15 October 1944, *WSC*/VII, p.1010.

72. WSC to CSC, 13 October 1944, *SFT*, p.506.

73. *WSC*/VIII, pp. 991–992.

74. Jenkins, *Churchill*, p.760.

75. WSC (Hearty 167) to Attlee, 17 October 1944, CAB120/165; Reynolds, *Command of History*, p.463.

76. For example, Herken, *Winning Weapon*, p.12; Bernstein, 'Quest for Security', p.1003.

77. Bernstein, 'Uneasy Alliance', pp.202, 214, 225, and 'Quest for Security', p.1003; Sherwin, *World Destroyed*, pp.7, 82–83; Farmelo, *Churchill's Bomb*, p.292; Dallek, *Lost Peace*, p.52; Kimball, *Juggler*, p.267; Kimball, 'The Bomb and the Special Relationship', pp.37–42.

78. WSC (M.117/4) to Eden, 14 February 1944, CHAR 20/152/2 (image 12).

79. Lindemann to WSC, 26 January 1945, PREM3/139/11A.

80. Halifax to Anderson, recounting meeting with Groves, 6 March 1945, CHAD IV/3/1.

81. *USAEC*/I, p.328.

82. Anderson to WSC, 26 January 1945 and Campbell telegrams ANCAM179, 188 and 191 to Anderson, 20 and 25 January 1945, CAB126/30.

Notes

83. Bush to Conant, 25 September 1944, NARA/RG227/OSRD/M1392/Bush-Conant file; Hershberg, *Conant,* p.210; Dallek, *Roosevelt,* p.471.

84. Lindemann to WSC, 26 January 1945, and WSC (M.(Arg)16/5) to Anderson, 16 February 1945, PREM3/139/11A; Goudsmit, *ALSOS,* p.71.

85. WSC (T.2068/4) to FDR, 8 November 1944, CHAR20/184/5 (image 6).

Chapter 6 Bolsheviks, Bombs and Bad Omens

1. WSC (T.4/5) to FDR, 1 January 1945, CHAR20/225/1 (image 2).

2. WSC (T.54/3) to FDR, 8 January 1945, CHAR20/225/1 (image 5).

3. Lascelles diary, 23 February 1945, in Hart-Davis, ed., *King's Counsellor,* p.297.

4. Sarah Oliver to CSC, 4 February 1945, in Churchill, *Keep on Dancing,* p.74.

5. Beevor, *Second World War,* p.674.

6. Kern, 'How "Uncle Joe" bugged FDR', pp.19–31.

7. Groves to Marshall, 30 December 1944, *FR1945/Malta/Yalta,* pp.383–384; Stimson diary, 31 December 1944.

8. US–UK plenary meeting, Anfa, 18 January 1943, *WSC/VII,* p.299.

9. See in general Bell, 'Singapore Strategy', pp.604–634.

10. WSC, *Grand Alliance,* p.551; Ismay, *Memoirs,* p.241.

11. WSC, *Hinge of Fate,* p.81.

12. Ramsden, *Churchill,* p.206; Keegan, 'Churchill's Strategy', pp.340–341.

13. WSC to Baldwin, 15 December 1924, CHAR18/4 (image 9); WSC memorandum to Chamberlain, 25 March 1939, PREM1/345.

14. Thorne, *Allies of a Kind,* p.724; WSC, *Gathering Storm,* p.372; WSC (M.745/1) to Ismay, 16 July 1941, PREM3/252/6A.

15. Toye, *Churchill's Empire,* p.218.

16. WSC (D(6a)7/4) to Ismay, 12 September 1944, PREM3/160/6; Thorne, *Allies of a Kind,* p.401.

17. WSC (T.566/3) to Arnold, 22 April 1943, CHAR20/110/74 (image 92).

18. WSC speech to US Congress, 19 May 1943, CHAR 9/162 (images 91–96).

19. Eden (PM/44/91) to WSC, 21 February 1944, PREM3/160/7; Eden (PM/45/205) to WSC, 26 May 1945, PREM3/252/6A; Brooke, 25 February 1944 and 18 May 1944, *War Diaries,* pp. 526, 548.

20. Ismay, *Memoirs,* p.374.

21. Leahy diary, 13 September 1944, LEAHY/6/p82; COS(Oct.)1st plenary meeting, 13 September 1944, PREM3/329/4; WSC (T.1786/4) to Curtin, 18 September 1944, PREM3/160/6.

22. Winant to Hopkins, 1 September 1944, *FR1944/Quebec,* pp.254–257.

23. CCS meeting, Quebec, 13 September 1944, *FR1944/Quebec,* pp.312–319; Ismay, *Memoirs,* p.374; Brooke, 14 September 1944, *War Diaries,* pp.592–593.

24. Frank, 'Ending the Pacific War', p.230.

25. FDR–WSC news conference, Casablanca, 24 January 1943, *PPP.*

26. For example, *HCD* Vol. 397, col. 699, 22 February 1944 and Vol. 407, cols 423–424, 18 January 1945.

27. WSC Note, 10 January 1944, PREM3/197/2; WSC (M.446/4) to Cadogan, 19 April 1944, CHAR 20/152/4 (image 16).

28. US-UK 2nd plenary meeting, 9 February 1945, PREM3/51/4.

29. WSC Note, Tehran, 29 November 1943, PREM3/136/12.

30. WSC (M.458/4) to Cadogan, 23 April 1944, CHAR20/152/4 (image 19); WSC (T.1828/A/4) to Stalin, 27 September 1944, CHAR20/184/3 (image 12).

31. Yalta agreement on the Far East, 11 February 1945, PREM3/397/4

32. Eden (PM/45/58) to WSC, 27 January 1945, PREM3/397/3; Eden to WSC, 28 January 1945, *Reckoning,* p.509; WSC (M.190/5) to Eden, 10 March 1945, CHAR20/209/3 (image 8).

33. Colville diary, 23 January 1945, *FOP*, p.555.

34. Reynolds, *Command of History*, p.467.

35. Declaration on Liberated Europe, 11 February 1945, *Avalon project*; WSC (JASON 376) to CSC, 12 February 1945, PREM4/78/1; WM(45)22nd conclusions, 19 February 1945, CAB65/51.

36. For a discussion of the Yalta controversy, see Harbutt, *Yalta,* pp.1–21.

37. Beria, *Beria My Father*, p.106; FDR (telegram 714) to WSC, 11 March 1945, CHAR20/212 (images 111–112).

38. Miscamble, *Roosevelt to Truman*, p.68, note 150.

39. FDR address to Congress, 1 March 1945, *PPP*.

40. WM(45)22nd conclusions, 19 February 1945, CAB65/51; Dalton, 23 February 1945, *War Diary*, p.836.

41. *HCD*, 27 February 1945, Vol. 408, cols 1283–1284.

42. Coote recollection, *WSC*/VII, p.664.

43. Gellately, *Stalin's Curse*, p.101; Reynolds, *World War to Cold War*, pp.242–248; Lunghi, 'Tribute to Churchill', 1 March 1997, CAC/LUNG/1/4.

44. WSC (M(S)31/4) to Eden, 16 January 1944, CHAR20/152/1 (image 5); Young, *Last Campaign*, p.14.

45. Moran diary, 11 February 1945, *CSFS,* p.232; Nicolson diary, 27 February 1945, in Nicolson, ed., *Diaries*/II, p.437.

46. Colville diary, 27 February 1945, *FOP*, p.565.

47. Zubok and Pleshakov, *Inside the Kremlin's Cold War*, pp.6, 17.

48. Muggeridge diary, 23 August 1950, in Bright-Holmes, ed., *Like It Was*, p.410.

49. Sarah Churchill to CSC, 7 February 1945, *WSC*/VII, p.1187.

50. WSC (M.(Arg.)16/5) to Anderson and Lindemann, 16 February 1945, PREM3/139/11A; Anderson (CANAM258) to Halifax, 23 February 1945, FO800/533/4.

51. Frankfurter to FDR, 8 September 1944, FDRL, Atomic-03/pp162–163; Stimson diary, 31 December 1944; Anderson to Eden, 1 February 1945, CAB126/30; Anderson to WSC, 7 March 1945, PREM3/139/11A.

52. WSC minute to Eden, draft and final, 25 March and 8 April 1945, PREM3/139/6.

53. Sherwin, *World Destroyed*, p.136, original emphasis.

54. King diary, 9 March 1945, MACK/Library and Archives Canada online.

55. WSC to WM(45)26th meeting, 6 March 1945, CAB65/51; WSC (T.260/5) to FDR, 8 March 1945, CHAR20/225/3 (image 3).

56. Colville diary, 23 February 1945, *FOP*, p.563.

57. WSC to WM(45)26th meeting, 6 March 1945, CAB65/51.

58. Colville diary, 28 February 1945, *FOP*, p.566.

59. WSC (T.250/5) to FDR, 8 March 1945, CHUR20/225/3 (images 3–5).

60. FDR (telegrams 714 and 718) to WSC, 11 March 1945, CHAR20/212 (images 111–112, 129); also WSC (M.255/5) to Eden, 24 March 1945, CHAR20/209/3 (image 16).

61. Hensel to Forrestal, notes on Cabinet meeting, 16 March 1945, in Millis, ed., *Forrestal Diaries*, pp.36–37.

62. Zubok and Pleshakov, *Kremlin's Cold War*, p.17; WSC, *HCD* Vol. 403, col. 492, 28 September 1944; WSC statement, WM(45)12th conclusions, 29 January 1945, and WM(45)22nd conclusions, 19 February 1945, CAB65/51.

63. Miscamble, *Roosevelt to Truman*, p.41, also pp.19, 31.

64. Maisky diary, 9 February 1943, in Gorodetsky, ed., *Maisky Diaries*, p.482; WSC, 'Epilogue', p.958; *WSC/VII*, p. 702.

65. Dalton diary, n.d., 1948, in Pimlott, ed., *Political Diary*, p.446.

66. FDR to Spellman, 3 September 1943, in Gannon, *Spellman Story*, pp.222–224; Dallek, *Roosevelt*, pp.541–543.

67. McNeal, *Stalin*, p.250.

68. WSC (T.371/5) to FDR, 31 March 1945, CHAR20/225/3 (image 14); FDR (telegram 732) to WSC, 31 March 1945, in Loewenheim *et al.*, eds, *Roosevelt and Churchill*, pp.695–696.

69. FDR to Stalin, 1 April 1945, *FR1945*/V, pp.194–197.

70. Ryan, *Anglo-America*, p.94.

71. WSC (T.379/5) to Stalin, 1 April 1945, CHAR20/225/4 (image 2).

72. Stalin to FDR, 9 April 1945, *FR1945*/V, pp.201–204; Stalin to WSC, text in WSC (T.444/5) to FDR, 11 April 1945, CHAR20/225/4 (image 10).

73. Anderson to Eden, 1 February 1945, and Eden reply, 7 February 1945, CAB126/30.

74. Anderson to WSC, 2 and 18 January 1945, PREM3/139/5 and -/6; Anderson-Joliot meeting, 23 February 1945, and Anderson (CANAM262) to Washington, 1 March 1945, CAB126/30.

75. Anderson to Halifax, 13 March 1945, CAB126/133; Ehrman, *Atomic Bomb*, p.175.

76. Cooper diary, 4 May 1945, in Norwich, ed., *Cooper Diaries*, p.364.

77. Anderson to Eden, 26 and 27 January 1945, and Eden response, 28 January 1945, Anderson (CANAM269) to Washington, 9 March 1945, Anderson to Eden, 14 March 1945, CAB126/30.

78. Eden to WSC, 20 March 1945, CAB126/183.

79. WSC to Eden, draft and final (M.262/5A), 25 March 1945, and WSC (M.312/5) to Eden, 8 April 1945, PREM3/139/6; Harvey, 19 April 1945, in Harvey, ed., *War Diaries*, pp.378–379.

80. WSC (T.374/5) to Eisenhower, 31 March 1945, CHAR20/225/3 (image 15); WSC (T.381/5 and T.406/5) to FDR, 1 and 5 April 1945, CHAR20/225/4 (images 3 and 6).

81. WSC to CSC, 13 April 1945, *SFT*, p.525.

82. Dallek, *Roosevelt*, p.528.

83. WSC telegram (T.298/5) to Roosevelt, 17 March 1945, CHAR20/225/3 (image 9).

84. WSC to George VI, 13 April 1945, CHAR20/193A-B (image 192–193).

85. Air miles in Reynolds, *Summits*, p.105.

86. Jenkins, *Churchill*, p.785.

87. WSC (M.315/5) to Eden, 8 April 1945, CHAR20/209 (image 14).

88. FDR (telegram 742) to WSC, 11 April 1945, *FR1945*/V, p.210.

89. Moran, diary, 15 October 1951, *CSFS*, p.347.

90. Truman to reporters, 13 April 1945, HSTL online.

91. Truman diary, 12 April 1945, *OTR*, p.16.

92. WSC (T.556/5) to Eden, 20 April 1945, CHAR20/225/4 (images 21–22).

93. WSC (T.675/5) to Stalin, 29 April 1945, CHAR20/225/4 (images 28–30).

94. Miscamble, *Roosevelt to Truman*, p.98.

95. Beevor, *Second World War*, p.725.

96. Moran, diary, 7 May 1945, *CSFS*, p.250.

97. WSC to CSC, 5 May 1945, *SFT*, p.530.

98. Channon diary, 8 May 1945, *Chips*, p.405.

99. WSC broadcast, 3:00 pm, 8 May 1945, *churchill.org*.

100. WSC speech, 10:30 pm, 8 May 1945, *churchill.org*.

101. WSC broadcast, BBC, 13 May 1945, *Listener*, 17 May 1945, pp.535–537.

102. Nicolson, 27 May 1945, *Diaries*/II, p.455; Hastings, *Finest Years*, p.577.

103. This sequencing had been agreed by the CCS at Yalta. WSC (T.223/5) to Dominions PMs, 26 February 1945, CHAR20/225/2 (image 5).

104. In general see Hobbs, *British Pacific Fleet*.

105. WSC (T.1216/5 and T.1217/5) to Australian and New Zealand PMs, 4 July 1945, CHAR20/225 (image 109); WSC (AMSSO 3698) to Marshall, 12 June 1945, CHAR20/221/18 (image 1), and WSC (DO135) to King, 16 June 1945, -/48 (images 1–2).

106. WSC (AMSSO 3698) to Marshall, 12 June 1945, CHAR20/221/18 (image 1); CCS report (COS 900/2) to Truman and Churchill, 23 July 1945, PREM3/430/4.

Chapter 7 Trinity and Potsdam

1. *USAEC*/I, pp.6, 374–376.

2. Lindemann memorandum, 28 January 1953, PREM11/565.

3. Clarke to Gorell Barnes, 25 April 1945, views of Lindemann, CAB126/48; Malloy, *Atomic Tragedy*, pp.93–95.

4. Chadwick to Anderson, 22 February 1945, CHAD/IV/2/1; Chadwick memorandum, 23 March 1945; Akers memorandum, 3 April 1945, TA(45)1st meeting, 9 April 1945, CAB98/47.

5. Halifax (ANCAM256) to Anderson, 20 April 1945, CAB126/183; Hyde Park agreement, 18 September 1944, PREM3/139/10.

6. Wilson (ANCAM264) to Anderson, 30 April 1945, CAB126/183.

Notes

7.   Yergin, *Shattered Peace*, p.110; Walker, *Prompt and Utter Destruction*, p.4.

8.   Truman, *Memoirs/I*, p.87; *USAEC/I*, pp.354–357; Offner, *Another Such Victory*, pp.62–64.

9.   Wilson obituary, *Times*, 1 January 1965.

10. Wilson (ANCAM259) to Anderson, 30 April 1945, CAB126/183.

11. Harvey, 13 March 1943, in *Diaries 1941–1945*, p.229.

12. Wilson to Stimson, 20 June 1945, PREM3/139/9.

13. Stimson diary, 25 June 1945.

14. Sherwin, *World Destroyed*, p.144.

15. Anderson to Eden, 14 May 1945, CAB126/183.

16. Anderson to WSC, 2 May 1945, PREM3/139/11A.

17. WSC (M.512/5), 21 May 1945, PREM3/139/11A.

18. Interim Committee, 1 June 1945, HSTL online.

19. Sherwin, *World Destroyed*, p.215.

20. Interim Committee, 21 June 1945, HSTL online.

21. Anderson to Churchill, 29 June 1945, PREM3/139/8A.

22. Wilson (ANCAM294 and 298) to Anderson, 22 June 1945, CAB126/146, and 23 June 1945, CAB126/188.

23. Halifax/Wilson (ANCAM313) to Anderson, 28 June 1945, CAB126/146.

24. Anderson to WSC, 29 June 1945, separate minutes, PREM3/139/8A and 11A; Rickett to Anderson, 28 June 1945, and Anderson annotated response, 29 June 1945, CAB126/188; Anderson (CANAM343) to Halifax/Wilson, 30 June 1945, CAB126/46.

25. Anderson to WSC, 29 June 1945, approved by WSC 2 July 1945, PREM3/139/8A and 11A.

26. WSC, 'Mass Effects in Modern Life', *Strand*, 1925, reprinted May 1931.

27. Anderson (CANAM350) to Halifax/Wilson, 2 July 1945, CAB126/146.

28. CPC(45)3rd meeting, 4 July 1945, CAB126/146.

29. FO memorandum, n.d. November 1945, CHAD/I/15/I.

30. Taylor, *English History*, p.601; Gilbert, *Churchill and America*, p.362.

31. Hymans, 'Britain and Hiroshima', pp.769–770.

32. Burk, *Old World, New World*, p.514.

33. *HCD*, Vol. 413, col. 79, 16 August 1945.

34. Ehrman, *Atomic Bomb*, pp.256–258.

35. *BAE*, pp.370–371.

36. WSC (M.312/5) to Eden, 8 April 1945, PREM3/139/6.

37. Aage Bohr memorandum, 25 June 1945, BOHR/6.2.

38. Hymans, 'Britain and Hiroshima', p.787; *BAE*, p.381; Hastings, *Nemesis*, p.496

39. Clark, *Greatest Power*, p.72.

40. Farmelo, *Churchill's Bomb*, p.286.

41. See Chapter 2, note 87.

42. Lindemann memorandum, 28 January 1953, PREM11/565.

43. *HCD* Vol. 413, col. 78, 16 August 1945.

44. Farmelo, *Churchill's Bomb*, p. 292.

45. WSC to Eden, (T.771/5) 5 May 1945, (T.874/5) 11 May 1945, and (T.891/5) 13 May 1945, CHAR20/225 (images 73, 79, and 81); Roberts, *Stalin's Wars*, pp.268–270.

46. WSC (T.876/5, T.895/5, T.982/5 and T.1027/5) to Truman, 11, 12, 21 and 31 May 1945, CHAR20/225 (images 79–80, 88, 90); Reynolds, *Command of History*, p.470.

47. WSC (T.515/5) to Truman, 18 April 1945, CHAR20/225/4 (image 16).

48. WSC (T.754/5) to Eden, 4 May 1945, CHAR20/225/5 (images 71–72).

49. Truman to Eleanor Roosevelt, 10 May 1945, and diary, 19 May 1945, *OTR,* pp.21–22, 31l; Truman (telegram 70) to WSC, 12 June 1945, CHAR20/221 (images 21–22); WSC, *Triumph and Tragedy*, p.525; Carlton, *Churchill*, p.138.

50. For example, WSC (T.876/5) to Truman, 11 May 1945, CHAR20/225/5 (image 12); WSC (T.1034/5) to Truman, 1 June 1945, CHAR20/225/6 (image 2).

51. On this see Edmonds, 'Yalta and Potsdam', p.208; Walker, *Prompt and Utter Destruction*, p.18.

52. Stimson diary, 15 May 1945.

53. Bird and Sherwin, *American Prometheus*, p.304.

54. Reynolds, *World War to Cold War*, p.239.

55. Leahy diary, 4 June 1945, LEAHY/6/p92; WSC (D149/5) to Ismay, 9 June 1945, CHAR20/209/6 (image 5).

56. Brooke, 13 May 1945, *War Diaries*, p.690.

57. Lascelles diary, 21 May 1945, in Hart-Davis ed., *King's Counsellor*, p.327.

58. Hastings, *Finest Years*, p.583.

59. JPS report, 'Operation Unthinkable', 22 May 1945, CAB120/691.

60. Brooke, 24 May 1945, *War Diaries*, and later annotations, pp.693–694; Ismay to Churchill, enclosing COS comments, 8 June 1945, CAB120/691.

61. WSC to Ismay, 10 June 1945, CAB120/691; Brooke, 11 June 1945, *War Diaries*, p.697.

62. Lukacs, *Churchill*, p.45; Beevor, *Second World War*, p.762.

63. WSC (D.145/5) to Ismay, 27 May 1945, CHAR20/209/5 (image 16); WSC (D.160/5) to Ismay, 1 July 1945, CHAR20/209/6 (image 16).

64. JPS revised report, 11 July 1945, CAB120/691.

65. It was briefly reopened in August 1946 at a moment of acute Anglo–Soviet tension. Dilks, *Churchill and Company*, p.222.

66. Moran, diary, 2 September 1953, *CSFS*, p.467; Colville diary, 1 January 1953, *FOP*, p.658.

67. Roberts, *Stalin's Wars*, pp.270–272.

68. Eden diary, 4 July 1945, *Reckoning*, p.544.

69. WSC (T.1210/5) to Truman, 3 July 1945, CHAR20/225 (image 109); WSC (M.676/5) to Cadogan, 5 July 1945, CHAR20/209/6 (image 17); Raczynski, *In Allied London*, p.296.

70. WSC (T.1195/5) to Mikolajczyk, 26 June 1945, CHAR20/225/6 (image 15).

71. Truman diary, 16 July 1945, *OTR*, p.52.

72. Moran, diary, 20 July 1945, *CSFS*, p.277.

73. Mallaby, *From My Level*, p.51.

74. WSC (T.1147/5) to Dominion PMs, 16 June 1945, CHAR20/225 (image 103).

75. Truman diary, 16 July 1945, *OTR*, p.50

76. Mary Churchill to CSC, 16 July 1945, in Soames, *Daughter's Tale*, p.449.

77. On this delineation see Lukacs, *Churchill*, pp.22–24.

78. Hayter, *Double Life*, pp.75–76; Cadogan to Theodosia, 18 July 1945, in Dilks, ed., *Diaries of Sir Alexander Cadogan*, p.765; Eden, *Reckoning*, p.414.

79. Eden diary, 17 July 1945, *WSC*/VIII, p.65; Moran, diary, 9 February 1945, *CSFS*, p.227.

80. WSC, *Triumph and Tragedy*, pp.272–273.

81. DeGroot, *Bomb*, p.62.

82. Frisch memorandum, 16 July 1945, CAB126/250; Chadwick to Anderson, 23 July 1945, CHAD/IV/12/5; Ham, *Hiroshima-Nagasaki*, p.223.

83. Bird and Sherwin, *American Prometheus*, p.309

84. Ham, *Hiroshima-Nagasaki*, p.225.

85. Stimson diary, 17 July 1945.

86. WSC, *Triumph and Tragedy*, p.552.

87. Truman to Bess, 18 July 1945, in Ferrell, ed., *Dear Bess*, p.519.

88. Truman diary, 17 July 1945, *OTR*, p.53.

89. See in general Frank, *Downfall*.

90. For example, Truman to Congress, 16 April 1945, *PPP*, and Truman statement, 8 May 1945, *PPP*.

91. WSC note, 18 July 1945, PREM3/430/8.

92. WSC–Stalin meeting, 18 July 1945, PREM3/430/6.

93. Truman diary, 18 July 1945, *OTR*, pp.53–54.

94. Stimson diary, 21 July 1945.

95. Truman diary, 25 July 1945, *OTR*, p.55.

96. Stimson diary, 22 July 1945; Bundy, 'Remembered Words', pp.56–57.

97. WSC (M.Ter.11/5) to Eden, 23 July 1945, CHAR20/209/6 (image 20).

98. WSC, *Triumph and Tragedy*, p.553.

99. Truman diary, 7 July 1945, *OTR*, p.49; Craig and Radchenko, *Atomic Bomb*, pp.79–80.

100. Handy to Spaatz, 25 July 1945, *dannen.com*.

101. Brooke, 17 July 1945, *Diaries*, p.706.

102. *WSC*/VIII, p.70.

103. Groves, *Now It Can Be Told*, p.265.

104. Handy to Spaatz, 25 July 1945, *dannen.com*.

105. Truman diary, 25 July 1945, *OTR*, p.55.

106. Stimson to Truman, 2 July 1945, *nuclearfiles.org*; Walker, *Prompt and Utter Destruction*, p.44; Malloy, *Atomic Tragedy*, p.119.

107. WSC, *Triumph and Tragedy*, p.553.

108. *HCD* Vol. 413, col. 79, 16 August 1945.

109. Groves to Stimson, 18 July 1945, *gatewaycoalition.org*, received in Potsdam 21 July 1945.

110. The accepted figure is $2 billion – or $24 billion in 2010 terms. Ham, *Hiroshima-Nagasaki*, p.74.

111. Moran, diary, 23 July 1945, *CSFS*, pp.280–81.

112. Brooke, 23 July 1945, original emphasis, and later commentary, *War Diaries*, pp.709–710.

Chapter 8 Heavy Metal, Iron Curtain

1. Note of WSC–Truman meeting, 18 July 1945, PREM3/139/11A; Stimson diary, 17 July 1945; Lindemann to WSC, 12 July 1945, PREM3/139/9.
2. Cunningham diary, 23 July 1945, *WSC*/VIII, p.90.
3. Montefiore, *Stalin*, p.442.
4. WSC, *Triumph and Tragedy*, pp.579–580.
5. Gordin, *Red Cloud*, p.9.
6. Hastings, *Secret War*, pp.524–535; Holloway, *Stalin and the Bomb*, pp.87–89; Montefiore, *Stalin*, p.441.
7. Dallek, *Lost Peace*, p.122; *USAEC*/I, p.388.
8. Malloy, *Atomic Tragedy*, p.10.
9. Truman diary, 16 July 1945, *OTR* p.49; *USAEC*/I, p.384.
10. Brown diary, 24 July 1945, in Miscamble, *Roosevelt to Truman*, p.201, note 116; Rotter, *Hiroshima*, pp.162–163; Hastings, *Nemesis*, p.436.
11. Potsdam proclamation, 26 July 1945, *atomicarchive.com*.
12. Ham, *Hiroshima-Nagasaki*, pps. 204–209, 237–239; Bernstein, 'Understanding the Atomic Bomb', p.250.
13. Truman diary, 25 July 1945, *OTR*, p.56.
14. On this point, Walker, *Prompt and Utter Destruction*, p.72.
15. Rhodes, *Atomic Bomb*, p.693.
16. Khrushchev, ed., *Memoirs of Nikita Khrushchev*, Vol. I, p.679; Glantz, *Soviet Strategic Offensive*, pp.138–140.
17. Mary Churchill diary, 26 July 1945, in Soames, *Daughter's Tale*, p.460.
18. Moran diary, 27 July and 8 August 1945, *CSFS* pps. 287, 289.
19. WSC–Stalin meeting, 18 July 1945, PREM3/430/6; Molotov to Chuev, 27 July 1972, Resis, ed., *Molotov Remembers*, p.59.
20. Pim recollection, *WSC*/VIII, p.111.
21. Truman to WSC, 30 July 1945, *WSC*/VIII, p.123.
22. Attlee to WSC, 1 August 1945, CHUR2/3 (images 46–48).
23. 'Mr. Churchill's regrets', *Times*, 27 July 1945.
24. Truman to Bess, 31 July 1945, in Ferrell, ed., *Dear Bess*, p.523.
25. Lascelles diary, 2 August 1945, *King's Counsellor*, pp.347–348; Nicolson diary, 8 August 1945, in Nicolson, ed. *Diaries*/III, p.31.
26. Gardner, *Churchill in His Time*, p.311.
27. Rotter, *Hiroshima*, p.1.
28. Truman statement, 6 August 1945, *PPP*.
29. Truman, *Year of Decisions*, p.420.

30. Truman radio address, 9 August 1945, *PPP*.

31. Truman radio address, 9 August 1945, *PPP*.

32. Hastings, *All Hell Let Loose*, p.650; Rotter, *Hiroshima*, p.146; Walker, *Prompt and Utter Destruction*, pps. 77, 80.

33. Miscamble, *Most Controversial Decision*, p.117.

34. Bernstein, 'Understanding the Atomic Bomb', pp.257–259; Malloy, *Atomic Tragedy*, p.4.

35. Colville to WSC, 1 August 1945, PREM3/139/9; Colville to Montague Browne, 6 October 1959, CHUR2/506 (image 84).

36. Lindemann to WSC, 26 July 1945, Colville telegram 278 to Rowan (Potsdam), 29 July 1945, PREM3/139/9.

37. *Times*, 7 August 1945.

38. FORD memorandum, 4 September 1945, CAB126/191; Hogg, *British Nuclear Culture*, p.59.

39. *Times*, 20 August 1945. In general, Willis, 'God and the Atom', pp.422–457.

40. Marshall, 'Atomic Bomb', p.458.

41. Hasegawa, *Racing the Enemy*, p.213.

42. DeGroot, *Bomb*, p.102.

43. CSC to Mary Churchill, 18 August 1945, in Soames, *Clementine Churchill*, pp.514–515.

44. Walker, *Prompt and Utter Destruction*, pp.84–85.

45. Hirohito broadcast, 15 August 1945 (Tokyo time), *mtholyoke.edu*.

46. Frank, 'Ending the Pacific War', p.245.

47. *HCD* Vol. 413, col. 79, 16 August 1945.

48. Stimson diary, 21 September 1945.

49. Walker, 'Decision to Use the Bomb', p.102, has described Byrnes as 'the most unabashed proponent of atomic diplomacy'.

50. WSC, *Triumph and Tragedy*, p.582.

51. WSC–Camrose meeting, 7 August 1945, *WSC/VIII*, p.119.

52. Holloway, *Stalin and the Bomb*, pp.114–118.

53. Gromyko, *Memoirs*, p.110.

54. Montefiore, *Stalin*, pps. 443, 445.

55. Resis, ed., *Molotov Remembers*, p.58.

56. Montefiore, *Stalin*, p.445; Holloway, *Stalin and the Bomb*, p.132.

57. Wheeler-Bennett, *Anderson*, pp.298–299.

58. *Times*, 11 August 1945.

59. Statement by UK scientists, n.d., August 1945, JRO/171/11.

60. *HCD* Vol. 413, cols 442–443, 21 August 1945.

61. Cited in Greenwood, *Britain and the Cold War*, p.13.

62. WSC to Anderson, 22 August 1945 and 7 September 1945, Anderson to WSC, 31 August 1945, CHUR2/3 (images 140–141 and 135–137).

63. *HLD* Vol. 137, col. 285–294, 16 October 1945.

64. WSC to CSC, 5 September 1945, *SFT*, p.535.

65. WSC to CSC, 24 September 1945, *SFT*, pp.540–541.

66. Harold Edwards recollection, *WSC*/VIII, pp.140–141.

67. Moran, diary, 2 September 1945, *CSFS*, p.294.

68. Attlee memorandum 28 August 1945, CAB130/2 GEN.75/1; Attlee, 'The Hiroshima Choice', *Observer*, 6 September 1959.

69. Attlee to WSC, and enclosure, 15 September 1945, CHUR2/3 (images 116–123); Greenwood, *Britain and the Cold War*, p.6.

70. WSC to Attlee, n.d., September 1945, CHUR2/3 (images 112–114).

71. Attlee to WSC, 4 October 1945, enclosing copy of letter to Truman as sent, 25 September 1945, CHUR2/3 (images 101–111).

72. Truman to Congress, 3 October 1945, *PPP*.

73. Truman news conference, 8 October 1945, *PPP*.

74. WSC *HCD*, Vol. 415, cols 1296–1300, 7 November 1945.

75. Churchill, *Tapestry*, p.91.

76. Thorpe, *Eden*, pp.335–336.

77. McCluer to WSC, and Truman handwritten note, 3 October 1945, CHUR2/230 (image 431).

78. WSC to Truman, 29 January 1946, CHUR2/158 (images 78–79).

79. King diary, 26 October 1945, MACK/LAC-online.

80. *WSC*/VIII, p.183.

81. See for example Harbutt, *Iron Curtain*; Muller, ed., *Churchill's Iron Curtain Speech*; Ramsden, *Churchill*, Chapter 4.

82. WSC, 'The Sinews of Peace', 5 March 1946, *winstonchurchill.org*; Ramsden, *Churchill*, pp.160, 168.

83. Washington Declaration, 15 November 1945, *nuclearfiles.org*, and CAB126/276.

84. UN General Assembly Resolution, 24 January 1946, *UN online archive*.

85. WSC, 'Sinews of Peace', 5 March 1946, *winstonchurchill.org*.

86. See on this point, Carlton, *Churchill*, p.153.

87. *Times*, 12 March 1946.

88. *New York Times*, 14 March 1946; Holloway, *Stalin and the Bomb*, p.153.

89. *WSC*/VIII, p.205; Addison, *Churchill*, p.223; Reynolds, *Command of History*, p.43; Steel, *Lippmann*, p.429.

90. WSC to Attlee, 7 March 1946, CHUR2/4 (images 7–9); Truman news conference, 8 March 1946, *PPP*; *WSC*/VIII, pp.205–206.

91. Moscow telegram 511 to Washington, 22 February 1946, *nsarchiv/coldwar*.

92. Truman to Byrnes (unsent), 5 January 1946, *OTR*, p.80.

93. Howard, 'Prophet of Détente', p.178.

94. *Times*, 6 March 1946; Bullock, *Bevin*, p.225.

95. *WSC*/VIII, p.208; Jenkins, *Churchill*, p.812.

96. Dutton, *Eden*, p.320; Reynolds, *World War to Cold War*, p.262; Thorpe, *Eden*, p.336.

97. Bracken to Beaverbrook, 16 October 1946, in Carlton, *Eden*, p.267.

Chapter 9 Warmongering and Peacemongering

1. *Times*, 8 May 1946; *HCD* Vol. 423, cols 2011–2033, 5 June 1946.

2. Cooper, 15 July 1946, in Norwich ed., *Diaries*, p.416.

3. Dutton, *Eden*, p.233.

4. Nicolson, 22 October 1946, *Diaries*/III, p.79.

5. Young, *Last Campaign*, p.32.

6. *HCD* Vol. 427, cols 1687–90, 23 October 1946; *WSC*/VIII, p.280.

7. *Times*, 30 October 1946.

8. WSC to Attlee, 10 October 1946, CHUR2/4 (images 51–53).

9. Pierre, *Nuclear Politics*, pp.88–89.

10. King diary, 26 October 1945, MACK/LAC-online; Moran diary, 24 October 1946, *CSFS*, p.316.

11. Moran, diary, 8 August 1946, *CSFS*, p.315.

12. Dallek, *Lost Peace*, p.212.

13. Jenkins, *Churchill*, p.834. Moran, in publishing his diary in 1966, controversially judged the oath to be relevant only during the lifetime of the patient.

14. Ladd to Hoover, 5 December 1947, FBI document release, *icij.org*.

15. King diary, 25–26 November 1947, MACK/LAC-online; *WSC*/VIII, pp.362–363.

16. Farmelo, *Churchill's Bomb*, p.339.

17. Acheson–Lilienthal Report, 16 March 1946, *fissilematerials.org*; Bohr to Oppenheimer, 17 April 1946, JRO/21/1.

18. Byrnes, *Speaking Frankly*, p.269.

19. *New York Times*, 19 March 1946; WSC to Attlee, 19 March 1946, *WSC*/VIII p.210; WSC to Baruch, 6 October 1946, CHUR2/210A-B (images 848–849); Colville, *Churchillians*, pp.86–88.

20. Bird and Sherwin, *American Prometheus*, p.343; Lilienthal diary, 19 March 1946, in Lilienthal, *Journal*/II, p.30.

21. Gordin, *Red Cloud*, p.52.

22. In general, Kearn, 'Baruch Plan', pp.41–67.

23. Holloway, *Stalin and the Bomb*, p.161; Craig and Radchenko, *Atomic Bomb*, pp.105–106; Notes on Stalin–Kurchatov meeting, 25 January 1946, *wilsoncenter.org*.

24. Herken, *Winning Weapon*, pp.153, 170.

25. Baruch address, UNAEC, 14 June 1946, *atomicarchive.com*; 'Atom Diplomacy and its Manoeuvres', *Pravda*, 14 July 1946, CAB126/220.

26. Gromyko statement, *BAS*, Vol. 2, Nos. 5–6 (September 1946), pp.11–18.

27. Zaloga, *Kremlin's Nuclear Shield*, pp.8–9, 13, 18; Holloway, *Stalin and the Bomb*, pp.133, 162; Gordin, *Red Cloud*, pp.160–161.

28. DeGroot, *Bomb*, p.123.

29. Kearn, 'Baruch Plan', pp.57–58.

30. Bernstein, 'Quest for Security', p.1044.

31. Baruch to Bush, 22 December 1946, BUSH/10/2; Baruch to Oppenheimer, 15 January 1947, JRO/19/7.

32. DeGroot, *Bomb*, p.123; Craig and Radchenko, *Atomic Bomb*, pp.125–130.

33. Truman diary, 16 March 1946, *OTR*, p.87; Holloway, *Stalin and the Bomb*, p.166.

34. Zubok, 'Stalin and the Nuclear Age', p.51.

35. WSC to Eden, 12 December 1951, PREM11/1682.

36. Truman, *Memoirs*/II, p.11. Also on this point, Harbutt, *Iron Curtain*, p.177.

37. Cited in Herken, *Winning Weapon*, p.178

38. WSC to Clarke, 28 March 1948, *WSC*/VIII, p.404.

39. Truman address, 12 March 1947, *Avalon Project online*; Marshall, Harvard address, 5 June 1947, *OECD online*.

40. The literature on the origins of the Cold War is vast and no attempt will be made here to summarize it. However, four works in particular have been relied on in producing a distillation of events, namely: Greenwood, *Britain and the Cold War*; Gaddis, *Cold War*; Reynolds, *World War to Cold War*; Roberts, *Stalin's Wars*. In addition, on the left-turn, see Kramer, 'Stalin', pp.264–294.

41. Graebner, *Churchill*, p.4.

42. WSC to Truman, 27 September 1947, CHUR2/158 (image 55).

43. *HCD* Vol. 481, col. 1331, 30 November 1950.

44. Atomic Energy Act (Public Law 595), 1946, *osti.gov*; Gordin, *Red Cloud*, p.41.

45. Williams, *Prime Minister Remembers*, pp.109–110, 118–119.

46. Hennessy, *Cabinets and the Bomb*, p.43; Clark and Wheeler, *Origins of Nuclear Strategy*, p 10.

47. Portal memorandum, 31 December 1946, PREM8/911; GEN.163(47)1st meeting, Confidential Annex, 8 January 1947, CAB130/16; Hennessy, *Cabinets and the Bomb*, pp.40–59.

48. Bevin to Attlee, 1 March 1948, ATTLEE/dep.68/fol7.

49. *USAEC*/II, p.55.

50. WSC to Eisenhower, 12 January 1955, CHUR6/3A/9–12 (images 1–4).

51. Reynolds, *Command of History*, pp.482–483.

52. Truman to WSC, 14 October 1947, CHUR2/158 (images 53–54).

53. *HCD* Vol. 446, col. 560, 23 January 1948.

54. *HCD*, Vol. 448, col. 1245, 10 March 1948 and 17 March 1948, col. 2137; WSC, WSC, 'The Highroad of the Future', *Collier's Magazine*, 4 January 1947, p.64, CHUR2/21A–B (image 394); WSC speech, 9 October 1948, CHUR5/21A–B (image 344).

55. Douglas to Lovett, 17 April 1948, *FR1948*/II, pp.895–896.

56. US Department of Energy, Declassified Stockpile Data, 1945–1994, *osti.gov*.

57. *Times*, 2 June 1948.

58. Greenwood, *Britain and the Cold War*, p.63.

59. *Times*, 12 July 1948; WSC to Montgomery, 18 July 1948, *WSC*/VIII, p.421, note 2; WSC to Eisenhower, 27 July 1948, CHUR2/148 (images 361–362).

60. Soames, *Clementine*, p.536.

61. Boothby, *My Yesterday*, p.212.

62. WSC to Eden, 12 September 1948, CHUR2/68 (images 1–6).

63. *HCD* Vol. 484, col. 208W, 21 February 1951; Ball, 'Military nuclear relations', pp.442–445.

Notes

64. Ball, 'Military nuclear relations', and more generally Young, 'Anglo-American (Mis) Understandings', pp.1133–1167.

65. WSC to Eden, 12 September 1948, CHUR2/68 (images 1–6).

66. *Times*, 11 October 1948.

67. WSC speech, 9 October 1948, CHUR5/21A-B (images 342–349). On the three circles, see Toye, *Churchill's Empire*, pp.263–264.

68. Editorial, *Times*, 11 October 1948; Dutton, *Eden*, p.321.

69. Sarah Churchill to WSC, 11 October 1948, CHUR1/45 (image 123)

70. *Times*, 22 October 1948; Bardens, *Churchill in Parliament*, p.328; BBC Monitoring Report 3139, 14 October 1948, CHUR2/69A–B (images 189–190).

71. *Times*, 11 October 1948.

72. *HCD* Vol. 457, col. 257, 28 October 1948.

73. Gomulka memorandum, 14 November 1945, *Wilsoncenter,org*; Craig and Radchenko, *Atomic Bomb*, p.96.

74. *Times*, 25 September 1946.

75. Gromyko, *Memoirs*, pp.391–392.

76. Nenni diary, July 1952, in Nenni, *Tempo di Guerra Freda* p.537. My thanks to Geoffrey Warner for pointing out this source.

77. Holloway, *Stalin and the Bomb*, pp.250, 271; Khlevniuk, *Stalin*, p.293.

78. Trachtenberg, 'A "Wasting Asset"', p.5; Gaddis, *Strategies of Containment*, p.4.

79. Hamby, *Man of the People*, p.444. There is some evidence that Truman reprised the Berlin B-29 ploy in 1950–1951 during the Korean War. Dingman, 'Atomic Diplomacy', pp.50–91.

80. Lilienthal dairy, 21 July 1948, *Journals*/II, p.391; Truman to WSC, 10 July 1948, CHUR2/158 (images 47–49).

81. Forrestal diary, 12 November 1948, *Diaries*, pp.523–524; WSC *HCD*, Vol. 459, col. 721, 10 December 1948; WSC to Montgomery, unsent letter, February 1949, CHUR2/31 (image 110).

82. WSC to Truman, 8 November 1948, *WSC*/VIII, pp.444–445; WSC to Barchard, 6 March 1949, CHUR2/265 (images 29–30).

83. WSC speech, 25 March 1949, *WSC*/VIII, p.463.

84. Sulzberger to WSC, 22 March 1949, CHUR2/266 (image 17); Reston, *Deadline*, pp.179–180.

85. Lindemann to WSC, 13 March 1949, CHUR2/81A–B (images 184–188).

86. WSC speech, 31 March 1949, CHUR5/24A–E (images 574–602); *Christian Science Monitor*, 1 April 1949.

87. *WSC*/VIII, p.467; *Daily Herald, Times* and *Manchester Guardian,* 1 April 1949.

88. CSC to WSC, n.d., early April 1949, *SFT*, p.552; Truman to WSC, 2 February 1949, CHUR2/266 (image 243).

89. WSC to Baruch, n.d., March 1949 (unsent), CHUR2/210A–B (images 1053–1055); *New York Times*, 22 March 1949.

90. The original signatories were the USA, UK, Canada, France, the Netherlands, Belgium, Luxembourg, Norway, Italy, Portugal, Iceland and Denmark.

91. Gilbert, *Churchill and America*, p.389.

92. Truman remarks, 6 April 1949, HSTL online.

93. WSC to Truman, 29 June 1949, and Truman reply, 2 July 1949, CHUR2/158 (images 16–17, 19–20).

94. US Department of Energy, Declassified Stockpile Data, 1945–1994, *osti.gov.*

95. Roberts, *Stalin's Wars*, p.355.

96. *HCD* Vol. 464, cols 2029–2031, 12 May 1949.

97. WSC to Attlee, 24 July 1949, CHUR2/29A-B (images 273–277); also WSC memorandum, 9 March 1949, and WSC to Attlee, 27 May 1949 (images 102–119, 191–192); WSC to Attlee, 21 July 1948, CHUR2/68A-B (images 162–163).

Chapter 10 To the Summit

1. Burr, ed., 'US Intelligence', *nsarchiv/nukevault.*

2. Truman statement, 23 September 1949, *PPP.*

3. Nicolson, 24 September 1949, *Diaries*, p.175.

4. *Times*, 26 September 1949; Holloway, *Stalin and the Bomb*, pp.267–269; Gordin, *Red Cloud*, p.244.

5. Montefiore, *Stalin*, p.533.

6. DeGroot, *Bomb*, p.147.

7. Truman statement, 31 January 1950, *PPP.*

8. Hamby, *Truman*, p.526.

9. McMahon to Truman, 21 November 1949, MJS/65/5.

10. Rhodes, *Dark Sun*, p.404.

11. Ayers diary, 4 February 1950, in Ferrell, ed., *Truman in the White House*, pp.340–341.

12. DeGroot, *Bomb*, pp.171–172.

13. Lilienthal diary, 31 January 1950, *Journals*/II, p.633.

14. Kennan note, 18 November 1949, JRO/43/15; Bradley/JCS memorandum, 13 January 1950, *FR1950*/I, pp.503–511.

15. *Times*, 2 February 1950.

16. *Illustrated London News*, 4 February 1950.

17. Cantaur, letter, *Times*, 24 February 1950.

18. WSC speech, 14 February 1950, CHUR5/32A–C (images 567–579).

19. *Times*, 15 February 1950.

20. Swinton to WSC, 18 February 1950, CHUR2/101A–B (images 497–498); *Times*, 16 and 17 February 1950; Young, *Last Campaign*, pp.29–31.

21. Nicolson to Vita Sackville-West, 16 February 1950, *Diaries*/III, p.186.

22. Addison, *Churchill*, pp. 225, 231; Farmelo, *Churchill's Bomb*, p.355. Also Young, *Last Campaign*, p.29; Carlton, *Churchill*, p.162; Best, *Churchill*, p.289; Rose, *Literary Churchill*, p.404; Jenkins, *Churchill*, p.834.

23. 'Parley at the Summit', *Spectator*, 17 February 1950, p.1; Trachtenberg, '"Wasting Asset"', p.21.

24. Smuts–McGhee meeting, 7 March 1950, *FR1950*/I, p.189; *Times*, 6 February 1950.

25. Beaverbrook to Bracken, 13 December 1950, in Cockett, ed., *My Dear Max*, p.117.

26. See note 22.

27. WSC to Lascelles, 27 February 1950, CHUR2/171 (images 176–178); Editorial, *Economist*, 4 March 1950.

28. *HCD* Vol. 472, cols 1295, 1297–1298, 16 March 1950.

29. Younger diary, 6 July 1950, in Warner, ed., *Midst of Events*, pp.26–28; WSC, *Triumph and Tragedy*, p.545.

30. Younger diary, 8 April 1950, in Warner, ed., *Midst of Events*, p.11; *HCD* Vol. 473, cols 201–202, 28 March 1950.

31. See on this point, Carlton, *Churchill*, p.153

32. *Times*, 28 August 1950.

33. *Times*, 23 February 1950; Roberts, *Stalin's Wars*, p.329.

34. NSC-68, 7 April 1950, *fas.org*.

35. See Larres, *Churchill's Cold War*, pp.127–128, 132–137.

36. WSC to Attlee, 24 May 1950, CHUR2/29A–B (images 338–340).

37. Greenwood, *Britain and the Cold War*, p.85; Bennett, *Six Moments of Crisis*, p.15.

38. R. H. Scott, note, n.d, SCOTT.Acc.8181, box 2; Hamby, *Man of the People*, p.540.

39. In general on these themes see Hennessey, *Britain's Korean War*; Ruane, 'Issue of "Limited War" with China'.

40. WSC *HCD*, Vol. 477, cols. 495–496, 5 July 1950; WSC speech, London, 4 July 1950, CHUR5/36A–C (images 3–20); *WSC/VIII*, p.535; Nicolson, 28 June 1950, reporting Butler on shadow Cabinet meeting, *Diaries/III*, p.191.

41. Chen Jian, 'Name of Revolution', p.104.

42. WSC, *HCD* Vol. 481, cols 1332–1335, 30 November 1950.

43. WSC, *HCD* Vol. 477, cols 495, 501–503, 5 July 1950.

44. WSC, *HCD* Vol. 478, cols 699–714, 27 July 1950.

45. *Times*, 28 July 1950.

46. Nicholson, 28 July 1950, *Diaries/III*, p.192.

47. Macmillan, 12 September 1950, *Diaries/I*, p.19.

48. Macmillan, 12 September 1950, *Diaries/I*, pp.3–4, 6 August 1950.

49. WSC to Attlee and enclosure, 6 August 1950, CHUR2/28 (images 187–191).

50. Lindemann Note, August 1950, CHUR2/28 (images 192–193).

51. *HCD* Vol. 450, col. 2117, 12 May 1948.

52. Hennessey, *Cabinets and the Bomb*, p.69; Cathcart, *Test of Greatness*, p.89.

53. WSC press release, n.d., August 1950, *WSC/VIII*, p.538.

54. *Reynold's News*, 2 July 1950; Attlee to Tom Attlee, 29 September 1950, ATTLEE/ms.Eng.c.4794.

55. *HCD* Vol. 478, col. 988, 12 September 1950.

56. Pak, *Korea and the United Nations*, pp.213–214.

57. Dallek, *Lost Peace*, p.318.

58. Ruane, 'Issue of "Limited War"', pp.62–65; Stueck, *Rethinking the Korean War*, p.125.

59. *HCD* Vol. 481, cols 1332–34, 30 November 1950.

60. Truman news conference, 30 November 1950, HSTL online; Macmillan, 30 November 1950, *Diaries*/I, p.33; Hamby, *Man of the People*, p.552.

61. Labour petition, and Dalton to Attlee, 30 November 1950, ATTLEE/dep.114/fol.154–158; *HCD* Vol. 481, col. 1440, 30 November 1950; *Times*, 1 December 1950.

62. Attlee to WSC and enclosure, 3 December 1950, CHUR/2/28 (images 263–266).

63. Attlee to WSC and enclosure, 3 December 1950, CHUR/2/28 (images 263–266).

64. *ID*/I, p.406.

65. Hennessey, *Cabinets and the Bomb*, p.77.

66. Brinkley, *Acheson*, p.24; BJSM Washington (ANCAM263) to Cabinet Office, 8 February 1950, and Bevin (CANAM127) to BJSM, 9 February 1950, CAB126/305.

67. *HCD* Vol. 472, col. 71, 6 March 1950; Williams, *Prime Minister Remembers*, p.118.

68. Goodman, *Nuclear Bear*, pp.63–64.

69. WSC to Lindemann, 3 December 1953, CAB21/3074; *ID*/I, p.407.

70. Macmillan, 6 December 1950, *Diaries*/I, pp.34–35.

71. *Washington Post*, 14 December 1950; Joe Alsop to Slessor, 11 December 1950, and to Salisbury, 28 December 1950, ALSOP/6/2; Macmillan, 20 December 1950, *Diaries*/I, p.37.

72. Slessor to Joe Alsop, 28 December 1950, ALSOP/7/4.

73. Brandon, *Special Relationships*, p.68.

74. Washington telegram 3330, 7 December 1950, and Dixon to Bevin, 8 December 1950, FO371/83019/13G.

75. COS(50)206th meeting, 14 December 1950, DEFE4/38.

76. *Times*, 9 December 1950.

77. *HCD* Vol. 482, cols 1357–1370, 14 December 1950.

78. *HCD* Vol. 482, cols 1357–1370, 14 December 1950.

79. WSC to CSC, 19 December 1950, CHUR/1/47 (images 210–213).

80. WSC to CSC, 25 December 1950 (images 223–228).

81. WSC to MacArthur, 27 December 1950, CHUR/2/173 (image 236).

82. Macmillan, 11 December 1950, *Diaries*/I, p.35; *HCD* Vol. 481, col. 1336, 30 November 1950.

83. WSC to Attlee, 8 February 1951, CHUR2/28 (image 257).

84. Jenkins, *Churchill*, pp.836–837.

85. Attlee to WSC, 9 February 1951, CHUR2/28 (image 256).

86. WSC to Attlee, 12 February 1951, CHUR2/28 (image 252), WSC to Truman, 12 February 1951 (images 274–277), Attlee to WSC, 14 February 1951 (image 251).

87. *HCD* Vol. 484, cols 623–641, 15 February 1951.

88. Ruane, *European Defence Community*, pp.4–5.

89. *HCD* Vol. 484, cols 623–641, 15 February 1951; *WSC*/VIII, p.590.

90. Truman to WSC, 16 February 1951, CHUR2/28 (images 269–270).

91. Attlee to WSC, 22 February 1951, CHUR2/28 (images 253–254).

92. Truman to WSC, 24 March 1951, CHUR2/28 (image 268).

93. WSC to Truman, 11 April 1951, CHUR2/28 (image 267).

94. Miller, *Plain Speaking*, p.287.

95. WSC to Truman, 11 April 1951, CHUR2/28 (image 267).

96. *WSC*/V III, p.605.

97. *HCD* Vol. 487, cols 2155–2168, 10 May 1951.

98. Macmillan, 25 April 1951, in Catterall ed., *Diaries*/I, p.67.

99. *Times*, 26 April 1951.

100. *Daily Mirror*, 9 October 1951.

101. Amery diary, 28 September 1951, in Toye, *Churchill's Empire*, p.282.

102. Macmillan, 20 October 1951, in Catterall ed., *Diaries*/I, p.109; Macmillan, *Tides of Fortune*, p.360.

103. Young, *Last Campaign*, p.39.

104. *Times*, 9, 10 and 24 October 1951.

105. Press release, 19 October 1951, CHUR2/221/64 (image 112); *Daily Mirror*, 25 October 1951.

106. Macmillan, *Tides of Fortune*, pp.360–362; King to WSC, n.d., May 1952, CHUR2/221 (image 186).

107. Cited in Hennessy, *Having It So Good*, p.185.

Chapter 11 Atomic Angles

1. Colville diary, *FOP*, p.633.

2. Jenkins, *Churchill*, p.843.

3. Colville diary, *FOP*, p.632.

4. WSC in Hennessy, *Prime Minister*, p.178; Soames, *Clementine*, p.566.

5. Jenkins, 'Churchill', p.492.

6. WSC, *HCD* Vol. 493, col. 79, 6 November 1951. Historians who question Churchill's motives include Carlton, *Churchill*, pp.170, 187; Hennessy, *Having It So Good*, p.134; and John Young, 'Cold War and Détente', p.75.

7. Addison, *Churchill*, p.246.

8. Fort, *Prof*, p.318.

9. Lindemann to WSC, 22 October 1951, LIND/A56/3–5.

10. Birkenhead, *Prof*, p.279.

11. WSC to Bowra, 28 October 1951, LIND/A56/6.

12. Lindemann to WSC, 1 August 1950, CHUR2/28 (images 228–230); Lindemann to Attlee, 6 March 1951, PREM8/1556; *HLD* Vol. 172, cols 682–707, 5 July 1951.

13. Lindemann to WSC, 17 June 1951, CHUR2/113A–B (images 83–84); Lindemann to WSC, 6 November 1951 and 12 February 1952, LIND/J110/55 and J122/340–348.

14. Ava Waverley notes, 1951, WAVE/ms.Eng.c.6661.

15. Moran diary, 1 June 1952, *CSFS*, p.387; Cynthia Jebb diary, 21 February 1947 and 14 January 1948, in Jebb, ed., *Diaries*, pp.33, 75; Wheeler-Bennett, *Anderson*, pp.353–354.

16. Butler, *Art of the Possible*, pp.156–157.

17. Butler memorandum, C(51)1, 31 October 1951, CAB129/48; Butler, *HCD* Vol. 493, cols 191–196, 7 November 1951; Cairncross, *Years of Recovery*, pp.220–225; Moran diary, 1 and 4 January 1952, *CSFS*, pp.352–353.

18. *ID*/I, pp.405–407.

19. Lindemann to WSC, 13 November 1951, PREM11/292.

20. WSC to Lindemann, 15 November 1951, PREM11/292.

21. *HCD* Vol. 415, cols. 1299–1300, 7 November 1945.

22. WSC to Attlee, 6 and 10 October 1946, CHUR2/4 (images 64–67 and 51–53).

23. See CHUR2/28 (images 236–250), February 1951.

24. Lindemann to WSC and enclosures, 21 November 1951, PREM11/292; Acheson testimony to JCAE, 12 May 1947, *FR1947*/I, pp.806–811.

25. Lindemann to WSC and enclosures, 21 November 1951, PREM11/292.

26. WSC to Lindemann, 14 December 1951, PREM11/292; WSC to Menzies, 27 December 1951, DEFE32/2.

27. WSC (M.140C/51) to Bridges, 8 December 1951, and Bridges response, 12 December 1951, PREM11/297; Moran diary, 31 December 1951, *CSFS*, p.352; ID/I, p.406.

28. *HCD* Vol. 494, cols 2591–2609, 6 December 1951; *Daily Telegraph*, 23 November 1951.

29. Colville diary, 25 November 1951, *FOP*, p.636.

30. Gordin, *Red Cloud*, pp.291–293; Arnold, *Britain and the H-Bomb*, p.16; Jones, 'Consultation over Use of the Atomic Bomb', pp.814–816.

31. Lloyd (UN) telegram 61, 3 December 1951, WSC (M.131C/51) to Eden, 5 December 1951, and Eden (PM.51/141) to WSC, 5 December 1951 (and WSC annotation, 7 December 1951), PREM11/1682.

32. Moran diary, 30 December 1951, *CSFS*, p.351.

33. Colville diary, *FOP*, p.637.

34. McCullough, *Truman*, p.1042.

35. Allison, *Ambassador*, p.181.

36. US press comment, 27 December 1951, FO371/97593/22; Young, *Last Campaign*, p.72.

37. Truman, *Years of Trial and Hope*, p.259.

38. Briefing paper D2–1b, December 1951, HSTL/PSF/General file, box 116.

39. Bohlen memorandum, 5 December 1951, NARA/RG59/Box 2911/641.61/12–551.

40. Rome telegrams 653 and 654, 29 November 1951, FO371/125000/1G; Cook, 'Sir John Slessor', p.46.

41. Eden (PM/52/3) to WSC, 6 January 1952, CHUR2/517A–B (images 145–146); US–UK talks, White House, 8 January 1952, *FR1952–54*/VI, p.784; Moran diary, 5 January 1952, *CSFS*, p.355.

42. Shuckburgh diary, January 1952, *DTS*, p.32.

43. Slessor Note, 23 December 1951, AIR75/25.

44. Lindemann to WSC, 31 December 1951, PREM11/291.

45. US–UK talks, White House, 7 January 1952, *FR1952–54*/VI, pp.763–766, and UK record, PREM11/161.

46. Lindemann to WSC, 7 January 1952, PREM11/291; *AEC*/II, pp.575–576.

47. WSC–McMahon meeting, 8 January 1952, PREM11/291; Moran diary, 8 January 1952, *CSFS*, p.359.

48. Young, 'English Airbases', p.1166; Paul, *Nuclear Rivals*, pp.189–194; Truman–Churchill communiqué, 9 January 1952, *FR1952–54*/VI, p.837.

49. Jones, 'Consultation over Use of the Atomic Bomb', p.814.

50. Moran diary, 9 January 1952, *CSFS*, p.361.

51. Churchill address to Congress, 17 January 1952, CHUR5/46A–C (images 74–77).

52. Lindemann–AEC–Pentagon meeting, 10 January 1952, FO371/99376/4G; Lindemann to WSC, 16 January 1952, and WSC annotation, PREM2/291.

53. COS brief for WSC, 19 December 1951, DEFE20/2, COS(71)763; Ball, 'Military Nuclear Relations', p.446; Paul, *Nuclear Rivals*, pp.166–188.

54. MOD (COS(E)92) to BJSM Washington, 24 August 1951, DEFE20/1.

55. Elliot telegrams ELL252 and 257 to MOD, 23–24 January 1952, DEFE20/1; *Daily Telegraph*, 23 November 1951.

56. *ID*/I, p.414.

57. Lovett obituary, *New York Times*, 8 May 1986.

58. WSC to CSC, 20 January 1952, *SFT*, p.563.

59. WSC–Truman talks, 5th plenary session, 18 January 1952, and WSC to Canadian Cabinet, 14 January 1952, PREM11/161.

60. Moran diary, 19 January 1952, *CSFS*, p.369.

61. Shuckburgh diary, January 1952, *DTS*, p.32.

62. Macmillan, 17 January 1952, *Diaries*/I, p.133.

63. WSC–Truman talks, 5th plenary session, 18 January 1952, PREM11/161.

64. Young, *Last Campaign*, p.85.

65. Truman desk diary, 27 January 1952, HSTL/PSF, Longhand Notes File, box 333.

66. Gaddis, *Strategies of Containment*, pp.145–146.

67. *Times* and *Manchester Guardian*, 18 January 1952; FO American (North) Department minutes, 23–25 January 1952 on press reaction, FO371/97529/20.

68. Richard Crossman, 'Churchill Comes to Washington', *New Statesman*, 19 January 1952.

69. Addison, *Churchill*, p.247; Hennessy, *Having It So Good*, p.185.

70. Lindemann to WSC, 19 February 1952, LIND/J122/338–340.

71. *HCD* Vol. 496, cols 964–982, 26 February 1952.

72. Nigel to Harold Nicolson, 3 March 1952, *Diaries*/III, p.222.

73. Colville diary, February 1952, *FOP*, p.652; Moran diary, 29 February 1952, *CSFS*, p.380.

74. Montague Browne, *Long Sunset*, p.127.

75. Lindemann to WSC, 4, 10 and 11 March 1952, LIND/J122/295–299, 283, 281; Birkenhead, *Prof*, p.305; Farmelo, *Churchill's Bomb*, p.387.

76. Colville diary, 16 and 22–23 March 1952, *FOP*, p.643.

77. WSC to Lindemann, 20 March 1952, PREM11/295.

78. Cathcart, *Test of Greatness*, p.172; Lindemann to WSC, 4 March 1952, LIND/J122/295–299.

79. Soames, *Clementine*, p.543.

80. WSC to Lindemann, 20 March 1952, PREM11/295.

81. Birkenhead, *Prof*, p.305.

82. WSC directive, 10 April 1952, CAB129/51, C(62)119.

83. Birkenhead, *Prof*, pp.279, 306.

84. Morrison, *Autobiography*, pp.192–193.

85. Lindemann to Attlee, 6 March 1951, PREM8/1556.

86. Farmelo, *Churchill's Bomb*, pp.366–372

87. Cathcart, *Test of Greatness*, pps. 22–24, 42–45; Hennessy, *Having It So Good*, pps. 153, 182.

88. A(52)1st meeting, 26 March 1952, CAB134/734.

89. *Times*, 18 February 1952; Lindemann to WSC, 18 February 1952, LIND/J122/344.

90. Morgan, *Peace and War*, p.297.

91. Colville to Crawley, 24 March 1952, FO371/99737/36G.

92. Cathcart, *Test of Greatness*, p.173.

93. A(52)1st meeting, 26 March 1952, CAB134/734.

Chapter 12 Hurricane Warning

1. Salisbury to WSC, 24 April 1952, CHUR2/198 (image 22); Cathcart, *Test of Greatness*, p.172.

2. *Times*, 15 May 1952.

3. Moyce obituary, *Independent*, 12 September 1996.

4. 'Defence Policy and Global Strategy' (GSP), D(52)26, 17 June 1952, and Defence Committee meeting, 9 July 1952, D(52)8th meeting, CAB131/12.

5. D(52)26, 17 June 1952, CAB131/12.

6. D(52)26, 17 June 1952, CAB131/12.

7. D(52)26, 17 June 1952, CAB131/12.

8. D(52)26, 17 June 1952, CAB131/12.

9. D(52)26, 17 June 1952, and Defence Committee meeting, 9 July 1952, D(52)8th meeting, CAB131/12.

10. Baylis and Stoddart, *British Nuclear Experience*, p.44; Colville diary, 20 June 1952, *FOP*, pp.651–652.

11. Brook to Attlee, 12 July 1951, PREM8/1547; 'Operation Hurricane', Ministry of Supply, Central Office of Information documentary, 1953.

12. Lindemann to WSC, 17 September 1952, and WSC annotation, 20 September 1952, LIND/J122/122–123.

13. Hennessy, *Having It So Good*, pp.182–183.

14. Alexander to WSC, 9 April 1952, PREM11/292.

15. DeGroot, *Bomb*, p.220.

16. Penney, BBC broadcast, 7 November 1952, AB16/543.

17. *Times*, 3 October 1952, and editorial, 4 October 1952; Hennessy, *Prime Ministers*, p.202.

18. *HCD* Vol. 505, cols 1268–1271, 23 October 1952; *Times*, 24 October 1952.

19. Morgan to WSC (and enclosure), 18 October 1952, PREM11/292; Cathcart, *Test of Greatness*, pp.261–265.

20. *ID*/I, pp.449–450.

21. AEC press release 56, 16 November 1952, FO371/99748/92.

22. *New York Times*, 17 November 1952; *Times*, 17 November 1952.

23. *USAEC*/III, p.3 Arnold, *H-Bomb*, p.17.

24. *WSC*/VIII, p.772.

25. Farmelo, *Churchill's Bomb*, pp.388–389; *ID*/I, pp.438–439.

26. Lindemann memorandum, C(52)317, 30 September 1952, CAB129/55; Lindemann to WSC, 26 September 1952, LIND/J122/99–100

27. Lindemann to WSC, 24 October 1952, LIND/J122/81–83, and WSC reply, 25 October 1952, *ID*/I, p.434.

28. Moran diary, 22 February 1952, *CSFS*, p.376.

29. *DNB*, 'Normanbrook'.

30. Brook minute (original emphases) and attachment to WSC, 27 October 1952, PREM11/779.

31. Colville diary, 9 November 1952, *FOP*, p.654.

32. CC(52)93, 6 November 1952, CAB128/25; Brook to WSC, 5 November 1952, PREM11/789. £40 million = approximately £930 million today.

33. Lindemann to WSC, 30 September 1952, LIND/J122/98; WSC to Defence Committee, 11 December 1952, CAB131/12, D(52)12th meeting.

34. Horne, *Macmillan*/I, p.347.

35. Colville diary, 13–15 June 1952, *FOP*, p.650.

36. PUSD paper, 6 November 1952, FO371/125009/4; Boyle, 'Special Relationship', p.36.

37. *WSC*/VIII, p.773; Colville diary, 9 November 1952, *FOP*, p.654.

38. Best, *Churchill and War*, p.239.

39. Immerman, *Dulles*, pp.44–45; Shuckburgh diary, 23 November 1952, *DTS*, p.58; Young, *Last Campaign*, p.106.

40. *WSC*/VIII, p.774.

41. Defence Committee, 11 December 1952, CAB131/12, D(52)12th meeting, and papers D(52)51 and 52, 6 and 8 December 1952.

42. Lindemann to WSC, 'Future UK Programme', 29 December 1952, PREM11/290.

43. Lindemann to WSC, 'Atomic Energy: Future of Anglo-American Relations', and 'Post-War Anglo-American Negotiations', 29 December 1952, PREM11/561.

44. New York telegrams 7 and 8 to FO, 6 January 1953, PREM11/404 and PREM11/561; Colville diary, 31 December 1952, *FOP*, pp.657–658.

45. FO telegram 14 to Washington, 7 January 1953, PREM11/561.

46. Makins to Eden, 9 January 1952, AVON/AP20/16/21; Colville diary, 7 January 1953, *FOP*, pp.661–662; Shuckburgh diary, 16 January 1953, *DTS*, p.74.

47. *WSC*/VIII, p.792.

48. Beaverbrook to Bracken, 15 January 1953, in Cockett, ed., *My Dear Max*, p.139.

49. Colville note, 6 January 1953, FO371/103519/1G Eisenhower diary, 6 January 1953, in Ferrell, ed., *Diaries*, pp.222–224.

50. WSC telegram 34 to Eden, 9 January 1953, FO800/838/1; Shuckburgh diary, 16 January 1953, *DTS*, p.74; Colville, 24 July 1953, *FOP*, p.672.

51. Carlton, *Churchill*, p.175.

52. Macmillan, 22 February 1953, in Catterall, ed., *Diaries*/I, p.215.

53. 'Note by the Prime Minister', January 1953, PREM11/49.

54. HDC(53)5(Revise), CAB134/942, May 1953, Hennessy, *Having It So Good*, p.165.

55. Zaloga, *Nuclear Shield*, pp.18, 21. In mid-1953, the USSR possessed less than a dozen atomic bombs while the USA had 1,350 bombs at its disposal.

56. Goodman, *Nuclear Bear*, pp.160–161; Sergey Radchenko, 'Shadows in the Nuclear Cave', *H-Net Reviews*, October 2008.

57. Gordin, *Red Cloud*, p.259.

58. WSC to Eisenhower, 7 February 1953, CHUR6/3 (images 155–157).

59. Eisenhower–Eden meeting, 9 March 1953, EG1/39.

60. Eisenhower to Dulles, 7 March 1953, Botti, *Long Wait*, p.115.

61. Lindemann to WSC, 19 March 1953, Eden minute, 31 March 1953, PREM11/561.

62. Lindemann to WSC, 1950, n.d., LIND/J97/8; Lindemann minutes to WSC, 29 December 1952, PREM11/561; Lindemann to WSC, 30 April 1953, and WSC annotation, 3 May 1953, LIND/J138/81; Dalton diary, 7 December 1946, *Political Diaries*, p.364, note 4.

63. C(53)8, 7 January 1953, CAB129/58.

64. CC(53)2, 14 January 1953, CAB128/26; Eden to WSC, 16 January 1953, PREM11/789.

65. Lindemann referred to this decision in the Defence Committee on 21 July 1953, CAB131/13, D(53)11th meeting, Confidential Annex, but the record of the meeting of 25 February 1953 (D(53)3rd meeting) at which agreement was reached is redacted.

66. CC(53)27 and 28, 16 and 21 April 1953, CAB128/26 and CAB195/11, 21 April 1953. The talks with the Australians made little headway.

67. WSC (M.125/3) to Lindemann, 1 May 1953, PREM11/561.

68. Lindemann to WSC, 4 May 1953, PREM11/561.

69. Montefiore, *Stalin*, pp.564–566.

70. *HCD* Vol. 512, col. 569, 5 March 1953.

71. Moran diary, 7 March 1953, *CSFS*, p.403.

72. Dixon, *Double Diploma*, p.165.

73. WSC to Eisenhower, and Eisenhower reply, 11 March 1953, *CEC*, pp.31–32.

74. Calvocoressi, *Survey 1953*, pp.17–18; Plowden to Alsop, 2 April 1953, ALSOP/9/1.

75. WSC to Eisenhower, 5 April 1953, CHUR6/3 (image 41).

76. Eisenhower to WSC, 6 April 1953, CHUR6/3 (images 298–299); also Eisenhower to WSC, 11 and 13 April 1953, and WSC to Eisenhower, 11 April 1953, *CEC*, pps. 42–43, 45.

77. Eisenhower, 'The Chance for Peace', 16 April 1953, *PPP*.

78. Macmillan, 14 April 1953, in Catterall, ed.,*Diaries*/I, p.222; *HCD* Vol. 514, col. 649, 17 April 1953; *Times*, 18 April 1953; Strang to Makins, 9 May 1953, SHER.ms.527.

79. *Times*, 18 April 1953.

80. Macmillan, 14 June 1953, in Catterall, ed., *Diaries*/I, p.237; Thorpe, *Supermac*, p.289.

81. Shuckburgh diary, 1 April 1953, *DTS*, pp.83–84; *WSC*/VIII, p.817.

82. Nutting, 'Eden', p.334.

83. Nutting, *Europe Will Not Wait*, p.50; Strang to Makins, 15 April and 8 May 1953, SHER/Ms.527.

84. Macmillan, 12 May 1953, in Catterall, ed.,*Diaries*/I, p.231.

85. *HCD* Vol. 515, cols 893–898, 11 May 1953.

86. Swinton to WSC, 12 May 1953, CHUR2/200 (image 91).

87. Aldrich telegram 6041 to State, 12 May 1953, *FR1952–54*/VI, pp.985–986.

88. Macmillan, 12 May 1953, in Catterall, ed., *Diaries*/I, pp.231–232.

89. Aldrich telegram 6041 to State, 12 May 1953, *FR1952–54*/VI, pp.985–986.

90. Macmillan, 12 May 1953, in Catterall, ed., *Diaries*/I, pp.231–232; Young, *Last Campaign*, pp.159–169.

91. Eden diary, 17 November 1953, AVON/AP20/1/30.

92. Ruane, *European Defence Community*, p.8.

93. Macmillan, 1–7 June 1953, in Catterall, ed., *Diaries*/I, p.236.

94. Clarissa Eden diary, 27 July 1953, in Clarissa Eden, *Memoir*, p.142; Colville diary, 24 and 27 July 1953, *FOP*, pp.672–673.

Chapter 13 A Pill to End It All

1. Moran diary, 16 June 1953, *CSFS*, p.406.

2. WSC to Eisenhower, 21 June 1953, *CEC*, p.78.

3. *WSC*/VIII, p.848.

4. *CEC*, pp.81–82.

5. Jenkins, *Churchill*, p.863.

6. Churchill, *Keep on Dancing*, pp.146–147; WSC to Eisenhower, 1 July 1953, CHUR6/3 (images 102–103).

7. Shuckburgh diary, 21 July 1953, *DTS*, p.89.

8. Macmillan, 3 and 31 July 1953, in Catterall, ed., *Diaries*/I, pp.242, 248.

9. Montague Browne to Priestman, detailing WSC's views, 30 July 1953, FO371/106519/41.

10. Moran diary, 25 June, 10, 12 and 27 July 1953, *CSFS*, pp.410, 428, 431, 447.

11. Gascoigne memorandum, 20 August 1953, FO371/106527/108G.

12. Bonham-Carter diary, 6 August 1953, in Pottle, ed., *Daring to Hope*, p.127.

13. Colville diary, 19 July 1953, *FOP*, p.671.

14. Macmillan to Ava Waverley, 22 July 1953, MAC/ms.Eng.c.4778.

15. D(53)11th meeting, 21 July 1953, CAB131/13.

16. Waverley Report, July 1953, ES1/427.

17. Lindemann to WSC, 24 July 1953, PREM11/779.

18. WSC draft minute to Butler, 9 August 1953, and Colville note, n.d., PREM11/779; CC(53)48, 10 August 1953, CAB128/26; Brook to WSC, 24 August 1953, PREM11/779.

19. Macmillan, 16 August 1953, in Catterall, ed., *Diaries/*I, p.254.

20. CC(53)50, 25 August 1953, CAB128/26.

21. WSC (M.295/53) to Bridges, 9 September 1953, PREM11/779; Colville, *Churchillians*, p.41; Birkenhead, *Prof*, p.315; *ID/*I, pp.435–436.

22. WSC to Sandys, n.d., October 1953, and M.309/53 to Salisbury, 21 October 1953, PREM11/779; Lindemann to WSC, 1 December 1953, EG1/39.

23. Pitblado to WSC, 9 November 1953, PREM11/779; *Times*, 11 November 1953; Atomic Energy Authority Act, 1954, legislation.gov.uk.

24. Moran diary, 16 August 1953, *CSFS*, p.451.

25. *Times*, 21 August 1953; *USAEC/*III, pp.58–59.

26. Holloway, *Stalin and the Bomb*, p.307. On the hybrid/true H-bomb differences see Arnold, *H-Bomb*, pp.40–41.

27. Colville diary, August 1953, *FOP*, pp.675–676.

28. Macmillan, 1 September 1953, MAC/dep.c.15.

29. Grey (Moscow) to Mason, 27 August 1953, FO371/106527/103.

30. Shuckburgh to Strang, 4 August 1953, AVON/AP20/16/7D; Salisbury to Eden, 6 September 1953, AVON/AP20/16/145; Colville diary, October 1953, *FOP*, p.680.

31. Moran diary, 27 July, 16 August 1953 and 2 September 1953, *CSFS*, pp.446, 452, 465.

32. Clarissa Eden diary, 27 July 1953, *Memoir*, p.142; Macmillan, 4 August 1953, *Diaries/*I, p.249.

33. WSC speech, 10 October 1953, CHUR5/51A–C (images 528–541); Macmillan, 11 October 1953, *Diaries/*I, p.269; Moran diary, 10 and 21 October 1953, *CSFS*, pp.477, 485.

34. Eisenhower news conference, 8 October 1953, *PPP*.

35. *HCD* Vol. 520, cols 28–31, 3 November 1953.

36. Channon diary, 3 November 1953, *Chips*, p.479.

37. *Times*, 4 November 1953.

38. Macmillan, 5 November 1953, in Catterall, ed., *Diaries/*I, p.272.

39. Moran diary, 3 November 1953, *CSFS*, p.494.

40. Salisbury to Emrys-Evans, 9 August 1953, EMRYS.add.mss.58235; Shuckburgh diary, 21 July 1953, *DTS*, p.89.

41. Colville diary, n.d., October 1953, *FOP*, p.680.

42. Woolton note, 1 October 1953, WOOL/3.

43. Moran diary, 14 July 1953, *CSFS*, p.433.

44. WSC to Eisenhower, 5 November 1953, *CEC*, p.93.

45. Moran diary, 10 November 1953, *CSFS*, p.497.

46. Moran diary, 3 December 1953, *CSFS*, p.503.

47. Botti, *Long Wait*, pp.115–119.

48. Elliot memorandum, 19 October 1953, and Makins to Dixon, 23 October 1953, FO371/105715/147; Lindemann to WSC, 12 November 1953, LIND/J138/66.

49. *New York Herald Tribune*, 24 November 1953; *Times*, 30 November 1953.

50. Strauss, *Men and Decisions*, pp.371–372; Eisenhower diary, 6 December 1953, DDEL/AWF/ International Series, box 3, file 1.

Notes

51. WSC to Eisenhower and Eisenhower reply, 12 November 1953, *CEC*, pp.97–98.

52. *Times*, 9 December 1953.

53. Sulzberger diary, 8 December 1953, in Sulzberger, *Long Row of Candles*, p.779.

54. Shuckburgh diary, 1, 3 and 5 December 1953, *DTS,* pp.111–114; Moran diary, 2 and 7 December 1953, *CSFS*, pp.501–502, 508; C. D. Jackson 'log', December 1953, JACK/DDEL/box 68.

55. Eden to Clarissa, 2, 5 and 6 December 1953, AVON/AP20/45/31, 33 and 34.

56. Eisenhower notes, 4 December 1953, and diary entry, 6 December 1953, DDEL/AWF/International Series, box 3, file 1.

57. *WSC*/VIII, pp.920–923.

58. Eden to Clarissa, 5 December 1953, AVON/AP20/45/33.

59. Eden to Clarissa, 5 December 1953, AVON/AP20/45/33; Colville diary, 4 December 1953, *FOP,* p.683.

60. Young, *Last Campaign*, p.223.

61. Eisenhower notes, 4 December 1953, DDEL/AWF/International Series, box 3, file 1; US record of meeting, 4 December 1953, *FR1952–54*/V, pp.1739–1740.

62. Moran diary, 3 December 1953, *CSFS*, pp.503–504.

63. *WSC*/VIII, p.924; Shuckburgh diary, 5 December 1953, *DTS*, p.114.

64. Jones, 'Consultation on Use of the Atomic Bomb, 1950–1954', p.819.

65. Eden (despatch 1193) to Washington, 16 November 1953, FO371/105534/437; BC(P)(53)4th meeting, 7 December 1953, FO371/105540/9G.

66. Eden to WSC, 4 December 1953 (PM53/337) and 7 December 1953 (PM53/339), AVON/AP20/16/90 and 91.

67. Eden note, n.d., Bermuda, AVON/AP20/1/29.

68. Strauss notes, 5 December 1953, DDEL online. The UK record is at EG1/36.

69. *WSC*/VIII, p.928.

70. UK record of meeting, 5 December 1953, FO371/105574/1G; US record of meeting, 5 December 1953, *FR1952–54*/V, p.1786.

71. Eden to Clarissa, 5 and 6 December 1953, and Eden diary, 5 December 1953, AVON/AP20/45/33–34 and -/1/29; Jones, 'Targeting China', p.47.

72. Colville diary, 6 December 1953, *FOP*, p.687.

73. Eisenhower diary, 6 December 1953, DDEL/AWF/International Series, box 3, file 1.

74. Colville diary, 6 December 1953, *FOP*, p.685.

75. Shuckburgh diary, 6 December 1953, *DTS*, p.115.

76. WSC to Eisenhower, 6 December 1953, *CEC*, p.110.

77. Eden note, n.d., Bermuda, AVON/AP20/1/29; Colville diary, 6 December 1953, *FOP*, pp.685–686.

78. WSC to Eisenhower, 6 December 1953, *CEC*, p.110.

79. Colville diary, 6 December 1953, *FOP*, pp.685–686.

80. Shuckburgh diary, 6 December 1953, *DTS*, p.115.

81. WSC to the Queen, 11 December 1953, CAB21/3074.

82. Eden to WSC, 4 and 7 December 1953, AVON/AP20/16/90 and 91; D(54)8, 1 February 1954, CAB131/14.

83. BC(P)(53)4th meeting, 7 December 1953, PREM11/2856.

84. Moran diary, 9–10 December 1953, *CSFS*, pp.510–511.

85. *WSC*/VIII, p.938.

86. 'Atoms for Peace', 8 December 1953, *PPP*.

87. Shuckburgh diary, 6 December 1953, *DTS*, p.115.

88. Ambrose, *Eisenhower*, p.149; *HCD* Vol. 522, col. 584, 17 December 1953.

89. Young, *Last Campaign*, pp.232–233.

90. WSC (M.6/54) to Eden, 8 January 1954, FO371/110691/20.

91. *USAEC*/III, p.221; Eden minute, 16 June 1954, FO371/110694/83G; CC(54)43, 22 June 1954, CAB128/27.

92. Staff conference, President's Office, 22 December 1953, DDEL online; see also Gaddis, *Strategies of Containment*, p.147.

93. Eisenhower diary, 4–8 December 1953, DDEL/AWF/International Series, box 3, file 2.

94. NSC 174th meeting, 10 December 1953, DDEL/AWF/NSC Series, Box 5; Cutler memorandum, 10 December 1953 (containing Dulles' views), JACK/DDEL/box 2.

95. *Times*, 15 December 1953; Eisenhower, State of the Union, 7 January 1954, *PPP*.

96. Folliot, ed., *Documents 1954*, pp.265–267. When Truman left office, the United States had 832 nuclear weapons of varying power. Within a year, that figure had increased to 1,161; within two years to 1,630, and within three years to 2,280. Gordin, *Red Cloud*, p.288.

97. Wenner minute, 18 January 1954, Maitland letter, 2 February 1954, FO371/109135/1.

98. D(54)8, 1 February 1954, CAB131/14.

99. WSC telegram 5290 to Washington, 16 December 1953, CHUR6/3A (image 83).

100. Eisenhower budget statement, 21 January 1954, *PPP* and Eisenhower 'Special Message to the Congress', 17 February 1954, *PPP*.

101. *Times*, 3 February 1954.

102. Eisenhower to WSC, 9 February 1954, *FR1952–54*/VI, pp.1012–1014.

103. Macmillan diary, 27 February 1954, MAC/dep.c.16.

104. Shuckburgh diary, 1 March 1954, *DTS*, p.137; Greenwood, *Britain and the Cold War*, p.111.

105. Eden to WSC, 2 March 1954, PREM11/1074.

Chapter 14 H-bomb Fever

1. WSC draft letter, February 1954, PREM11/1074.

2. Bullard minute, 11 February 1954, FO371/105540/9G.

3. *Manchester Guardian*, 18 February 1954.

4. Colville in Wheeler-Bennett, ed., *Action This Day*, p.122.

5. *HCD* Vol. 530, cols 34–36, 12 July 1954, and Vol, 537, col. 1895, 1 March 1955.

6. Cabot Lodge–Churchill meeting, 26 June 1954, *FR1952–1954*/VI, pp.1107–1110.

7. WSC to Eisenhower, 9 March 1954, *CEC*, pp.122–123.

8. Shuckburgh diary, 12 March 1954, *DTS*, p.147.

9. Eisenhower news conference, 10 March 1954, *PPP*.

10. Eisenhower to WSC, 19 March 1954, CHUR6/3B (images 219–220).

11. Macmillan diary, 9 July 1954, MAC/dep.c.16; Butler note, 11 March 1954, BUTLER/G27/18–19.

12. *Times*, 2 March 1954; Rosenbluth obituary, *Guardian*, 4 October 2003.

13. *USAEC*/III, p.165.

14. Divine, *Blowing on the Wind*, pp.4–11; Saloff, 'Lucky Dragon', pp.21–23; *Times*, 20 March 1954.

15. 'An Agenda for the Hydrogen Age', *Life*, 12 April 1954, p.38.

16. Jones, *After Hiroshima*, p.196; Arnold, *H-Bomb*, p.44; *Times*, 27 March 1954.

17. Eisenhower news conference, 24 March 1954, *PPP*; Divine, *Blowing on the Wind*, pp.8–9.

18. *Times*, 30 March 1954; *New York Times*, 3 April 1954; *Life*, 12 April 1954.

19. Macmillan, 22 March 1954, in Catterall, ed., *Diaries*/I, p.301; CC(52)31, 22 March 1954, CAB128/27.

20. *HCD* Vol. 525, cols 1052–1054, 23 March 1954.

21. WSC to Eisenhower, 24 March 1954, CHUR6/3A (images 69–73).

22. *Times*, 30 March 1954.

23. *USAEC*/III, pp.225, 275–276.

24. *USAEC*/III, p.178; *HLD* Vol. 186, col. 651, 24 March 1954.

25. 'The H-Bomb and World Opinion', *BAS*, Vol. 10, No. 5 (May 1954), p.165; *Daily Mirror*, 2 April 1954.

26. Shuckburgh diary, 26 March 1954, *DTS*, pp.153–154.

27. Kynaston, *Family Britain*, p.372; *Times*, 24 May 1954; *Chicago Tribune*, 4 April 1954.

28. *Times*, 31 March 1954.

29. Baruch to WSC, 31 March 1954, CHUR21/210A–B (image 431).

30. *Daily Mirror*, 1 April 1954.

31. *Times*, 31 March 1954.

32. *Punch,* 3 February 1954, *photoshelter.com*; Moran diary, 4 February 1954, *CSFS*, p.523.

33. Macmillan, 31 March 1954, in Catterall, ed., *Diaries*/I, p.303.

34. CC(54)23, 31 March 1954, CAB128/27.

35. Moran diary, 1 and 5 April 1954, *CSFS*, pps. 531–532, 537.

36. Dulles-Strauss telcon, 29 March 1954, *FR1952–54*/II, pp.1379–1380.

37. Eisenhower–Strauss news conference, 31 March 1954, *PPP*; Hagerty, 31 March 1954, Ferrell, ed., *Diary of James C. Hagerty*, p.36.

38. *New York Times*, 1 April 1954.

39. Divine, *Blowing on the Wind*, p.13. According to AEC estimates at this time, a H-bomb dropped on Washington 'might ravage the entire north-eastern seaboard with radiation'. *USAEC*/III, p.273.

40. Bush to Conant, 29 March 1954, BUSH/27/5.

41. Macmillan diary, 3 April 1954, MAC/dep.c.16.

42. WSC to Eisenhower, 1 April 1954, CHUR6/3A (images 64–65).

43. Eisenhower to WSC, 1 April 1954, *FR1952–54*/VI, p.1022.

44. Macmillan, 6 April 1954, in Catterall, ed., *Diaries*/I, p.304.

45. *HCD* Vol. 526, cols 36–153, 5 April 1954; Moran diary, 5 April 1954, *CSFS*, p.535.

46. Woolton diary, 6 April 1954, WOOL/3.

47. Shuckburgh diary, 5 April 1954, *DTS*, p.160.

48. Macmillan diary, 5 April 1954, MAC/dep.c.16.

49. Jenkins, *Churchill*, p.876.

50. *Times, Manchester Guardian, Daily Mirror* and *Daily Express*, 6 April 1954.

51. Attlee to Tom Attlee, 8 April 1954, ATTLEE/ms.Eng.c.4795.

52. Brook to WSC, 21 May 1954, PREM11/2856.

53. Jenkins, *Churchill*, p.876; Moran diary, 5 and 6 April 1954, *CSFS*, pps. 536, 538.

54. Macmillan, 6 April 1954, *Diaries*/I, p.304.

55. Thorpe, *Eden*, p.400.

56. The classic account of the battle remains Fall, *Hell in a Very Small Place*, but see also Windrow, *Last Valley*. On American support for France and general US involvement in Indo-China see Logevall, *Embers of War* and Lawrence, *Assuming the Burden*.

57. Dulles–Radford telcon, 24 March 1954, *FR1952–54*/XIII, p.1151; Eisenhower news conference, 7 April 1954, *PPP*.

58. On the Eisenhower administration's policy, see Anderson, *Trapped by Success*.

59. Gaddis, *Strategies of Containment*, pp.176–177.

60. Dulles speech, New York, 29 March 1954, *Avalon project*; Dulles to Eisenhower, 26 March 1954, Dulles Papers, Princeton, DULLES/box 80.

61. Macmillan, 9 April 1954, in Catterall, ed., *Diaries*/I, p.305.

62. CC(54)21st conclusions, 22 March 1954, CAB195/12, original emphases; also D(54)8, 1 February 1954, CAB131/14.

63. Dulles–Makins meeting, 2 April 1954, FO 371/112050/134G; Washington telegram 579, 3 April 1954, FO 371/112049/121; Dulles–Munro meeting, 4 April 1954, *FR1952–54*/XIII, pp.1231–1235.

64. Wilkinson letter to Maitland, 11 March 1953, FO 371/103513/31.

65. 'Policy towards Indo-China', 31 March 1954, and Eden minute, 1 April 1954, FO 371/112049/103G; COS(54)36th meeting, 31 March 1954, DEFE 4/69.

66. CC(54)26, 7 April 1954, CAB128/27 and CAB195/12; Eden memorandum, C(54)134, 7 April 1954, CAB129/67.

67. Ruane, 'Containing America', pp.141–142.

68. WSC to Eden, 3 September 1952, CHUR2/517 (image 342).

69. Eisenhower to WSC, 4 April 1954, pp.136–138.

70. Moran diary, 26 March 1954, *CSFS*, p.530.

71. WSC to Eisenhower, 6 April 1954, *CEC*, p.138

72. Hagerty, 1 April 1954, *Diary*, p.39; Divine, *Blowing on the Wind*, p.22.

73. British Pathé, 'H-Bomb', 8 April 1954.

74. Schlosser, *Command and Control*, pp.140–141.

75. *Manchester Guardian*, 1 May 1954; Barnett, 'Coventry Civil Defence Controversy', pp.1–2.

76. Paris telegram 257, 23 April 1954, FO371/112055/305G.

77. Clarissa Eden diary, 24 April 1954, *Memoir*, p.157.

78. Cabinet meeting, C(54)155, 25 April 1954, 11.00 am, CAB129/68 and CAB195/12.

79. Cabinet meeting, C(54)155, 25 April 1954, 4:00 pm, CAB129/68 and CAB195/12.

80. Shuckburgh diary, 26 April 1954, *DTS*, p.176; Geneva telegram 7, 26 April 1954, FO371/112055/309G.

81. Clarissa Eden diary, 24 April 1954, *Memoir*, p.157; Colville letters to Makins, 28 April 1954, PREM11/666 and FO371/112060/454G.

82. Eisenhower–Smith telcon, 24 April 1954, *FR1952–54*/XIII, pp.1381–1383.

83. Colville memorandum, 26 April 1954, FO371/112057/360G; Trachtenberg, 'Wasting Asset', p.42, note 154.

84. Radford (JCS-960578) to Dulles, 27 April 1954, *FR1952–54*/XIII, p.1416, note 3; Makins to Colville, 29 April 1954, PREM11/666.

85. Eden minute, n.d., FO371/112057/360G.

86. GEN464/1st meeting, 13 April 1954, CAB130/101; WSC (M.70/54) to Salisbury, 9 April 1954, PREM11/784.

87. GEN.465/1st and 2nd meetings, 12 and 19 March 1954, CAB130/101; Brook to WSC, 22 and 23 March 1954, PREM11/797.

88. *DNB*, 'Normanbrook'.

89. DP(54)1st meeting, 4 May 1954, CAB134/808.

90. DP(54)1st and 2nd meetings, 4 and 19 May 1954, and DP(54)1, 13 April 1954, CAB134/808.

91. Farmelo, *Churchill's Bomb*, p.426, for a recent example.

92. Plowden in Hennessy, *Secret State*, p.93.

93. Geneva telegrams 293 and 294, 15 May 1954, FO371/112065/540G; Eden to Salisbury, 16 May 1954, AVON/AP20/17/118A.

Chapter 15 The July Days

1. *HCD* Vol. 526, cols 1455–1456, 27 April 1954.

2. Geneva telegrams 110 and 113, 2 May 1954, FO371/112058/379G; Shuckburgh diary, 2 May 1954, *DTS*, p.196.

3. CC(54)31st conclusion, 3 May 1954, CAB128/27; Moran diary, 4 May 1954, *CSFS*, p.545.

4. Hoopes, *Dulles*, p.222.

5. Clarissa Eden, diary 1 and 3 May 1954, *Memoirs*, p.160.

6. Geneva telegram 144, 5 May 1954, AVON/AP20/17/35A; Statler, *Replacing France*, pp.95–99.

7. Logevall, *Embers of War*, p.534.

8. FO telegrams 286 and 298 to Geneva, 8 May 1954, FO800/785/35 and 36.

9. Draft Congressional resolution, 17 May 1954, and Washington telegram 4184 to Paris, 21 May 1954, *FR1952–54/XIII*, pps. 1585, 1594.

10. Eden to Clarissa, 22 May 1954, AVON/AP20/45/49.

11. Eden diary, 16 June 1954, AVON/AP20/17/231.

12. Rioux, *Fourth Republic*, pp.224–225.

13. Eden, *Full Circle*, p.130.

14. *HCD* Vol. 529, col. 441, 23 June 1954.

15. Geneva telegram 540, 1 June 1954, PREM11/646.

16. DP(54)6, COS memorandum, 1 June 1954, CAB134/808; GEN.465/2nd meeting, 19 March 1954, CAB130/101; Hennessy, *Having It So Good*, p.337.

17. DP(54)3rd meeting, 16 June 1954, and DP(54)7, COS memorandum, 9 June 1954, CAB134/808.

18. *Manchester Guardian*, 14 May 1954.

19. *Daily Telegraph*, 8 July 1954.

20. DP(54)1st meeting, 4 May 1954, CAB134/808.

21. WSC to Eisenhower, 22 April 1954, *CEC*, p.139; Colville diary, 24 June 1954, *FOP*, p.691.

22. WSC to Eisenhower, 24 May 1954 and 22 June 1954, *CEC*, pp.142, 148; Colville to WSC, 22 June 1954, PREM11/797.

23. CC(54)39, 5 June 1954, CAB128/27; Macmillan, 6 June 1954, in Catterall, ed., *Diaries*/I, p.316.

24. Eden to Clarissa, 28 June 1954, AVON/AP20/45/60.

25. Hagerty, 26 June 1954, *Diary*, pp.77–78.

26. US–UK meeting, 25 June 1954, *FR1952–4*/VI, pp.1085–1086; *USAEC*/III, p.276.

27. Strauss record of US–UK meeting, 26 June 1954, *FR1952–4*/VI, pp.1096–1097.

28. Hagerty, 24 June 1954, *Diary*, p.76.

29. Strauss record of US–UK meeting, 26 June 1954, *FR1952–4*/VI, pp.1096–1097, original emphasis; Lindemann to WSC, 26 June 1954, PREM11/797; de L'Isle and Dudley, to WSC, 24 June 1954 and 10 January 1955, PREM11/763.

30. Joint statement, 29 June 1954, *FR1952–4*/VI, pp.1132–1133.

31. Atomic Energy Act, 1954, Public Law 83–703, *nrc.gov*; Makins to Caccia, 22 April 1954; EG1/40; Pierre, *Nuclear Politics*, p.159.

32. Colville diary, 25–26 June 1954, *FOP*, p.692.

33. Moran diary, 26 June 1954, *CSFS*, p.562.

34. Jones, 'Consultation on Use of the Atomic Bomb, 1950–1954', p.826.

35. Jones, 'Consultation on Use of the Atomic Bomb, 1950–1954', p.826.

36. Young, *Last Campaign*, pp.266–270.

37. US–UK meeting, White House, 25 June 1954, and Dulles memorandum, 27 June 1954, *FR1952–4*/VI, pp.1079–1084, 1111–1112; Colville diary, 25–27 June 1954, *FOP*, pp.692–693.

38. Hagerty diary, 23 June 1954, *Diary*, p.73.

39. Moran diary, 26 June 1954, *CSFS*, p.562.

40. Macmillan diary, 31 July and 24 August 1954, MAC/dep.c.16.

41. WSC (T.240/54) to Molotov, 4 July 1954, and Molotov reply, 5 July 1954, PREM11/669.

42. *Yorkshire Post*, 1 July 1954; *Times*, 1 July 1954.

43. Moran diary, 2–3 and 5 July 1954, *CSFS*, pps. 572–574, 578.

44. Nicolson, *Public Faces*; Colville diary, 3–4 July 1954, p.699.

45. Moran diary, 3 July 1954, *CSFS*, p.573.

46. Arnold, *H-Bomb*, p.40.

47. Mallaby, *From My Level*, pp.16–17.

48. Macmillan diary, 10 July 1954, MAC/dep.c.16.

49. CC(54)47, 7 July 1954, CAB128/27 and CAB195/12; Macmillan diary, 7 July 1954, MAC/dep.c.16; WSC to Eisenhower, 7 July 1954, *CEC*, pp.152–153.

50. WSC, *Hinge of Fate*, p.78.

51. CC(54)47, 7 July 1954, CAB128/27 and CAB 195/12.

52. Macmillan diary, 7 July 1954, MAC/dep.c.16.

53. Crookshank to WSC, 7 July 1954, CHUR2/183 (image 240).

54. CC(54)48, 8 July 1954, CAB128/27 and CAB195/12.

55. Crookshank diary, 8 July 1954, CROOK/ms.Eng/d361.

56. WSC to the Queen, 16 July 1954, PREM11/747.

57. Macmillan diary, 8 July 1954, MAC/dep.c.16.

58. Among the few historians to recognize the linkage are Hennessy, *Having It So Good*, p.321, and Young, *Last Campaign*, p.259.

59. Eisenhower to WSC, 7 July 1954, CHUR6/3C (images 254–255).

60. WSC to Eisenhower, 8 July 1954, *CEC*, pp.154–155.

61. CC(54)48, 8 July 1954, CAB128/27 and CAB195/12.

62. CC(54)48, 8 July 1954, CAB128/27 and CAB195/12. See also Butler to WSC, 21 July 1954, PREM11/669, defending his conduct.

63. Macmillan diary, 9 July 1954, MAC/dep.c.16.

64. CC(54)48, 8 July 1954, CAB195/12.

65. Macmillan diary, 9 July 1954, MAC/dep.c.16.

66. CC(54)49, 9 July 1954, CAB128/27 and CAB195/12.

67. Macmillan diary, 9 July 1954, MAC/dep.c.16.

68. CC(54)49, 9 July 1954, CAB128/27.

69. WSC to Eisenhower, 9 July 1954, *CEC*, p.p.137–138.

70. Macmillan diary, 10 July 1954, MAC/dep.c.16.

71. Clarissa Eden diary, 20 July 1954, *Memoir*, p.167.

72. *HCD* Vol. 530, cols 34–49, 12 July 1954.

73. Eisenhower to WSC, 12 July 1954, CHUR/6/3B (images 200–207).

74. CC(54)50, 13 July 1954, CAB128/27.

75. Macmillan, 13 July 1954, in Catterall, ed., *Diaries*/I, p.333.

76. Colville diary, 2 and 16 July 1954, and August 1954 reflection, *FOP*, pp.698, 702.

77. Final Declaration of the Geneva Conference, 21 July 1954, *fordham.edu*. In general, Cable, *Geneva Conference*.

78. Adamthwaite, 'The Foreign Office', p.1; Thorpe, *Eden*, p.415; James, *Eden*, pp.389–390.

79. NSC 195th meeting, 6 May 1954, *FR1952–54*/II, p.1428.

80. Young, *Last Campaign*, p.277.

81. Smith–Eisenhower telcon, 23 July 1954, DDEL/AWF/DDE diary series, box 7.

82.   Eden (T.260/54) to WSC, 17 July 1954, PREM11/669.

83.   Colville diary, 7 July 1954, *FOP*, p.701.

84.   Macmillan diary, 16 July 1954, MAC/dep.c.16.

85.   Moran diary, 23 July 1954, *CSFS*, p.581.

86.   Eisenhower to WSC, 22 July 1954, CHUR/6/3B (images 195–199).

87.   CC(54)52, 23 July 1954, CAB128/27 and CAB195/12; Macmillan diary, 23 July 1954, MAC/dep.c.16.

88.   CC(54)52, 23 July 1954, CAB128/27 and CAB195/12; Macmillan diary, 23 July 1954, MAC/dep.c.16.

89.   Macmillan, 23 July 1954, in Catterall, ed., *Diaries/*I, p.337.

90.   Crookshank diary, 23 July 1954, CROOK/ms.Eng/d361.

91.   Macmillan diary, 23 July 1953, MAC/dep.c.16; Clarissa Eden diary, 25 July 1953, *Memoir*, p.169.

92.   Seldon, *Churchill's Indian Summer*, p.407.

93.   Aldrich telegram 709 to State, 10 August 1954, *FR1952–54/*VI, pp.1054–1055.

94.   Moran, commentary, *CSFS*, p.247; Hennessy, *Having It So Good*, Chapter 4, *passim*.

95.   Carlton, *Churchill*, pp.191–193.

96.   Young, *Last Campaign*, p.272.

97.   Colville, *Churchillians*, p.179.

98.   'United Kingdom Defence Policy', C(54)249, 23 July 1954, CAB129/69, and DPC report, C(54)250, 24 July 1954, CAB129/69.

99.   *Times*, 26 July 1954.

100. CC(54)53, 26 July 1954, CAB128/27 and CAB195/12; Crookshank diary, 26 July 1954, CROOK/ms.Eng/d361.

101. CC(54)53, 26 July 1954, CAB128/27 and CAB195/12; Crookshank diary, 26 July 1954, CROOK/ms.Eng/d361.

102. CC(54)54, 27 July 1954, CAB128/27 and CAB195/12.

Chapter 16 Sturdy Child of Terror

1.   Hennessey, 'Churchill and the Premiership', p.217.

2.   Graebner, *Churchill*, pp.18–19.

3.   *HCD* Vol. 531, cols 231–233, 27 July 1954.

4.   Molotov to WSC, 31 July 1954, and WSC (T.275/54) to Molotov, 5 August 1954, PREM11/669.

5.   *WSC/*VIII, p.1035.

6.   Moran diary, 30 July 1954, *CSFS*, p.586.

7.   Moran diary, 6 August 1954, *CSFS*, p.589.

8.   C(54)263, WSC memorandum, 2 August 1954, CAB129/70.

9.   Moran diary, 6 August 1954, *CSFS*, p.589.

Notes

10. WSC to Eden, n.d., August 1954, BUTLER/G27/108–113.

11. WSC to Eisenhower, 8 August 1954, CHUR/6/3A (image 34).

12. US–UK meeting, White House, 25 June 1954, *FR1952–4*/VI, pp.1085–1086; WSC, 'Epilogue', p.965.

13. WSC, 'Shall We All Commit Suicide?', *Nash's Pall Mall*, 1924, CHAR 8/200A–B (images 225–229).

14. Smith memorandum, 26 July 1954, *FR1952–4*/VI, pp.1049–1050.

15. WSC to Baruch, 29 August 1954, CHUR/2/210A–B (images 458–460).

16. Clarissa Eden diary, 27 August 1954, *Memoir*, p.170; WSC to Eden, 24 August 1954, CHUR6/4 (images 25–28).

17. Wheeler-Bennett, ed., *Action This Day*, pp.44–45.

18. WSC speech, Blackpool, 9 October 1954, CHUR5/56A–B (images 86–97).

19. Ruane, *European Defence Community*, pp.111–152.

20. WSC to Eisenhower, 18 September 1954, CHUR6/3A (images 24–25).

21. WSC to Eisenhower, 7 December 1954, *CEC*, pp.179–180.

22. Eisenhower to WSC, 14 December 1954, CHUR6/3A (images 180–183).

23. WSC (M1/55) to Eden, 1 January 1955, PREM11/1052; WSC to Eisenhower, 12 January 1955, CHUR2/217 (images 20–23).

24. Lindemann to WSC, 18 November 1954, LIND/J146/36–37.

25. WSC (M1.55) to Eden, 1 January 1955, PREM11/1052.

26. Ministerial meeting, 9 December 1954, CAB21/4054.

27. Macmillan to WSC, 10 and 13 December 1954, WSC annotation, 12 December 1954, PREM11/1066.

28. Brook to WSC, 1 December 1954, FO telegram 5954 to Washington, 3 December 1954, PREM11/849.

29. Macmillan, 25 November 1954, in Catterall, ed., *Diaries*/I, p.367, original emphases.

30. Larres, *Churchill's Cold War*, p.365.

31. FO estimate, 18 October 1954, PREM11/2546.

32. Macmillan diary, 11 December 1954, MAC/dep.c.16.

33. Woolton diary, 22 December 1954, WOOL/3.

34. Soames diary, 19 March 1955, in Soames, *Clementine*, p.594.

35. Carlton, *Churchill*, pp.170, 187; Hennessy, *Having It So Good*, p.134; Jenkins, *Churchill*, p.869; Addison, *Churchill*, p.235.

36. James, 'Enigma', p.22.

37. WSC, 'Notes on Tube Alloys', C(54)390, 14 December 1954, CAB129/72.

38. WSC, 'Notes on Tube Alloys', C(54)390, 14 December 1954, CAB129/72.

39. Young, *Last Campaign*, p.308.

40. Attlee to WSC, 20 December 1954, Ismay to WSC, 18 December 1954, and Montgomery to WSC, 22 December 1954, PREM11/1066.

41. Colville to Adeane, 16 December 1954, PREM11/747.

42. WSC to Eisenhower, 12 January 1955, CHUR2/217 (images 20–23).

43. Eisenhower to Churchill, 25 January 1955, CHUR 6/3B (images 176–179).

44. CC(54)81 and 86, CAB195/13, 2 and 14 December 1954; FO despatch 263 (draft) to Washington, 17 December 1954, FO371/125105/7; *Times*, 16 March 1955.

45. Cmd. 9391, *Statement on Defence*, pp.3–4.

46. Macmillan to WSC, 1 February 1955, PREM11/1066; Macmillan diary, 2 February 1955, in Catterall, ed., *Diaries/I*, p.389.

47. Pearson diary, 2 February 1955, in Pearson, *Mike*, pp.86–87.

48. *Times*, 9 February 1955; Macmillan, 11 February 1955, in Catterall, ed., *Diaries/I*, p.394; Young, *Last Campaign*, pp.300–306.

49. Moran diary, 1 March 1955, *CSFS*, p.634.

50. WSC to Adeane, 28 February 1955, CHUR6/6 9 (image 103).

51. Moran diary, 21 February and 1 March 1955, *CSFS*, pp.633–634.

52. Macmillan diary, 25 February 1955, in Catterall, ed., *Diaries/I*, p.397.

53. Macmillan to WSC, 28 February 1955, PREM11/1055; *Economist*, 6 November 1954.

54. Moran diary, 1 March 1955, *CSFS*, pp.633–634.

55. WSC minute, 12 December 1954, PREM11/1066.

56. For the work of the Strath committee and its final report, 25 March 1955, see CAB134/1174. An ad hoc Cabinet committee, GEN.491, was established in late March 1955 to weigh up the conclusions of the report; see CAB130/109. For discussion, Hennessy, *Secret State*, pp.167–178; Hughes, 'Strath Report', pp.257–275.

57. Moran diary, 1 March 1955, *CSFS*, p.634.

58. *HCD* Vol. 537, cols 1893–1905, 1 March 1955.

59. Warren Dockter, 'Winston Churchill's 10 Most Important Speeches', *Daily Telegraph*, 26 January 2015.

60. Press digest, Best, *Churchill and War*, pp.242–243; *Times*, 3 March 1955; Moran diary, 3 March 1955, *CSFS*, p.638.

61. *HCD* Vol. 537, col. 1894, 1 March 1955; Crossman diary, 2 March 1955, in Morgan, ed., *Diaries*, p.392.

62. *HCD* Vol. 537, cols 1907–1917, 1 March 1955.

63. WSC to Eisenhower, 4 March 1955, *CEC*, p.199.

64. *Times*, 3 March 1955. Nor did the H-bomb prove especially controversial in the June 1955 General Election. Pierre, *Nuclear Politics*, p.102.

65. *HCD* Vol. 537, col. 1909, 1 March 1955.

66. *HCD* Vol. 537, col. 2116, 2 March 1955.

67. *HCD* Vol. 537, Vol. 538, col. 964, 14 March 1955.

68. Soames, *Clementine*, p.596.

69. Colville diary, March–April 1955, *FOP*, p.708.

70. Macmillan diary, 5 May 1955, in Catterall, ed., *Diaries/I*, p.420.

71. C(55)83, 26 March 1955, CAB129/74.

72. Bar-Noi, *Cold War*, pp.6–8.

73. Eisenhower to WSC, 15 July 1955, CHUR2/217 (image 85).

74. WSC to Eisenhower, 18 July 1955, CHUR2/217 (images 81–84).

75. McDonald, *A Man of the Times*, p.140.

76. Eisenhower speech, 24 August 1955, *PPP*.

77. WSC to Eisenhower, 18 July 1955, CHUR2/217 (images 81–84).

78. WSC to Eisenhower, 16 April 1956, CHUR2/217 (images 99–103).

79. Eisenhower to WSC, 27 April 1956, CHUR2/217 (images 128–130).

80. Moran diary, 6 December 1959, *CSFS*, p.763.

81. Lees-Milne diary, 12 September 1957, *Mingled Measure*, p.68.

Conclusion: '. . . If God Wearied of Mankind'

1. Divine, *Blowing on the Wind*, p.11.

2. Craig and Radchenko, *Atomic Bomb*, p.81.

3. *Times*, 7 August 1945; WSC, *Triumph and Tragedy*, pp.552–553.

4. *Times*, 16 August 1945.

5. Thicknesse obituary, *Times*, 3 June 1971.

6. Kynaston, *Austerity Britain*, p.85, original emphasis.

7. Wyndham diary, 6 and 10 August 1945, in Wyndham, *Love is Blue*, pp.189–190.

8. WSC 16 August 1945, Hansard, *HCD*, Vol. 413, col. 79.

9. WSC, *Gathering Storm*, p.16.

10. *BAS*, Vol. 9, No. 1 (1953), pp.4–6.

11. *Era of Atomic Power: Report of a Commission appointed by the British Council of Churches* (London: SCM, 1946); Willis, 'God and the Atom', pp.422–457; Ham, *Hiroshima Nagasaki*, p.310.

12. WSC, *Triumph and Tragedy*, pp.552–553.

13. Reynolds, *Command of History*, pp.xxi, xxiv.

14. WSC, 16 August 1945, *HCD* Vol. 413, col. 79; WSC, *Triumph and Tragedy*, p. 552.

15. Ramsden, 'Churchill', pp.30–31.

16. WSC to Lady Randolph, 14 January 1897, CHAR28/23 (images 24–28); Rose, *Literary Churchill*, pp.28–29.

17. WSC to Lady Randolph, 24 August 1898, *WSC*/I, p.406.

18. Ramsden, *Churchill*, p.145.

19. Toye, *Roar of the Lion*, p.46.

20. *HCD* Vol. 537, col. 1895, 1 March 1955.

21. Jenkins, *Churchill*, p.893.

22. Strauss, *Men and Decisions*, p.186; *Times*, 7 August 1945; WSC, 'The Sinews of Peace', 5 March 1946, winstonchurchill.org; *HCD* Vol. 472, cols 1295, 1297–1298, 16 March 1950.

23. *HCD* Vol. 520, cols 28–31, 3 November 1953 and Vol. 530, cols 34–49, 12 July 1954.

24. Roberts, 'Churchill and Religion', pp.52–59.

25. WSC to Lady Randolph, March 1898, in Rose, *Literary Churchill*, p.29.

26. Moran diary, 2 July 1953, *CSFS*, p.417.

27. King diary, 22 May 1946, MACK/Library and Archives Canada online.

28. Churchill–Mountbatten meeting, 30 July 1946, *WSC*/VIII, p.249.

29. *Life*, 1 December 1972, pp.69–70.

30. Aikman, *Billy Graham*, pp.91–93; WSC to CSC, 25 May 1954, CHUR1/50A–B (images 427–431); *Chicago Tribune*, 4 April 1954.

31. *New York Times*, 10 November 2007.

32. WSC, *Marlborough*, pp.822–823.

33. DeGroot, *Bomb*, pp. 28–29. McGeorge Bundy later argued strongly, but unconvincingly, that the USA, not the UK, was the real progenitor: *Danger and Survival*, pp.4, 27–29.

34. Channon diary, 11 November 1941, *Chips*, pp.312–313.

35. See note 87 on p.36.

36. Taylor, 'War in Our Time', pp.8–9,

37. Bohr, 'War Years', p.204; Jones, 'Meetings in Wartime', p.281.

38. Rose, *Churchill*, p.197.

39. See p.92 including note 77.

40. According to Colville, in June 1945 Truman confirmed to Churchill that the test would happen my mid-July. Colville to Montague-Browne, 6 October 1959, Churchill Papers, CHUR 2/506 (image 84).

41. On this point, Ryan, *Anglo-America*, pp.1–3.

42. Quebec Agreement, 19 August 1943, PREM3/139/10.

43. WSC (M.662/4) to Lindemann, 27 May 1944, PREM3/139/11A; WSC–McMahon meeting, 8 January 1952, PREM11/291; Moran diary, 8 January 1952, *CSFS*, p.359.

44. Kissinger, *Diplomacy*, p. 507.

45. Macmillan, 27 October 1951, in Catterall, ed., *Diaries*, Vol. I, p. 111.

46. Lukacs, *Churchill*, p. 73.

47. Colville diary, 29 March 1955, *FOP*, pp. 706–707.

48. See p.288 including note 35.

49. Eisenhower news conference, 11 August 1954, *PPP*.

50. *HCD* Vol. 537, cols 1893–1905, 1 March 1955.

51. May, *Love and Will*, p.122.

BIBLIOGRAPHY

Unless otherwise stated, original publication has been consulted in this book.

Archival/manuscript sources

Bodleian Library, Oxford
  Papers of Earl (Clement) Attlee (ATTLEE).
  Papers of Lord (Harry) Crookshank (CROOK).
  Papers of Harold Macmillan, Earl of Stockton (MAC).
  Papers of Sir Rudolf Peierls (NCUACS).
  Papers of Lord Sherfield (SHER).
  Papers of Lady Ava Waverley (WAVE).
  Papers of Lord Woolton (WOOL).
Bohr Archive, Copenhagen
  Papers of Niels and Aage Bohr (BOHR).
British Library, London
  Papers of Paul Emrys-Evans.
Churchill Archives Centre, Churchill College, Cambridge
  Papers of Sir James Chadwick (CHAD).
  Papers of Sir Winston Churchill, Chartwell (CHAR) and Churchill (CHUR) collections,
    online version courtesy of Bloomsbury Publishers, London: http://www.churchillarchive.
    com/
  Papers of Hugh Lunghi (LUNG).
  Papers of John Martin (MART).
  Papers of Sir George Paget Thomson (TMSN).
Dwight D. Eisenhower Presidential Library (DDEL), *Abilene, Kansas*
  Papers of John Foster Dulles.
  Papers of James. C. Hagerty.
  Papers of C. D. Jackson.
  Whitman (Anne) file: Eisenhower diary, International and NSC series.
  DDEL online documents archive: http://www.eisenhower.archives.gov/research/online_
    documents/
Library and Archives of Canada, online collections
  The diary of William Mackenzie King: https://www.collectionscanada.gc.ca/king/index-e.
    html
Library of Congress, Washington DC
  Papers of Joseph and Stewart Alsop (ALSOP).
  Papers of Vannevar Bush (BUSH).
  Papers of Felix Frankfurter (FRANK).
  Papers of Admiral William D. Leahy (LEAHY).
  Papers of J. Robert Oppenheimer (JRO).
  Papers of Martin J. Sherwin (MJS).

Bibliography

Princeton University, New Jersey: Mudd Library
  Papers of John Foster Dulles (DULLES).
National Library of Scotland, Edinburgh
  Papers of R. H. Scott (SCOTT).
Nuffield College, Oxford
  Papers of Lord Cherwell, Professor F. A. Lindemann (LIND).
Franklin D. Roosevelt Presidential Library (FDRL), *Hyde Park, New York, online collections*
  Atomic Bomb collection.
  Diaries of Henry Morgenthau, Jr.
  Papers of Harry L. Hopkins.
  Map Room papers.
  President's Secretary's File.
  Papers of Alexander Sachs.
  All available at: http://www.fdrlibrary.marist.edu/archives/collections/franklin/index.
    php?p=collections/findingaid&id=309
Harry S. Truman Library (HSTL), *Independence, Missouri*
  President's Secretary's files.
  Online documents archive: https://www.trumanlibrary.org/photos/av-photo.htm
  White House Central files.
Trinity College, Cambridge
  Papers of R. A. Butler (BUTLER).
UK National Archives, Kew, London
  AB, Atomic Energy Authority files.
  AIR, Air Ministry files.
  CAB, Cabinet Office files.
  DEFE, Ministry of Defence files.
  DO, Dominions Office files.
  EG, Atomic Energy Policy files.
  ES, Atomic Weapons Research Establishment files.
  HO, Home Office files.
  KV, Security Service, Personal files series.
  PREM, Prime Minister's Private Office files.
  T, Treasury files.
US National Archives and Records Administration (NARA), *College Park, Maryland: Archives II*
  OSRD, RG227, Bush-Conant file, Microfilm M1392.
  State Department, RG59, decimal and lot files.
Yale University Library, New Haven, Connecticut
  The diary of Henry L. Stimson (microfilm).

Primary sources (published)

Ferrell, Robert H., ed., *Off the Record: The Private Papers of Harry S. Truman* (New York: Harper and Row, 1980).
Folliot, Denise, ed., *Documents on International Affairs, 1954* (Oxford: Oxford University Press, 1957).
Foreign Relations of the United States (Washington DC: State Department, Government Printing Office, various volumes, see full online collection at the University of Wisconsin: http://digicoll.library.wisc.edu/FRUS/Browse.htmlhttp://digicoll.library.wisc.edu/FRUS/Browse.html).

Gilbert, Martin, ed., *Winston S. Churchill, Volume V Companion Part 3, Documents – the Coming of War, 1936–1939* (London: Heinemann, 1982).

Hansard, *House of Commons Debates* and *House of Lords Debates*, online at: http://hansard.millbanksystems.com/index.html

Loewenheim, Francis L., Harold D. Langley and Manfred Jonas, eds, *Roosevelt and Churchill: Their Secret Wartime Correspondence* (London: Barrie and Jenkins, 1975).

Public Papers of the Presidents of the United States, various volumes, online at: http://www.presidency.ucsb.edu/ws/

Sherwood, Robert E., ed., *The White House Papers of Harry L. Hopkins*, Vol. I (London: Eyre and Spottiswoode, 1948).

United States Atomic Energy Commission, *In the Matter of J. Robert Oppenheimer*, full transcript of 1954 hearings, online at: https://archive.org/stream/unitedstatesatom007206mbp/unitedstatesatom007206mbp_djvu.txt

Works by Churchill

My Early Life, 1874–1904 (New York: Touchstone, 1996 edition).

Marlborough: His Life and Times, Volume I (Chicago: University of Chicago Press, 2002 edition).

The World Crisis, 1911–1918, abridged, 2 volumes (London: Odhams, 1938 edition).

Thoughts and Adventures (London: Odhams, 1948 edition).

Great Contemporaries (London: Odhams, 1949 edition).

The Second World War, 6 volumes (London: Penguin, 1985 editions, listing below with year of original UK publication):
    The Gathering Storm (1948).
    Their Finest Hour (1949).
    The Grand Alliance (1950).
    The Hinge of Fate (1951).
    Closing the Ring (1952).
    Triumph and Tragedy (1954).

The Second World War: Abridged One-Volume Edition with a New Epilogue on the Years 1945 to 1957 (London: Cassell, 1965).

'Shall We All Commit Suicide?', *Nash's Pall Mall*, 24 September 1924.

'Mass Effects in Modern Life', *Strand*, 1925, reprinted May 1931.

'H. G. Wells', *Sunday Pictorial*, 23 August 1931.

'Fifty Years Hence', *Strand*, December 1931.

'The Highroad of the Future', *Collier's Magazine*, 4 January 1947.

Biographies and studies of Churchill

Addison, Paul, *Churchill: The Unexpected Hero* (Oxford: Oxford University Press, 2005).

Bar-Noi, Uri, *The Cold War and Soviet Mistrust of Churchill's Pursuit of Détente, 1951–1955* (Brighton: Sussex Academic Press, 2008).

Bardens, Dennis, *Churchill in Parliament* (New York: Barnes, 1969).

Best, Geoffrey, *Churchill: A Study in Greatness* (London: Hambledon, 2001).

Best, Geoffrey, *Churchill and War* (London: Hambledon, 2005).

Carlton, David, *Churchill and the Soviet Union* (Manchester: Manchester University Press, 2000).

Charmley, John, *Churchill: The End of Glory* (London: Hodder and Stoughton, 1993).

Bibliography

Churchill, Randolph (first two volumes) and Gilbert, Martin, *Winston S. Churchill* (London: Heinemann, dates as below).

　Volume I, *Youth, 1874–1900* (1966).
　Volume II, *Young Statesman, 1900–1914* (1967).
　Volume III, *1914–1916* (1971).
　Volume IV, *1917–1922* (1975).
　Volume V, *1922–1939* (1976).
　Volume VI, *1939–1941, Finest Hour* (1983).
　Volume VII, *1941–1945, Road to Victory* (1986).
　Volume VIII, *1945–1965, Never Despair* (1988).

Colville, John, *The Churchillians* (London: Weidenfeld and Nicolson, 1981).

Dilks, David, *Churchill and Company: Allies and Rivals in War and Peace* (London: Tauris, 2012).

Eade, Charles, ed., *Churchill by His Contemporaries* (London: Reprint Society, 1955 edition).

Farmelo, Graham, *Churchill's Bomb: A Hidden History of Science, War and Politics* (London: Faber & Faber, 2013).

Gardner, Brian, *Churchill in His Time: A Study in a Reputation, 1939–1945* (London: Methuen, 1948).

Gilbert, Martin, *Churchill: A Life* (London: Heinemann, 1991).

Gilbert, Martin, *Churchill and America* (London: Free Press, 2005).

Graebner, Walter, *My Dear Mr. Churchill* (Boston: Houghton Mifflin, 1965).

Halle, Kay, ed., *The Irrepressible Churchill: Through His Own Words and the Eyes of his Contemporaries* (London: Robson, 1988 edition).

Harbutt, Fraser J., *Iron Curtain: Churchill, America and the Origins of the Cold War* (Oxford: Oxford University Press, 1988).

Hastings, Max, *Finest Years: Churchill as Warlord, 1940–45* (London: Harper Press, 2009).

Jenkins, Roy, *Churchill* (London: Macmillan, 2001).

Kemper III, R. Crosby, ed., *Winston Churchill: Resolution, Defiance, Magnanimity, Good Will* (Columbia, MO: University of Missouri Press, 1996).

Kimball, Warren F., *The Juggler: Franklin Roosevelt as Wartime Statesman* (Princeton, NJ: Princeton University Press, 1991)

Kimball, Warren F., *Forged in War: Churchill, Roosevelt and the Second World War* (London: Harper Press, 1997).

Larres, Klaus, *Churchill's Cold War: The Politics of Personal Diplomacy* (New Haven, CT: Yale University Press, 2002).

Leaming, Barbara, *Churchill Defiant: Fighting On, 1945–1955* (London: Harper Press, 2010).

Lough, David, *No More Champagne: Churchill and his Money* (London: Head of Zeus, 2015).

Louis, William Roger and Robert Blake, eds, *Churchill: A Major New Assessment of his Life in Peace and War* (Oxford: Oxford University Press, 1996).

Lukacs, John, *Churchill: Visionary, Statesman, Historian* (New Haven, CT: Yale University Press, 2004 edition).

McCrae, Stuart, *Winston Churchill's Toyshop* (Kineton: Roundwood Press, 1971).

Muller, James W., ed., *Churchill as Peacemaker* (Cambridge: Cambridge University Press, 1997).

Muller, James W., ed., *Churchill's Iron Curtain Speech Fifty Years Later* (Columbia, MO: University of Missouri Press, 1999).

Ramsden, John, *Man of the Century: Winston Churchill and his Legend since 1945* (London: Harper Collins, 2002).

Reynolds, David, *In Command of History: Churchill Fighting and Writing the Second World War* (London: Allen Lane, 2004).

Rose, Jonathan, *The Literary Churchill: Author, Reader, Actor* (New Haven, CT: Yale University Press, 2014).

Rose, Norman, *Churchill: An Unruly Life* (London: Tauris Parke, 2009 edition).

Seldon, Anthony, *Churchill's Indian Summer: The Conservative Government, 1951–55* (London: Hodder and Stoughton, 1981).

Soames, Mary, *Clementine Churchill: The Biography of a Marriage* (Boston, MA: Houghton Mifflin, 1979).

Soames, Mary, ed., *Speaking for Themselves: The Personal Letters of Winston and Clementine Churchill* (London: Black Swan, 1999 edition).

Soames, Mary, *A Daughter's Tale: The Memoir of Winston and Clementine Churchill's Youngest Child* (London: Black Swan, 2012 edition).

Toye, Richard, *The Roar of the Lion: The Untold Story of Churchill's World War II Speeches* (Oxford: Oxford University Press, 2013).

Toye, Richard, *Churchill's Empire: The World that Made Him and the World He Made*, (Basingstoke: Macmillan, 2010).

Trory, Ernie, *Churchill and the Bomb: A Study in Pragmatism* (Hove: Crabtree, 1984).

Wheeler-Bennett, John, *Action This Day: Working with Churchill* (London: Macmillan, 1968).

Young, John, *Winston Churchill's Last Campaign: Britain and the Cold War 1951–55* (Oxford: Clarendon Press, 1996).

Zoller, Curtis J., *Annotated Bibliography of Works about Sir Winston Churchill* (Abingdon: Routledge, 2015 edition).

Published diaries and correspondence

Bond, Brian, ed., *Chief of Staff: The Diaries of Lieutenant-General Sir Henry Pownall* (London: Cooper, 1974).

Boyle, Peter, ed., *The Churchill–Eisenhower Correspondence, 1953–1955* (Chapel Hill, NC: University of North Carolina Press, 1990).

Bright-Holmes, John, ed., *Like It Was: The Diaries of Malcolm Muggeridge* (London: Collins, 1981).

Butler, Susan, ed., *My Dear Mr Stalin: The Complete Correspondence of Franklin D. Roosevelt and Joseph V. Stalin* (New Haven, CT: Yale University Press, 2005).

Catterall, Peter, ed., *The Macmillan Diaries: Volume I, the Cabinet Years 1950–1957* (London: Macmillan, 2003).

Cockett, Richard, ed., *My Dear Max: The Letters of Brendan Bracken to Lord Beaverbrook, 1925–1958* (London: Historian's Press, 1990).

Colville, John, *The Fringes of Power: Downing Street Diaries, 1939–1955* (London: Hodder and Stoughton, 1985).

Danchev, Alex and Daniel Todman, eds, *The War Diaries of Field Marshal Lord Alanbrooke, 1939–1945* (London: Weidenfeld and Nicolson, 2001).

Dilks, David, ed., *The Diaries of Sir Alexander Cadogan* (London: Cassell, 1971).

Ferrell, Robert H., ed., *The Eisenhower Diaries* (New York: Norton, 1981).

Ferrell, Robert H., ed., *The Diary of James C. Hagerty: Eisenhower in Mid-Course, 1954–1955* (Bloomington, IN: Indiana University Press, 1983).

Ferrell, Robert H., ed., *Dear Bess – the Letters from Harry to Bess Truman, 1910–1959* (New York: Norton, 1984).

Ferrell, Robert H., ed., *Truman in the White House: The Diary of Eben A. Ayers* (Columbia, MO: University of Missouri Press, 1991).

Hart-Davis, Duff, ed., *King's Counsellor: Abdication and War – The Diaries of Sir Alan Lascelles* (London: Weidenfeld and Nicolson, 2006).

Gorodetsky, Gabriel, ed., *The Maisky Diaries: Red Ambassador to the Court of St. James's, 1932–1943* (New Haven, CT: Yale University Press, 2015).

Bibliography

Harvey, John, ed., *The War Diaries of Oliver Harvey, 1941–1945* (London: Collins, 1978).

James, Robert Rhodes, ed., *'Chips': The Diaries of Sir Henry Channon* (London: Phoenix, 1996 edition).

Jebb, Miles, ed., *The Diaries of Cynthia Jebb* (London: Constable, 1991).

Jones, Thomas, *A Diary With Letters, 1931–1950* (Oxford: Oxford University Press, 1954).

Lilienthal, David, *Journals Volume II: The Atomic Energy Years* (New York: Harper and Row, 1964).

Millis, Walter, ed., *The Forrestal Diaries* (New York: Viking, 1951).

Milne, James Lees, *Mingled Measure: Diaries 1953–1972* (London: Murray, 1994).

Moran, Lord, *Winston Churchill: The Struggle for Survival* (London: Constable, 1966).

Morgan, Janet, ed., *The Backbench Diaries of Richard Crossman* (London: Hamilton and Cape, 1981).

Nenni, Pietro, *Tempo di Guerra Freda: Diari 1943–1956* (Milan: Sugar, 1981).

Nicolson, Nigel, ed., *Harold Nicolson: Diaries and Letters, Volume II – The War Years, 1939–1945* (New York: Atheneum, 1967).

Nicolson, Nigel, *Harold Nicolson: Diaries and Letters, Volume III, 1945–1962* (London: Collins, 1968).

Norwich, John Julius, ed., *The Duff Cooper Diaries* (London: Phoenix, 2006 edition).

Pickersgill, J. W., ed., *The Mackenzie King Record: Volume I, 1939–1944* (Toronto: University of Toronto Press, 1960).

Pimlott, Ben, ed., *The Second World War Diary of Hugh Dalton, 1940–1945* (London: Cape, 1986).

Pimlott, Ben, ed., *The Political Diary of Hugh Dalton, 1918–40, 1945–60* (London: Cape, 1987).

Pottle, Mark, ed., *Champion Redoubtable: The Diaries and Letters of Violet Bonham Carter, 1914–1945* (London: Weidenfeld and Nicolson, 1998).

Pottle, Mark, ed., *Daring to Hope: The Diaries and Letters of Violet Bonham-Carter, 1946–1969* (London: Weidenfeld and Nicolson, 2000).

Shuckburgh, Evelyn, *Descent to Suez: Diaries, 1951–56* (London: Weidenfeld and Nicolson, 1986).

Stuart, Charles, ed., *The Reith Diaries* (London: HarperCollins, 1975).

Sulzberger, C. L., *A Long Row of Candles: Memoirs and Diaries, 1934–1954* (Toronto: Macmillan, 1969).

Warner, Geoffrey, ed., *In the Midst of Events: The Foreign Office Diaries and Papers of Kenneth Younger, February 1950–October 1951* (London: Routledge, 2005).

Wyndham, Joan, *Love is Blue: A Wartime Diary* (London: Flamingo, 1987 edition).

Memoirs

Allison, John, *Ambassador from the Prairie* (Boston, MA: Houghton Mifflin, 1973).

Attlee, Clement, *As It Happened* (London: Heinemann, 1954).

Beria, Sergo, *Beria My Father: Inside Stalin's Kremlin* (London: Duckworth, 2003 edition).

Boothby, Lord, *My Yesterday, Your Tomorrow* (London: Quality Book Club, 1962).

Brandon, Henry, *Special Relationships: A Foreign Correspondent's Memoirs from Roosevelt to Reagan* (New York: Atheneum, 1988).

Bush, Vannevar, *Pieces of the Action* (London: Cassell, 1972).

Butler, R. A., *The Art of the Possible* (London: Hamish Hamilton, 1971).

Byrnes, James F., *Speaking Frankly* (London: Heinemann, 1947).

Churchill, Sarah, *A Thread in the Tapestry* (London: Deutsch, 1967).

Churchill, Sarah, *Keep on Dancing: An Autobiography* (London: Weidenfeld and Nicolson, 1981).

Conant, James B., *My Several Lives* (New York: Harper and Row, 1970).

Eden, Anthony, *Memoirs: Full Circle* (London: Cassell, 1960).

Eden, Anthony, *Memoirs: The Reckoning* (London: Cassell, 1965).

Eden, Clarissa (with Cate Haste), *Clarissa Eden: A Memoir from Churchill to Eden* (London: Weidenfeld and Nicolson, 2007).

Frisch, Otto, *What Little I Remember* (Cambridge: Cambridge University Press, 1980).

Gromyko, Andrei, *Memoirs* (New York: Doubleday, 1989).

Groves, Leslie R., *Now It Can Be Told* (London: Deutsch, 1963).

Harrod, Roy, *The Prof: A Personal Memoir of Lord Cherwell* (London: Macmillan, 1959).

Hayter, William, *A Double Life: The Memoirs of Sir William Hayter* (London: Hamish Hamilton, 1974).

Ismay, Lord, *The Memoirs of General the Lord Ismay* (London: Heinemann, 1960).

Khrushchev, Sergei, ed., *The Memoirs of Nikita Khrushchev, Vol. I* (University Park, PA: Pennsylvania State University Press, 2004).

Macmillan, Harold, *Tides of Fortune, 1945–1955* (London: Macmillan, 1969).

Mallaby, George, *From My Level: Unwritten Minutes* (London: Hutchinson, 1965).

McDonald, Iverach, *A Man of the Times* (London: Hamilton, 1976).

Montague Browne, Anthony, *Long Sunset: Memoirs of Winston Churchill's Last Private Secretary* (London: Cassell, 1995).

Morgan, General Sir Frederick, *Peace and War: A Soldier's Life* (London: Hodder and Stoughton, 1961).

Morrison, Herbert, *An Autobiography* (London: Odhams, 1960).

Peierls, Rudolph, *Bird of Passage: Recollections of a Physicist* (Princeton, NJ: Princeton University Press, 1985).

Raczynski, Count Edward, *In Allied London* (London: Weidenfeld and Nicolson, 1962).

Reston, James, *Deadline: A Memoir* (New York: Random House, 1991).

Scott, Harold, *Your Obedient Servant* (London: Deutsch, 1959).

Stimson, Henry L. (with McGeorge Bundy), *On Active Service in Peace and War* (New York: Harper and Brothers, 1948).

Strauss, Lewis L., *Men and Decisions* (New York: Doubleday, 1962).

Truman, Harry S., *Memoirs: Year of Decisions* (New York: Doubleday, 1955).

Truman, Harry S., *Memoirs: Years of Trial and Hope* (New York: Doubleday, 1956).

Williams, Francis, *A Prime Minister Remembers: The War and Post-War Memoirs of the Rt Hon. Earl Attlee* (London: Heinemann, 1961).

Winant, John G., *A Letter from Grosvenor Square: An Account of a Stewardship* (London: Hodder and Stoughton, 1948 edition).

General works

Aikman, David, *Billy Graham: His Life and Influence* (Nashville, TN: Nelson, 2007).

Alperovitz, Gar, *The Decision to Use the Atomic Bomb and the Architecture of an American Myth* (London: Harper Collins, 1995).

Ambrose, Stephen E., *Eisenhower the President, 1952–1969* (London: Allen and Unwin, 1984).

Anderson, David L., *Trapped by Success: The Eisenhower Administration and Vietnam, 1953–1961* (New York: Columbia University Press, 1991).

Arnold, Lorna, *Britain and the H-Bomb* (Basingstoke: Palgrave, 2001).

Barker, Elisabeth, *Churchill and Eden at War* (London: Macmillan, 1978).

Baylis, John and Kristan Stoddart, *The British Nuclear Experience: The Role of Beliefs, Culture and Identity* (Oxford: Oxford University Press, 2015).

Beevor, Antony, *The Second World War* (London: Weidenfeld and Nicolson, 2012).

Bennett, Gill, *Six Moments of Crisis: Inside British Foreign Policy* (Oxford: Oxford University Press, 2013).

Bibliography

Beschloss, Michael, *The Conquerors: Roosevelt, Truman and the Destruction of Hitler's Germany* (New York: Simon and Schuster, 2002).

Bird, Kai and Martin Sherwin, *American Prometheus: The Triumph and Tragedy of J. Robert Oppenheimer* (London: Atlantic, 2008).

Birkenhead, Lord, *The Prof in Two Worlds: The Official Life of Professor F. A. Lindemann, Viscount Cherwell* (London: Collins, 1961).

Botti, Timothy J., *The Long Wait: The Forging of the Anglo-American Nuclear Alliance, 1945–1958* (New York: Greenwood Press, 1987).

Brinkley, Douglas, *Dean Acheson: The Cold War Years, 1953–1971* (New Haven: Yale University Press, 1992).

Bullock, Alan, *Ernest Bevin: Foreign Secretary* (New York: Norton, 1983).

Bundy, McGeorge, *Danger and Survival: Choices about the Bomb in the First Fifty Years* (New York: Random House, 1988).

Burk, Kathleen, *Old World, New World: The Story of Britain and America* (London: Abacus, 2009).

Byron, Lord, *Don Juan* (1819).

Cable, James, *The Geneva Conference of 1954 on Indochina* (London: Macmillan, 1986).

Cairncross, Alec, *Years of Recovery: British Economic Policy, 1945–51* (London: Methuen, 1985).

Calvocoressi, Peter, *Survey of International Affairs, 1953* (Oxford: Oxford University Press, 1956).

Cathcart, Brian, *Test of Greatness: Britain's Struggle for the Atomic Bomb* (London: John Murray, 1994).

Clark, Ian and Nicholas J. Wheeler, *The British Origins of Nuclear Strategy, 1945–1955* (Oxford; Clarendon Press, 1989).

Clark, Ronald, *The Greatest Power on* Earth (London: Sidgwick and Jackson, 1980).

Clark, Ronald, *Tizard* (London: Methuen, 1965).

Clymer, Kenton J., *Quest for Freedom: The United States and India's Independence* (New York: Columbia University Press, 1995).

Costigliola, Frank, *Roosevelt's Lost Alliances: How Personal Politics Helped Start the Cold War* (Princeton, NJ: Princeton University Press, 2012).

Craig, Campbell and Sergey Radchenko, *The Atomic Bomb and the Origins of the Cold War* (New Haven, CT: Yale University Press, 2008).

Dallek, Robert, *Franklin D. Roosevelt and American Foreign Policy, 1932–1945* (New York: Oxford University Press, 1995 edition).

Dallek, Robert, *The Lost Peace: Leadership in a Time of Horror and Hope, 1945–1953* (New York: Harper, 2005).

DeGroot, Gerard, *The Bomb: A Life* (Cambridge, MA: Harvard University Press, 2005).

De Ropp, Robert S. *The New Prometheans: Creative and Destructive Forces in Modern Science* (New York: Delacorte, 1972).

Dickens, Charles, *The Adventures of Oliver Twist* (Boston: Ticknor and Fields, 1866 edition).

Divine, Robert A., *Blowing on the Wind: The Nuclear Test Ban Debate, 1954–1968* (New York: Oxford University Press, 1978).

Dixon, Piers, *Double Diploma: The Life of Sir Pierson Dixon, Don and Diplomat* (London: Hutchison, 1968).

Dutton, David, *Anthony Eden: A Life and Reputation* (London: Arnold, 1997).

Edgerton, David, *Britain's War Machine* (London: Penguin, 2012 edition).

Eggleston, Albert, *Canada's Nuclear Story* (Toronto: Clarke and Irwin, 1965).

Ehrman, John, *The Atomic Bomb: An Account of British Policy in the Second World War* (London: Cabinet Office, 1954).

Fall, Bernard, *Hell in a Very Small Place: The Siege of Dien Bien Phu* (Philadelphia: Lippincott, 1966).

Forster, E. M., *Howards End* (London: Arnold, 1910).

Fort, Adrian, *Prof: The Life of Frederick Lindemann* (London: Jonathan Cape, 2003).

Frank, Richard, *Downfall: The End of the Imperial Japanese Empire* (New York: Random House, 1999).

French, A. and P. Kennedy, eds, *Niels Bohr: A Centenary Volume* (Cambridge, MA: Harvard University Press, 1985).

Gaddis, John Lewis, *The Cold War* (London: Allen Lane, 2005).

Gaddis, John Lewis, *Strategies of Containment: A Critical Appraisal of American National Security Policy during the Cold War* (Oxford: Oxford University Press, 2005 edition).

Gaddis, John Lewis, Philip H. Gordon, Ernest R. May and Jonathan Rosenberg, eds, *Cold War Statesmen Confront the Bomb* (Oxford: Oxford University Press, 1999).

Gannon, Robert, *The Cardinal Spellman Story* (Garden City: Doubleday, 1962).

Gellately, Robert, *Stalin's Curse: Battling for Communism in War and Cold War* (Oxford: Oxford University Press, 2013).

Glantz, David, *The Soviet Strategic Offensive against Manchuria, 1945: 'August Storm'* (London: Cass, 2003).

Goodman, Michael S., *Spying on the Nuclear Bear: Anglo-American Intelligence and the Soviet Bomb* (Stanford, CA: Stanford University Press, 2007).

Goodwin, Doris Kearns, *No Ordinary Time: Franklin and Eleanor Roosevelt – The Home Front in World War II* (New York: Simon and Schuster, 1994).

Gordin, Michael, *Red Cloud at Dawn: Truman, Stalin, and the End of the Atomic Monopoly* (New York: FSG, 2009).

Goudsmit, Samuel A., *ALSOS* (Woodbury, NY: AIP, 1996 edition).

Gowing, Margaret, *Britain and Atomic Energy, 1939–1945* (London: Macmillan, 1964).

Gowing, Margaret, *Independence and Deterrence: Britain and Atomic Energy, 1945–1952 – Volume I, Policy Making* (London: Macmillan, 1974).

Greenwood, Sean, *Britain and the Cold War, 1945–91* (Basingstoke: Macmillan, 2000).

Ham, Paul, *Hiroshima-Nagasaki* (London: Transworld, 2011).

Hamby, Alonzo L., *Man of the People: A Life of Harry S. Truman* (Oxford: Oxford University Press, 1995).

Harbutt, Fraser J., *Yalta 1945: Europe and America at the Crossroads* (Cambridge: Cambridge University Press, 2010).

Hasegawa, Tsuyoshi, *Racing the Enemy: Stalin, Truman, and the Surrender of Japan* (Cambridge, MA: Belknap, 2005).

Hastings, Max, *Nemesis: The Battle for Japan, 1944–46* (London: Harper Press, 2007).

Hastings, Max, *All Hell Let Loose: The World at War, 1939–1945* (London: Harper Press, 2011)

Hastings, Max, *The Secret War: Spies, Codes and Guerrillas, 1939–1945* (London: Collins, 2015).

Hennessey, Thomas, *Britain's Korean War: Cold War Diplomacy, Strategy and Security, 1950–1953* (Manchester: Manchester University Press, 2013).

Hennessy, Peter, *The Prime Minister: The Office and its Holders since 1945* (London: Penguin, 2001 edition).

Hennessy, Peter, *Having It So Good: Britain in the Fifties* (London: Allen Lane, 2006).

Hennessy, Peter, *Cabinets and the Bomb* (Oxford: Oxford University Press/British Academy, 2007).

Hennessy, Peter, *Secret State: Preparing for the Worst, 1945–2010* (London: Penguin, 2010 edition).

Herken, Gregg, *The Winning Weapon: The Atomic Bomb in the Cold War, 1945–1950* (New York: Knopf, 1980).

Hershberg, James G., *James B. Conant: Harvard to Hiroshima and the Making of the Nuclear Age* (New York: Knopf, 1993).

Hewlett, Richard G. and Oscar E. Anderson, *A History of the United States Atomic Energy Commission: Volume I, The New World, 1939–1946* (University Park, PA: Pennsylvania State University Press, 1962).

Bibliography

Hewlett, Richard G. and Francis Duncan, *A History of the United States Atomic Energy Commission: Volume II, Atomic Shield, 1947–1952* (University Park, PA: Pennsylvania State University Press, 1969).

Hewlett, Richard G. and Jack M. Holl, *A History of the United States Atomic Energy Commission: Volume III, Atoms for Peace and War, 1953–1961* (Berkeley: University of California Press, 1989).

Hilderbrand, Robert C., *Dumbarton Oaks: The Origins of the United Nations and the Search for Postwar Security* (Chapel Hill, NC: University of North Carolina Press, 1990).

Hobbs, David, *The British Pacific Fleet: The Royal Navy's Most Powerful Strike Force* (Annapolis, MD: Naval Institute Press, 2011).

Hogg, Jonathan, *British Nuclear Culture: Official and Unofficial Narratives in the Long 20th Century* (London: Bloomsbury, 2016).

Holloway, David, *Stalin and the Bomb* (New Haven: Yale University Press, 1994).

Hoopes, Townsend, *The Devil and John Foster Dulles* (Boston: Little, Brown, 1973).

Horne, Alistair, *Macmillan: Volume I, 1894–1956* (London: Macmillan, 1988).

Howard, Anthony, *RAB: The Life of R. A. Butler* (London: Cape, 1987).

Immerman, Richard H., *John Foster Dulles: Piety, Pragmatism and Power in US Foreign Policy* (Wilmington, DE: Scholarly Resources, 1990).

James, Laylin K., *Nobel Laureates in Chemistry, 1901–1992* (Washington, DC: American Chemical Society, 1993).

James, Robert Rhodes, *Churchill: A Study in Failure, 1900–1939* (London: Pelican, 1973 edition).

James, Robert Rhodes, *Anthony Eden* (London: Weidenfeld and Nicolson, 1986).

James, Robert Rhodes, *A Spirit Undaunted: The Political Role of George VI* (London: Abacus, 1999).

Jones, Matthew, *After Hiroshima: The United States, Race and Nuclear Weapons in Asia, 1945–1965* (Cambridge: Cambridge University Press, 2012 edition).

Khlevniuk, Oleg V., *Stalin: New Biography of a Dictator* (New Haven, CT: Yale University Press, 2015).

Kinvig, Clifford, *Churchill's Crusade: The British Invasion of Russia, 1918–1920* (London: Hambledon Continuum, 2006).

Kissinger, Henry, *Diplomacy* (London: Simon and Schuster, 1994).

Kynaston, David, *Austerity Britain, 1945–51* (London: Bloomsbury, 2007).

Kynaston, David, *Family Britain, 1951–1957* (London: Bloomsbury, 2009).

Laucht, Christoph, *Elemental Germans: Klaus Fuchs, Rudolf Peierls, and the Making of British Nuclear Culture, 1939–59* (Basingstoke: Palgrave Macmillan, 2012).

Lawrence, Mark, *Assuming the Burden: Europe and the American Commitment to War in Vietnam* (Berkeley, CA: University of California Press, 2005).

Logevall, Frederik, *Embers of War: The Fall of an Empire and the Making of America's Vietnam* (New York: Random House, 2012).

Louis, William Roger and Hedley Bull, eds, *The Special Relationship: Anglo-American Relations since 1945* (Oxford: Oxford University Press, 1989 edition).

Malloy, Sean, *Atomic Tragedy: Henry L. Stimson and the Decision to Use the Bomb against Japan* (Ithaca, NY: Cornell University Press, 2008).

Marston, Daniel, ed., *The Pacific War Companion* (Oxford: Osprey, 2005).

May, Rollo, *Love and Will* (New York: Delta, 1969).

McCullough, David, *Truman* (New York: Simon and Schuster, 1992).

McNeal, Robert, *Stalin: Man and Ruler* (London: Macmillan, 1988).

Miller, Merle, *Plain Speaking: An Oral Biography of Harry S. Truman* (New York: Berkeley, 1973).

Milton, Giles, *Russian Roulette: How British Spies Thwarted Lenin's Bid for Global Revolution* (London: Sceptre, 2013).

Miscamble, Wilson D., *From Roosevelt to Truman: Potsdam, Hiroshima, and the Cold War* (Cambridge: Cambridge University Press, 2007).

Miscamble, Wilson D., *The Most Controversial Decision: Truman, the Atomic Bombs, and the Defeat of Japan* (Cambridge: Cambridge University Press, 2011 edition).

Montefiore, Simon Sebag, *Stalin: The Court of the Red Tsar* (London: Weidenfeld and Nicolson, 2003).

Newhouse, John, *War and Peace in the Nuclear Age* (New York: Knopf, 1989).

Nicolson, Harold, *Public Faces* (London: Constable, 1932).

Nutting, Anthony, *Europe Will Not Wait* (London: Chatto and Windus, 1960).

Offner, Arnold, *Another Such Victory: President Truman and the Cold War, 1945–1953* (Stanford: Stanford University Press, 2002).

Overy, Richard, *The Bombing War: Europe 1939–1945* (London: Allen Lane, 2013).

Pak, Chi Young, *Korea and the United Nations* (The Hague: Kluwer Law International, 2000).

Paul, Septimus H., *Nuclear Rivals: Anglo-American Atomic Relations, 1941–1952* (Columbus: Ohio State University Press, 2000).

Pierre, Andrew, *Nuclear Politics: The British Experience with an Independent Strategic Force, 1939–1970* (Oxford: Oxford University Press, 1972).

Powers, Thomas, *Heisenberg's War: The Secret History of the German Bomb* (New York: Knopf, 1993).

Reader, W. J., *Imperial Chemical Industries: A History, Vol. II* (London: Oxford University Press, 1975).

Resis, A., ed., *Molotov Remembers: Conversations with Felix Chuev* (Chicago, IL: Ivan R. Dee, 1993).

Reynolds, David, *Britannia Overruled: British Policy and Power in the 20th Century* (Harlow: Longman, 1991).

Reynolds, David, *From World War to Cold War: Churchill, Roosevelt, and the International History of the 1940s* (Oxford: Oxford University Press, 2006).

Reynolds, David, *Summits: Six Meetings that Shaped the Twentieth Century* (New York: Basic Books, 2009 edition).

Rhodes, Richard, *The Making of the Atomic Bomb* (New York: Simon and Schuster, 1986).

Rhodes, Richard, *Dark Sun: The Making of the Hydrogen Bomb* (New York: Simon and Schuster, 1995).

Richardson, Charles, *From Churchill's Secret Circle to the BBC: The Biography of Lieutenant General Sir Ian Jacob* (London: Brassey's, 1991).

Rioux, Jean-Pierre, *The Fourth Republic, 1944–1958* (Cambridge: Cambridge University Press, 1989 edition, trans.).

Roberts, Geoffrey, *Stalin's Wars: From World War to Cold War, 1939–1953* (New Haven, CT: Yale University Press, 2006).

Roosevelt, Elliott, *As He Saw It* (New York: Duell, Sloan and Pearce, 1946).

Rose, Paul, *Heisenberg and the Nazi Atomic Bomb Project: A Study in German Culture* (Berkeley: University of California Press, 1998).

Rotter, Andrew, *Hiroshima: The World's Bomb* (Oxford: Oxford University Press, 2008).

Rozental, Stefan, ed., *Niels Bohr: His Life and Work as Seen by His Friends and Colleagues* (Amsterdam: North Holland Publishing Company, 1967).

Ruane, Kevin, *The Rise and Fall of the European Defence Community: Anglo-American Relations and the Crisis of European Defence, 1950–1955* (Basingstoke: Macmillan, 2000).

Ryan, Henry B., *The Vision of Anglo-America: The US–UK Alliance and the Emerging Cold War, 1943–1946* (Cambridge: Cambridge University Press, 1987).

Sainsbury, Keith, *The Turning Point: Roosevelt, Stalin, Churchill and Chiang Kai-shek, 1943* (Oxford: Oxford University Press, 1986).

Sanger, Clyde, *Malcolm MacDonald: Bringing an End to Empire* (Liverpool: Liverpool University Press, 1995).

Schlosser, Eric, *Command and Control* (London: Penguin, 2013).

Sherwin, Martin J., *A World Destroyed: The Atomic Bomb and the Grand Alliance* (New York: Vintage, 1977 edition).

Bibliography

Snow, C. P., *Science and Government* (Cambridge, MA: Harvard University Press, 1961).

Snyder, Timothy and Ray Brandon, eds, *Stalin and Europe: Imitation and Domination, 1928–1953* (Oxford: Oxford University Press, 2014).

Statler, Katherine, *Replacing France: The Origins of American Intervention in Vietnam* (Lexington, KY: University Press of Kentucky, 2007).

Steel, Ronald, *Walter Lippmann and the American Century* (New Brunswick, NJ: Transaction, 1999 edition).

Stueck, William, *Rethinking the Korean War: A New Diplomatic and Strategic History* Princeton, NJ: Princeton University Press, 2002).

Stueck, William, ed., *The Korean War in World History* (Lexington, KY: University of Kentucky Press, 2004).

Szasz, Ferenc, *British Scientists and the Manhattan Project: The Los Alamos Years* (Basingstoke: Palgrave Macmillan, 1992).

Taylor, A. J. P., *English History, 1914–1945* (Oxford: Clarendon Press, 1965).

Taylor, A. J. P., *Essays in English History* (London: Penguin, 1976).

Thorpe, D. R., *Eden: The Life and Times of Anthony Eden, First Early of Avon, 1897–1977* (London: Chatto and Windus, 2003).

Thorpe, D. R., *Supermac: The Life of Harold Macmillan* (London: Chatto and Windus, 2010).

Thorne, Christopher, *Allies of a Kind: The United States, Britain and the War against Japan, 1941–1945* (Oxford: Oxford University Press, 1978).

Van Thal, Herbert, ed., *The Prime Ministers, Vol. II* (London: Allen and Unwin, 1975).

Walker, J. Samuel, *Prompt and Utter Destruction: Truman and the Use of the Atomic Bombs against Japan* (Chapel Hill, NC: University of North Carolina Press, 2005).

Walker, Mark, *German National Socialism and the Quest for Nuclear Power* (Cambridge: Cambridge University Press, 1989).

Wells, H. G., *The World Set Free* (London: Odhams, 1948 edition).

Wheeler-Bennett, John, *John Anderson: Viscount Waverley* (London: Macmillan, 1962).

Windrow, Martin, *The Last Valley: Dien Bien Phu and the French Defeat in Vietnam* (London: Weidenfeld and Nicolson, 2004).

Woods, Randall B., *A Changing of the Guard: Anglo-American Relations, 1941–1946* (Chapel Hill: University of North Carolina Press, 1990).

Yergin, Daniel, *Shattered Peace: The Origins of the Cold War and the National Security State* (London: Deutsch, 1978).

Young, John, ed., *The Foreign Policy of Churchill's Peacetime Administration, 1951–1955* (Leicester: Leicester University Press, 1988).

Young, John, Effie Pedaliu and Michael Kandiah, eds, *Britain in Global Politics: Vol. 2, From Churchill to Blair* (Basingstoke: Palgrave Macmillan, 2013).

Zachary, G. Pascal, *Endless Frontier: Vannevar Bush, Engineer of the American Century* (New York: Free Press, 1997).

Zaloga, Steven J., *The Kremlin's Nuclear Shield: The Rise and Fall of Russia's Strategic Nuclear Forces, 1945–2000* (Washington, DC: Smithsonian, 2014).

Zubok, Vladislav and Constantine Pleshakov, *Inside the Kremlin's Cold War: From Stalin to Khrushchev* (Cambridge, MA: Harvard University Press, 1997 edition).

Academic/professional journal articles and chapters in edited collections

Aaserud, Finn, 'The Scientist and the Statesman: Niels Bohr's Political Crusade during World War II', *Historical Studies in the Physical and Biological Sciences*, Vol. 30, No. 1 (1999), pp.1–47.

Adamthwaite, Anthony, 'The Foreign Office and Policy-making', in Young, ed., *Peacetime Administration*, 'Introduction'.

Addison, Paul, 'The Three Careers of Winston Churchill', *TRHS*, Vol. 11 (2001), pp.183–200.

Ball, S. J., 'Military Nuclear Relations between the United States and Great Britain under the Terms of the McMahon Act, 1946–1958', *Historical Journal*, Vol. 38, No. 2 (1995), pp.439–454.

Barnett, Nicholas, '"No Protection against the H-bomb": Press and Popular Reactions to the Coventry Civil Defence Controversy', *Cold War History*, Vol. 15, No. 3 (2015), pp.277–300.

Bell, Christopher, 'The Singapore Strategy and the Deterrence of Japan: Winston Churchill, the Admiralty, and the Dispatch of Force Z', *English Historical Review*, Vol. 116, No. 467 (2001), pp.604–34.

Bernstein, Barton J., 'The Quest for Security: American Foreign Policy and International Control of Atomic Energy, 1942–1946', *Journal of American History*, Vol. 60, No. 4 (1974), pp.1003–1044.

Bernstein, Barton J., 'Roosevelt, Truman, and the Atomic Bomb, 1941–1945: A Reinterpretation', *Political Science Quarterly*, Vol. 90, No. 1 (1975), pp.23–69.

Bernstein, Barton J., 'The Uneasy Alliance: Roosevelt, Churchill, and the Atomic Bomb, 1940–1945', *Western Political Quarterly*, Vol. 29, No. 2 (1976), pp.202–230.

Bernstein, Barton J., 'The Atomic Bombings Revisited', *Foreign Affairs*, Vol. 74, No. 1 (1995), pp.135–152.

Bernstein, Barton J., 'Understanding the Atomic Bomb and the Japanese Surrender: Missed Opportunities, Little-Known Near Disasters, and Modern Memory', *Diplomatic History*, Vol. 19, No. 2 (1995), pp.227–273.

Bernstein, Barton J., 'Reconsidering the "Atomic General": Leslie R. Groves', *Journal of Military History*, Vol. 67, No. 3 (2003), pp.883–920.

Bohr, Aage, 'The War Years and the Prospects Raised by the Atomic Weapons', in Rozental, ed., *Bohr*, pp.191–214.

Bohr, Niels and John Wheeler, 'The Mechanism of Nuclear Fission', *Physical Review*, Vol. 56, No. 5 (September 1939), pp.426–450.

Boyle, Peter, 'The "Special Relationship" with Washington' in Young, ed., *Churchill's Peacetime Administration*, chapter 1.

Bridges, Lord and Henry Dale, 'John Anderson', *BMFRS*, Vol. 4 (1958), pp.306–325.

Carlton, David, 'Churchill and the two "Evil Empires"', *TRHS*, Vol. 11 (2001), pp.331–352.

Dingman, Roger, 'Atomic Diplomacy during the Korean War', *International Security*, Vol. 13, No. 3 (1988–1989), pp.50–91.

Edmonds, Robin, 'Churchill and Stalin', in Blake and Louis, eds, *Churchill*, chapter 18.

Edmonds, Robin, 'Yalta and Potsdam: Forty Years After', *International Affairs*, Vol. 62, No. 2 (1986), pp.197–216.

Farren, William S., 'Henry Thomas Tizard', *BMFRS*, Vol. 7 (1961).

Frank, Richard B., 'Ending the Pacific War', in Marston, ed., *Pacific War Companion*, chapter 13.

Gilbert, Martin, 'Churchill and Bombing Policy', Fifth Churchill Centre lecture, Washington DC, October 2005, available at: http://www.winstonchurchill.org/images/pdfs/for_educators/ Gilbert TCC Lecture CHURCHILL AND BOMBING POLICY.pdf

Goldberg, Stanley, 'Groves Takes the Reins', *BAS*, Vol. 48, No. 10 (1992), pp.32–39.

Gowing, Margaret, 'Niels Bohr and Nuclear Weapons', in French and Kennedy, eds, *Bohr*, pp.266–278.

Harbutt, Fraser, 'Churchill, Hopkins, and the "Other" Americans: An Alternative Perspective on Anglo-American Relations, 1941–1945', *International History Review*, Vol. 8, No. 2 (1986), pp.236–262.

Hennessey, Peter, 'Churchill and the Premiership', *TRHS*, Vol. 11 (2001), pp.295–306.

Howard, Michael, 'Churchill and the First World War', in Louis and Blake, eds, *Churchill*, chapter 8.

Bibliography

Howard, Michael, 'Churchill: Prophet of Détente', in Kemper, ed., *Churchill*, chapter 8.
Hughes, Jeff, 'The Strath Report: Britain Confronts the H-bomb, 1954–1955', *History and Technology*, Vol. 19, No. 3 (2003), pp.257–275.
Hymans, Jacques E., 'Britain and Hiroshima', *Journal of Strategic Studies*, Vol. 32, No. 5 (2009), pp.767–797.
James, Robert Rhodes, 'The Enigma', in Muller, ed., *Churchill as Peacemaker*, chapter 1.
Jones, Matthew, 'Targeting China: US Nuclear Planning and "Massive Retaliation" in East Asia, 1953–1955', *Journal of Cold War Studies*, Vol. 10, No. 4, pp.37–65.
Jones, Matthew, 'Great Britain, the United States, and Consultation over Use of the Atomic Bomb, 1950–1954', *Historical Journal*, Vol. 54, No. 3 (2011), pp.797–828.
Jones, R. V., Lord Cherwell obituary, *Nature*, Vol. 180 (September 1957), pp.579–580.
Jones, R. V., 'Churchill and Science', in Blake and Louis, eds, *Churchill*, chapter 24.
Jones, R. V., 'Meetings in Wartime and After', in French and Kennedy, *Bohr*, pp.278–287.
Jenkins, Roy, 'Churchill: The Government of 1951–1955', in Blake and Louis, *Churchill*, chapter 28.
Jian, Chen, 'In the Name of Revolution: China's Road to the Korean War Revisited', in Stueck, ed., *Korean War*, chapter 3.
Kaiser, David, 'Churchill, Roosevelt and the Limits of Power: A Review Essay', *International Security*, Vol. 10, No. 1 (1985), pp.204–221.
Kearn, David W., 'The Baruch Plan and the Quest for Atomic Disarmament', *Diplomacy & Statecraft*, Vol. 21, No. 1 (2010), pp.41–67.
Keas, Michael N., 'Ernest Rutherford', in James, ed., *Nobel Laureates*, pp.49–60.
Keegan, John, 'Churchill's Strategy', in Blake and Louis, eds, *Churchill*, chapter 19.
Kern, Gary, 'How "Uncle Joe" bugged FDR', *Studies in Intelligence*, Vol. 47, No. 1 (2007), pp.19–31.
Kimball, Warren F., 'Wheel within a Wheel: Churchill, Roosevelt and the Special Relationship', in Louis and Blake, eds, *Churchill*, chapter 17.
Kort, Michael, 'The Historiography of Hiroshima: The Rise and Fall of Revisionism', *The New England Journal of History*, Vol. 64, No. 1 (2007), pp.31–48.
Kramer, Mark, 'Stalin, Soviet Policy, and the Establishment of the Communist Bloc in Eastern Europe, 1941–1948', in Snyder and Brandon, eds, *Stalin and Europe*, pp.264–294.
Low, A. M., 'Churchill and Science', in Eade, ed., *Churchill By His Contemporaries*, pp.305–312.
Marshall, Robert, 'The Atomic Bomb – and the Lag in Historical Understanding', *Intelligence and National Security*, Vol. 6, No. 2 (1991), pp.458–466.
Moore, Ruth, 'Niels Bohr as a Political Figure', in French and Kennedy, eds, *Bohr*, pp.253–260.
Nutting, Anthony, 'Sir Anthony Eden', in Van Thal, ed., *The Prime Ministers*, Vol. II.
Oliphant, Mark, 'The Beginning: Chadwick and the Neutron', *BAS*, Vol. 38, No. 10 (1982), pp.14–18.
Perkins Jr., Ray, 'Bertrand Russell and Preventive War', *Russell: The Journal of the Bertrand Russell Archives*, Vol. 14 (1994–1995), pp.135–153.
Polanyi, Michael, 'The Republic of Science: Its Political and Economic Theory', *Minerva*, No. 1 (1962), pp.54–74.
Reynolds, David, '1940: The Worst and Finest Hour', in Blake and Louis, eds, *Churchill*, chapter 14.
Reynolds, David, 'Rethinking Anglo-American Relations', *International Affairs*, Vol. 65, No. 1 (1988–1989), pp.89–111.
Rosenberg, Jonathan, 'Before the Bomb and After: Winston Churchill and the Use of Force', in Gaddis et al., eds, *Cold War Statesmen Confront the Bomb*, chapter 8.
Ruane, Kevin, 'Britain, the United States and the Issue of "Limited War" with China, 1950–54', in Young et al., eds, *Churchill to Blair*, chapter 4.
Ruane, Kevin, 'Containing America; Aspects of British Foreign Policy and the Cold War in South-East Asia, 1951–54', *Diplomacy and Statecraft*, Vol. 7, No. 1 (1996), pp.141–174.

Russell, Bertrand, 'The Atomic Bomb and the Prevention of War', *BAS*, Vol. 2, No. 7–8 (1946), pp.19–21.

Saloff, Stephen, '*Lucky Dragon*', *BAS*, Vol. 34, No. 5 (1978), pp.21–23.

Sherwin, Martin J., 'Old Issues in New Editions', *BAS*, Vol. 41, No. 11 (1985), pp.40–44

Sherwin, Martin J., 'Niels Bohr: Spurned Prophet of Arms Control', *BAS*, Vol. 42, No. 9 (1986), pp.41–45.

Taylor, A. J. P., 'Daddy, What Was Winston Churchill?', in Taylor, *Essays*, pp.295–307.

Toye, Richard, 'H. G. Wells and Winston Churchill: A Reassessment', in Steven McLean, ed., *H. G. Wells: Interdisciplinary Essays* (Newcastle: Cambridge Scholars Publishing, 2009), pp.147–161

Trachtenberg, Marc, 'A "Wasting Asset": American Strategy and the Shifting Nuclear Balance, 1949–1954', *International Security*, Vol. 13, No. 3 (1988–89), pp.5–49.

Walker, J. Samuel, 'The Decision to Use the Bomb: A Historiographical Update', *Diplomatic History*, Vol. 14, No. 1 (1990), pp.97–114.

Walker, J. Samuel, 'Recent Literature on Truman's Atomic Bomb Decision: A Search for Middle Ground', *Diplomatic History*, Vol. 29, No. 2 (2005), pp.311–334.

Waverley, Lord and Alexander Fleck, 'Akers', *BMFRS*, Vol. I (1955), pp.1–4.

Willis, Kirk, '"God and the Atom": British Churchmen and the Challenge of Nuclear Power 1945–1950', *Albion*, Vol. 29, No. 3 (1997), pp.422–457.

Yagami, Kazuo, 'Bombing Hiroshima and Nagasaki – Gar Alperovitz and his Critics', *Southeast Review of Asian Studies*, Vol. 31 (2009), pp.301–307.

Young, John, 'Cold War and Détente with Moscow', in Young, ed., *Churchill's Peacetime Administration*, chapter 2.

Young, Ken, 'Anglo-American (Mis)Understandings and the Use of the English Airbases', *Journal of Military History*, Vol. 71, No. 4 (2007), pp.1133–1167.

Zubok, Vladislav, 'Stalin and the Nuclear Age', in Gaddis et al., eds, *Cold War Statesmen*, chapter 3.

Selected press, magazine and web publications

Addison, Paul, 'Naked Except For a Bath Towel', *LRB*, Vol. 7, No. 1 (1985).

Amrine, Michael, 'The Day the Sun Rose Twice', *Washington Post* (*Book Week* section), 18 July 1965.

Best, Geoffrey, 'Momentous Conjecture', *LRB*, Vol. 26, No. 6 (March 2004).

Best, Geoffrey, 'Winston Churchill, the H-Bomb and Nuclear Disarmament', *History Today*, Vol. 55, No. 10 (2005), pp.37–50.

Bundy, Harvey H., 'Remembered Words', *The Atlantic*, March 1957, pp.56–57.

Burr, William ed., 'US Intelligence and the Detection of the First Soviet Nuclear Test, September 1949', *National Security Archive*, September 2009, available at: http://www2.gwu.edu/~nsarchiv/nukevault/ebb286/

Capet, Antoine. '"The Creeds of the Devil": Churchill between the Two Totalitarianisms, 1917–1945', *Finest Hour* (2009) online edition, available at: http://www.winstonchurchill.org/support/the-churchill-centre/publications/finest-hour-online

Charlton, Michael, 'The Eagle and the Small Birds: I, the Spectre of Yalta', *Encounter* (June 1983), pp.7–23.

Chartwell Bulletin, No. 58 (2013), 'New Colour Film of Churchill with Royal Family', available at:. http://www.winstonchurchill.org/publications/chartwell-bulletin/bulletin-58-apr-2013/release-of-rare-colour-film-of-churchill-with-royal-family

Heffer, Simon, 'The Churchill Myth', *New Statesman*, 9–15 January 2015, pp.18–23.

Kimball, Warren F., 'The Bomb and the Special Relationship', *Finest Hour*, No. 137 (2007–2008), pp.37–42.

Bibliography

Kimball, Warren F., 'Sheriffs and Constables: Churchill's and Roosevelt's Postwar World', *Finest Hour*, No. 141 (2008–2009), pp.36–42.

Murphy, Charles J. V. and John Davenport, 'The Lives of Winston Churchill', *Life*, 21 May 1945. pp.92–108.

Oppenheimer, J. Robert, 'Niels Bohr and Atomic Weapons', *NYRB*, 17 December 1964.

Orwell, George, 'You and the Atomic Bomb', *Tribune*, 19 October 1945.

Radchenko, Sergey, 'Shadows in the Nuclear Cave', *H-Net Reviews*, October 2008, available at: https://networks.h-net.org/node/28443/reviews/30355/radchenko-goodman-spying-nuclear-bear-anglo-american-intelligence-and

Ramsden, John, 'Churchill: A Man Who Believed', *Finest Hour*, No. 129 (2005–2006), pp.30–31.

Reynolds, David, 'Had He Not Run', *LRB*, Vol. 27, No. 11 (2005), pp.29–31.

Roberts, Andrew, 'Winston Churchill and Religion: A Comfortable Relationship with the Almighty', *Finest Hour*, No. 163 (2014), pp.52–59.

Schama, Simon 'Rescuing Churchill', *NYRB*, 28 February 2002.

Taylor, A. J. P., 'War in Our Time', *LRB*, Vol. 4, No. 14 (1982).

Truman, Margaret, 'After the Presidency', *Life*, 1 December 1972, pp.69–70.

Newspapers and magazines

Bulletin of the Atomic Scientists; Chartwell Bulletin; Chicago Tribune; Christian Science Monitor; Daily Express; Daily Herald; Daily Mail; Daily Mirror; Economist; Finest Hour; Guardian; Life; Illustrated London News; Independent; Listener; London Review of Books; Manchester Guardian; Morning Post; Nash's Pall Mall; New Statesman; New York Herald Tribune; New York Times; News Chronicle; Observer; Punch; Reynold's News; Spectator; Strand; Sunday Pictorial; Sunday Times; Times; Tribune; Washington Post; Yorkshire Post.

Miscellaneous

Archive on 4, BBC Radio 4, 'Destroyer of Worlds', broadcast 11 July 2015, available at: http://www.bbc.co.uk/programmes/b061pchg

British Pathé, 'H-Bomb', 8 April 1954, available at: http://www.britishpathe.com/video/h-bomb/query/scientists

Cannadine, David, *Churchill's Other Lives: Money* (BBC Radio 4, first broadcast 2011), available at: https://soundcloud.com/churchillcentre/churchills-other-lives-4

Command paper, Cmd. 9391, *Statement on Defence* (London: HMSO, 1955).

Cook, Matthew, 'Sir John Slessor, the Chiefs of Staff and the Evolution of British Strategic Thinking on Nuclear Weapons, 1945–1952', unpublished M.Res., Canterbury Christ Church University (2012).

Ministry of Supply, Central Office of Information 'Operation Hurricane', 1953, available at: http://media.nationalarchives.gov.uk/index.php/operation-hurricane-2/

Oxford Dictionary of National Biography (DNB), online, various named entries, available at: http://www.oxforddnb.com/

Wimbledon online archives, 1920 tournament, available at: http://www.wimbledon.com/en_GB/scores/draws/archive/1920/MS/r1s1.html

INDEX

Note: Entries in italics refer to images.

Index

Index

Index

Index

Mitsubishi Corporation 138
Molotov, Vyacheslav 105, 136, 144, 224
  all-European conference (1954) 283, 285
  Churchill, personal attack on 290
  Churchill–Malenkov meeting (mooted 1954)
    269, 271–2, 274–7, 281, 283, 285
Monckton, Walter 272
monopoly (US) of A-bomb, US 57–8, 75, 93, 115,
    157, 159, 223; *see also* Churchill,
    Winston, atomic monopolist
Montebello islands xii, 212, 214
Montgomery, General (later Field Marshal) Bernard
    121–2, 289
Moon, Philip 24
Moore-Brabazon, J.P.C. 29
morality of nuclear weapons 299–305
  right to use A-bomb, US 237–9
Moran, Lord (Charles Wilson) 32, 37–8, 68, 89, 110,
    136, 194, 199, 227–8, 230, 251, 253,
    257, 270, 278, 290–1
  A-bomb 128–9, 134, 146, 156
  stimulants provided to Churchill 231
Morgan, General (Sir) Frederick 209
Morgenthau, Henry, Jr. 81
Morning Post 4
Morrison, Herbert 175–6, 208
Moscow conference (1944) *see* 'Tolstoy'
Mosley, Oswald 9
Mountbatten, Admiral (Lord) Louis 110, 304
Moyce, Bill 211, 214
Munich agreement (1938) 18, 21, 164, 184, 225,
    230, 259
Mussolini, Benito xiv, 13, 109, 256
Mutual Assured Destruction (MAD) xiii, 231,
    284–5, 288, 293, 296, 314–15

Nagasaki, atomic bombing of 12, 23, 71, 76, 96, 120,
    141, 173, 219, 309
  death toll xiii, 139, 245
  decision to bomb xv, 96, 120, 127–9, 219
  destruction 138–9, 141, 245
  morality of 299–305
  size of bomb xv, 28, 138, 264
  See also 'Fat Man'
Nagoya 139
Nash's Pall Mall 11
Napoleon Bonaparte 5, 21
Nation, The 152
National Academy of Sciences (US) 35
National Bureau of Standards (US) 34
National Defense Research Committee (NDRC) 34
National Security Council (NSC) 200, 248, 268, 278
NATO *see* North Atlantic Treaty Organization
Nazi-Soviet Pact (1939) 38
Nehru, Jawaharlal 248
Nenni, Pietro 167

neutron, discovery of 15–16
New Look, US national security strategy 240–1,
    254–5, 278, 301
New Statesman 205
New York Herald Tribune 169
New York Times 168, 251
News Chronicle 249, 294
Nicolson, Harold 110, 173, 175–6
  Public Faces (1932) 270–1
Nicolson, Nigel 206
Niigata 127
Nobel Prize 16, 239
Normandy campaign (1944) 67, 88
  See also Operation 'Overlord'
North Africa, Allied campaign in 38, 43, 46, 50–1
North Atlantic Treaty (1949) 168–9
North Atlantic Treaty Organization (NATO) 183,
    189, 191–2, 203, 232–3, 251
  conventional arms build-up 212–13, 224–5,
    265, 288
  destabilization of 276, 284
  foundation of 169, 219
  Korean War 182
  New Look 241
  nuclearization of 287, 289
  West European Union (WEU) and 286
  West German troops, use of 178, 190
  West Germany, admission to 286, 294–5, 312
Norway 21, 25
NSC-68 179, 189
nuclear (atomic) arms race 14, 62, 74–5, 145, 147,
    150, 158, 170, 215, 231, 239, 245, 264,
    296, 308
nuclear deterrence xv, 24, 156, 212, 265, 270, 273,
    289, 293–4, 314
nuclear fission xiv, 15–18, 23, 27, 33, 35, 41, 54, 113,
    203, 230, 240
nuclear fusion xiv
nuclear weapons xii–xvi *passim*, 74, 86, 117, 145, 181,
    197, 205, 213, 232, 238, 240–1, 245,
    255, 258, 264–5, 268, 272–3, 281, 286,
    292, 301, 312
  See also A-bomb projects, various
Nunn May, Alan 71

Oak Ridge, Tennessee 70–1, 113
'Octagon' conference (Quebec 1944) 81–4, 87, 91, 97
Office of Scientific Research and Development
    (OSRD) 34–5, 44
Okinawa 110, 135
Oldham 4–5
Oliphant, Mark 24, 34, 71
Oliver Twist (1837), Charles Dickens 31
Operation 'Barbarossa' (1941) 38, 87, 91
Operation 'Castle' (1954) 247–8, 255, 288, 301, 312
Operation 'Downfall' (1945–6) 110, 125